P9-CRF-092

Neurobiology

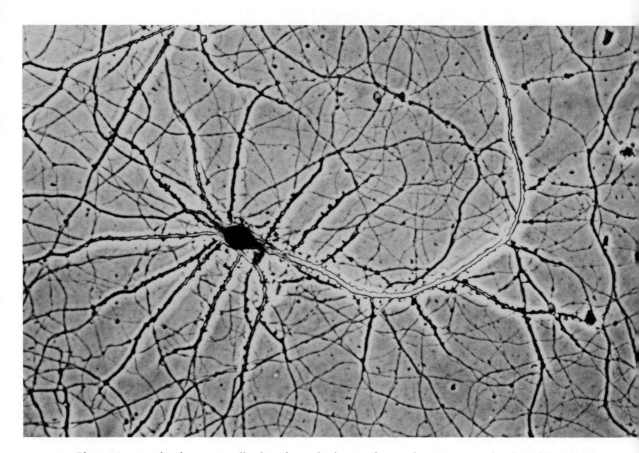

Photomicrograph of a nerve cell taken from the brain of an embryonic rat and cultured in a petri dish for three weeks. Arising from the darkly stained cell body are several dendritic branches; the largest extends to the right and describes a graceful arc as it leaves the top of the field of view. On its surface are many tiny spines. Fibers from other cells criss-cross within the field of view and make synapses on the dendrites and spines. The cells have been stained with a monoclonal antibody to Microtubule-associated Protein 2 (MAP 2), which is related to the cytoskeleton: the reaction makes the cell body appear dark and large dendrites bright. Magnification X400. (Courtesy of Gary Banker and Aaron Waxman, Albany Medical College)

NEUROBIOLOGY

SECOND EDITION

GORDON M. SHEPHERD, M.D., D. Phil.
Professor of Neuroscience
Yale University

New York   Oxford
OXFORD UNIVERSITY PRESS
1988

Oxford University Press

Oxford   New York   Toronto
Delhi   Bombay   Calcutta   Madras   Karachi
Petaling Jaya   Singapore   Hong Kong   Tokyo
Nairobi   Dar es Salaam   Cape Town
Melbourne   Auckland

and associated companies in
Beirut   Berlin   Ibadan   Nicosia

Copyright © 1988 by Oxford University Press, Inc.

Published by Oxford University Press, Inc.,
200 Madison Avenue, New York, New York 10016

Oxford is a registered trademark of Oxford University Press

All rights reserved. No part of this publication may be reproduced,
stored in a retrieval system, or transmitted, in any form or by any means,
electronic, mechanical, photocopying, recording, or otherwise,
without the prior permission of Oxford University Press.

Library of Congress Cataloging-in-Publication Data
Shepherd, Gordon M., 1933–
Neurobiology.
Includes bibliographies and index.
1. Neurobiology.   2. Molecular neurobiology.   I. Title.
[DNLM: 1. Neurobiology.   WL 102 S548n]
QP355.2.S52   1988   612.8   87-7930
ISBN 0-19-505171-8
ISBN 0-19-505172-6 (pbk.)

8 9 7

Printed in the United States of America
on acid-free paper

for Grethe

Preface

The field of neurobiology continues to grow at a rapid pace, and this new edition is necessitated by advances in many vital areas. Most significant is the arrival of methods of molecular biology. In recognition of this, the book treats molecular neurobiology as the foundation for the study of the nervous system, and provides at the outset an orientation to these methods and a summary of their application to a model synapse. This innovation will give the student an early familiarity with the molecular approach and will reflect the central importance of the synapse in nervous organization as well. These themes are part of the warp and woof of all the subsequent chapters.

Although molecular methods have thus opened a new era in the study of the nervous system, it has quickly become apparent that by themselves they are not enough, and are in fact only a beginning. We are constantly reminded that the essence of the nervous system is organization; neural mediation of behavior requires coordination of a hierarchy of levels of organization. This is the necessary conceptual framework for understanding the significance of any particular molecule or any other component of the brain. This fundamental concept, of successive levels of organization, is made explicit in the first chapter, and throughout the text I have tried to relate experimental results to their appropriate level.

In addition to molecular biology and levels of organization, a third major theme is phylogenetic comparison. Although beginning students are interested mainly in learning about the human brain, there are compelling reasons at this stage to avoid an exclusive preoccupation with the human. One reason is that many of our most important insights into neural properties come from studies of invertebrates and submammalian vertebrates. Even more persuasive is the fact that the only way to appreciate the evolution of the human brain is to understand how neural organization has evolved in the other phyla. My own feeling is that the importance of invertebrates will lie increasingly in the testing and demonstration of universal principles of neural organization. To reflect that belief, I have continued the organization of this book along the lines of Plutarch's *Lives*, substituting for paired biographies of great Greeks and Romans the parallel accounts of invertebrates and vertebrates in each chapter.

Although its basic structure and goals

are thus retained, the book has been extensively revised and updated to incorporate new work and integrate the results more coherently into the molecular, hierarchical, and phylogenetic frameworks. Among the main changes, two introductory chapters summarizing invertebrate and vertebrate nervous systems have been deleted on the grounds that this material is adequately covered in introductory biology texts. In addition to the new chapter on molecular neurobiology, recent data on proteins critical for neural functions are discussed in many places, and homologies indicating evolutionary conservation and common principles of function are emphasized. Considerable attention is given to the proliferation of knowledge about neuropeptides, membrane channels, and second messenger systems that provide for the diversity of interactions between neurons. At the circuit and systems levels, traditional concepts such as the command neuron and feeding centers are reassessed, and several new models for mechanisms underlying learning and memory in the mammal are discussed. A new section on neuroimmunology introduces the student to this fascinating field concerned with the relationship between the immune system and the brain. The final chapter on the human cortex has been extensively revised; the basic plan of the cortex is presented in terms of the levels of organization introduced in the first chapter.

Throughout the revisions I have attempted to incorporate the latest research findings while extracting from them the simplest unifying principles. The latter enterprise, of course, is the more difficult, and I have had occasion to admit ruefully to myself the old saying, that "If I had had more time, I would have written a shorter book."

A number of readers have provided valuable suggestions and constructive criticisms based on their teaching experience with the book. I have responded by trimming the number of examples of different systems, and filling out the descriptions of those that are considered. Most of the figure legends now provide extensive coverage of the experiments that are illustrated.

The book contains enough material for a year-long, broadly based course in neurobiology and behavior. I believe that this is the direction that will be taken in undergraduate teaching as the field continues to expand. However, in the United States at present, neurobiology is usually taught as a one-semester course that follows a year of introductory biology. A few teachers have therefore suggested that the book should be shorter. There are two reasons for not cutting its length. One is that this book represents an attempt "to see the nervous system steadily, and see it whole"; what is included is, in my view, the minimum necessary to understand the range of behavior in which the nervous system is critically involved. The other, related answer is that the one-semester courses now taught vary widely. Different instructors have indicated to me that their courses emphasize human neuroanatomy, or the electrophysiology of ion channels, or sensory systems, or invertebrates, or the psychobiology of behavior. To cover all these needs, I have kept my sights firmly on the nervous system as a whole, and invite instructors to extract the material for their specific types of courses. Toward this end, a study guide to topics covered in different chapters is included as an Appendix.

The labor of carrying out this revision has already been repaid by the generosity of many colleagues in rendering assistance and advice. At an early stage, Jurgen Boeckh reviewed the entire book, correcting errors and helping to shape the strategy of the revision. Vera Boeckh has gone over the text with great care, helping enormously with this revision while preparing the German translation. Several instructors shared their experiences in using the book in undergraduate teaching; I am particularly grateful to Miriam LeGare in this regard. Among individual chapters, molecular biology was read by Toni Claudio, the chapter on development by Karl Herrup and Alain Prochiantz, parts of the chapter on action potentials by Stephen Smith, and on synaptic potentials by George Aghajanian. Anonymous reviewers provided valuable comments on the entire sections of molecular and cellular mechanisms and of motor systems. I am most grateful to these colleagues for their careful readings and constructive criticism.

I am deeply indebted to a number of colleagues who helped with specific topics and in a number of cases generously provided illustrations from their work. These include George Aghajanian, William Agnew, Peter Anderson, Philipe Ascher, Tim Bliss, William Carr, Toni Claudio, Jack Cooper, Brian Curtis, Peter Dallos, Yves Gallifret, Patricia Goldman-Rakic, Charles Greer, Robert Guy, Bartley Hoebel, Roland Johansson, Tom Lentz, Dennis Lincoln, Owen Lockerbie, Neil MacLusky, Alain Marty, Charles Michael, Mortimer Mishkin, Dennis Noble, Alan Peters, Pasko Rakic, Thomas Reese, Aryeh Routenberg, Stephen Smith, Richard Thompson, Didier Trotier, Åke Vallbo, David van Essen, and Charles Woody.

Balancing the demands of this book against the ongoing research in my laboratory has been difficult. I could not have managed without the continued collaboration of William Stewart and Charles Greer, the efforts of colleagues Patricia Pedersen and Leona Masukawa, and of students Ben Strowbridge, Tom Woolf, Shridar Ganesan, and Jessica Hopfield. Our research has been generously supported by grants from the National Institute of Neurological and Communicative Disorders and Stroke, and the Office of Naval Research. I am very grateful to them, and to my program directors, Jack Pearl and Joel Davis.

It is a pleasure to acknowledge the hospitality of Professors Jacques Glowinski and Yves Laporte at the College de France during the autumn of 1986, and the kind invitation to deliver a series of *leçons* on "Principles of Synaptic Organization." The synthesis attempted there is reflected throughout this book, particularly in the final chapter on the cerebral cortex.

As in the previous edition, special care has been taken with the illustrations; of 445 total, 85 have been revised and 109 are completely new. A number of them are composites, to illustrate several experiments focused on a common problem. Many of these constitute attempts to interpret recent findings and synthesize new concepts. I apologize to colleagues whose work has been oversimplified in the interest of clarity for the introductory student. Once again I am much indebted to Virginia Simon and the staff of the Medical Illustration Department at Yale for the artwork. Wendolyn Hill, aided by Sharon Schmiedel, did a beautiful job of converting my pencil drawings into finished illustrations.

The references are relatively extensive for an introductory text. Each author of an original illustration is credited in the figure legend, and cited either in the original publication or, in some instances, in a secondary source that would be more accessible to students. Within the text I have liberally cited key contributions, but have held the number of actual references to an absolute minimum. I beg the indulgence of my colleagues in this attempt to be accurate without overloading the text with references. Even so, the list of Literature Cited consists of over 500 entries. A shorter list for Further Reading is also provided. In both lists, I have tried to include both historically important contributions and the latest research results. I thank the many authors and publishers who have kindly granted permission to reproduce copyrighted material.

I have received much help in dealing with the enormous volume of work involved in this revision. Jeffrey House has remained committed to his belief in this single-author text, and has kept up the spirits of the single author during the times the task seemed too overwhelming. Rosalind Corman has been incredibly efficient in editing the text, and countenanced no compromises in striving for accuracy and consistency. Leslie Phillips, Ellen Fuchs and Mindy Schulman have coordinated the whole en-

terprise most efficiently. Al Mueller and
Ellen Stanley have provided expert typing.

My family has been unstinting in its support. Gordon, Kirsten, and Lisbeth have
given numerous insights from students'
perspectives, and assisted with typing and

editing. My wife, Grethe, has seen the whole
project through to completion with her
unerring judgment and equanimity.

Hamden, Connecticut   G. M. S.
June, 1987

Contents

Neurobiology

1

Introduction

Why Study Neurobiology?

There are many reasons for studying neurobiology. First, we all learn from an early age that our behavior, and the behavior of all animal life, depends on the nervous system. As we grow older, we experience the full richness of human behavior—the ability to think and feel, to remember and create—and we wonder, if we have any wonder at all, how the brain makes this possible. How this comes about is the subject matter of neurobiology.

A second reason is simply that the brain is the most complex of all biological organs. Some therefore believe that understanding how it works offers the greatest challenge in all of biological science.

A third reason is that the brain is the organ through which we think. Some therefore believe that this offers the supreme philosophical challenge; understanding how the brain can enable us to understand how the brain enables us to understand. (If you already know the answer to this enigma, proceed directly to page 658!)

A fourth reason is that the brain is the organ that makes us human. Everything we learn about the brain gives us potential insight into the nature of being human. This makes neurobiology more than just a philosophical exercise or intellectual game; it could help to ensure that we have a future. Nations at present appear determined to evolve the means for mutual destruction, through the development of weapons with the power to annihilate life on this planet. Why do we have this in our brains, and how can we control it? In all of science and medicine, neurobiology is the only field that can ultimately address this critical issue. It could be the most urgent reason for studying the brain.

In addition to these special reasons, neurobiology is important as a field in biomedicine. Everything we learn about the nervous system, from the most primitive worms and slugs to the human, brings us closer to being able to prevent or relieve the suffering of nervous diseases such as epilepsy, Parkinson's disease, or senile dementia, and mental disorders such as drug addiction, depression, or schizophrenia.

Finally, as in every field of science, neurobiology can be pursued for the fun of using new technologies, the challenge of discovery, and the beauty of new insights into nature that scientific endeavors offer as their own reward.

What Is Neurobiology?

The things we experience about human behavior in our own lifetimes have been pondered over ever since the philosophers of ancient Greece first conceived the notion that human beings have a mind and a soul, and began to probe their nature. However, despite the strivings of humankind's profoundest thinkers in the more than 2,500 years since then, it is only very recently that we have begun to acquire any realistic idea at all about the true nature of the brain.

The relevant history may be briefly told. Only 100 years ago was it learned that the brain is composed of cells, and that the cells are connected together to form circuits. Scarcely 30 years ago were the main kinds of nerve cell activity directly recorded, and the junctions, called synapses, identified that allow nerve cells to communicate with each other. Only 10 years ago were we provided the means to analyze directly the molecular mechanisms that control the differentiation of nerve cells and the expression of their functional properties. These and other milestones along the way are summarized in Table 1.1.

It should be obvious therefore that neurobiology is a very young science, and is

Table 1.1 Some steps in acquiring knowledge about the basic mechanisms of the brain

600–400 B.C.	Greek philosophers describe the mind and soul; thinking depends on the brain (or heart?).
1543	Vesalius accurately describes gross anatomy of the human nervous system.
1637	Descartes characterizes the brain as a machinelike mechanism, independent of, but related to, the soul.
1798	Galvani discovers the electrical nature of nervous activity.
1891	Cajal and others determine that the nervous system is composed of independent nerve cells connected together to form pathways.
1897	Sherrington proposes that nerve cells form pathways by communicating with each other through junctions called synapses.
1920s	Langley, Loewi, Dale, and others identify chemical substances (neurotransmitters) that function as messengers which act on receptors at the synapses.
1940s	Shannon, Weaver, and Weiner introduce concepts of information processing and control systems (cybernetics).
1950s	Hodgkin, Huxley, Katz, and Eccles make precise recordings of electrical signals with microelectrodes. Electron microscopy reveals synapses and neuronal fine structure.
1950s	Single cell analysis by Mountcastle, Lettvin, Hubel, and Wiesel of brain circuits for feature abstraction.
1960s	Integrative functions of dendrites are recognized: synaptic circuits and synaptic interactions without impulses are identified.
1970s	Neuromodulator substances and second messengers are found that greatly extend the duration and complexity of neuronal interactions.
1970s	Computerized imaging techniques permit visualization of brain activity patterns in relation to sensation and cognition.
1970s	Molecular methods are introduced for analyzing genetic mechanisms (recombinant DNA technologies) and single membrane proteins (patch clamping).
1980s	Advances in computers and artificial intelligence begin to promise realistic models of nervous system functions (vision, language, memory, logic).

acquiring new knowledge at a very rapid rate. What you will learn about the nervous system in the course of studying this book will far exceed even the wildest dreams that René Descartes might have had as he struggled to formulate the first concepts of the brain as a machine, in the early part of the seventeenth century. But will that vast amount of new and detailed knowledge you learn lead to understanding? —to a coherent view of how the nervous system mediates behavior?

In order for this to occur, it is not enough to learn the facts; the facts must be related to each other in ways that make them meaningful. For a fact to have meaning, it must be seen within the context of a general principle. The main aim of neurobiology, therefore, and the main aim of this book, is to identify the principles underlying the mechanisms through which the nervous system mediates behavior.

One of the ways in which principles are useful is that they force us to define the elementary units, the basic building blocks, of a field of knowledge. Thus, in physics, we understand matter in terms of elementary atomic particles and forces. Similarly, we can gain a good understanding of the heart in terms of the coordinated actions of cardiac cells. In neurobiology, the problem is much more complicated. We know that nerve cells process information, but we do not understand the different forms that this information takes within the nervous system. We also know that nervous function depends on the coordinated actions of nerve cells, but we do not understand the enormous variety of functions that the nervous system must have in order to mediate the different types of behavior. However, as our brief review of history revealed, there have been identified some of the structures, substances, and properties that must contribute to the elementary units that underlie those functions. These elementary units reflect different levels of organization, that range from the single molecule or ion, to the expression of a behavior such as feeding or thinking.

From these considerations we can deduce a basic premise, that an understanding of nervous function requires identifying the elementary units at different levels of organization, and understanding the relations between the different levels. We can summarize this view with a more precise definition of the subject matter of modern neurobiology, and of this book: *Neurobiology is the study of the molecular organization of the nerve cell, and the ways that nerve cells are organized, through synapses, into functional circuits that process information and mediate behavior.*

The Levels of Neural Organization

The importance of the different levels of organization for understanding the principles of neurobiology can be illustrated by an example. Let us consider a simple *behavior*, such as reading this page (see A in Fig. 1.1). We know, by observation, that this act has several component parts. First, there is our sensory perception of the page and the symbols printed upon it. Second, there is a process of comprehension, which gives those symbols meaning. Third, there is movement of our eyes so that we can scan the page.

These parts *describe* the behavior of reading the page. In order to *understand* how this occurs, we need to look inside the brain. Tracing fiber tracts through the brain has been one of the traditional concerns of neurobiologists. From these studies we can lay out the *pathways* within the brain that are involved in reading this page (B in Fig. 1.1). First, there is the sensory pathway, which starts within the eye and ends within the visual cortex at the back of the brain. Second, there are the central connections reaching forward to the frontal lobes of the brain, that underlie comprehension. Third, there are the descending motor pathways that control the movement of the eyes. In this way we identify the major sensory, central, and motor *systems* that are involved in this particular behavior. These

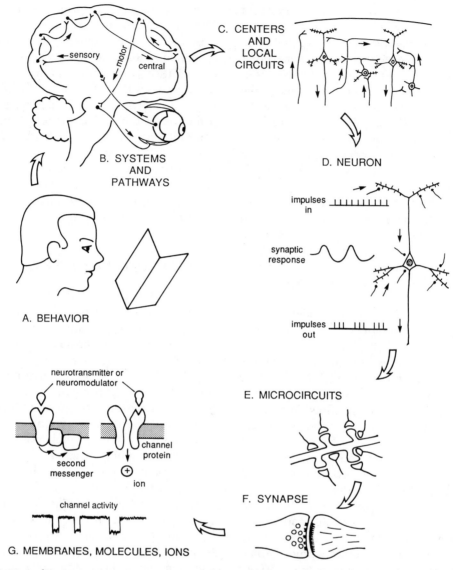

Fig. 1.1 A diagrammatic representation of the organization of the nervous system, from the behavioral to molecular level. **A.** The behavioral act of reading this page. **B.** A lateral view inside the brain, showing in schematic fashion the visual pathway from the eye, central pathway for comprehension, and motor pathway for eye movement. **C.** Neurons and their branches form local-circuit functional units within cortical areas. **D.** The neuron is a functional unit; impulses in arriving axons set up excitatory or inhibitory synaptic potentials, which are integrated in the neuron to control the impulse output to other neurons. **E.** Patterns of synaptic connections form microcircuits. **F.** The individual synapse is a complex input–output unit. **G.** Molecular mechanisms are responsible for transmitter reception, biochemical transmission, and amplification, and control of ionic current flow underlying the membrane response at a single synapse.

systems are at the highest level of brain organization.

To understand how a system works, we need to analyze the organization of the centers. Within each center are populations of nerve cells and satellite cells called glia. There are typically several different types of nerve cell. Neurons characteristically have short branches, called dendrites; many neurons, especially those connecting to other centers, also have a long branch called an axon. Each cell connects with other cells within the center in specific ways through its axon and/or dendrites. These connections form what are called *local circuits* (C in Fig. 1.1). Through these, the center receives information coming from other centers, performs some specific processing operations on it, and sends the output to other centers. Within the local circuits are usually certain patterns of connections that are stereotyped and distinctive. These are referred to as *microcircuits* (E in Fig. 1.1), which mediate the specific types of operations that are carried out in that center.

Local circuits are constructed of *neurons,* which represent an important level of organization (D in Fig. 1.1). The main function of the neuron is to generate a characteristic type of activity and integrate it with the activity it receives from other neurons through long distance and local circuit connections. One common pattern of organization of a neuron is for the dendrites to receive inputs and the axon to send outputs. The output is characteristically carried in a discharge of brief electrical changes, termed impulses, which can travel long distances along the outer membrane of the axon without diminishing in amplitude.

In order for neurons to communicate with each other and form circuits, they need to have points of contact with each other. These are called *synapses* (F in Fig. 1.1). A single neuron may send its output through hundreds of synapses on other neurons; conversely, it may receive inputs through hundreds or thousands of synapses made upon it by other neurons. Each synapse

may be considered as a semi-independent input–output unit. Synapses are therefore critical building blocks of microcircuits and local circuits.

At the *molecular* level, the synapse is a complicated structural and functional unit. The chemical type of synapse involves release of a neurotransmitter substance from a presynaptic process, which causes an increase or decrease in the flow of ions through a channel protein in the membrane of a postsynaptic process. The substance may act directly on the channel protein, or indirectly, through second messengers, as indicated in G of Fig. 1.1. The molecular structure of the different channel proteins, and the ways they are expressed by the genome are elucidated using biochemical methods and recombinant DNA technologies.

Also indicated in G is the fact that the action of a channel protein in allowing ions to flow across the membrane may be recorded by special electrophysiological methods, called patch clamping. Analysis by these methods enables one to show how single-channel events are triggered by the neurotransmitter at a synapse to generate the synaptic potentials which control the firing by the neuron. Similar methods permit analysis of the single-channel events that underlie the nerve impulse.

Figure 1.1 summarizes most of the levels of organization that are present in the nervous system. If you turn back to the definition of neurobiology, you will see that it embraces most of these levels.

Figure 1.1 helps to show how one starts with a given behavior and works downward, so to speak, through successive levels of organization, to identify the units of function underlying that behavior. If we do that for the act of reading this page, we can at least begin to understand the mechanisms that enable us to do this act. However, the job is not complete until we compare this analysis with the results from other systems, and are able to generalize the levels of organization and their functional units across all systems. Only then may we say that we can begin to understand the general principles that apply across all systems.

This book is founded on the premise that these general principles are present and are being revealed by modern neurobiological investigations; our task is to identify them and weld them into a coherent framework.

Figure 1.1 not only helps us to see that behavior emerges out of a hierarchy of functional units; it also implies that a functional unit can be understood only within the context of the behavior that it mediates. Thus, no matter how complex a neural circuit may appear, we can be confident that it is efficiently designed to mediate specific naturally occurring behaviors. This same principle must apply, no matter how deeply one delves into the hierarchy of organizational levels, even down to the individual molecule gating a flow of ions. We may summarize this principle with the proposition that "Nothing in neurobiology makes sense except in the light of behavior."

From this discussion, you can begin to appreciate that behavior is a product of nervous organization, and is also an agent in molding that organization.

The Plan of This Book

The principles summarized in Fig. 1.1 indicate the plan of this book. Instead of working our way down, we will start at the bottom, at the molecular level, and work our way upward toward behavior.

In the remaining chapters of this section, we will discuss the molecular and cellular organization of the neuron, and how they provide for the basic functions that apply generally throughout the entire nervous system. We will then consider the organization of different systems. We will first study the sensory systems that are responsible for our sensations and perceptions of the world around and within us. Next we will consider the motor systems that enable us to act on our environment. Finally, we learn about the central systems that not only mediate sensorimotor coordination, but also provide the complex circuits that underlie the highest nervous functions such as memory, emotions, and cognition.

In this book, special emphasis will be placed on the ways in which nerve cells are connected through their synapses to form functional circuits. The synaptic circuit will be shown to be a key concept in enabling us to understand how nerve cells are organized to process information and mediate behavior.

We will see that this requires certain modifications in the classical concept of the neuron as an independent functional unit. For example, many neurons, like many other cells, have the continuity of their plasma membrane interrupted by gap junctions (electrical synapses), which allow small molecules to pass freely between cells. It has been argued that "It is the coupled cell ensemble, and not the single cell, that is the functional compartmental unit for the smaller cytoplasmic molecules" (Loewenstein, 1981).

Studies of chemical synapses have similarly changed our views. In place of the old idea that each neuron is a simple functional unit, receiving synaptic inputs in its dendrites and emitting signals through its axon, is an enlarged view in which the neuron

Fig. 1.2 An affectionate view of Stephen Kuffler from the early years of modern neurobiology. Armed with his trusty microelectrode, Don Quixote seeks the secrets of the neuron. (From Kuffler, 1958)

can provide multiple sites for input–output units in both its dendrites and axon. In this view, synaptic units, organized into multineuronal circuits and assemblies, provide the basis for nervous organization (Shepherd, 1972). One of the main purposes of this book is to identify these circuits that underlie different behaviors.

A second purpose of this book is to compare the circuits in invertebrates and vertebrates, in order to identify basic principles of organization. For those pursuing biology in its broadest aspects, the invertebrates represent solutions to adaptation that are of interest in their own right, quite apart from their relevance to vertebrates. Those who are primarily interested in the vertebrates should heed the warning of E. J. W. Barrington (1979):

Vertebrate studies by themselves . . . tell us little, if anything of the origin of vertebrates, or of the origin of the principles of biological organization that have determined the course of their adaptive evolution. Indeed, the appeal that the vertebrates make to our anthropocentric tendencies can be dangerously deceptive. It can easily lead to over-optimistic generalization from limited data, obtained from some laboratory mammal that has nothing to recommend it for the purposes other than its convenience and its compliant behaviour. If, therefore, we are to evaluate and exploit the dramatic advances of contemporary biology . . . we need as one essential condition the widest possible extension of our understanding of the principles of animal organization.

Those whose interests are confined mainly to humans will see, when we come to consider higher mental functions in the final chapters, that our understanding is drawn from a wide perspective on the principles of organization of neuronal circuits that has been built up in the preceding chapters.

I
Molecular and
Cellular Mechanisms

2

Molecular Neurobiology

Until recently, our knowledge of nerve cells at the molecular level was limited by the difficulty of applying traditional biochemical methods to nervous tissue. Most of our understanding had to be inferred from studies of more accessible cells, such as blood cells or gland cells. Modern methods of molecular biology have changed all this, because now we can analyze molecular mechanisms directly in the brain itself. Because of these advances, we can for the first time begin the study of neurobiology on a foundation of the molecular biology of the nerve cell.

This new field of investigation has the name of molecular neurobiology. It is concerned with three fundamental questions. First, what is the molecular composition of nerve cells? In order to answer this question, we will review briefly the main types of biological molecules and their functions within cells. We will then consider methods for analyzing how the chemical composition of nerve cells is determined by the flow of information from the genes, taking as examples the development of the hybridoma and recombinant DNA technologies.

Second, how does the molecular composition of nerve cells provide the basis for their special functional properties? The most characteristic function of nerve cells is their ability to transmit signals at specialized junctions called synapses. This involves the secretion of signal molecules, called neurotransmitters, which bind to receptor molecules in the membrane of the receiving cell. The best understood synapse is the neuromuscular junction, where transmission of the nerve signals that tell a muscle to contract takes place. We will see how application of a variety of modern methods is permitting a unified picture to be built up at the molecular level, showing how a nerve signal is transmitted at this model synapse.

The third fundamental question concerns how nerve cells are assembled into functional circuits during development. For this we need to understand the mechanisms of gene expression, as they relate to the unfolding structure and function of a given neuron, and the way this is orchestrated with similar or complementary events in neighboring neurons with which it interacts. In addition, we need to know how the particular environment and experience of the organism at each stage of development interact with the products of gene expression to determine the neural basis of behavior. We will consider this question

13

later in Chap. 9, and at many other places in this book.

Molecular Biology of the Neuron

The Biomolecular Quartet

One of the beautiful simplifying principles in biology is that all living organisms have been constructed of just four main types of molecules. Each type is composed of carbon atoms, linked together by covalent bonds (see Fig. 2.1). Simplest among these are the *fatty acids;* these consist of straight chains of carbon atoms, ending in carboxyl (—COOH) groups. A second type is the *sugars* (also called carbohydrates); these contain hydroxyl groups (—C—OH), and aldehyde (—CHO) or ketone (—CO—) groups. In larger sugars, such as glucose, a hydroxyl group near one end combines with the aldehyde or ketone group at the other end to form a ring structure. A third type is the *amino acids*. These consist of a carbon atom which is bound to four different moieties: a hydrogen atom (—H), an amino group (—$^+NH_3$), a carboxyl group (—COO^-), and a variable side chain (—R). Finally, a fourth main type is the *nucleotides*. These consist of a pentose (5—carbon) sugar linked to a nitrogen-containing ring structure called a base.

Simple versions of these four basic types of molecule were formed at an early stage in earth's evolution. The next steps occurred when single units of a given type of molecule combined with each other to form larger units, called polymers. Thus, *lipid* polymers were built of repeated fatty acid molecules. *Carbohydrate* polymers, built of sugar molecules, are called saccharides; glycogen, for example, is a polysaccharide composed of repeated glucose molecules. Amino acids were linked by peptide bonds to form *peptides;* long peptides formed *proteins*. These basic steps in building polymers are illustrated in Fig. 2.1 (we will consider nucleotide polymers later).

Each of these main categories of molecule is suited for a particular range of functions. Within each category, different sizes and compositions of the molecules bestow specific properties. These different properties were the crucial basis for the evolution, first, of simple cells, and then of multicellular organisms. The different types of molecules in each of the categories are summarized in Table 2.1. With regard to the nervous system, this table conveys two important points. One is that, with the exception of fat storage and the immune response, cells of the nervous system (neurons and their satellite cells, glia) express most of the main types of molecules and functions found in other cells. This is particularly true of such basic cell processes as metabolism, second messenger systems, and secretion. In addition, they express certain

Table 2.1 Types of biomolecules and their functions[a]

	Lipids	Sugars	Amino acids	Nucleotides
Small molecules	fatty acids energy transfer (acetyl-CoA) hormones	energy (glucose)	metabolism neurotransmitters hormones	energy transfer (ATP) second messengers (cAMP)
Large molecules	membranes fat storage (triacylglycerols)	energy storage (glycogen) molecular recognition (glycolipids, glycoproteins)	cell structure enzymes receptors antibodies	coenzymes DNA and RNA

[a]Note the difference between the functions of small and large molecules (formed by polymerization of small molecules). All of these functions are found in nerve cells and/or their satellite cells (neuroglia), with the exception of fat storage.

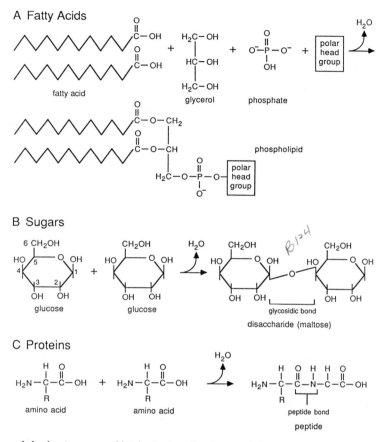

Fig. 2.1 Three of the basic types of biological molecules, and the ways they are built into polymers by different types of chemical bonds.

A. In *fatty acids,* the hydrophilic carboxyl group at one end is very reactive. These groups readily interact with hydroxyl groups of other molecules to form esters, which in turn can become covalently linked to phosphate groups and other molecules to build up complicated molecules. As an example in the nervous system, fatty acids are important constituents of myelin, a special membrane that enwraps some nerve axons.

B. *Sugar* molecules in ring conformation, such as glucose, are joined by two hydroxyl (OH) groups to form a glycosidic (-C-O-C-) bond. In this manner disaccharides (two sugars), oligosaccharides (several sugars), and polysaccharides (many sugars) can be built up. Polysaccharides are important constituents of recognition molecules at the surfaces of nerve cell membranes.

C. *Amino acids* are linked by joining the amino (-$^+NH_3$) group of one to the carboxyl (-COO^-) group of the other to form an amide (-CONH-) bond, also called a *peptide bond.* Two amino acids thus joined are called a *peptide;* longer chains of amino acids are called oligopeptides and polypeptides. Long peptide polymers form proteins; they become folded in complex ways, as a result of weak interactions (such as hydrogen bonds) between different parts of the chains. Small amino acids and peptides can function as neurotransmitters and neuromodulators; larger polypeptides and proteins function as their receptors.

molecules and functions to a greater degree, or uniquely. These lie particularly in the categories of membranes, signaling molecules (neurotransmitters and hormones and their receptors), and recognition molecules that are crucial to the assembly of synaptic circuits during development. These general and special molecular properties of nerve cells will be the subject of Chap. 3.

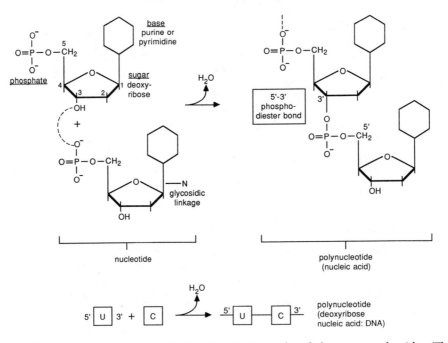

Fig. 2.2 Nucleic acids are polymers built by phosphodiester bonds between nucleotides. This may be summarized by a block diagram, in which the nucleotides are represented by single letters (U for uracil and C for cytosine). In a chain of nucleotides, the 5′ carbon end is shown on the left, and the 3′ carbon end is on the right. Single-ring bases are called pyrimidines, and double-ring bases are called purines. A sugar plus its base is called a nucleoside; a nucleoside with a phosphate (PO₄) group attached to the sugar is called a nucleotide.

Nucleic Acids Encode Molecular Information

The evolution of lipid, sugar, and protein molecules provided for most of the functions of cells, including nerve cells, but a crucial function is still to be accounted for: how did the different molecules get assembled in a reliable and efficient manner? This was especially important for proteins, with their long chains of amino acids arranged in highly specific sequences.

This capacity for assembling polymers was in fact probably one of the first properties of molecules to arise. It was a property well suited to the fourth major category of molecule, the *nucleic acids*. As shown in Fig. 2.2, nucleic acids are built up of units called nucleotides, consisting of a sugar, a nitrogenous base and a phosphate group. The phosphate group is quite reactive, and two nucleotides can be readily joined together by the formation of a bond between the phosphate group of one nucleotide and the sugar of the other. Thus, for the case of deoxyribonucleotide, an oxygen of the phosphate group attached to the number 5 carbon of one deoxyribose molecule is covalently bonded to the hydroxyl group of the number 3 carbon of the second deoxyribose molecule. As shown in Fig. 2.2, this results in the formation of a phosphodiester bond linking the two. Polynucleotides, consisting of long chains of nucleotides, can thus be easily built up. A polynucleotide containing ribose as the sugar is called ribonucleic acid (RNA); one containing deoxyribose is called deoxyribonucleic acid (DNA).

In addition to the functions we have already noted, such as serving structural uses and providing reactive sites, polymers also have another inherent property, that of being able to serve as templates for the assembly of additional polymers (see Fig.

2.3). This is due to the ability of each nucleotide unit to form a weak bond with an identical or complementary nucleotide unit that is brought into register with it. This unit can then form phosphodiester bonds with neighboring units also brought into register, so that a new chain is formed. The key is to have the weak bonds strong enough to bring the new units into register, but weak enough so that the new chain can be easily separated from the first as soon as it is assembled. In early evolution this process of assembly was probably quite slow, but eventually it came to be catalyzed by specific enzymes and could proceed quite rapidly.

The ability of nucleic acids to serve as templates in this fashion conferred upon them the ability to perform three functions which were crucial for the evolution of living organisms (see Fig. 2.3). The first was *replication,* the ability of the nucleic acid polymer to reproduce itself. A single strand of RNA or DNA could produce a double strand, and a double strand could reproduce itself as another double strand. This made it possible for a cell to divide into two daughter cells, each receiving exact copies of the original RNA or DNA. By this means, cells could increase their populations, and a species could perpetuate itself through successive generations. The second function was *transcription.* A single strand of DNA could serve as a template for assembling RNA, and this RNA could then serve as a template elsewhere in the cell. Thus there could be communication or transfer of the information throughout a cell. The third crucial function that could be served by this template was in the construction, not simply of more nucleic acids, but of proteins. This process, of converting information from nucleic acids to proteins, is termed *translation.*

DNA and RNA have particular properties which resulted in their being selected during evolution to perform these functions. These properties were first recognized in the model of James Watson and Francis Crick in England in 1953. They showed that the DNA polymer takes the form of a double helix, in which the pentose sugars and phosphates constitute two intertwining backbones and the bases project toward the interior, where the bases of one strand are constrained by hydrogen bonds to be in perfect register with the bases of the other. Because of this perfect register, DNA can act as a reliable repository of the precise information needed to encode for protein synthesis. RNA, on the other hand, has become specialized for receiving the transcribed code and translating it into the proper sequences of amino acids to form proteins; as we shall see, several types of RNA cooperate in this task.

The unit of information for protein synthesis is a triplet of successive nucleotides in the RNA; each successive triplet constitutes a code "name," a codon which specifies a particular amino acid (see Fig. 2.3). The RNA nucleotide triplet is encoded and stored in the DNA by the complementary nucleotide triplet. The chain of DNA nucleotides that specifies one polypeptide molecule, such as a structural protein or an enzyme, is called a gene; the total amount of DNA constitutes the genome of the organism.

The genome of the mammal is believed to consist of approximately 100,000 genes. The complexity of the brain is reflected in the fact that more of the genes are devoted to encoding proteins in the nervous system than in any other organ. The brain may express over 50,000 different mRNA species, whereas the kidney probably expresses only 10,000 or so. As many as 30,000 of the total number of genes may be specific for the brain. However, there is not a direct relation between the uniqueness of brain genes and the special functions of the brain. As pointed out by Lois Lampson (1984) at the University of Pennsylvania, neurons may express specialized forms of proteins that serve general functions (such as different types of cytoskeletal filaments: see Chap. 3). On the other hand, some proteins serve functions that are unique to certain neurons or neuronal subpopulations. An im-

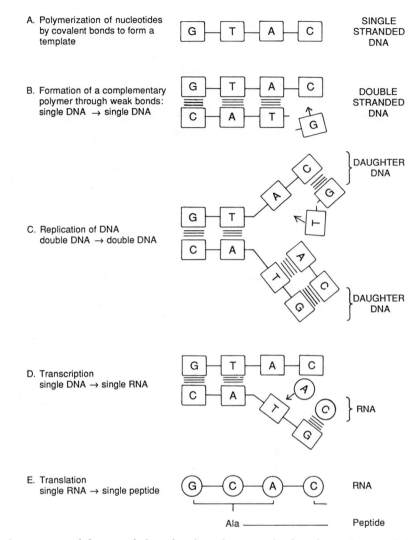

Fig. 2.3   A summary of the steps believed to have been involved in the evolution of the nucleotide system for the storage and utilization of genetic information.

portant principle is that many of the proteins crucial for neuronal function are produced by multigene families. These proteins are related through common amino acid sequences, indicating their common evolutionary origins. They can be adapted to different functions through diversity of amino acid sequences generated at different levels of transcription and translation.

Development of Molecular Biology

It is not necessary to review the history of the development of our present concepts of the molecular biology of the cell; for this the student is referred to the appropriate textbooks (e.g., Alberts et al., 1983). Our aim here is to provide sufficient orientation so that the student can understand the soil that nurtured the roots of molecular neurobiology.

The basic scheme, for replication of DNA, and for transfer of the genetic information from DNA to RNA for the manufacture of proteins, as outlined above, was worked out in only about a dozen years. By 1965, the genetic code had been broken, and the

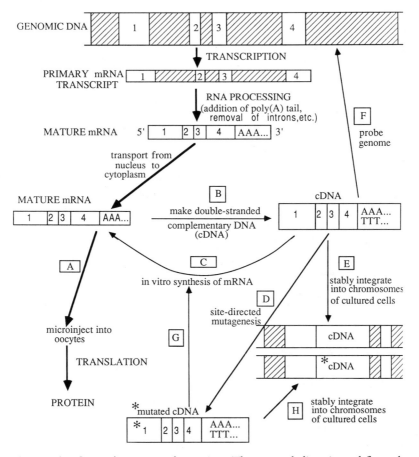

Fig. 2.4 Pathways for flow of genetic information. The normal direction of flow, from genomic DNA to RNA to protein, is shown by thick arrows on the left. Pathways utilized in recombinant DNA methods are shown by thin arrows. **A.** Injection of mRNA coding for a membrane channel protein, into oocytes; the protein is then studied with patch-recording methods (see Fig. 2.13, below). **B.** Reverse transcriptase makes cDNA. **C.** cDNA can be used to synthesize mRNA directly. **D.** cDNA can be subjected to site-directed mutagenesis to produce mutation of a specific gene locus. **E.** cDNA can be integrated into chromosomes of cultured cells. **F.** cDNA can be used to probe DNA by means of hybridization screening (see Fig. 2.5, below). **G.** Mutated cDNA can be used to synthesize mRNA. **H.** Mutated cDNA can be integrated into chromosomes of cultured cells. (From Claudio, 1986)

codons for all essential amino acids had been recognized. Synthesis of the amino acids into proteins was shown to require three types of RNA, each specialized for a different task. *messenger RNA* (mRNA), to read specific lengths of the DNA base code and bring it to the cytoplasm; *transfer RNA* (tRNA), to bring the individual amino acids to be connected; and *ribosomal RNA* (rRNA), to serve as the site of synthesis. We will have more to say about these

steps in neurons in later chapters (Chaps. 3 and 8).

There is thus a flow of genetic information, from DNA to DNA for replication, and from DNA to RNA to proteins for protein synthesis. These simple paths for flow of genetic information within the cell became established as a "Central Dogma" of molecular biology. This is represented in Fig. 2.4, together with an expanded view in which the normal directions of flow in eukaryotic cells, including neurons, are shown by the thick arrows.

In the early years of molecular biology, the main focus was on gaining an understanding of normal genetic mechanisms involved in the processes of replication and protein synthesis in viruses, bacteria, and animal cells. Very soon, however, the results began to reveal specific enzymes which not only provided explanations for these processes, but also put into scientists' hands the means to manipulate the genetic mechanisms themselves.

These methods have been crucial for the development of molecular neurobiology. Their use is now widespread in the analysis of neural systems, and we will study their applications throughout this book. It will therefore be important to review briefly the principles involved. The methods fall into two main groups: recombinant DNA technology and hybridoma technology.

Recombinant DNA Technology. One of the first steps toward gene manipulation was the discovery in the late 1960s of *restriction endonucleases.* These are enzymes that protect a bacterium against an infecting bacterial virus (phage) by cleaving the viral DNA at specific sites and thereby inactivating it. Different bacteria have restriction endonucleases which recognize and bind to different sequences of nucleotide bases; the most common types recognize four or six base sequences. The resulting *restriction fragments* are then separated on the basis of size (number of bases) by agarose gel electrophoresis. By combining the information obtained from exposing DNA to different restriction endonucleases, a *restriction map* of the DNA can be constructed. When combined with other procedures, this approach provides the basis for the methods used in the rapid sequencing of DNA or RNA; these methods became widely available in the late 1970s.

Restriction endonucleases commonly cleave a double helix asymmetrically, leaving the single-stranded tails of one to four bases at the site of cleavage. These ends are "sticky"; that is, they tend to associate by base pairing to any complementary sequence of bases. Around 1970, it was found that strands associated in this way can be annealed and then sealed by the action of *DNA ligase,* an enzyme that joins the ends of two DNA strands by forming phosphodiester bonds between the 5′ carbon atom of one deoxyribose molecule and the 3′ carbon of the other (see Fig. 2.2). This made it possible to apply a particular restriction endonuclease to two different species of DNA and then combine the fragments together to yield a *recombinant DNA.* Thus, one had the means in principle for recombining segments of DNA in any desired manner.

In order to make these methods practical, it was necessary to be able to generate large amounts of the desired DNA sequences. This was done by taking advantage of the ability of bacteria to reproduce quickly (once every 20 minutes or so), and to yield progeny that are genetically identical; such a population is called a *clone.* In addition, bacteria can contain selfreplicating DNA in the form of a plasmid or a phage, that is separate from the bacterial chromosome. This can be used as a *vector* for transmission within the bacterium of a desired DNA fragment.

These and other mechanisms are the basis for *recombinant DNA technology.* The principles of the procedures are outlined in Fig. 2.5A. First is the construction of a recombinant DNA molecule, by snipping out DNA fragments of interest with restriction endonucleases and sealing them into a vector with DNA ligase. Second is the introduction of the vector into host bacterial cells by transformation or viral infection. Third is selection or screening of the cells for those that contain the recombinant DNA. Selection can be done by incorporating the DNA into plasmids that carry genes that confer resistance of the bacterium to a specific antibiotic; only these will survive exposure to that antibiotic. Fourth is cloning of the recombinant DNA by continued divisions of the resistant cells. Finally there is recovery of the cloned DNA fragment by restriction nuclease cleavage and electrophoretic separation.

In the above process it can be appreciated that the purer the preparation of DNA fragments to start with, the easier it is to screen the population and clone the specific fragment of interest. An effective way of preparing purer fragments was provided by the discovery that in RNA tumor viruses, the viral enzyme *reverse transcriptase* enables the RNA of the virus to be transcribed into DNA, which then becomes incorporated into the genome of the host cell and can make it cancerous. This special case therefore stands as an exception to the unidirectional flow of genetic information stated in the Central Dogma (see Fig. 2.4). Although this reverse flow does not occur in eukaryotes, it does provide molecular biologists with another powerful tool for recombinant technology. Thus, one can begin with a purified preparation of mRNA for a specific protein and use reverse transcriptase to transcribe it into a *complementary DNA* copy (cDNA; see Figs. 2.4 and 2.5B). This single strand of cDNA can then be copied into a double helix by DNA polymerase and cloned by the procedures indicated in Fig. 2.5A. This is especially useful for cloning genes coding for proteins that are present in only small amounts. Since, as noted above, this is often the case for proteins of interest in brain cells, this is an especially powerful method for neurobiology.

How does one identify specific RNA or DNA base sequences? An effective method for accomplishing this began with the simple observation that DNA that has been denatured by boiling, so that the two strands of the double helix dissociate into separate single strands, can re-form a double helix under continued moderate heating. Furthermore, a single strand will re-form a double helix with any other nucleic acid strand that is complementary to it. This second strand can be from another cell, or be artificially synthesized; thus, the two strands can be DNA:DNA, DNA:RNA, or

RNA:RNA. This process is called *hybridization*.

Hybridization provides endless possibilities for manipulating different parts of the genome. A typical example consists of radioactively labeling a specific DNA fragment and hybridizing it to a mixture of DNA, in order to determine how much of that specific DNA sequence is present in the mixture. DNA fragments used in this way are called *DNA probes*, because they function to probe an unknown sample for specific nucleic acid sequences. In this way, a probe functions somewhat like an antibody does in attaching to a specific antigen molecule. Probes can be applied to samples in which fragments have been separated by gel electrophoresis, using various blotting procedures, or they can be applied directly to sections of tissue, a procedure referred to as *in situ hybridization*. As we shall see, this approach has widespread applications to nerve cells.

Monoclonal Antibodies. Antibodies are proteins secreted by B lymphocytes in response to infection or invasion of the body by a foreign substance, called an antigen. Antibodies can be used by molecular biologists to identify specific molecules in a sample run on a gel. In order to do this, the cell or molecule of interest is first purified, and then injected as an antigen into an animal such as a rabbit. The rabbit's B lymphocytes, in response, secrete antibodies. The antiserum containing these antibodies can then be applied to the sample of interest, where the antibodies bind to the particular antigenic sites. The sample is then exposed to another antiserum previously prepared against these antibodies; the second antibodies are in turn visualized by attaching a marker molecule to them (see Fig. 2.6A). This is known as the *indirect immunocytochemical method*.

Antibodies prepared in this way are heterogeneous; each lymphocyte responding to the antigen secretes an antibody that reacts with a different part of the antigenic molecule. In addition, there may be cross-

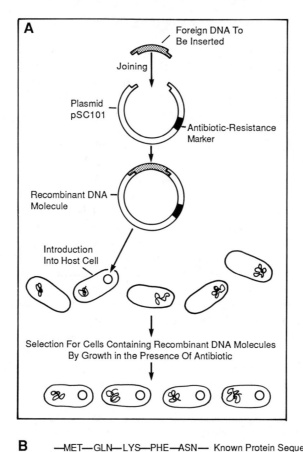

A

Foreign DNA To Be Inserted

Joining

Plasmid pSC101

Antibiotic-Resistance Marker

Recombinant DNA Molecule

Introduction Into Host Cell

Selection For Cells Containing Recombinant DNA Molecules By Growth in the Presence Of Antibiotic

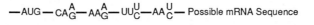

B —MET—GLN—LYS—PHE—ASN— Known Protein Sequence

—AUG—CA^A_G—AA^A_G—UU^U_C—AA^U_C— Possible mRNA Sequence

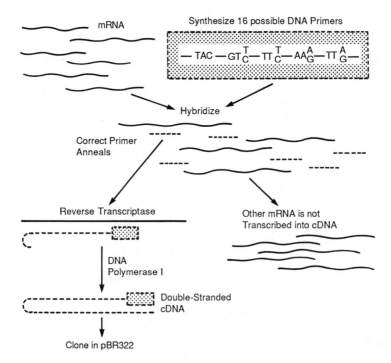

mRNA

Synthesize 16 possible DNA Primers

—TAC—GT^T_C—TT^T_C—AA^A_G—TT^A_G—

Hybridize

Correct Primer Anneals

Reverse Transcriptase

Other mRNA is not Transcribed into cDNA

DNA Polymerase I

Double-Stranded cDNA

Clone in pBR322

22

reactivity with parts of other types of antigens. Heterogeneous antisera therefore lack sufficient specificity to be of much value for cytochemical localization of molecules of interest.

What one needs is to be able to select a single antibody molecule and amplify it. The methods for achieving this goal had their origins around 1960 in the finding that certain viruses have the ability to induce cells in culture to fuse together. This produces hybrid cells which contain chromosomes from both parents and can undergo normal mitosis. It was then found that if one of the parents is from a myeloma (a type of lymphocyte tumor), the hybrid cells will retain the ability of the myeloma parent to continue multiplying indefinitely. Hybrid cells with this capacity are termed *hybridomas*. After fusion, the preparation can be exposed to selective media in which the parent cells die. The surviving cells consist of clones of the original fused cells.

By the late 1960s, it was shown that parent cells from different species (for example, human cells and mouse myeloma cells) could be fused. In addition, methods were developed for identification of individual chromosomes. Thus it became possible to construct gene maps, in which specific genes introduced from a parent line could be identified. Of great interest was the possibility that immunoglobulin-secreting hybridomas could be made, and by the early 1970s this had been achieved. Hybridomas prepared in this way were still heterogeneous in their production of antibodies. The last step was therefore to obtain a homogeneous antibody population. In 1975, George Kohler and Cesar Milstein in Cambridge showed that antibodies of a particular specificity could be obtained by screening the supernatants of individual hybridoma cells with the antigen in question, and isolating and propagating the positive cells. Those cells constituted single clonal lines secreting one type of antibody, which therefore were called *monoclonal antibodies* (see Fig. 2.6B).

These methods together constitute *hybridoma technology*. Like recombinant DNA technology, its power resides in its ability to make precise identifications of individual genes and gene products. It was quickly realized that monoclonal antibodies (mAbs) are a particularly powerful tool in the investigation of the nervous system. In some of the earliest work, Susan Hockfield and her colleagues (1983) at Cold Spring Harbor showed that mAbs not only can be used to identify specific neuronal types in the brain, but also can provide the means for analyzing the differential expression of specific gene products during development and in relation to different activity states.

Emergence of Molecular Neurobiology

Scientific fields are usually defined by their technology. The hybridoma and recombinant DNA technologies have been crucial for enabling the methods of molecular biology to be applied to the nervous system.

Fig. 2.5 Recombinant DNA procedures. **A.** DNA can be cloned, using a plasmid as a vector. **B.** Method for identifying and cloning the gene for a peptide that is present in small amounts, as is common in neurons. The known amino acid sequence of a part of the peptide is used to predict the possible sequences of the mRNA (there are alternative nucleotides for some codons). Complementary nucleotide chains to all these mRNA sequences are then synthesized by biochemical methods. This mixture is then exposed to mRNA extracted from the cells of interest; the mRNA anneals to the precise complementary nucleotide chain. This permits reverse transcription of the mRNA into cDNA, which can then be cloned by the procedure in A. This method is particularly applicable to the nervous system, where the mRNA of interest will often be present in small amounts and in a complex mixture of other mRNAs. The method was employed to make the probes needed for probing the cDNA libraries used to clone the acetylcholine receptor gene (see below). (Modified from Watson et al., 1983)

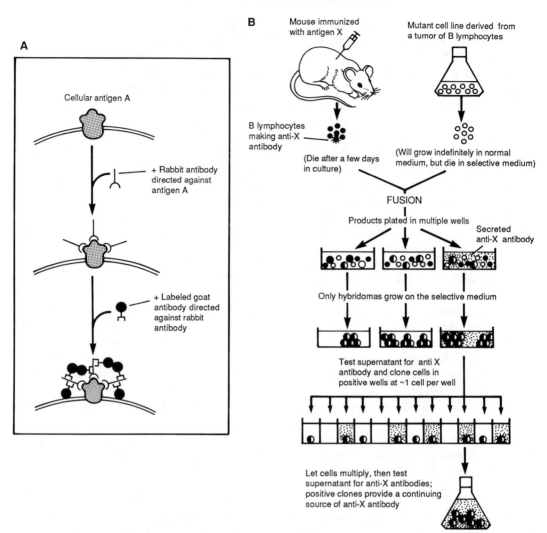

Fig. 2.6 The use of antibodies for identifying molecules in cells. **A.** The molecule of interest is used to make antibodies; these antibodies are then applied to tissue. In order to vizualise the antibodies, they are used as antigens to make antibodies to themselves; these antibodies, conjugated with a marker such as horseradish peroxidase (HRP) or fluorescein, permit the original antibody–antigen complex to be visualized. This is referred to as the indirect immunocytochemistry method. **B.** Preparation of monoclonal antibodies. This shows a summary of the main steps: initial production of polyclonal antibodies; fusion with tumor lymphocytes to produce hybridomas; screening and isolation of specific hybridoma cells; cloning of specific cells to obtain monoclonal antibodies. This method is widely applied in studies of specific molecules in the nervous system. (From Alberts et al., 1983)

Among related approaches has been the use of mutations to identify genes coding for specific proteins. For example, in *Drosophila*, mutated genes can be tagged by attachment to a movable gene segment (transposon tagging); subsequent mating produces a *dysgenic hybrid* which has high levels of the mutation. One can use this method to screen for resulting transposons and their neighboring genes which may code for proteins of interest, such as specific types of membrane channel proteins.

A related technique is *site-directed muta-genesis,* in which mutations are induced in genes or cDNAs that code for subunits of a membrane protein; in this way, the expression of these genes through corresponding mRNAs, and the contributions of peptide sequences within each subunit to specific properties of the whole protein (such as ion movements through a membrane channel), can be assessed.

While these methods provide the means to identify genes and gene products, other methods are needed to characterize their three-dimensional structures and their functions. In *anatomy,* the electron microscope has revealed images of genes undergoing transcription into RNA, as well as RNA undergoing translation into polypeptides. Methods for negative staining and low-angle diffraction have been developed to permit image reconstruction of the three-dimensional shapes of membrane proteins. In *electrophysiology,* the glass micropipette has been refined into a tool for patch-clamping cell membranes, which permits recording of the electrical properties of a single-channel-forming protein within the membrane of a neuron or other type of cell (see below). In *neurochemistry,* a variety of histochemical methods are permitting the identification of specific enzymes, transmitters, second messengers, and other substances that mediate the functions of neurons. In addition, radioactive isotopes are being tagged onto neuroactive molecules and used to construct maps of ligand binding sites and functional activity throughout the entire brain. Computer technology plays an important role in many of these advances, by permitting automation of cell and molecular screening procedures, acquisition and analysis of patch-clamp data, and reconstruction of images from electron microscopy and tomography.

We will have frequent occasion to refer to these methods, and explain them in further detail, later in this chapter, and in every subsequent chapter in this book. It is exhilarating to realize that these represent only a beginning; that new methods, drawing on the entire range of technologies being developed to explore physical and biological materials, will be applied at an increasing rate in the months and years ahead for unraveling the molecular basis of nervous activity.

Mechanisms of a Receptor Molecule

Thus far, we have considered the techniques of molecular neurobiology on an individual basis. However, the real power comes when several of them are applied to a particular problem, so that a coherent picture, correlating molecular structure and function, can emerge.

The best example thus far in which this has been possible is the mechanism of transmission of signals from a motor nerve fiber to a muscle. This takes place at a specialized site of apposition between the nerve fiber and the muscle, called the neuromuscular junction. Since the 1940s, it has been studied as a model synapse, and in recent years it has been a primary focus for the application of the new tools of molecular neurobiology. We will therefore summarize briefly the ways that these methods have been applied, and the model they have produced for the way that a chemical signal brings about a response at the molecular level of a synapse.

Overview of the Neuromuscular Junction

When we move our muscles to perform a motor act, the signal to do so has to pass from our nervous system to the muscle fibers to be contracted. The signals are conveyed by nerve cells called motoneurons, situated with their cell bodies in the spinal cord and brainstem. The signals are in the form of nerve impulses, carried in the long fiber, called an axon, of the motoneuron (see Fig. 2.7A). Each muscle in our body is composed of many individual muscle fibers. At the muscle, the motor axon divides a number of times, and each terminal branch finds its way to an individual muscle fiber. There the terminal runs along a length of the muscle fiber, forming

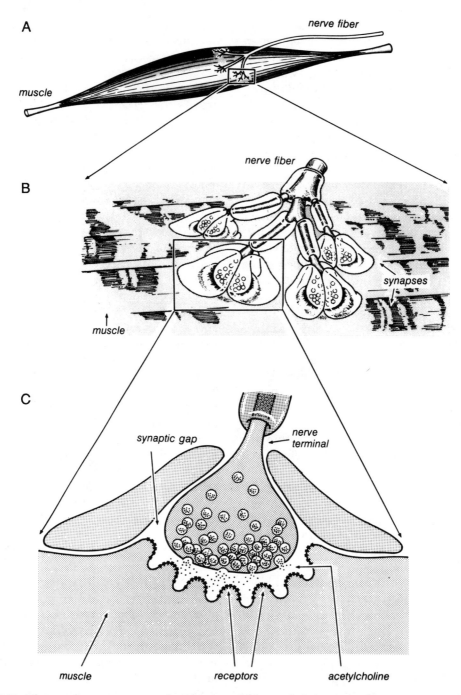

Fig. 2.7 The vertebrate neuromuscular junction. **A.** A muscle is innervated by a motor nerve fiber. **B.** The nerve fiber branches to form synaptic junctions with individual muscle fibers. **C.** Each neuromuscular junction consists of a presynaptic nerve terminal from which neurotransmitter (acetylcholine) is released; a synaptic cleft; a postsynaptic area on the muscle containing the acetylcholine receptors; and a surrounding envelope of glia. (From Miller, 1983)

the specialized region of contact with the underlying muscle membrane called the neuromuscular junction (see Fig. 2.7B).

Like every other synapse, the neuromuscular junction is made up of a presynaptic process (the axon terminal, in this case) and a postsynaptic process (the muscle). The nerve impulse traveling down the motoneuron axon spreads into the terminals, as shown in B, where it triggers the release of a chemical substance called a neurotransmitter, in this case, a small molecule named acetylcholine (ACh). There is considerable evidence that most of the release is associated with tiny spheres, called vesicles, that fuse with the terminal membrane facing the narrow space, or cleft, between the two processes (Fig. 2.7C). The ACh diffuses the short distance (approximately 60 nm) across the cleft to reach receptor molecules in the specialized endplate region of the muscle membrane. Activation of these receptors causes ions to flow through them across the membrane, thereby initiating the electrical response of the muscle, called the endplate potential (EPP). This in turn spreads from the endplate region to the surrounding muscle membrane, initiating the impulse response of the muscle that finally leads to muscle contraction.

All of the steps just described, from the nerve impulse in the motoneuron axon through the steps of synaptic transmission at the neuromuscular junction to the contraction of the muscle fibers, will be discussed in detail later (Chaps. 6, 7, 8, and 17).

It can be appreciated that, among the steps involved in nervous transmission described above, the action of the neurotransmitter substance on this molecular receptor is the crucial link that provides for communication of information between cells. Because of its importance, and because it is accessible to physiological analysis and can be obtained in large quantities for biochemical analysis, the ACh receptor at the neuromuscular junction has become the most thoroughly studied and best understood of all receptor proteins at the molecular level.

We will therefore focus on this receptor, and ask: what is its molecular composition, how is it encoded in the genome, and how does it function at the molecular level?

Amino Acid Sequence of the Acetycholine Receptor Molecule

The first question to ask about the ACh receptor is, what kind of macromolecule is it? Over the years, there were speculations that it was a lipid or an enzyme. However, by the 1960s, it was generally agreed that it was a receptor protein. By around 1980, it was established that it is a pentameric protein, that is, made up of five separate polypeptide chains, or subunits. One chain, labeled α (alpha), is double, and there are single copies of β (beta), γ (gamma), and δ (delta). The total molecular weight, as determined biochemically by polyacrylamide gel electrophoresis (PAGE), was approximately 250,000; the recent revised estimate (see below) is approximately 270,000, with molecular weights for the four subunits of approximately 40,000, 48,000, 58,000 and 64,000 respectively. It has been known for some time that the α subunits are the sites of binding of the ACh.

In order to characterize this protein biochemically, it was an advantage to find a tissue where it was present in high concentration; this is a common strategy for any biochemical analysis. Such a tissue is present in the electric ray, *Torpedo*. This species of cartilaginous fish has an electric organ, composed of flattened modified muscle cells arranged in parallel columns called electroplaques. Each cell has a neuromuscular junction that covers much of one face of the cell. Transmission takes place at the junction in the usual manner described above. However, because of the flattened geometry of the cells and their innervation on only one side, there is an electrical asymmetry of the cell so that there is a net electrical potential between the two faces. The stacked arrangement of the cells further means that the voltages of the cells add together like batteries connected in series. Thus, an electroplaque containing a

Table 2.2   Steps for identifying primary structure of α subunit precursor of ACh receptor

Step 1. Determine an initial sequence of 54 amino acids at the amino-terminal end of all 4 polypeptide subunits derived from *Torpedo californica,* using amino acid sequencing methods; this step was done by Raftery, Hood, and colleagues in 1980.

Step 2. Obtain poly(A) mRNA from an electric organ by extracting total RNA and subjecting it to oligo(dT)-cellulose chromatography.

Step 3. Mix poly(A) mRNA with vector–primer DNA and avian myeloblastosis virus reverse transcriptase to produce cDNA transcripts.

Step 4. Insert cDNA into DNA of χ1776 or HB101 plasmid vector.

Step 5. Infect and transform *Escherichia coli* bacteria with these plasmids.

Step 6. Grow transformed ampicillin-resistant *E. coli* clones to produce a plasmid cDNA "library." Steps 4–6 were performed according to the method of Okayama and Berg.

Step 7. Screen a library of some 200,000 clones by hybridization to an oligonucleotide probe, which included all possible cDNA sequences for a known short peptide sequence (positions 25–29 in Fig. 2.8) within the previously determined amino-terminal region (see step 1 above). This yielded 57 hybridization-positive clones.

Step 8. Rescreen these 57 clones by hybridization with a second probe, which included cDNA sequences for a second peptide sequence (residues at positions 13–18 in Fig. 2.8). This narrowed the field to 20 clones.

Step 9. Map these clones with restriction endonucleases, to show the presence of common restriction sites in all clones, suggesting that they represent a single mRNA species.

Step 10. Select two of these clones with the largest cDNA inserts and carry out rapid nucleotide sequence analysis by the method of Maxam and Gilbert, to obtain the nucleotide sequence for the entire α-subunit precursor molecule.

Step 11. Begin with the known reading frames for the initial 54 amino-terminal amino acids and read off the triplet codons in the nucleotide sequence, to give the amino acid sequence for the entire α-subunit precursor molecule.

---

column of 500 cells can generate a potential of 500 times 150 mV = 75 volts. The fish uses this to stun its prey. This is a good example of how cells and cell mechanisms are adapted for specialized functions; the neuromuscular junction in this tissue functions in the normal manner, but it activates musclelike cells that have lost their contractile apparatus and have become specialized for voltage generation. Since as much as half of the innervated membrane of the cell may be occupied by ACh receptors, the electroplaque has been an excellent source of this protein for many of the biochemical studies that have been carried out to date.

Using this preparation, it was possible to apply recombinant DNA technology to clone and sequence the DNA that codes for each of the polypeptide subunits of the ACh receptor. This was first accomplished by Toni Claudio and her colleagues (1983) at the Salk Institute in California for the γ subunit. At about the same time, Shosaku Numa's laboratory at Kyoto University worked out the sequences for the α subunit,

and shortly thereafter for the other subunits.

Earlier in this chapter we summarized the main principles involved in this type of analysis. The application of these principles is illustrated in Table 2.2, which summarizes the main steps in obtaining the amino acid sequence for the α subunit of the ACh receptor protein. The student can work through these steps in reference to the sequence displayed previously in Fig. 2.5.

From this analysis it was concluded that the α-subunit precursor is composed of 461 amino acids, with the sequence indicated in Fig. 2.8. This subunit is referred to as "precursor" because it represents the molecule before it is processed and joined to the other subunits and inserted into the postsynaptic membrane. After an initial 5' amino-terminal untranslated sequence of 160 nucleotides, there is a 24-residue sequence containing mostly hydrophobic amino acids, thus resembling the signal peptide of secretory proteins (see Chap. 8). This hydrophobic sequence is cleaved and may be involved in translocation of the

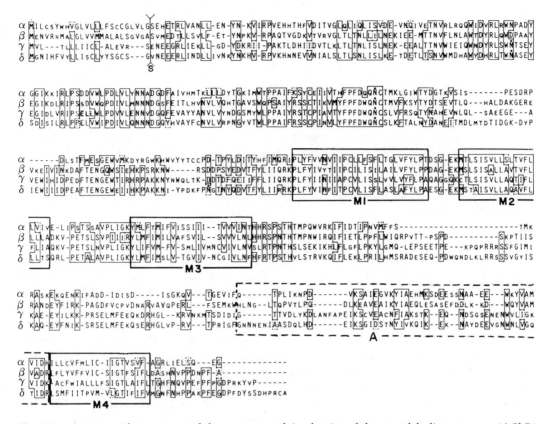

Fig. 2.8 Amino acid sequences of the α, β, γ, and δ subunits of the acetylcholine receptor (AChR) of *Torpedo californica*, as deduced from cDNA clones. Amino acids that are identical in at least three of the subunits at a given position are enclosed in solid lines. Amino acids at a given position which have opposite hydrophilic or hydrophobic properties are enclosed in dotted lines. The four transmembrane α-helices originally proposed by Claudio et al. (1983) and Numa et al. (1983) are indicated by heavily lined boxes. The amphipathic α-helix (see text) is indicated by a dashed line box. The cleavage site of the signal protein is indicated by S. Recent studies show that other types of ligand-binding channels, such as those for the neurotransmitters γ-aminobutyric acid (GABA) and glycine, share sequence homologies with the nicotinic ACh receptor. (From Numa et al, 1983, in Changeux et al. 1984)

subunit into the synaptic site at the plasma membrane.

In further work, the primary sequence of the *mammalian* ACh receptor α subunit was obtained, using a cDNA fragment for the *Torpedo* α subunit to probe a library of cloned cDNA from newborn calf muscle. This showed exactly the same number of amino acids, and over 80% sequence homology. In addition, a *human* genomic DNA library was screened by hybridization with a calf α-subunit cDNA probe. By nucleotide analysis of the cloned human DNA, it

was possible to show the structure of the human gene for the ACh receptor α-subunit. As shown in Fig. 2.9 this has the common form of a split gene, with eight introns separating nine exons. The exons appear to correspond to some degree with different functional domains of the subunit (see below). The complete sequence of the human α subunit consists of 457 amino acids, showing 97% homology with the α subunit of the calf. This presumably reflects the closeness of the cow and human on the evolutionary scale. The other subunits (β,

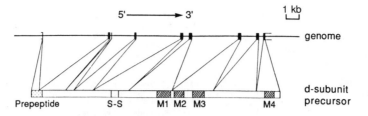

Fig. 2.9 Arrangement of the gene that codes for the ACh receptor α-subunit peptide in the human. The 5′ to 3′ orientation of the chromosomal DNA is indicated above; the scale shows 1 kilobase (kb). M1–4 represent the membrane-spanning segments of the α-subunit peptide as originally proposed; S–S, disulfide bonds near the ACh binding site. Note that nine exons code for the α-subunit precursor peptide; several exons appear to code for different structural and functional domains. (From Numa et al, 1983)

γ, δ) have also been sequenced, and show considerable homologies with the α-subunits (see Fig. 2.8).

Functional Organization of the Acetylcholine Receptor Molecule

The acetylcholine receptor molecule does not exist as a straight chain of amino acids; like DNA and other macromolecules, it has a three-dimensional, or secondary, structure, determined by the angles of the covalent bonding and the weak bonds between nearby parts of the chain. The weak forces are particularly important for the α-helical structure of DNA and RNA, and the secondary structure of all proteins. Interactions between distant parts of the chain determine the overall, tertiary, structure of the molecule.

A variety of methods have been used to obtain evidence regarding the tertiary structure of the ACh receptor. To begin with, some clues can be gathered from the primary structure itself. There are several regions of the molecule in which many of the amino acids are uncharged and nonpolar. These regions are therefore hydrophobic; they do not form weak bonds with water molecules, and in fact repel them. Previous studies of bacteriorhodopsin, the light-sensitive membrane protein of bacteria, had shown that such hydrophobic sequences are contained within the plasma membrane, where the interior is also hydrophobic because of the lipid tails of the phospholipids. In the ACh receptor (AChR)

subunits, four of these sequences were originally identified (Figs. 2.8 and 2.10A); in the α subunit they were labeled M1–M4 (see Fig. 2.8). Each sequence was 19–27 amino acids in length. Assuming that they are arranged in an α-helix, this is sufficient to span the membrane (approximately 4 nm thick). Subsequently, evidence was obtained in the α subunit for an additional intramembranous sequence, M5, between M3 and M4 (see Figs. 2.8 and 2.10B). The precise conformations of the receptor subunits are still controversial; a current view is shown in Fig. 2.10B.

The α subunit of the ACh receptor molecule thus appears to thread its way back and forth across the plasma membrane in the manner illustrated in Fig. 2.10B. As can be seen, this leaves almost half of the length of the molecule (from the 5′ amino terminal to residue 210) protruding into the extracellular space outside the membrane. Within this segment are several sequences believed to be arranged in α-helices, and several folded into β-sheets. On the inside, there is a relatively long sequence protruding into the cytoplasm between M3 and M4 (see Fig. 2.10B). Since it is known that the amino-terminal portion lies outside, the presence of five membrane-spanning segments requires that the carboxy-terminal portion lie inside, and this is in accord with recent experiments. The other subunits are similar in their primary structure, and are also believed to be similar in their secondary structure.

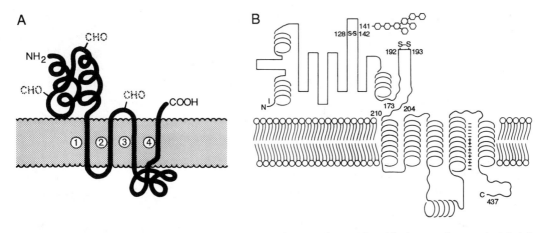

Fig. 2.10   Tertiary structure of the ACh receptor subunit polypeptide with the membrane. **A.** Model of Claudio et al. (1983) for the γ subunit. Possible membrane spanning segments are indicated by ① to ④. Possible glycosylation sites are indicated by hatched CHO groups. **B.** Model of the α-subunit according to Finer-Moore and Stroud (1984). The site of binding of ACh is believed to be near the disulfide bond linking the cysteine residues at positions 192 and 193. The neurotoxin α-bungarotoxin binds to the 32-residue peptide 173–204. The asparagine residue 141 is shown as the site of N-glycosylation, from which the carbohydrate moiety of this glycoprotein arises and extends into the extracellular space. In this model there are five transmembrane segments; one of these is an amphipathic helix which is believed to form the wall of the ionic channel (see text). (Drawing by Tom Lentz, after Finer-Moore and Stroud, 1984) For an alternative view of the folding of the ACh receptor molecule within the membrane, based on monoclonal antibodies directed against extracellular and intracellular segments of the peptide rather than deductions based on hydrophobicity, see Ratnam et al. (1986).

Each subunit is encoded by a separate gene. Gene expression therefore must be coordinated within this gene family in order for the entire ACh receptor to be assembled. It is presently envisioned that each subunit is translated from its mRNA by rRNA in the endoplasmic reticulum (see Chap. 3), where the M1–M3 segments anchor the newly formed molecule within the endoplasmic membrane. Posttranslational processing includes the infolding of segments M4 and M5 within the membrane. The five subunits then come together and are inserted into the postsynaptic plasma membrane in a circular arrangement, in the sequence α-β-α-γ-δ or α-γ-α-β-δ in clockwise rotation as one looks down on it from outside. The resulting three-dimensional structure is depicted in Fig. 2.11.

How does this structure provide for ACh binding and generation of an electrical signal? Let us consider each step briefly.

The sites of ACh binding are known to be on the α subunits. The main binding site is near the disulfide bridge (residues 192–193 in Fig. 2.10B.) Acetylcholine acts as a ligand for the receptor, interacting with

Fig. 2.11   Three-dimensional representations of the ACh receptor, showing arrangement of the two α and single β, γ, and δ subunits around a central channel. There is controversy about whether the α subunits are separated by a β (as shown) or a γ subunit. Each α subunit has an ACh binding site. (Based on Kistler et al., 1982)

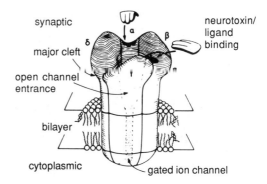

these sites by means of relatively weak bonds, such as hydrogen and hydrophobic bonds.

The circular arrangement of the subunits provides for the formation of a central pore, or channel. The structure of the channel has been the subject of lively debate. It is generally agreed that the channel is shaped like a funnel, with a large, cone-shaped vestibule facing outward, formed by the long external amino-terminal sequences of the subunits. The narrow part of the channel lies within the membrane; in one current view, its walls are formed by the M5 sequences of each of the subunits. These sequences contain charged amino acids, and computerized analysis has shown that their positive and negative charges line up on one side of the α-helices in which they are contained whereas hydrophobic side chains line up on the other side. A helix with these properties is called amphipathic. This provides the channel walls with a mixture of positive and negative charges that makes the appropriate interface with the water molecules filling the channel.

The biochemical and structural studies thus suggest the following mechanism. Acetylcholine binds to receptor sites on the external amino-terminal portions of the α subunits of the ACh receptor protein. This binding is signaled to the rest of the α subunits by means of changes in the secondary structure of the intramembranous parts of the subunits and the other subunit polypeptides. Such intramolecular changes are termed allosteric, and are a common consequence of the binding of a protein or enzyme to its ligand or substrate. At rest, the diameter of the channel and the distribution of charges lining it are such that few ions can pass through. The allosteric changes induced by ACh binding cause a slight widening of the diameter and a shift in the charge distribution lining the wall such that positively charged ions, called cations, can pass through. The channel is said to be selective for these ions. The main ions that move are K^+, from inside to outside, and Na^+, from outside to inside.

This movement of ions changes the electrical charge across the membrane, generating the electrical response termed the synaptic potential. This response in turn initiates the events that lead to contraction of the muscle.

Physiological Action of the Receptor Molecule

The mechanism postulated from the molecular structure of the ACh receptor described above must be tested by physiological recordings of the receptor in action. Since the function of the receptor is to control the movement of ions through the channel, one wants to measure this as an electrical current by using electrophysiological recording techniques.

The fact that the receptor protein is embedded in a membrane turns out to be of great practical value in this respect. Beginning in the late 1960s, scientists found that they could measure the electrical current through single channel-forming proteins that had been inserted into artificial membrane bilayers. This approach was extended to living cells by a method called patch clamping. In this method, developed by Erwin Neher and Bert Sakmann in West Germany in the late 1970s (see Sakmann and Neher, 1983), a fine glass tube is pulled out to form a micropipette with a tip diameter of 2–3 μm, and filled with an electrically conducting salt solution. If great care is taken to make the tip very clean, and the surface of a cell, such as a muscle cell, is also very clean, the tip can be gently placed on the cell surface and it will seal very tightly to the membrane. When this happens, the resistance from the inside of the pipette to ground increases dramatically, from the range of thousands of ohms (kilohms) to billions of ohms (gigohms = 10^9 ohms). The membrane encircled by the tip is called a patch; analysis can be carried out with the electrical potential across the membrane clamped at different values in order to obtain the currents that flow through the patch, hence the term patch-clamp recording.

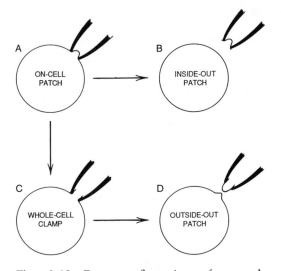

Fig. 2.12 Four configurations for patch clamping. **A.** An on-cell or cell-attached patch is studied with the cell intact. **B.** By withdrawing the patch pipette, one can isolate the patch of membrane under the pipette; this is termed an "inside-out patch" because the inside of the membrane faces the bath. **C.** If additional suction is applied to the cell-attached patch to rupture the membrane under the pipette, the whole-cell membrane potential may be controlled through the pipette, enabling study of the cell with a whole-cell clamp. **D.** From the whole-cell patch, the pipette can be slowly withdrawn to form a tube of membrane, which pinches off to create an outside-out patch. (From Corey, 1983)

Patch recordings can be carried out with different relations between the tip and the cell membrane. Several of the basic configurations are indicated in the diagram of Fig. 2.12. The *whole-cell recording* is similar to the traditional mode of intracellular recording. The *on-cell* (cell-attached) *patch* is the simplest and most direct mode of single-channel analysis. This patch can be removed directly to give an *inside-out patch*. Alternatively, the electrode can be gently withdrawn from a whole-cell configuration, pulling the membrane into an *outside-out patch*. Each of these configurations has advantages and disadvantages for analyzing particular properties of channel proteins, as summarized in Table 2.3. The

student may refer to these configurations when studying results discussed in later chapters.

The information that one can obtain about the functional properties of the ACh receptor protein is in the form of recording traces, as illustrated in Fig. 2.13. The properties may be summarized as follows. The channel opens abruptly (activates) ①, has a constant open conductance ②, and closes abruptly (inactivates) ③. These are general properties of all channel proteins thus far studied, and suggest that the protein jumps from one conformation to another. There are different open times ④; the shorter open times may be due to binding of a single ACh molecule, whereas the longer open times may be due to binding of two or more molecules. The open states are often interrupted by brief closings ⑤; the molecule thus appears to "flicker" between the open and closed states. This may occur several times while the ACh molecule unbinds slowly from its binding site. The channel can flicker between the open state and other partially closed states ⑥, indicating that there may be substates between the two. Finally, the noise level during the open state is often higher than at rest ⑦. This channel noise has implied that the open channel "quivers" as a result of the motion of water or neighboring lipid molecules in the membrane.

These remarkable recordings thus give us an immediate sense of looking directly at the action of a single molecule; in the words of the poet Wordsworth, it is as if "we see into the life of things." The protein undergoes abrupt changes in its molecular conformation, which cause abrupt changes in the channel conductance states. This seems to be a fundamental property of channel proteins, whether they are neurotransmitter receptors activated by different ligands, or excitable channels activated by changes in membrane voltage, and regardless of what kinds of ions are controlled. Further studies are presently being pursued, using methods such as site-directed mutagenesis, to alter different parts of the polypeptide

Table 2.3 Advantages and disadvantages of four configurations for patch clamping

Method	Advantages	Disadvantages
On-cell patch (single channels)	no perfusion needed does not disturb cytoplasm modulatory systems intact	cannot change intracellular medium must measure membrane potential with another electrode
Excised inside-out patch (single channels)	access to both sides of membrane can change concentration of intracellular ions or regulatory substances, or apply enzymes to inner surface of membrane	cannot change outside medium during experiment must have low-Ca^{2+}-concentration bath perfusion to prevent vesiculation
Whole-cell clamp (average current through many channels)	can change internal medium to isolate currents low access resistance allows single-pipette voltage clamp with good speed (<0.5 msec)	necessary to exchange internal medium hard to clamp cells much bigger than 30–40 μm in diameter
Excised outside-out patch (single channels)	access to both sides of membrane no bath perfusion needed can change concentration of extracellular substances such as neurotransmitters	cannot change inside medium during experiment must have low Ca^{2+} in pipette to prevent vesiculation

(From Corey, 1983)

Fig. 2.13 Patch recordings of ionic current through single acetylcholine receptor channels. The main characteristics of the channel activity are labeled ① through ⑦, and are described in the text. **A** and **B** are from a cell-attached patch on a myoball preparation from rat myotubes (embryonic muscle cells); **C** is from an outside-out patch. (From F. J. Sigworth, in Corey, 1983)

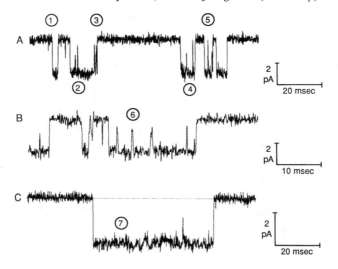

chains, to understand the contribution of each part to binding selectivity, ionic selectivity, and channel kinetics.

Mechanism of Neuromuscular Transmission

Let us now see how these single-channel conductances are related to the sequence of events during neuromuscular transmission that we outlined in connection with Fig. 2.7. Our description will serve also as an introduction to many molecular and cellular properties underlying synaptic transmission that will be subjects of closer study in later chapters.

Transmission from the nerve ending at the neuromuscular junction takes place at localized sites called *active zones*. As shown in Fig. 2.14A, these are characterized by a density of the cytoplasm; an accumulation of small spheres, called vesicles; and an outward bulging of the cell membrane. The elegant experiments of John Heuser and Tom Reese have shown that stimulation of the nerve ending causes the vesicles to fuse with the cell membrane. This process, known

Fig. 2.14 Morphology of the neuromuscular junction of a frog. **A.** Electron micrograph of frog neuromuscular junction. (From Heuser and Reese, 1977) **B.** Freeze-fracture electron micrograph of synaptic vesicles, showing two sites where vesicles are about to fuse with the plasmalemma. Note absence of intramembranous particles at these sites. (From Heuser, 1977) **C.** Diagrams of proposed mechanisms for fusion of vesicle with plasma membrane. Fusion occurs only when fluidity of membrane lipids is raised, allowing lateral displacement (b) of membrane proteins (intramembranous particles) so that fusion can occur (c). (From Maddrell and Nordmann, 1979) Enzymes involved in vesicle fusion are discussed further in Chap. 4.

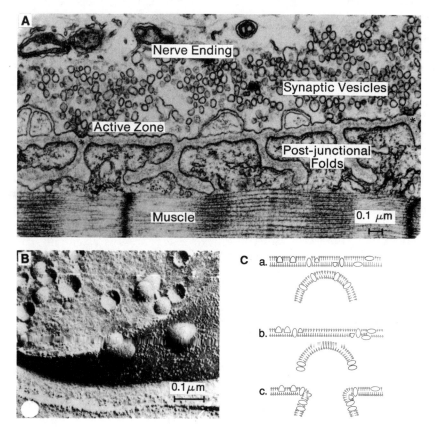

as exocytosis, is widely used in cells to release substances contained in the vesicles. The mechanism of vesicle fusion has been the subject of intensive study by a variety of methods. Fig. 2.14B shows an image obtained by the freeze-fracture technique, which will be described further in Chap. 4. The molecular mechanisms that bring vesicles to the surface and allow them to fuse with the cell membrane (see Fig. 2.14C) will be discussed further in Chap. 4.

Our understanding of the process for release of ACh from the nerve terminal and the subsequent events that give rise to a response in the muscle membrane is based on the brilliant investigations of Bernard Katz and his co-workers, beginning in the early 1950s. We can incorporate these classical findings with the newer results by starting with the molecular events and building up to the muscle response in the following way.

At the molecular level, the effect of ACh is to open conductance channels in the endplate membrane, as shown in Fig. 2.15D. When channels open together, they change the electrical potential across the endplate membrane. The smallest change is an increase in "noise," due to slow "leaking" of ACh from the nerve terminal. The next larger change is caused by a number of channels opening in synchrony. This is called a miniature end-plate potential (MEPP in Fig. 2.15C). It was discovered by del Castilo and Katz in 1954. The unitary nature of the MEPP indicates that it is due to a packet, or quantum, of ACh. Somewhere between 1000 and 10,000 ACh molecules are contained in each quantum. The quantal nature of transmitter release and action has been fundamental to our understanding of synaptic transmission. It has been tempting to equate one quantum with one vesicle, but this has turned out to be a complicated problem, which will be discussed further in Chap. 7.

A single MEPP is due to a quantum released at a single active zone. When several quanta occur at or about the same time, their effects summate to produce a larger potential, as shown in Fig. 2.15B. When the motoneuron wants to signal the muscle to contract, the impulse it sends through the axon invades the terminal and depolarizes the membrane of the nerve terminal. There are approximately 1000 active zones in a typical ending. They do not all automatically release their quanta when depolarized by the impulse. Each one has a certain probability of release, so that the total number of quanta released, m, is equal to the number, n, of possible quanta (i.e., roughly the number of active zones) times the average probability of release, p, so that one has the following relationship:

$$m = n \, p$$

This simple equation summarizes the quantal hypothesis, and was used by del Castillo, Katz, Martin, and subsequent workers to develop the idea that quantal release is a statistical, probabilistic process, not a deterministic process. An impulse releases 100–200 quanta, implying a p of .1–.2. The quanta are released in synchrony by the impulse, and their effects summate to give a large potential, called the endplate potential (EPP), which can be recorded by an electrode with its tip inserted inside the muscle fiber near the endplate. As shown in Fig. 2.15A, the EPP spreads from the endplate to initiate the muscle impulse, that leads to muscle contraction.

The release of transmitter molecules in quanta has been found at several types of synapses, and may apply to most chemical synapses. It is important to realize that the release process is essentially controlled by the amount of depolarization of the nerve terminal membrane; as shown in Fig. 2.16, the more the applied depolarization in the terminal, the more the depolarizing response in the endplate membrane. This is an expression of a generalization linking depolarization with Ca^{2+} entry and transmitter release (see Chap. 7). Special note should be made of the fact that the nerve terminal depolarization increases the frequency (probability of occurrence) of the MEPPs; the individual amplitudes remain

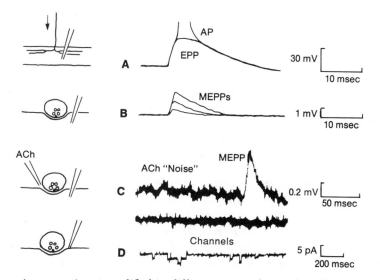

Fig. 2.15 Synaptic properties exemplified in different types of recordings from the neuromuscular junction. **A.** Intracellular recording of endplate potential (EPP) giving rise to an action potential (AP) in the muscle cell: experimental setup shown at left. **B.** High-gain recording, showing summation of miniature endplate potentials (MEPPs). **C.** Very high gain recording, showing noise induced by ionophoresis of ACh (compare with control trace below). **D.** Extracellular "patch clamp" recording from junctional site, showing currents passing through single AChR channels. This was one of the first reports of single-channel activity, using a subgigohm (<10^9 ohms) recording seal. (A–C from Katz, Miledi, and colleagues (see text); D from Neher and Steinbach, 1978)

Fig. 2.16 Presynaptic control of the frequency of miniature endplate potentials (MEPPs). **A.** Recordings at three levels of depolarization of terminals. Recordings (upper traces) were made as in Fig. 2.15B, while current (bottom traces) was applied to the presynaptic nerves through an extracellular electrode. (From del Castillo and Katz, in Katz, 1962). **B.** Graph showing dependence of MEPP frequency on relative polarization of presynaptic terminals (From Liley, in Katz, 1962)

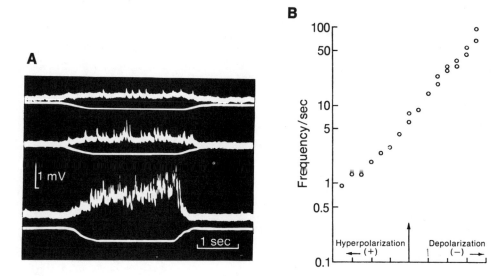

the same. The experiment in Fig. 2.16 shows clearly how the depolarizing response is due to the summation of MEPPs overlapping in time.

Grading of postsynaptic responses with the amount of presynaptic depolarization is a crucial property for synapses in many central regions. A synapse from an incoming axon terminal is normally activated by an impulse invading the terminal, but a synapse from a dendrite may be activated by the graded depolarizations of synaptic potentials within that dendrite. The grading of depolarizations, and the differing probabilities of release, are properties that add to the complexity of operation of synaptic circuits in a number of regions of the nervous system, and need to be kept in mind as we apply the neuromuscular junction model to other synapse.

This completes our introduction to the molecular mechanisms of a model synapse. There is more to learn about the neuromuscular junction: We will study how the receptors are translated from the genome and inserted in the membrane (Chap. 3), and how the junction is formed during development (Chap. 9). We will also compare the junction with other synapses, and see how biochemical mechanisms can come into play to provide for more complex and long-lasting effects that enable synapses in different parts of the nervous system to contribute to such higher functions as memory (Chaps. 8 and 29).

3

The Neuron

The Cellular Basis of Neurobiology: A Brief History

Until about 100 years ago, it was not known whether the cell theory applied to the nervous system. As early as 1836, Jan Purkinje, the great Czech anatomist, had published observations of cells (which later would bear his name) in the cerebellum, but, as can be seen in Fig. 3.1A, these showed little more than the nucleus and surrounding cytoplasm. An important advance was made in 1865, when the observations of Otto Deiters of Bonn were published. In his diagram of a large motor neuron of the spinal cord (Fig. 3.1B), he distinguished between two kinds of fiber arising from the cell body. One kind consisted of a number of branches which appeared to be extensions of the cell body, and which he termed "protoplasmic prolongations," *protoplasm* being the traditional term for the living substance of the cell. The other kind consisted of a single, unbranched, tubular process, or "axis cylinder," which arose from a small, conical mound on the cell body, and in turn became the fiber which left the spinal cord and entered the peripheral nerve that supplied the muscles. The protoplasmic pro-

longations came eventually to be called "dendrites," a term borrowed from botany, meaning, simply, branches. The axis cylinder came to be called "axon." You should be able to distinguish axon from dendrites in Fig. 3.1B.

Despite these advances, a single nerve cell had not yet been seen in its entirety. One could therefore only speculate as to how nerve cells were organized. Many believed that when an axon split up into fine branches within the brain, those branches became continuous with the finest branches of dendrites of other cells, in much the same way that the smallest arteries and veins in the body communicate through capillaries. This became known as the "reticular theory" of nervous organization, in opposition to the cell theory, in which each nerve cell was conceived of as a separate entity whose branches terminate in "free nerve endings."

It seemed almost impossible to resolve this issue, because even if a method could be found that made it possible to stain the finest branches, they would be obscured by the thousands of other branches around them. What was needed was a method that would stain only a few percent of the cells, but stain them in their entirety. And that

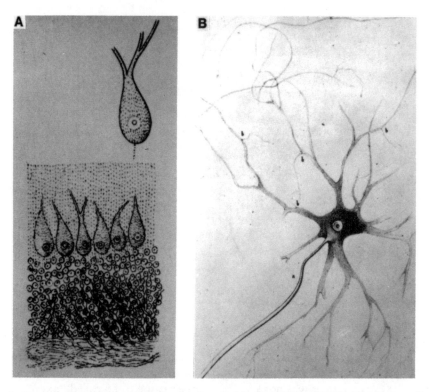

Fig. 3.1 **A.** Nerve cells in the cerebellum, as observed by Purkinje in 1837. The large cells are now known as Purkinje cells; the small cells packed tightly below are granule cells. The cerebellum is discussed in Chap. 21. **B.** A large motoneuron in the spinal cord, as observed by Deiters in 1865. Note the single long, smooth axon, which is distinctly different in appearance from the branching dendrites. The spinal cord is discussed in Chap. 20. (From Liddell, 1960)

is exactly what happened! In 1873, an impoverished doctor, Camillo Golgi of Pavia, was carrying out experiments by candlelight in his kitchen, trying to find a better way to visualize nerve cells. Among the many different methods he tried was a combination of potassium dichromate fixation and silver impregnation. To his astonishment, in nervous tissue this method revealed, here and there, a few cells with their cell bodies and dendrites stained completely black, out to the finest terminal branches. Golgi applied his method to a number of different parts of the nervous system, and published his results in 1885, in a comprehensive work in Italian. At first it aroused little interest among anatomists, and the full implications of the results were not realized until a Spanish histologist, Santiago Ramón y Cajal, working in a small laboratory in Barcelona, stumbled on the

method in 1888. The effect of this new vision of the nervous system is best described in his own words (as translated by Sherrington, 1935):

Against a clear background stood black threadlets, some slender and smooth, some thick and thorny, in a pattern punctuated by small dense spots, stellate or fusiform. All was sharp as a sketch with Chinese ink on transparent Japanpaper. And to think that that was the same tissue which when stained with carmine or logwood left the eye in a tangled thicket where sight may stare and grope for ever fruitlessly, baffled in its effort to unravel confusion and lost for ever in a twilit doubt. Here, on the contrary, all was clear and plain as a diagram. A look was enough. Dumbfounded, I could not take my eye from the microscope.

Cajal worked feverishly, developing the Golgi method and applying it to many parts of the nervous system in many animal spe-

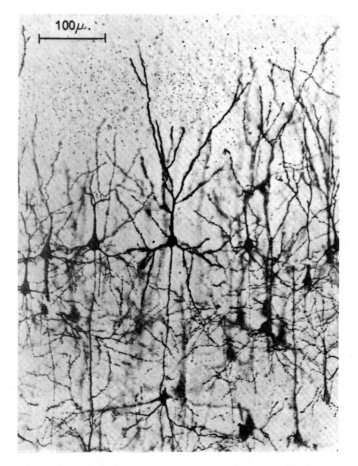

Fig. 3.2 Neurons in the visual cortex of the cat impregnated by the Golgi method. Can you identify the cell bodies, apical dendrites, basal dendrites, and axons of these neurons? (From Sholl, 1956)

cies. Figure 3.2 shows some cells in the cerebral cortex. Cajal had the genius to realize that the entity stained by the method was, in fact, the entire nerve cell, and that this procedure provided the long-sought proof that each nerve cell is an entity, separate from the others. He also deduced the basic principles that nervous signals pass through the dendrites as well as the axon of a cell, and that transmission between cells takes place where their axons and dendrites contact each other.

Cajal's outpouring of publications between 1888 and 1891 attracted a number of other anatomists, and most of them agreed with his interpretations. These ideas also fit with conclusions that had been reached from studies of the embryological devel-

opment of nerve cells by Wilhelm His, of Leipzig, in 1887, and of the way that nerve cells respond individually to injury by August Forel, of Zurich, in 1888. It remained only for someone to assemble all the evidence in a convincing way, and this was done by Wilhelm Waldeyer, a distinguished professor of anatomy and pathology in Berlin, in 1891. Waldeyer's extensive review in a German medical journal finally showed, after a 50-year delay, that the cell theory applied to the nervous system, too. Waldeyer suggested the term "neuron" for the nerve cell, and the cell theory as applied to the nervous system became known as the "neuron doctrine." Cajal, for his part, never quite forgave Waldeyer for being credited with the doctrine he considered his own.

Ironically, Golgi himself never accepted the individuality of the nerve cell, clinging bitterly to the reticular theory, even on the occasion of his Nobel lecture when he and Cajal shared the award in 1906.

Although the neuron doctrine became widely accepted, final proof required a method that could demonstrate that nerve cell membranes remain everywhere distinct from each other. This is beyond the power of resolution of the light microscope, and the question awaited the advent of the electron microscope. This instrument was first applied to physical materials in the 1940s, and to biological tissues around 1950. Its application to the nervous system was delayed by the same problems of fixing and staining the tissue that we have already noted. However, by the mid-1950s, the investigations of David Robertson in London, Eduardo de Robertis in Argentina, and Sanford Palay and George Palade in New York showed that the nerve cell membrane resembles the basic "unit membrane" of other cells, and that it appears to be continuous around each nerve cell (see Fig. 3.3). This supported the neuron theory in its proposition that each nerve cell is a genetic and anatomical unit like other cells of the body, and its corollary that nervous tissue consists of populations of these units organized into functional systems.

Today the modern study of cellular structure and function is called *cell biology*. It is based on the use of the electron microscope to reveal the fine structural elements of the cell and, in combination with special methods of biochemistry and molecular biology, give evidence of their functions. The general theme that has emerged is that the fine structural elements, or organelles, reflect a beautifully orchestrated division of labor within the cell, enabling it to carry out the different functions necessary to sustain its life by means of specific interactions with neighboring cells.

Studies of cellular organelles have traditionally been done in organs other than the brain, such as the liver or pancreas, and one has had to infer their applicability to nerve cells. With the advent of molecular neurobiology, this situation has begun to change, and it is increasingly possible to obtain information directly from nerve cells themselves.

The neuron is the most fundamental of the building blocks of the nervous system, and the way its functions arise out of the properties of its organelles is essential for grasping the principles of neurobiology. Figure 3.4 is a summary view of the main organelles and their distribution within the different parts of the neuron. We will briefly describe each organelle. It will be seen that the divisions of labor resemble those in other cells of the body, but there are specializations that are adapted for the unique functions of nerve cells. The specializations relating to the synapse will be considered in the following chapter.

The Plasma Membrane

The nerve cell, like all other cells of the body, is bounded by a plasma membrane. In cross sections of electron micrographs at low magnification, (for example, as in Fig. 3.3), the membrane appears as a single dark line. At higher magnification it can be seen that there are, in fact, two dark lines with a light space between them. This gives the membrane a two-layered structure, with inner and outer leaflets.

In the early 1970s, it was proposed that the two layers are two sheets of oppositely oriented phospholipid molecules; the hydrophilic phosphorylated heads lie at the exterior surface of the membrane, and the hydrophobic lipid tails lie at the water-free interior of the membrane. It is an inherent property of phospholipid molecules to form such a membrane (see Chap. 2). The hydrocarbon tails within the membrane set up a barrier to passage of polar charged molecules. Water molecules, being small uncharged dipoles, cross this barrier readily, but ions of salts do not, nor do the water-soluble molecules contained within

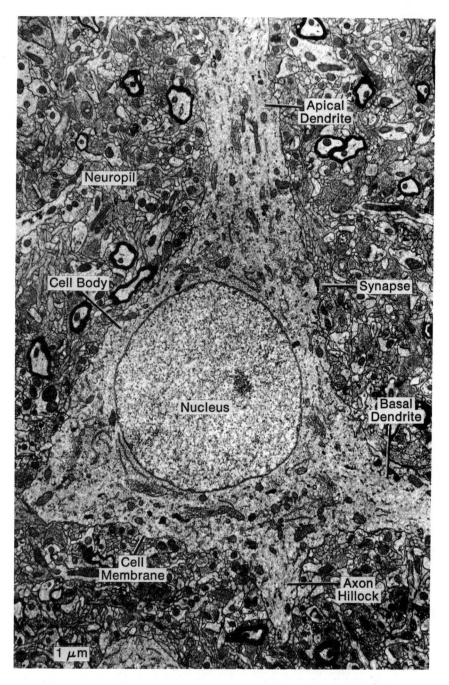

Fig. 3.3 Electron micrograph of a pyramidal cell in the visual cortex of the rat. Use the labels on the micrograph to check your identification of the parts of the neuron as seen with the Golgi stain in Fig. 3.2. Magnification, approximately ×5000. (Courtesy of Steven Hersch and Alan Peters)

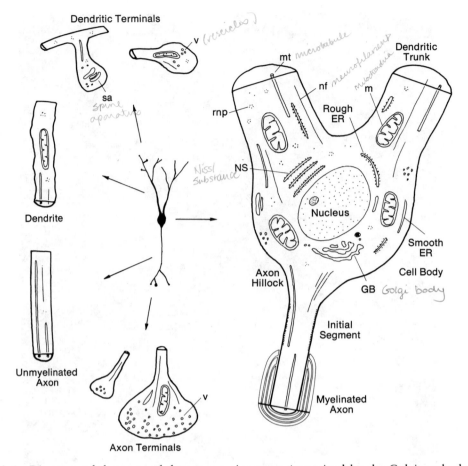

Fig. 3.4 Diagrams of the parts of the neuron. A neuron (as stained by the Golgi method or by intracellular injection of dyes), shown at center, is surrounded by schematic drawings of fine structure (as viewed in the electron microscope) of the different parts. ER, endoplasmic reticulum; GB, Golgi body, NS, Nissl substance; mt, microtubule; nf, neurofilament; rnp, ribonuclear protein particles; sa, spine apparatus; v, vesicles; m, mitochondria. Compare the parts of the neuron with the stained cells in Fig. 3.2, and the fine structure with Fig. 3.3. (From Shepherd, 1979)

the cell cytoplasm. The lipids of the membrane thus form a natural barrier to retain the cytoplasm. However, the cell has to pay for this by needing special mechanisms for transporting across the membrane the ions and water-soluble molecules essential for metabolism. This is provided by proteins embedded in the membrane.

The lipids form a fluid matrix within which the protein molecules are embedded. This is known as the *fluid mosaic membrane model*. The membrane has been shown to be quite fluid; in some cells the lipids can move laterally at rates of 2 μm/sec.

Protein molecules move about 40 times more slowly (50 nm/sec, or 3 μm/min).

Membrane Lipids

The *lipid* moiety imparts an electrical capacitance to the membrane, which stores the charge involved in the membrane potential (Chap. 5). In addition it has other properties, as indicated in the diagram of Fig. 3.5. The phospholipid bilayer is not, in fact, symmetrical; in the outer layer the head groups contain mostly choline, whereas in the inner layer they contain mostly amino acids. These head groups may interact with

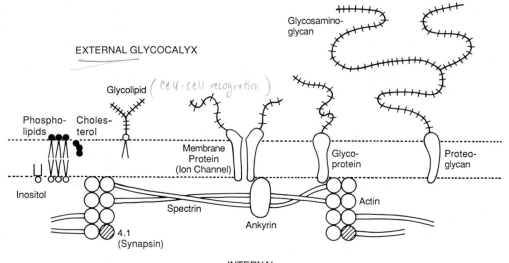

Fig. 3.5 Diagram of the structure of the plasma membrane, showing the types of molecules that are characteristic of the membrane and its associated intracellular and extracellular domains. (Adapted from Alberts et al, 1983)

the membrane proteins in ways that are essential for the proper functioning of the proteins. Among the phospholipids of the inner layer is phosphatidylinositol, composed of two fatty acid chains linked through glycerol to a phosphorylated six-carbon ring molecule called inositol. Phosphatidylinositol is the source of an important intracellular second-messenger system, as we shall see in Chap. 8.

The outer layer contains fatty acids giving rise to head groups of short chains of sugar molecules. These are called *glycolipids*. The most complex glycolipids are gangliosides, whose head groups contain a complex sugar called sialic acid. They are present in high amounts in neurons. These short-chain sugars (called oligosaccharides) protrude into the extracellular space, and are believed to perform some function in cell–cell recognition.

Membrane Proteins

The *protein* moiety is crucial to many functions of the cell. These functions depend on the parts of the proteins that lie outside, across, and inside the membrane. Let us consider each briefly.

Surface Proteins. The *outside* of the membrane fairly bristles with *carbohydrate* molecules arising from, or attached to, certain of the membrane protein molecules (see Fig. 3.5). *Glycoproteins* give rise to oligosaccharide moieties, characteristically containing sialic acid. One of these is fibronectin, which is present in regions of cell migration during development. Another example is a neural cell adhesion molecule (N—CAM). This is a high-molecular-weight (~200,000) glycopeptide, with the carbohydrate accounting for about one-third of the weight. As its name suggests, it is believed to be important for the adhesion between neurons that takes place during development.

Some membrane proteins give rise to extremely long sugar chains. These are *proteoglycans;* the carbohydrate moieties are called *glycosaminoglycans*. The carbohydrate may constitute 95% of these molecules. This long branching structure is like a long test-tube brush, or a centipede wriggling its way through the extracellular space. It attracts water, imparting a spongy turgor to the extracellular space. The branching structure contains complex sequences of reactive saccharides, which are believed to play an important role in cell–cell recognition that must take place during development.

Together, the extracellular carbohydrates form a layer around the cell that is called the *glycocalyx;* in addition to being important for structural support, cell adhesion, and cell recognition, it appears also to regulate the diffusion of molecules through the extracellular space.

Intrinsic Proteins. The parts of the proteins that lie *within* or *across* the membrane are called intrinsic membrane proteins; they have several distinct functions. Some provide sites for reception of neurotransmitters and other neuroactive molecules. Some provide channels for ion movements across the membrane. Some provide carriers for movement of molecules involved in the metabolism of the cell, such as glucose and amino acids, whereas others pump ions inward or outward, or both. Finally, proteins that are attached to molecules in both the extracellular and intacellular spaces serve to anchor the cell. These different types of intrinsic membrane proteins are represented in Fig. 3.5.

Cytoplasmic Proteins. On the *cytoplasmic* side, certain of the membrane proteins attach to other proteins that form a complicated latticework near the inner surface of the membrane. These are called *membrane skeletal proteins.* Most of our information has come from studies of the red blood cell. David Anderson's (1984) comment—

Although the biconcave erythrocyte seems an unlikely model for the neuron with its complex architecture, it has proved to be surprisingly relevant.

—nicely catches the spirit of modern times, when our understanding of molecular biology is drawn from a variety of cells.

The current view of the relations between membrane proteins and membrane skeletal proteins is summarized in the diagram of Fig. 3.5. Several types of proteins, including a short-chain *actin,* form nodal points under the membrane; in addition, a protein called *ankyrin* is bound to an intrinsic membrane protein (in erythrocytes, this is band 3, an anion channel). Forming the links between these nodes is a type of filamentous protein called *fodrin.* There are several types of fodrin. The first to be characterized was found in red cells; called spectrin, it is a heterodimer (that is, its peptide subunits are different) consisting of α and β subunits of molecular weights (MW) 240,000 and 222,000 respectively. The cross-links between spectrin and actin are responsible for giving the red cell its characteristic biconcave shape.

In the brain, spectrin is found only in cell bodies, and only in fully differentiated neurons. There is, in addition, a brain-specific fodrin, a heterodimer of an α and a γ (MW = 235,000) subunit; this fodrin is present in both developing and mature neurons, and is transported into the axon and dendrites. These differing distributions have suggested that the fodrins may be part of the mechanism that generates the different parts of the neuron, as well as microdomains within those parts. The evidence in the red cell implies that they may be important in determining the shape of axonal and dendritic branches. The linkage of spectrin to the red cell anion channel limits lateral diffusion of the channel in the membrane. In neurons, similar linkages to channel proteins appear to play a role in organizing the subsynaptic membrane (Chap. 4), or be subject to activity-dependent changes underlying memory (see Chap. 29). A role in vesicle exocytosis has also been suggested.

The Nucleus

Each nerve cell contains a nucleus. As in other eukaryotic cells, the nucleus contains the genes, consisting of DNA and its asso-

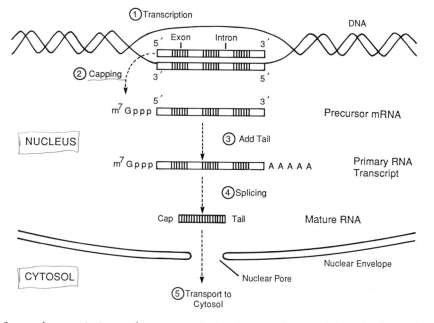

Fig. 3.6 Steps of transcription and posttranscriptional processing carried out in the nucleus. Some transcripts for brain proteins in the fetus lack poly(A) tails (step ③). For further details, see text. (Modified from Watson et al., 1983)

ciated proteins. Through its DNA, the nucleus plays two essential roles. One is to provide for DNA replication during mitosis. Mitotic activity is essential to the functioning of many body cells (for example, two million red blood cells are produced every second!). This function is present in the nervous system during development, but is lost in most mature neurons (exceptions are the olfactory receptor neuron in vertebrates, and certain cells in the avian brain). The other role is to transcribe DNA into RNA in order to synthesize proteins, especially the enzymes which then synthesize the macromolecules of the cell. By this means the nucleus generates the instructions for controlling the differentiation and growth of the neuron during development, and maintaining its integrity during maturity.

The mechanisms of DNA replication and RNA transcription have been mentioned in Chap. 2 and are covered in detail in many textbooks of biochemistry and molecular biology (see Alberts et al., 1983). Our in-

terest here will be in nuclear mechanisms for RNA transcription that are especially important for neurons.

DNA is transcribed into RNA in the nucleus by one of several RNA polymerases. Transcription into messenger RNA (mRNA) takes place in several steps, as summarized in Fig. 3.6. As transcription ① proceeds, a methylated guanosine residue is added to the 5' end of the RNA by a triphosphate bridge. This is called the cap ②. It signals the ribosomes where protein synthesis is to be initiated. When transcription is finished, a chain of adenylate residues is added to the 3' end. This is called the poly(A) tail ③. The tail may contain as many as 200 residues. The function of the tail is not yet clear. However, an interesting finding is that in the rat brain, there is a population of mRNA that lacks the poly(A) tail. Absent in the fetus, this population begins to appear soon after birth, but does not reach a maximum until young adulthood. It has been speculated that these mRNAs may code for proteins that are important for the development of nerve cells.

Attired in cap and tail, the RNA is termed a primary transcript. It is also known as heterogeneous nuclear RNA (hnRNA) because of its highly variable length. The primary transcript contains coding regions (exons) and noncoding regions (introns). The last step is to remove the introns and connect the ends of the exons together to form mature RNA. This is called RNA splicing ④. The result is mature mRNA that is ready for transport from the nucleus to the cytoplasm ⑤. The nuclear envelope appears to function to prevent the mRNA from being translated in the cytosol until the coding regions are in perfect uninterrupted sequence.

Ribosomal RNA (rRNA) is transcribed from DNA in a special part of the nucleus called the nucleolus (see Fig. 3.4). A large and a small subunit are immediately joined to special proteins to create a ribonuclear protein particle, called a ribosome. Processing of the particle is not completed until the mature ribosome is leaving the nucleus, so that it does not interact prematurely with mRNA.

The proteins involved in the assembly operations within the nucleus come from the cytoplasm, so there is a busy two-way traffic through the nuclear pores (see below). The molecular machinery contained in the nucleus can be affected in several ways. For example, the nucleus is the prime target of one of the major classes of hormones, the steroid hormones. Estrogen and testosterone bind to cytoplasmic receptors to form a complex which is transported to the nucleus, where it stimulates an increase in mRNA synthesis that leads to synthesis of specific proteins in the cytoplasm. This underlies the actions of these hormones on the reproductive organs and their associated tissues, and also their actions on nerve cells in the hypothalamus and related regions of the limbic brain (Chaps. 8, 24, and 27). Certain chromosomal aberrations lead to deficits or malfunctioning in nerve cells, as in Down's syndrome (mongolism).

Finally, the nucleus may be the site of action of environmental toxins; for example, certain mushroom toxins inhibit the nuclear polymerases that produce mRNA. These actions on nuclear mechanisms offer the opportunity to neurobiologists for experimental manipulations that can provide insight into the relations between gene expression, neuronal properties, and behavior.

As in other cells, the position of the nucleus defines the location of the *cell body* (also called soma); the cell body, in other words, is the part of the neuron that contains the nucleus. The size of the nucleus varies with the size of the cell body. In the largest neurons the cell body may reach 100 μm or more in diameter, and the nucleus may be as large as 20 μm. The smallest nerve cell bodies are around 5 μm in diameter. In these cells the nucleus may almost fill the cell body, leaving only a very thin rim of cytoplasm. The fact that processes may extend for long distances poses a special problem for the nucleus in controlling protein synthesis in all parts of the nerve cell (see below).

Ribosomes and the Rough Endoplasmic Reticulum

The nucleus is separated from the cytoplasm by a nuclear envelope composed of a double membrane formed by folds of the endoplasmic reticulum (see Fig. 3.7). Within the folds are numerous pores, which provide for transport of proteins into the nucleus and RNA out of the nucleus. When the ribosomes reach the cytoplasm they are sorted into two populations. Some remain "free" within the cytoplasm, either singly or in clusters ("polyribosomes"). In most cells of the body these ribosomes manufacture proteins that remain within the cell. The other population of ribosomes is attached to the *endoplasmic reticulum* (ER). This extends throughout the cytoplasm of the cell body as a system of sheets, channels, and membrane-enclosed spaces (large, flat spaces called cysternae, small spaces

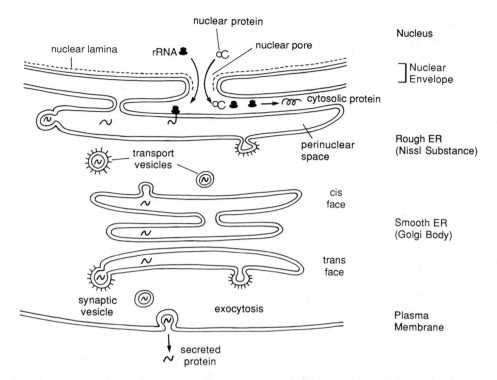

Fig. 3.7 Proteins synthesized by ribosomes (rRNA) are sorted through different compartments of the neuron. *Nuclear proteins* return through the nuclear pore. *Cytosolic proteins* are synthesized within the cytosol and remain there. *Secretory proteins* are synthesized within the endoplasmic lumen, which is continuous with the space between the inner nuclear membrane and outer nuclear membrane of the nuclear envelope (see diagram). Buds from the rough endoplasmic reticulum (ER) form transport (shuttle) vesicles which fuse with the cis face of the Golgi smooth ER. The contents of the smooth ER are transferred by continuity or vesicles to the trans face of the Golgi body, where synaptic vesicles are formed. Secretion occurs by exocytosis. (Based on Palade and Farquhar, 1981, and others)

called vesicles). The part of this system that has attached ribosomes is called the *rough ER*. The membrane-bound ribosomes of the rough ER synthesize proteins that in most cells are destined for insertion into the plasmalemma or secretion from the cell.

Synthesis of proteins depends on the third type of RNA called *transfer RNA (tRNA)*. This combines with a given amino acid to "activate" it, so that it is ready to be assembled into place. The assembly is directed by mRNA. The mRNA attaches to the ribosomes and moves across them, bringing its template into position to select *(translate)* the right sequence of activated amino acids to form a given polypeptide.

By suitable foldings of the chain, the polypeptide becomes a protein.

In nerve cells there is a characteristic accumulation of rough ER near the nucleus that is termed the *Nissl substance* (see Figs. 3.4, 3.7). This is obviously a site of intense protein-synthesizing activity. In large neurons the Nissl substance is large and dense; in small neurons it may consist only of scattered particles. Close examination reveals that many of the ribosomes within the Nissl substance are not attached to the ER membrane, but lie between the membranes as polyribosomes. It has been speculated that these clusters may be involved in synthesizing complex proteins specific for nerve cells, perhaps specific for different types of nerve cells. Some of the protein synthesized in the Nissl substance may be destined for secretion in the form of transmitter substances. However, it has been speculated that most proteins are probably used for maintenance of the large expanses of branching processes of the neuron.

The ribosomes manufacture the molecular machinery for most of the characteristic functions of cells: enzymes, regulators, carriers, receptors, transducers, contractile and structural elements, and membranes. As in the case of the nucleus, this machinery is susceptible to modification or disruption by various influences. For example, antibiotics exert their effects by interfering at various specific steps in transcription or translation. In nerve cells, diphtheria toxin inactivates one of the elongation factors responsible for assembly of polypeptides.

Secretion and the Golgi Complex

We have described the rough ER; what about the other part of the endoplasmic reticulum, that lacks attached ribosomes? This is called the *smooth ER*. It is an extremely versatile structure, which is put in the service of cells in a variety of ways. With regard to other cells of the body we will note only two examples. At one extreme, the smooth ER may form a rigidly defined inner system of sheets and channels, as in the skeletal muscle fiber. In muscle, it is called the sarcoplasmic reticulum; this forms the T-system, which has as its primary functions the conduction of the impulse into the interior of fiber, and the regulation of the calcium level there in relation to muscle contraction. This will be discussed further in Chap. 17.

A second function of the smooth ER is to prepare proteins for insertion into the plasmalemma. This mechanism has been worked out by Jon Lindstrom (1983) and his colleagues for the ACh receptor in muscle, and is summarized in Fig. 3.8. The receptor subunits are synthesized by membrane-bound ribosomes. Approxi-

mately two-thirds of the newly formed α subunits are degraded and disappear. The surviving one-third of the α-subunit monomers develop toward their mature conformation, and then are assembled to form the pentameric receptor-channel protein. These are transported from the Golgi body in the membranes of transport vesicles to the cell surface, where they are inserted into the plasmalemma by vesicle fusion. During development of muscle cells, the ACh receptors are first distributed widely in the muscle membrane, and become localized at the neuromuscular junction in association with the arrival of the ingrowing motor nerve terminals. This sequence of events may be correlated with the molecular details of the ACh receptor discussed in Chap. 2. It serves as a model for the insertion of receptor molecules in membranes of nerve, muscle, and glial cells, and also for mechanisms of synaptogenesis discussed in Chap. 9.

In contrast to the muscle fiber, a secretory cell such as that of the pancreas employs its smooth ER in a different manner. As indicated in Fig. 3.7, the proteins manufactured by the rough ER are transferred (via shuttle vesicles) to the system of flattened pancakelike sacks, or cysternae, called the *Golgi complex*. The membranes here are called transitional ER. The Golgi complex has an orientation, there being an internal, *forming* face (cis) and an external, *releasing* face (trans). From the latter, vesicles bud off to form secretory granules. The secretory granules remain within the cytoplasm of the cell until the cell is stimulated with the appropriate factors. The granules then move to the apical surface where their membranes fuse with the plasma membrane and discharge their contents. This process, called *exocytosis*, requires energy and the presence of free calcium ions.

In nerve cells, the Golgi complex is represented by smaller accumulations of cysternae that are not clearly polarized and that tend to be dispersed in the cytoplasm and extend out even into the dendrites (but not the axon). In the neighborhood of the

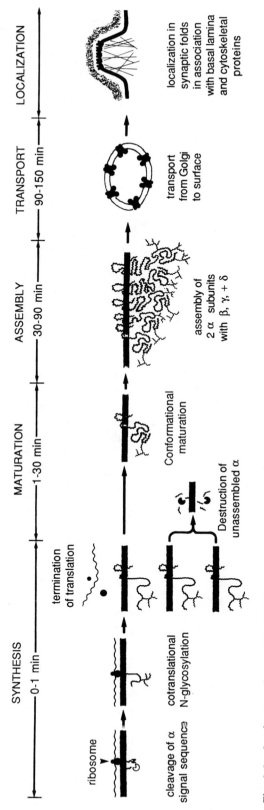

Fig. 3.8 Synthesis and assembly of ACh receptor subunits in developing muscle cells in tissue culture. Monoclonal antibodies (mAbs) were developed against α subunits at different stages of development. Coprecipitation of other subunits permitted determination of the time course of assembly of the entire receptor protein. Immunoprecipitation results were correlated with binding of α-bungarotoxin to the receptor. (From Merlie et al., 1983)

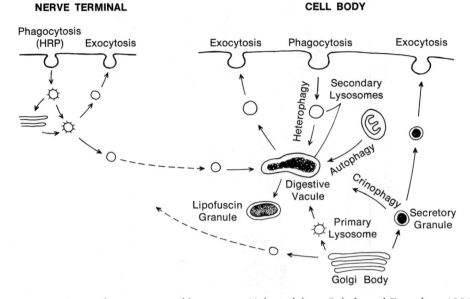

Fig. 3.9 Formation and movements of lysosomes. (Adapted from Palade and Farquhar, 1981)

Golgi complex are clouds of small vesicles which may well be analogous to the shuttle vesicles in a secretory cell (see Fig. 3.7). However, most neurons do not secrete large granules like those of secretory cells. The relation of the smooth ER and the Golgi complex to the secretion of transmitter and neuromodulatory substances is still being worked out.

Lysosomes

In addition to systems for manufacture and transport of substances, the cell also has an internal digestive system comprised of *lysosomes*. Like the smooth ER, lysosomes are membrane-bound structures. They differ, however, in having no particular shape. They vary in size from small vesicles to large, rounded sacks; and they contain a variety of hydrolytic enzymes that degrade and digest a wide range of substances that originate both inside and outside the cell.

Some of the functions of lysosomes, and the complex interrelations with other cell constituents, are indicated in Fig. 3.9. *Primary lysosomes* are formed from the Golgi complex by the budding off of vesicles which

then acquire a dense matrix about them; these are termed *alveolate vesicles*. They contain acid hydrolases specific for different digestive tasks. When these processes begin, the vesicle becomes a *secondary lysosome*, and may assume a variety of forms as a digestive vacuole. The material that is digested may come from within the cell (digestion of these substances is called *autophagy*), or from outside the cell (this is called *heterophagy*). A third type of action occurs in some secretory cells; the number of secretory granules stored in the cytoplasm may be reduced and regulated by a process of *crinophagy*. The contents of the vacuoles are disposed of by diffusion of the breakdown products into the cytoplasm, or by exocytosis.

This general scheme appears to apply to nerve cells, but with some interesting differences. Because of the long distances between many nerve terminals and their cell body, the terminals must carry out some functions in semiautonomy. Nerve stimulation causes alveolate vesicles to appear in the terminal, and Fig. 3.9 indicates that there is a cycle of pinocytosis and exocytosis within the terminal that shares some

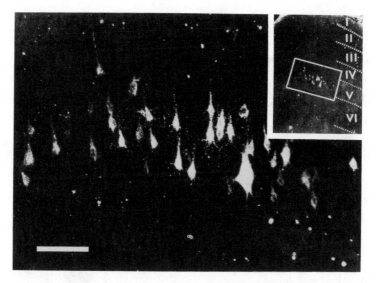

Fig. 3.10 Uptake and transport of the enzyme horseradish peroxidase (HRP) in nerve cells. The HRP was injected into the superior colliculus of the cat; it was taken up by nerve terminals and retrogradely transported to their cell bodies located in layer V (see inset) of area 19 of the visual cortex. Bar indicates 100 μm. (From Gilbert and Kelly, 1975)

common features with the sequence of steps that occurs through the lysosomal system in the cell body.

Figure 3.9 also indicates that alveolate vesicles are in communication with a transport system from the terminal to the cell body. This system is believed to provide the structural basis for experimental methods for tracing nerve connections. An enzyme, *horseradish peroxidase* (HRP), that is injected into a region of terminals will be taken up by the terminals and transported back to the cell bodies. Appropriate staining procedures can visualize the transported HRP, thus establishing the connection between the site of injection and the cell bodies that send fibers to that site (see Fig. 3.10). Various dyes, as well as artificial microspheres, are also transported in this manner, with differential uptake in dendrites, cell bodies, axons, and axonal terminals. We will refer to these methods often in discussing central nervous system pathways in later chapters.

A distinctive feature of nerve cells is the presence of *lipofuscin granules*. These form during adult life, and gradually increase with age. For this reason they are believed to represent the effects of "wear and tear" on the cell. They also are implicated in certain diseases. As Fig. 3.9 indicates, there is evidence that these granules are derived from lysosomes.

Mitochondria

Most of the cellular functions we have described require energy, and most of this energy comes from *mitochondria*. Apart from the nucleus, this is the most complex organelle within the cell. As indicated in Fig. 3.4, it is cigar-shaped, with a smooth outer membrane and an inner membrane that is thrown into internal folds called cristae. In general, the higher the energy demands in a particular cell, the more tightly packed the cristae. The inner membrane is relatively impermeable, so movement of substances across this membrane requires special transport mechanisms. The outer membrane is freely permeable to ions and water. Electron microscopic observations indicate that the outer membrane is contin-

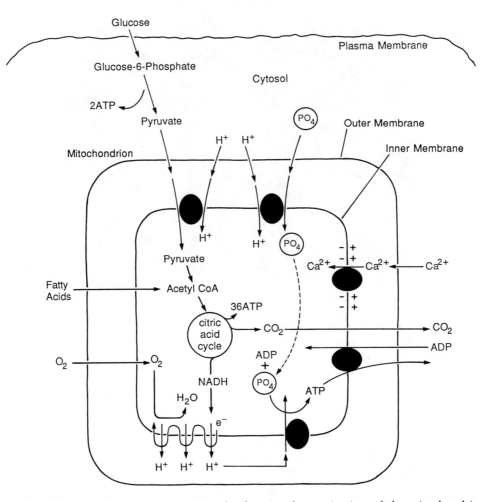

Fig. 3.11 Schematic diagram summarizing the functional organization of the mitochondrion. In normal neurons of the adult vertebrate nervous system, the main and probably exclusive source of energy is glucose. The metabolic pathway for energy metabolism begins with breakdown of glucose in the glycolytic chain to pyruvate, which takes place in the cytosol. This is followed by aerobic metabolism, by the citric acid cycle inside the mitochondrion, yielding 36 ATP molecules for each molecule of glucose. The energy is generated by the proton pump in the inner membrane, as shown in the diagram. Also shown in the diagram are sequestration of Ca^{2+}, utilization of O_2, and production of CO_2.

uous with the smooth endoplasmic reticulum.

The mechanisms for production of energy are summarized in Fig. 3.11. One source of energy is *glycolysis,* the chain of reactions that breaks down glucose by *anaerobic metabolism* to yield, for each molecule of glucose, a net of two molecules of *adenosine triphosphate* (ATP) with its high-energy phosphate bonds. All the glycolytic enzymes in the chain are soluble proteins which exist free within the cytoplasm. In contrast, *aerobic metabolism,* involving the acetylation of pyruvic acid and the reactions of the *citric acid cycle,* yields a net from each glucose molecule of 36 molecules of ATP, obviously a much more efficient source. All of the citric acid cycle enzymes are contained within the inner matrix of the mitochondria. The enzymes of the associated electron transport chain are components of the inner mitochondrial membrane. It is believed that electron transfer sets up a gradient of H^+ across the inner membrane, and the potential energy in this gradient is used to form ATP from ADP (see Fig. 3.11). The ATP is then available for the various energy-requiring processes of the cell.

In most cells of the body a variety of sugars can be taken up by the cell and metabolized to yield energy, or be stored within the cell as glycogen. However, nerve cells in the vertebrate brain are special, in that they are almost exclusively dependent on glucose. (In invertebrates the corresponding substance for supplying energy is trehalose.) Other substances are excluded by the blood–brain barrier, as described in the next chapter. Most nerve cells also lack the ability to store glycogen, further increasing their dependence for energy on circulating glucose, as well as the oxygen needed for its aerobic metabolism. This is why we lose consciousness if the blood supply to our brains is interrupted for only a few seconds. Among the other functions of mitochondria is the ability to store calcium, which, as we shall see, can be a factor in regulating calcium in nerve terminals.

Mitochondria also contain small ribosomes and even a few strands of DNA. This indicates that the mitochondrion itself has most of the features of a cell, and, indeed, mitochondria probably originated from a prokaryotic microbelike ancestor. It is hypothesized that this aerobic microorganism developed a symbiotic relation with the anerobic eukaryotic cell and became incorporated into it, to the mutual benefit of both.

The Cytoskeleton

If the neuron contained only the organelles discussed so far, it would be a stationary, simple sack of genetic and metabolic machinery. However, the neuron grows in size and moves during development, sends out branches, transports substances and organ-

elles within those branches, and makes synapses with other cells. There are thus demanding requirements for maintaining a complicated structure that yet provides for flexibility and movement.

These requirements are met by three types of filamentous proteins that form an internal network called the *cytoskeleton*. Figure 3.12 shows how this can be visualized in neural tissue that has been specially prepared for electron microscopy by the quick-freeze, deep-etch procedure. In this view of the interior of an axon, the larger elongated structures are *microtubules;* the smaller, more beaded structures are *neurofilaments*. The smallest of the filamentous proteins, *microfilaments* (actin), are not seen. Also present are vesicles and mitochondria. Let us discuss each of the filament types.

Microtubules and Neurofilaments

Microtubules. These are long, unbranched tubes of approximately 20 nm in diameter. The walls are composed of subunits of tubulin. The globular polypeptide monomer has a molecular weight of approximately 50,000. Assembly into microtubules begins with the formation of a heterodimer of α- and β-tubulin subunits containing similar amino acid sequences. These then polymerize into thin protofilaments of alternating subunits. The microtubule consists of 13 protofilaments arranged around the central core (note the protofilaments in the walls of the microtubules in Fig. 3.12). Polymerization depends on the presence of guanosine triphosphate (GTP), which is hydrolyzed during assembly. Associated with the microtubules are two types of special proteins. Tau (τ) proteins (MW = 60,000) appear to enhance polymerization. Microtubule-associated proteins (MAPs) (MW = 200,000–300,000) also enhance polymerization; in addition, they make bonds that link the microtubules to neighboring structures.

Microtubules are employed in various ways. In all cells undergoing mitotic division, the mitotic spindle consists of microtubules. In motile cilia, and in the tails of

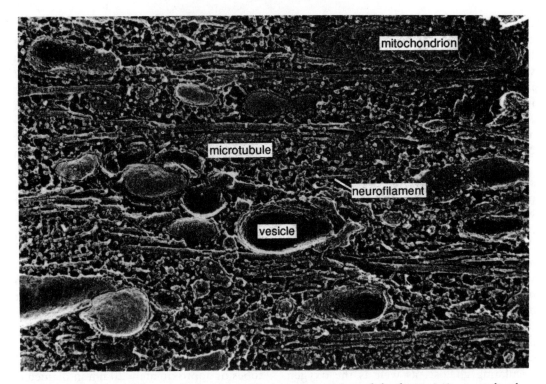

Fig. 3.12 Elements of the cytoskeleton, as seen in a preparation of the frog sciatic axon that has been quick-frozen and deep-etched. (Modified from Hirokawa et al., 1982, in Baitinger et al., 1983)

spermatozoa, they are arranged in a rigid pattern, consisting of a ring of nine pairs (doublets) around a central pair. This appears to provide an internal skeleton for the cilium, as well as mediating the forces that move it. In contrast, in many cells the microtubules are structural elements that lack any obvious orientation. In nerve cells they are present in the cell body singly or in groups that weave their way through the cytoplasm and out into the axon and dendrites. Certain plant alkaloids, such as *colchicine,* bind with the microtubules to depolymerize them, stopping mitosis in metaphase and also inhibiting the transport of substances in the axon (see below).

Neurofilaments. These are long solid filaments approximately 10 nm in diameter. They belong to the class of structure which in other cells is called *intermediate filament* (because it is intermediate in diameter between microtubules and microfilaments).

In contrast to microtubules and microfilaments, which have been conserved across phyla, intermediate filaments are composed of proteins showing considerable polymorphism, varying with different types of cells, and also within cell types. Thus, the proteins in neurofilaments differ from muscle or epithelial cell intermediate filaments. In neurofilaments three main polypeptides have been identified, with molecular weights of about 70,000, 140,000, and 210,000. Glial cells are also rich in these filaments, where they are composed of a polypeptide called vimentin (present in fibroblasts) and, in some glial cells (see below), a glial fibrillary acidic protein (GFAP) with a molecular weight of 50,000.

Neurofilaments are especially prominent in large axons, where they outnumber the microtubules; on the other hand, in small axons and dendrites the proportions are reversed. Neurofilaments, and their relation to microtubules, change during aging, and extreme changes, such as the development of tangles and placques in neurons within the cerebral cortex, appear to be associated with the progressive senility seen in Alzheimer's disease.

Intracellular Transport. The presence of microtubules and neurofilaments in axons and dendrites has naturally suggested that they might be involved in the transport of substances, and a variety of biochemical studies, including those with colchicine (see above), have supported this notion. Intracellular transport between cell body and outlying processes is vital to the economy of the nerve cell, and we have already noted one example of this in the transport of substances (including HRP) from nerve terminals to the cell body. This direction is referred to as *retrograde.* Transport from cell body to terminals, on the other hand, is in the *orthograde* direction.

One of the most vivid demonstrations of these movements has been by the use of video-enhanced microscopy. In this method, axoplasm of a large axon, such as the squid giant axon, is spread out in a dish. The light microscopic image is recorded by a video camera under high power. The ability to set the level of light and contrast in the image (the same way one can on a television screen) enables one to visualize objects that would otherwise be below the resolving power of the light microscope. In addition, the image can be digitized and fed to a "frame-grabbing" computer for further enhancement. The result is an image in which particles (vesicles) can be seen moving along tubular structures (microtubules). Astonishingly, particles move in either the orthograde or retrograde direction along the same tubule, or change from one tubule to another. Recent experiments suggest that the motive force for the movement comes not from the microtubules, but from the vesicle itself, through the action of a polypeptide called kinesin. The mechanism as presently envisaged is illustrated in Fig. 3.13.

When radioactively labeled amino acids are injected in the vicinity of cell bodies, the amino acids are taken up by the cell bodies and incorporated into protein, which is then transported down the axon to the terminals. These experiments have identified two general types of *axonal transport:*

Fig. 3.13 High-resolution video-enhanced microscopy shows that vesicles can move along microtubules in either direction. A mechanism proposed for mediating this movement is illustrated in this diagram. In this model, kinesin, a 110- to 134-kdalton polypeptide, interacts with both a vesicle and a microtubule to bring about movement towards the (+) end of the microtubule (to the right). Conversely, kinesin interacts with the microtubule and a substrate (for example, a glass coverslip, as shown) to move the microtubule in the opposite direction. Evidence that movement is not imparted by the vesicle or the microtubule is shown by the fact that artificial beads can be induced to move along a microtubule in the presence of kinesin. Movement in the other direction is believed to be mediated by a complementary kinesin-like polypeptide. (From Vale et al., 1985)

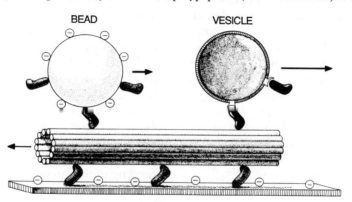

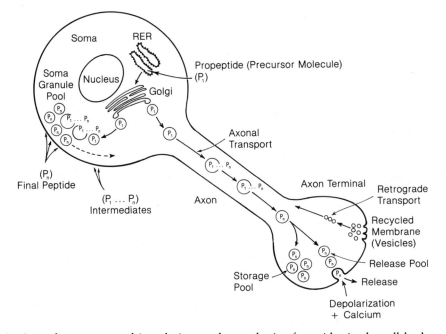

Fig. 3.14 Axonal transport and its relation to the synthesis of peptides in the cell body and their release from terminals. Propeptides (P_1) are synthesized in the rough endoplasmic reticulum and transported through the Golgi body. Transfer of intermediates or final peptide (P_n) then takes place to storage (soma granule pool), or by axonal transport to their terminals for release. Not shown is dendritic transport for release from dendritic synapses. (From Mains et al., in Gainer and Brownstein, 1981)

slow transport at a rate of about one millimeter per day, and *fast* (rapid) *transport* at rates of several hundred millimeters per day. Many of the substances transported are intimately related to functions involved in synaptic transmission. The transport of peptides is illustrated in Fig. 3.14. The relation of transport to synaptic functions will be discussed in Chap. 8.

Intracellular transport has provided the basis for a valuable method for demonstrating nerve connections in the central nervous system. The location of labeled substances after an injection can be ascertained by making sections of the tissue and exposing them to photographic film, a method known as *autoradiography* (the tissue takes its own photograph, so to speak). An example of this method is shown in Fig. 3.15A. In later chapters, we will often refer to results obtained in this way.

Equally important is the transport of substances in dendrites. In 1968, Tony Stretton and Ed Kravitz at Harvard showed that a dye (Procion Yellow) injected from a micropipette into the cell body of a neuron is transported into the dendrites and can be visualized by fluorescence microscopy. This was a key discovery for cellular neurobiology, for it enabled an investigator to see the whole dendritic tree of the cell that was being recorded. It was like having a Golgi stain of the very neuron one wished to study. Since then, a host of substances have been used for this purpose, including HRP and dyes such as Lucifer Yellow; visualization of radioactively labeled amino acids in motoneuronal dendrites by autoradiography is illustrated in Fig. 3.15B. The ability to correlate physiological properties with the morphology of the cell revealed in this way is the basis of much of our understanding of the integrative functions of neurons.

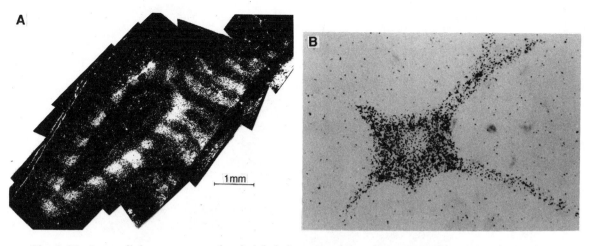

Fig. 3.15 Intracellular transport of radiolabeled compunds, as demonstrated by autoradiography. **A.** Transport of [³H]proline into visual cortex of monkey. Injection was made into one eye; [³H]proline was incorporated into protein in retinal ganglion cells, transported to their terminals in the lateral geniculate nucleus, and transferred to cells therein which project to the cortex. The alternating bands demonstrate ocular dominance columns (see Chap. 16). (From Wiesel et al., 1974) **B.** Transport of [³H]fucose into dendrites of a motoneuron after intracellular injection into the cell body, where it is incorporated into glycoprotein. (From Kreutzberg et al., 1975)

Microfilaments

The third type of fibrillar structure in the cell is the *microfilament*. The best understood of these are in skeletal muscle, where thick filaments (12-nm diameter, composed of myosin) and thin filaments (5-nm diameter, composed of actin) are arranged in a highly geometrical array to provide the mechanism for muscle contraction (Chap. 17). Even in many nonmuscular cells, actin surprisingly accounts for up to 10% of the total cell protein, and most or all of this may be in the form of microfilaments. Microfilaments are abundant in growing nerve processes (Chap 9). They are also abundant in neuroglia, as discussed in the next section, and they are involved in certain kinds of neuronal junctions (next chapter). In many freely moving cells they are present just beneath the plasma membrane, where it is believed they control movement of the membrane and fluidity of the underlying cytoplasm. Evidence for this has been obtained by observing the inhibition of movements of macrophages after treatment with cytochalasin B, a substance obtained from

fungi that disrupts microfilaments. In the neuron, interactions between fodrin and actin and other elements provide the means for controlling the form and movement of the plasma membrane, the membrane skeletal proteins, and the cytoskeleton.

Neuroglia and Nerve Sheaths

The nervous system contains other types of cells besides nerve cells. These are important, because they help to control the environment of the nerve cells, and they play an essential role in many of their functions.

Neuroglia

At any given site on a nerve cell there may be two kinds of neighbors facing it across the extracellular cleft. One may be the process of another nerve cell of fiber. The other may be a nonnervous cell. These are termed *neuroglia,* or simply *glia*. Their name comes from the famous German neuropathologist, Rudolf Virchow, who, in 1856, observed that there was an amorphous kind of substance that appeared to surround

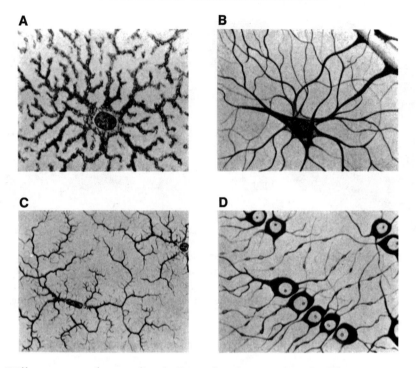

Fig. 3.16   Different types of neuroglia. **A.** Protoplasmic astrocytes. **B.** Fibrous astrocytes. **C.** Microglia. **D.** Oligodendrocytes. (After del Rio-Hortega, in Bloom and Fawcett, 1975)

nerve cells, and he bestowed on it a name—neuroglia—meaning "nerve glue." A number of studies with the light microscope in the early part of this century suggested that the neuroglia are composed of specific kinds of cells (see Fig. 3.16). Studies with the electron microscope have proven this, and have fully characterized the different types.

Neuroglial cells are very numerous; in some parts of the nervous system they outnumber the nerve cells by 10 to 1. They have been most closely studied and classified in the vertebrate nervous system. One of the main types is the *astrocyte*. These have many processes which radiate out in all directions from the cell body, giving the cell a star-shaped appearance. Within the central nervous system some of the processes terminate as end-feet on the surfaces of blood vessels. Astrocytes located in the white matter of the brain are called *fibrous* astrocytes, by virtue of the large numbers of fibrils present in the cytoplasm of their

cell bodies and branches. Those located in the gray matter have fewer fibrils, and are called *protoplasmic* astrocytes. In the electron microscope, astrocytes are seen to have a somewhat dark cytoplasmic matrix and large numbers of neurofilaments (these are the fibrils seen in the light microscope) as well as glycogen granules in the cytoplasm, all characteristics that are different from those of nerve cells. Astrocytes also are interconnected by gap junctions (Chap. 4).

The functions of astrocytes are believed to include: (1) providing structural support for nerve cells; (2) proliferation and repair following injury to nerves; (3) isolation and grouping of nerve fibers and terminals; and (4) participating in metabolic pathways which modulate the ions, transmitters, and metabolites involved in functions of nerve cells and their synapses. Earlier speculations, that they form part of the blood–brain barrier, or that they are involved in the transport of nutrients from the blood vessels to the nerve cells, seem now to be largely discounted. In the vertebrate central nervous system, a special kind of cell, called radial glia, appears only during embryonic life, and provides guidelines for migrating neurons to follow (Chaps. 9 and 30).

Some glial cells have distinctly fewer and thinner branches than astrocytes, and these are termed *oligodendrocytes* (oligo = few, dendro = branches). In the electron microscope, they are seen to contain few neurofilaments and glycogen granules, but numerous microtubules. The branches are often hard to distinguish from those of nerve cells, but can be differentiated because they never take part in synaptic connections. The functions of oligodendrocytes include the formation of the myelin around axons in the central nervous system (see below), and it has also been proposed that they have a symbiotic relation with certain nerve cells, involving complex metabolic exchanges.

A third main type of glial cell is termed *microglia*. These are small cells scattered throughout the nervous system. Wherever there is injury or degeneration, these cells proliferate, move to the site, and transform into large macrophages that remove and phagocytize the debris. They thus appear to be the nervous system representatives of the macrophages of the reticuloendothelial system, which defend against inflammation and infection in the body.

Nerve Sheaths

A very important function of neuroglia is to provide special sheaths around the long axons that interconnect different parts of the nervous system. These sheaths not only protect the axons, but are also intimately involved in structural modifications of the axons needed to conduct signals over long distances.

The simplest arrangement is one in which a single axon, or group of axons, is embedded in a glial cell, as shown in Fig. 3.17A. This is the common situation for very small-diameter fibers, in both invertebrates and vertebrates. The cells that provide these sheaths in peripheral nerves are modified glial cells, called *Schwann cells*. The point at which the Schwann cell membranes come together to enclose the axon or axons is called the *mesaxon* (it is analogous to the mesentery that encloses the intestines in the abdomen). The axons ensheathed in this manner are termed *unmyelinated,* for reasons that will become apparent below.

A somewhat more complicated arrangement is found where there are several loose folds of Schwann cell membrane around a given axon. This is characteristic of many larger invertebrate axons (see Fig. 3.17B).

The most complicated arrangement is one in which there are a number of layers of Schwann cell membranes tightly packed around a single axon. The layers are formed by the wrapping around of the Schwann cell membrane in a spiral manner during development, as indicated in Fig. 3.17C. By virtue of their tight packing and modified composition, these layers form a special tissue called *myelin*. This is such an important structure that all nerve fibers can be generally classified as either *unmyelinated* (see above), or *myelinated*.

Myelinated tissue has a fatty consistency and, to the naked eye, a white appearance (as in the white matter of the brain). The fibers are revealed in the light microscope as *black* structures when treated with the common lipid stains. Biochemical studies have been carried out on myelin isolated by various cell fractionation procedures. These have shown that myelin is about 80% lipid and 20% protein; cholesterol is one of the major lipids, with various other substances such as cerebrosides and phospholipids present in variable amounts in different tissues and species. An important proteolipid is called *myelin basic protein;* it has a molecular weight of approximately 10,000, and is found in both peripheral and central myelin. X-ray diffraction data show that myelin consists of repeating units with a period of about 18nm. In the electron microscope, myelin is clearly recog-

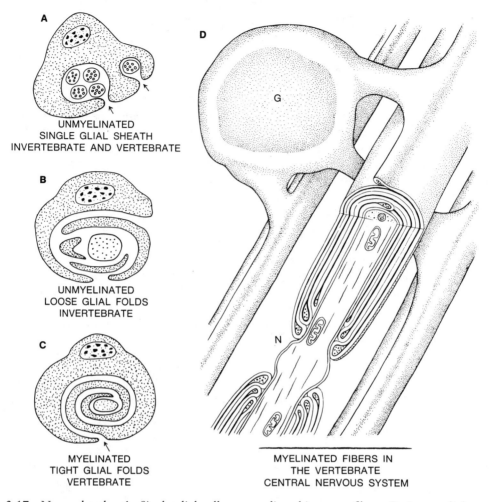

A

UNMYELINATED
SINGLE GLIAL SHEATH
INVERTEBRATE AND VERTEBRATE

B

UNMYELINATED
LOOSE GLIAL FOLDS
INVERTEBRATE

C

MYELINATED
TIGHT GLIAL FOLDS
VERTEBRATE

D

MYELINATED FIBERS IN
THE VERTEBRATE
CENTRAL NERVOUS SYSTEM

Fig. 3.17 Nerve sheaths. **A.** Single glial cell surrounding thin nerve fibers. **B.** Loose glial wrappings. **C.** Tight glial wrapping, forming myelin. **D.** Relation of glial (G) cell to myelin folds around nerve fiber and node (N) of Ranvier. (From Bunge, 1968).

nized as repeating light and dark layers with a period of about 18 nm, which, after allowing for shrinkage during preparation of the tissue, corresponds to two thicknesses of compressed plasma membrane.

A single Schwann cell in peripheral nerve supplies myelin for a length of about 1 mm of axon. At the borders of this region, the myelin layers overlap progressively in the manner shown in Fig. 3.17D. There is a gap of 1–2 μm between neighboring myelinated regions that is known as the *node of Ranvier*. Here the plasma membrane of the axon is unsheathed; in its place are

hair-like microvilli arising from satellite cells. A myelinated fiber thus consists of *nodes* of naked (unsheathed) nerve membrane alternating with *internodes* of myelinated membrane. The manner in which this imparts special properties for efficient conduction of nerve impulses is explained in Chap. 6.

Myelin is found almost exclusively in vertebrates. It would be possible to think of myelin, therefore, as an essential element in the higher nervous functions of which vertebrates are capable. The main contribution of myelin is probably that it permits efficient signal conduction over long distances. This allows precise integration of information from widely separated regions, which may be presumed to be necessary for the evolution of higher nervous functions. Loss of this precision has a disastrous effect on brain function, as when myelin undergoes degeneration in multiple sclerosis.

Neuron Terminology

Neurons are so various in form that students may find the terminology applied to different parts of a neuron and to different types of neuron somewhat confusing. Here are some simple rules for applying different terms.

To begin with, the cell body is that region of the cell around the nucleus. In nerve cells, as in other cells, the main organelles of the cytoplasm are gathered here in order to interact with the nucleus and with each other. These include the Golgi body and (in nerve cells) the Nissl substance, in addition to large numbers of mitochondria, rough and smooth ER, polysomes, and fibrillar structures.

Next are the branches. One of the cardinal features of neurons is that their branches have widely different patterns. Like trees, neurons acquire different names on the basis of different branching patterns. However, the branching patterns are so diverse that it is sometimes difficult to make the distinction between what is an axon and what is a dendrite. Let us see if we can take some logical steps toward making these distinctions.

Some nerve cells have long fibers that connect to other regions of the nervous system. These are called *projection neurons, principal neurons,* or *relay cells.* They characteristically have a single, long axon that makes the distant connections. This process can be recognized in Golgi-stained material because the fiber arises from a cone-shaped part (axon hillock) of the cell body or a dendritic trunk. It usually (but not always) maintains the same diameter throughout its length, despite giving off branches. The branches usually arise at right angles. Large axons and their branches may have a myelin covering. Under the electron microscope, the origin of the axon at the hillock can usually be recognized by a dense undercoating of the plasma membrane, and a funneling of microfilaments. Many of these points are represented in the diagram of Fig. 3.4.

Thus, in projection neurons, an axon can nearly always be identified by one or another (often all) of the above criteria. Then, all the other processes of the cell are dendrites. Thus, *dendrites are all those branches of a nerve cell that do not fulfill the criteria for being an axon.* Figure 3.18A shows several examples of projection neurons in which these definitions have been applied. Note that despite the specializations of the dorsal root ganglion cell and the invertebrate neuron, the definition can be applied with ease. The term "neurite" is sometimes used to refer to the dendritic branches of invertebrate neurons.

The other main type of nerve cell is contained wholly within one region of the nervous system. These are called *intrinsic neurons,* or *interneurons.* Examples of these are shown in Fig. 3.18B. The problem that arises here is that many intrinsic neurons do not require an axon for their functions. Thus, some have almost no processes whatever (the hair cell); others have only short processes (the bipolar cell); some have no process qualifying as an axon (the granule cell). The latter are usually called *anaxonal,* or *amacrine* (a = no, macrine = long process) cells; their processes may thus all be called dendrites. Only in the case of a cell with a short axon (short-axon cell) does one have an interneuron in which one can make the usual distinctions that apply to the projection neuron.

As noted earlier, dendrites were originally termed "protoplasmic prolongations," and the modern studies with the electron

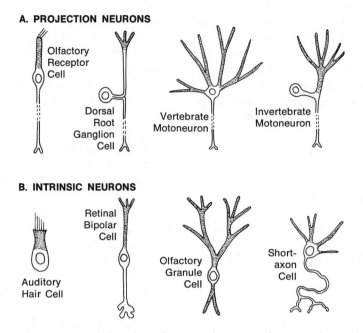

Fig. 3.18 Types of neurons and their branches. Dendrites are shown with stippling, axons with clear profiles.

microscope have fully confirmed the correctness of that idea. As indicated in Fig. 3.4, the main organelles of the cell body extend without any sharp boundaries into the trunks of the dendrites. Thus, large dendrites can be clearly distinguished from large axons. However, small axons and small dendrites are not so dissimilar in their fine structure. The terminals of axons are often characterized by a large number of synaptic vesicles (see next chapter), but small axon terminals differ little from small dendritic branches and terminals in their fine structure. The sites of synapses on axons and dendrites will be considered in the next chapter.

4

The Synapse

The Synapse: A Brief History

In Chap. 1, we saw that the main business of neurobiology is to understand how individual neuronal elements are organized into functional systems. The principal means of organization is through connections between the neurons called *synapses*. As Sanford Palay, a modern scholar of the nervous system, has expressed it: "The concept of the synapse lies at the heart of the neuron doctrine." Let us take a brief excursion into history to see how our knowledge of synapses has come about.

The origin of the idea of the synapse is particularly associated with one man, Charles Sherrington, an English physiologist. Around 1890, when Cajal and his contemporaries were establishing the anatomical evidence for the neuron as a cell, Sherrington was just beginning his study of the reflex functions of the spinal cord. His work involved a painstaking analysis of the anatomy and physiology of the spinal nerves and spinal cord, and the results provided the foundation for all subsequent concepts of the reflex as a basic unit of function in the spinal cord as well as in other parts of the nervous system, as will be discussed in Chap. 19.

Sherrington's results also set him to thinking about how activity conducted in the sensory fibers to the spinal cord is transferred to the motor cells that innervate the muscles. His studies had convinced him that the transfer involved properties different from those involved in the conducting of signals in the fibers themselves. If Cajal and his colleagues were right, and the sensory nerves arborize and terminate in free endings, then these different properties must be associated with some kind of special contact between those endings and the motor cells. And so it was, when Michael Foster came in 1897 to revise his standard physiology textbook of the day, and asked Sherrington to contribute the chapters on the spinal cord, that Sherrington advanced the following simple proposal:

So far as our present knowledge goes, we are led to think that the tip of a twig of the arborescence is not continuous with but merely in contact with the substance of the dendrite or cell body on which it impinges. Such a special connection of one nerve cell with another might be called a *synapse*.

The term *synapse* is derived from the Greek, meaning to clasp, connect, or join.

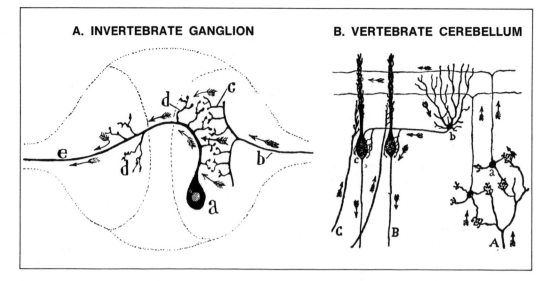

Fig. 4.1 Diagrams by Cajal, to show the direction of transmission of signals in nerve cells and nerve circuits according to his law of dynamic polarization. **A.** Invertebrate ganglion. Abbreviations: a, cell body of ganglion cell; b, incoming axon; c, axon terminal; d, neurite (dendritic) terminal; e, projection axon of ganglion cell. **B.** Vertebrate cerebellum. Abbreviations: A, incoming axon (mossy fiber); B, output axon of Purkinje cell; C, second type of incoming axon (climbing fiber); a, granule cell; b, basket cell; c, Purkinje cell. (From Cajal, 1911)

Sherrington thought of it, anatomically, as a site of "surfaces of separation," but he always emphasized that it was first and foremost a *functional* connection. He conceived of the possible functions very broadly, as shown in a passage from his famous book, *The Integrative Action of the Nervous System,* published in 1906:

> Such a surface might restrain diffusion, bank up osmotic pressure, restrict the movement of ions, accumulate electric charges, support a double electric layer, alter in shape and surface-tension with changes in difference of potential . . . or intervene as a membrane between dilute solutions of electrolytes of different concentration or colloidal suspensions with different sign of charge.

We will see that a broad framework of this kind is very much needed to embrace the varieties of interactions between nerve cells shown by modern studies.

One of the important properties of spinal reflexes is that they always proceed from sensory to motor, never in the reverse direction. Sherrington suggested that this is imparted by a one-way valvelike property of the synapses. This seemed to fit with another idea, that the dendrites and cell body of a neuron are its *receptor* parts, where signals are received, and the axon and its terminals are the *effector* parts, where signals are emitted. This had been deduced around 1890 by Cajal and a Belgian anatomist, Arthur van Gehuchten, who had taken up the Golgi method very soon after Cajal, and it was christened the *Law of Dynamic Polarization.* Figure 4.1 illustrates how this concept applied to the flow of activity in neurons in invertebrates (A) and vertebrates (B).

This "law" was soon accepted as a corollary to the neuron doctrine, and provided an attractive and logical framework for understanding how individual nerve cells could be connected into groups and chains for transmitting nerve signals. However, in the 1960s, methods for analyzing single nerve cells showed that in many parts of the nervous system, axons interact with other axons, and dendrites interact with other dendrites, or with axons. Thus, the Law of Dynamic Polarization describes the overall flow of information through a nervous center, but at any site on any neuron within that center there are opportunities for complex interactions (with neighboring axons, cell bodies, or dendrites) that enhance the ability to process information (Bodian, 1972; Shepherd, 1972).

Modern research in neurobiology has focused much of its attention on the synapse and its role in the functioning of the nervous system. This is not by accident, for it is possible to regard the synapse as the essential and defining property of the neuron. Thus, one can suggest that a *neuron is a cell connected to other cells by synapses that mediate specific signals involved in behavior.* Note how this parallels rather closely our definition of the subject matter of neurobiology in Chap. 1.

Having stated the importance of the synapse, we also want to recognize that it is not the only means by which nerve cells can interact with each other. Interactions, in fact, take many forms, and the organization of neurons is built on these as well. Our study therefore requires a broad view of the nature of interneuronal relations.

In any relations between two nerve cells, there are three components. One is the cell or cell process from which activity is sent. This is called the *presynaptic* process. Another is the cell or cell process which receives the activity; this is the *postsynaptic* process. The third component is whatever *intervenes* between the two processes. This may be just as important in determining the nature of the interaction as the other two components. In fact, on the basis of this intervening component, we can identify three main degrees of relatedness between the other two: the two may be at a *distance* from each other; they may be next to (*juxtaposed* to) each other; and they may be actually in contact or joined to each other to form a morphological *junction.* Let us organize our discussion in terms of these three degrees of relatedness.

Distant Relations Between Neurons

The most distant relation is between two cells that are in two different animal bodies. Specific interactions of this type are those in which a particular substance is secreted into the air or water by one member of a species, and is detected and responded to by another member of that same species (see Fig. 4.2). Such a substance is called a *pheromone,* and is an important factor in the behavior of many species, as will be described in Chaps. 11 and 27. Dietrich Schneider, one of the pioneers in studies of pheromones, has suggested humorously that this situation can be thought of as a "giant synapse."

This idea is not so farfetched as it may seem. Many years ago, the great biologist J. B. S. Haldane suggested that substances that act as transmitters between cells within an organism may have their evolutionary origins as substances that act as chemical messengers between organisms. Table 4.1 summarizes the evidence for such transmit-

Fig. 4.2 Types of long-distance, chemically mediated interactions between cells.

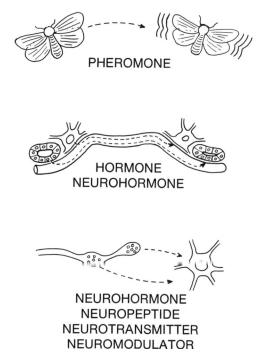

PHEROMONE

HORMONE
NEUROHORMONE

NEUROHORMONE
NEUROPEPTIDE
NEUROTRANSMITTER
NEUROMODULATOR

Table 4.1   Internal neuroactive substances for which external chemoreceptors also exist

Substances having internal neuroactive role	Organism with external chemoreceptors for the substance	Behavior stimulated by activation of external receptor
1. AMP	shrimp, spiny lobster, mosquito larvae	attractant for shrimp, mosquito larvae
2. Cyclic AMP	slime mold	attractant following exhaustion of food supply
3. ATP	mosquito (insect)	gorge on liquid
4. Acetylcholine	*Tetrahymena* (ciliated protozoan)	reduction in forward swimming velocity
5. γ-Aminobutyric acid (GABA)	abalone larvae (mollusk)	induces settlement and metamorphosis
6. Glutamate	American lobster	prey detection
7. Glycine	snail	extend proboscis
8. Taurine	spiny lobster	attraction
9. α, β-Ecdysone	spiny lobster	not known
10. Prostaglandin A$_2$	reef fish	rejection of food

From Carr (1986)

ter substances that have been shown to function also as external chemical messengers. One may speculate that the differentiation of membrane receptors for the external messenger was a step toward enabling the same substance to act as an internal transmitter. The ability of an external messenger to elicit an entire behavior pattern may also carry over to the capacity of some substances to elicit behavior patterns when they act as neurotransmitters or neurohormones (an example is serotonin; see Chap. 20).

Within the same body, two cells in different organs may interact with each other over long distances. This occurs when one of them secretes a *hormone,* which is carried in the bloodstream to elicit a specific response in cells of another organ. Hormones play essential roles in the economy of the body, as we will note in later chapters. In some cases, hormones are secreted by gland cells and act on other gland cells or on smooth muscle cells of various internal organs. However, some hormones are secreted by nerve cells to act on glands or muscles, and some are secreted by glands to act on nerve cells. Most important, an enormous amount of evidence is accumulating for a variety of hormonelike substances secreted by neurons and acting on other neurons. These are called *neurohormones* or *neuroactive peptides.* The neurons that synthesize and secrete these substances are called *neuroendocrine* cells. It is becoming increasingly difficult to make the distinction between a neuroendocrine cell and a nerve cell that, in addition to the usual types of nerve signaling, also secretes a neuroactive peptide or hormone. Neuroendocrine cells are very common in virtually all the invertebrate phyla as well as in vertebrates. As indicated in Fig. 4.2, in the case of a neurohormone, one has the three components of a synapse, but with the intervening component comprised of interstitial fluid or the bloodstream.

The similarities that may exist between hormonal and synaptic actions are exemplified by adrenaline (epinephrine). Epinephrine has been traditionally regarded as a hormone, secreted by the adrenal medulla and preparing the body for "fight or flight." The secretion is stimulated by nerves of the sympathetic nervous system. Epinephrine is derived from norepinephrine (noradrenaline), which has many similar actions and, in addition, is a transmitter substance at some synapses. Furthermore, epinephrine acts on some of the same receptors that norepinephrine acts on, and the receptors in turn activate the "second messenger," cyclic AMP, in the postsynaptic responses at some synapses. Thus, there is a great deal of overlap between some kinds of hormonal and synaptic actions (see Chap. 8).

Within a given part of the nervous system, a terminal or other part of a neuron may release substances that diffuse through the intercellular clefts and affect neurons not actually in contact with it. Cells in the midbrain of vertebrates, for example, project their axons diffusely to many parts of the nervous system, where they ramify and terminate, in many cases, without making definite contacts with specific structures. The branches and terminals nonetheless contain vesicles and neurotransmitter substances, and it is therefore believed that such axons release these substances to act on nearby neuronal processes, as indicated in Fig. 4.2. Similar release appears to occur from dendrites in certain areas. The range of action of such substances is limited by diffusion, as well as other factors. These substances may act as *neuromodulators* as well as specific *neurotransmitters,* as discussed in Chap. 8.

Membrane Juxtapositions

Let us now consider the situation in which the membranes of two neurons come close together, separated only by the ubiquitous extracellular space, or cleft, of about 20 nm. We term this a *juxtaposition* (juxta = next to) of the two membranes. This relationship is a very common one in the nervous system; in fact, one can say as a general rule that neurons usually are

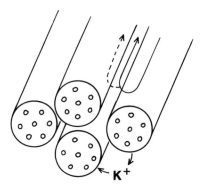

Fig. 4.3 Membrane juxtapositions, as exemplified by a bundle of unmyelinated axons, which provide for interactions through ions (K^+) or electric current (--). The current flows indicated in the diagram occur during an impulse, increasing the excitability of neighboring axons; accumulation of extracellular K^+ following an impulse peak depolarizes neighboring axons, also increasing their excitability.

crowded against each other, with their membranes in juxtaposition to each other, except where glial membranes are intruded in order to keep particular processes apart. As indicated in Fig. 4.3, certain types of fine, unmyelinated axons (for example, the axons of the olfactory nerve, or the parallel fibers of the cerebellum) have this membrane-to-membrane relationship with each other. It also occurs throughout the neuropil of the local regions of the nervous system, between the terminals of axons and dendrites. The membranes of neurons and glia are juxtaposed nearly everywhere they occur together.

This juxtaposition of membranes provides for several possible functions. Any movement of substances, such as ions or metabolites, out of one cell into the intervening cleft may have effects on that same cell as well as on all the juxtaposed processes of other cells. Uptake of substances may occur by this route, as for example the uptake of K^+ (see Fig. 4.3) or the uptake of the neurotransmitter γ-aminobutyric acid (GABA) by glial cells. Juxtaposed membranes also provide for electrical interactions between neighboring

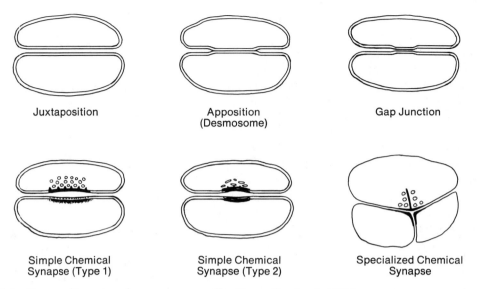

Fig. 4.4   Types of junctions between nerve cells. (From Shepherd, 1979)

processes under some conditions (Fig. 4.3); the sites at which such interactions occur are called ephapses (see Chap. 7).

Membrane Junctions

The closest stage of relatedness between neurons is a specific contact of their membranes. This occurs at sites where (1) the two membranes come close together or are fused, and/or (2) the membranes appear more dense. Such sites are found between cells throughout the body. Depending on details of structure, they are called occluding junctions, desmosomes, tight junctions, gap junctions, septate junctions, or zonulae adherens. They vary widely in size and form, ranging from small spots to long strips or patches. Such junctions provide for several possible functions: simple adhesion; transfer of substances during metabolism or embryological development; restriction of movement of substances in the extracellular compartment.

An instance of the latter function is provided by the *tight junctions* between the cells that line the blood vessels and ventricles of the brain. The two outer leaflets of the unit membrane of these junctions, as illustrated in Fig. 4.4, are completely fused, to form a five-layered complex. These tight junctions restrict the movement of substances in the extracellular space and are responsible for the so-called *blood–brain barrier,* which limits transport from brain capillaries and thereby protects the brain from circulating toxic substances.

An important type of membrane junction is the *gap junction.* Here, the outer leaflets are separated by a gap of 2–4 nm, to form a seven-layered complex (Figs. 4.4 and 4.5). In many cases, the presence of these junctions has been correlated with the physiological finding of a low-resistance electrical pathway between two neurons. On this basis they have been categorized as *electrical synapses* (we will study these electrical interactions in Chap. 7). The junction varies in diameter from 0.1 to 10 μm. At high resolution, dense material is seen beneath each apposed membrane, and it can be shown that the membranes are part of two systems of channels, the one continuous with the extracellular space, the other connecting the two cells. This arrangement is shown in Fig. 4.5A. The molecular structure of the gap junction polypeptide inferred from DNA cloning is shown in B. Recently it has been possible to make patch recordings from two adjacent cells (C), and

A. Gap junction structure

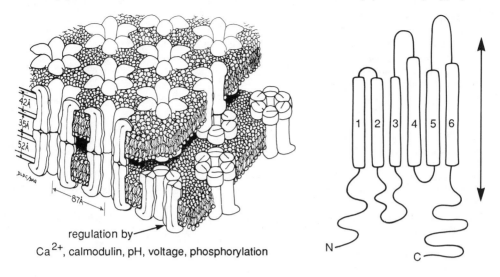

regulation by
Ca^{2+}, calmodulin, pH, voltage, phosphorylation

B. Gap junction polypeptide

C. Recording set-up

D. Single channel events

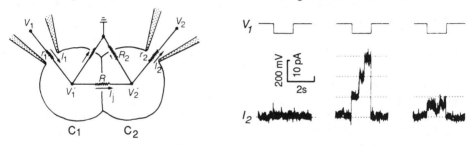

Fig. 4.5 **A.** Diagram of a gap junction (electrical synapse). Channels provide for intercellular exchange of low-molecular-weight substances and electric current. Some gap junctions pass current in only one direction (rectifying junctions); this is regulated by several factors as indicated in the diagram. Channel walls are composed of six protein subunits (referred to collectively as a connexon) which span the lipid bilayer of each plasma membrane. Because of the gap between the membranes, extracellular substances can percolate between the channels. (From Makowski et al., 1977) **B.** Tertiary structure of gap junction polypeptide deduced from amino acid sequence. Each polypeptide has six hydrophobic α-helices which span the membrane (membrane thickness indicated by arrows). Segment 6 is amphipathic, and might form part of the channel wall. **C.** Method for double patch-clamp recording of single-channel currents at a gap junction. Diagram illustrates the whole-cell patch recordings from two rat lacrimal gland cells (C_1, C_2). Abbreviations: V_1, V_2, command voltages in C_1, C_2; I_1, I_2, recorded currents; r_1, r_2, access resistances for the two electrodes; R_2, resistance across cell membrane; R, resistance of gap junction channels; I_j, current through gap junction channels. In the experiment, a small command voltage V_1 is imposed in C_1, and the junctional current I_j is calculated by the equation $I_j = \Delta I_2 (1 + r_2/R_2)$. From this, the gap junction conductance (G_j) is calculated by $G_j = I_j/V_j$, where V_j equals the difference between the holding and command values of V_1 and V_2. **D.** Recordings of single-channel events. V_1, step voltage commands in cell C_1; I_2, currents recorded in cell C_2. The three recordings show typical variations, due to channel activity near the threshold for activation. Note in the middle trace the three steps, representing either successive openings of three identical channels, or different substates of one channel. Some partial openings are also seen (far right). The quantal conductance calculated for a single event in these recordings is approximately 120 pS; this is the elementary conductance of a fully open channel. (B–D from Neyton and Trautmann, 1985)

71

Table 4.2 Physiological roles of cell-to-cell channels

A. Tissue homeostasis
   1. Equilibration of individual cell differences in electrical potential
   2. Equilibration and buffering of individual cell differences in small molecules
   3. Transport of nutrient substances from cell to cell
B. Regulating signal transmission
   1. Signals affecting cytoplasmic processes
      a. Chemical signals: cyclic nucleotides, various metabolites
      b. Electrical signals: propagation of electrical activity in heart, smooth muscle, electrical synapses
   2. Signals affecting genetic processes
      a. Cellular differentiation: ubiquity of cell-to-cell channels in embryonic tissue
      b. Cellular growth: channels are necessary for control of growth and prevention of unregulated (cancerous) growth
C. Cellular organization
   1. Amplification of cell responses through diffusable messenger modules (such as cyclic nucleotides) or voltage-sensitive electrical responses
   2. Hierarchical interactions: driving of secondary cells by a primary pacemaker, as in the heart and some neural circuits

Adapted from Loewenstein (1981)

observe the single channel currents (D). The single channel conductance is relatively large (120pS) compared with voltage-gated (Chap. 6) and ligand-gated channels (see below). As indicated in Fig. 4.5A, the gap junction channels may be gated (activated or modulated) by several factors: the concentration of intracellular free Ca^{2+}; intracellular pH; membrane voltage (as in C,D); calmodulin, or phosphorylation.

Gap junctions are widely distributed throughout the body, and are the most common type of junction between cells in most body organs. Through these junctions multicellular functional units are formed for interchanges of small molecules that are important during embryonic development, and into adult life, as was mentioned in Chap. 1. Some of the many functions proposed for gap junctions and related cell-to-cell channels are listed in Table 4.2. In the nervous system, gap junctions are especially common between glial cells. They are common between neurons in invertebrates and lower vertebrates, and have been found between certain types of neurons in the mammalian brain (see Chap. 7). The relatively low incidence of gap junctions in the mature mammalian brain is noteworthy. This reduction could reflect a mechanism to increase the metabolic and functional

independence of individual neurons, in order to permit more complex information processing.

Chemical Synapses

The most complicated type of junction in the nervous system, and the type considered to be the most characteristic, is the chemical synapse (Fig. 4.4). It differs morphologically from other types of membrane appositions in being oriented, or polarized, from one neuron to the other. This polarization is determined mainly by two features: (1) There is usually a group of small vesicles near the site of contact, and (2) there is an increased density associated with the apposed membranes, which in some synapses is particularly marked opposite the vesicle-containing process. In certain cases (e.g., the neuromuscular junction), it can be shown unequivocally that transmission is from the vesicle-containing process to the other process, so that one can identify the *presynaptic* and *postsynaptic* process with confidence.

Molecular Components of the Synapse

The concept of the synapse as a site of small vesicles and membrane-associated

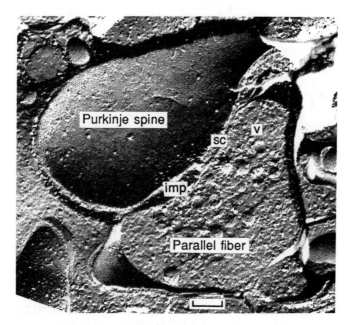

Fig. 4.6 A freeze-fractured specimen of synaptic terminals in the cerebellum. The line of cleavage is such that one sees the inner surface of an outer leaflet of a Purkinje cell dendritic spine; it also cuts across a synaptic terminal of a parallel fiber. Note the vesicles (v) in the presynaptic terminal, the widened synaptic cleft (sc), and the accumulation of small particles (imp) in the postsynaptic terminal membrane. Bracket, 0.1 μm. (From Landis and Reese, 1974)

densities originated in the first electron microscopical studies of Palay, Palade, and others in the 1950s (see above). Since that time, this concept has been universally accepted as the morphological definition when the synapse is viewed at relatively low magnification.

Further details have been produced by a variety of methods. Among these, one of the most useful has been the freeze-fracturing technique, in which a tiny block of tissue is frozen and then fractured by a swift blow with a sharp blade. A micrograph of a specimen prepared in this way is shown in Fig. 4.6. The lines of cleavage are not between the membranes of the two neighboring neurons, but between the inner and outer leaflets of the same membrane. As can be seen, the fracture line jumps from one membrane to the next, or cuts entirely through a process, in its course through the tissue. In this view, the fracture line has cut through a synapse between a pre- and a postsynaptic process. There is a collection of intramembranous particles (IMPs) on the inner surface of the outer leaflet of the postsynaptic membrane. IMPs are found widely in the membranes of cells, where they generally appear to be the electron microscopic images of membrane proteins. At synapses, they may represent channels for Ca^{2+}, an important ion in synaptic transmission and cell metabolism (Chaps. 7 and 8). When IMPs are present in high density, they serve as an additional morphological component for defining a synapse. However, they are present only in certain types of synapses, mainly those believed to have an excitatory action (see below).

The concept of the synapse has been greatly expanded by a variety of biochemical studies. The picture that has emerged is summarized in Fig. 4.7, which combines morphological and biochemical results. One of the earliest studies employed special stains to reveal dense projections into the cytoplasm, forming a gridwork in the presyn-

MORPHOLOGY   BIOCHEMISTRY

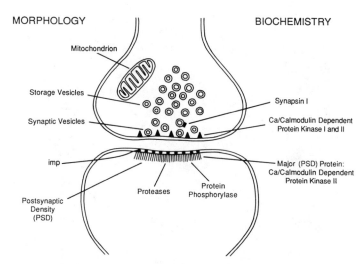

Fig. 4.7 Some of the morphological and biochemical properties of a chemical synapse. Abbreviations: imp, intramembranous particle; PSD, postsynaptic density. A major biochemical constituent of the synapse is Ca^{2+}/calmodulin protein kinase II (CaM, II); it is present in the presynaptic terminal and is especially concentrated in the PSD. It is one of a family of homologous kinases, consisting of large multimeric proteins composed of approximately 12 50–60kd subunits. One of the main actions of this enzyme is autophosphorylation of its own subunits. According to Miller and Kennedy (1986), changes produced by autophosphorylation enable the kinase to function as a molecular switch, so that it can remain active after an initial brief calcium signal; this may contribute to long-term activity dependent changes at synapses (cf. Fig. 29.15). Other cytoskeletal proteins present in the postsynaptic membrane include actin, which may contribute to receptor clustering, and a 43K protein, which may be a kinase, and which appears to be present in an activity-dependent manner. See text.

aptic terminal; the synaptic vesicles appear to move between these projections to fuse with the membrane during neurotransmitter release. The points at which the vesicles actually contact the plasma membrane to undergo exocytosis are called vesicle attachment sites.

A basic tool for analysis has been cell fractionation, in which the brain is homogenized to obtain suspensions of cells and cell organelles, which are then separated by means of centrifugation. In addition to nuclei, mitochondria, vesicles, etc., one obtains synaptosomes, consisting of pre- and postsynaptic terminals whose membranes seal over. Biochemical analysis can then be carried out on these preparations in which the biochemical components of the synapse are present in high concentration.

The main advances made with these and related methods have been the identifica-

tion of a number of proteins that are specific for the synapse. On the *presynaptic side,* one of the most important is synapsin I. Discovered by Paul Greengard and his collaborators at Yale and Rockefeller universities, synapsin I is found in virtually all nerve cells, where it is concentrated in synaptic terminals, mainly on the presynaptic side. It is a heterodimer of 166 kilodaltons, and is very similar to the band 4.1 protein of the red blood cell membrane cytoskeleton (see Fig. 3.5). As shown in Fig. 4.7, synapsin I is essentially associated with synaptic vesicles. When synapsin I is phosphorylated, it dissociates from the vesicle membrane, allowing the vesicle to move through the cytoskeleton and fuse with the plasma membrane so that exocytosis can take place and neurotransmitter can be released. Phosphorylation is believed to be due to an enzyme called Ca/calmodulin dependent protein kinase I. This enzyme is activated by Ca^{2+} influx, as a result of depolarization of the terminal by an impulse spreading into it from the axon. Vesicle fusion is a complex event, in which there is lateral movement of proteins within the vesicular and plasma membranes as they approach each other, as well as interactions of the two membranes with their associated cytoskeletal elements, as indicated in Fig. 4.7 (see also Fig. 2.14).

On the *postsynaptic side,* the main elements identified thus far are the membrane receptors that bind the neurotransmitter molecules and allow ion movements through channels; the postsynaptic density (PSD); and the enzymes that phosphorylate and dephosphorylate the PSD proteins. Let us consider each of these briefly.

Membrane receptors are of two types. One consists of a channel protein that itself binds the neurotransmitter molecule, inducing an allosteric change in the channel to allow ions to flow; the ACh receptor belongs to this class, as discussed in Chap. 2. Alternatively, the neurotransmitter may bind to a nonchannel protein. In either case, there may ensue further reactions, such as phosphorylation of nearby enzymes and proteins, which ultimately affect the membrane properties, cytoskeleton, or metabolism of the terminal or rest of the neuron. These receptor mechanisms thus allow for a wide range of brief or long-lasting effects on the postsynaptic terminal or neuron.

The postsynaptic density has been the subject of numerous investigations, using subcellular fractionation in combination with other biochemical methods. Much of the density is due to the membrane cytoskeleton, whose basic organization we have already discussed (Chap. 3). In addition, the PSD is enriched in certain components. Microtubules and neurofilaments and their associated proteins are anchored in the PSD. Proteolytic enzymes are present; they act to degrade components of the membrane cytoskeleton, particularly fodrin and microtubule-associated proteins. The pos-

sible role of one such enzyme, calpain, in a mechanism for memory is discussed in Chap. 29. The most abundant protein is a 50-kdalton polypeptide, called the major PSD protein because it accounts for up to 50% of the total PSD protein. These elements, and their possible interrelations, are indicated in the diagram of Fig. 4.7.

Protein phosphorylation, as already mentioned, is important in presynaptic release mechanisms, and it is also important in postsynaptic responses. Recent work has shown that the major PSD protein is virtually identical to the 50-kdalton subunit of Ca/calmodulin-dependent protein kinase II. PSDs are enriched in several types of phosphoproteins which are substrates for this kinase, and the number is growing. In addition, PSDs are enriched in protein phosphatases, as they must be if the proteins are to be able to undergo dephosphorylation. In Chap. 8, we will learn how these phosphorylation and dephosphorylation reactions control the physiological responses of neurons to their synaptic inputs.

Molecular Mechanism of the Synapse

How do these molecular components function together as a coordinated mechanism to provide for synaptic transmission? A summary of the basic steps involved is shown in Fig. 4.8. Although this scheme appears daunting at first, it can easily be broken down into several main types of mechanisms. These are as follows:

1. *Metabolic machinery.* These include biosynthesis (A), transport (B), and storage (C) of transmitters and vesicles, insertion of membrane proteins (D), and assembly of elements of the terminal. Corresponding events take place in the postsynaptic terminal (A', B', etc.).
2. *Presynaptic release.* Rapid release of transmitter, such as occurs at the neuromuscular junction, is achieved by presynaptic depolarization ①, causing Ca^{2+} influx ②, which leads directly, or indi-

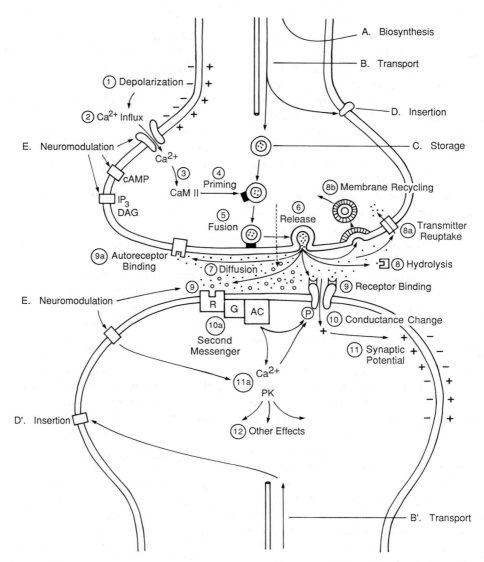

Fig. 4.8 A summary of some of the main biochemical mechanisms that have been identified at chemical synapses. **A–E.** Long-term steps in synthesis, transport, and storage of neurotransmitters and neuromodulators; insertion of membrane channel proteins and receptors; and neuromodulatory effects. ①–⑫. These summarize the more rapid steps involved in immediate signaling at the synapse. These steps are described in the text, and are further discussed for different types of synapses in Chapter 8. Abbreviations: IP_3, inositol triphosphate; CAM II, Ca/calmodulin-dependent protein kinase II; DAG, diacylglycerol; PK, protein kinase; R, receptor; G, G protein; AC, adenylate cyclase.

rectly via intermediary second messengers ③, to priming of vesicles ④, fusion ⑤, and release ⑥. Transmitters may also be released from the cytoplasm, as indicated.

3. *Presynaptic restitution.* Transmitter re-

lease activates mechanisms to restore the presynaptic terminal. These include transmitter reuptake in some cases (8a), and membrane recycling (8b).

4. *Presynaptic modulation.* The release process is subject to modulation by neu-

romodulators (E), acting either directly on membrane channels or indirectly through internal second messengers; it can also be modulated by action of the released transmitter on autoreceptors ⑨.

5. *Cleft mechanisms.* The transmitter diffuses across the cleft to act on its receptors. Diffusion ⑦ is controlled by the cleft extracellular matrix. The action of the transmitter is terminated by diffusion, and in some cases by hydrolysis ⑧ or by reuptake (8a).

6. *Postsynaptic receptors.* The transmitter may act directly on channel proteins in the postsynaptic membrane ⑨, causing a conductance change ⑩ and a consequent postsynaptic potential response ⑪ which spreads along the membrane in decrementing fashion (see next chapter). This is the mechanism at the neuromuscular junction. Alternatively, the transmitter may bind to receptors ⑨ linked to second messenger systems (10a). These may in turn act on membrane channels directly, or indirectly through kinases (11a) or other enzymes. These enzymes may also have many other effects on the molecular machinery of the neuron ⑫ related to motility, growth, and metabolism.

7. *Postsynaptic modulation.* The postsynaptic site may be modulated in several ways. First, peptides released from the presynaptic terminal (see small circles in the diagram) may bind to postsynaptic receptors, affecting binding of their neurotransmitter ligand ⑨. Second, neuroactive substances from other sources (neighboring terminals, blood-borne hormones, etc.) may bind to membrane channels ⑨ or second-messenger receptors (10a). Third, peptides may act internally on protein kinases (11a) and other enzymes or components of the postsynaptic process.

The student should work carefully through this diagram to be able to understand each step as a part of a basic type of molecular mechanism, and as a part of the whole

synapse. It should be emphasized that no synapse is likely to have all of these individual components; they provide rather a roster of players, from which each synapse selects a cast of characters for its contribution to the drama of behavior. We will see the roles that these characters play when we study the biochemistry of different synapses in Chap. 8.

Two Types of Synapses

In 1959, E. G. Gray of London, working on the cerebral cortex, obtained evidence for two morphological types of synapses. There is a consensus that, despite many local variations and gradations between the two, this division has some validity. The two types are illustrated in Fig. 4.4. The distinguishing features may be summarized as follows:

Type 1: synaptic cleft approximately 30 nm; junctional area relatively large (up to 1–2 μm in diameter); prominent accumulation of dense material next to the postsynaptic membrane (i.e., an asymmetric densification related to the two apposed membranes).

Type II: synaptic cleft approximately 20 nm; junctional area relatively small (less than 1 μm in diameter); membrane-associated densifications modest and symmetrical.

Following the recognition of these types, evidence was obtained in 1965 by Uchizono of Japan that, in many parts of the brain, type I synapses are associated with spherical vesicles (diameter approximately 30–60 nm) which are usually present in considerable numbers. Type II synapses, on the other hand, are associated with smaller (diameter 10–30 nm) vesicles, which are less numerous and which, significantly, take on various ellipsoidal and flattened shapes. The distinction between round and flat types of vesicles is by no means a sharp one; in many synapses a vesicle simply tends to the one shape or the other.

In addition to the membrane-related

PRESYNAPTIC

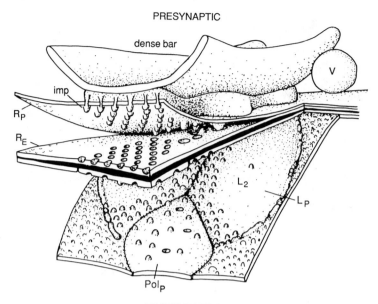

POSTSYNAPTIC

Fig. 4.9 Structural specializations at the synapses of the photoreceptor within the optic lamina of the fly, *Musca domestica*. Within the presynaptic process is a dense bar and associated synaptic vesicles (v). Intramembranous particles (imp) are embedded in the protoplasmic leaflet of the presynaptic receptor cell membrane (R_P), their protrusions form pits in the external leaflet of the receptor cell membrane (R_E), as seen in freeze-fractured specimens. The synaptic cleft is shown in black (c). There are four postsynaptic processes at this synapse, two from monopolar cells (L_1 and L_2); imp's are embedded in the P face (L_P) of these membranes near their inner boundary, leaving the rest of the membrane relatively particle-free. The other two postsynaptic processes are from polar elements (Pol_P). Note that the postsynaptic imp's fracture with the P face, as is characteristic of many GABAergic, inhibitory synapses; this is in contrast to fracture of imps with the E face at many glutamatergic, excitatory synapses. (Modified from Frohlich, 1985)

densities and the vesicle shapes, a third distinction is the distribution of intramembranous particles. Type I synapses tend to have a dense collection of IMPs in the postsynaptic membrane, as already shown in Fig. 4.6; by contrast, this is lacking at many type II synapses, at least in the vertebrate nervous system.

In invertebrate synapses, recent studies have shown that arrays of IMPs may be present in both pre- and postsynaptic membranes. An example of an invertebrate synapse is shown in Fig. 4.9; this shows a common pattern, in which the presynaptic terminal contains a dense bar, and makes synaptic contact with several (in this case, four) different postsynaptic terminals (see also this pattern in Fig. 4.4). In this ex-

ample, the postsynaptic IMPs are found in the internal leaflet (P-face) of the plasma membrane. Freeze-fracture studies have shown that IMPs appear to have this location at inhibitory synapses (many of which use GABA as a transmitter), whereas IMPs fracture predominantly with the external leaflet (E-face) at excitatory synapses (many of which use glutamate as a transmitter). It appears that these differing IMP distributions are correlated with the excitatory (depolarizing) or inhibitory (hyperpolarizing) actions at the synapse, rather than with the particular transmitter involved. These are intriguing glimpses into structure–function relations at the molecular level of the synapse, which we will explore further in Chaps. 7 and 8.

The recognition of the two types of synapse has provided anatomists with a useful tool to unravel the synaptic organization of local brain regions. Much of this usefulness has been based on the premise that all the synapses made by a given neuron onto other neurons are either of one type or the other. This is commonly called the *morphological corollary of Dale's Law,* Dale's Law being usually understood as stating that a given neuron has the same physiological action at all its synapses. As we will see in Chap. 8, this is neither what Dale, in fact, put forward nor what electrophysiology reveals. Nor has it been proven that the morphological corollary has universal validity.

Many neuroanatomists have been skeptical of the validity of the two types of synapse on the basis of the fact that the flattening of vesicles has been shown to depend on the osmolarity of solutions used in preparing the tissue for electron microscopy. But, in a sense, everything the electron microscopist sees is a distortion of the true dynamic living state. The interpretation of electron micrographs, and of any preparations of anatomical specimens, must be made with this constantly in mind. Despite these reservations, the recognition of the two types of synapse has been the basis for remarkable progress in the understanding of the synaptic organization of the brain.

Vesicles

Synaptic vesicles are a subject in themselves. They come, in the felicitous phraseology of Sanford Palay, like chocolates, in a variety of shapes and sizes, and are stuffed with different kinds of filling. Small vesicles (20–40 nm in diameter) are the most common; they are the ones we have discussed in regard to type I and type II synapses (see Fig. 1.10). At some synapses, there is evidence that acetylcholine is bound to, or contained within, the vesicles; such synapses are, therefore, called cholinergic. At other synapses, the vesicles appear to be

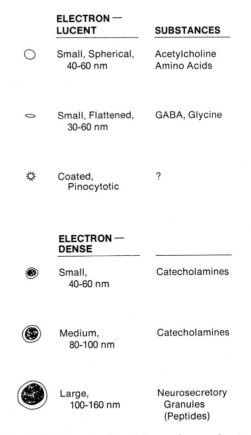

ELECTRON — LUCENT		SUBSTANCES
○	Small, Spherical, 40-60 nm	Acetylcholine Amino Acids
⌒	Small, Flattened, 30-60 nm	GABA, Glycine
☼	Coated, Pinocytotic	?

ELECTRON — DENSE		
◉	Small, 40-60 nm	Catecholamines
◉	Medium, 80-100 nm	Catecholamines
◉	Large, 100-160 nm	Neurosecretory Granules (Peptides)

Fig. 4.10 Types of vesicles and granules in nerve cells.

associated with certain amino acids. These are the transmitter substances that are released by the presynaptic terminal when it is activated and that mediate the synaptic action onto the postsynaptic membrane, as will be described in Chaps. 7 and 8.

Another type of vesicle is medium sized (50–90 nm in diameter) and contains a dense granule; these vesicles are associated with monoamines. Large vesicles (120–150 nm in diameter) are characteristically found in neurosecretory cells, for example, in the nerve endings of hypothalamic neurons, which send their axons to the pituitary. A large, dense droplet within these vesicles contains a polypeptide hormone, which is released in response to the appropriate behavioral stimulus. A neuron, or indeed a single terminal, may contain more than one type of vesicle, possibly for transport and storage, or for immediate release at the synapse.

This very brief account only scratches the surface of the subject of synaptic vesicles. The main point to be made here is that the vesicles are structural evidence of the fact that chemical synapses are a type of neurosecretory apparatus. Like other secretory mechanisms, they are activated by specific stimuli, have specific targets, and exert particular actions on those targets. The dynamics of these mechanisms are the subject of Chaps. 7 and 8.

Synapses and Terminals

Types I and II synapses provide relatively small areas of contact between neurons. They may be characterized as *simple* synapses. They are typical of the contacts made by small terminals, both axonal and dendritic, and they are also the type of contact made by most cell bodies and dendrites when those structures occupy presynaptic positions. It is probably fair to say that they make up the majority of synapses in the brain. This, in itself, bespeaks an important principle of brain organization, that the output of a neuron is fractionated, as it were, through many synapses onto many other neurons, and, conversely, that synapses from many sources play onto a given neuron. This is referred to as divergence and convergence, respectively. It is an essential aspect of the complexity of information processing in the brain.

In addition, there are, in many regions, much more extensive contacts with more elaborate structure that may be characterized as *specialized synapses*. The neuromuscular junction is an example in the peripheral nervous system. We have already discussed an example in the invertebrate nervous system (Fig. 4.9). In the vertebrate central nervous system, we find an example in the retina, where the large terminal of a receptor cell makes contact with several postsynaptic neurons; within the terminal, the synaptic vesicles are grouped around a special small dense bar. This arrangement is shown very schematically in Fig. 4.4 and is described further in Chap. 16.

One may also characterize the terminals that bear the synapses. A terminal may be small and have a single synapse onto a single postsynaptic structure, as shown in most of the diagrams of Fig. 4.4. These may be characterized as *simple terminals*. On the other hand, a large terminal, with complicated geometry, may be characterized as a *specialized terminal*: examples are the neuromuscular junction and the basket cell endings around the Purkinje cell (Chap. 21). In many regions of the brain, large terminals have synapses onto more than one postsynaptic structure; the receptor terminal in the retina mentioned above is an example. Another example is the large terminal rosette of the mossy fiber in the cerebellum, which has as many as 300 synaptic contacts onto postsynaptic structures (see below).

Within the brain are all possible combinations of synapses and terminals. Simple synapses may be established by any of the parts of the neuron: terminals, trunks, or the cell body. Simple synapses may also be made by specialized terminals, as in the case of the mossy fiber of the cerebellum. On the other hand, specialized synapses may be made by small terminals, as in the spinule synapses of the hippocampus, and, finally, specialized synapses may arise from specialized terminals, as in the case of the retinal receptor.

Patterns of Synaptic Connections

Synapses are also categorized by the kinds of processes that take part in the synapse. Thus, for example, a contact from an axon onto a cell body is termed an *axosomatic* synapse, whereas that onto a dendrite is termed an *axodendritic* synapse (Fig. 4.11A). Similarly, a contact between two axons is termed an *axoaxonic* synapse (C, E), and a contact between two dendrites is termed a *dendrodendritic* synapse (B).

A single synapse seldom occurs in isola-

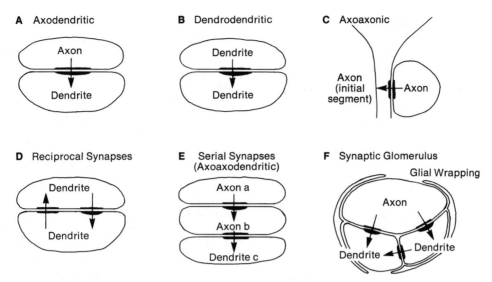

Fig. 4.11 Types of synaptic arrangements.

tion in the brain; it is usually one of a number of synapses that together make up a larger pattern of interconnecting synapses. In Chap. 1, these were referred to as microcircuits. The simplest of these patterns is that formed by two or more synapses situated near each other and oriented in the same direction; they are all axodendritic. A more complicated pattern is one in which there is a synapse from process (a) to process (b), and another from (b) to (c). Such a situation is diagramed in Fig. 4.11E. These are referred to as *serial* synapses; examples are axoaxodendritic sequences and axodendrodendritic sequences.

Another pattern has a synapse from process (a) to process (b), and a return synapse from (b) to (a). This is diagramed in Fig. 4.11D. It is referred to as a *reciprocal* synapse. If the two synapses are side by side, they are called a *reciprocal pair*. If the two synapses are far apart, a *reciprocal arrangement* results. Finally, there are patterns of synaptic connections between tightly grouped clusters of terminals, called *synaptic glomeruli* (Fig. 4.11F).

The first synapses identified by electron microscopists were simple contacts made by simple terminals, of the axosomatic and axodendritic type. Since these simple arrangements were in accord with the idea of a "polarized" neuron, they came to be regarded as "classical" synapses. The axoaxonic and dendrodendritic types were identified later, as were the serial and reciprocal arrangements and the various types of specialized synaptic contacts and terminals. Since these synapses, terminals, and patterns did not fit classical concepts, the practice grew up of referring to the simple synapses as "conventional" and to all the other synapses as "unconventional" or even "nonusual."

In recent years, so many examples of complex synaptic arrangements have come to light that we are in danger of believing that most parts of the nervous system, in invertebrates and vertebrates, are organized in unconventional ways! This of course is absurd. It simple shows that nature does not always work according to our simple preconceptions. Certainly the nervous system does not put these labels on its synapses. We may conceive that, in any given region, it is faced with specific tasks of information processing, and it assembles the necessary circuits from the available neuronal components. Thus, far from being unconventional, the complex synaptic arrangements, in fact, give expression to the extraordinary flexibility of the nerve cell as the fundamental anatomical unit of the nervous system. This has undoubtedly been crucial to the evolution of synaptic circuits that meet the needs placed on them by adaptive pressures for processing information, sometimes with competing priorities, in the most efficient ways possible. After considering the multitude of synaptic patterns that have emerged, David Bodian (1972) summarized the situation in the following eloquent manner:

> In synaptic systems . . . we see not a stereotyped mechanism for the transfer of information from cell to cell, but another display of the fact that every conceivable capability of living organisms to solve adaptive problems is likely to be put to the test in the evolution of life.

Identification of Synaptic Connections

If the synaptic connections between neurons are so complex, how do we identify which neuronal processes contribute to a given synapse or synaptic cluster? Neuroanatomists have developed many methods for doing this. Sometimes the fine structure differs sufficiently enough to identify the processes in single sections, as in the case of the retina shown in Fig. 4.12A. As a general rule, however, three-dimensional reconstructions from serial sections are necessary, as illustrated in the olfactory bulb in Fig. 4.12B. Another method is to treat the tissue with antibodies to an enzyme that is involved in the synthesis of a neurotransmitter. Figure 14.12C shows that, in olfactory bulb tissue treated with antibodies to glutamic acid decarboxylase (the enzyme that synthesizes GABA), the granule cell gemules are positive, whereas the mitral cell dendrites are not. This is consistent with other evidence that the granule cell dendrites inhibit the mitral cell dendrites by the action of GABA at the dendrodendritic synapses. A fourth method is to inject a cell with Lucifer Yellow, or HRP which under EM is electron-dense. A fifth method is to transect a bundle of input

fibers and identify the synapses made by degenerating terminals. A final method is to impregnate tissue by the Golgi method and then partially deimpregnate and examine the synapses made by or onto partially deimpregnated cells and terminals.

The examples above are all taken from vertebrates. An example from invertebrates is shown in Fig. 4.13. Here (4.13A) the cell bodies of two neurons in the stomatogastric ganglion of the lobster were injected with the dye Procion Yellow. The neurons were visualized under light microscopy in whole mounts of the ganglion, and precisely reconstructed from serial sections made through the cells. In the EM, serial reconstructions of ultrathin sections show that the dendritic trees that arise from the axons of these cells have numerous expansions (varicosities) where synapses are present. A typical reconstruction is shown in Fig. 4.13B. The results have been summarized by Allen Selverston, Don Russell, John Miller, and David King of San Diego as follows (Selverston et al., 1976):

> Each synaptic varicosity is functionally bipolar . . . ; it both projects synapses onto and receives synapses from many other processes. These bifunctional varicosities are found on all of the dendrites of the neuron. Hence input and output are each distributed over the entire dendritic arborization. Although neuronal input and output are traditionally thought of as segregated onto polarized regions of the neuron (onto "dendrite" and "axons"), this does not seem to be the case in stomatogastric ganglion neurons. In this, the stomatogastric ganglion may show functional similarity to those regions of vertebrate central nervous system (such as olfactory bulb and retina) where dendrodendritic interactions are important.

From Synapses to Circuits

From these considerations it is obvious that the flow of information through a neuron and between neurons is much more complicated than depicted in the diagrams of Cajal in Fig. 4.1. Although this seems perplexing at first, some relatively simple general principles about how synapses are or-

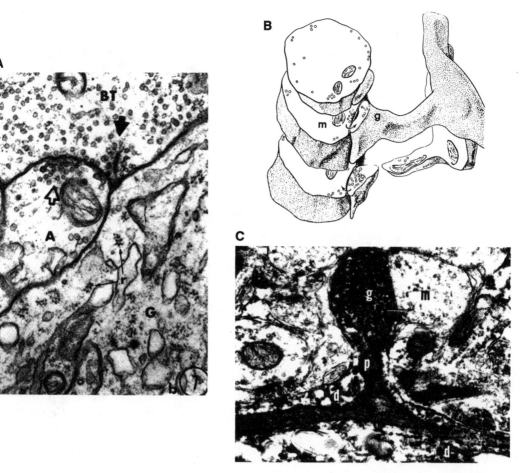

Fig. 4.12 Examples of synaptic arrangements. **A.** Human retina, showing ribbon synapse (dark arrow) between bipolar terminal (BT) and amacrine (A) and ganglion (G) cells. Also shown is a reciprocal synapse from amacrine to bipolar cell (open arrow). r, ribosomes. (From Dowling and Boycott, 1966) **B.** Olfactory bulb, reconstruction in three dimensions from serial EM sections, showing reciprocal synapses between mitral (m) and granule (g) cell dendrites. (From Rall et al., 1966) **C.** Rat olfactory bulb, treated with antibodies for glutamic acid decarboxylase (GAD), the enzyme that synthesizes GABA. Reaction product is found in granule cell spine (g), pedicle (p), and dendrite (d), but not in mitral cell dendrite (m). Arrow indicates site of granule-to-mitral dendrodendritic synapse. (From Ribak et al., 1977)

ganized into circuits have begun to emerge.

A useful generalization to begin with is that synapses are usually made by one of three types of neuronal element. First are the *inputs* coming from other regions, usually ending as axon terminals. Second are the *relay neurons* of the given region. Third are the *intrinsic neurons* within that region. Thus, as shown in Fig. 4.14, a given synapse can be made by any one of these elements, and a complex synaptic arrange-

ment generally involves some specific way in which the three elements are interrelated. We call these three elements the *synaptic triad*. Sometimes the elements are very tightly organized, as in serial or reciprocal synapses. Sometimes they are loosely organized, as in spread-out regions like the ventral horn of the spinal cord or the cerebral cortex. Sometimes the interneuronal elements may be lacking, as in some simple relay structures. Or perhaps the output

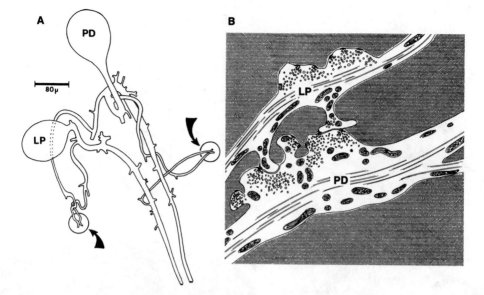

Fig. 4.13 Lobster stomatogastric ganglion. **A.** Two cells [pyloric dilator (PD) and lateral pyloric (LP)] have been reconstructed from serial sections. Circles show sites of synaptic connection between the cells. **B.** Synaptic connections, as reconstructed from serial EM sections, at right-hand site in A. (From Selverston et al., 1976)

neuron is lacking, if the output is humoral, or the cell body is situated elsewhere. In the face of all this diversity, it is useful to use the synaptic triad as a general framework for identifying the main kinds of connections present in a region, and comparing them with those of other regions.

With the identification of patterns of syn-

aptic connections, we are in a position to begin to identify circuits at different levels of organization (see Fig. 4.15). We will take as an example the pathway for the sense of smell, and see if we can identify its levels of organization in vertebrates and invertebrates. We will apply the same principles introduced in Chap. 1.

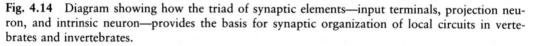

Fig. 4.14 Diagram showing how the triad of synaptic elements—input terminals, projection neuron, and intrinsic neuron—provides the basis for synaptic organization of local circuits in vertebrates and invertebrates.

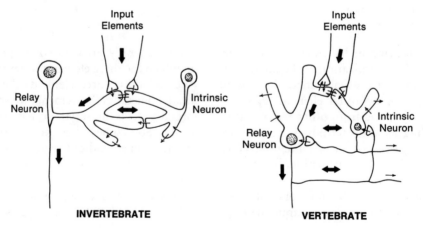

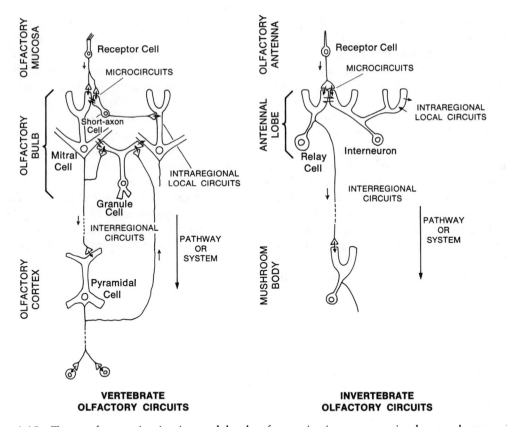

Fig. 4.15 Types of synaptic circuits, and levels of organization, as seen in the vertebrate and invertebrate olfactory pathways.

At the first level of synaptic organization is the arrangement of synapses at a local site on a cell body, dendrite, or axon terminal. This may involve simple *convergence* of several inputs onto that site, or simple *divergence* to several output sites. In addition, it may involve *serial* relays of information, or *reciprocal* interactions. In all these cases, there is a set of synaptic connections that acts as an *integrative unit*. These local patterns of connections have been termed microcircuits (Shepherd, 1978). It is very common for a particular type of microcircuit to be repeated throughout a given layer or on a given cell type, thus acting as a *module* for a specific kind of information processing or memory storage. The microcircuits on a computer chip represent the same operating principle.

At the next level of organization is the circuit that connects different neurons over longer distances within a given region. This transmission may take place through a dendritic branch or dendritic trunk, or it may take place through the axon of an interneuron, or the axon collateral of an output neuron. The key point about all of these pathways is that they remain within a given region (see Fig. 4.15). The term introduced for all these types is *local circuit* (Rakic, 1976). The most restricted local circuits include microcircuits; the most extensive involve interlaminar and intraregional axonal connections. The functions of these different types vary widely. Some provide for reexcitatory spread of activity from neuron to neuron; others provide for antagonistic interactions between neighboring integrative units within a region.

The next highest level of organization

involves connections of one region with another. Usually a region receives input from more than one other region, and usually a region projects output to more than one other region. Thus, the same principles of convergence, divergence, and integration of different kinds of information operate at this level, too. It is also common for there to be feedback from one region to another. Note that feedback loops are present at all levels. The more local feedback loops can be regarded as *nested* within the more extensive loops (see Fig. 4.15).

At a still higher level are sequences of connections through several regions. These are said to constitute a *pathway* or *system*. The function is usually to transmit infor-mation from the periphery into the central nervous system (as in a sensory system), or from central to periphery (as in a motor system). However, in any pathway there are often connections running in the opposite direction to provide for *descending*, *ascending*, or *centrifugal* control.

Finally, at the highest level (at least the highest thus far identified) are sets of connections between a number of regions, which together mediate a behavior that involves to some extent the whole organism. These are called *distributed systems*. They are characteristic of higher functions of motor and sensory systems, and of many central systems.

5

The Membrane Potential

We have seen that a nerve cell, like other cells of the body, contains a number of organelles for carrying out different basic functions. In addition, a neuron has unique modifications—synapses—that provide for specific interactions with its neighbors. We now want to consider the types of activity that enable a nerve cell to use its synapses. The activity may be very quick, in which case it is mediated by electrical currents, or it may be slow, in which case it may involve movements of chemical substances as well as slow electrical changes. In this chapter, we will begin to consider the mechanisms of the electrical signals. In order to do so, we will first consider some basic aspects of the physicochemical milieu of the neuron.

Nerve Cells and Their Ions

The organelles of a neuron are embedded in a cytoplasm that is made up mostly of *water*, *protein*, and *inorganic salts*, as shown schematically in Fig. 5.1. The proteins range from structural macromolecules and enzymes of high molecular weights, down through smaller subunits like polypeptides and peptides, all the way to the various amino acids. Many of these molecules have terminal groups that are dissociated in the

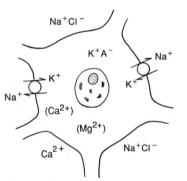

Fig. 5.1 A nerve cell and its ions. A, organic anions; Cl, chloride; K, potassium; Na, sodium; Ca, calcium; Mg, magnesium.

aqueous medium of the cytoplasm, and their net electrical charge makes them *ions*. In the squid giant axon these *organic ions* can be determined simply by squeezing out the axoplasm and assaying it. The main organic ion is isethionate; it has a net negative charge, and is therefore an organic *anion*, represented by A^- in Fig. 5.1. Glutamate, aspartate, and organic phosphates have been suggested to be present in other nerves. Whatever their identity, the net charge on these molecules makes them anions.

In addition to organic ions there are *in-*

87

Table 5.1 Ionic concentrations for squid axon and mammalian muscle fiber

Ions	Invertebrate Squid Axon (seawater ≈ blood)		Vertebrate Muscle (neurons) (interstitial fluid)	
	Internal	External	Internal	External
Cations				
K^+	400	(10)	124	2
Na^+	50	460	10	(125)
Ca^{2+}	(.4)	10	5	2
Mg^{2+}	10	54	14	1
other	—	—	—	—
Total	460	534	153	130
Anions				
Cl^-	40–150	560	2	77
HCO_3^-	—	—	12	27
$(A)^-$	345	—	74	13
other	—	—	(65)	(13)
Total	460	560	153	130

Concentrations in mM. The values for the mammalian muscle fiber are believed to be representative of neurons. ( ) indicates estimates, to give electroneutrality between cations and anions. Note lack of osmotic equilibrium across the membrane (between internal and external medium).

After Aidley (1978)

organic ions. These are needed for the operation of many enzymes; for maintaining electrical, chemical, and osmotic equilibrium within the cell and between it and the outside; and for other functions. The main intracellular *cation* is potassium, as shown by K^+ in Fig. 5.1. Also present in smaller but significant amounts are calcium and magnesium. The inorganic *anions* include chloride, phosphate, and sulfate. Outside the cell, the main *extracellular cation* is sodium (Na^+) and the main *anion* is chloride (Cl^-).

It can be seen at a glance in Fig. 5.1 that the electrolyte composition inside and outside the cell is quite different. This is summarized more quantitatively in Fig. 5.2 and Table 5.1, for the case of an invertebrate cell (the squid giant axon) and a vertebrate cell. The latter is exemplified by frog mus-

Fig. 5.2 Ionic concentrations for an invertebrate neuron (squid axon) and a mammalian muscle fiber. (Based on from Aidley, 1978)

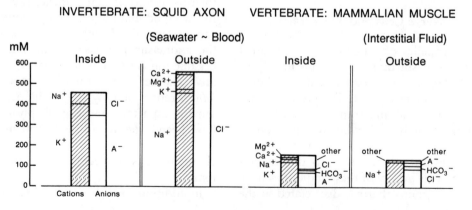

cle fibers, which have been well studied, and are believed to be similar to vertebrate neurons in these respects.

The electrical activity of nerve cells is derived from the unequal distribution of electrolytes across the cell membrane, as depicted in Figs. 5.1 and 5.2. There are two steps we want to understand: first, how the unequal distribution comes about, and second, how it gives rise to an electrical potential.

The Donnan Equilibrium

Our understanding of the first step is based on a classical paper by F. G. Donnan in 1924, entitled "The Theory of Membrane Equilibria." Many studies in the later nineteenth and early twentieth century had established the physicochemical properties of substances in solution—in particular, the dissociation of salts into ions, and the passive diffusion of ions through a solution from a region of high concentration to a region of low concentration. If two such regions are separated by a membrane, the diffusion will take place at a rate depending on how *permeable* (i.e., permissive) the membrane is in allowing the specific type of ion to pass through it. Eventually, the diffusion results in equal concentrations of all the diffusible and permeable ions on either side of the membrane. However, Donnan showed that if a large *impermeable organic ion* is present on one side, the permeable ions distribute themselves unequally on either side of the membrane. Donnan, being a physical chemist, used an artificial collodion membrane for his experiments, together with an organic electrolyte like phenol red that could serve as a convenient visual marker.

The application of the Donnan model to the case of the biological cell is illustrated by the hypothetical experiment shown in the diagram of Fig. 5.3. We begin with solutions of the salt KCl, which dissociates into K^+ and Cl^- ions, and a membrane that has a small but significant permeability to both ions. As shown in ①, the concentration of KCl on either side will be equal, in order to preserve *chemical equilibrium* across the membrane, and the concentrations of K^+ and Cl^- will be equal on each side, in order to preserve *electrical neutrality* on each side.

Next (step ②) we add to one side a large concentration of organic anions (A^-), to which the membrane is completely impermeable. The anions are accompanied by an equal charge of cations (K^+). Although the K^+ preserves electroneutrality inside, it upsets the chemical concentration balance across the membrane. Therefore, diffusion of K^+ and Cl^- to the outside occurs, because K^+ moves down its concentration gradient and Cl^- accompanies it to preserve electroneutrality. Donnan showed that this diffusion continues until an equilibrium is reached that is defined by the following relation:

$$\frac{[K^+]_{OUT}}{[K^+]_{IN}} = \frac{[Cl^-]_{IN}}{[Cl^-]_{OUT}} \qquad (5.1)$$

In the example of Fig. 5.2, this occurs when the original concentrations of KCl (3 units

Fig. 5.3 Steps in the establishment of a Donnan equilibrium. See text.

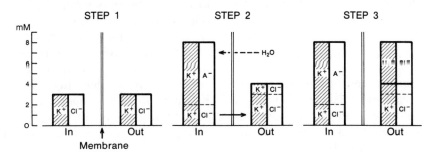

on each side) are replaced by 2 units inside and 4 outside. Thus, the equation defining equilibrium changes from

$$\frac{3}{3} = \frac{3}{3}$$

in step ① to

$$\frac{4}{8} = \frac{2}{4}$$

in step ②.

This defines a *Donnan equilibrium,* with electroneutrality on both sides. However, the system is not in *osmotic equilibrium,* because of the excess of total electrolyte inside, which has the effect of drawing water into the cell to dilute the electrolyte. In model systems this excess water builds up a pressure that can be measured as *hydrostatic,* or *osmotic, pressure.* In plant cells, a certain amount of such pressure can be sustained without bursting the cell because the cell wall is reinforced with cellulose. While this is fine for the sedentary lives of plants, it is not well suited to the mobile, active lives of animals. Thus, in animals, osmotic equilibrium across the cell wall is achieved by making up the electrolyte deficit on the outside with NaCl (step ③). In order to ensure the exclusion of Na^+ from within the cell, the membrane is *relatively impermeable* to Na^+. The external Na^+, in effect, balances the osmotic effect of the internal organic anions. This is an economical strategy for a marine invertebrate cell, because of the abundance of NaCl in the surrounding sea. In terrestrial invertebrates and vertebrates, an internal sea has been created by preserving the approximate saline composition of the interstitial fluid (see Fig. 5.2 and Table 5.1).

The Nernst Potential

We have seen that ions diffuse through the membrane to achieve a balance of chemical forces, and now we can discuss how this gives rise to an electrical difference. In order to do this, we will delve a bit deeper

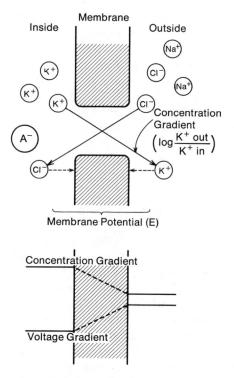

Fig. 5.4 Relations between electrical and chemical gradients across the membrane. (Modified from Woodbury, 1965)

into the nature of diffusion processes; the diagram of Fig. 5.4 serves as an intuitive guide to the following discussion.

When a substance diffuses in a solution, the force that moves the molecules from a region of high concentration to one of low concentration is a *chemical force.* We say that this force moves the molecules down their *concentration gradient,* like gravity makes marbles roll down an inclined plane. This can be described mathematically in several ways, for example, in terms of how fast the substance moves (called the *flux*), or how much *work* would be necessary to oppose the movement of the substance. If we consider our system of two regions separated by a membrane permeable to K^+, then the unequal concentrations of K^+ on either side mean that there is a force on K^+ that moves it *outward,* down its concentration gradient. In terms of the work (W_C) to oppose this chemical force, we have

$$W_C = 2.3 \ RT \ \log \frac{[K^+]_{OUT}}{[K^+]_{IN}} \qquad (5.2)$$

where R = gas constant (a measure of the energy of the substance), T = absolute temperature (a substance is more active as the temperature is raised), and the concentrations of K^+ inside and outside are in moles. For present purposes we will not worry about the units of these parameters, but only concern ourselves with gaining an intuitive grasp of the relations.

Now, as K^+ diffuses outward through the membrane, Cl^- is diffusing *inward*, down *its* concentration gradient (see again Fig. 5.3 as well as Fig. 5.4). This means there is a tendency for K^+ to become separated from its accompanying negative ion. However, since opposite charges attract, there is an *electrical force* tending to pull the K^+ back inside toward the inwardly diffusing Cl^- ions. The work (W_E) required to oppose this electrical force is given simply by

$$W_E = FE \qquad (5.3)$$

where F = Faraday's constant (a measure of electrical charge per mole of substance) and E = electrical potential difference, due to the charge separation across the membrane, measured in volts.

When the system is at equilibrium, there will be no net movement of K^+ or any other substance, and the chemical force tending to move K^+ out will be just balanced by the electrical force tending to move it in. The two forces are therefore equal, and that means we can set Eq. (5.2) equal to Eq. (5.3), thus

$$W_E = W_C$$

$$FE = RT \ \log \frac{[K^+]_{OUT}}{[K^+]_{IN}}$$

$$E = 2.3 \ \frac{RT}{F} \ \log \frac{[K^+]_{OUT}}{[K^+]_{IN}} \qquad (5.4)$$

This is the *Nernst equation,* named for its discovered, W. Nernst. We refer to *(E)* as the *Nernst potential,* or the *diffusion potential.* For the case of the squid axon at room temperature (18°C) the constant $2.3 \ RT/F = 58$ mV, and, for the concentration of K outside and inside, we have

$$E_K = 58 \ \log \frac{[K^+]_{OUT}}{[K^+]_{IN}} \ mV$$

$$= 58 \ \log \frac{20}{400} \ mV$$

$$= -75 \ mV$$

If you learn only one equation in your study of neurobiology, the Nernst equation is the one to learn, because it is fundamental to the nature of electrical potentials in all cells, as well as the electrical activity in neurons. For any given ion species, E is the potential at which there is no net flux of ions across the membrane; it is therefore referred to as the *equilibrium potential* for that ion. In other words, it is the potential that the membrane tends toward when the membrane is permeable to that particular ion. Since the potential E exists across the cell membrane, it is called the *membrane potential.* When we take up the specific kinds of electrical activity that are associated with synapses and with impulses, we will see that they all take the form of changes in the membrane potential.

The Membrane Potential

Sir Arthur Eddington, the British astronomer, once remarked that "You cannot believe in astronomical observations before they are confirmed by theory." Much the same applies to the experiments we do in biology: we can begin to believe in results only if we have an adequate grasp of the theories that seek to explain the nature of the systems we study. That is why some of the theoretical basis of the membrane potential has been presented. With an understanding of how a membrane potential *might* arise, we are ready to set up an experiment that will tell us the actual value of the membrane potential, and how it fits with the theory.

The aim of this experiment will be to measure the electrical potential across a nerve membrane, using the giant axon of the squid as our test subject. All electrical measurements involve recording the difference between some quantities of electricity at two electrodes. In this case, one electrode is outside the axon, and the other is inside. The squid axon is so large (up to 1 mm in diameter) that the internal electrode can be a fine wire inserted longitudinally through a cut end. Generally, however, a nerve cell is much smaller, and in order to insert the electrode through the membrane, one uses a microelectrode, fabricated especially for this purpose.

Intracellular Recordings

The method used for making a microelectrode for *intracellular* recording is to take a length of glass capillary or pipette tubing, heat it in the middle, and quickly pull it apart so that one obtains tips which are very fine but still open; they are called *micropipettes*. The first ones, made around 1950, were pulled by hand over a small Bunsen burner flame (it took a steady hand and eye to do it!), but machines (microelectrode pullers) were soon devised to make them automatically. A salt solution is placed in the tubing at the large end; if the tubing contains a fine glass thread, the solution will fill the pipette to the tip by capillary action (Fig. 5.5). The micropipette is now a microelectrode. When the pipette tip is inserted into the axon, the salt solution serves as an electrical conductor between the axoplasm at the tip and a wire in the large end, connected to a suitable electronic amplifier and recorder. The most convenient recorder is a *cathode ray oscilloscope*. The cathode ray tube is constructed on the same principle as a television tube, except that it has only a single beam that travels across the screen, to register electrical changes at different speeds and at different amplifications (see Fig. 5.5).

When both electrodes are outside the nerve, there is naturally no signal registered on the oscilloscope (the beam just keeps moving across and being reset at the same level). However, when the pipette tip is delicately pushed through the axonal membrane (sometimes a gentle tap on the table will help), the oscilloscope beam is abruptly deflected in a direction that indicates that the pipette tip has become electrically *negative* relative to the outside electrode (this

Fig. 5.5 The micropipette is used for electrical recording (extracellular, intracellular, patch), electrical stimulation (current or voltage clamp), or delivery of substances (microionophoresis or pressure ejection). Preparation of an intracellular recording micropipette is shown on the left. The diagram on the right shows the arrangement for recording from a squid axon, and observing potentials on a cathode ray oscilloscope (CRO).

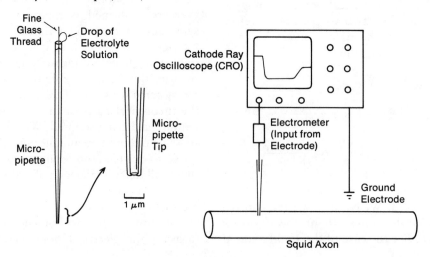

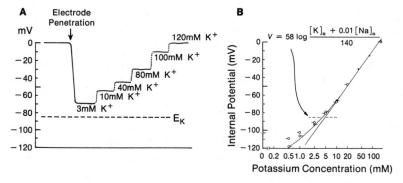

Fig. 5.6 A. The resting membrane potential and its dependence on K^+ outside the membrane. **B.** Graph of experimental results (open circles), and comparison with theoretical curves assuming dependence solely on K^+ (straight line) and including Na^+ (curved line). (From Hodgkin and Horowicz, 1959)

occurs at the arrow shown in Fig. 5.6A). If it is a "good" penetration, the membrane seals around the pipette, and, if nobody trips over a cord in the dark or slams a door (!), the recording may be stable for many minutes or even hours.

Under these conditions, the stable negative potential that is recorded is the *resting membrane potential;* we assume that all the potential difference between the two electrodes is due to the potential difference across the membrane. The value of the resting membrane potential in a typical experiment is in the range of -60 to -70 mV. Because of this internal negativity, we say that the membrane has a negative polarity. If the membrane potential moves toward zero, we say that it becomes *depolarized;* if it increases above the resting value, we say it becomes *hyperpolarized.* The significance of such changes in polarization will soon become apparent.

Identifying Ionic Conductances

The recorded membrane potential is close to the value predicted by the Nernst equation for potassium, but it is not exactly the same. To test further the correspondence between theory and experiment, the concentration of $[K^+]_{OUT}$ in the bathing medium can be varied and the effects on the membrane potential observed. This is illustrated in Fig. 5.6A. As $[K^+]_{OUT}$ increases,

the concentration gradient across the membrane decreases, as does the membrane potential; the membrane thus becomes progressively depolarized. The results are plotted in B and compared with those expected from the Nernst equation. It can be seen that there is a good fit for higher potassium concentrations, but the experimental curve deviates from the theoretical one at low concentrations, the prevailing situation under natural conditions.

These experiments suggest that normally the membrane potential reflects the presence of other ions besides K^+, and indeed, in our discussion of the Donnan equilibrium, we assumed that the membrane is also slightly permeable to both Cl^- and Na^+. We can calculate individual Nernst potentials for these ions as well; for Na, we have

$$E_{Na} = 58 \log \frac{[Na^+]_{OUT}}{[Na^+]_{IN}} \qquad (5.5)$$

$$= 58 \log \frac{460}{50}$$

$$= +55 \text{ mV}$$

Thus, the equilibrium potential for Na^+ has a polarity opposite to that for K^+, in accord with their opposing concentration gradients (see Fig. 5.2). If the permeability of the membrane for Na^+ were equal to that for K^+, then the two equilibrium potentials would tend to cancel each other out, and the membrane potential would be near zero. However, the permeability to Na^+ has been shown to be only about 1/25 of that of K^+, so that the effect of Na^+ is to decrease (depolarize) only slightly the membrane potential from the K^+ equilibrium potential.

The combined effects on the membrane potential of more than one ionic species can be expressed in a single large equation as follows:

$$V_m = 58 \log$$

$$\frac{P_K[K^+]_{OUT} + P_{Na}[Na^+]_{OUT} + P_{Cl}[Cl^-]_{IN}}{P_K[K^+]_{IN} + P_{Na}[Na^+]_{IN} + P_{Cl}[Cl^-]_{OUT}}$$

$$(5.6)$$

in which V_m = membrane potential, and P = relative membrane permeability. This equation was derived by David Goldman of Bethesda in 1943. One of the premises on which it is based is that the potential gradient, or electrical field, within the membrane is constant; hence it is referred to as the *constant-field equation*. It lets us take account of the contribution of any

ionic gradient to the membrane potential by simply weighting its effect in accord with the permeability.

For present purposes we neglect the contribution of Cl^- (it is near equilibrium across the membrane) and focus on the effect of Na^+. Using the weighting factor of $1/25 = 0.04$ for P_{Na} (and neglecting Cl^-), Eq. (5.5) yields a value of -60 mV for V_m, and the curve for different values of (K^+_{OUT}) now falls very closely on the curve obtained from the experimental data (Fig. 5.6B).

The Equivalent Circuit

We thus have a reasonable explanation for the membrane potential, and we would like to have a convenient way to represent it. Representing the various factors with diagrams is cumbersome, and carrying around equations in one's head is too abstract. The most convenient form is an electrical analogue, or model, as shown in Fig. 5.7. This little electrical circuit represents the membrane, or more correctly, a membrane site. Each equilibrium potential is represented by a *battery* across the membrane, which has the appropriate polarity and voltage

Fig. 5.7 Equivalent electrical circuit for the electrical properties of the nerve membrane.

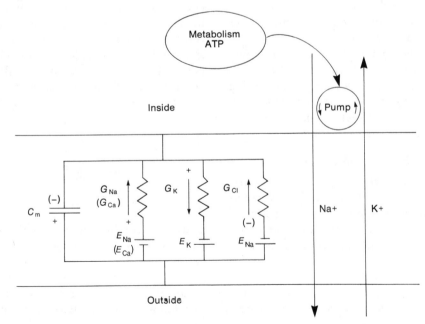

(E) for that ion. In series with the battery is a *resistance (R)* which is related to the membrane permeability for that ion. The relation is a bit indirect. First, what we are really interested in is the *conductance,* which is the reciprocal of the resistance *(R = 1/G).* Second, electrical conductance *(G)* is related to membrane permeability *(P)* as follows (using K^+ as the ion in question):

$$G_K \propto P_K \frac{[K^+]_{OUT}}{[K^+]_{IN}} \qquad (5.7)$$

Thus, theoretically the membrane could be quite permeable to K^+, but if there are no K^+ ions outside, the conductance would be zero (there would be no ions to carry the current through the permeability channels). Under physiological conditions, however, Eq. (5.7) is a reasonable approximation.

The "channels" for each ionic species are separate and independent, as shown in Fig. 5.7. In addition, the lipids of the membrane impart an electrical *capacitance (C)* to it; that is, they are poor conductors, and are able to store electrical charges on either side of the membrane. In fact, the membrane potential we record, representing the algebraic sum of the ionic batteries, is the potential due to the separation and storage of charge across the membrane capacitance *(C),* as illustrated in the circuit of Fig. 5.7. When changes in the membrane potential occur slowly, we can neglect the effects of the storage of charge across the capacitance, but when changes are rapid, the time course over which the capacitance charges or discharges is a very important factor in shaping the signals. We will see later how this comes about during synaptic and impulse activity.

The Membrane Potential and Metabolism

The fact that we can account for our experimental recording of the membrane potential as a combination of diffusion potentials does not mean the end of our interest in how this potential arises. In many ways it is only the beginning. In our theoretical discussion we simply assumed a high concentration of K^+ inside the cell to begin with. But during life, the cell is supplied with nutrients and substances through the blood and interstitial fluid, where the K^+ concentration is, as we have seen, very low. How does the cell actually obtain K^+, and replenish the small amounts that are continually lost by leakage due to outward diffusion through the permeability channels? It cannot be by passive diffusion, because the concentration gradient is only in the direction of *outward* diffusion. A similar problem concerns Na^+; how does the cell prevent a buildup of Na^+ at rest, and particularly as a consequence of impulse activity (see next chapter). And, in the face of these ion movements, how does the cell maintain osmotic equilibrium, so that it does not swell up and burst?

From these considerations it is clear that the cell is more than a mere bag of salt solution. The cell must contain metabolic mechanisms that can maintain and adjust ion concentrations under resting as well as changing conditions, and against ion concentration gradients. More specifically, there must be mechanisms in or at the membrane to pump ions across the membrane against their concentration gradients, and a source of energy in the cell to keep the pumps going. The process of moving substances in this way is called *active transport,* and the mechanism for doing it is called a *metabolic pump.* There is an obvious analogy with the raising of well-water by a good old-fashioned barnyard pump, worked by an energetic farm kid.

The first step in identifying this mechanism was to show that ion transport across the membrane requires energy. This was revealed in experiments on the squid giant axon, in which the rate of efflux of radioactive Na^+ was measured. Under resting conditions the rate is relatively low, but it can be raised by stimulating the axon repetitively, which loads the axon because of Na^+ influx during the impulse (see next chapter). Following such stimulation, the rate of Na^+ efflux is relatively high (see Fig. 5.8). The efflux is blocked when the

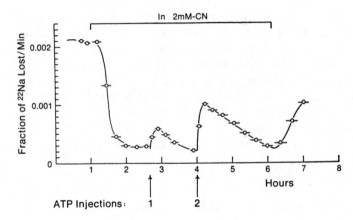

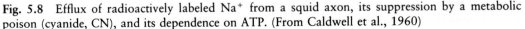

Fig. 5.8 Efflux of radioactively labeled Na$^+$ from a squid axon, its suppression by a metabolic poison (cyanide, CN), and its dependence on ATP. (From Caldwell et al., 1960)

axon is poisoned with cyanide, a well-known metabolic inhibitor. Injection of ATP partially restores the efflux (see Fig. 5.8), suggesting that the energy supply comes through ATP.

Direct evidence has subsequently been obtained that the membrane pump produces an actual current flow across the membrane. Such currents are called *membrane currents*. In order to demonstrate

them, electrophysiologists use a method called a *voltage clamp*. This method will be explained in Chap. 6. An elegant experiment demonstrating pump currents with the voltage clamp was carried out by Roger Thomas of England in 1972. He used a giant cell of the snail *Helix*, in which four electrodes (one a double-barreled electrode) could be inserted. The arrangement is shown in Fig. 5.9. Electrode ① was used to mea-

Fig. 5.9 Experimental setup for carrying out voltage-clamp experiments in a snail neuron. To the right are shown (**A**) the steady membrane potential recorded by electrode ① while the membrane is voltage-clamped by electrode ②; (**B**) the injection of Na$^+$ by microionophoresis through electrode ③, measured in milliamperes (mA) of injection current; (**C**) the current due to the action of the Na$^+$ pump, recorded by electrode ⑤ under the voltage-clamp conditions maintained by electrode ②. Injection of K$^+$ could be done through electrode ④. See Chap. 6 for further details of the voltage-clamp method. (Modified from Thomas, 1972)

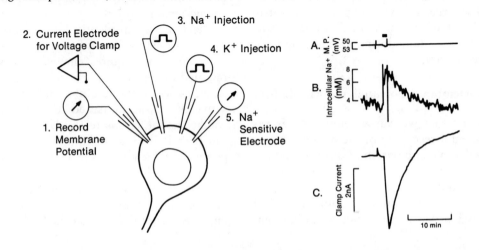

sure the membrane potential. Electrode ②
was used to "clamp" the membrane potential at a preset value and record the current
necessary to hold it at that value. Electrode
③ was used to inject Na^+ into the cell, and
electrode ④ was used to complete the circuit, by injecting K^+, so that this current
would not cross the membrane. Electrode
⑤ was an ion-sensitive electrode that monitored the Na^+ concentration in the cell.
The results in Fig. 5.9 showed that when
Na^+ was injected, it was necessary to pass
an inward current to hold the membrane
potential "clamped." This implied that there
was an equal and opposite outward current
associated with the raised Na^+ concentration, due to the action of the pump. The
net current represented movement of only
about one-third of the injected Na ions,
implying that the pump ejects three Na ions
for every two K ions that enter the cell.

The Membrane Pump

Because of the ions it transports, the pump
is known as the $Na^+ - K^+$ pump; because
it requires high energy from the hydrolysis
of ATP to ADP, it is also a (Na^+, K^+)-
ATPase. Studies in red cell ghosts, in which
the intracellular and extracellular conditions could be precisely controlled, showed
that the pump works only when Na^+ and
ATP are present on the inside and K^+ is
present on the outside. The glycoside ouabain inhibits the pump by competing for
the K^+ binding site on the outside.

Biochemical analysis has shown that the
purified enzyme consists of a catalytic subunit (α) of approximately 100,000 daltons,
coupled to a glycoprotein subunit (β) of
approximately 45,000 daltons. The binding sites are on the catalytic subunit; the
function of the glycoprotein is as yet unknown.

Recently, the complete amino acid sequence of the α-unit has been obtained by
gene cloning. Analysis of hydrophobic regions in the sequence has suggested that
there are eight transmembrane regions, giving the tertiary structure shown in Fig.

5.10. Of interest is the larger number of
transmembrane regions as compared with
the acetylcholine receptor (cf. Chap. 2).
Between transmembrane regions 4 and 5,
there is a large cytosolic domain, which
contains the ATPase hydrolysis site. Binding sites for Na^+ and K^+ have been identified on cytosolic domains (see Fig. 5.10),
but not yet on the extracellular domains.
As indicated in the diagram, the α subunit
shows considerable sequence homologies
with Ca^{2+}-ATPase, which pumps Ca^{2+} out
of the sarcoplasmic reticulum (see Chap.
17) as well as a bacterial K^+-ATPase, suggesting a common gene origin for these
membrane proteins with similar enzymatic
functions.

The pump functions as an antiport, because it transports two different ions in
opposite directions across the membrane.
The mechanism as presently understood is
represented in Fig. 5.11. In A, the catalytic
subunit binds K^+ on the outside; this is
followed by dephosphorylation, which
causes a conformational change in the protein, resulting in transfer of K^+ into the
cytoplasm. This leads to B, where Na^+
binding to its internal site is followed by
phosphorylation, which induces another
conformational change that transfers Na^+
to the outside. The protein is then ready to
bind K^+ on the outside again, and the cycle
repeats itself.

The $Na^+ - K^+$ pump is found in all cells.
It normally accounts for as much as one-
third of the total energy consumed by the
cell. This can rise to two-thirds in nerve
cells after periods of electrical activity, when
ion gradients are being restored (see Chap.
6). In some cells the ratio of Na^+ to K^+
transported is 1:1, in which case the pump
simply helps to maintain the passive gradients of ions that determine the resting
membrane potential. However, if the ratio
of exchange is not 1:1, the pump makes its
own additional contribution to the membrane potential. Such pumps are called
electrogenic. In the cell illustrated in Fig.
5.9, the pump is electrogenic, because the
ratio of Na:K movements is 3:2. In this

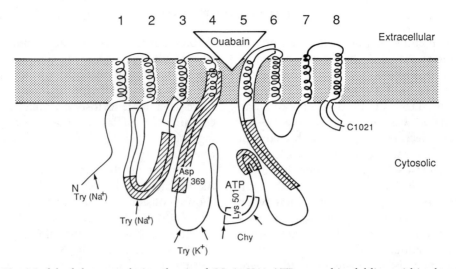

Fig. 5.10 Model of the α catalytic subunit of (Na⁺, K⁺)-ATPase and its folding within the plasma membrane, based on amino acid sequencing from cDNA clones. Numbers 1–8 indicate the hydrophobic regions that cross the interior of the membrane. Most of the molecule forms loops within the cytosol. Hydrolysis of ATP occurs at the lysine (Lys) residue site 501, coupled with an intermediate step of phosphorylation of aspartate (Asp) residue site 369. Na⁺ and K⁺ binding sites, determined by trypsin (Try) cleavage, are indicated in the diagram (Chy = chymotrypsin cleavage site). The chemical energy released by ATP hydrolysis is coupled to transport of Na⁺ and K⁺ across the membrane. The drugs ouabain and digitalis inhibit ion transport, leading to decrease of the membrane potential, by binding to a site(s) on the external surface of the α (or β) subunit. Sequence homologies with the Ca²⁺-ATPase of the sarcoplasmic reticulum in muscle are indicated by open (clear) boxes, and further homologies with bacterial K⁺-ATPase are shown by shaded boxes. (Based on Cantley, 1986)

Fig. 5.11 Mechanism of the Na⁺–K⁺ pump. **A.** In the presence of external K⁺, there is an allosteric conformational change which causes dephosphorylation at the ATP binding site. In this conformation, there is transport of K⁺ to the inside, against the K⁺ gradient across the membrane. **B.** When Na⁺ binds to its specific site(s) on the inside, there is a conformational change which favors phosphorylation at the ATP binding site. This favors transport of Na⁺ to the outside, against the Na⁺ gradient. The transport occurs in the stoichiometric ratio of 3 Na⁺ for 2 K⁺. The molecule alternates between these two phosphorylation states and associated conformations to carry out its pumping function. (Based on Alberts et al., 1983; Cantley, 1986; Shull et al., 1986)

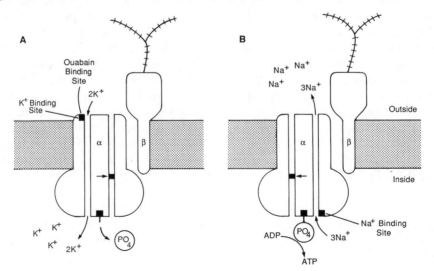

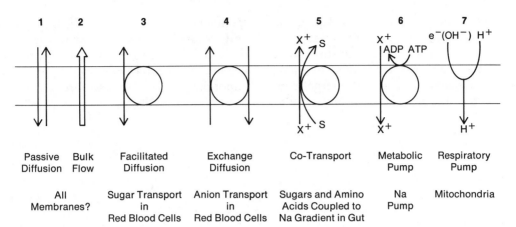

Fig. 5.12 Main categories of transport mechanisms in biological membranes. (Diagram adapted from C. L. Slayman)

cell, the pump is normally activated only after impulse activity. However, there are by now many examples of cells in which an electrogenic pump contributes to the normal resting potential.

Membrane Transport Mechanisms

In this discussion we have focused on one possible mechanism for carrier-mediated transport of ions. This is only one of the many ways that substances can move across a membrane. Figure 5.12 summarizes some of the main categories of transport mechanisms that have been identified in biological membranes. Beginning at the left are the simplest cases, of ① passive diffusion of ions and ② simple bulk flow. Next is carrier-mediated passive diffusion, in one direction ③ or in both directions ④. A very common passive mechanism is the linking of one substance to another; thus ⑤ sugars and amino acids are cotransported along with Na⁺ down its concentration gradient in many cells. Finally, we have the systems requiring energy. These include the active pump just discussed ⑥, driven by high-energy phosphate, and the proton pump ⑦, driven by respiratory enzymes, that is present in the inner membrane of the mitochondrion, as discussed in Chap. 3. While these mechanisms are all

present in biological membranes, most of them have also been demonstrated in artificial membranes composed of various organic substances. This has provided a powerful tool for experimental analysis, and has suggested that transport phenomena are to a large extent inherent in the properties of organic molecules and macromolecular complexes, when arranged in monolayers or very thin membranes.

In conclusion, both passive and active properties contribute to the membrane potential. These properties are present in different combinations in different cells. As a reflection of this, it is being recognized that the membrane potential does not have the same value in all neurons, nor do neurons respond in the same ways to change brought about by activity. In some cells or fibers the membrane potential may have a relatively high value, around −80 mV, inside negative. In other cells, the value may be lower, as low as −40 mV. A low value is found, for example, in vertebrate retinal receptor cells, where it is associated with a large resting leak of Na ions (see Chap. 16). The metabolic mechanisms for active transport are *temperature dependent*, which means that their contribution to the membrane potential in poikilothermic animals will vary according to temperature changes during the day, or in different seasons. The amount of pumping will also depend on the *size* of a nerve process. The smaller the process, the higher the surface-to-volume ratio, and the higher the rate of pumping activity required to maintain internal concentrations. If a neuron has a high level of spontaneous impulse firing, there may not be a "resting" membrane potential between the successive action potentials. Thus, the membrane potential, even at rest, is a very important variable for the different functions of nerve cells.

6

The Action Potential

The Nerve Impulse: A Brief History

The earliest ideas about the nature of the signals in the nervous system, going back to the Greeks, involved notions that the brain secretes fluids or "spirits" that flow through the nerves to the muscles. However, a new era opened in 1791 when Luigi Galvani of Bologna showed that frog muscles can be stimulated by electricity. His postulate of the existence of "animal electricity" in nerves and muscles soon led to a focus of attention almost exclusively on electrical mechanisms in nerve signaling.

In the 1840s, Galvani's countryman, Carlo Matteuci, who also had a distinguished career in Italian government, obtained the first evidence for the electrical nature of the nerve impulse. This was soon followed up and put on a sound and systematic basis by the extensive studies of Emil du Bois Reymond of Berlin. In 1850, Reymond's colleague, Herman von Helmholtz, later to be the famous physicist, was able to measure the speed of conduction of the nerve impulse, and showed for the first time that, though fast, it is not all *that* fast. In the large nerves of the frog, it is about 40 meters per second, which is about 140 kilometers per hour. This was another land-mark finding, for it showed that the mechanism of the nerve impulse has to involve something more than merely the physical passage of electricity as through a wire; it has to involve an *active biological process*. The impulse therefore came to be called the *action potential*.

The ability of a nerve to respond to an electrical shock with an impulse is a property referred to as *excitation*, and we say that the nerve is *excitable*. In the early experiments there were no instruments that could record the impulse directly; it could be detected only by the fact that, if a nerve was connected to its muscle, the shock was followed (after a brief period for conduction in the nerve) by a twitch of the muscle. The brief nature of the twitch indicated that an impulse must also occur in the muscle, so that the muscle was also recognized as having the property of excitability.

The electrical nature of the nerve impulse and its finite speed of conduction were important discoveries for physiology in general, and indeed for all science, because they constituted the first direct evidence for the kind of activity present in the nervous system. It appeared that, just as the heart pumps blood and the kidney makes urine, so now one could say that the nervous system produces impulses. In addition, the fact that the impulse moves at only a moderate speed had tremendous implications for psychology, for it seemed to separate the mind from the actions that the mind wills—in effect, it provided a basis for separating mind from body. It therefore was one of the stepping stones toward development of modern psychology and the study of behavior, as well as contributing to the debate on the nature of the mind and the body.

The Sodium Impulse

There are several essential facts about the impulse in nerve (or in any other cell, for that matter) that we start with in analyzing the underlying mechanism. First, the action potential is a *membrane event;* it consists of a transient change in the *membrane potential.* This was already suspected in the nineteenth century, and it has been elegantly demonstrated in squid axons, where impulses continue to be conducted even though all the axoplasm has been squeezed out.

The second important fact about the action potential is that it consists of a transient *depolarization* of the membrane potential. This had also been suggested by the

experiments of the nineteenth century, but direct demonstration was first obtained with intracellular recordings from the squid axon. The basic experimental setup for recording the membrane potential in the squid axon has been described in Chap. 5 (see Fig. 5.5), and the similar arrangement for recording the impulse is shown in Fig. 6.1. The earliest results, by K. C. Cole and H. J. Curtis at Woods Hole in 1939, showed that not only does the membrane depolarize (in other words, become less negative inside), but it passes zero and actually becomes almost 50 mV positive inside at the peak of the action potential.

What can account for this finding? It cannot be simply a transient breakdown in permeability to allow all ions to move across the membrane, because that would only depolarize the membrane to zero, not beyond. The clue is provided by a third key fact, that in squid axons the action potential depends on the presence of *sodium ions* in the external medium. If they are removed, the action potential is reduced in amplitude, as illustrated by the recordings and the graph in Fig. 6.2. It may be remembered that changing sodium has very little effect on the resting membrane potential, in accord with its low permeability relative to potassium in the resting membrane (see

Fig. 6.1   The impulse in the squid axon. The impulse has been triggered by a brief depolarization at A. Note that the impulse has the ability to spread in both directions when elicited experimentally in the middle of a nerve.

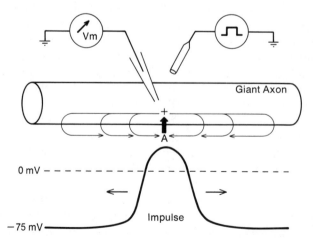

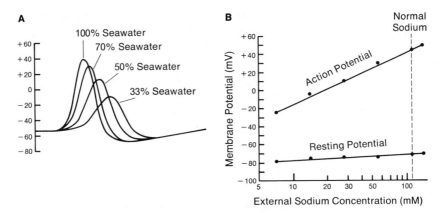

Fig. 6.2 Dependence of the action potential on Na ions. **A.** Impulse in normal (100%) seawater, and reduction in amplitude of impulse when external Na^+ is reduced to one-third normal concentration. **B.** Graph of effect of different external $[Na^+]$ on action potential amplitude. (From Hodgkin and Katz, 1949)

Fig. 5.6). The results of Fig. 6.2 indicate that, in contrast, the sodium permeability, and hence the sodium conductance, is very high at the peak of the action potential. That the sodium conductance can account for the peak is confirmed by the fourth fact, that the peak is near the Na equilibrium potential of approximately $+55$ mV, positive inside.

These facts thus suggest that the action potential in the squid axon involves a transient increase in the conductance of the membrane for sodium, providing for an inward rush of positively charged Na ions down their concentration gradient. This reduces the charge difference across the membrane and actually reverses it, as the membrane potential tends toward the sodium equilibrium potential of about $+55$ mV, positive inside.

What is the mechanism that produces this inward rush of sodium ions in response to a small depolarization of the membrane? We have seen that the usual means for moving ions across the plasma membrane is an integral membrane protein. For many years it was postulated that a channel protein is responsible for the sodium impulse, and this has been confirmed by recent advances using techniques of molecular biology.

These advances mean that, for the first time, the student can learn the mechanism of the impulse in a direct and logical way. We will begin with the molecular structure of the sodium channel. Then we will discuss the properties of single-channel events; the synchronous actions of many channels that give rise to the sodium impulse; and finally the variety of channel types that control impulse generation in different types of cells.

Molecular Structure of the Sodium Channel

The first information about the composition of the sodium channel came from biochemical studies. Certain toxins, such as tetrodotoxin (TTX), act by specifically binding to and blocking the sodium channel, and the impulse. Biochemists took advantage of this property of TTX to do binding assays and obtain the channel protein in purified form. This work was first done in the electric eel, *Electrophorus electricus,* the same animal in which the initial work on the acetylcholine (ACh) receptor was done. As we noted in Chap. 2, the high density of neuromuscular junctions in the electric organ (electroplaque) provided a rich source of ACh receptors; by the same token, the high density of modified muscle cells, whose summed action potentials generate the electric current which stuns the prey, provides a rich source of sodium channels. It was found that the *Electrophorus* sodium channel consists of a single continuous polypeptide with a molecular weight of 260,000–300,000, similar to the molecular weight of the ACh receptor.

The amino acid sequence of the polypeptide was determined by recombinant DNA techniques resembling those used to sequence the ACh receptor; in fact, the first work was carried out in the same laboratory of Shosaku Numa in Japan, this time by a team of 18 collaborators! The methods included the following key steps: microsequence analysis of purified polypeptide segments of the complete protein; preparation of a cDNA library from electroplaque mRNA; obtaining a cDNA complementary to one of these segments; use of this clone to screen a cDNA library to obtain seven longer overlapping clones; sequence analysis of these oligonucleotides, leading to the complete sequence of the entire cDNA coding for the sodium channel protein (Noda et al., 1986).

The entire cDNA consists of a chain of 7230 nucleotides, containing the triplet codes for a polypeptide chain of 1820 amino acids, giving a calculated molecular weight of approximately 208,000. Interestingly, the chain lacks the signal peptide at the amino terminal that is characteristic of a transmembrane protein translated by the ribosome on the endoplasmic reticulum (recall Chap. 3). It resembles other exceptions, such as the erythrocyte anion (chloride) channel (Chap. 3), certain ion pumps (Chap. 3), and rhodopsin (Chap. 16), in this regard.

In order to determine how this polypeptide chain forms a secondary structure that is inserted into the plasma membrane, the pattern of amino acid sequences was analyzed in a fashion similar to that used for the ACh receptor. First, a computer analysis showed that there is a pattern of about 300 amino acids forming a unit which is repeated four times. This repetition is called

internal sequence homology. Second, the entire chain was analyzed for the hydrophobic or hydrophilic properties of the amino acids. This showed a pattern of six segments with each homology unit. Finally, the tertiary structure of the polypeptide was deduced from this analysis. The structure is shown diagrammatically in Fig. 6.3; the legend may be consulted for details.

The structure of the functioning channel protein is formed by arranging the four units in a cylindrical fashion within the membrane. The channel within this structure must have a cross section no larger than 3×5 Ångströms if it is selectively to permit Na^+ to pass through. This indicates that the walls of the channel are probably formed by the faces of only one segment from each unit.

Movement of ions through the channel is normally blocked in the resting membrane, but occurs when the resting membrane potential is reduced (i.e., depolarized). This implies that there is a part of the channel protein that is sensitive to a change of electric charge across the membrane. In the middle of the sequence, between units II and III (see Fig. 6.3), there is a stretch of 200 amino acids that has four sequences containing negatively charged amino acids. It is believed that interactions between these negative charges and the positive charges of segment IV serve as a sensor of changes in transmembrane voltage. In fact, these interactions had previously been detected experimentally, by electrodes placed across the membrane, as a tiny *gating current* when the membrane potential was changed. This change in electric charge is believed to bring about allosteric changes in the conformation of the channel protein, which opens the channel slightly and allows Na ions to flow though it toward the inside of the membrane, down their concentration gradient. The interaction between the sensor and the conformation of the channel protein thus contains the heart of the impulse mechanism.

At this point, the student should review the fundamental principles underlying the

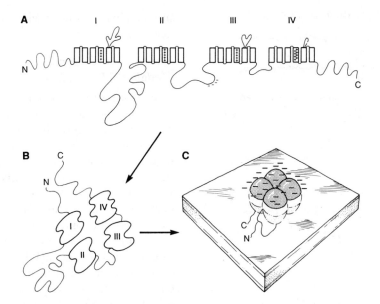

Fig. 6.3 Molecular structure of the sodium channel. This model is based on cDNA clones derived from rat brain mRNAs (Noda et al., 1986). **A.** Topology of the channel polypeptide, showing four repeated units (I–IV), each consisting of six homologous transmembrane segments. The segments labeled (+) contain a high proportion of positively charged residues, and are believed to function as the voltage sensor; upon transmembrane depolarization, these segments are believed to move outward, bringing about conformational change and transfer of ions (Armstrong, 1981). **B, C.** Views of the channel, to show arrangement of repeating units (I–IV), and their constituent transmembrane segments in relation to the central channel. (Diagrams courtesy of W. Agnew)

structure of the sodium channel protein in comparison with other channel-forming proteins. The sodium channel protein forms its channel by alignment of segments from subunits within a single polypeptide. The channel of the ACh receptor and other examples such as the gap junction channel also form their channels by the faces of single segments, but these come from independent polypeptide subunits coded by separate genes. The sodium channel is gated by transmembrane voltage, whereas the ACh receptor is gated by binding of its chemical ligand (ACh). We will see that these two types of gating may overlap to some extent in some channel proteins.

Single Channel Function

The physiological action of a single sodium channel polypeptide can be recorded by the patch-clamp technique. This was first accomplished in immature muscle cells (my-otubes) grown in tissue culture. Typical recordings are shown in Fig. 6.4A. In this experiment, the potential across the membrane patch was controlled by a command voltage step from a hyperpolarized level to a depolarized level. The recording shows that the depolarization induced an immediate response, consisting of a square pulse of current. The response to a depolarization shows that these are voltage-gated events, in contrast to the action of the ACh receptor, which responds only to the presence of its ligand, ACh (see Chap. 2). The responses are immediate, as expected if the voltage sensor in the polypeptide induces an immediate conformational change in the channel wall to allow Na ions to begin to flow through the channel. The inward direction of the current across the membrane is in accord with the flow of Na ions down their concentration gradient.

The responses have some of the same

A. SINGLE CHANNEL CURRENTS

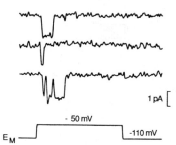

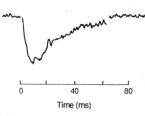

B. SUMMED CURRENTS

Time (ms)

Fig. 6.4 Recordings of single voltage-gated Na channels. **A.** Three traces showing single channel activity in response to a depolarizing step from -110 mV to -50 mV (monitor of clamped membrane potential (E_m) is shown below). Note the abrupt channel openings and closings, similar to the activity of ligand-gated channels such as AChR (Chap. 2). **B.** Smooth record obtained by summing or averaging the responses in 144 traces. These are referred to as macroscopic, as contrasted with microscopic (single channel), currents. They resemble the results seen in intracellular and whole-cell patch recordings. (From Patlak and Horn, 1982)

general characteristics of single channel events that we have previously noted for the ACh receptor. These include rapid opening to a constant plateau, rapid closing, and flickering of the open channel. When many of these single channel events are summed and averaged, one obtains, as in Fig. 6.4B, a smooth time course of the Na current. In these combined records, one refers to the onset as *activation* of the sodium channels, and the decay from the peak as *inactivation*. It can be seen that the Na channels undergo rapid activation, immediately followed by inactivation, in response to a depolarization of the mem-

brane. This is exactly what is required for generating an impulse.

The Sodium Channel: Hodgkin–Huxley Model

The information about single channels in a patch of membrane must next be interpreted in relation to the actual situation, in which many sodium channels are distributed in the membrane of an axon such as the squid giant axon. In this analysis, we want to know the time course of the ionic conductance change and current flow across the membrane, and we want to know also if any other ions might be involved. To do this we must set the membrane potential at different levels and determine how the ionic currents vary. This requires a technique for achieving a *space clamp* of the membrane, so that the impulse is held stationary over a length of the axon, together with a *voltage clamp* of that membrane, which enables the membrane potential to be set and held at a particular value and the response of the membrane measured in terms of the transmembrane current. The basic setup is illustrated in Fig. 6.5A, and the principles of measuring the ionic currents are explained in the legend.

This method was applied by Alan Hodgkin and Andrew Huxley of Cambridge University in a famous series of experiments that was published in 1952. The way they went about the analysis is indicated in Fig. 6.6. They set the membrane potential at different levels and recorded the membrane currents during voltage clamping; as shown in Fig. 6.6A,a, the currents consisted of an early inward phase and a later outward phase. They then repeated the experiments while replacing the Na in the external medium. This produced recordings, as in Fig. 6.6A,b, consisting of only a later outward phase, which increased in amplitude as the membrane was set at more depolarized levels. They postulated and confirmed that this component of the current is carried by K^+; the current is stronger the further the membrane is depolarized away from the

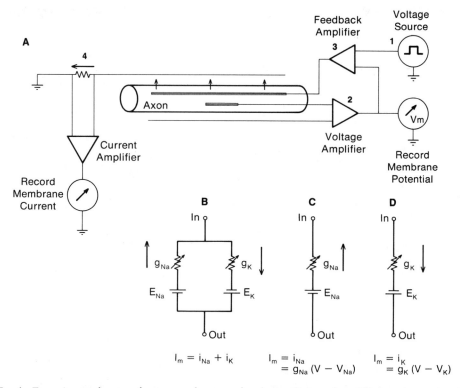

Fig. 6.5 A. Experimental setup for space-clamp and voltage-clamp of squid giant axon. A voltage source ① sets the membrane at a given level, which is recorded by an amplifier ②. This amplifier is connected to a feedback amplifier ③, that feeds back current across the membrane that just balances off the ionic current induced by the imposed voltage. The current is measured across a resistance ④. (After Kandel, 1976) **B–D.** Simplified equivalent circuits for flow of ionic currents under conditions of space and voltage clamp. **B.** In the clamped membrane, capacitative currents can be ignored, and the equivalent circuit reduces to conductance pathways for ionic currents driven by their electrochemical voltage sources. **C.** When K conductance is blocked, the membrane current (I_m) is due only to Na ionic flow (i_{Na}). **D.** When Na conductance is blocked, I_m is due only to i_K. (Modified from Hubbard et al., 1969)

K^+ equilibrium potential. When this component was subtracted from the control recording, they obtained an early component, as in Fig. 6.6A,c; this began to appear with small depolarizations, was largest at around zero potential, and reversed to an opposite polarity around +55 mV Fig. 6.6B,c. This is what would be expected if this component was carried by Na^+, driven by the Na^+ equilibrium potential of around +55 mV.

Subsequent experiments using poisons that selectively block Na^+ and K^+ conductances have confirmed these basic results.

As shown in Fig. 6.6B,c, when K^+ conductance is blocked by adding tetraethylammonium (TEA) to the external medium, only the early, Na^+ component remains. When, on the other hand, the Na^+ conductance is blocked, by adding tetrodotoxin (TTX), a poison found in the ovary of the puffer fish, only the late, K^+ component is present.

From measurements of the ionic currents, Hodgkin and Huxley were able to obtain the Na^+ and K^+ conductances by the application of Ohm's law to the reduced circuits for the membrane, as illus-

A. ION REPLACEMENT

B. PHARMACOLOGICAL BLOCKAGE

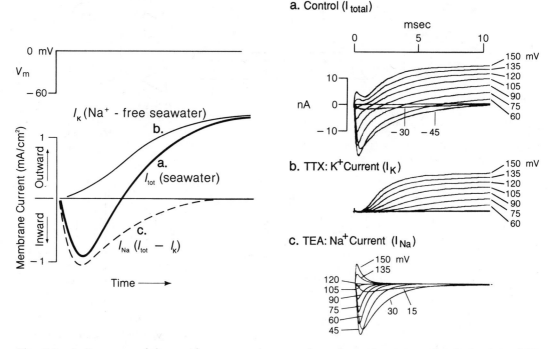

Fig. 6.6   A. Response of the squid axon membrane under voltage clamp, to a depolarization of 60 mV. a. Response in normal seawater. b. Response due to potassium current (I_K) when extracellular Na^+ is replaced by choline (a nonpolar molecule that maintains the osmotic pressure of the solution). c. Calculated response due to Na^+ current ($I_{Na} = I_{total} - I_K$). (From the original study of Hodgkin and Huxley, 1952) **B.** Separation of ionic currents by use of nerve poisons. a. Response in normal seawater, Different amplitudes of voltage steps are indicated on the right (in millivolts). b. Response due to I_K when I_{Na} is blocked by tetrodotoxin (TTX). c. Response due to I_{Na} when I_K is blocked by tetraethylammonium (TEA). (From Hille, 1977)

trated in Fig. 6.5B–D. They then derived equations that describe the turning on of these conductances. The only remaining piece of the puzzle was to account for the fact that, after rising rapidly, the Na^+ conductance quickly falls. This was described by a process of Na inactivation; in subsequent experiments it has been possible to block this selectively by application of the enzyme pronase within the axon.

The interrelations between these three factors—*Na$^+$ conductance, K$^+$ conductance*, and *Na$^+$ inactivation*—are shown in Fig. 6.7. This figure also brings out a crucial property of the Na conductance—that it is involved in a positive feedback relation with the membrane depolarization. When

the membrane begins to be depolarized, it causes the Na^+ conductance to begin to increase, which depolarizes the membrane further, which increases Na^+ conductance, and so on. This is the kind of self-reinforcing, *regenerative* relation that characterizes various kinds of devices; for example, a similar relation between heat and chemical reaction underlies the explosion of gunpowder. One can say that it is the property that puts the "action" in the action potential! It gives the impulse a *threshold*, below which it fails to fire, above which it is fully successful; one says that it is "all or nothing." This property is due to the interaction between Na and K conductances. Below threshold, the constant outward flow of K

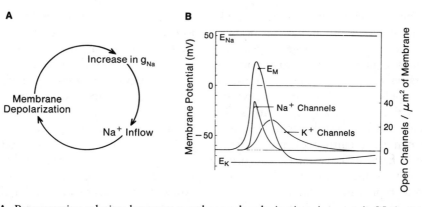

Fig. 6.7 **A.** Regenerative relation between membrane depolarization, increase in Na$^+$ permeability and conductance, and Na$^+$ current that underlies the action potential. **B.** Reconstruction of changes in ionic conductance underlying the action potential according to the Hodgkin-Huxley model; scale for the membrane potential (E_m) is shown on the left. The equilibrium potentials for Na and K are also indicated on the left ($E_{Na} = +50$ mV, $E_K = -77$ mV). Changes in Na and K ionic conductances are scaled on the right in terms of calculated open channels per square micrometer of membrane. The time courses of these changes are controlled by a set of equations that constitutes the Hodgkin-Huxley model. (For further details, see Hodgkin and Huxley, 1952; Hille, 1984.)

across the resting membrane prevents depolarization by small increases in Na conductance; "threshold" is the amount of depolarization at which inward Na flow exceeds the passive outward K flow, so that the regenerative mechanism takes over. The nerve is briefly *refractory* to restimulation, because of the Na inactivation during the peak and the high K conductance that keeps the membrane hyperpolarized during the afterpotential. The regenerative property also allows the impulse to propagate at a *constant amplitude* for long distances, properties that we will discuss further in later sections. This nonlinear, regenerative behavior, in which the Na$^+$ and K$^+$ conductances occur in *sequence,* rather than simultaneously, is the key way in which the mechanism of the action potential differs from the mechanism of the synaptic potential.

Based on their analysis of the experimental results, Hodgkin and Huxley were able to finish their study by deriving equations for the variables controlling the conductances, and, using these equations, construct a model that reproduced the action potential. As implied in Fig. 6.7, the fit of experiment and theory is very close. Further

details of the model are given in the legend, and in the references.

The Hodgkin-Huxley model of the nerve impulse is a consummate matching of experiment and theory, and is one of the great achievements of modern neurobiology and, indeed, of modern science. Its importance for neurobiology in general, and the study of membrane mechanisms in nerve cells in particular, cannot be overemphasized; it has been the solid touchstone for all subsequent research.

The Orchestra of Ionic Channels

The Hodgkin-Huxley model of the squid axon impulse received widespread support, and during the 1950s and 1960s it was extended to mammalian peripheral nerve and, by implication, to central neurons of both invertebrates and vertebrates. However, it soon became apparent that, whereas the Na$^+$–K$^+$ mechanism of the model could account for a single impulse, it could not provide for the complex patterns of impulse discharge that characterize the firing of most neurons.

During the 1970s, a variety of new types of ionic channel were recognized that could mediate these patterns. The early work took advantage of molluscan nerve cell bodies, which present invitingly large targets for the methods required in intracellular voltage-clamp analysis. However, these limitations need not apply to patch recordings, which can be carried out on any cell with sufficiently clean and accessible membrane surface, grown in a culture dish or freshly dissociated from a tissue slice. The properties of the cell membrane revealed in this work may represent to some extent the properties of synaptic terminals, and thus give clues to the membrane properties controlling synaptic outputs and synaptic responses, especially as they relate to mechanisms in development and learning (see Chap. 29).

The number of ionic conductances identified has grown rapidly, and it is impossible in an introductory account to describe them all. There are, however, certain main types that appear to play major roles in controlling nerve cell excitability and synaptic output. These fall into three groups: Na, Ca, and K conductances. The Na and Ca conductances are related, because Na and Ca both have inward concentration gradients across the membrane. Inside the membrane, Na is in low concentration according to the Donnan equilibrium (see Chap. 5), and Ca concentration is held very low by a variety of mechanism (see Chap. 8). As in the case of Na channels, voltage-gated Ca channels open in response to an initial membrane depolarization, letting Ca ions rush into the cell, and there is a regenerative relation between increasing conductance and increasing depolarization, similar to that for Na in the Hodgkin-Huxley model (see Fig. 6.7, above). Although Na and Ca conductances share these properties, their functions in the neuron are distinct. The Na conductances tend to be involved in generating fast action potentials in axons. As noted by Hille (1984), Na action potentials are not known outside metazoan animals; they thus appear to be an evolutionary specialization for rapid long-distance communication. By contrast, voltage-gated Ca channels (as well as various of the K channels) arose at earlier stages of evolution, among single-celled animals. They subserve several crucial functions: coupling membrane excitability to intracellular processes, shaping prolonged impulses, and controlling neurotransmitter release at sites of synapses.

The other main group of voltage-gated conductances is represented by channels that permit the flow of K ions. Since the concentration gradient for K is in the opposite direction to that for Na and Ca, opening this channel type by depolarizing the membrane causes K ions to move out of the cell. As we have seen, in the squid axon this tends to return the membrane potential to its relatively polarized resting level.

It turns out that there are many different types of K channels. This diversity may be partly due to the fact that K channels appear to survive better the patch-clamp procedures, but the variety is also real. Although it was at first bewildering, there seems to be logic behind the diversity. The nerve cell is ceaselessly active in a variety of ways, and the K channels constitute one of the main mechanisms for maintaining the equilibrium of the cell in the face of these demands. Since the potassium equilibrium potential is usually near the resting membrane potential, activation of K channels tends to return the membrane potential to this level during and following periods of Na or Ca impulse activity. Without this mechanism, the cell would tend to go into excessive electrical activity and the organism would have persistent seizures. Build-ups of Ca are especially to be avoided because of the critical role of Ca in many intracellular processes; therefore, it would be sensible for the cell to have a mechanism for turning on a K conductance after a Ca conductance. Also, some impulses are quite prolonged, in which case it would be an advantage to turn off the K conductance during the impulse so that it would not oppose the prolonged depolarization.

An orientation to the mechanisms of each

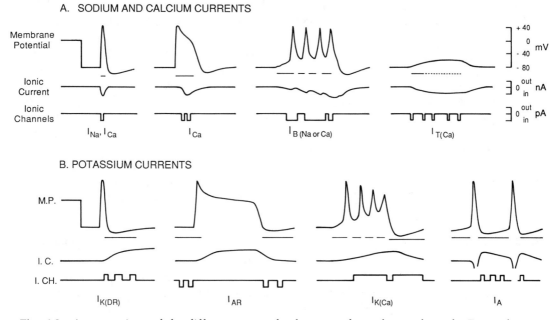

Fig. 6.8 A comparison of the different types of voltage-gated membrane channels. For each type are shown the membrane potential change to which it is related, the period during which it is active (horizontal lines), the macroscopic ionic currents producing that potential charge, and the channel activity underlying the macroscopic currents (this involves summation of activity of many channels, as shown in Fig. 6.4, above). **A.** Sodium and calcium currents. From left to right: the cation channel (I_{Na}, I_{Ca}), calcium channel (I_{Ca}), channel generating burst firing (I_B), channel passing transient Ca current (I_T). At right, voltage scale is in millivolts; current scales are in arbitrary units. **B.** Potassium currents. From left to right: the classical H–H delayed rectifier channel (I_{DR}); the anomalous rectifier channel (I_{AR}), so called because it passes inward current when the membrane is hyperpolarized (also called the inward rectifier (I_{IR}), in contrast to the outward rectifier (I_{DR}); the calcium-activated potassium channel ($I_{K(Ca)}$); the A channel, or transient K channel (I_A). Not depicted is the M channel, which acts like a noninactivating delayed rectifier during membrane depolarization (see text and Chaps. 7 and 19). (Based on data in Hille, 1984, and many other sources)

main type of channel and the relations between them can be obtained by study of Fig. 6.8, in which idealized recordings show the relation between membrane potential, summed ionic currents, and individual channel events, for the three main groups. We will discuss briefly each of the main types of conductances. S. J. Smith has assisted with the following overview.

Sodium (Na) Channels

Activation Characteristics. As discussed above, Na channels are closed at the resting potential, but open within 1 msec or less upon membrane depolarization. Na channels remain open for a maximum of a few

milliseconds, even if depolarization is maintained, because of the characteristic inactivation process inherent in the channels' voltage-gating mechanism. When the membrane is returned to the resting potential range, Na channels are reprimed for subsequent activation cycles. The unitary conductance of the channel is small, approximately 10 pS.

Pharmacology. A broad range of naturally occurring toxins block or otherwise modify Na channel function. The guanidinium toxins, represented by tetrodotoxin (TTX) and saxitoxin (STX), are strong blocking agents which have been widely used to block Na

Table 6.1 Densities per μm^2 of channels, pumps, and receptor proteins in membranes of neurons and other cells

Sodium channels	
Garfish olfactory nerves	1–35
Squid giant axon	100–600
Rabbit vagus nerve	100
Rabbit myelinated nodes of Ranvier	12,000
Sodium pumping sites	
Garfish olfactory nerve	300
Rabbit vagus nerve	750
Receptor molecules	
Muscle endplate: acetylcholine receptors	10,000
Rhodopsin in photoreceptors	50,000
(fat cells: insulin receptors)	1

For references, see Hille (1984)

currents in physiological studies and to label channel proteins for molecular analysis (see Fig. 6.3) or determination of density (see Table 6.1).

Diversity. There are subtypes that activate and inactivate more slowly, or show little inactivation; they are found particularly in cell bodies and dendrites of the CNS (see Fig. 25.11).

Calcium (Ca) Channels

Activation Characteristics. Ca channels are normally closed at the resting membrane potential and opened reversibly by depolarization to more positive potentials. The opening and closing occurs within a few milliseconds in most instances. Ca channels are also subject to inactivation during prolonged depolarizations. Some instances of Ca channel inactivation are secondary to intracellular Ca ion accumulation; others are a direct effect of membrane depolarization. The subject of Ca channels is complex (see Augustine et al., 1987.)

Pharmacology. Agents used to block Ca channel conduction include a number of inorganic cations: Cd^{2+}, Co^{2+}, Mn^{2+}, Ni^{2+}, and La^{2+} are commonly used. Organic Ca channel blocking agents include verapamil, diltiazem, and the dihydropyridines (nife-dipine, nitrendipine, nisoldipine, etc.). Recently, a number of protein toxins from snails of the genus *Conus* and some spiders also have been found to block certain Ca channels. Certain dihydropyridines, such as Bay-K 8644, have been found actually to promote the opening of some Ca channels. Ba^{2+} and Sr^{2+} ions can permeate through Ca channels and are sometimes substituted for Ca^{2+} ions in studies where investigators wish to eliminate other specific actions of the Ca^{2+} ion, such as intracellular activation of second messengers or vesicle release.

Diversity. Multiple Ca channel subtypes have been distinguished on the basis of activation voltage threshold, inactivation characteristics, single-channel conductance, and pharmacological sensitivities. In many instances, multiple subtypes are present on individual cells.

I_C type. This type is highly diverse in function; it triggers secretion of neurotransmitters by vesicle release, regulates cytoplasmic enzymes, and contributes to upstrokes and plateaus of some action potentials. It has a unitary conductance of 20–40 pS. The common pharmacological blockers are Co, Mn, Cd, Ni, and La.

L type. This is one of several new types of Ca^{2+} channel recently identified in neurons by Richard Tsien and his colleagues at Yale (Nowycky et al., 1985). The *L* (long-lasting) channel has a high threshold; it is opened by strong depolarization and is noninactivating. Its unitary conductance is 25 pS. It is blocked by dihydropyridines and by omega toxin from *Conus*.

T type. This type, by contrast, has a very small unitary conductance (9 pS). It has a low threshold, around a membrane potential of -70 mV, and is rapidly inactivating (hence *T* for transient) (see Fig. 6.8). Low threshold Ca spikes of this type may be important in boosting weak signals in dendrites, contributing significantly thereby to subthreshold synaptic integration.

N type. *N* stands for "neither" (*T* nor *L*). This channel has a high threshold, requiring strong depolarizations (around -30

mV) to activate it. In response to continued depolarization, it slowly inactivates. It has a unitary conductance of 13 pS, and is blocked by omega toxin. There is evidence that it may regulate neurotransmitter release from presynaptic terminals.

I_B type. In addition to Ca^{2+} current during the impulse, a separate Ca^{2+} current has been identified that is very slow (I_B in Fig. 6.8A). This current provides for a slow depolarization that underlies the generation of bursts of impulses in certain kinds of pacemaker neurons, and in neuroendocrine cells when they secrete their neurohormones.

K Conductances

The action of all K channels is to stabilize the membrane potential at a relatively polarized level (near E_K), and thus to oppose depolarization which would lead to increased impulse firing or neurotransmitter output. This is obviously extremely important, and K channels are thus diversified into many types to control the variety of excitatory influences on the cell.

I_K Type. This is perhaps the most ubiquitous of the K channels. It activates extremely slowly with small depolarizations. It is thus well suited for maintaining the resting membrane potential, and also contributes to the repolarizing phase of the action potential, impulse frequency coding, and subthreshold synaptic integration. It also serves to link intracellular metabolism to membrane excitability via protein phosphorylation and Ca^{2+}. The unitary conductance is approximately 20 pS. It is blocked by TEA, 4-aminopyridine (4-AP), Ba, and Co.

Delayed Rectifier (I_{DR}). This is the classical conductance of the squid axon. It is activated after a brief delay by strong depolarization, and inactivates very slowly. The unitary conductance is approximately 10 pS in squid axon, and the blockers are similar to those for I_K. At some sites this late K conductance may be absent (this appears to be the case at the node of Ranvier). At these sites, repolarization of the membrane occurs as a consequence of Na^+ inactivation.

Calcium-Dependent K Channel (I_C, $I_{K(Ca)}$). The voltage dependence of this current is mostly secondary to activation of voltage-dependent Ca channels. The inflow and cytoplasmic accumulation of Ca leads to opening of this type of K channel. The resulting slow hyperpolarization is important in shaping action potentials in neuronal cell bodies, and controlling slow rates of impulse firing by opposing increases in excitability associated with increase in Ca influences. The unitary conductance in snail neurons is 10–20 pS. It is blocked by apamin.

Early K (I_A). This type is also called fast transient K. It is rapidly activated and inactivated by small depolarizations, and is turned on particularly after being deinactivated by hyperpolarizations such as follow an impulse. It therefore is well suited for opposing interimpulse depolarizations, thus contributing to control of slow impulse firing rates. The unitary conductance is approximately 20 pS, and is blocked by 4-AP.

Anomalous Rectifier (I_{AR}). All of the K conductances considered thus far turn on with depolarization, to help return the membrane to its resting potential level. There is, however, a K conductance that turns off with depolarization, and turns on only when the membrane is hyperpolarized above its resting level. In this range, the K current is inward (to drive the membrane toward E_K), and this channel is therefore called the inward rectifier, or anomalous rectifier (I_{AR} in Fig. 6.8B). Since this conductance is turned off during depolarization, it helps to maintain prolonged depolarization of the membrane, as during the depolarized plateaus of long-lasting impulses. This is important in the cardiac action potential (see Chap.

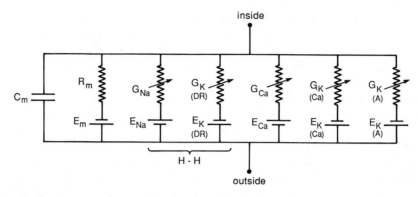

Fig. 6.9 Equivalent circuit of a patch of neuronal membrane which includes different types of voltage-gated ionic channels discussed in the text, and illustrated in Figs. 6.8 and 6.10. This is an expanded version of the single equivalent circuit in Fig. 5.7. Leak resistance of the membrane is R_m. H–H refers to the Na and K conductances of the Hodgkin-Huxley model. Other conductances shown are calcium (G_{Ca}), calcium-activated K ($G_{K(Ca)}$), and transient K ($G_{K(A)}$). For other abbreviations, see Fig. 5.7.

17), in the prolonged action potential generated by many egg cells in association with fertilization, and during the Na action potentials generated in the electroplaque (in this case their function is presumably to enhance the depolarization by the Na action potential, in order to generate the greatest possible amount of electric current by the electroplaque organ).

M Current (I_M). A final interesting type of current to be noted is I_M. This is activated by depolarization, but, unlike I_{DR}, it does not inactivate. This constant current can be affected by neurotransmitters, and appears to provide a mechanism for adjusting the sensitivity of a neuron to synaptic inputs. We will discuss it further in relation to synaptic potentials (Chap. 7) and sympathetic neurons (Chap. 18).

In the electrical analogue of the membrane, these ionic conductances are present as elements in parallel with the others. Fig. 6.9 shows how they can be incorporated into the electrical circuit analogue of the membrane previously shown in Fig. 5.7.

Some rather sophisticated computer models of nerve cells have been constructed which incorporate these ionic conductances. An example of a neuron in *Aplysia*

is shown in Fig. 6.10. It can be seen that the model provides a relatively close approximation to the burst firing pattern recorded from the neuron.

Channel Densities and Local Excitability

Using the fact that the nerve poison tetrodotoxin (TTX) selectively blocks Na$^+$ channels, studies have been carried out to determine the amount of binding of radioactively labeled TTX (and related poisons) to nerve fibers, in order to obtain an estimate of the density of Na$^+$ channels per area of membrane. Studies of this type have revealed that the density varies considerably in different neurons, and in different parts of the neuron. Table 6.1 summarizes some results, together with estimates for related properties such as pumping sites and receptors. The extremely high density of Na$^+$ channels in the node of Ranvier (see Chap. 3) presumably reflects the specialization of this small patch of membrane for generation of the action potential during saltatory conduction (see below). The differences among the nerves shown may reflect in part their differing sizes; for example, olfactory nerves are among the thinnest fibers in the nervous system (diameter = 0.2 μm), with correspondingly very high surface-to-volume ratio.

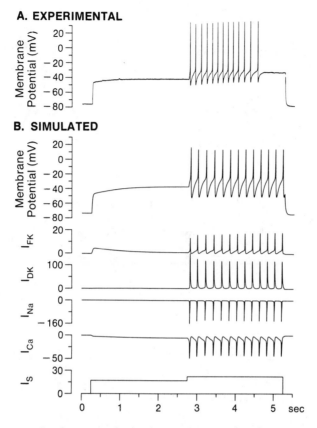

Fig. 6.10 Repetitive impulse firing in ink-gland motoneuron of *Aplysia*. **A.** Experimental recording, of impulse burst response to steps of injected stimulating current (I_S monitor below). **B.** Simulation of the voltage response in A by a computational model comprising four types of voltage-gated current (below): fast K or A current (I_{FK}); delayed rectifier K current (I_{DK}), Na current (I_{Na}), and calcium current (I_{Ca}). Current scales are in nanoamperes (nA); inward currents down, outward currents up. Note the close correspondence between the simulated burst and the experimentally recorded burst. (From Byrne, 1980)

These studies make it clear that the density of voltage-dependent ion channels varies widely, as an expression of the functional specialization of the nerve membrane. Local regions of a neuron may thus have different excitable properties; this is an extension of our discussion of membrane microdomains in Chap. 3, and is an important principle underlying the complexity of neuronal organization.

Voltage Dependence and Neurotransmitter Sensitivity

Thus far we have considered the ion channel to be formed by a macromolecular complex which permits ions to pass through according to the potential difference across the membrane. This is a purely "voltage-dependent" channel. Traditionally it has been believed that this property makes impulse channels distinct from synaptic channels, which are presumed to be sensitive only to the action of a chemical transmitter substance liberated from another neuron. However, it has been found that in many cases the voltage-dependent channels are also sensitive to neurotransmitters.

A nice demonstration of this was provided by the experiments of Kathleen Dunlap and Gerald Fischbach, then at Harvard.

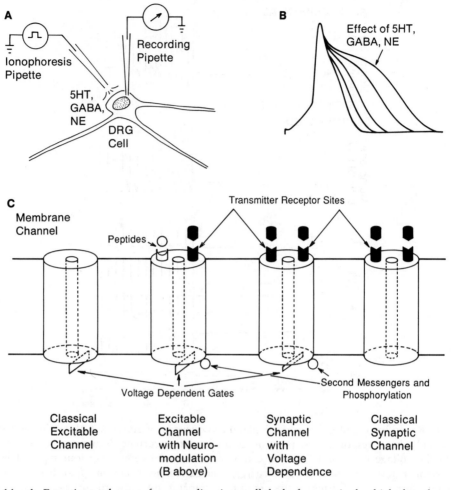

Fig. 6.11 **A.** Experimental setup for recording intracellularly from a single chick dorsal root ganglion cell in culture while ionophoresing neurotransmitter substances. **B.** Effects of different substances on impulses. Long-duration spikes before, short-duration spikes after, ionophoresis of substances. **C.** Simple models to illustrate different types of voltage-sensitive and ligand (neurotransmitter)-sensitive channels. In addition to neurotransmitters, ligand-gating also occurs externally by neuromodulators and internally by phosphorylation and other second-messenger actions, as indicated in C. (Diagram B redrawn from Dunlap and Fischbach, 1978)

They made intracellular recordings from disseminated cell cultures of the chick dorsal root ganglion (Fig. 6.11A). These cells have a prolonged action potential, with an early peak that is due to Na^+ current, and a later component that is carried by Ca^{2+}. Neurotransmitter substances were ionophoresed onto the cells from extracellular micropipettes. As shown in Fig. 6.11B, several of these substances (serotonin, γ-aminobutyric acid, and norepinephrine) re-

duced the slow Ca^{2+} component of the impulse. Other substances, such as dopamine or various peptides, had no effect.

These cells lack dendrites and receive no synapses onto their cell bodies. However, their axon terminals in the spinal cord receive synapses from several types of fibers (these belong to the category of axoaxonic synapses). It has been suggested that these fibers may release one or another of the above transmitters to depress the Ca^{2+}

component of the impulse and thereby reduce the amount of transmitter released by the dorsal root fibers onto motoneurons and other spinal cord cells. This mechanism of reducing the input to motoneurons is called presynaptic inhibition. A similar mechanism has been invoked to explain plastic changes of synapses underlying learning in *Aplysia,* as we will discuss in Chap. 29.

These experiments have made it clear that, at specific sites on a neuron, excitable channels may have receptors for neurotransmitters which permit modulation of the excitable properties. Complementing this work are the findings of those working on synapses that, in many cases, the responses to a neurotransmitter may depend on the level of the resting membrane potential. The situation is summarized in Fig. 6.11C. At the far left is the traditional impulse channel, with only a voltage-dependent property, while at the right is the traditional synaptic channel, with only transmitter receptor sites. Between are channels that contain some degree of the other property, as well as sites for modulation by peptides and by second messengers. These channels obviously provide the nervous system with much greater flexibility in modifying trains of impulses, on the one hand, or integration of synaptic inputs, on the other, depending on the ongoing state of the organism and level of activity in its neural circuits. This should be kept in mind when we discuss the properties of synapses in Chaps. 7 and 8.

Conduction of the Action Potential

We have seen that, during the action potential, positive current carried by Na^+ or Ca^{2+} flows into the cell. Where does it go from there? As shown in Fig. 6.12, the current will have to flow back out through the membrane to complete the circuit. It cannot all return at the point of entry, and it therefore spreads out along the fiber, seeking pathways of least resistance to get outside. How far it extends down the fiber depends on the ratio of the resistance of the cytoplasm to the resistance of the membrane. The higher the membrane resistance (or the lower the cytoplasm resistance), the further the current will tend to flow along the fiber.

Local Currents

This spread of electric current through the constant resistance and capacitance properties of the nerve is called *electrotonus*. It was first studied in the late nineteenth century. At that time, electric cables for long-distance telephone communication were being laid down, and it was recognized that the equations used to describe the spread of electricity in the cables were similar to those that applied to nerve. From that time, the electrotonic properties of nerve cells have been referred to as *cable properties*. The simple cable equations for the spread of electrotonic potentials are described in the legend of Fig. 6.12.

We will consider the spread of electrotonic potentials, and their crucial role in the integrative functions of dendrites, in the next chapter. Here we simply point out that whenever an impulse is set up, electrotonic currents flow through the neighboring membrane. These currents, also called *local currents,* spread the depolarization of an impulse to neighboring membrane sites where, if threshold is reached, the impulse is also generated. The process continues along the fiber, at a rate determined by the size of the fiber: the larger the fiber, the faster the rate, other things being equal. This is a function of the cable properties; the larger the axon, the smaller the internal resistance and the farther the spread of the local currents (see Fig. 6.12). We say that the local currents spread *passively*, whereas the impulse is *conducted*, or *propagates*.

Continuous propagation of the impulse, as just described, occurs in unmyelinated axons. These may be very large, in certain invertebrate axons like the squid giant axon. In vertebrates, they are the smallest fibers, from several micrometers in diameter down to around 0.2 μm.

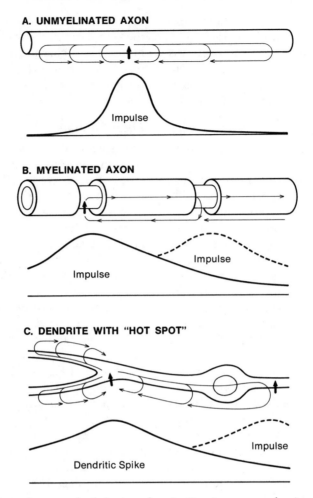

Fig. 6.12 Mechanisms for spread of the impulse. **A.** Continuous conduction in an unmyelinated axon. Amplitude scale is in millivolts. **B.** Discontinuous (saltatory) conduction from node to node in a myelinated axon. **C.** Discontinuous spread from "hot spot" to "hot spot" in a dendrite. In all diagrams, the impulses are shown in their spatial extent along the fiber at an instant of time. The extent of current spread is governed by the cable properties of the fiber. For an orientation to these properties, see Jack et al. (1975) and Shepherd (1979).

Saltatory Conduction

Myelinated fibers, as we have seen, have a coating of many membranes that is interrupted at intervals by nodes of Ranvier. The nodes are the sites of impulse generation; here, the Na^+ channels are packed together at a density of some $12,000/\mu m^2$ (see Table 6.1), the highest density yet known in the nervous system. In contrast, the intervening membrane under the myelin has few voltage-dependent conductance channels, and spread through the interno-

Table 6.2 Functions of excitability in cells

Development	Motility
in fertilization	ciliary
in cell division	vascular
in morphogenesis	muscle
Ion transfers across membranes	Nerve signaling
Bioluminescence	propagation
Secretion	other functions
hormonal	
glandular	
synaptic	

From Shepherd (1981), Hille (1984)

dal segments is therefore purely electrotonic (see Fig. 6.12B). It is very effective, because the myelin wrapping has a high resistance and low capacitance that makes the current tend to flow down the fiber to the next node rather than leak back across the membrane. The impulse in effect jumps from node to node, and this form of propagation is therefore called *saltatory conduction*. It is an efficient mechanism that achieves maximum conduction speed with a minimum of active membrane, metabolic machinery, and fiber size. It is especially prevalent in vertebrates, where it has been an important factor in making possible high-speed conduction over many fibers between many nerve centers.

A variation on this type of conduction is present in the dendrites of some neurons. As shown in Fig. 6.12C, there are patches of active membrane in the dendritic tree. These patches are separated from the site of impulse initiation in the cell body and axon by passive dendritic membrane. The active patches are called "hot spots." They are believed to boost the response to synaptic inputs in the dendrites, thereby enhancing the effect of distant dendritic inputs in affecting impulse generation at or near the cell body. As already noted, hot spots may generate impulses by Na^+ conductance mechanisms, whereas other parts of the dendritic tree may have slower Ca^{2+} conductances. In addition to their role in conductance, dendritic spikes may have significance for other functions of dendrites, especially those concerned with synaptic integration and control of output from presynaptic dendrites, as discussed in the next chapter.

The Many Functions of the Impulse

Traditionally, the impulse has been regarded as the characteristic functional property of the nerve cell. It has been assumed that this property of peripheral nerves can be generalized to all nerve cells within the brain. This has led to two common beliefs: first, that the nerve cell can be defined as a cell that generates impulses, and second, that impulses are the only means by which nerve cells communicate with each other. These beliefs are widespread today, but neither is correct.

The idea that nerve cells communicate only through impulses was perhaps natural—after all, it is the only means by which signals can travel rapidly over a long stretch of peripheral nerve. It therefore seems reasonable to suppose that rapid signaling over long axons between regions within the brain similarly depends on impulses. However, within brain regions much of the communication takes place over short distances, and in these cases the electrotonic spread of synaptic potentials within nerve cells can be sufficient, without need of action potentials. We will describe this type of signaling in the next chapter, where we will see that many nerve cells are able to carry out nervous functions without generating action potentials.

A second reason for doubting that the impulse is the one defining property of the neuron is that the neuron is not the only kind of cell that can generate impulses. As mentioned above, skeletal muscle was recognized to have this property, and so was cardiac muscle. As so often happens in science, these were easily regarded as exceptions to the rule. However, it was soon found that they were not the only exceptions; in the 1870s John Burdon-Sanderson, one of the leading British physiologists, showed that, when a Venus flytrap is touched by an insect (or by an experimenter), impulses can be recorded in association with the rapid closing of its leaves around the prey. This experiment showed that the impulse is not exclusive to nerve cells, or even to the Animal Kingdom.

These results have been confirmed and amplified in recent years, particularly since the advent of the microelectrode and the development of techniques to record intracellularly from cells in a variety of organisms, and most recently, to make patch recordings of single channel activities. The surprising finding has been that many very

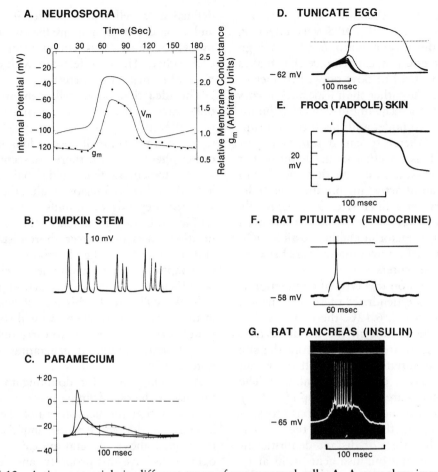

Fig. 6.13 Action potentials in different types of nonneuronal cells. **A.** A very slow impulse in the elongated cells of the giant alga. **B.** Impulse bursts in vascular cells of the pumpkin stem. **C.** Ca²⁺ action potential in a protozoan. **D.** Example of slow action potential characteristic of many types of ova. **E.** Impulse typical of several types of epithelial cell. **F.** Action potential of a pituitary cell that secretes melanocyte stimulating hormone (MSH). **G.** Characteristic impulse burst associated with secretion of insulin from β cells of the pancreas. (A from Slayman et al., B from Sinyuhkin and Gorchakov, C from Eckert et al., D from Hagiwara and Miyazaki, E from Roberts and Stirling, F from Douglas and Taraskevich, G from Dean et al.) (From Shepherd, 1981, which includes full references; see also review in Hille, 1984)

different kinds of cells show the ability to generate impulses. Some examples are illustrated in Fig. 6.13. In the giant cells of the fungus *Neurospora* (A), impulses are very slow, lasting over one minute. By comparison, a number of higher plants have cells that generate impulses in bursts (B); these cells are found especially in long-stemmed plants like peas and pumpkins, where they appear to be involved in pump-

ing sap through the vasculature. In single-cell organisms like the *Paramecium* (C), impulses are involved in sensory responses as well as in the control of ciliary movement.

Within the Animal Kingdom, a number of studies have shown that oocytes of many species respond to an electric shock with an impulse; the example in D is from a primitive chordate *(Tunicata)*, and similar findings have been reported in invertebrates (for example, the oocyte of annelid worms) and in higher vertebrates (for example, the rat). Impulses have also been recorded in the skin of tadpoles (E). In mammals, a number of types of gland cells have been found to generate impulses; two examples are the cells of the anterior pituitary that secrete pituitary hormones (F) and the islet cells of the pancreas that secrete insulin (G).

These examples by no means exhaust the list; one might mention, for instance, the finding of voltage-gated channels in cells of the immune system, and impulses in certain kinds of cancer cells. However, they are sufficient to indicate that voltage-gated channels are present in a wide variety of cells throughout the plant and animal kingdoms. This is a good illustration of why it is important to take a broad molecular and cellular approach to the functions of nerve cells. In line with that approach, we would say that *excitability*—the ability to generate impulses by means of voltage-gated channels—*is a property expressed to a greater or lesser extent in many different cells, depending on their particular functions.*

In later chapters, we will study the function of the impulse in embryonic cells (Chap. 9), in gland cells (Chap. 18), and in muscle cells (Chap. 17).

Some of the functions of impulses that have been identified in plant and animal cells are summarized in Table 6.2. Some of these, such as bioluminescence or fertilization, are obviously special for certain types of nonnervous cells. However, some of them have implications for nerve cells as well. These include the possible role of excitability in cell division and morphogenesis; in transfer of ions across membranes; in control of transmembrane movements of various substances; or in motility of nerve processes underlying growth and plasticity.

In addition to these general properties, we have noted certain functions of excitability already identified in neurons, such as prolonged effects on impulse firing, complex integration in dendrites, and control of output from presynaptic dendrites. Many of these functions are likely to be of increased importance in smaller processes such as axon terminals and dendritic spines, where even small conductance changes may have very large effects on membrane potential, internal ion concentrations, and associated metabolic machinery.

Excitability can thus be seen to play many possible roles in nerve cells. Some of these involve general properties common to many other cells. From this perspective, the impulse can be regarded as an expression of the cell biology of the neuron. We will see another aspect of this unity within cell biology when we discuss interactions between neurons that take place without impulses, in the next chapter.

7

Synaptic Potentials and Synaptic Integration

Synaptic Potentials: A Brief History

By the early years of this century, the idea of the synapse was firmly established. Cajal had demonstrated that nerve cells are individual entities, requiring that transmission between them takes place, as he phrased it, "by contiguity, not continuity." Sherrington had made contiguity explicit in his concept of the synapse. Sherrington also provided evidence for some of the physiological properties of the synapses in his studies of transmission through reflex arcs in the spinal cord. He showed that reflex discharges were graded in strength, showed summation without refractoriness, displayed inhibition as well as excitation, and often long outlasted the stimulus, all properties that are clearly differentiated from those of impulses in the nerves.

We have seen that during this time, biochemists like Dale and Loewi were laying the foundations for the view that synaptic transmission takes place through chemical messengers. However, the opposite view, that synaptic transmission occurs by means of electrical current passing from one neuron to the next, was held by many neurophysiologists. They objected that many of the biochemical experiments involved collecting substances in perfusates of isolated organs that were stimulated at high rates, so that the results admitted of more than one interpretation. It was also difficult to generalize from these peripheral organs to synapses in the central nervous system where experimental methods, both physiological and biochemical, were at that time almost completely lacking. It was a situation that gave rise to much heated debate, from the 1920s to the early 1950s; some sense of it can be gained from the remarks of Alexander Forbes (one of the few who was able to maintain his good humor) of Harvard, summing up a symposium on the synapse that was held in 1939:

> So goes the controversy. Dale in discussing it remarked that it was unreasonable to suppose that nature would provide for the liberation in the ganglion of acetylcholine, the most powerful known stimulant of ganglion cells, for the sole purpose of fooling physiologists. To this Monnier replied that it was likewise unreasonable to suppose action potentials would be delivered at the synapses with voltages apparently adequate for exciting the ganglion cells merely to fool physiologists.

All this confusion was swept away by the advent of the microelectrode and the electron microscope in the 1950s. The old controversy was supplanted by the clear evidence that some synapses are chemical and some electrical (and some are mixed).

The first synapses studied with intracellular methods were the neuromuscular junction, by Bernard Katz and his colleagues in London, and the motoneuron, by John Eccles and his colleagues in New Zealand and Australia. Since that time, neurophysiologists have characterized the action at a synapse in terms of the electrical responses which they could record when a presynaptic process acts through the synapse on a postsynaptic process. The postsynaptic electrical response usually takes the form of a transient change in membrane potential, and this change is referred to as a *postsynaptic potential,* or simply *synaptic potential.*

The study of synaptic actions is therefore largely concerned with the mechanisms for producing synaptic potentials, and the preceding chapters have prepared the way for this study. The student should therefore review Chap. 2, to appreciate how it is that many single channel conductances acting together give rise to the postsynaptic potential. The molecular mechanisms underlying transmitter release and postsynaptic responses will be covered in the next chapter. We will learn that there are multiple actions at most synapses, lasting over different periods of time. Not all of these are associated with postsynaptic potentials. However, these are the responses we understand best. The brief synaptic actions must be critical for all the sensory perceptions, motor acts, and cognitive processes that happen quickly. In order for this to occur, neurons must not only generate these responses but also integrate them, in order to process information in a coordinated manner. Our aim therefore will be to put this information together with the structure of the nerve cell and its ability to generate impulses, in order to understand how synaptic potentials are involved in the integrative behavior of the neuron.

Electric Fields

The simplest mechanism for effecting a change in the membrane potential is through the flow of current from a neighboring cell. Consider the situation diagramed in Fig. 7.1A. An active site exists in the upper cell

Fig. 7.1 Types of electrical interactions. **A.** Field potential effects through membrane juxtapositions. **B.** Representative recordings from pre- and postsynaptic processes in A. **C.** Current flows through gap junction (electrical synapse). **D.** Representative recordings from C. Note much larger loss in transmission in B than D.

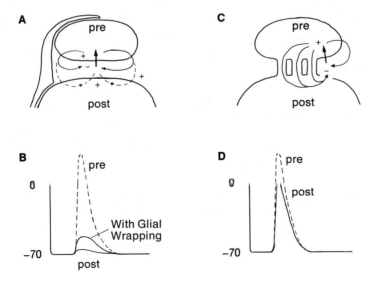

which causes current to flow inward at that site (as, for example, by the inward flow of Na ions). Associated with this is an outward flow of current to complete the circuit through the neighboring membrane. For the present, we recognize that as the current emerges from the membrane it can flow directly back to the active site through the low-resistance extracellular space (solid arrow), or it can pass through the high-resistance membrane of the neighboring cell (dotted line). Naturally it will prefer the path of low resistance, but a small amount will pass through the membrane. If the points of entry and exit are sufficiently separate, there will be a net flow of current at each point, and one can record a corresponding small change in the membrane potential. A nonspecific electrical interaction of this type is sometimes referred to as an *ephapse*.

Representative recordings for this case are illustrated in Fig. 7.1B. While this seems like a very inefficient mechanism, it can be enhanced in several ways. A large number of tightly packed active processes will heighten the effect, as could occur in the case of unmyelinated axons running together; olfactory nerves and cerebellar parallel fibers are possible sites for this. Large populations of synchronously active cells in the cerebral cortex generate currents sufficient to give rise to the waves of the electroencephalogram (EEG); this might also involve field effects between the cells, particularly between their dendrites. A glial wrapping can restrict the extracellular current flow and increase the amount of current crossing neighboring membrane; this has, in fact, been demonstrated for one of the input terminals onto the Mauthner cell in lower vertebrates (see Chap. 19).

An advantage of this type of interaction is that it requires no extra energy. The disadvantages are that the effects are minimal, diffuse, and nonspecific without structural constraints, and the membrane potential changes are rigidly locked to the original activity.

Electrical Synapses

Effective electrical coupling between cells is achieved through gap junctions. As we have described in detail in Chap. 4 (see Fig. 4.5), the intercellular channels at these junctions have a very low resistance to current passing between the two neurons, and at the same time they prevent loss by leakage to the extracellular space. Thus, a potential change in a presynaptic terminal may be transmitted to a postsynaptic terminal with little attenuation, as shown in Fig. 7.1C,D. Experimentally this is the direct test for the presence of an electrical synapse, and was first reported by Ed Furshpan and David Potter in 1959 at a synapse between two nerve fibers in the crayfish. The synapse they studied is made by the lateral giant fiber onto the giant motor fiber in the abdominal ganglion; it mediates rapid flip movements of the tail that are used for defensive reflexes (see Chap. 19). As shown in Fig. 7.2, an action potential in the presynaptic fiber spreads with little attenuation into the postsynaptic fiber (A), whereas spread in the reverse direction (B) is very limited. This directionality of current flow is called *rectification*.

Electrical synapses (and their morphological substrates, gap junctions) have been found between neurons at many sites in the nervous systems of invertebrates and lower vertebrates.

Three sites have been found in the mammalian brainstem. These are illustrated in Fig. 7.3. In the mesencephalic nucleus of the fifth cranial nerve, there are electrical synapses between cell bodies and between cell bodies and initial axonal segments (A). In the vestibular (Deiter's) nucleus the synapses occur between cell bodies and axon terminals. A spike initiated in one cell is transmitted to a neighboring cell as a short-latency depolarization by current flow through the axon terminals and branches, as shown in (B). In the inferior olive, dendritic spines are interconnected by electrical synapses. The spines also receive chemical

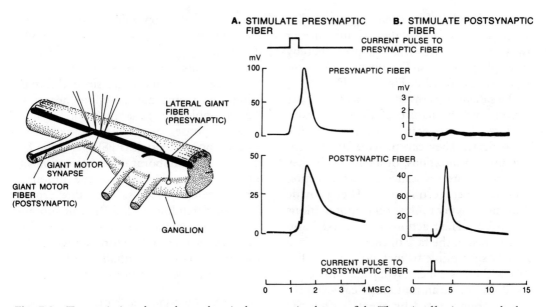

A. STIMULATE PRESYNAPTIC FIBER **B.** STIMULATE POSTSYNAPTIC FIBER

CURRENT PULSE TO PRESYNAPTIC FIBER

PRESYNAPTIC FIBER

POSTSYNAPTIC FIBER

CURRENT PULSE TO POSTSYNAPTIC FIBER

LATERAL GIANT FIBER (PRESYNAPTIC)

GIANT MOTOR SYNAPSE

GIANT MOTOR FIBER (POSTSYNAPTIC)

GANGLION

Fig. 7.2 Transmission through an electrical synapse in the crayfish. There is effective spread of an impulse from the lateral giant fiber into the giant motor fiber (**A**). The lack of spread in the opposite direction is called *rectification* (**B**). (After Furshpan and Potter, 1959, in Kuffler et al., 1976)

Fig. 7.3 Three examples of electrical synapses in the mammalian brain. **A.** Mesencephalic nucleus of the fifth cranial nerve. (Baker and Llinas, 1971) **B.** Deiter's nucleus, in the vestibular complex of the eighth cranial nerve. (Korn et al., 1973) **C, D.** Inferior olivary nucleus, in the medulla oblongata. (Llinas et al., 1974)

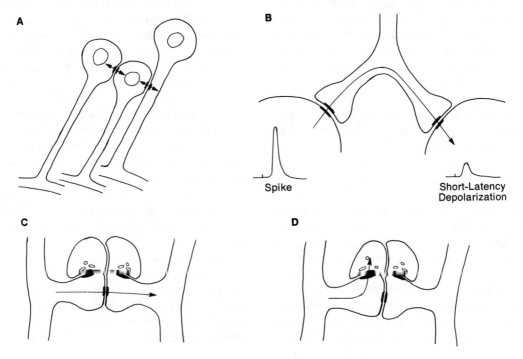

Spike

Short-Latency Depolarization

synapses, and it has been suggested that when they are active they shunt current away from the electrical synapses, thereby uncoupling the cells. The postulated mechanism is illustrated in Fig. 7.3C,D.

The salient features of electrical synapses derive from the nature of the direct connections. They operate quickly, with little or no delay. They can provide for current flow in both directions, or alternatively they can offer more resistance in one direction than the other (rectification). They provide a means of synchronization of populations of neurons. Their actions can be fixed and stereotyped in the face of repeated use, and are less susceptible to metabolic and other effects than chemical synapses. However, this does not mean that electrical synapses cannot be influenced by events within the cytoplasm. Experiments in salivary gland cells have shown that increases in internal Ca^{2+} block the ability of a small molecule (fluorescein) to pass through gap junctions. This uncoupling effect may depend on a concomitant fall in intracellular pH. There is evidence from freeze-fracture studies that the uncoupling involves changes in the geometrical arrays of intramembranous particles at the gap junction. Whether this mechanism is operative in the modulation of electrical coupling between nerve cells has not been determined. In addition to mediating electrical transmission, gap junctions are also important in other ways for intercellular communication and the organization of cells into multicellular ensembles as discussed in Chap. 4.

Chemical Synapses

Chemical synapses, operating through the release of a neurotransmitter, are the predominant type throughout the nervous system. The main short-term effect on the postsynaptic neuron is the setting up of a postsynaptic potential (PSP). This is the basis for rapid information reception and integration in the neuron, and thus an understanding of its mechanism is impor-

tant. Our discussion will build directly on the neuromuscular junction as a model (Chap. 2).

Synaptic potentials are of two main types. One type is depolarizing; since this type brings the membrane potential nearer to the threshold for generating an impulse, these responses were termed excitatory postsynaptic potentials (EPSPs) by John Eccles and his collaborators in their pioneering microelectrode studies of the motoneuron in the early 1950s. The other type is polarizing, tending to hold the membrane potential away from generating an impulse; these responses are therefore termed inhibitory postsynaptic potentials (IPSPs). Let us consider the mechanism of each.

Excitatory Postsynaptic Potentials

In many cases, EPSPs at central synapses appear to be generated by mechanisms very similar to those at the neuromuscular junction. As summarized in Fig. 7.4A, the transmitter released from the presynaptic terminal binds to membrane receptors in the postsynaptic terminal, opening channels that are relatively nonspecific for cations (Na^+, Ca^{2+}, K^+). The predominance of Na^+ and Ca^{2+} ion flows produces a net inward current. The individual channel openings are indicated in B; the summed ionic current they produce has a larger and longer-duration envelope, as shown in C. This envelope constitutes the unitary PSP due to the action of one quantum of transmitter. A number of these unitary PSPs, acting together at the same or neighboring synapses, produce a larger summed synaptic current which depolarizes the membrane to produce the EPSPs, as shown in D. These steps should be compared with the similar steps at the neuromuscular junction (see Fig. 2.16).

The student should note the key properties by which this synaptic potential differs from an action potential. First, the channel is ligand-gated, rather than voltage-gated. Second, the Na and K currents are simultaneous, not sequential as in the case

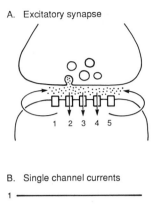

A. Excitatory synapse

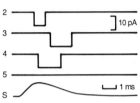

B. Single channel currents

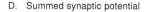

10 pA

1 ms

C. Summed synaptic current

10 nA

D. Summed synaptic potential

0

mV

-70

Fig. 7.4 Steps in generation of an EPSP. **A.** Transmitter, released from presynaptic vesicle, diffuses across cleft and binds to some postsynaptic receptors (2–4). This opens conductance channels, causing inward positive ion flow, and outward flow across neighboring membrane to complete the circuit. **B.** Patch-clamp recordings would reveal openings of channels 2–4, correlated with wave of diffusing transmitter (stimulus, S). **C.** Many active channels give summed current at the synapse (compare with summed voltage-gated currents underlying impulse in Fig. 6.4). **D.** Summed excitatory postsynaptic potential (EPSP) is generated by summed synaptic currents; the time course is slowed by the charging of the membrane capacitance (compare equivalent circuit diagram in Fig. 6.9).

of the impulse. Third, the amplitude of the potential lacks the nonlinear properties of a threshold and the regenerative response that characterize the impulse. For this reason, synaptic potentials are also called *graded potentials*. A comparison of the single-channel conductances at several types of synapses is given in Table 7.1. The different types of neurotransmitters will be discussed in the next chapter.

As mentioned above, depolarizing PSPs are called excitatory because they lead to generation of impulses. What about neurons that do not generate impulses; what should we call a depolarizing PSP in them? Here we are helped by the fact that, as far as is known, transmitter release occurs only by means of membrane depolarization. Thus, a more general definition of an EPSP is that it is excitatory because it leads to impulse generation and/or transmitter release.

Excitatory Reversal (Equilibrium) Potential

The amplitude of the EPSP not only is graded by the number of open channels, but also depends on the relation between the membrane potential and the equilibrium potentials of the ions that flow through the channels. This is such an important concept for understanding the generation of synaptic potentials that we will consider it more closely.

From our previous discussion in Chap. 5, we know that the potential across the membrane depends on the relative permeabilities of the ion channels in the membrane. When a channel is open, the current through it depends on the driving force deriving from the electrochemical gradient for that ion. Let us consider how this driving force would vary for the case of the Na current that flows through a cation channel at a synapse. At the normal resting membrane potential of -80 mV, opening of the channels causes depolarization of the membrane (Fig. 7.5A,a), because Na ions flow through the channels, down their concentration gradient from outside to inside (see

Table 7.1 Single-channel conductances of neurotransmitter-activated channels

Preparation	Agonist	Method	γ (pS)	T (°C)
Cation-permeable excitatory channels				
Amphibian, reptile, bird, and mammalian endplate	ACh	SF	20–40	8–27
Bovine chromaffin cells	ACh	UC	44	21
Aplysia ganglion	ACh	SF	8	27
Locust muscle	Glutamate	UC	130	21
Mammalian neurons	Glutamate (Q, K)	UC	15	21
Mammalian neurons	Glutamate (NMDA)	UC	50	21
Chloride-permeable inhibitory channels				
Lamprey brainstem neurons	Glycine	SF	73	4
Cultured mouse spinal neurons	Glycine	SF	30	26
Cultured mouse spinal neurons	GABA	SF	18	26
Crayfish muscle	GABA	SF	9	23

Abbreviations: NMDA, N-methyl-D-aspartate; SF, stationary fluctuations; UC, unitary currents.

Adapted from Hille (1984) and C. F. Stevens (personal communication)

Fig. 7.5 Principles underlying the generation of an excitatory postsynaptic potential (EPSP) by an increase in membrane conductance to Na. **A.** Intracellular recordings from the postsynaptic neuron, showing the EPSPs at different levels of membrane potential (MP). a. MP at −80 mV and −40 mV. Note large EPSP at −80 mV; note also action potential (AP) arising from the EPSPs. b. MP set at E_{Na}; synaptic change in Na conductance (arrow) gives no change in MP. c. MP set above E_{Na}; synaptic potential reverses polarization toward E_{Na}. d. Similar test when EPSP is due to increase in conductance for both Na and K, so that the excitatory reversal potential (E_e) is near zero. **B.** Diagrammatic representation of Na conductance channel and ion flows underlying recordings, in a–c. **C.** Equivalent circuit representation of ion flows in a–c.

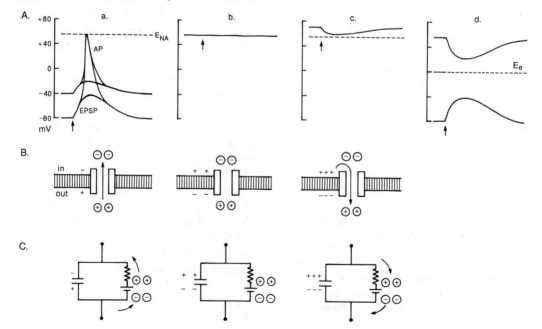

B below a). If the membrane potential is initially at a lower value, say -40 mV (see A,a), the EPSP is still present, but it has a smaller amplitude. This is because there are relatively more positive charges on the inside of the membrane, and these oppose the effect of the Na concentration gradient. This is seen most clearly if the membrane is experimentally held at a value of $+55$ mV inside by injection of positive current (see A,b); now, as shown in (B,b), the potential gradient across the membrane exactly balances out the driving force due to the Na^+ concentration gradient; no Na^+ current flows, and there is no EPSP (even though the Na^+ channels are wide open!). This would be the *equilibrium potential* for Na current (E_{Na}). It is also called the *reversal potential*, because if the membrane is made more positive inside by injecting more current, opening the Na^+ channels produces a polarizing response (Fig. 7.5A,c). This is due to the excess of inside positive charge, which flows outward through the Na^+ channel to attempt to restore equilibrium (B,c).

The reverse potential is very useful to neurophysiologists, because by obtaining this information they gain insight into the types of channels involved in a synapse or in the impulse, as we saw in Chap. 6. At the neuromuscular junction, and at most other excitatory synapses, the reversal potential is near zero; in other words, it is as if a short-circuit has been placed across the membrane. Some other ion flow must be involved to keep the membrane from going all the way to E_{Na} of $+55$ mV. This ion is usually K^+. Thus, the EPSP is due to channels that allow the simultaneous flows of Na^+ inward and K^+ outward, in roughly equal proportions, so that the combined E_{EPSP} lies between E_{Na} and E_K, or approximately zero (see A,d).

Inhibitory Postsynaptic Potentials

Many inhibitory synapses generate their IPSPs by a mechanism that is similar in principle to that of the EPSP just described, but which achieves the inhibitory effect by means of ion currents with different equilibrium potentials.

As summarized in Fig. 7.6, the inhibitory transmitter (for example, GABA or glycine) binds to postsynaptic receptors (A). At the usual resting membrane potential, the flow of positive current through the inhibitory channels is outward (in the opposite direction to the inward flow of EPSPs). These single channel currents are indicated in B, and the summed current is shown in C. As in the case of EPSPs, inhibitory transmitters appear to be released in quanta. Summation of quanta, at the same or at neighboring synapses, produces graded IPSPs, as shown in D.

Let us now set up an experiment to determine the conductance involved in the IPSP, building on the principles described above. First, we record the IPSP at different levels of membrane depolarization and note, as in Fig. 7.7A,a, that near rest the IPSP is hyperpolarizing (opposite to the EPSP at these levels: see Fig. 7.5 above), and that its amplitude is smaller with more polarized membrane levels. At -90 mV, the inhibitory response generates no potential (b), and at even more polarized levels, the IPSP becomes depolarizing (c). The reversal potential in (b) is close to the equilibrium potential for K^+ (E_K), and we conclude that the conductance channel that mediates the IPSP is K^+ selective. Some IPSPs are mediated by Cl^- channels. The same principles outlined in Fig. 7.7 apply, except that the negatively charged Cl ions, rather than positively charged K ions, carry the current. In these cases, the reversal potential would be intermediate between E_{Cl} and resting E_K.

The relationship between the membrane potential and the driving force for K^+ governs the strength of the current flow through the channel and its direction, just as in the case of Na^+ for the EPSP. You should work through the diagrams in Fig. 7.7B,C to be sure you understand this relationship. Although the resting membrane potential seldom gets down in the range of E_{Na}, it is normally close to E_K. This means that the inhibitory response may generate a hyper-

A. Inhibitory synapse

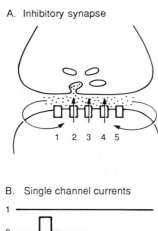

B. Single channel currents

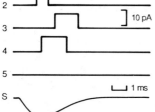

C. Summed synaptic current

D. Summed synaptic potential

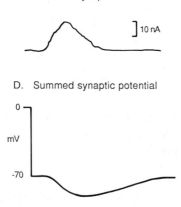

Fig. 7.6 Steps in generation of an inhibitory postsynaptic potential (IPSP). **A.** Transmitter, released from presynaptic vesicle, diffuses across cleft and binds to some postsynaptic receptors (2–4). This opens conductance channels, causing outward positive ion flow, and inward flow across neighboring membrane to complete the circuit. **B.** Patch-clamp recordings would reveal openings of channels 2–4, correlated with wave of diffusing transmitter (stimulus, S). **C.** Many active channels give summed current at the synapse. **D.** Summed inhibitory postsynaptic potential (IPSP) is generated by summed synaptic currents.

polarizing or a depolarizing response, or no detectable potential at all, depending on where the resting membrane potential is in relation to E_K. This has important consequences for understanding the nature of synaptic integration, as we shall see below.

It should be noted that the equilibrium potential for Cl^- (E_{Cl-}) is near E_K, and our experiment would need to include a means for discriminating between conductances for these two ions. This could be done by carrying out the experiments in excised tissue maintained in a recording chamber, so that drugs that block K or Cl conductance could be introduced in the bathing medium, or the Cl^- in the bath could be removed. This is one of the advantages of using slice preparations (see below).

Synaptic Integration

It is largely through the interaction between excitatory and inhibitory synapses that the competition for control of the membrane potential in different parts of the neuron is carried out. This competition lies at the heart of the study of the dynamics of synaptic organization. The principle goes back to Sherrington; following him, the process by which different synaptic inputs are combined within the neuron is termed *synaptic integration.*

The interaction of a single EPSP and IPSP serves as a paradigm for synaptic integration in neurons, and it will be useful to grasp certain essentials. Let us assume an excitatory synapse and a nearby inhibitory synapse, the activation of which individually produce an EPSP and IPSP, respectively, as shown in Fig. 7.8A. Assume now that the two are activated simultaneously. The effect of the IPSP is to reduce the amplitude of the EPSP, away from the threshold for impulse initiation, as is shown in Fig. 7.8A. The dotted line traces the resulting transient; it represents the "integrated" result of the two synaptic potentials.

Now it is commonly thought that this

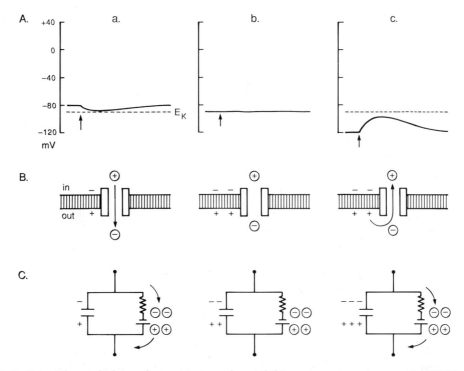

Fig. 7.7 Principles underlying the generation of an inhibitory postsynaptic potential (IPSP) by an increase in membrane conductance to K. **A.** Intracellular recordings from the postsynaptic neuron, showing the IPSPs at different levels of membrane potential (MP). a. MP at -80 mV (near rest); note that IPSP is hyperpolarizing, toward $E_K = -90$ mV. b. MP at level of E_K; synaptic change in K conductance (arrow) gives no change in MP. c. MP is below E_K; synaptic potential reverses toward E_K. **B.** Diagrammatic representation of K conductance channel and ion flows underlying recordings, in a–c. **C.** Equivalent circuit representation of ion flows, in a–c. Similar principles underlie IPSP due to increase in Cl conductance, but with electric charge carried by Cl$^-$.

Fig. 7.8 Integration of EPSP and IPSP at different resting membrane potentials. **A.** When the resting MP is below (less negative than) the inhibitory equilibrium potential (E_i), the conductance increase during the IPSP causes a hyperpolarization of the membrane. **B.** When the resting MP is equal to E_i, the inhibitory conductance increase causes no change in potential. **C.** When the resting MP is above (more negative than) E_i, the IPSP causes a depolarization of the membrane. In all cases, integrative summation of the EPSP and IPSP causes a decrease in amplitude of the EPSP (dashed line), making the neuron less excitable.

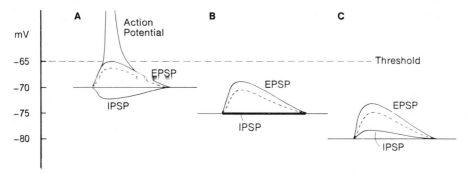

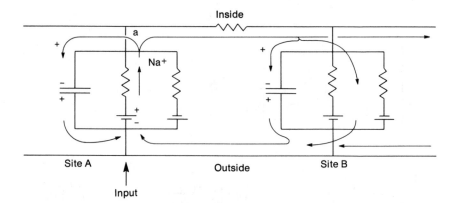

Fig. 7.9 Current flows underlying the depolarization of membrane patches. Initial input (as from an EPSP, applied current, or local potential) at site A causes inward current flow of positively charged Na ions. At (a), current can flow in two directions: outward, to depolarize membrane capacitance, or longitudinally and then outward to depolarize capacitance of neighboring membrane patch (site B). Thus membrane depolarization is brought about by both inward ionic current and outward capacitative current. Note that external current flow completes the circuit.

process of integration is a matter of simple algebraic addition of the two opposed synaptic potentials; to wit, "depolarization plus hyperpolarization equals membrane potential." However, this simple formula does not have general validity. As shown in Fig. 7.8B, when the resting potential is at the inhibitory equilibrium (reversal) potential, no IPSP is recorded, but there is still a reduction of a simultaneous EPSP, due to the shunting effect of the increased inhibitory conductance. And when the resting membrane is more polarized (Fig. 7.8C), the IPSP is in fact depolarizing (toward the inhibitory equilibrium potential), yet its effect is still to reduce the EPSP by virtue of the increased conductance. The essential inhibitory action is therefore not a hyperpolarization of the membrane, but rather an increase in ionic conductance that drives the membrane potential toward the equilibrium potential for those ions.

It is thus the opposition of synaptically activated conductances and ionic currents that controls the relative amounts of depolarization and hyperpolarization of the membrane potential. In addition, one must consider the geometrical relations between excitatory and inhibitory synaptic sites in a dendritic tree, and the electrotonic flow of current through the dendrites. Synaptic integration thus involves a complex interplay between ionic conductances and neuronal geometry (see below).

Ionic Currents

It will be useful at this point to consider more closely the relation between an ionic conductance change and the resultant change in membrane potential. For an example we take the case of a brief increase in conductance to Na ions. As shown in Fig. 7.9, Na^+ moves inward through its conductance channel at the active site (A). In the electrical circuit, the current reaches a point on the inside where it can travel in two directions. Some current passes onto the inner surface of the membrane capacitance, where it deposits positive charge that depolarizes the membrane. Some passes along the inside of the nerve cell to the next patch of membrane (site B), where it can follow three paths: onto the membrane capacitance, through the membrane resistance, or further along the fiber. Ultimately all the current must pass out across the membrane and pass back along the outside of the cell to the negative pole of the Na battery.

Careful study of the diagram and current flows will help answer two questions that are often puzzling to the student. The first is, how can inward and outward current both depolarize the membrane? As can be seen, the reason is that inward current at an active site and outward current at a neighboring site both have the same effect, of putting positive charge on the inside of the membrane capacitance. The same reasoning applies to the relation between oppositely directed current flows and hyperpolarization.

The second question is, what are the time relations between the current flows and the potential changes? When the flow is rapid the potential response is slower, because charge is transiently stored on the membrane capacitance. The amount of slowing depends on the time constant (τ_m) of the membrane, given by the product of the membrane capacitance (C_m) and membrane resistance (R_m): $\tau = RC$. The relation between the rapid synaptic current flows and the slower synaptic potentials was shown in Figs. 7.4 and 7.6. For very slow or constant changes in conductance, a steady state exists in which the capacitance becomes an open circuit and can be ignored, and the spread of current to the neighboring site is determined solely by the resistance along the paths.

These relations between current and potential underlie most of the electrophysiological properties of nerve cells. For instance, the diagram of Fig. 7.9 applies equally to the case of activation of an action potential and its propagation by local currents, as we discussed in Chap. 6. The slowing of potential responses and the decay of potential spread are both governed by electrotonic properties. The diagram also emphasizes that at any site on a nerve cell there can be two pathways for interactions: internally with other parts of the same cell, by means of electrotonic spread or impulse generation, or externally through synapses onto neighboring cells.

Conductance-Decrease Synapses

Thus far we have considered synaptic responses as being due to the opening of conductance channels. By contrast, there are responses that are produced by the closing of conductance channels. These are called conductance-decrease synapses. They were first described by Forrest Weight and his colleagues in sympathetic ganglion cells, and have been analyzed extensively in recent years by Paul Adams and his colleagues.

An excitatory response can be generated at a conductance-decrease synapse in the following manner. At rest, the membrane is somewhat depolarized (say, at -60 mV), representing a balance between a resting K conductance (g_K) and a significant amount of Na conductance (g_{Na}). When the synapse is activated (stimulated), the effect of the released transmitter is to turn off the resting g_K. The membrane moves toward the equilibrium potential of the remaining ion (Na^+) to which it is permeable, thus producing a depolarizing response.

This type of synaptic response has been demonstrated in sympathetic ganglion cells, in the slow EPSP and late, slow EPSP (we will discuss these in Chap. 18). The K current which is turned off is in fact the M current (I_m), previously discussed in Chap. 6. The mechanism is explained in Fig. 7.10 and legend.

You probably realize by now that the opposite effect could be produced by turning off a Na current, and you are right; Nature has not missed this opportunity. If both Na and K currents are present at rest, the membrane will be partially depolarized. The effect of turning off I_{Na} is thus to hyperpolarize the membrane toward E_K. This type of mechanism has been seen most clearly in the response of vertebrate photoreceptors to light; we will study this further below and in Chaps. 10 and 16.

Conductance-decrease synapses have several properties that are of interest. The decreased conductance raises the resistance of the membrane, thereby increasing the amplitude of any other synaptic responses nearby. However, this also increases the time constant of the membrane, and therefore slows any nearby responses. Conductance-decrease synapses thus help to increase the strength of neighboring re-

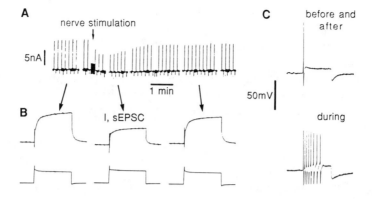

Fig. 7.10 Properties of the M current in bullfrog sympathetic neurons. **A.** Inhibition of the M current. Electrical stimulation of presynaptic fibers (22 Hz for 10 seconds) caused a late slow EPSP, associated with a depression followed by recovery of the M current, as shown by the height of the testing pulses. **B.** Fast sweeps show the time course of individual responses to test pulses before, during, and after stimulation. Cell was voltage-clamped; command pulses were from −70 mV to −30 mV. Note the relatively large M current elicited in the resting cell by a depolarizing pulse, and suppression of $I_{(sEPSP)}$ during the late slow EPSP. A similar result was obtained when LHRH was ejected onto the cell. **C.** Effect of the slow EPSP on excitability of the ganglion cell. The excitability was tested with a pulse of depolarizing injected current. At rest, this elicited a single impulse; during slow EPSP, it elicited a burst of impulses, due to the higher input resistance (when the M current is turned off), and the subsequently larger depolarization elicited by the current injection. (From Jones and Adams, 1987)

sponses, and, by slowing them, increase their chances of summation (see Fig. 7.10C). They thus can contribute significantly to enhancing the integrative properties of neurons.

Integrative Organization of the Nerve Cell

We are now in a position to ask: how do the graded potentials set up at the junctions of a cell carry information through the cell and produce a transfer of information to other cells? This function can be best understood by using as a model a well-studied nerve cell, the stretch receptor of the crayfish. This preparation was introduced to intracellular electrophysiology by Stephen Kuffler and Carlos Eyzaguirre in a classic series of experiments in the 1950s. We will use this model to bring together the different properties we have considered thus far.

A schematic diagram of the stretch receptor cell is shown in Fig. 7.11A. The cell

has several large dendritic trunks, which enter the muscle and terminate in fine branches. When stretch is applied to the muscle (Fig. 7.11B), a depolarization is set up in the dendritic branches, graded with the amount of stretch. This depolarization is due to an increase in permeability of the membrane to Na ions, and probably also other ions, which moves the membrane potential toward an equilibrium potential around zero. This *receptor potential* is thus similar to an EPSP. We will discuss mechanisms of transduction of the stimulus and other sensory properties in later chapters (Chaps. 10 and 13).

An intracellular electrode inserted into the cell body records the receptor potential together with the discharge of impulses that arise from it (Fig. 7.11B). In this situation, as in all recording experiments, the electrode is in one particular spot in the nerve cell, and we must deduce the sites where the different types of activity are actually initiated. With regard to the receptor po-

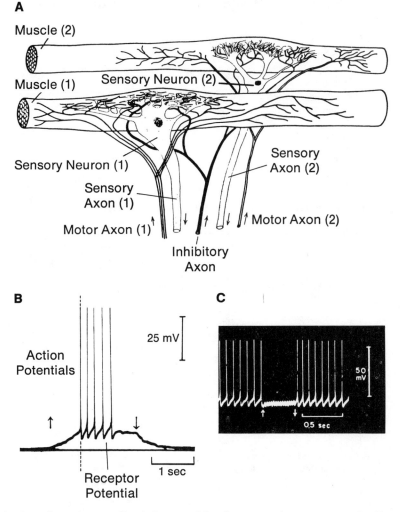

Fig. 7.11 A. Stretch receptor cell of the crayfish, showing relation to muscle fibers, inhibitory axon, and motor axons to muscles. **B.** Excitatory response of receptor cell to stretch of the muscle (arrows), as recorded by intracellular electrode inserted into cell body of sensory neuron (2). Dotted line indicates point in time for display of potentials in Fig. 7.12. **C.** Inhibition of the excitatory response by stimulation of the inhibitory axon (between arrows). (A from Burkhardt, B from Eyzaguirre and Kuffler, in Aidley, 1978; C from Kuffler and Eyzaguirre, 1955)

tential, the site of generation is in the dendritic terminals, which are 100–300 μm away from the cell body. We therefore know that our recording must represent an attenuated version of the true receptor potential, because of the leakage of current across the membrane of the dendritic trunk as the current flows toward the cell body and out into the axon, according to the cable properties of the dendrites. But what about the impulses? Where do they arise—in the dendrites, in the cell body, or in the axon? An elegant experiment by Charles Edwards and David Ottoson, working in Kuffler's laboratory in 1957, showed that, contrary to expectation, the site of impulse generation is in the axon, at a considerable distance from the cell body. To complete

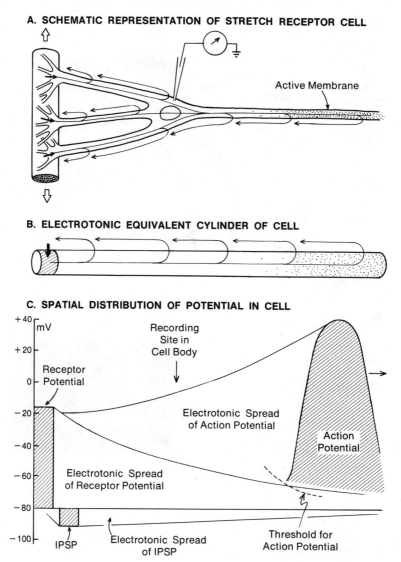

A. SCHEMATIC REPRESENTATION OF STRETCH RECEPTOR CELL

Active Membrane

B. ELECTROTONIC EQUIVALENT CYLINDER OF CELL

C. SPATIAL DISTRIBUTION OF POTENTIAL IN CELL

Recording
Site in
Cell Body

Receptor
Potential

Electrotonic Spread
of Action Potential

Action
Potential

Electrotonic Spread
of Receptor Potential

IPSP   Electrotonic Spread
of IPSP

Threshold for
Action Potential

Fig. 7.12 Diagrams illustrating the analysis of spread of electrical activity in the stretch receptor cell. See text.

the picture, there are inhibitory nerves which make synapses on the dendrites of these cells. Stimulation of these fibers produces IPSPs, as indicated in Fig. 7.11C. How do these responses interact with the other activity in the cell?

In order to appreciate these relationships we need to think about the nerve cell in its spatial dimension. We need to take a point in time during an impulse response (see dotted line in Fig. 7.11B), and ask: what is the distribution of potentials throughout

the cell at this point in time? We can answer this question in an intuitive way with the help of the diagram in Fig. 7.12. We will follow the methods of Wilfrid Rall, of the National Institutes of Health, who has developed most of the methods now used for describing the flow of electrical activity in dendritic systems.

Beginning with the dimensions of the cell in Fig. 7.12A, we construct a model of the cell in which its electrical cable properties are incorporated in a simple equivalent cylinder (B). In C, we plot the distribution of the different types of potentials in this equivalent cylinder. To begin with, the *receptor potential,* as we have already mentioned, is generated in the fine terminals, and spreads electrotonically through the cell, as indicated in the figure. The action potential, in contrast, is generated in the axon; it propagates in the axon toward the central nervous system and also spreads electrotonically back into the cell body and dendrites. The IPSP is generated in the distal dendrites, and spreads, also by electrotonic means, as indicated in the diagram.

The normal sequence of events is thus: stimulus→setting up of receptor potential in terminals→electrotonic spread through dendrites and cell body to axon→generation of action potential in axon when depolarization reaches threshold→propagation of action potential forward (orthodromically), and electrotonic spread backward (antidromically) into cell body and dendrites. The IPSP, acting during a response to stretch, opposes the response by making the membrane tend toward the relatively hyperpolarized inhibitory equilibrium potential.

Several questions often arise at this point in students' minds; let's see if we can anticipate and answer them.

Question 1: "It seems to me a funny way to organize a cell; how can the potentials spread so far?" *Answer:* As we noted in Chap. 6, electrotonic spread depends on just three factors: the resistance of the cytoplasm, the resistance of the cell membrane, and the diameter of the dendrite or axon. The two main ways that neurons control the effectiveness of spread is by means of the membrane resistance and the diameter. *The greater the membrane resistance,* the less current leaks out across the membrane, and the more effective is the spread of a receptor potential and synaptic potential (and also, as we saw earlier, the local currents spreading in front of an action potential). *The greater the diameter,* the easier it is for the current to spread through the interior (cytoplasm) of the cell.

Thus, stretch receptor neurons have a relatively *high* membrane resistance, and are sufficiently *large,* to provide for effective electrotonic spread of potentials within them.

Different neurons vary greatly in this respect. In many cases, there is effective spread throughout much of a dendritic tree, and this provides the basis for the integration of many synaptic inputs. In other cases, there is limitation of spread; one sees this, for example, in the thin necks of some spines that arise from dendrites, and in very thin processes that connect parts of cells. In these cases, it appears that there is an isolation of the activity at a given site from the ongoing activity in the rest of the cell, so that different parts of the cell can operate as independent or semi-independent functional units.

Question 2: "Is the electrotonic potential active or passive?" *Answer:* Recall that the electrotonic potential is a *passive* potential. It is the spread that occurs along a process when all of the electrical properties of that process remain constant, at their resting values. Strictly speaking, "active" is used only in reference to the regenerative property of the action potential. Any time there is a change in the membrane potential at some site (due to a receptor potential, synaptic potential, or action potential), current always flows electrotonically through neighboring regions to equalize the distribution of charge. Part of the strategy of the functional organization of a neuron is to restrict synaptic sites and action potential sites to different parts of the neuron, and link them all together with passive electrotonic spread.

Question 3: "I don't understand; is the electrode at the cell body recording directly the receptor potential and the action potential, or isn't it?" *Answer:* Strictly speaking, the electrode is recording the *electrotonically spread* receptor potential and action potential. If we wanted to record the receptor potential directly, we would have to put the electrode tip into the terminals. We would then record a very big depolarization, as indicated in the diagram. Similarly, the action potentials recorded in the cell body are attenuated versions of the action potentials in the axon, as shown by the lower amplitudes in the recordings of Fig. 7.11. This serves as a reminder of the fact that every recording gives a selective view of what is going on in a neuron, being weighted for events happening near at hand.

Question 4: "I thought there was a general rule in the nervous system that inhibition occurs at the cell body. Why does it occur in the dendrites in this cell?" *Answer:* The rule is one of the many that has had to be modified. It is true that many neurons receive inhibitory inputs to their cell bodies, and even initial segments. It is presumed that this provides for very effective control of impulse initiation at these sites. However, the stretch receptor cell shows that another effective placement is near the site of excitatory input. At this site, there is maximum opportunity for shunting of excitatory currents by the increased conductances of the inhibitory channels, thus depressing the receptor potential. Thus, the IPSP at this site tends to gate the receptor potential near its site of origin, rather than gating the impulse near *its* site of origin. The nervous system provides variations on these two themes in different regions, presumably reflecting needs for the interaction of excitation and inhibition in the processing of different kinds of information.

These questions and answers show how a model cell like the stretch receptor can illustrate basic properties that are involved in integrative actions of nerve cells. Many other cells demonstrate further these properties. For example, the motoneuron of the mammalian spinal cord shares many properties with the stretch receptor cells, such as the site of impulse initiation in the initial segment, but differs in others, such as the placement of inhibition (see Fig. 7.13A). In comparison, an insect motoneuron has quite a different morphology (Fig. 7.13B). The cell body is to one side, so to speak, and

has no significance for transmission of signals. Synaptic responses in the dendrites are integrated in the axon trunk; impulses generated in the spike-initiating zone are conducted into the axon and to the muscles. The synaptic potentials in the dendrites are believed also to activate synaptic outputs from the dendrites to neighboring processes. The diagram indicates the considerable amount of dendrodendritic processing through synaptic potentials (see next section) that is believed to take place in the neuropil, and the differentiation of the membrane of a single neuron into differing synaptic, inexcitable and excitable regions.

Nonimpulse Neurons

The stretch receptor and the vertebrate motoneuron are models for nerve cells that have axons, generate impulses, and have dendrites that are postsynaptic only. In the classical view, all neurons are of this type. However, beginning with studies of the vertebrate retina and olfactory bulb in 1966, a number of neurons have been found that do not fit this simple model.

Among the best-studied examples are the cells of the vertebrate retina (Fig. 7.14A). The photoreceptors respond to light with a slow potential. The effect of light is to turn off a resting Na^+ conductance, thereby allowing the membrane potential to move toward the more polarized K^+ equilibrium potential; we have already discussed this conductance-decrease mechanism above. Normally, the photoreceptor response consists solely of this slow hyperpolarizing potential (see Fig. 7.14B). This slow potential by itself brings about transmission of the light response, presumably by interrupting transmitter release from the photoreceptor terminals onto other retinal neurons. Because of the very short lengths of the photoreceptors, electrotonic spread through the cell is effective, in the absence of impulses. The cells to which the photoreceptors transmit, the bipolar cells and horizontal cells, also operate exclusively by graded

A. VERTEBRATE MOTONEURON

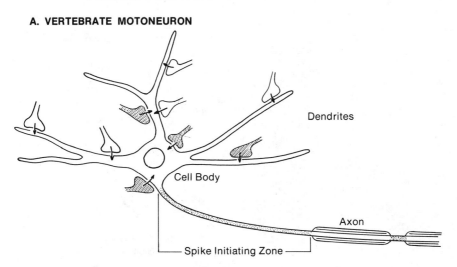

B. INVERTEBRATE MOTONEURON

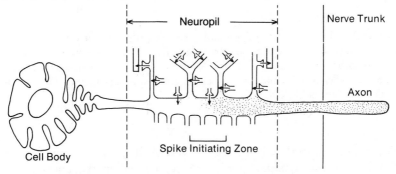

Fig. 7.13 A. Diagram of motoneuron in spinal cord of the cat, showing relation of excitatory (open profiles) and inhibitory (shaded profiles) synapses to each other and to the site of impulse output. **B.** Diagram of a motoneuron to a leg extensor muscle in the metathoracic ganglion of a locust. (From Gwilliam and Burrows, 1980)

potentials. The roles of these cells in visual processing will be discussed in Chap. 16.

An interesting aspect is that although the photoreceptors do not usually generate impulses, their membrane nonetheless has excitable properties; in other words, it contains voltage-sensitive channels. This has been shown in experiments in which the retina is treated with tetraethylammonium, which blocks K^+ currents (see Table 6.1). Under these conditions, the photoreceptors show spiking activity (see Fig. 7.14C). The spikes are blocked by treatment with cobalt

(D), indicating that they are due to a Ca^{2+} current. The interpretation is that normally the inward Ca^{2+} current is balanced or swamped by outward K^+ current, so that the excitability of the membrane is not expressed. This gives support to the idea that excitability is a widespread property of biological membranes, which is expressed only under specific conditions, as discussed in Chap. 6.

A second example that has contributed to a revision of our concepts of neuronal function is the vertebrate olfactory bulb.

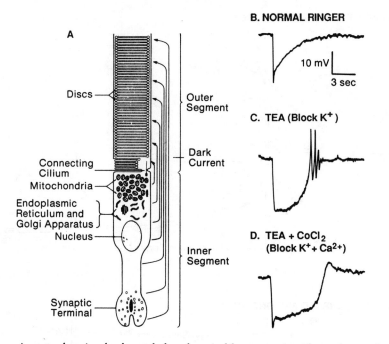

Fig. 7.14 Experiments showing both graded and excitable properties of vertebrate photoreceptors. **A.** Diagram of a rod receptor of the toad. **B.** Responses when retina was in normal Ringer solution. **C.** TEA was added to bathing medium to block K^+ conductance, revealing regenerative spikes. **D.** $CoCl_2$ was added to block Ca^{2+} conductance, eliminating spikes. (A from Fain, in Roberts and Bush, 1981; B–D from Fain et al., 1980)

Here, the relay neuron (mitral cell) makes reciprocal dendrodendritic synapses with the interneurons (granule cells) (Fig. 7.15; see also Chap. 4). This synaptic arrangement has implied that input and output through the granule cells can be mediated solely by the synaptic potentials in the granule cell dendrites, without need of transmission by an impulse. Electrophysiological recordings together with computer models have suggested that the spines act as semi-independent input–output units. The fact that mitral cells take part in these interactions shows that relay neurons that have long axons and generate impulses can also have local synaptic outputs through their dendrites. Thus, the presynaptic dendrites give the mitral cell added capabilities for local processing (see Chaps. 4 and 11).

Among invertebrates, many cells have been identified that show properties similar to those in the retina and olfactory bulb.

One of the earliest examples was a stretch receptor cell in the crab, which responds to stretch stimulation with only graded potentials. This is discussed further in Chap. 13. Other examples include several types of interneuron in the central ganglia of insects, which control motoneurons involved in producing coordinated movements of the legs (see Fig. 7.13B above, and Chap. 20). An example of this type of nonspiking interneuron is shown in Fig. 7.16. The neuron in A was filled with cobalt, and the $CoCl_2$ precipitate was intensified with silver. Note the cell body on the lower left, the lack of an axon, the extension of the dendritic tree throughout much of the neuropil, and the profuse branching of the dendrites. Nerve cells show their true beauty when stained like this, and we can sense some of the same feelings that Cajal had when he first beheld these sights under the microscope almost a century ago. The

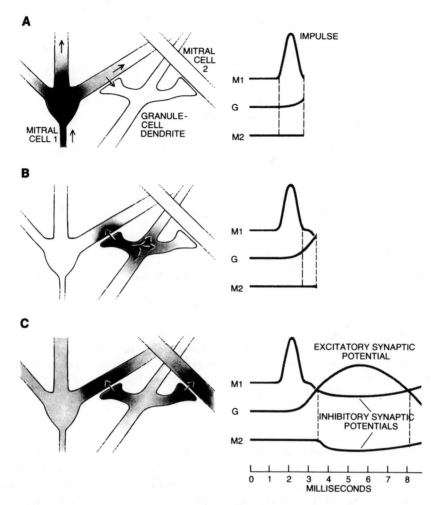

Fig. 7.15 Diagram illustrating local interactions between mitral and granule cells in the vertebrate olfactory bulb, by means of synapses between their dendrites. Sequence begins (A) with impulse in mitral cell (1); in (B) an EPSP has been initiated in the granule cell spine; in (C) the spine feeds back an IPSP onto mitral cell (1), and sends inhibition laterally onto mitral cell (2). All interactions are by dendrodendritic synapses. (From Shepherd, 1978, based on Rall and Shepherd, 1968)

dendrites are sites of both input and output synaptic connections with the dendrites of other intraneurons and motoneurons. Some interactions mediated through these synapses are shown in B. Depolarization of an interneuron by prolonged current injection (top trace) gives rise to a graded synaptic excitation of an extensor motoneuron to the leg (bottom trace) and inhibition of a flexor motoneuron (middle trace). The effect of this interneuron is to cause the leg to extend (f), through the connections indicated in (g). Malcolm Burrows and his colleagues at Cambridge have shown that there is an extensive network of interneurons, some nonspiking and some spiking, which control the leg motoneurons.

Isolated Preparations for Studying Synaptic Circuits

How do neurobiologists analyze the actions of synapses that are embedded in complicated local circuits? In the case of

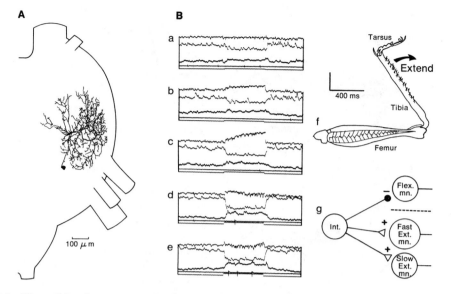

Fig. 7.16 Nonspiking interneurons in the metathoracic ganglion of the locust. **A.** Example of an interneuron filled with cobalt. (From Siegler and Burrows, 1979) **B.** Simultaneous recordings from another type of interneuron (upper trace) and two leg motoneurons: a flexor (middle trace) and an extensor (bottom trace). Current injection in interneuron (increasing intensity from a to e) causes graded depolarization in interneuron, which in turn synaptically hyperpolarizes flexor motoneuron and depolarizes extensor motoneuron. Resulting movement of leg shown in (f). Synaptic connections shown in (g). (From Burrows, 1978)

invertebrate ganglia, one can excise the intact ganglion, maintain it in a recording chamber, stimulate selected input and output pathways, and record the synaptic responses using intracellular electrodes. This ease of preparation, together with the large sizes of many of the cells, is why invertebrate ganglia are so attractive to electrophysiologists.

Studies in the mammalian brain were traditionally carried out in the intact anesthetized animal, with all its attendant problems of maintaining the proper levels of anesthesia, allowing for the depressant effects of the anesthetic agents, and controlling the respiratory and vascular pulsations that dislodge the electrode from its intracellular position. A big step forward was the discovery by Chosaburo Yamamoto and Henry McIlwain in London in 1966 that slices of the mammalian brain can be prepared and maintained in a recording chamber. Since that time, many

parts of the brain have been studied *in vitro,* including even slices of human cortex obtained in neurosurgical operations. Other preparations include the mammalian brainstem perfused through its blood vessels, and the entire brain of the turtle, from medulla to olfactory nerves, simply bathed in Ringer's solution.

These in vitro preparations allow investigation of individual synapses and synaptic circuits under conditions in which the region is completely stable, and pharmacological manipulations can be carried out with different drugs in the bathing medium. One of the first and best known preparations is the hippocampal slice, which we will describe briefly.

A summary diagram of the synaptic organization of the hippocampus is shown in Fig. 7.17. As can be seen, the cell layers form two C-shaped sheets, facing and overlapping each other. One of these sheets is the hippocampus proper, containing large

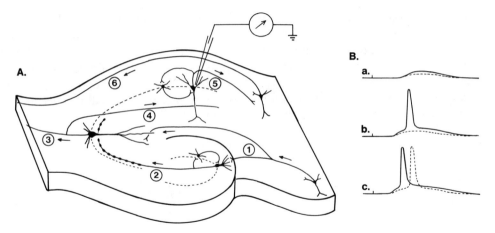

Fig. 7.17 **A.** Synaptic organization of hippocampus. The circuits are shown as they would be present in a slice of the hippocampus prepared for recording in an isolation chamber. Different parts of the circuits ①–⑥ are described in the text. **B.** Intracellular recordings from pyramidal cell showing plasticity of synaptic actions. a. Response to weak volleys in radiation fibers ④ before (dotted trace) and after (solid trace) tetanization of radiation fibers to produce long-term potentiation (LTP). b and c. Same, stronger volleys. (After Andersen et al., 1977)

pyramidal neurons, which are the main output cells. The other sheet is the dentate fascia, whose output neurons are called granule cells. By virtue of the main fiber pathways, there is a natural sequence of activity in these regions. The sequence actually begins in the entorhinal cortex, a region which receives and integrates multisensory inputs from the touch, auditory, olfactory, and visual pathways, as well as inputs from the cingulate gyrus as a part of limbic systems (see Chap. 28). The entorhinal cortical output fibers ① traverse ("perforate") the surrounding cortex and terminate mainly in the dentate fascia. The dentate granule cells have relatively short axons ("mossy fibers") which connect to the nearest part of the hippocampal pyramidal cell population ②. The axons of these pyramidal cells ③ project to the septum through the fornix; in addition, they send a collateral branch ④ to connect to the long apical dendrites of pyramidal cells in another part of the hippocampus. These cells project to a nearby cortical area, the subiculum ⑤, which in turn projects to the septum through the fornix ⑥.

The hippocampus is well suited for pre-paring in a slice, because it is constructed as a series of lamellae, each of which contains the whole circuit indicated in Fig. 7.17. In the chamber under the microscope, stimulating electrodes can be placed on each of the layers or pathways and recordings made from each of the types of cell with intracellular microelectrodes. These studies have provided direct confirmation of previous results in the intact animal, and have enabled more precise analyses to be carried out on neuronal properties and synaptic actions. For example, they have shown that the cell bodies of the pyramidal cells generate Na^+ action potentials, whereas their dendrites generate a combination of slow Ca^{2+} and fast Na^+ action potentials. All of the connections shown in Fig. 7.17 are excitatory; the input from the septum is also excitatory. In contrast, the interneurons in the hippocampus and dentate are inhibitory.

The hippocampus has a tendency to generate prolonged, uncontrolled discharges which are the cause of some kinds of epileptic seizures in humans. Analyses of the hippocampal slice are providing evidence for the mechanisms controlling the delicate balance between excitatory and inhibitory synaptic actions, that spell the difference between normal and abnormal function. Glutamate is believed to be the transmitter substance at the perforant pathway synapses, and GABA at the inhibitory interneuronal synapses; the balance between these two is obviously critical for normal function. We will discuss these and other transmitters in the next chapter. The synapses have plastic properties (see Fig. 7.17), which are believed to be involved in memory mechanisms, as will be discussed in Chap. 29.

8

Neurotransmitters and Neuromodulators

Biochemistry of the Synapse: A Brief History

In contrast to studies of electrical activity in the nervous system, studies of biochemistry had a slower beginning. The apparatus was primitive, and, throughout most of the nineteenth century, studies were limited to characterizing the presence of fats, proteins, and carbohydrates in ground-up samples of the brain.

A decisive step forward was taken around 1900 by a school of English physiologists under John Langley studying the autonomic nerves to the internal organs of the body. They found that electrical stimulation of these nerves produced characteristic bodily changes (increase in heart rate, increased blood pressure), and that these changes were mimicked by the injection of extracts of the adrenal gland. According to Masanori Otsuka and Zach Hall (1979):

> The idea that chemicals might mediate transmission between excitable cells is thought to have originated in 1903 during a conversation between two young scientists: Otto Loewi, a 29-year-old Austrian pharmacologist, and Thomas R. Elliot, a 25-year-old British medical student and physiologist.

In a preliminary communication to the Physiological Society in 1904, Elliott, a student under Langley, postulated that impulses in the autonomic nerves cause the release of an epinephrine-like substance from the nerve terminals onto the effector cells in the adrenal gland. In the same year, Langley further postulated that the cells in the gland have excitatory and inhibitory "receptive substances" which determine what the response and action will be. These were indeed far-reaching suggestions, for in their postulates of a *chemical link* between cells, its dependence on the amount of *electrical impulse activity,* and the presence of specific *molecular receptors,* they presaged many of the essential properties of synaptic transmission.

The culmination of this line of work was the demonstration in 1921 by Loewi that the vagus nerve inhibits the heart by liberating the substance acetylcholine. The work of Henry Dale and his collaborators in England in the 1930s provided evidence for acetylcholine as the transmitter substance in autonomic ganglia as well as at the junctions of nerves onto skeletal muscles.

As biochemists tackled the molecular mechanisms of the nervous system in the 1950s, they faced two main problems. One was that methods were lacking for getting at the molecular structure of accessible synapses such as the neuromuscular junction; this awaited the arrival of recombinant DNA technology, as we saw in Chap. 2. The other problem was how to study inaccessible synapses tucked away within the central nervous system. The main traditional method was to homogenize the brain and analyze the biochemical constituents of different fractions. Most of these whole-brain studies made little connection with the cellular anatomy and physiology of the time. It was not until the development of a method for visualization of biogenic amines by their fluorescence around 1960 that one had a tool for identifying neurotransmitter substances in individual neurons and neuron terminals. On the receptor side, it was realized by the 1970s that the response to a transmitter is not necessarily limited to an immediate change in membrane conductance, but can involve activation of second messenger systems with many effects within the neuron. A third main development, beginning in the 1970s, has been the identification of a wide variety of small peptides, which can have trophic actions on neuronal growth, modulate synaptic transmission or second messenger systems, or have other effects within the neuron.

The result of this work is that one can regard the neuromuscular junction and the central synapses with rapid excitatory and inhibitory actions as the simplest types of synapses. With these models in mind, we can turn to more complex types that include one or more of the following features: different first messengers (neurotransmitters and neuropeptides), acting at different receptors, activating different second messenger systems. These more complex and longer-lasting mechanisms are grouped under the term, *neuromodulation*. We will first consider the main types of second messenger systems, and then summarize the main types of synapses.

Second Messenger Systems

Second messengers are defined as molecules that serve as functional links between receptors of external (first) messengers, and effector mechanisms in the receptive cell

Table 8.1 Second messenger systems in neurons

Free calcium ions (Ca^{2+})
G-binding proteins
Phosphoinositide hydrolysis (IP_3, DAG)
Protein phosphorylation
Protein carboxymethylation
Phospholipid methylation
Arachidonic acid metabolites (prostaglandins, leukotrienes, thromboxanes)

Abbreviations: DAG, diacylglycerol; IP_3, inositol triphosphate.

Adapted from Cooper et al. (1987)

(metabolic processes, genes, ion channels). The number of these links is growing, and it is becoming obvious that there are third, fourth, and higher-order messengers in many reaction chains. In addition, the same molecule can be active at different steps in different chains. Thus, Ca^{2+} can be the trigger for a reaction chain, or the final objective that is modulated; as another example, G-binding proteins can be steps in modulation of cAMP levels, or they themselves can act directly on ion channels.

A list of second messenger systems in neurons is shown in Table 8.1. We will discuss several of the best understood of these.

Calcium as a Second Messenger

Over 30 years ago, the physiologist L. V. Heilbrunn stressed the importance of calcium for many cell functions. Modern research has amply confirmed this view, especially in relation to intracellular free ionized Ca. Several methods have been developed for determining these levels. One involves measurements of luminescence of aequorin, a protein isolated from jellyfish, which reacts with Ca^{2+} to emit light. Another method uses metallochromic dyes, such as arsenazo III; when this complexes with Ca^{2+} it changes its absorption spectrum, which can be measured by differential spectroscopy. Ion-exchange microelectrodes that are selective for Ca^{2+} have been developed, which give a direct measure of intracellular free Ca^{2+}. Electron microscopy combined with X-ray or protein microprobe spectroscopy has permitted localization of several ion species, including Ca^{2+}, in relation to cell organelles.

All of these methods, together with traditional biochemical methods of measuring radioactive Ca^{2+} fluxes, are in agreement in showing that the levels of free ionized Ca in nerve cells are extremely low. The levels are in the range of 10^{-6} to 10^{-8} M. This may be compared with estimates of about 10^{-4} M of total Ca^{2+}/kg of axoplasm for the case of the squid giant axon (and about 10^{-2} M in seawater; see Table 5.1). Thus, most of the Ca in a neuron (or any other body cell for that matter) is in the bound form, and only a very small proportion is free and ionized within the cytoplasm. This is critical for the second messenger functions of Ca, for it means that the cell can use small changes in local Ca^{2+} levels to promote large or significant effects. This is the basis for the crucial role that Ca^{2+} plays in such diverse functions as secretion, axoplasmic flow, motility, contraction, enzymatic reactions, and membrane permeability.

With regard to neurotransmitter release, the key event is the influx of Ca^{2+}. As was indicated in Chap. 4 (Fig. 4.8), binding of Ca^{2+} to Ca^{2+}/calmodulin-dependent protein kinase II is considered to be an essential step in priming of synaptic vesicles, and Ca^{2+} may also play a more direct role in bringing about vesicle fusion. The Ca ions enter the presynaptic terminal through voltage-gated channels when the terminal is depolarized by invading nerve impulses. The resultant transient elevation of cytosolic Ca concentration has been visualized at the giant synapse of the squid through combined use of indicator dye and video-enhanced microscopy. An experiment using the dye fura-2 is shown in Fig. 8.1. These results indicate that synaptic Ca^{2+} channels are highly localized to the region of synaptic contact, but that opening of the channels leads to transient increase of Ca^{2+} concentration throughout much of the presynaptic terminal. After the Ca^{2+} has participated in exocytosis and release of neurotransmitter, it must be cleared from the cytoplasm. The most important mechanisms for doing this are binding to calmodulin, and binding to endoplasmic reticulum and other organelles, sequestration in cisternae, uptake by mitochondria, and efflux by pumping. These mechanisms controlling the availability of free Ca are in turn linked in many ways to second messenger systems, protein phosphorylation steps, pathways for transmitter synthesis, and the general metabolism of the cell. Through these means, Ca^{2+} plays important roles in longer-term processes underlying synaptic plasticity, development, and memory and learning; these will be discussed in later chapters.

Cyclic Nucleotide System

The best understood of the enzymatic second messenger systems is the type that uses a cyclic nucleotide as the intracellular signal molecule. Most prevalent is the adenosine 3', 5'-cyclic monophosphate (cAMP) system. As shown in Fig. 8.2 (top), cAMP is synthesized by the enzyme adenylate cyclase, which removes the two outermost phosphate groups and creates an additional ester bond between the remaining phosphate group and the No. 3 carbon of the ribose molecule. The cyclic AMP is in turn hydrolyzed by phosphodiesterase (PDE) to the inactive AMP.

In order to function as a second messenger, the basal concentration of cAMP in the cytoplasm must be held at a low level. Normally this level is less than 10^{-6} M. When adenylate cyclase is stimulated, the synthesized cAMP has only a brief period during which it can act before it is degraded by PDE.

How is the synthesis of cAMP stimulated or inhibited? Recent studies have defined a three-component system of membrane-associated proteins, that consists of a receptor, a linking protein, and the adenylate cyclase. This triumvirate operates in the following manner (see Fig. 8.2, bottom). In step 1, the transmitter, hormone, or other

B. PRESYNAPTIC Ca IMAGE

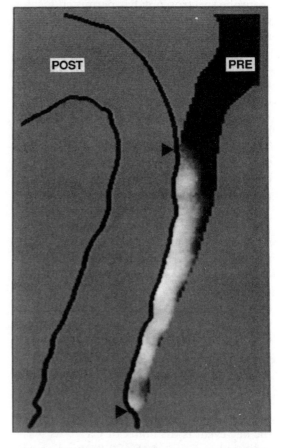

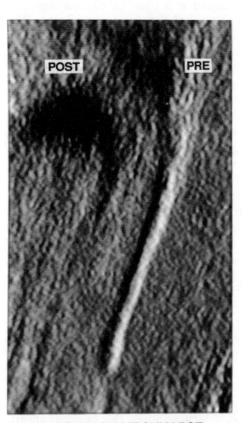

A. SQUID GIANT SYNAPSE

Fig. 8.1 Changes in intracellular Ca^{2+} at the squid giant synapse. **A.** The synaptic region was visualized by video-enhanced microscopy, using a combination of brightfield and fluorescence illumination. The tapered presynaptic (PRE) ending of the secondary giant fiber makes synaptic contact where it envelops a segment of the tertiary giant fiber (POST), which forms an inverted U in this view. The presynaptic fiber was injected with a fluorescent Ca^{2+} indicator dye (fura-2), and appears lighter. **B.** The spatial distribution of elevated Ca^{2+} during a train of 50 impulses stimulated at 100 Hz in the presynaptic fiber. The brighter areas of the presynaptic process indicate raised Ca^{2+} concentration. The gray-scale values reflect changes in fluorescence of fura-2 during stimulation divided by resting levels of fura-2 fluorescence. The physiology of the squid giant synapse is further considered in Fig. 8.4 and Figs. 19.3–19.5. (From Smith et al., 1987; illustration and description kindly provided by Dr. S. J. Smith)

first messenger binds to a receptor protein (R). This causes an allosteric change which activates the linking protein (called G protein, N protein, or transducing protein) to bind preferentially GTP instead of GDP. When this occurs, the G protein moves laterally in the membrane to associate with the adenylate cyclase molecule. This has two effects: It first activates adenylate cyclase to synthesize cAMP (step 2)and it also activates the GTPase activity of the G protein to hydrolyze GTP to GDP (step 3), returning the G protein and the membrane receptor to their base configurations (step 4), ready for another activation cycle.

The cAMP produces its effects as a sec-

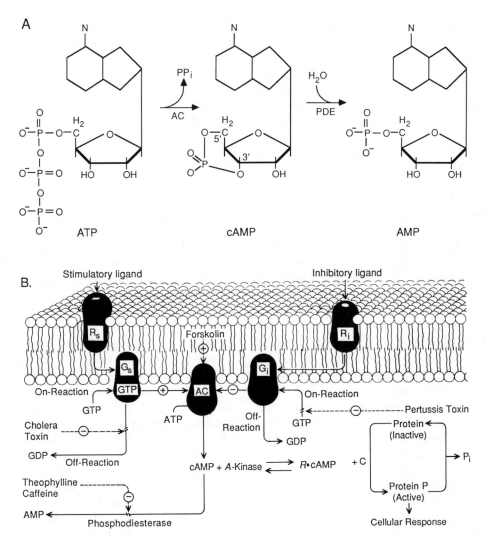

Fig. 8.2 Cyclic adenosine monophosphate (cAMP) second messenger system. **A.** Conversion of adenosine triphosphate (ATP) into cAMP, catalzyzed by adenylate cyclase, and hydrolysis by phosphodiesterase (PDE) to adenosine monophosphate (AMP). **B.** Signal pathways related to cAMP. Receptor proteins (R) act through GTP-binding proteins (G) to activate or inhibit adenylate cyclase (AC). The cAMP produced binds to the regulatory subunit of protein kinase A, releasing its catalytic unit to phosphorylate target proteins that produce cellular responses. The actions of drugs at various sites in the pathways are indicated.

External signal molecules that act at excitatory receptors (R_s) include epinephrine (at β-adrenoceptors), thyroid stimulating hormone (TSH), vasopressin, glucagon, serotonin, and dopamine. Molecules that act at inhibitory receptors (R_i) include epinephrine (at α_2-adrenoceptors), acetylcholine (M_1 receptors), opioids, angiotensin II, and dopamine (D_2 receptors). (Modified from Berridge, 1985)

ond messenger by binding to the regulatory unit of cAMP-dependent protein kinase, freeing the catalytic unit of this enzyme to phosphorylate specific proteins. These phosphorylated proteins may be involved in many different metabolic or physiological processes. An example is a membrane channel protein: phosphorylation may cause an allosteric change in the protein which alters the channel opening. Other types of metabolic and physiological effects are noted below.

The cAMP system is virtually universal in cells, but it appears to be particularly important in nerve cells; adenylate cyclase activity is very high in the brain. An adenylate cyclase-stimulating receptor has been purified; it consists of a 60-kdalton polypeptide, which may be present as a dimer. The G_s protein has also been purified; it is a 80-kdalton protein, composed of two or three subunits. An inhibiting protein, G_i, with a similar composition, inhibits adenylate cyclase when activated by β-adrenergic receptors and opiate receptors (see below). G_s and G_i turn out to be members of a family of GTP binding proteins, that includes transducin in photoreceptors (see Chap. 16) and GTP binding proteins that are involved in regulation of growth; some of these are products of oncogenes (see Chap. 9).

Another cyclic nucleotide that acts as a second messenger is guanosine $3'$, $5'$-cyclic monophosphate (cGMP). In general, it is present in much lower concentrations than cAMP. Its specific role in mediating responses to light in photoreceptors will be discussed in Chap. 16.

Why are several steps interposed in the linkage between the first messenger and the final effect of the second messenger? One reason is the multiple control points that this provides. Another reason is the amplification that is achieved. A single receptor protein activates not just one, but many G proteins; each adenylate cyclase molecule synthesizes many cAMP molecules, and there is similar multiplication at steps 7 and 8 in

Fig. 8.2. The enzyme cascade thus achieves effects that are specific, powerful, and under exquisite control.

G-Protein System

In addition to acting on adenylate cyclase, G-binding proteins can also act on other molecules; these actions include direct coupling to ion channels themselves. This evidence has come to light from experiments by Pfaffinger et al. (1985) and Breitwieser and Szabo (1985) on single cultured heart cells, in which whole-cell patch recordings were made of responses of K^+ currents to externally applied ACh with agents that affect G-binding proteins (see Noma, 1986, for review). The muscarinic cholinergic effect of ACh in activating K^+ conductance (thereby inhibiting the cell) was found to depend on G-binding proteins and GTP analogues. In addition, ACh stimulation of a whole cell does not activate channels isolated within an on-cell patch. This shows that a diffusible substance, such as cAMP, is not involved, and suggests that the G-binding protein is acting directly on the K^+ channels. And this is not all; the inhibitory G-protein can also block the action of adenylate cyclase in opening excitatory Ca^{2+} channels in response to β-adrenergic stimulation. The rationale for the double action is that the opening of the K^+ channels inhibits the cell by hyperpolarizing it toward the K^+ equilibrium potential, and the inhibition of adenylate cyclase prevents adrenergic stimulation of the cell through Ca^{2+} channel activation.

These mechanisms in heart cells have turned out, as has happened so often in the past, to have their counterparts in nerve cells. G-protein-stimulated opening of K^+ channels, coupled in some cases to inhibition of adenylate cyclase, has been reported at several types of synapses in the brain; we will review them later in this chapter. Through these actions, together with their role in controlling cAMP and cGMP, G proteins are crucial constituents of most synapses that have neuromodulatory prop-

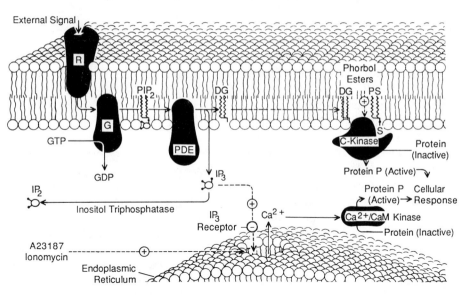

Fig. 8.3 Inositol-lipid second messenger system. Receptor proteins (R) activate a GTP-binding protein (G) which stimulates a phosphodiesterase (PDE) which hydrolyzes phosphatylinositol-4,5-bisphosphate (PIP$_2$) into two signal molecules: inositol triphosphate (IP$_3$) and diacylglycerol (DAG). IP$_3$ acts on the endoplasmic reticulum to release Ca^{2+}, which functions as a third messenger to activate Ca^{2+}/calmodulin-dependent protein kinase (Ca^{2+}/CaM kinase); this kinase, in turn, phosphorylates target proteins to produce cellular responses. DAG, on the other hand, activates a protein kinase C, which phosphorylates target proteins to produce cellular responses. Drugs can act at the sites indicated in the pathways. External signal molecules that activate the membrane receptors include acetylcholine, vasopressin, thyrotropin releasing hormone (TRH), serotonin, thrombin, and antigens. (Modified from Berridge, 1985)

erties. It is therefore not surprising that G-protein dysfunction is implicated in several types of mental disorders, and is a prime target for development of psychotropic therapeutic drugs; progress in this area is reviewed by Aghajanian and Rasmussen (1987).

Membrane Lipid System

In Chap. 3, we pointed out that membrane lipids play more roles than simply providing a fluid medium for proteins to float in. One of these additional roles is now known to be an important second messenger system. This begins with phosphatidylinositol, one of the phospholipids present in the inner membrane (cf. Chap 3). Phosphatidylinositol (PI) is phosphorylated in two steps to phosphatidylinositol-4,5-bisphosphate (PIP$_2$), which is a substrate for a phosphodiesterase called phospholipase C (PC). This enzyme can be activated by a membrane receptor protein when it binds to its appropriate lipid; present evidence suggests that this activation is probably mediated by a G protein (see Fig. 8.3).

The key effect of PC is to cleave off the lipid chains, producing inositol triphosphate (IP$_3$) and diacylglycerol (DAG). Both of these are second messengers.

IP$_3$ is water soluble and can diffuse into the cytoplasm. There it acts on receptors in the endoplasmic reticulum to increase efflux of Ca^{2+} from inside the ER to the cytoplasm (Fig. 8.3). The Ca^{2+} (which when mobilized in this way is really functioning as a third messenger), then exerts its various effects as indicated in Fig. 8.3.

The second compound produced by phospholipase C, diacyglycerol (DAG), consists of glycerol joined to two fatty acids (stearic and arachidonic acid). DAG appears only briefly in membranes, being incorporated again into phosphatidylinositol, or being enzymatically degraded (in which case the arachidonic acid can contribute to synthesis of prostaglandins). Associated with the appearance of DAG is activation of protein kinase C (PKC). This phosphorylating enzyme is found widely in cells, and is present with the highest specific activity in brain. In most cells it is present in the cytoplasm, whereas in the brain it appears to be preferentially associated with synaptic membranes, as previously noted in Chap. 4.

Protein kinase C has been shown to phosphorylate several proteins in the brain, including B50 (F1) protein associated with presynaptic membranes; synapsin I associated with synaptic vesicles; microtubule-associated proteins; and other cytoplasmic and membrane-associated proteins whose functions are still unknown. In many of its actions, PKC acts synergistically with the Ca^{2+} mobilized by IP_3; it may also act synergistically in other ways, as with cAMP and Ca/calmodulin-dependent protein kinase II on synaptic vesicles (see Chap. 4).

It appears, therefore, that in contrast to the vast array of transmitter and modulator "first messengers," there are relatively few "second messengers." Specificity in the activity of these second messengers is achieved in several ways: (1) by the specificity of receptors; (2) through specific synergistic effects between two or three of the systems; and (3) by kinases acting on target proteins that are specific for a given neuronal type, or for a given locus in a neuronal type.

Second Messengers and Protein Phosphorylation

A general conclusion arising from the study of second messenger systems is that protein phosphorylation is a common end result. A protein kinase catalyzes the transfer of the terminal phosphate group of ATP to a hydroxyl group on a substrate protein. As shown in Fig. 8.4A, the usual site of transfer is the hydroxyl group of a serine or threonine residue. Phosphorylation at these sites induces conformational changes which bring about short-term physiological changes. In addition to these sites, phosphorylation can also occur at tyrosine residues, through a tyrosine kinase (Fig. 8.4B). This type of phosphorylation is involved in control of normal growth, as well as the abnormal growth responses to oncogenes (see Chap. 9).

What kind of experiments can we do to study the effects of protein phosphorylation? A direct approach was taken by Rudolfo Llinas and Paul Greengard and their colleagues, who wished to test for the effects of protein phosphorylation on synaptic transmission. They used the giant synapse of the squid, in which the pre- and postsynaptic processes are large enough that one can insert microelectrode tips into them. By injecting Ca/calmodulin-dependent protein kinase (Ca/CaM PK) from one electrode, and recording the response from another electrode, they were able to test for the effect of this enzyme, and its site of action. As shown in Fig. 8.4C, injection of Ca/CaM PK into the postsynaptic terminal produced no physiological response, whereas injection into the presynaptic terminal induced a large increase in the postsynaptic response. The interpretation of these results was that the injection had enhanced the normal action of Ca/CaM PK in phosphorylating synapsin I, detaching it from the synaptic vesicles and allowing the vesicles to undergo exocytosis and release their transmitter. This has been part of the evidence supporting the sequence of events at the synapses we outlined in Chap. 4 (Fig. 4.8).

This is only one example of the kinds of proteins that are phosphorylated as a result of second messenger actions. Other types of proteins are listed in Table 8.2. We discuss some of these further below, as well as in other chapters.

A. Phosphorylation of threonine (or serine) residue

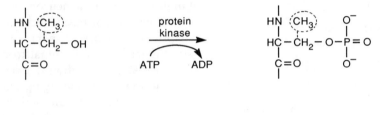

B. Phosphorylation of tyrosine residue

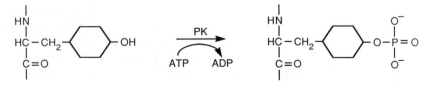

C. Test for protein phosphorylation at squid giant synapse

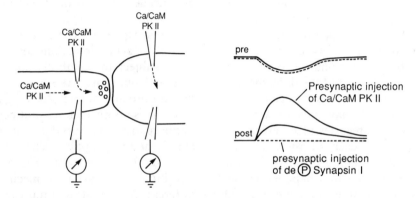

Fig. 8.4 Molecular mechanisms of protein phosphorylation. **A.** Some protein kinases catalyze the transfer of a phosphate group to a threonine or serine (additional carbon in serine indicated by dashed lines) residue of a substrate protein. This induces a conformational change which produces a rapid cellular response. **B.** Some protein kinases catalyze transfer of a phosphate group to a tyrosine residue of a substrate protein; this leads to a slower cellular response. Examples of such kinases are those involved in normal and abnormal (tumor) growth (see Chap. 9, Fig. 9.5). (After Nestler and Greengard, 1984) **C.** Experimental test for the functional role of protein phosphorylation in synaptic transmission. On the left, the experimental setup involved injecting Ca/calmodulin-dependent protein kinase (Ca/CaM PK) into either the pre- or postsynaptic terminal of the giant synapse of the squid, while recording intracellularly from those sites. The recordings, on the right, showed that neither presynaptic (dashed line) nor postsynaptic (solid line) injection of Ca/CaM PK had an effect on the presynaptic potential; however, pre- (but not post-) synaptic injection greatly enhanced the postsynaptic potential. Presynaptic injection of dephosphorylated synapsin I had no effect on the postsynaptic potential. (Adapted from Llinás et al., 1985)

Table 8.2 Types of proteins that are targets for phosphorylation

1. Regulatory proteins (G proteins)
2. Cytoskeletal proteins (microtubule-associated proteins or neurofilaments)
3. Synaptic vesicle proteins (synapsin I)
4. Neurotransmitter-synthesizing enzymes (tyrosine hydroxylase)
5. Neurotransmitter receptors (ACh receptor or β-adrenergic receptor)
6. Ion channel proteins (Na^+ or Ca^{2+} channels)

From Nestler and Greengard (1984)

Main Types of Synapses

We are now in a position to consider the functional organization of different types of synapses. Synapses are commonly grouped into types, according to the transmitter released by the presynaptic process. They are further divided into subtype on the basis of binding by different pharmacological agonists or antagonists, and the different types of postsynaptic responses associated with each. These criteria have given rise to several traditional categories of synapses, and we will consider each of these in turn. Building on the common framework for all synapses introduced in Chap. 4, we will show how it is adapted to achieve a wide variety of functional effects between neurons.

Acetylcholine

Acetylcholine (ACh) is unique as a small transmitter molecule in that it does not appear to belong to a larger clan of related compounds.

Ever since the work of Langley, Dale, and Loewi early in this century, it has been known that synapses that use ACh as a transmitter can be divided into two main classes, depending on whether they are blocked by the application of the substance nicotine or muscarine. The two classes are therefore called nicotinic and muscarinic cholinergic synapses. The neuromuscular junction is a nicotinic synapse.

By now we have become well acquainted with the function of ACh as a transmitter of motoneurons at the neuromuscular junction (Chap. 2). The basic mechanism at this synapse is summarized in Fig. 8.5A. ACh is synthesized in the terminal from choline and acetyl-CoA by choline acetylase ①; this is followed by packaging and mobilization ②, release ③, and action on postsynaptic ④ and presynaptic receptors ⑤. Brief action of the ACh is ensured by the presence in the cleft of acetylcholinesterase, an enzyme that rapidly hydrolyzes ACh into acetate and choline ⑥; the choline is taken up again by the presynaptic terminal ⑦ for resynthesis into ACh. It can be seen that direct binding of ACh to the channel protein and the rapid hydrolysis of ACh in the cleft are adaptations for quick action, as is needed for control of skeletal muscles.

In contrast to nicotinic synapses, muscarinic synapses are characteristically found where the synaptic actions are slower and more subject to metabolic and other factors; examples are the synapses of motor nerves onto autonomic ganglia, glands, cardiac and smooth muscle, and certain sites in the central nervous system. At these synapses, the presynaptic mechanisms involve the same basic steps (see Fig. 8.5B, ① to ③), but the postsynaptic mechanisms are different. ACh binds to a muscarinic receptor (mAChR) molecule that is distinct from the channel protein. The muscarinic receptor is not soluble in detergents, so progress in understanding its molecular structure by traditional biochemical methods has been slow. Recently, however, a cDNA for a muscarinic cholinergic receptor in the pig brain has been cloned and expressed by Shosaku Numa's laboratory (Kubo et al., 1986). The polypeptide consists of 460 amino acid residues, with a molecular weight of 51,000. Analysis of hydrophobicity suggests the presence of seven membrane-spanning segments. A pleasant surprise is that this pattern is similar to that of the visual protein rhodospin (see Chap. 16) and the β-adrenergic receptor (see below), a result supported by a high degree of amino acid sequence homologies. A com-

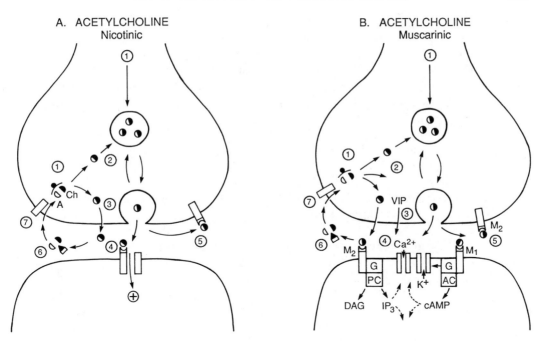

Fig. 8.5 Molecular mechanisms of cholinergic synapses. **A.** Nicotinic cholinergic synapse. The main steps are indicated by numbers ① to ⑦ in this and the following diagrams: ① synthesis of acetylcholine (ACh) from acetate and choline (catalyzed by choline acetylase) in the cell body or the synaptic terminal; ② transport and storage in vesicles; ③ release by exocytosis, or from the cytosol (recycling of vesicle membrane indicated by dashed arrow); diffusion in the synaptic cleft (release is blocked by botulinum toxin or high Mg^{2+}); ④ binding of ACh to the nicotinic cholinergic receptor molecule, which opens the channel for net inward cationic flow, depolarizing the membrane (nicotine is an agonist at this receptor); ⑤ binding of ACh to the presynaptic receptor; ⑥ hydrolysis of ACh into acetate and choline by acetylcholinesterase; ⑦ reuptake of choline into presynaptic terminal. (Modified from Dunant and Israel, 1985) **B.** Muscarinic cholinergic synapse: ① synthesis; ② transport and storage; ③ release (corelease with a peptide, such as vasoactive intestinal peptide, VIP); ④ binding to M_1 postsynaptic receptor activates a G protein which directly modulates K^+ channel. Additional G protein modulation of cAMP second messenger system leads to complementary effects on Ca^{2+} channels. Other types of mAChRs are coupled to IP_3 second messenger system. This is shown as M_2 receptor in B, but M_1 and M_2 receptors may be coupled to different second messenger systems at particular synapses. ⑤ binding to presynaptic M_2 receptor; ⑥ hydrolysis by acetylcholinesterase; ⑦ reuptake of choline.

mon ancestor for the genes encoding these three proteins of diverse function is thus implied.

The binding sites for ACh are not yet identified, but there are several types of receptors (M_1, M_2) based on affinities for different ligands and the postsynaptic effects they produce. Muscarinic responses are slow because the receptor molecule is coupled to ion channels by second messenger systems. In different types of nerve,

muscle, and gland cells, responses to receptor stimulation have been found to be associated with activation of G proteins (brain), inhibition of cAMP formation (heart), stimulation of cGMP formation, and increased turnover of inositol phosphates (glands). The second messenger generated by these responses may lead to one or several of the actions discussed previously, including phosphorylation of a membrane channel protein to produce an electrical response, and phosphorylation of a membrane or cytosolic protein to produce a longer-term metabolic response. As shown in Fig. 8.5B ④, a common mechanism at many muscarinic cholinergic synapses is for the mAChR to activate a G protein which modulates a K^+ channel; opening the channel polarizes the membrane and inhibits the cell, whereas closing the channel makes the cell more excitable (see M current in sympathetic ganglion cells: Chaps. 7 and 18). The G protein may also modulate adenylate cyclase production of cAMP, which in turn modulates Ca^{2+} channels, usually in a way that complements the effects on K^+ channels (i.e., closing Ca^{2+} channels would reinforce the inhibitory effect of opening K^+ channels).

We have considered nicotinic and muscarinic synapses as separate entities for convenience of explanation, but the two types of receptors may be intermingled so that the neuron can give a more complex response. Additional degrees of complexity are provided by the corelease at some muscarinic synapses of a peptide, such as vasoactive intestinal peptide (VIP; see below), which can modulate the ACh response, and by the presence of autoreceptors on the presynaptic terminal, which can modulate the presynaptic release processes (see Fig. 8.5B).

Biogenic Amines

Several types of small molecules have an amine group and can affect a variety of cells, from platelets to neurons; they are classified as monoamines, or biogenic amines. They form several subgroups: these are (1) the catecholamines (dopamine, norepinephrine, and epinephrine), all of which contain a catechol nucleus and share a common synthetic pathway; (2) serotonin, or 5-hydroxytryptamine (5HT); and (3) histamine. Let us consider the most important of them as far as the nervous system is concerned.

Adrenergic Synapses. This term can apply to synapses that use either norepinephrine (NE) or epinephrine (E); of these, NE is the most prevalent in the nervous system, being the main neurotransmitter of ganglion cells in the sympathetic nervous system (Chap. 18), and also of locus ceruleus cells that project widely throughout the vertebrate brain (Chap. 24).

As indicated in Fig. 8.6A, synthesis of catecholamines ① begins with the amino acid tyrosine (Tyr), which is taken up by nerve cells from the blood. NE synthesis takes place in the cell body or in the synaptic terminals themselves; it is packaged into vesicles that enter a storage pool as shown in ②. With depolarization and Ca^{2+} influx, the NE is released by exocytosis ③, and acts on postsynaptic receptors ④, termed α_1-adrenergic receptors. The primary effect, mediated through second messengers, is on Ca^{2+} channels. In addition, the released NE acts on α_2 receptors, located primarily on the presynaptic terminal ⑤. Through second messengers and protein phosphorylation, α_2 receptors exert diverse controls on the state of the synapse, including changes in the gating of K^+ channels. This may take place by the direct action of a G protein, as in the case of the mAChR. Termination of NE action occurs by reuptake ⑥ into the presynaptic terminal, where the level of NE is controlled through enzymatic degradation or inactivation ⑦.

A second type of adrenergic receptor is the β receptor. As shown in Fig. 8.6B, this differs from the α receptor mainly in being primarily postsynaptic, and linked to the cAMP second messenger system. One effect of this system is to decrease the membrane conductance of the postsynaptic cell and inhibit its firing. This was first shown in 1971 by George Siggins, Barry Hoffer and Floyd Bloom, then in Washington, D.C. They used a multibarrel pipette which allowed them to record the impulse activity of a Purkinje cell in the cerebellum (Chap. 22) from one barrel while ejecting different drugs from the other barrels (a technique called microionophoresis). They showed that ionophoresis of NE or cAMP produced a

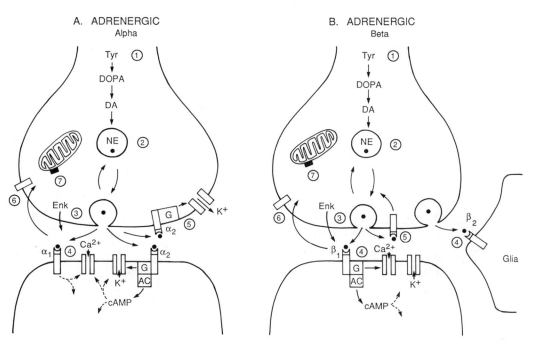

Fig. 8.6 Molecular mechanism of adrenergic synapses. **A.** α-Adrenergic synapse: ① synthetic pathway is through tyrosine (Tyr) to 3,4-dihydroxyphenylalanine (DOPA; catalyzed by tyrosine hydroxylase) to dopamine (DA; catalyzed by DOPA decarboxylase) to norepinephrine (NE; catalyzed by dopamine-β-hydroxylase); ② transport and storage (storage is blocked by reserpine); ③ release by exocytosis (increased by amphetamine); corelease with neuropeptides such as enkephalin, Enk; ④ binding of NE to postsynaptic receptors. Examples are shown of binding to α_1 receptor which leads to modulation of Ca^{2+} channels, and binding to α_2 receptors, which are linked to adenylate cyclase and modulate K^+ channels; there may also be direct actions of G proteins on K^+ channels; ⑤ binding of NE to presynaptic α_2 receptors; ⑥ reuptake, which terminates NE action (blocked by tricyclic antidepressant drugs); ⑦ degradation by monoamine oxidase (MAO) [there may also be inactivation by catechol-O-methyltransferase (COMT)]. **B.** β-Adrenergic synapse: ①–③ synthesis, transport, storage, and release as in A above; ④ binding of NE to β_1 receptor which leads to phosphorylation of ionic channels through cAMP; β_2 receptors are also found on glia; ⑤–⑦ presynaptic receptors, reuptake, degradation, and inactivation, as in A above. (Based on Cooper et al., 1987; Aghajanian and Rasmussen, 1987; Tsien, 1987; and others)

suppression of impulse firing similar to that produced by stimulation of the noradrenergic fibers of the locus ceruleus that innervate the cerebellum. These actions were blocked by ionophoresis of β-receptor blockers such as antipsychotic drugs (chlorpromazine) and prostaglandins, or by drugs that block activation of adenylate cyclase.

Subsequent studies have supported the idea that β receptors act through the cAMP second messenger system. The actions are different in different cells; for example, in heart cells NE and E act mainly through β receptors and cAMP, whereas in dorsal root ganglion neurons they act through α receptors and DAG (Tsien, 1987). A β_2 receptor has been characterized which, in the brain, appears to be more localized in glial cells. Also indicated in Fig. 8.6A, B is the fact that adrenergic endings may corelease neuroactive peptides such as enkephalin (see below).

Dopamine Synapses. In neurons that utilize dopamine (DA) as their transmitter, the biogenic amine synthetic pathway stops

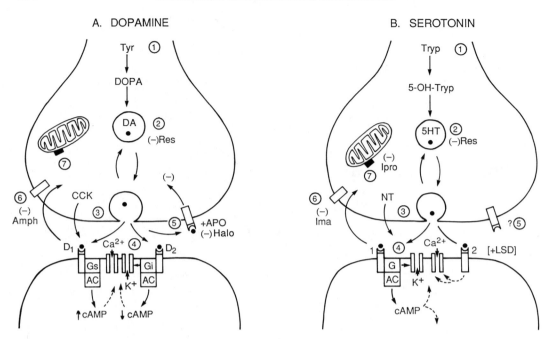

Fig. 8.7 **A.** Molecular mechanism of dopaminergic synapses: ① synthesis by enzymatic pathway from Tyr to DOPA to DA (see legend, Fig. 8.6); ② transport and storage (storage inhibited by reserpine, Res); ③ release of DA by exocytosis; corelease of a neuropeptide such as cholecystokinin (CCK); ④ binding to D_1 receptor, acting through stimulatory G protein (G_s) to increase levels of cAMP, or to D_2 receptor, acting through inhibitory G protein to lower levels of cAMP (antipsychotic drugs such as butyrophenones block D_2 receptors); G protein can also have a direct action on K^+ channels at some synapses; ⑤ binding of DA to presynaptic receptors [typically D_2; DA receptors are stimulated by psychoactive drugs such as apomorphine (APO), blocked by haloperidol (Halo)]; ⑥ reuptake terminates DA action; ⑦ degradation by MAO and inactivation by COMT. **B.** Molecular mechanism of serotonergic synapses: ① synthetic pathway is from tryptophan to 5-hydroxytryptophan (catalyzed by tryptophan hydroxylase) to 5-hydroxytryptamine (5HT, or serotonin) (catalyzed by 5-hydroxytryptophan decarboxylase); ② transport and storage (blocked by reserpine, Res); ③ release of 5HT by exocytosis; corelease with a neuropeptide, e.g. neurotensin, NT ; ④ binding to a $5HT_1$ postsynaptic receptor (coupled to G protein and cAMP), or to a $5HT_2$ receptor (LSD is an agonist/antagonist); ?⑤ possible binding to presynaptic receptors; ⑥ reuptake terminates 5HT action (blocked by tricylic antidepressant drugs such as imipramine, Ima); ⑦ degraded by MAO. (Based on Cooper et al., 1987; Aghajanian and Rasmussen, 1987; and others)

with DOPA decarboxylase, the enzyme that synthesizes DA (see ① in Fig. 8.7A). Storage ② and release ③ mechanisms appear to be similar to those for NE discussed above. DA acts on two types of receptors ④, both of which are linked to adenylate cyclase–cAMP second messenger systems. Stimulation of D_1-receptors causes an increase in cAMP levels, whereas stimulation of D_2 receptors cause a decrease in cAMP, in the postsynaptic neuron. There are also

autoreceptors ⑤ on the presynaptic terminal, which are thought to exert an inhibitory feedback effect on the DA neuron. The action of DA is terminated largely by reuptake ⑥. Mechanisms for degradation and inactivation ⑦ are similar to those for NE.

Dopaminergic synapses have been of great interest because of the evidence, beginning in the 1960s, that antipsychotic drugs that are effective in alleviating the symptoms of schizophrenia have the common effect of interfering with transmission at dopaminergic synapses in the brain. Recent studies indicate that the primary mode of action of antipsychotic drugs is to bind to, and block, the D_2 receptors. In contrast to these blocking actions of antipsychotic drugs, it is known that drugs that are DA agonists such as amphetamine, that enhance or mimic the actions of DA, can induce schizophrenia-like behavior. It has been tempting therefore to believe that schizophrenia is due to overactivity of DA neurons in the brain. Although malfunction of DA synapses is likely to be important in schizophrenia, there is general agreement that other mechanisms and other transmitter systems must be involved, too. We will return to this question in Chap. 24 when we consider the location of transmitter pathways in the brain.

Serotonin Synapses. Serotonin (5-hydroxytryptamine: 5HT) differs from the catecholamines in having, in addition to the catechole ring, an indole ring, from which the alkyl group with its terminal amine group arises. The precursor for 5HT is tryptophan, which is taken up from the bloodstream, as indicated in ① of Fig. 8.7B. The 5HT synthesized is stored in vesicles ② and released ③ by mechanisms similar to those for other biogenic amines. Serotonin receptors are divided into two types, depending on whether they preferentially bind 5HT (5HT-1) or a central stimulatory drug (neuroleptic) called spiperine (5HT-2). The 5HT-1 receptors are linked to G-protein and/or cAMP second messenger systems which regulate K^+ and Ca^{2+} channels. We will study an example of this in a molluscan neuron (Chap. 29), where a serotonin receptor can mediate sensitization of a synapse. There is little evidence for 5HT autoreceptors ⑤. Reuptake ⑥ is believed to be the main mechanism for terminating 5HT action, and degradation occurs in the presynaptic terminal ⑦.

Interest in the behavioral actions of 5HT began around 1950 with the realization that its molecular structure resembled that of lysergic acid diethylamide (LSD), a hallucinogenic drug, and the finding that the stimulatory action of 5HT on the smooth muscles of the gut was antagonized by LSD. From this observation arose the theory that the hallucinations associated with LSD are due to blockade of 5HT receptors in the central nervous system (see step ④ in Fig. 8.7B), and that this receptor blockade might be a mechanism underlying some psychoses. As in the case of the DA theory of schizophrenia, this theory has been considerably modified. We will discuss these matters further in Chap. 24.

Other Biogenic Amines. Closely related to norepinephrine is epinephrine (E), which is synthesized by carboxylation of the terminal nitrogen group of norepinephrine. Epinephrine is produced mainly in the adrenal medulla, and is the main circulating hormone released during "fight or flight" stress reactions. It has a limited distribution in the brain (Chap. 24).

Histamine is another monoamine, synthesized from histidine which has been taken up from the blood. Histamine is found primarily in mast cells, which release it as part of their reactions to allergens. If you suffer from hay fever, you know that an antihistamine tablet not only relieves your stuffy nose, but also produces drowsiness; this may be due to an action on histamine receptors in the brain, which have been found mostly in the hypothalamus. Different types of histamine receptors have been identified; one type is found in the neocortex and hippocampus, where stimulation leads to changes in neuronal metabolism believed to be mediated by cAMP.

The biogenic amines discussed above are found in invertebrates as well as vertebrates. In addition, a common transmitter in some invertebrates is octopamine, a biogenic amine formed by an alternative synthetic pathway from tyrosine. In the lobster, octopamine is believed to act through cAMP and protein phosphorylation to prime extensor muscles to respond more vigorously when stimulated. This underlies the extensor posture assumed by the lobster in defensive behavior, in contrast to the flexion posture of aggressive behavior that is mediated by 5HT (as we will learn in Chap. 19). Both of these priming actions are characteristic of neuromodulatory transmitter actions (see below).

Amino Acids

At first consideration, amino acids that are involved in intermediary metabolism would seem to be unlikely to fulfill in addition the kinds of specific signaling functions that are required of a neurotransmitter substance. However, since the 1950s, several amino acids have been identified that do satisfy these requirements and in fact appear to account for some of the most prevalent types of excitatory and inhibitory actions in the nervous system.

Glutamate. It has been known for many years that glutamic acid (Glu) is found in high concentrations in the whole brain. Recent studies have shown that it is found in certain specific neurons in the vertebrate brain (see Chap. 24), as well as in invertebrate neuron systems (see Chap. 17).

Less is known about glutamatergic mechanisms compared with the other types of synapses we have discussed thus far but new information is accumulating rapidly (see Fig. 8.8A). Glu is synthesized from glutamine ①; it is stored ② and released ③ in a Ca^{2+}-dependent manner. Glu acts on postsynaptic receptors that appear to be linked directly to conductance channels that depolarize the membrane. The receptors are presently believed to fall into two main groups. One type binds quisqualate (Q) and kainate (K), and the other type binds a compound called N-methyl-D-aspartate (NMDA). Patch-clamp recordings (Jahr and Stevens, 1987; Cull-Candy and Usowicz, 1987) have suggested that both types are part of the same receptor-channel complex. Glu (and Q and K) normally activates multiple conductance states in this complex, to permit Na^+ and K^+ to flow through the channel to depolarize the membrane. The

NMDA receptor is linked to a larger conductance state that also permits Ca^{2+} influx; as shown in Fig. 8.8A, step ④, this is normally blocked by external magnesium, and is unblocked when the postsynaptic membrane is depolarized (Nowak et al., 1984). This voltage-dependent property, combined with second messenger actions of the Ca^{2+}, is believed to play a role in mechanisms underlying learning and memory (see Chap. 29).

The receptor mechanisms illustrated in Fig. 8.8A represent only the simplest types. Future work will undoubtedly reveal additional linkages to other second messenger systems.

Kainic acid has been found to be an extremely powerful agonist for Glu; in fact, in high concentrations it has a cytotoxic effect on neurons, and can be used this way to lesion selectively glutamatergic pathways. To complete its actions at a synapse, Glu may act on autoreceptors ⑤ and be taken up again into the presynaptic terminal by a high-affinity reuptake system ⑥.

Ionophoresis of Glu onto neurons at glutamatergic synapses causes depolarization and excitation, mimicking the actions of those synapses and supporting its role as the transmitter. The main problem in assessing this role has been that Glu has the same effect on most other neurons as well, suggesting that its excitatory effects may to some extent be nonspecific.

Other Amino Acids Related to Glutamate. Aspartate (Asp) is present in the brain in high concentration, and has been closely associated with glutamate as a possible transmitter substance at many glutamatergic synapses. The mechanisms appear to be similar to those summarized in Fig. 8.8A. Like Glu, Asp generally has a depolarizing, excitatory action on neurons.

In addition to their relatively nonspecific actions, Glu and Asp have been puzzling because of the inconsistent effects of various blocking agents at different presumed Glu/Asp synapses. It has been suggested that the transmitter at some of these syn-

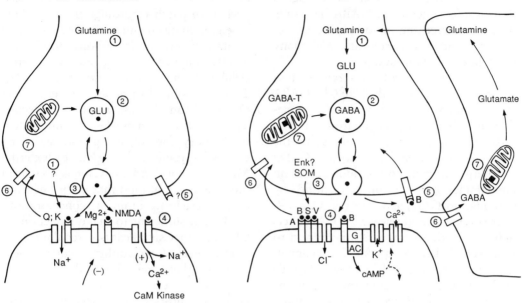

Fig. 8.8 Molecular mechanisms of amino acid synapses. **A.** Glutamatergic synapses: ?① synthesis of glutamate (GLU) from glutamine; ② transport and storage; ③ release of GLU by exocytosis or from cytosol; ④ binding of GLU to several types of receptors identified by specific antagonists [N-methyl-D-aspartate (NMDA), kainate (K), quisqualate (Q)]. The Q and K receptors gate Na^+ and K^+ flux; the NMDA receptor regulates a Ca^{2+}-permeable conductance state which is normally blocked by Mg^{2+} and high resting membrane potential $(-)$; when this block is relieved by membrane depolarization $(+)$, Ca^{2+} flows in to depolarize the membrane further and activate other second messenger systems. The three receptor mechanisms illustrated in the figure represent different conductance states of the same receptor-channel complex. ?⑤ binding to presynaptic receptors; ⑥ reuptake; ⑦ degradation. A similar sequence is involved at synapses utilizing aspartate. (Based on Cooper et al., 1987; Jahr and Stevens, 1987; Cull-Candy and Usowicz, 1987) **B.** GABAergic synapse. ① Synthesis of γ-aminobutyric acid (GABA) from glutamine (catalyzed by glutamic acid decarboxylase); ② transport and storage of GABA; ③ release of GABA by exocytosis [corelease with a neuropeptide such as enkephalin (Enk) or somatostatin (SOM)]; ④ binding to a GABA-A receptor blocked by bicuculline (B), picrotoxin, or strychnine (S), which are coupled to a chloride channel; the GABA receptor also has a site for binding of benzodiazepines, such as valium (V); GABA-B receptors, by contrast, are linked via a G protein and/or cAMP to K^+ and Ca^{2+} channels: these are blocked by baclofen; ⑤ binding to presynaptic receptors; ⑥ reuptake in presynaptic terminal, and uptake by glia; ⑦ transamination of GABA to α-ketoglutarate (catalyzed by GABA transaminase, GABA-T, regenerating glutamate and glutamine; glial glutamine then reenters the neuron. (Modified from Cooper et al., 1987; Aghajanian and Rasmussen, 1987; Nicoll, 1982)

apses may be aspartyl-glutamate, a dipeptide composed of precisely these two amino acids!

GABA. The best-studied amino acid transmitter is γ-aminobutyric acid (GABA). Whereas Glu and Asp are generally associated with excitatory actions on nerve cells, GABA is generally associated with inhibitory actions.

GABA is almost uniquely present in the nervous system, and was therefore long suspected of being a neurotransmitter. Ernst Florey in Oregon first suggested its inhibitory function in the lobster; proof that it is a specific transmitter awaited exhaustive analysis by Ed Kravitz and his colleagues in the 1960s. Since then, GABA has come to be considered the main specific inhibitory transmitter in vertebrate, and many invertebrate, nervous systems.

The mechanism of a GABAergic synapse is summarized in Fig. 8.8B. Like Glu, GABA arises from common pathways of intermediary metabolism in the neuron; in fact, GABA is synthesized from Glu ①, by the enzyme glutamic acid decarboxylase (GAD). GABAergic neurons do not fluoresce, as do monoamines, but they can be identified by antibodies to GAD, as we saw in Chap. 4. After storage ② and release ③, GABA acts on postsynaptic receptors ④ that appear to be closely linked to a chloride channel; opening of this channel increases chloride conductance (g_C), causing the membrane potential to stay, or become, relatively hyperpolarized (see Chap. 7). The GABA receptor, a membrane protein, is actually quite complicated; there are separate low- and high-affinity binding sites for GABA, as well as separate sites, linked to the GABA sites and to the Cl^- channel, where different blocking agents act (see Fig. 8.8B). A basic distinction is made between GABA-A receptors, linked directly to the Cl^- channel, and GABA-B receptors, linked via the G protein of cAMP to K^+ and Ca^{2+} channels (see figure). The B-type receptors are also present on presynaptic terminals ⑤, where they may modulate transmission by parallel fibers in the cerebellum and dorsal root fibers in the spinal cord. There are also high-affinity uptake systems in both presynaptic terminals ⑥ and glia ⑥. GABA is degraded by transamination in mitochondria ⑦. Note the active participation of glia in the uptake and resynthesis of this neurotransmitter.

Glycine. Glycine (Gly) is found in the vertebrate, but not the invertebrate, nervous system. Classically it has been considered to be an inhibitory transmitter, like GABA, but with a more limited distribution (see Chap. 24). Recent work, however, has indicated that glycine has more interesting and subtle actions than heretofore suspected. In patch recordings from NMDA-type glutamate channels, the single-channel excitatory currents in response to Glu are greatly enhanced in the presence of extracellular glycine (Johnson and Ascher, 1987). This is presumed to be an allosteric effect of glycine on the Glu receptor molecule. The Glu NMDA channel is thus under dual modulatory control, being potentiated by external glycine and blocked by external Mg^{2+} (see Fig. 8.8A). Glycine is present in the cerebrospinal fluid that bathes neurons of the vertebrate brain, at concentrations ($> 1 \ \mu M$) sufficient to make its action on Glu receptors significant in regulating the normal level of excitability in cortical neurons. Another interesting finding has been that glycine receptors are present among GABA receptors in the postsynaptic membranes of GABAergic synapses, suggesting that glycine may also have a role in modulating excitability or responsiveness at GABAergic synapses (Triller et al., 1987).

Purines

In recent years, evidence has grown that nucleosides may function at some synapses as transmitters. Most attention has been focused on adenosine, which is composed of a nitrogenous base (in this case, the purine adenine) and a ribose sugar; adenosine is already familiar to us as it is one of the building blocks of the genetic code, has a role through ATP in energy metabolism, and has a role through cAMP as a second messenger.

Evidence that adenosine or ATP may function as a first messenger comes from several sources. Various studies have indicated that adenosine or ATP may exert excitatory or inhibitory influences on neurons. Binding studies of adenosine-analogues have permitted identification of adenosine receptors in the brain. Two types of receptor, one that inhibits adenylate cyclase (A_1) and one that stimulates adenylate cyclase (A_2), have been identified. We will discuss the distribution of purinergic systems further in Chaps. 18 and 24.

Dale's Principle

Although the nervous system as a whole can use different substances at different synapses, this is not necessarily true for an individual neuron. The metabolic unity of the neuron would seem to require that it release the same transmitter substance at all its synapses. This is *Dale's Principle* and, since it can be easily misunderstood, it is well to quote the original formulation. In a review of synaptic transmission in the autonomic nervous system many years ago, Dale (1935) wrote

. . . the phenomena of regeneration appear to indicate that the nature of the chemical function, whether cholinergic or adrenergic, is characteristic for each particular neurone, and unchangeable. When we are dealing with two different endings of the same sensory neurone, the one peripheral and concerned with vasodilatation and the other at a central synapse, can we suppose that the discovery and identification of a chemical transmitter of axon-reflex dilation would furnish a hint as to the nature of the transmission process at a central synapse? The possibility has at least some value as a stimulus to further experiment.

The principle implies that during development some process of differentiation determines the particular secretory product a given neuron will manufacture, store, and release (see Chap. 9). The usefulness of the principle in the analysis of synaptic circuits is explicit in Dale's statement, for, if a substance can be established as the transmitter at one synapse, it can be inferred to be the transmitter at all other synapses made by that neuron.

Dale's law applies only to the presynaptic unity of the neuron; it does not apply to the postsynaptic actions the transmitter will have at the synapses made by the neuron onto different target neurons. These actions may be similar, or they may be different. Several possibilities for diversity of action exist for the transmitter released from a single neuron. Such neurons have been termed *multiaction cells,* and have been particularly well studied in inverte-

brates. Eric Kandel (1976) has summarized the conclusions from this work as follows:

1. The sign of the synaptic action is not determined by the transmitter but by the properties of the receptors on the postsynaptic cell.
2. The receptors in the follower [postsynaptic] cells of a single presynaptic neuron can be pharmacologically distinct and can control different ionic channels.
3. A single follower cell may have more than one kind of receptor for a given transmitter, with each receptor controlling a different ionic conductance mechanism.

As a result of these three features, cells can mediate opposite synaptic actions to different follower cells or to a single follower cell.

These may be regarded as corollaries to Dale's Principle.

What of the possibility of cells with multiple transmitters? Among invertebrates, four putative transmitters have been reported in single neurons of *Aplysia.* In the vertebrate, there is increasing evidence, especially from the extensive studies of Tomas Hökfelt and his co-workers in Stockholm, for the presence of more than one transmitter substance in single nerve terminals in many parts of the nervous system. As we have already discussed above, a common pattern appears to be the presence of one or more peptides within a monoamine-containing terminal (an example of the way this has been demonstrated is shown in Fig. 8.9). The fact that some synaptic terminals contain more than one type of synaptic vesicle is also suggestive in this regard.

These findings do not negate the idea expressed by Dale that the neuron has a metabolic unity; the fact that the unity subsumes the ability of a neuron to manufacture and release more than one kind of neuroactive substance may therefore be recognized as Dale's Modified Principle. However, if different substances could be released at different sites (for example, one substance from dendrites and another from axons), this would violate the *functional* unity of the neuron implied by Dale's Principle. Since the functional unity of the neuron has already been disproved by the evi-

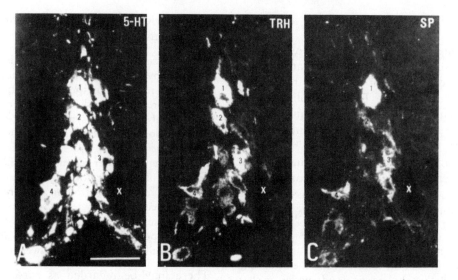

Fig. 8.9 Immunocytochemical demonstration of neuroactive peptides. Parts A–C are consecutive thin sections of the raphe nucleus in the medulla oblongata, treated with antisera to serotonin (**A**), thyroid hormone releasing hormone (**B**), and substance P (**C**). Several cells (1–4), identifiable in all three sections, can be seen to be immunoreactive to all three antisera. X marks a blood vessel, used to orient the slides. Arrows point to a process emanating from cell 1. (From Johansson et al., 1981)

dence for semi-independent synaptic input–output units within the dendritic trees of many neurons (see Chap. 4), it would not be unreasonable to expect that some of these units might release different neuroactive substances, or combinations of substances. The possibility could at least serve as a stimulus to further experiment.

Neuropeptides

One of the most important developments of recent years in neurobiology has been recognition of the widespread distribution of *neuroactive peptides* in the nervous system. Many of these compounds were identified in other organs by biochemists working over the past 50 years or so, and were only recently identified in the nervous system. The names of these compounds, such as vasopressin or prostaglandin, reflect the organ in which they were first found or the physiological action that was first studied. Similarly, some have names, like luteinizing hormone releasing hormone (LHRH), reflecting one specific function of the nervous

system. A number of peptides previously identified in the gut have turned up in the central nervous system. Thus, the nomenclature for these substances can be somewhat confusing.

Like neurotransmitters, peptides can be identified as neuroactive substances only by meeting certain criteria. Although there is no set number of these, the list in Table 8.3 can serve as a useful guide. It begins with a bioassay, which involves procedures for extraction and testing which are actually quite stringent. Separation and purification of the peptide have traditionally depended on a number of chromatographic techniques and other standard and advanced biochemical methodologies. However, these have been largely replaced by recombinant DNA technology, because it is now much faster to sequence the cDNA and synthesize the protein from it than to sequence the protein itself. The localization of peptides in neural tissue relies on immunological methods; the high sensitivity and high specificity of monoclonal antibodies has been of great advantage in this

Table 8.3 Steps in identification of neurotransmitters and neuropeptides

Neurotransmitters	Neuropeptides
1. *Anatomical:* presence of the substance in appropriate amounts in presynaptic processes.	1. Development of a quantitative bioassay.
2. *Biochemical:* presence and operation of enzymes that synthesize the substance in the presynaptic neuron and processes, and remove or inactivate the substance at the synapse.	2. Evidence that the biologically active material is peptidic in nature.
3. *Physiological:* demonstration that physiological stimulation causes the presynaptic terminal to release the substance, and that ionophoretic application of the substance to the synapse in appropriate amounts mimics the natural response.	3. Development of extraction and separation procedures for maximum yields of the purified peptide.
4. *Pharmacological:* drugs that affect the different enzymatic or biophysical steps have their expected effects on synthesis, storage, release, action, inactivation, and reuptake of the substance.	4. Chemical and physical characterization of the pure peptide (e.g., molecular weight determination and amino acid composition).
	5. Determination of amino acid sequence of the peptide.
	6. Chemical synthesis of the peptide (which is then tested for bioactivity using quantitative bioassay).
	7. Production of antibodies to peptide.
	8. Characterization of antibodies using synthetic analogues of the peptide (purification of antibodies).
	9. Development of immunological assays and procedures for use on neural tissues (e.g., radioimmunoassay and immunocytochemistry).

From Gainer and Brownstein (1981)

work. The ability of a substance to evoke a response when experimentally applied to a neuron is a final, and important, criterion in the identification of a peptide as being involved in the normal function of a given type of synapse or neuron.

Some of the best known neuroactive peptides are summarized in Fig. 8.10. This represents only a modest proportion of the neuroactive peptides in the brain which probably total over 50, and may reach 100 or more. There is, in fact, no definitive list; a recent review of peptides (Cooper et al., 1987) prompted the comment: "We write with pencil in one hand and eraser in the other!" It can be seen that many of the peptides contain 2–10 amino acids, and thus overlap in size with small amino acid transmitters, on the one hand, and hormones on the other.

The large numbers of peptides, and their idiosyncratic names, give the impression that this is a heterogeneous collection of substances. However, the more that is learned about them, the more it is possible to discern some powerful unifying principles underlying their functions. First, neuroendocrine cells, secreting peptides, were among the first kinds of neurons to appear in the evolution of primitive nervous systems. Second, neuropeptides are strongly conserved in phylogeny, so that similar substances or similar amino acid sequences appear in different species, both invertebrate and vertebrate. Third, many peptides of the nervous system are also found in other tissues of the body, such as the gut, as already mentioned. This has suggested that many peptidergic neurons may derive embryologically from a common type of neuroectodermal precursor cell, a cell characterized biochemically by "amine precursor uptake and decarboxylation: APUD." Finally, neuroactive peptides as a class share certain biochemical and physiological properties. Table 8.1 summarizes some of these, and contrasts them with properties of neurotransmitters.

With this as a general orientation to neuroactive peptides, let us consider in more detail the main aspects of their synthesis and mechanism of action.

CARNOSINE
(Ala)(His)

THYROTROPIN RELEASING HORMONE (TRH)
p(Glu)(His)(Pro) NH₂

Met-ENKEPHALIN
(Tyr)(Gly)(Gly)(Phe)(Met)

Leu-ENKEPHALIN
(Tyr)(Gly)(Gly)(Phe)(Leu)

ANGIOTENSIN II
(Asp)(Arg)(Val)(Tyr)(Ile)(His)(Pro)(Phe) NH₂

CHOLECYSTOKININ-LIKE PEPTIDE
(Asp)(Tyr)(Met)(Gly)(Trp)(Met)(Asp)(Phe) NH₂
SO₃H

Ala	ALANINE	Leu	LEUCINE
Arg	ARGININE	Lys	LYSINE
Asn	ASPARAGINE	Met	METHIONINE
Asp	ASPARTIC ACID	Phe	PHENYLALANINE
Cys	CYSTEINE	Pro	PROLINE
Gln	GLUTAMINE	Ser	SERINE
Glu	GLUTAMIC ACID	Thr	THREONINE
Gly	GLYCINE	Trp	TRYPTOPHAN
His	HISTIDINE	Tyr	TYROSINE
Ile	ISOLEUCINE	Val	VALINE

OXYTOCIN
(Ile) (Tyr)(Cys)
(Gln)(Asn)(Cys)(Pro)(Leu)(Gly) NH₂

VASOPRESSIN
(Phe) (Tyr)(Cys)
(Gln)(Asn)(Cys)(Pro)(Arg)(Gly) NH₂

LUTEINIZING-HORMONE RELEASING HORMONE (LHRH)
p(Glu)(His)(Trp)(Ser)(Tyr)(Gly)(Leu)(Arg)(Pro)(Gly) NH₂

SUBSTANCE P
(Arg)(Pro)(Lys)(Pro)(Gln)(Gln)(Phe)(Phe)(Gly)(Leu)(Met) NH₂

NEUROTENSIN
p(Glu)(Leu)(Tyr)(Glu)(Asn)(Lys)(Pro)(Arg)(Arg)(Pro)(Tyr)(Ile)(Leu)

BOMBESIN
p(Glu)(Gln)(Arg)(Leu)(Gly)(Asn)(Gln)(Trp)(Ala)(Val)(Gly)(His)(Leu)(Met) NH₂

SOMATOSTATIN
(Ala)(Gly)(Cys)(Lys)(Asn)(Phe)(Phe) (Trp)
(Cys)(Ser)(Thr)(Phe)(Thr) (Lys)

VASOACTIVE INTESTINAL POLYPEPTIDE (VIP)
(His)(Ser)(Asp)(Ala)(Val)(Phe)(Thr)(Asp)(Asn)(Tyr)(Thr)(Arg)(Leu)(Arg)(Lys)(Gln)(Met)(Ala)(Val)(Lys)(Lys)(Tyr)(Leu)(Asn)(Ser)(Ile)(Leu)(Asn) NH₂

β-ENDORPHIN
(Tyr)(Gly)(Gly)(Phe)(Met)(Thr)(Ser)(Glu)(Lys)(Ser)(Gln)(Thr)(Pro)(Leu)(Val)(Thr)(Leu)(Phe)(Lys)(Asn)(Ala)(Ile)(Val)(Lys)(Asn)(Ala)(His)(Lys)(Lys)(Gly)(Gln)

ACTH (CORTICOTROPIN)
(Ser)(Tyr)(Ser)(Met)(Glu)(His)(Phe)(Arg)(Tyr)(Gly)(Lys)(Pro)(Val)(Gly)(Lys)(Lys)(Arg)(Arg)(Pro)(Val)(Lys)(Val)(Tyr)(Pro)(Asp)(Gly)(Ala)(Glu)(Asp)(Glu)(Leu)(Ala)(Glu)(Ala)(Phe)(Pro)(Leu)(Glu)(Phe) NH₂

Fig. 8.10 Neuroactive peptides, arranged in order of increasing number of carbon atoms. (Modified from Iversen, 1979)

Table 8.4 Properties of neurotransmitters and neuropeptides

Properties of neurotransmitters	Properties of neuropeptides
medium to high concentration	extremely low concentration
high-affinity binding to receptors	low-affinity binding to receptors
low potency	extremely high potency
high specificity	high specificity
moderate rate of synthesis	low rate of synthesis (*in vitro*)
small molecules (2–10 carbons)	small to medium-size molecules (2–100 carbons)

Adapted in part from Reichelt and Edminson (1977)

Synthesis

In comparison with the transmitter substances discussed above, synthesis of neuroactive peptides is more complicated. Let us take the opioid peptides as an example. Synthesis of these molecules (see Fig. 8.11) follows the plan for peptide hormones in which amino acids are first assembled by the ribosomes into a large polypeptide *prehormone*. This is then reduced in the Golgi body to a somewhat smaller *prohormone*, which in turn is cleaved into fragments that are the active peptides, and secreted in vesicles. This general sequence has been shown to apply to the manufacture of most neuroactive peptides. Note that, as a general rule, synthesis of neuropeptides requires gene activation, DNA transcription, and RNA translation, with the final peptide being transported from soma to release sites, as previously reviewed in Chap. 3. This is an important distinction, as compared with most transmitter substances which can be synthesized immediately by cytosolic enzymes, often at synaptic sites, more under the influence of local activity states than global genetic control.

Receptors

We have seen that most neurotransmitters can bind to and activate more than one kind of receptor; the same applies to neuropeptides. The opiate receptors illustrate very nicely this principle of multiple receptor types.

In 1975, several laboratories reported biochemical studies showing that there are receptors in the brain that specifically bind morphine, the substance known since time immemorial as both pain-killing and addicting. Did the brain evolve receptors just to bind this substance, or are there neurons that secrete morphinelike substances (called "endorphins")? This was soon answered, still in 1975, by the finding in brain extracts of two small pentapeptides, called enkephalins, that had appropriate biochemical specificity in binding assays and analgesic effects when injected into animals. Both enkephalin and endorphin amino acid sequences are contained within the precursor molecule β-lipotropin. It is only recently with the application of recombinant DNA methods that we know that the enkephalins and endorphins and related peptides arise not from one but from three separate genes, in the manner already indicated in Fig. 8.11.

It did not take long after the identification of different opioid peptides for different types of receptors to be postulated and analyzed. Receptors were characterized by the physiological responses of different peripheral tissues such as the vas deferens, to morphine agonists and antagonists. These tissues then served as bioassay systems for testing for opioid peptides in extracts of different brain regions. From such studies it became apparent that there are several types of receptors. These types have been

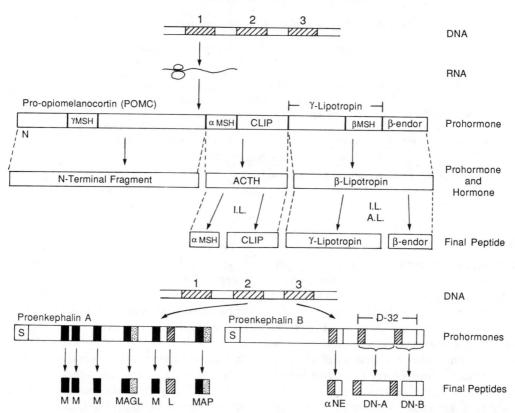

Fig. 8.11 Pathways for biosynthesis of opioid peptides. These arise from three genes. Gene 1 (above) gives rise to a precursor molecule termed pro-opiomelanocortin (POMC). Posttranslational processing produces the peptides shown: α-, β-, and γ-melanophore stimulating hormone (MSH); β-endorphin; ACTH; and corticotropin-like intermediate lobe peptide (CLIP). The enkephalins (below) arise from two other genes that code for proenkephalins A and B: M, met-enkephalin (Tyr-Gly-Gly-Phe-Met); L, leu-enkephalin (Tyr-Gly-Gly-Phe-Leu); MAGL (M-Arg-Gly-Leu; MAP (M-Arg-Phe); α-neoendorphin (OLNE); dynorphin A (DN-A); dynorphin B (DN-B); dynorphin 32 (D-32). I.L., intermediate lobe of pituitary; A.L., anterior lobe of pituitary. (Based on Marx, 1983)

further analyzed in brain slice preparations, in which single-neuron activity can be recorded during application of different pharmacological agents, as explained in Chap. 6.

A summary of three main types of opioid receptors and their mechanisms of action is provided in Fig. 8.12. The mechanism at this peptidergic synapse begins in the presynaptic neuron with the synthesis ①, storage ②, and release ③ of the opioid peptide. The different types of receptors ④ are shown as if they are all on one postsynaptic neuron, though of course in ac-

tuality each is specific for different types of postsynaptic neurons.

The mu (μ) receptor is defined by the fact that it preferentially binds morphine and its antagonist, naloxone, with a dissociation equilibrium constant (K_d) of around 1 nM. Activation of this receptor leads, through a cAMP second messenger system, to opening of K^+ channels, which reduces the excitability and the impulse firing rate of the postsynaptic cell or neuron. The sigma (σ) receptor similarly opens K^+ channels; it differs from the μ receptor in having different binding characteristics

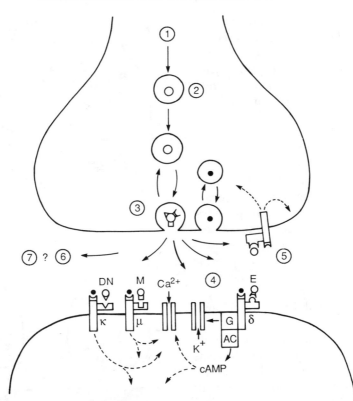

Fig. 8.12 Molecular mechanism of a peptidergic synapse, as exemplified by opioid peptides: ①, synthesis in cell body; ②, transport and storage in vesicles (see Fig. 3.14); ③, release by exocytosis; corelease with neurotransmitters at many synapses; ④, binding to one of several types of receptor. M (μ) receptor preferentially binds morphine; it activates cAMP to open K^+ channels and close Ca^{2+} channels. Delta (δ) receptor is similar but binds enkephalin preferentially. K (κ) receptor preferentially binds dynorphin (DN), and acts through second messenger to close Ca^{2+} channels. Not shown are two other types, γ and ϵ. (Based on Snyder, 1983; Cooper et al., 1987; Aghajanian and Rasmussen, 1987; and other sources)

for agonists, particularly enkephalins (see Fig. 8.12 and legend). The kappa (κ) receptor preferentially binds the endorphin substance dynorphin (DN). Activation of this receptor leads to a closing of Ca^{2+} channels and a reduction in Ca^{2+} current. This has the effect of shortening Ca^{2+} impulses and reduces the amount of transmitter released from the postsynaptic cell. Thus, different receptor types can achieve similar effects on cell excitability and transmitter release by controlling different ionic channels. As Alan North of the Massachusetts Institute of Technology has observed, these actions are not unique to opioid peptides; they are also produced by acetylcholine and monoamines in different cells. The opioid peptides may also act on presynaptic receptors at some synapses, to bring about negative feedback through modulation of presynaptic Ca^{2+} channels, as indicated in Fig. 8.12.

The distribution of the different types of opioid receptors in the brain, and their behavioral effects, will be discussed in Chap. 24.

The mechanisms illustrated in Fig. 8.12 are examples of the variety of mechanisms in which neuropeptides are involved. In these examples, the effect on the receptors is to inhibit the postsynaptic cell; by contrast, the actions of other peptides bring about a decrease in the K^+ currents, which renders the postsynaptic cell more excitable (see Chaps. 17 and 18).

Multiple Messenger Mechanisms

From our discussion of Dale's Modified Principle, we have learned that a single neuron may secrete both a neurotransmitter and one or more neuroactive peptides. In recent years, it has been realized that corelease combined with multiple receptors provides the means for greatly amplifying the complexity of actions and the levels of control at a single synapse.

Some of these possibilities are summarized in the diagrams of Fig. 8.13. In A is shown the classical view: this synapse functions through a single transmitter that acts at a postsynaptic receptor and an autoreceptor, when driven by depolarizing input (arrow). Now take the case of a terminal in which there is coexistence of a peptide. Assume, as in B, that at a given level of input (say, a slightly higher frequency of impulses travelling down the axon and invading the terminal) there is corelease of the peptide. There are several sites at which this peptide may act. As shown in B, it may act on the presynaptic side, to block the autoreceptors for the transmitter, thus freeing the terminal from feedback inhibition, and leading to increased transmitter release and increased postsynaptic response. Alternatively, it may act on the postsynaptic terminal, as shown in C. Here it could change the affinity of the transmitter receptor, or it could act on a separate receptor that is linked to a common second messenger system. Finally, as shown in D, the peptide may have independent actions on membrane receptors, or on cytosolic receptors which in turn act on the nucleus (this applies especially to steroid hormones), and there may also be direct actions in the nucleus.

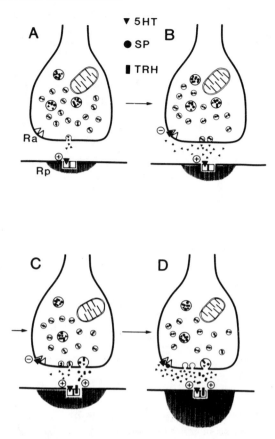

Fig. 8.13 Schematic representation of a nerve ending in the ventral horn containing 5HT, TRH, and substance P (SP), whereby the small vesicles (diameter about 500 Å) contain only 5HT and the larger vesicles (diameter about 1000 Å) contain, in addition, substance P and TRH. An attempt is made to illustrate a sequence of events occurring hypothetically when presynaptic nervous impulse activity is increased. **A.** At low frequency, small numbers of 5HT molecules, released from small synaptic vesicles, cause a small activation ⊕ of the postsynaptic receptor (R_p). **B.** Increased release of 5HT results in activation of the presynaptic autoreceptor (R_a) ⊖, which inhibits further 5HT release and prevents a larger postsynaptic response. Further increase in impulse traffic may activate large vesicles and release TRH and substance P, whereby (**C**) TRH acts together with 5HT on postsynaptic receptors, and (**D**) substance P blocks the inhibitory 5HT autoreceptor, resulting in a profound postsynaptic activation. (Figure and legend from Hökfelt et al., 1984)

These cover only a few of the possible actions of peptides and their relations with transmitters. An important point is that the action of a peptide may not be manifest by itself, but rather in its interaction with the neurotransmitter. The student should be sure to see this point in working through the examples of Fig. 8.13B and C. This means that experimentally it tends to be difficult to demonstrate the physiological function of a peptide unless the experimental conditions are precisely right. Also, the action of a peptide may involve effects on metabolism or growth, as implied in D, and therefore be on a time scale different from that being examined in an acute experiment in which one is looking at a neuronal response to rapid application of a substance.

The Synapse as a Multicellular Organelle

The general conclusion arising out of these considerations is that the synapse is not a simple link or valve between two neurons. Rather, it is a complex organelle in its own right, unique, among cellular organelles, in being constructed by the coordinated interaction of two or more cells. This fact puts developmental constraints on its construction, as we shall see in Chap. 9. However, it also confers an enormous flexibility in construction. As we have seen, the key sources of this flexibility are the multiple messengers that may be released from the presynaptic side, the multiple receptors that may be present on the postsynaptic and presynaptic side, and the multiple second-messenger systems that link the receptors to the electromechanical, metabolic, and genetic machinery of the postsynaptic (and presynaptic) neuron.

In view of these considerations, it seems appropriate to recognize the synapse as a multicellular organelle. Like other organelles, such as the mitochondrion or the nucleus, it satisfies certain basic criteria: it is an anatomical entity, it has a distinct biochemical composition, and it has specific functions. An important point, which can be appreciated in Fig. 8.13, is that it has multiple points of control, a property that is essential for coordinated function. As an organelle, it has intrinsic functions of synthesis, storage, and reception, driven by local processes of metabolism and growth in its participating neurons, as well as evoked functions prompted by more rapid electrical signals.

This view helps us to appreciate the synapse as a building block of nervous circuits, as we discussed in Chaps. 1 and 4. It will help us to understand how synaptogenesis is a main goal of neuronal development (Chap. 9), and how the synapse is adapted for different information-processing functions in the sensory, motor, and central systems we will study in the remainder of this book.

Time Courses of Action

As is obvious from our discussion above, the time courses of action of neuroactive substances vary over a wide range. This is summarized schematically in Fig. 8.14. The time courses of action of the classical neurotransmitters, such as acetylcholine, represent the briefest types. The slower actions of neurotransmitters overlap with the periods of facilitation and depression that occur in the aftermath of activity, and with the effects mediated by peptides and hormones. These in turn overlap with trophic effects, and with the neuronal interactions that underlie such processes as development and plasticity.

Figure 8.14 illustrates further the problem that can arise in defining a neurotransmitter. Thus, to the traditional criteria mentioned previously, one must now add another dimension: the time course of action. Brief actions are more characteristic of neurotransmitters, whereas long-term effects are more representative of neuromodulators. For substances, such as the monoamines, whose actions generally fall between

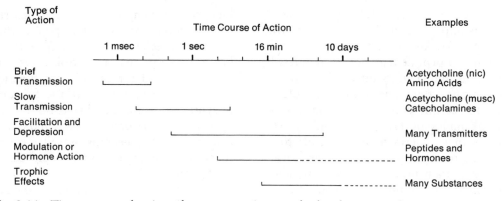

Fig. 8.14 Time courses of action of neurotransmitters and related compounds.

these two extremes, the term neurotransmodulator has even been suggested!

Although this profusion of time courses of action thus complicates our terminology, it is nonetheless telling us something very important about how the nervous system works. Animal behavior involves a wide range of time courses of action. Sensory systems are organized to receive and process information extremely quickly, often within milliseconds. Motor systems similarly provide for very rapid movements, also in the millisecond range, such as those made in typewriting or playing a piano. On the other hand, some movements are very slow; examples are the maintenance of a standing posture, or the prolonged contraction of muscles of a clam that close the shell. The same applies to central systems, from the quick initiation of a voluntary movement, to the slow modulation of states of sleep or arousal during the day and night, to the gradual changes that occur during development, maturation, and aging. One of the most profound questions about the nervous system is how it coordinates all these activities taking place simultaneously within the same neurons and neural circuits. At least part of the answer appears to be that it utilizes different substances with actions on different receptors with different time courses, as we have discussed above.

Transport of Substances

Closely related to synaptic transmission and its associated metabolic processes is the transport of substances within the nerve cell. Far from being the static structure visualized in microscopic sections, the neuron at the molecular level is in constant motion. As noted in the discussion of cell organelles in Chap. 3, there is ongoing synthesis of transmitter molecules, macromolecules, and vesicle membranes in the cell body, and movement out into the axon and dendrites (see Fig. 8.15). Some of these substances pass out of axon terminals and are taken up by postsynaptic cells, as shown by transneuronal transport of labeled amino acids incorporated into protein. Proteins and small enzymes also are taken up by axon terminals and move in the axon toward the cell body; this is the basis of the mapping of axonal projections by the horseradish peroxidase technique. A similar movement of substances takes place in dendrites, involving transmitters, enzymes, and even such large molecules as nucleoside derivatives. Some of these substances are those taken up from neighboring terminals by transneuronal transport. Ions and small molecules move directly between cells through the channels of gap junctions. Thus, there is constant biochemical transport and communication between all parts of the

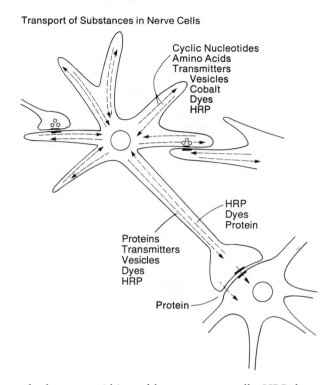

Transport of Substances in Nerve Cells

Cyclic Nucleotides
Amino Acids
Transmitters
Vesicles
Cobalt
Dyes
HRP

HRP
Dyes
Protein

Proteins
Transmitters
Vesicles
Dyes
HRP

Protein

Fig. 8.15   Transport of substances within and between nerve cells. HRP, horseradish peroxidase.

neuron and between neighboring neurons.

These movements take place at different rates. Axoplasmic transport, in mammals, as noted in Chap. 3, ranges from slow (about 1 mm/day) to fast (100–400 mm/day). What do these rates tell us about how quickly events are taking place at the molecular level? This can be answered if we plot distance against time on logarithmic scales, as in Fig. 8.16. The fastest transport in axons, of 400 mm/day, thus translates to a rate of about 5 μm/sec. Surprisingly, this is similar to the rate that has been estimated for diffusion of phospholipids in the cell membrane, as shown in the graph. Slow transport is at a rate of 0.01 μm (10 nm)/sec; this is even slower than the estimated rate of diffusion of proteins in the cell membrane. These values serve to emphasize that the membrane, as well as the internal cell substance, is in dynamic flux.

With regard to transport of synaptic transmitters across the vesicular membrane, this would take many minutes even by fast transport in the shortest axons (that are a millimeter or less in length), and would be a matter of hours in the longest axons. This helps to explain why axonal terminals contain some of their own metabolic machinery for transmitter synthesis and reuptake. In the case of output synapses from dendrites, however, the distances from the cell body are characteristically less than one millimeter, and the synapses could seem to be able to draw more directly on the metabolic resources of the cell body for sustaining their activity. For output synapses from the cell body itself, this of course becomes obvious.

Other rates are also shown in Fig. 8.16, for comparison. Note that the slowest rate of nerve conduction is more than five orders of magnitude faster than the fastest axonal transport; even the slowest impulses travel a micron in less than a microsecond. Synaptic transmitter diffusion through the cleft (see earlier in this chapter) works out

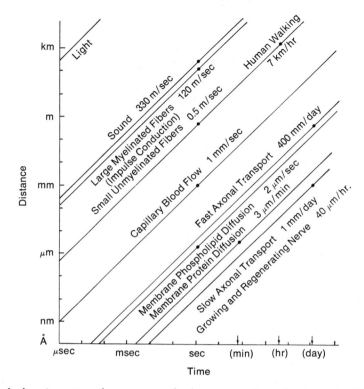

Fig. 8.16 Graph showing rates of movement of substances and conduction of activity for different dimensions of time and space. Small dots indicate values used for common expressions for rates.

to a rate about one micron (micrometer) per millisecond, similar to the rate of capillary blood flow. The reader can insert other rates and relations as well. The general principle, that physiological processes at molecular levels take place in incredibly short times, is readily apparent. It is also the reason why the time domain for microelectrode and single-channel analysis of synaptic functions commonly falls into the range of milliseconds.

Energy Metabolism and 2-Deoxyglucose Mapping

The vertebrate brain is virtually completely dependent on glucose for energy metabolism. Glucose is taken up by neurons and phosphorylated by hexokinase to glucose-6-phosphate. As in other cells of the body, it is then metabolized in the cytosol through the glycolytic chain to pyruvate, which enters the mitochondria and undergoes oxi-

dative metabolism by the Krebs cycle to yield high-energy phosphates. The initial steps in this sequence are indicated in Fig. 8.17. The high-energy phosphate is incorporated into adenosine triphosphate (ATP) and made available for the ongoing metabolism of the neuron and for the immediate demands related to nervous activity.

What types of activity require energy? We have seen that ions move passively through their conductance channels in the membrane; however, the concentration gradients are maintained by the metabolic pump, which requires energy. The squid giant axon can continue to generate action potentials for hours after metabolic poisoning, because the passive ion flows are small compared with the large amounts of available ions. The flows are proportionately larger in smaller fibers, with their larger surface-to-volume ratios; in the finest unmyelinated fibers, impulse activity therefore places immediate demands on the met-

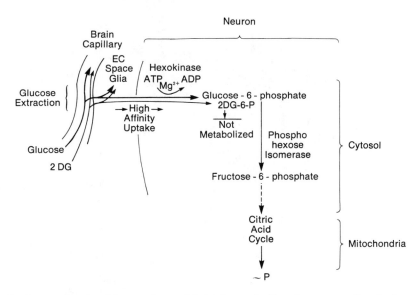

Fig. 8.17 Pathways involved in uptake and initial metabolism in nerve cells of glucose and the analogue, 2-deoxyglucose.

abolic pump. Similar factors are involved at synapses; the ion flows themselves may be passive, but the restoration and maintenance of ion concentrations require energy, as does the synthesis of transmitters and the recycling of membrane. Also, higher rates of ion pumping may be expected at sites where the resting membrane potential is relatively low because of an increased permeability to Na (as at nodes of Ranvier, and in retinal receptors). The high density of mitochondria in the small processes of axons and dendrites reflects to a large extent the energy demands of synapses at those sites.

These types of activity thus have immediate energy demands, and there is a method that uses this property to map the distribution of activity in the brain during different functional states. The method was introduced by Louis Sokoloff and his colleagues at the National Institutes of Health, and makes use of an analogue of glucose, 2-deoxyglucose (2DG), which simply lacks an oxygen on the second carbon atom. As shown in Fig. 8.17, 2DG is taken up like glucose and, is phosphorylated by hexokinase. However, the resulting 2DG-6-P is

not a substrate for phosphoglucose isomerase and cannot be metabolized further; it is trapped in the tissue. Sokoloff and his colleagues reasoned that if 2DG was labeled with radioactive carbon (^{14}C) and injected in tracer amounts into an animal, the sites of increased [14C] 2DG-6-P could be marked by exposing sections of the brain tissue to X-ray film. As many sections can be made as desired, so that the activity pattern associated with a particular functional state can be mapped throughout the entire brain.

The method has been applied to many systems. Among the most dramatic results are those that have been obtained in the visual system. A monkey is injected a day after one eye has been removed. The autoradiograms of the visual cortex show alternating dark and light stripes, which represent the ocular dominance columns that had previously been demonstrated by elec trophysiology and anatomical methods (see Chap. 16). These results are shown in Fig. 8.18A. For comparison, the method has also been successfully applied to the olfactory system, where relatively little was known about spatial activity patterns. Sur-

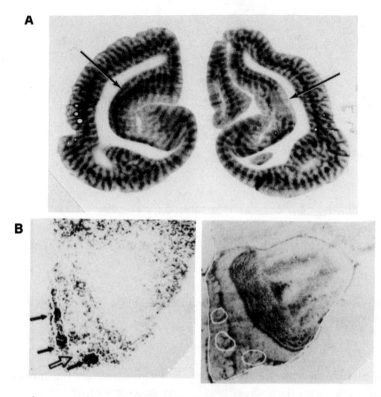

Fig. 8.18   Autoradiograms obtained using the [^{14}C]2-deoxyglucose method. **A.** Monkey visual cortex after removal of one eye. Arrows indicate blind spots. (From Sokoloff, 1977) **B.** Rat olfactory bulb after exposure to odor of amyl acetate. *Left:* Autoradiogram showing three small dense foci (arrows) and intervening light region (open arrow). *Right:* Outlines of dense foci fall precisely on small groups of glomeruli when superimposed on Nissl-stained section of bulb. (From Stewart et al., 1979)

prisingly, after an injection into a rat breathing an odor, small intense foci of activity are found in the olfactory bulb over the glomerular layer, where the axons from the olfactory receptor cells terminate. These results are shown in Fig. 8.18B (see Chap. 11 for further discussion of olfactory bulb function).

These results indicate the power of this method for confirming and extending our previous knowledge about particular systems, and for providing new insights into systems in which information about spatial activity patterns has not been obtainable by other methods. The applications of this and related methods range from the analysis of local circuit organization to the identification of activity patterns underlying cognition, as we shall see in Chap. 30.

9

Developmental
Neurobiology

How do the structures and functions of the nervous system develop? This is a fascinating subject that addresses the age-old question of how the organism arises out of the interplay between nature and nurture, between genes and environment. In addition, it is of practical importance, because knowledge of how the nervous system is assembled often gives insight into the mature system, and it also tells us what goes wrong in nervous and mental diseases that have a genetic basis. The new tools of molecular biology make developmental mechanisms accessible as never before, and provide thereby the hope not only of understanding normal development, but also of intervening to correct for genetic disorders.

A Brief History

The study of the developing nervous system began with the first microscopic investigations of the nineteenth century. One of the greatest of the early pioneers was Wilhelm His, a Swiss who worked in Leipzig. Much of the work, with many young colleagues, was carried out in his home. It is said that His's microscopic material was of inferior quality, but his ideas were clear and pro-

found. In the 1880s, his description of the axon as an outgrowth from the developing nerve cell was an important step toward the concept of the neuron as a cell and the formulation of the neuron theory. To him also we owe such terms as dendrite, for the branches from the cell body, and neuropil, cell-free regions containing connections between axons and dendrites.

In his abundant investigations of the nervous system, Cajal was fascinated by the development of nerve cells and their connections. He combined study of Golgi-impregnated neurons in the adult with studies of their forms and movements in embryonic tissue, and thus laid the basis for the modern approach to the subject at the cellular level. Figure 9.1 is from his study in the 1890s of the development of granule cells in the vertebrate cerebellum.

This diagram provides a useful summary of the main steps that, from this early date, have been recognized to be involved in neuronal development, or *neurogenesis*. The first step is the sequence of cell divisions that ends with the birth of the neuron (1–2 in Fig. 9.1). This is followed by three types of mechanisms: differentiation of branches, synapses, and functional properties (3–10); growth in size (5–10); and

177

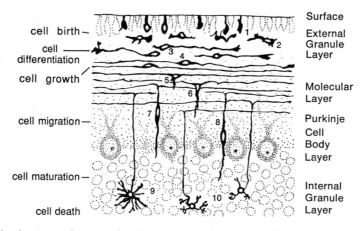

Fig. 9.1   Cajal's diagrams showing the development of granule cells in the mammalian cerebellum. Onset of developmental steps: cell birth and lineage, ①–②; cell differentiation and synaptogenesis, ③–④; cell growth, ⑤–⑥; cell migration, ⑦–⑧; cell maturation, ⑨–⑩; cell death (not shown). After cell birth, the other steps overlap considerably in duration (see text)

migration of the cell to a final position (7–9). These three mechanisms characteristically overlap in time. Maturation of the cell into its final form and function (9–10) is a process that in many animals, especially humans, may last over considerable periods of time. Cell death is an important factor in early maturation as well as in old age.

Early studies were carried out within the field of histology (the light-microscopic study of tissues), and the events in the formation of different tissues were called *histogenesis*. Today, our focus is on the molecular and cellular mechanisms that are involved, and the study of neurogenesis is therefore becoming a branch of molecular and cell biology. Neurogenesis was originally thought to occur primarily during embryonic life, and was therefore regarded as a part of *embryology*. We now realize that events related to neurogenesis and the laying down of neural circuits continue into early life; moreover, as noted above, many of the properties underlying the development of neurons and their functional capacities continue to be expressed throughout life, under normal conditions or in response to injury or aging. We therefore gather all these aspects under the term *developmental neurobiology*, and regard development as

a process that extends throughout most of the life of the animal.

In this chapter, we will consider the mechanisms underlying each of the steps indicated in Fig. 9.1.

Neuronal Birth and Gene Expression

The first step in building a nervous system is to generate nerve cells. An important principle that applies, with few exceptions, is that neurons once generated cannot be replaced; in this regard, the nervous system differs from the liver, skin, or immune system, and resembles other more highly differented organs like the heart and lungs. This means that the determination of whether a cell is to become a neuron, and what type of neuron in which part of the nervous system, must be completed once and for all, relatively early in development. This determination depends on the genes, by the selective process called *gene expression*.

Since every cell in the body carries in its DNA the same complete instructions for the entire body, how is gene expression in neuron precursors selectively controlled to yield cells different from those destined to build other organs? This process, the *reg-*

ulation of gene expression, is thus central to understanding neurogenesis.

The model for this process in prokaryotes goes back to the classical studies of bacteria by François Jacob and Jacques Monod in France in the early 1960s. When bacteria are in an environment rich in galactose (one of their principal nutrient sugars), the enzyme for utilizing this sugar is synthesized in abundance. Jacob and Monod showed that normally the gene for this enzyme is repressed; galactose relieves this repression, so that the gene can be expressed.

At present, it is not clear whether this model applies to the regulation of genes in laying down nerve cells in eukaryotes. One approach has been to look for RNAs that are specific for brain cells. It has been proposed, for example, that brain-specific RNAs could interact with "identifier" sequences of DNA to direct tissue-specific transcription of genes for nerve cells (Sutcliffe et al., 1984).

Another approach has been to analyze cell lineage, from the earliest precursor cells (neuroblasts) to the final mature neurons. In a tiny roundworm, *Caenorhabditis elegans,* the number of neurons is so small (302) that it has been possible to make serial electron microscopic sections through the entire nervous system at every stage of development and trace the lineage of every neuron back to the zygote. This work has been carried out by Sidney Brenner and his colleagues (see Sulston et al., 1983). Partial studies of this nature have been extended to neurons of other species, such as insects (see below), and to certain vertebrate species (for example, studies of Kimmel and his colleagues on cell lineages of motoneurons in the zebra fish: see Kimmel and Warga, 1986).

The results of the studies in invertebrates have been summarized as follows (Purves and Lichtman, 1985):

. . . these studies of lineage underscore the relative stereotyped and programmatic development of invertebrates. Invertebrate cells seem to differentiate nearly immediately—after all,

they have only a few divisions in which to create the finished product . . . Consistent with rapid differentiation is the . . . limited ability of invertebrate embryos to replace missing cell lines following ablation. A variety of experiments . . . on developing vertebrates . . . indicate that cells at early stages have a much broader range of fates. This raises the interesting question of whether vertebrates and invertebrates are fundamentally different in this respect.

A general conclusion arising from these studies is that larger brains require many successive cell divisions in order to generate the requisite large number of neurons. This protracted series of cell divisions gives an opportunity for many factors to be involved in determining gene expression and ultimate neuronal phenotype. As pointed out by Easter et al. (1985), these factors include competition between neurons, trophic interactions, and modification by functional activity. One may postulate that these dynamic factors are present to different degrees in the development of most nervous systems, invertebrate and vertebrate, and reach their greatest importance in the human.

Thus, at every developmental stage there is interaction of the genome with the internal state and environment of the cell, which in turn depend on interactions with neighboring cells. An important general conclusion to be drawn from this phenomenon is that development is not simply a reading out of the genetic code. The code probably contains an economical minimum of instructions; as Gunther Stent (1981) has pointed out, they probably serve mainly to set neurons along general paths, with final forms and functions determined by cellular interactions.

Cell Migration

A general rule in the vertebrate nervous system is that neurons do not remain at their site of origin, but rather migrate to their final position. This is a necessary consequence of the fact that the nervous system starts as a thin tube of ectoderm within the embryo (the neural tube), and the final product is a much larger structure (the nervous system). Also, the initial relations between the sites of origin of neurons may be very different from their final relations, as already indicated in the diagrams from Cajal (Fig. 9.1).

An overview of the way that cells differentiate and migrate from their sites of origin is shown in Fig. 9.2. Cells derived from the *neural tube* may be either neuronal precursors destined to be neurons, or glial precursors destined to be glial cells. The neuronal precursors give rise to the different types of neurons—long-axon cells, short-axon cells, and anaxon cells—as indicated at the bottom of the figure. In cortical structures of the vertebrate brain, the neurons migrate to their final positions along radial glia, a type of glia that is transiently expressed during development in order to play this specific guiding role. Mature astrocytes may derive from these or from other glial precursors. The origins of the glial cells responsible for making myelin sheaths—Schwann cells in the periphery and oligodendroglia in the central nervous system—are less well understood. Also associated with the neural tube is a collection of cells called the *neural crest*. The neuroblasts of the neural crest migrate through peripheral tissue and give rise to several types of neurons in the peripheral nervous system, as shown in the figure.

Growth Cones

The considerable displacements that occur during development imply that the cells and their processes actively move. There was keen interest in this question among early investigators. Cajal, with his genius for preparing the right material and drawing the right conclusions, studied single growing fibers in Golgi-impregnated specimens. He saw enlargements at the ends of the fibers, and called them "growth cones." He imagined that the growth cone is endowed with ameboid movements, which enable it to push aside obstacles in its way until it reaches its destination.

The evidence that this in fact is true soon came from the experiments of Ross Harrison at Yale in 1907. Harrison introduced the technique of tissue culture to biology. In pieces of neural tissue excised from the developing nervous system and maintained in artificial media in a dish, he observed the growth cones and the movements that Cajal had hypothesized. The results illustrated in Fig. 9.3A have been repeated and confirmed many times since.

It may be noted that tissue culture methods have become one of the most powerful tools for analysis of neuronal properties. There is always a problem of interpreting the results, because a cell grown under artificial conditions has a form much simpler than its normal counterpart, and its properties may be significantly altered. This problem was discussed at a meeting of the Society for Neuroscience, and drew the cheerful comment from Richard Bunge, one of the leaders in this field, that "There are no artefacts in the culture dish!" This seemingly outrageous claim was made only partly in fun, for it carried the reminder that what one sees in the culture dish is indeed a property of the neuron, perhaps only accessible or expressed under culture conditions.

Detailed studies have begun to reveal the special properties of the growth cone. The molecular organization of the growth cone, as revealed by recent findings, is summarized in Fig. 9.3B. Clockwise, starting at left, we see the nerve process (axon or dendrite: ①) that extends from the cell body. Within are microtubules (MT) and microtubule-associated proteins (MAP-2), which transport vesicles to the cone; the MT are assembled from tubulin monomers (T). The process also contains neurofilaments (NF). Associated with the cytoskeleton ② are actin and myosin, which provide contractility for moving the growth cone. Various membrane receptors ③ are present for GABA, norepinephrine (NE), and certain proteases; through these, target cells can affect growth cone membrane excitability, which is mainly due to voltage-

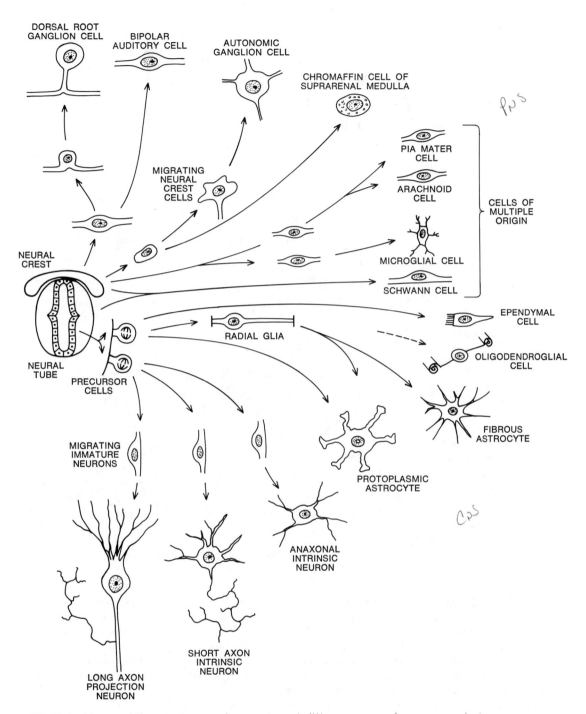

Fig. 9.2 Origin, differentiation, and migration of different types of neurons and glia. (Modified from Crelin, 1974) In this figure, neurons of the peripheral nervous system are shown above, glial cells are shown in the middle, and neurons of the central nervous system are shown below. Note that precursor cells (in the ventricular zone) give rise directly to glial and neuronal lines before these cells migrate during development to their final positions and assume their final forms (Rakic, 1981).

181

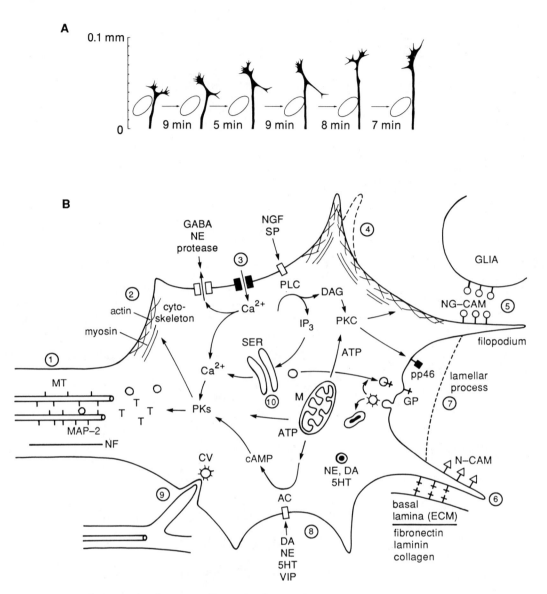

Fig. 9.3 **A.** The growth of a nerve fiber of a frog embryo in tissue culture, as observed under a microscope at intervals of time indicated. Ellipse indicates red blood cell, which did not move. **B.** Molecular organization of the neuronal growth cone, as summarized from recent research. Numbers ① to ⑨ indicate different functional domains and molecular mechanisms. Abbreviations (clockwise from ①): MT, microtubules; MAP-2, microtubule-associated proteins; NF, neurofilaments; NGF, nerve growth factor; SP, substance P; components of the phospholipid second messenger system (PLC, phospholipase C; IP$_3$ inositol triphosphate; DAG, diacylglycerol; PKC, proteinkinase C); NG-CAM, nerve-glia cell adhesion molecule; pp 46, phosphoprotein 46; GP, glycoprotein; N-CAM, nerve cell adhesion molecule; ECM, extracellular matrix; AC, adenylate cyclase; VIP, vasoactive intestinal peptide; CV, coated vesicle; M, mitochondria; SER, smooth endoplasmic reticulum; PK, protein kinases. Abbreviations for neurotransmitters (NE, DA, 5HT) as in Chap. 8. (A from Harrison, 1907; B based on Pfenninger, 1986; Lockerbie, 1987, and personal communication; and many others)

dependent Ca^{2+} channels (see below). Other receptors, for nerve growth factor (NGF) and substance P (SP), are coupled to phospholipase C (PLC). Their activation thus results in changes in concentration of the second messengers inositol triphosphate (IP_3) and diacylglycerol (DAG). These in turn exert their actions through changes in Ca^{2+} and protein kinase C (PKC), respectively. Changes in contractility of the cytoskeleton, bringing about movement of the filopodia ④, may be produced by these second messengers.

The growth cone membrane interacts with its environment through several types of cell-surface molecules. One type is neuron–glia cell adhesion molecule (NG-CAM) ⑤; another is neuron-CAM (N-CAM) ⑥. These and other glycoproteins also interact with constituents of the extracellular matrix (ECM), such as laminin, fibronectin, and collagen. These interactions control the movement of the growth cone through its immediate environment, and the recognition of its target. The various types of membrane glycoproteins (GP) are delivered to the plasmalemma by exocytosis, recycled by endocytosis, and degraded in lysosomes.

Forward moment of the growth cone occurs by extension of filopodia on or through the substrate, followed by formation of lamellar processes which fill in the spaces between the filopodia ⑦. Various kinds of neurotransmitters and neuromodulators act on receptors that use cAMP as a second messenger ⑧. Interactions with other processes appear to include invaginations and budding off of coated vesicles (CV).

Within the growth cone ⑩, organelles perform the basic cell functions described in Chap. 3: mitochondria supply ATP, and the smooth endoplasmic reticulum (SER) sequesters Ca^{2+} and packages vesicles. Various phosphokinases (PK) activate target substrates. Of particular interest is protein pp46, isolated by Karl Pfenninger (1986) at Colorado; this is a major growth-associated membrane protein that is phosphorylated by Ca^{2+}/calmodulin-dependent kinase and PKC. It appears to be identical to phosphoprotein F1, which has been implicated in synaptic plasticity and memory mechanisms (see Chap. 29).

Recent studies have suggested that the growth cone membrane generates Ca^{2+}-mediated action potentials. A nice demonstration of this has been provided by treating cells in culture with voltage-sensitive dyes, and measuring the voltage changes in different parts using a laser microbeam. The results in Fig. 9.4 show that the optical recordings and electrical recordings of presumed Ca^{2+} action potentials are very similar. It is believed that the Ca^{2+} that flows into the cell during the action potential controls the contractility of the actin filaments and the shape and movement of the growth cone and other parts of the neuron.

Cell Growth and Growth Factors

It is clear from the preceding sections that interactions between neurons are critical for many aspects of development. We next inquire how these interactions take place.

Nerve Growth Factor

The first evidence for a specific chemical substance that could stimulate or control neuronal development came from experiments conducted around 1950, which showed that implantation of a type of soft-tissue tumor (sarcoma) from a mouse on one side of the vertebral column of a chick embryo caused enlargement of the spinal ganglion on that side. It was soon established, by Rita Levi-Montalcini, working with Viktor Hamburger in St. Louis, that a humoral agent was involved, and that it specifically stimulated the growth of cells derived from the neural crest. As shown in Fig. 9.2, these include sympathetic ganglion cells, and some dorsal root ganglion cells.

This humoral substance was termed nerve growth factor (NGF). NGF is one of a class of trophic substances, meaning that it affects the general metabolism of neurons. It has been found that NGF's influences come after the mitotic phase of cell proliferation,

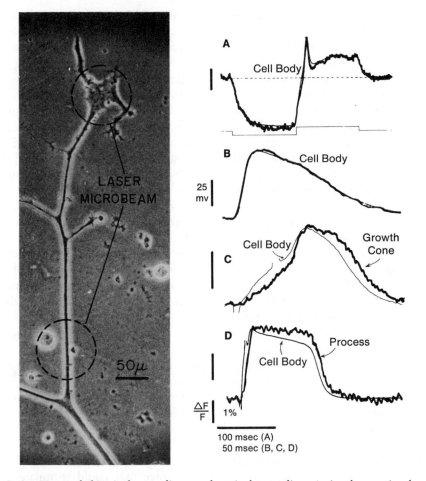

Fig. 9.4 Comparison of electrical recordings and optical recordings (using laser microbeam) from different parts of a neuroblastoma cell growing in culture. Intracellular recordings are shown by thin lines; optical recordings of fluorescence changes obtained by use of oxonal dye in the bathing medium are shown by thick traces. (From Grinvald and Farber, 1981)

and potentially could be exerted on phases of growth, elaboration of processes, maturation, or survival. For example, sympathetic ganglion cells grown in tissue culture show almost no growth in a medium lacking NGF, and ultimately die. If, instead, NGF is added, there is vigorous growth of cell bodies and neurites beginning within a few hours.

These kinds of experiments showed that NGF is produced by target cells, such as gland, muscle, or skin cells. What is the time of NGF production in relation to the ingrowth of the developing nerve fiber, and the time of expression of NGF receptors

on the ingrowing fibers? These questions have been addressed by Hans Thoenen and his colleagues in Munich (Davies et al., 1987), using as a model the developing sensory innervation of the skin surrounding the whiskers in the snout of a fetal rat. First they used in situ hybridization for NGF messenger RNA (see Chap. 2), and found that the onset of transcription in the target skin cells does not precede, but is precisely coincident with, the arrival of the sensory fibers of the trigeminal nerve. Then they assessed the time of expression of NGF receptors by observing binding of radioactively labeled NGF to the sensory neurons;

they found that binding does not occur until after the fibers reach the whisker skin. These results thus suggest that other factors must be primarily responsible for controlling outgrowth and guidance of fibers to their targets, and that NGF is mainly important in the survival of axons during the period in which they compete for target innervation.

What is the molecular basis for the ability of NGF to stimulate nerve fibers and maintain survival? NGF is a peptide, one of the first neuroactive peptides to be sequenced (in 1971). It has a molecular weight of 130,000, and consists of three subunits (α, β, γ), in the ratio 2 : 1 : 2. The neurally active subunit is β; this subunit consists of two monomers, each of MW 13,000. The monomers are 118 amino acids long, and share sequence homologies with insulin and growth factors related to insulin. NGF and insulin may therefore have a common evolutionary precursor. There is evidence that binding of the β subunit to surface receptors on axonal and dendritic membranes enables it to have local effects on the growth of these processes. There is also evidence that NGF is taken up by endocytosis, packaged into vesicles, and retrogradely transported back to the cell body by axoplasmic transport mechanisms (see Fig. 3.9). Within the soma, NGF may affect protein synthesis through several levels of posttranscriptional and posttranslational control; these somatic actions may be responsible for the ability of NGF to promote overall cell growth and survival.

Oncogenes and Neuronal Growth

A separate line of research on factors involved in neuronal development has emerged from the study of genes that control cell growth. Knowledge of these genes originated in studies of viruses. The simplest cases are found in retroviruses. These consist of RNA and reverse transcriptase; when the virus infects a cell, the reverse transcriptase makes first a single complementary DNA followed by a second DNA strand to form a double helix, which is then integrated into a host chromosome (recall that reverse transcriptase is an important tool in recombinant DNA techniques: Chap. 2). The virally derived DNA functions as an oncogene (v-onc); its gene products stimulate unrestrained cell divisions, transforming the normal cell into a cancer cell. The action of oncogenes is therefore mainly on cell proliferation. The use of molecular probes against v-onc has permitted demonstration of the existence of similar DNA sequences in normal cells. These are therefore called proto-oncogenes (or c-onc for cell oncogene), and have control sequences and DNA associated proteins that provide for the orderly and self-terminating gene expression that characterizes normal cell proliferation and growth. We also know that the activity of some of these proto-oncogenes may be related to differentiation and maturation in postmitotic cells. Among these, two called c-fos and c-myc appear to be good candidates.

What is the molecular basis for the mechanism of proto-oncogenes? Of the 100,000 or so functional genes in the human genome, perhaps 100 are involved in the control of growth. This small number suggests that many proto-oncogenes may function like regulator genes, exerting their control by throwing developmental switches or activating families of genes that express different gene products which, acting together, are necessary for coordinated growth.

One of the important developments in recent years is the discovery of relationships that exist between the products of proto-oncogenes, homeotic genes, and various types of growth factors (see Bender, 1985). A key link was forged by experiments to obtain the DNA sequence for a homeotic gene in Drosophila (called Notch) and the nematode Caenorhabditis (called lin-12). The surprising result was that the predicted amino acid sequences of the two gene products from these unrelated animals (showing quite different phenotypes for these gene loci) were similar. Even more surprising, each contained a number of repeated

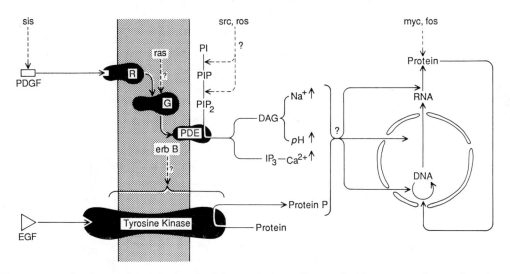

Fig. 9.5 Molecular mechanisms involved in regulating cell growth. Two types of control pathways are shown in the diagram. In one type, activated by platelet-derived growth factor (PDGF), there is a membrane receptor (R) coupled to a common second-messenger cascade, exemplified by a GTP-binding protein (G), phosphodiesterase (PDE), and the second messengers, diacylglycerol (DAG) and inositol triphosphate (IP$_3$). In another type, the extracellular signal, such as epidermal growth factor (EGF), activates a membrane-spanning tyrosine kinase, which phosphorylates a tyrosine residue in a target protein (cf. Fig. 8.4). The actions of these second messengers lead to regulation of DNA replication (mitosis), DNA translation into RNA, or RNA translation into protein, as indicated by the arrows. Several types of oncogenes have disruptive effects at different sties in these growth-regulatory pathways, as indicated by the dashed arrows. Other abbreviations: PI, phosphatidylinositol; PIP, phosphatidylinositol-4-phosphate; PIP$_2$, phosphatidylinositol-4,5-bisphosphate; sis, ras, erb B, src, ros, myc, fos: oncogenes. (Modified from Berridge, 1985)

sequences that showed homology with epidermal growth factor (EGF).

EGF is well-known as a peptide of 53 amino acids. It is derived, in the manner of most peptides (see Chap. 8), from a longer precursor of some 1,200 amino acids, which resembles the precursors for Notch and lin-12 peptides in having multiple EGF-like repeats. EGF binds to an external receptor site on an integral membrane protein that acts as a tyrosine kinase. As we noted in discussing second messengers in Chap. 8, phosphorylation of tyrosine residues appears to be specifically involved in cell growth. Binding of EGF leads to phosphorylation of tyrosine residues in the receptor itself, as well as in other proteins; this acts as a signal to bring about proliferation of several cell types, including fibroblasts and

glia. Virally derived oncogenes bring about proliferation of transformed cells by phosphorylating tyrosine residues in these same proteins.

The evidence from these experiments points to the plasma membrane as the site for reception of peptides involved in regulating neuronal proliferation and growth. Recent work has suggested that several proto-oncogene products act on membrane receptors that are involved in the inositol–diacylglycerol second messenger system. The reader should review this system in Chap. 8 (see Fig. 8.3). Figure 9.5 shows how EGF appears to act on a receptor coupled through a G-type protein to PLC, thereby exerting control over cell proliferation via several actions, including an increase in CA^{2+} concentration and a rise in pH. Other growth factors, proto-oncogene products, and tumor-promoting agents may act at other control points, as indicated in the diagram.

The importance of this work is that it is aimed at the genetic mechanisms that control neuronal development. Some of these mechanisms are concerned with stimulation of cell division, and switching the cell from one developmental fate to another. Others are concerned with stimulation of growth and differentiation, whereas still others are concerned with turning off growth and differentiation when the mature state is reached. Of great interest is the mechanism by which neuronal cell division is finally turned off, never to return. This permanent switch may explain why tumors of the brain arise in glial cells but rarely in nerve cells. We pay dearly for this benefit by losing the ability (with certain exceptions: see below) to generate new neurons to replace those lost to injury or aging. It is hoped that a deeper understanding of proto-oncogenes and growth factors will allow us eventually to achieve that goal.

Cell Differentiation

The third step in neuronal development is the differentiation of specific structures, properties, and connections. This overlaps greatly with other steps; in some cases differentiation is well underway before migration starts. The term is also used by some workers to refer to the whole process of generation of the sequence of neuroblast precursors as well as the events that bring about the final neuronal form. Let us consider several examples that illustrate principles underlying neuronal differentiation.

Cell Fate and Pioneer Fibers

The central nervous system of the grasshopper has been favorable for studies of neural development. The embryonic nerve cord is relatively thin and translucent, which has allowed individual cells and even their growth cones to be visualized under the microscope in the living animal, and intra-cellular electrodes have been introduced for recording and dye injection. The entire sequence of steps, from precursor cell to mature form, has been analyzed for several types of neuron. As illustrated in Fig. 9.6A,B, a ganglion, such as the third thoracic ganglion, contains a specific set of precursor cells. There is a lateral group of 30 neuroblasts (NB), and a midline group of medial precursors (MP) plus a single medial neuroblast (MNB). To the right in the figure, the pattern of cell divisions is indicated. Each MP divides only once. Each NB divides several times to give rise to a chain of ganglion mother cells (GMC); each of these divides into a ganglion cell (GC), which then differentiates to reach its final form as a mature neuron (N). Each NB generates from 10 to 100 progeny according to this fixed pattern, after which it degenerates and dies.

By making intracellular injections of fluorescent dyes at different stages, it has been possible to study the development of axons and dendrites of individual identified neurons. The earliest axonal pathways, connecting neighboring ganglia, are made by "pioneer" cells. One of these is the MP2 cell, as illustrated in Fig. 9.6C. Similarly, sensory neurons in the periphery (PN1) send pioneer fibers to the ganglion. Within the ganglion, later differentiating cells send their axons along the paths laid down by the pioneer axon. As an example, the MP3 cell, which initially lacks any processes, first differentiates an axon at day 6 (see Fig. 9.6D). From day 6 to day 12, there follows an elaboration of the dendritic branches, to reach the final form characteristic of the mature neuron, called an H neuron.

Excitable Properties

Correlated with the differentiation of neuronal form is the acquisition of specific physiological properties. This has been studied in a variety of systems, including muscle cells, neuroblastoma cells in tissue culture, large identified neurons such as

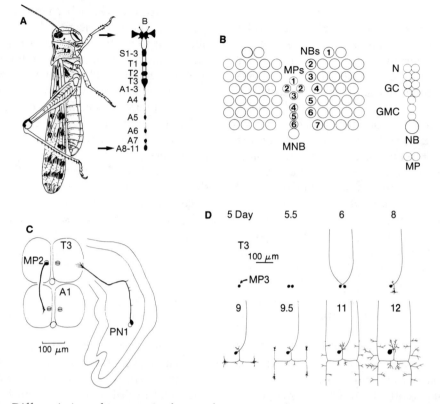

Fig. 9.6 Differentiation of neurons in the grasshopper central nervous system. **A.** Lateral view of grasshopper. Central nervous system, showing brain (B) and associated anterior segmental (S), thoracic (T), and abdominal (A) ganglia. **B.** Identified precursor cells in T3 ganglion, including lateral neuroblasts (NB), medial neuroblast (MNB), and midline precursors (MP). *To the right:* Sequence of cell divisions: MP cells give rise to neurons by a single division; NB cells give rise to sequence of cells, from ganglion mother cells (GMC) to ganglion cells (GC), which differentiate into neurons (N). **C.** "Pioneer" axons laid down by the MP2 cell and a peripheral pioneer neuron (PN1). **D.** Differentiation of MP3 cell into an H neuron from 5 to 12 days of age; drawn from cells injected with Lucifer Yellow. (A–C from Goodman and Bate, 1981; D from Goodman et al., 1981)

Rohon-Beard cells in the frog, and several types of cell in the grasshopper.

A common finding in many studies has been that cells are excitable at early stages of development, and that the inward (depolarizing) current is carried by Ca^{2+}. This has already been pointed out in Chap. 6. At these early stages, the cells are characteristically coupled by gap junctions. The Ca^{2+} spike may be localized in the cell body, or in the growth cone, as discussed above. In some cells the Ca^{2+} spike persists into maturity (for example, in muscle cells). In many systems there is a change to a spike with both a Na^+ and a Ca^{2+} component, and finally one with only a Na^+ component. This particularly applies to projection neurons with long axons. In contrast, many nonspiking cells have inexcitable membranes at all stages of development: alternatively, some pass through earlier stages of excitability.

Some of these relationships are indicated in Fig. 9.7. It should be emphasized that any of these properties may be localized to a particular site in a neuron, a particular stage of development, or in relation to a particular birth date. Thus, there is a pop-

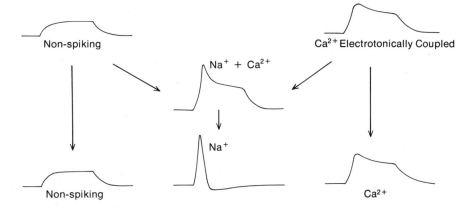

Fig. 9.7 Diagram illustrating some sequences of excitable and nonexcitable properties that have been identified in developing neurons. (Based on Spitzer, 1979)

ulation of dorsal unpaired median (DUM) neurons in grasshoppers, which contains subpopulations of cells depending on their dates of birth from the median neuroblast. The earliest cells to be born have both soma and axon spikes; later come cells with spikes in the dendrites and axon, then cells with only axon spikes, and finally nonspiking neurons. This last cell type is a local-circuit neuron. This is consistent with the pattern, found in many vertebrates, showing that small interneurons are the last to differentiate, and are thus most susceptible to shaping by environmental and other factors (see below).

The presence of Ca^{2+} spikes at early stages of development may be important for the control of the motility of growth cones, as already noted above. In addition, Ca^{2+} must be important in relation to the neurosecretory activity of the developing neuron, and it could also play a role in controlling the insertion of neurotransmitter receptor proteins into the surface membrane. These and other possible functions of Ca^{2+} in the developing neuron may be reviewed in relation to the discussion of Ca^{2+} as a second messenger in Chap. 8.

Transmitter Determination

When and how does a neuron become committed to the neurotransmitter it will use?

Experiments on sympathetic ganglion cells have thrown light on this question. The background for these studies was the demonstration that when "trunk" regions of the neural crest, that normally give rise to sympathetic ganglion cells, were transplanted to anterior regions that normally give rise to vagal (parasympathetic) cells, the normal adrenergic character of the trunk cells was lost. These divisions of the autonomic system are considered in Chap. 18. In cell cultures it was found that if the sympathetic ganglion neurons are maintained in the absence of any other cell type, they develop adrenergic properties; that is, they take up, store, synthesize, and release norepinephrine from their terminals. Furthermore, they form morphological synapses that contain small granular vesicles, like normal adult adrenergic synapses.

In contrast, when the neurons are maintained together (cocultured) with other kinds of cells such as cardiac cells, they develop cholinergic properties. They synthesize up to 1000 times as much acetylcholine as the tiny amounts found in isolated cultured neurons; they make cholinergic synapses onto other neurons or onto muscle cells; and the amount of NE and the number of granular vesicles are greatly reduced. This can occur solely in the presence of medium that contained the cardiac cells or other nonneuronal cells. The medium is thus called *conditioned medium,* and is believed to

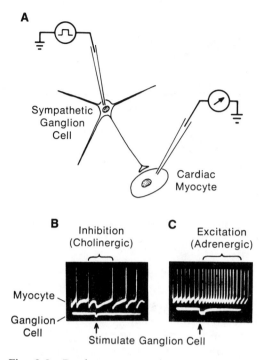

Fig. 9.8 Dual transmitter function of developing sympathetic ganglion cells of the rat. **A.** Schematic diagram showing ganglion cell and cardiac muscle cell. **B.** Normal bathing medium; stimulation of neuron causes inhibition of muscle cell impulse discharge. **C.** Addition of atropine to medium; this blocks inhibition (showing its cholinergic nature), leaving excitation. This was blocked by addition of propranolol to medium (not shown), showing its adrenergic nature. (After Potter et al., 1981)

contain a substance or substances that mediate the effect. By varying the amount of exposure to other cells or conditioned medium, a balance between adrenergic and cholinergic properties in the same cell can be achieved (see Fig. 9.8).

These results show that neural crest cells are potentially "dual function" neurons. Very early in development, these cells may actually synthesize and release both types of transmitter simultaneously. They retain this ability to be adrenergic or cholinergic past the last mitosis, and the expression of one trait or the other is determined by chemical factors in the environment of the cell. These experiments therefore provide evidence at the single-cell level for the ways in which the cell genotype interacts with the environment to produce the cell phenotype.

Development of the Synapse

Making the correct synaptic connections requires a precise coordination between the synaptic nerve process and its postsynaptic target. The factors involved in this coordination have been best studied in the neuromuscular junction, and we will therefore consider this first as a model for the individual synapse. We will then take up the mechanisms for formation of synaptic circuits in the central nervous system.

Studies of the development of neuromuscular junction and of its reaction to nerve transection have made it possible to identify some of the molecular mechanisms that guide the nerve to its target and control the differentiation of the junctional complex. There are four main types of interaction that take place between nerve and muscle, and these are summarized in Fig. 9.9.

Presynaptic Factors

The most obvious factor is the activity of the presynaptic nerve. As indicated in A and B, this may have several effects on the postsynaptic target. It may contribute to the differentiation of the myotube and development into a mature muscle cell, either by release of transmitter or through electrical junctions; it may also help to shape other membrane properties of the muscle. At the junction, the release of transmitter (acetylcholine) by presynaptic activity affects the distribution of extrajunctional ACh receptor molecules, and encourages stable deposition of the degradating enzyme acetylcholinesterase.

The dense clustering of ACh receptor molecules that occurs in the postsynaptic membrane depends on the presence of the presynaptic terminal. Although it is attractive to think that the clustering might be induced by presynaptic motoneuron activ-

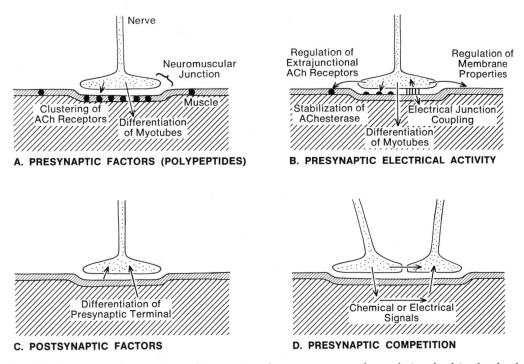

Fig. 9.9 Summary of main types of interactions between nerve and muscle involved in the development of the vertebrate neuromuscular junction. (Based on Lømo and Rosenthal, 1972; Thompson et al., 1979; Frank and Fischbach, 1979; Landmesser, 1980; Hopkins and Brown, 1984; and many others)

ity, in fact it has been shown to be independent of this. It appears instead that clustering is induced by release of one or more substances, probably polypeptides, which also may have other actions on the developing myotube.

Postsynaptic Factors

If the presynaptic axon is crucial for the development of the postsynaptic muscle, the same can be said of the importance of the muscle for the nerve (C in Fig. 9.9). When the motor axon terminal first arrives at the muscle it has a very primitive form, and most of the morphological differentiation of the terminal occurs after a synaptic contact has been established, under the influence of the postsynaptic muscle. This appears to be mediated by several factors, which include specific molecules from three possible areas: molecules (1) contained within the extracellular matrix around the

terminal, (2) projecting from postsynaptic membrane, or (3) released from the muscle cytoplasm.

Competition Between Axon Terminals

A fourth factor is that the axons interact among themselves. A given muscle first receives axons from several motoneurons (polyneuronal innervation); in the course of development, all the synapses except those from one motoneuron are eliminated. This appears to reflect competition between the axons. The signals mediating this competition may be either chemical or electrical. They may pass directly between the axons, or indirectly by first affecting the muscle, as shown in Fig. 9.9D.

It thus seems clear that the development of specific synaptic sites, as exemplified by the neuromuscular junction, depends not on one factor, but on multiple factors. The presynaptic process, extracellular matrix, and postsynaptic process each contribute, in a carefully programed sequence of mutual interactions. Both chemical and electrical factors are involved. Axons from several presynaptic cells compete for input to one postsynaptic cell. In these basic mechanisms, the neuromuscular junction exemplifies many of the properties of development of synapses, and many of the plastic properties involved in regeneration and learning (see Chap. 29).

Establishment of Synaptic Connections

The essence of nervous organization is the establishment of synaptic circuits. Normal behavior requires precision in assembling these circuits, and it is not surprising, therefore, that many of the disorders of behavior that occur in humans and other animals are due to abnormalities in the development of the circuit connections (see Chap. 30). In development, as in politics, timing is all. From the experimental evidence it is possible to begin to identify the intricate sequence of steps that is involved in establishing specific connections. Table 9.1 provides a summary of the main steps that have been identified so far. As can be seen, the entire process spans the time from the birth of a neuron, through migration and differentiation, to the final maturation of each part of the cell.

Retinotectal Pathway

The ways in which neuronal populations interact in forming circuits has been studied in many systems, under many experimental conditions. Present thinking has been much influenced by the pioneering experiments of Roger Sperry of the California Institute of Technology. This work was carried out in amphibians, in the retinotectal pathway, which is composed of the axons of retinal ganglion cells that project to the optic tectum, the main relay center for visual information in the lower vertebrate brain (see Chap. 16). Sperry cut one optic nerve and rotated the eye through 180°. When regeneration of the optic nerve was complete, he

Table 9.1 Steps in establishing specific synaptic connections

1. The neuron must leave the cell cycle at a set time.
2. It must migrate to the appropriate region.
3. It may develop a spatial identity with respect to its neighbors.
4. Dendrites must develop in a characteristic shape and orientation.
5. The axon must leave the cell body and grow in the right direction toward its region of termination.
6. The axon must direct its branches to the appropriate side of the brain.
7. The axon must direct branches to the right region or regions.
8. Within a region, the axon must ramify in the right subdivision or layer.
9. The terminal field of the axon must be ordered in a particular topographic relationship with the cell bodies in the regions of its origin and termination.
10. The axon terminals may end only on certain cell types within the terminal distribution area.
11. The axon terminals may end only on certain parts of these cells (parts of the dendritic surface, for example).

After Lund (1978)

found that the axons grew back to their previous target sites; the map of the retina onto the tectum was preserved, despite the rotation of the eye and the disorganization and regrowth produced by the transection (Fig. 9.10). He therefore postulated that individual axons and their individual target cells have matching biochemical "identification tags," so that they establish synaptic connections by a *chemical affinity* between them. He suggested that this affinity is responsible not only for the reestablishment of connections during regeneration, but also for the establishment of connections during normal development.

Because of the precision with which the retina is mapped onto the tectum, this system has been the object of considerable study. Subsequent work has confirmed and greatly extended Sperry's original finding. It has also somewhat qualified the interpretation. The original hypothesis stressed rigid genetic mechanisms in laying down the patterns of synaptic connections in the nervous

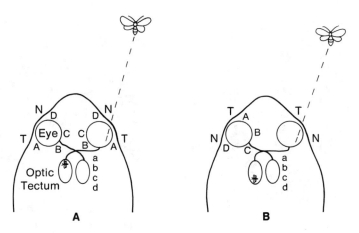

Fig. 9.10 Visual projection of image of a fly onto the retina of a normal frog (A) and a frog in which the eyes have been rotated through 180° (B). Note retinal points A–D and their projections onto the optic tectum. (From Lund, 1978)

system, whereas in most systems it appears that additional factors operate during development (*epigenetic* factors, such as conditioning by experience) and are essential to the final connection patterns.

Genetic Mutations

The formation of synaptic circuits has also been studied under abnormal conditions induced by genetic mutations. In invertebrates, the most studied species from this point of view are the nematode roundworm *Caenorhabditis elegans,* and the fruit fly *Drosophila melanogaster.* The strategy of these experiments is to produce a single mutation by X-irradiation, characterize the behavioral abnormality produced, and then identify the underlying abnormality in synaptic connection.

In vertebrates, mutant species have been particularly useful in studying the ways that cortical structures are formed. The earliest and most complete studies have been carried out in mutant strains of mice by Richard Sidman, Pasko Rakic, and their colleagues at Harvard. Most of these strains have been identified by the effects of the mutation on locomotion, and the cellular mechanisms have been analyzed especially in the cerebellum. Depending on the kind of locomotor disorder, the mutant strains have acquired names of reeler, staggerer,

weaver, nervous, jumpy, and so on. Each type of disorder is associated with a particular way in which the cerebellar cortex is disorganized.

The results are summarized in Fig. 9.11 for three mutant strains—weaver, reeler, and staggerer—and compared with the normal. In brief, the normal cerebellar cortex (A) consists of an orderly layering of the main neuronal types, and sets of specific connections between them (we will examine these in more detail in Chap. 21). In the homozygous weaver (B), most of the granule cells degenerate prior to the time of their migration from the surface layer to the deeper position they occupy in the normal adult. Also affected is a type of radial glial cell called a *Bergmann glia,* which normally serves as a guide for the migration of the granule cell bodies during development. Serum cholesterol and related lipids are abnormally high in weavers; this may have deleterious effects on the granule and glial cells.

In the reeler mutant (C), the main abnormality is a lack of granule cells, which remain in a layer at the surface, so that the normal relations between the layers in the adult are reversed. As a consequence, there are few parallel fibers, and the Purkinje cells lack their characteristic branching pattern. The effects on the Purkinje cell are

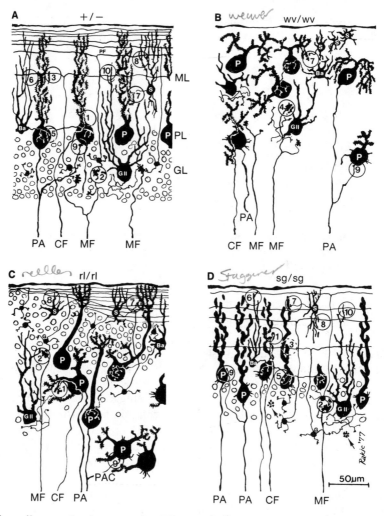

Fig. 9.11 The cell types in the normal mouse cerebellum (A) and in the cerebellum of several mutant strains (B–D). Abbreviations: Ba, basket cell; CF, climbing fiber; G, granule cell; GII, Golgi type II cell; MF, mossy fiber; P, Purkinje cell; PA, Purkinje cell axon; PAC, Purkinje cell axon collateral; PF, parallel fiber; S, stellate cell. Layers in A: ML, molecular layer; PL, Purkinje cell body layer; GL, granule cell layer. Circled numbers indicate corresponding types of synapses: ① climbing fiber synapses on P cell dendrites; ② mossy fiber synapses on G cells; ③ parallel fiber synapses on P cells; ④ mossy fiber synapses on GII cell basal dendrites; ⑤ climbing fiber synapses on P cell bodies; ⑥ parallel fiber synapses on Ba cell dendrites; ⑦ S cell synapses on P cell dendrites; ⑧ parallel fiber synapses on S cell dendrites; ⑨ P cell axon collateral synapses on P cell bodies; ⑩ parallel fiber synapses on GII cell apical dendrites. See text for explanations. (From Caviness and Rakic, 1978)

taken to indicate that the maturation of dendritic branches and dendritic spines into their final form is under control of the granule cell axons in their normal arrangement as parallel fibers.

As a final example, in the staggerer mutant (D), the main site of gene action appears to be the Purkinje cells, which fail to develop their mature dendritic tree, and retain several embryonic characteristics. The granule cells migrate, leaving behind their axons as parallel fibers in the normal manner. However, in the absence of their normal Purkinje cell dendritic targets, the granule cells degenerate. This occurs despite the fact that postsynaptic specializations (submembranous densities) are present in the malformed Purkinje cell dendrites.

These studies thus give evidence of the multiple factors involved in the establishment of neuronal circuits. A problem in interpretation is that there is rarely an isolated site of gene action; on the contrary, each mutant exhibits a mixture of effects. The effects are not confined to the cerebellum, but involve a variety of abnormalities throughout the nervous system. Despite these complications, some of the gene actions are surprisingly specific, as already discussed. In addition, electrophysiological recordings from the Purkinje cells in weaver and reeler indicate that these cells, despite their grossly abnormal morphology, have relatively normal excitable membrane properties. The picture one obtains clearly shows the profound effects of genetic abnormalities on development, and the resourcefulness of the developmental process in attempting to assemble its circuits despite the abnormalities which may occur. The functions of the cerebellum will be discussed in Chap. 21.

Maturation

Maturation refers to the process by which neurons and circuits achieve their final form. It is difficult to specify precisely as a distinct process because it is continuous with the preceding steps of differentiation, and involves the finalization of many of the processes listed in Table 9.1. Of these various steps, we will discuss three of special interest.

The first point is that the elements that make up a synapse may be assembled first in immature form before being "fine-tuned" to their mature form by posttranslational mechanisms. As noted above, this appears to be the case for the ACh receptor at the neuromuscular junction. Maturation may also involve a process of "stabilization" (see Changeux et al., 1984). It is possible that many synapses do not reach a final form, but are subject to a continuous process of activity-dependent remodeling; this has been postulated to be the synaptic basis for learning and memory (Chap. 29).

The second point is that the neurons in a given region do not all differentiate, migrate, and achieve maturation at the same time. We have seen in the cerebellar cortex, for example, that the granule cells migrate to their final positions and take on their final form long after the Purkinje cells have been in place. Studies in other regions have indicated that small interneurons similarly reach their final positions and shapes after the projection neurons. It has been postulated that this may be a general rule in the nervous system, making small neurons and local synaptic circuits more open to influence by the experience of the animal.

An important step in maturation is the acquisition of myelin. The ability to stain for myelin led the early histologists to focus their studies of development on the onset of myelination, and use this as a criterion of maturation. However, most axons in the brain are thin and unmyelinated or only thinly myelinated, and it is now recognized that the myelination of larger axons is only one among many steps in maturation. Nonetheless, it is true that different regions vary considerably in their times of myelination. It is one of the later stages of maturation, beginning usually late in embryonic life or early in postnatal life after the projection neurons are well in place, and continuing for considerable periods of time (into childhood, in the case of humans).

Cell Death

We tend to think of death as the end point of old age, but that is not the view from the perspective of development. From this perspective, degeneration and death of specific cells, fibers, and synaptic terminals are integral parts of the process of development. This was shown in the vertebrate

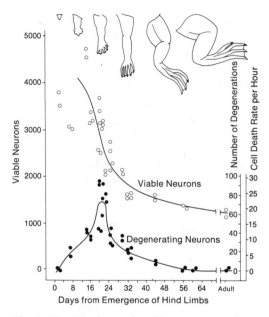

Fig. 9.12 Numbers of viable neurons and degenerating neurons in the ventral horn of the lumbar spinal cord of the frog at different times in relation to development of the hindlimbs. (Modified from Hughes, in Jacobson, 1978)

nervous system in 1949 by Viktor Hamburger and Rita Levi-Montalcini, at Washington University (see Lichtman and Purves, 1984, for a review). They found that in dorsal root ganglia and in the spinal cord motor regions, large numbers of cells degenerate during brief and specific time periods early in embryonic life. It was observed that this occurs approximately at the time when the peripheral fibers establish their connections in the periphery.

Like many important discoveries, this lay dormant for a time, but after a decade or so the question was taken up and pursued in a number of other regions. The results have shown that cell death is a common phenomenon in many regions. The amount of loss is considerable, reaching as high as 75% in some cases (see Fig. 9.12). In many cases there is a coincidence of cell death with the time at which the cells of that region are innervating their targets. From this observation, it has been hypothesized that there is a competition for innervation

of neuronal targets, and the cells that die are the ones that lose out in the competition. This, in turn, implies that the cells that survive receive some signal or sustaining trophic factor from the cells they innervate. There is recent evidence that NGF can play this role at sites in the periphery (see above). Thus, the establishment of synaptic connections appears, at least in some cases, to involve competition for targets, validation of successful connections, and elimination of unsuccessful or redundant connections.

These properties relating to cell death are seen at the level of individual terminals and synapses, too. For example, in spinal motoneurons there are synapses on the initial segment of the axon that disappear later in embryonic life. In the cerebellum, there is a time during early development when the Purkinje cell bodies bristle with small spines which receive climbing fiber synapses; later, these spines, and their synapses, completely disappear. Perhaps the early connections help to guide other synapses to their sites, or perhaps they provide for some control of excitability that is necessary at a particular stage of development.

Molting

Some of the clearest evidence for mechanisms governing the remodeling that takes place during development comes from studies of metamorphosis in insects. Emergence from the last larval stage in the development of insects is called *eclosion*, and it is under control of a hormone, manufactured in the brain and secreted from a neuroendocrine gland termed the corpora cardiaca. This is called, appropriately, *eclosion hormone*, a peptide with a molecular weight of approximately 8500. In addition to triggering eclosion, this hormone also appears to coordinate the timing of many developmental processes.

Certain of the neurons and muscles in the larva have functions that are specific only for the larva, and after eclosion they no longer are needed. James Truman and his colleagues in Seattle have shown that

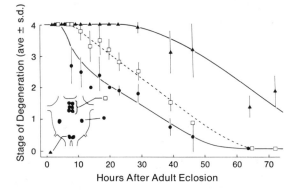

Fig. 9.13 Cell death occurring with different time course in three types of motoneuron in the abdominal ganglion during development of the sphinx moth *Manduca sexta*. (From Truman and Schwartz, 1980)

these neurons and muscles degenerate according to a sequence that is under the control of eclosion hormone. Figure 9.13 shows the time course of reduction and disappearance of motoneurons in the abdominal ganglion (the muscles they innervate show similar reductions). As in most invertebrate ganglia, many neurons have characteristic shapes and positions within the ganglion, so that the sequence of disappearance of cell types can be clearly demonstrated.

This type of cell loss is called *programmed cell death,* and serves as a model for this general phenomenon, including the examples we have previously discussed. It is presumed to be due in the insect to a direct action of the peptide hormone on the specific muscles and neurons. The process can be delayed by artificially stimulating the motoneurons. Truman has obtained evidence that the action of the hormone is associated with an elevation in intracellular levels of cGMP, and therefore appears to be mediated by this second messenger mechanism.

Metamorphosis in insects is thus controlled by a complex series of hormonal actions, which are in turn under control of the central nervous system. Similar principles apply to metamorphosis in lower vertebrates like the frog, and also the more continuous, less drastic changes during de-

velopment of higher vertebrates. We will discuss the actions of sex hormones on vertebrate development in Chaps. 23 and 27.

New Neurons in Old Brains?

Some tissues of the body retain the ability to form new cells from existing precursors during the life of the animal. For example, the cells in the skin are constantly turning over, and the liver can regenerate much of its substance. The nervous system is severely limited in this respect. It appears to be a general rule, in both invertebrates and vertebrates, that once the processes of development are complete there is little or no further generation of new nerve cells. This, of course, is the main reason why injuries to the nervous system have such devastating effects.

Despite this general rule, there are exceptions. One example is the vertebrate olfactory receptor neuron. As illustrated in Fig. 9.14A, precursor cells ① in the olfactory epithelium within the nasal cavity normally undergo a slow cycle of mitotic activity that generates immature neurons ②, which gradually mature ③ as they migrate toward the surface. Maturation consists of sending out a dendrite with cilia at the tip (the site of reception of odorous molecules: see Chap. 10), and an axon which establishes synap-

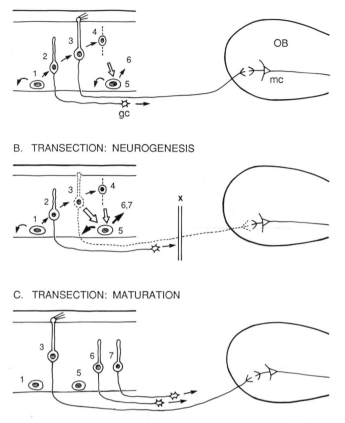

Fig. 9.14   Neurogenesis of the vertebrate olfactory receptor neuron. **A.** Normal sequence of neu-rogenesis: differentiation from stem cells (1), maturation (2,3), cell death (4), and stimulation of a new cycle (5,6). Abbreviations: gc, growth cone of the receptor axon; OB, olfactory bulb; mc, mitral cell. **B.** Transection (×) of the olfactory nerves causes die-back of receptor neurons (3), sending a powerful mitotic signal to stem cells to proliferate new neurons (6,7). **C.** Maturation of unaffected (3) and new (6,7) neurons leads to "regeneration" of the olfactory nerve and reestablish-ment of synaptic connections to the olfactory bulb. (Based on Graziadei and Monti-Graziadei, 1979; Farbman, 1986; and others)

tic contacts in the olfactory bulb, the first relay station of the olfactory pathway; see Chaps. 4 and 11). The mature receptor-neuron eventually dies ④, sending an as yet unknown signal to the precursor cells ⑤ to undergo mitosis again. This constant remodeling goes on at a low rate through-out adult life. The new neurons perform the amazing double feat of generating the correct receptors for receiving the odor-carrying molecules in the dendrites, and sending their axons to the right synaptic targets in the olfactory bulb. How they do this is completely unknown!

This process can be massively activated by cutting the olfactory nerves. As shown in Fig. 9.14B, transection causes immediate (within a few days) degeneration of all neurons (③) whose axons have been cut. This in turn sends a powerful signal to all the precursor cells ⑤ to differentiate new neurons. As a consequence, as shown in Fig. 9.14C, the olfactory bulb is reinner-vated by the neurons with uncut axons ② and the axons of the newly differentiated neurons (⑥ and ⑦).

The physiological properties of the neu-rons change at different stages of development. The ability to generate impulses appears already in young rats before birth; Robert Gesteland (1986) at Cincinnati has obtained evidence that immature neurons are first relatively nonspecific (responding to many different odors), showing more specific responses (to fewer odors) just before term, perhaps when their axons establish synaptic contacts in the olfactory bulb. Immature neurons (such as ② in the diagrams) lack the ability to generate sustained repetitive discharges, as would be required to transmit specific information about stimulating odors. This may be correlated with an increased membrane K^+ conductance, which opposes depolarization (see Chap. 7). An increase in K^+ channels is well known to accompany mitosis of lymphocytes in response to antigenic stimulation in the immune system. Comparisons like this may give clues to the molecular mechanisms controlling proliferation of olfactory receptor neurons. Presumably there are growth-regulating genes that are selectively expressed in these neurons. An understanding of these mechanisms could tell us how these genes might be expressed in other neurons, to permit neuron replacement during aging, degenerative diseases, or after injury.

A second example of the generation of new neurons in the adult vertebrate is in the brains of birds. We will consider this in Chap. 23.

Regeneration and Plasticity

The inability to generate new neurons might imply that the adult nervous system is a static, "hard-wired" machine. This is far from the truth. Although new neurons cannot be generated, each neuron retains the ability to form new processes and new synaptic connections. Thus, although the nerve cell body is a relatively fixed component within each center of the adult nervous system, the synaptic circuits it forms with the processes of other neurons are subject to ongoing modification. We learn new skills and new facts, remember them, and use them in different ways, which in itself ar-

gues strongly that our neural circuits are modifiable. Research at the cellular level has provided considerable evidence for changes of cellular properties that are dependent on use. These mechanisms will be discussed in several chapters, particularly in regard to cellular and molecular properties underlying memory of learning in Chap. 29, and functions of the cerebral cortex in Chap. 30.

What of the ability of nerve cells to respond to injury? Although the nervous system cannot generate new neurons to replace lost ones, each cell can proliferate new processes to replace those that have been lost or damaged. The experiments cited above on regeneration of the optic nerve demonstrate this capacity, as well as the ability to reestablish specific synaptic connections.

Nerve cells are primed to make new connections when other cells are lost. A key experiment was the study of William Chambers and John Liu, of the University of Pennsylvania, in 1958. They transected the pyramidal tract in the spinal cord, and several years later examined the fields of termination of dorsal root fibers within both sides of the cord. They found that the field of termination was larger on the side of the tract lesion, suggesting that the dorsal root fibers give off collateral sprouts that take over the vacated synaptic sites.

An elegant demonstration of this process at the synaptic level was provided by Geoffrey Raisman at Oxford in 1969. He studied the septal nucleus, a region in the forebrain that receives two well-defined inputs: one from the hippocampus, the other from the median forebrain bundle (MFB). Each makes characteristic synaptic connections onto septal neurons, as shown in Fig. 9.15. When the hippocampal input is cut, there is an increased incidence of large terminals making double synaptic contacts, presumably from MFB fibers. On the other hand, when the MFB is cut, the synaptic sites on the soma are taken over by hippocampal terminals.

These results reflect the same kind of competition for synaptic sites that occurs

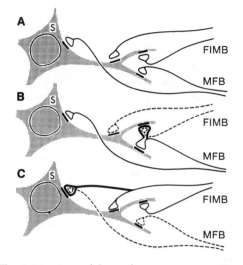

Fig. 9.15 Remodeling of synaptic connections in the septal nuclei of the rat. **A.** Normal inputs to septal (S) cell. Fimbria (FIMB) fibers terminate on dendrites, whereas medial forebrain bundle fibers (MFB) terminate on both dendrites and soma. **B.** Lesion of FIMB (degenerating fibers shown by dashed lines); MFB terminals occupy vacated synaptic sites on dendrites. **C.** Lesion of MFB; FIMB terminals occupy vacated sites on cell body. (From Raisman, 1969)

during normal development. Loss of a particular type of synaptic terminal stimulates the production of axonal *sprouts*, which have the *mobility* to move to the vacated sites, and the necessary *chemoaffinity* to establish new synaptic connections. In many respects the process involves reactivation of mechanisms that operated during development.

Similar experiments have now been carried out in a number of regions, demonstrating that when one input is transected, another input expands its terminal field into the vacated sites on cell bodies or dendrites. These include such regions as the hippocampus (Chap. 29), red nucleus, olfactory cortex, and superior colliculus in the vertebrate. In addition to specific pathways, nonspecific pathways also exhibit these properties. Thus, when the cerebellum is ablated, the amount of histofluorescence for norepinephrine increases in the forebrain. Cells in the locus ceruleus send

noradrenergic fibers to both cerebellum and forebrain (see Chap. 24), so it appears that loss of the cerebellar branches induces sprouting of the forebrain branches. This kind of *compensatory sprouting* has been seen in a number of cells, and suggests that a cell is programed to make a certain number of synapses, and reacts to injury in a way to compensate for the loss and try to restore its appropriate number of connections, even though those connections may be in uncharacteristic or inappropriate places.

Within the cerebral cortex, a vivid demonstration of regeneration has been provided by the experiments of Patricia Goldman-Rakic and her colleagues. They made injections of tritiated amino acids

Fig. 9.16 Diagram of frontal sections of the prefrontal lobes of the rhesus monkey. **A.** Injections of tritiated amino acids in the right hemisphere, showing pattern of projection through the corpus callosum to the left hemisphere. **B.** In this animal, the contralateral region of the prefrontal cortex was ablated two months previously. The regenerating fibers revealed by the injected amino acids innervate a new region of cortex. Note columnar patterns of innervation in both cases. (From Goldman-Rakic, 1981)

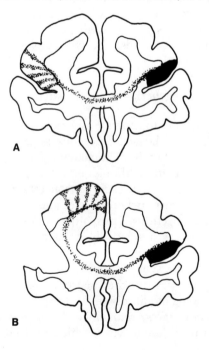

into the frontal association cortex of monkeys on one side, and found transport through fibers of the corpus callosum to the same region of the frontal cortex of the contralateral side (Fig. 9.16A). The experiment was then repeated in animals in which the contralateral site was ablated. The callosal fibers whose terminals were removed by these ablations regenerated; when they reached the contralateral side and found their normal target absent, they swerved and terminated in a neighboring region of cortex (Fig. 9.16B). Although it is not known whether these connections are functional or not, the results attest to the tremendous "force" operating within each neuron to grow out new axons and make new connections even when the normal targets for the axon are not available. A further point of interest in these experiments is the arrangement of the fiber terminations in columns, in both the normal and experimental situations. The column is one of the organ-izing principles of cortical synaptic circuits, as we shall discuss in later chapters.

These experiments thus give evidence of the ongoing competition to make synaptic connections that each neuron engages in during development and throughout adult life. This competition is the basis of much of the plasticity that is inherent in neural circuits.

Brain Transplants

Neurobiologists are only beginning to understand the potentials of this plasticity. For example, recent studies show that a region of the mammalian brain can be excised and grafted onto the brain of another animal. Two kinds of grafts have been tried. In one, a length of peripheral nerve is placed as a bridge across a site of transection (see Fig. 9.17A). Neurons whose axons have been cut by the transection regenerate new axons, which normally would be unable to penetrate the scar tissue at the site of tran-

Fig. 9.17 Transplantation procedures which demonstrate growth of grafted nerve cells. **A.** Diagram of the brainstem and spinal cord of a rat, showing a graft of a bridging section of peripheral nerve. The dots indicate cell bodies of neurons labeled retrogradely by HRP applied to the nerve bridge. The labeling shows that regenerating axons can move in both directions through the grafts. **B–D.** Procedures for transplantation of catecholamine-containing neurons into the striatum of the rat brain. **B.** Frontal section of the rat brain, showing placement of pipette tip in the striatum. A piece of substantia nigra, containing dopaminergic neurons which normally innervate the striatum, is deposited in the lateral ventricle and grows as indicated. **C.** A piece of substantia nigra is placed in an artificial cavity created on the surface of the striatum, from which it grows into the striatum. **D.** A suspension of fetal substantia nigra cells, or adrenal medulla containing chromaffin cells, is made (test tube insert) and injected into the striatum. (A from Aguayo, 1985; B from Olson, 1985)

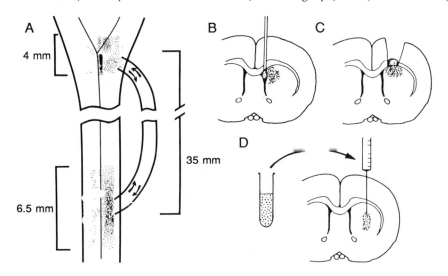

section; the graft gives them an alternative pathway through which they may grow. It has yet to be shown that such axons can establish functionally meaningful synaptic contacts on the other side of the transection. These experiments give hope of reestablishing some degree of neural function in patients with severe spinal cord trauma.

A second type of graft consists of introducing new neural tissue to replace neurons and transmitters lost due to disease. One aim of this kind of research is to replace the neurons whose degeneration causes Parkinson's disease. These neurons use dopamine as a transmitter at their synapses in a part of the brain called the striatum (see Chap. 21). Dopamine-synthesizing neurons (such as chromaffin cells: see Chap. 18) are introduced into the striatum (see Fig. 9.17B–D) with the hope that they will compensate for the degenerated neurons. Trials using this procedure are presently being pursued in a few selected patients.

These kinds of experiments thus carry the hope that we can not only reveal more of the plastic capabilities of nerve cells that are normally at work, but also eventually use them to compensate for the effects of injuries and disease in the human brain.

II
Sensory Systems

10

Introduction: From Receptors to Perceptions

From early childhood we are aware of the sensations and perceptions that occur as a part of the business of living. Those that are particularly painful or pleasurable become powerful factors in molding the way we develop, the kinds of personalities we acquire, and the goals we work toward. Since sensory experience is so immediate, it is much more readily understandable than many other aspects of nervous function. On the other hand, our senses not only inform us, but may often fool us; they constantly test our abilities to make judgments about things.

The fact that sensory perceptions are so accessible to our introspection means that when humans first acquired the ability to think and speculate about their own nature, they were very much aware of the importance of sensory experience. The early Greek philosophers of the sixth century B.C. were able to make the distinction between reason on the one hand, and the senses on the other. This is exemplified in the statement of Heraclitus, that "knowledge comes to man through the door of the senses." It was realized that different senses are mediated by different sense organs, but also that the different sensory impressions are united in our minds. Some of these

philosophers even suspected that the site of this integration is in the brain. In these ideas lay the origins of physiology and psychology.

Sensory Modalities

It would be fascinating to trace the development of concepts about the senses since then, but to understand the foundation of modern concepts we need go back only to the nineteenth century. In the 1830s, Johannes Muller of Berlin published a monumental *Handbook of Human Physiology*, which served as the definitive textbook of physiology in Europe and America for many years. In it he summarized the work on sensor physiology, and promulgated the *"law of specific nerve energies."* This states that we are aware, not of objects themselves, but of signals about them transmitted through our nerves, and that there are different kinds of nerves, each nerve having its own "specific nerve energy." The kinds of nerves considered by Muller corresponded to the five primary senses that Aristotle had recognized: seeing, hearing, touch, smell, and taste. The specific nerve energy represented the *sensory modality* that each type of nerve transmitted. The key point is that the nerve transmits this modality no matter how it is stimulated. Thus, an electric shock or a blow on the head may stimulate the nerves of hearing, and elicit sounds in our ears.

The doctrine was applied in a famous law case in which Muller was called for expert testimony. A man had been assaulted at night, and had accused someone. When asked how he could identify the assailant since it was pitch dark, he replied that he caught a glimpse of him in the light caused by the blow to his head! Muller pointed out that pressure on the eye does indeed cause a light sensation—a phosphene—but this is an expression of the fact that the eye responds to any stimulation with a light sensation, and that this is an entirely internal phenomenon.

In modern terms, we recognize that there are specific *receptor cells* tuned to be sensitive to different forms of *energy* in the environment. The forms of energy serve as *stimuli* for the receptor cells. A summary of the main types of receptor cells in the human body, the organs in which they are located, and the forms of energy to which each is sensitive, is provided in Table 10.1. Note that there are many more modalities than the five senses that we think of in everyday life. Among the conscious senses, we must include pressure, temperature, and pain under "touch," and also joint position and the sense of balance. It is also evident from the list that we have specialized cells that are sensitive to many stimuli within our bodies that never reach consciousness. Particularly important in this group are stretch receptors in the vasculature and muscles, and a variety of receptors sensitive to different kinds of chemical factors. The receptors in the viscera and other internal organs are often called *interoceptors* or visceroceptors, to distinguish them from the olfactory, auditory, and visual *exteroceptors* that receive signals from outside the body (also called teleceptors: tele = distant). Taken as a whole, our array of receptors provides information that ranges from the minutest changes in the internal milieu of our bodies to the faintest signals that waft our way from the furthest reaches of our external world.

Within a modality there may be different submodalities, or *qualities*. Thus, we perceive different tastes and smells; we describe temperature sensations in terms of warmth and cold; we see different wavelengths of light as different colors. In general, just as a modality is determined mainly by a type of receptor, so is a sensory quality based on a differentiation of receptors into subtypes. Each receptor cell subtype is tuned to a more narrow spectrum of the stimulus band. Thus, odor qualities depend on receptor cells in the nose being differentially sensitive to different airborne molecules, and different colors depend on photoreceptors in the eye having different sensitivities to wavelengths of light.

The sense organs and modalities listed in Table 10.1 are those that are found in the human. If we look back over the course of evolution, we see that in general the main categories of modalities are present in most of the main animal groups. Perhaps the most basic are the chemical and touch modalities which are necessary aspects of the mere existence of an animal, together with some capacity for light sensitivity, which permits a sense of the cycles of night and day.

At the level of molecules and cell membranes, the basic receptor mechanisms within a given modality share many common features across different phyla and species. However, the receptor cells and sense organs show diversity of forms, as is evident from a survey of the diversity of body plans and nervous systems throughout the Animal Kingdom. Thus, it is not surprising that the eye of a flatworm or an insect should be different from our own. We could expect that some species should have sense organs that we lack, such as electric fish with their organs for sensing electric currents, or the mollusc with its osphradial organ for sensing water entering the mantle cavity. Nor is it surprising that many sense organs may be absent, as with the extreme

Table 10.1 Main types of sensory modalities

Sensory modality	Form of energy	Receptor organ	Receptor cell
Chemical			
common chemical	molecules	various	free nerve endings
arterial oxygen	O_2 tension	carotid body	cells and nerve endings
toxins (vomiting)	molecular	medulla	chemoreceptor cells
osmotic pressure	osmotic pressure	hypothalamus	osmoreceptors
glucose	glucose	hypothalamus	glucoreceptors
pH (cerebrospinal fluid)	ions	medulla	ventricle cells
Taste	ions and molecules	tongue and pharynx	taste bud cells
Smell	molecules	nose	olfactory receptors
Somatosensory			
touch	mechanical	skin	nerve terminals
pressure	mechanical	skin and deep tissue	encapsulated nerve endings
temperature	temperature	skin, hypothalamus	nerve terminals and central neurons
pain	various	skin and various organs	nerve terminals
Muscle			
vascular pressure	mechanical	blood vessels	nerve terminals
muscle stretch	mechanical	muscle spindle	nerve terminals
muscle tension	mechanical	tendon organs	nerve terminals
joint position	mechanical	joint capsule and ligaments	nerve terminals
Balance			
linear acceleration (gravity)	mechanical	vestibular organ	hair cells
angular acceleration	mechanical	vestibular organ	hair cells
Hearing	mechanical	inner ear (cochlea)	hair cells
Vision	electromagnetic (photons)	eye (retina)	photoreceptors

Modified from Ganong (1985)

adaptations of the tapeworm to a parasitic experience in the gut of its host. Finally, despite this diversity, we should not be surprised to learn that some sensory cells and organs are such successful adaptations that, like the vertebrate receptor cells for smell, or the vertebrate eye, they are present relatively unchanged across many different species.

In the six remaining chapters in this section, we will learn about the six main classes of sensory modalities and their respective sense organs and sensory systems. For each modality we will discuss examples from invertebrate and vertebrate species, and finish by considering the human.

It will be useful to recognize at the beginning that there are some *basic mechanisms* that are common to all the sensory modalities. These mechanisms operate at three main levels: the sensory receptors themselves, the pathways that transmit the information, and the systems that underlie sensory perception. Let us consider briefly these common mechanisms before proceeding to the individual sensory systems.

Sensory Receptors

In order to detect and discriminate different stimuli in the environment or within the body, the stimuli have to be converted from their different forms of energy into the common currency of nervous signals. The initial conversion is termed *transduction,* and the cells in which it takes place are, by definition, *sensory receptor cells.*

Transduction

Figure 10.1 represents schematically some of the main types of sensory receptors in the vertebrate. The sites at which transduction occurs are indicated in shading. As a general rule, the stimulus acts on membrane receptors. These may be distributed all over the plasmalemma of an entire cell, as in some chemical receptor cells such as those sensitive to oxygen tension in the blood (to the far left in the figure). In most cases, however, transduction takes place in the membrane of a specialized site in the sensory cell. The specializations may have many different forms. In some cases they

may be microvilli (as in taste); in others they may be cilia (smell or vision). In most receptors of the skin, viscera, and muscles, the sites of transduction are in the terminals of nerve fibers. The terminals may be free (naked nerve endings), as in the skin, or embedded in special structures, as in corpuscles or muscle spindles. Finally, the sites may be in special intracellular membranes as in visual receptors.

Despite the diversity of receptors, there are unifying principles that underly their mechanisms of operation. One of these principles is that there are three main types of sensory stimuli—chemical, mechanical, and electromagnetic (light)—and that most receptors can be grouped according to which of these types of energy they transduce. The receptor mechanisms within each group share certain basic properties, which are summarized in Fig. 10.2. Let us discuss each of these briefly.

Fig. 10.1   Different types of sensory receptor cells in vertebrates. Small arrows indicate sites where sensory stimuli act. Stippling indicates sites for transduction of the sensory stimuli, and also for synaptic transmission; both of these sites mediate graded signal transmission. Large arrows indicate sites of impulse initiation. (Adapted from Bodian, 1967)

| Oxygen | Taste | Smell | Somatosensory | Muscle | Hearing | Vision |

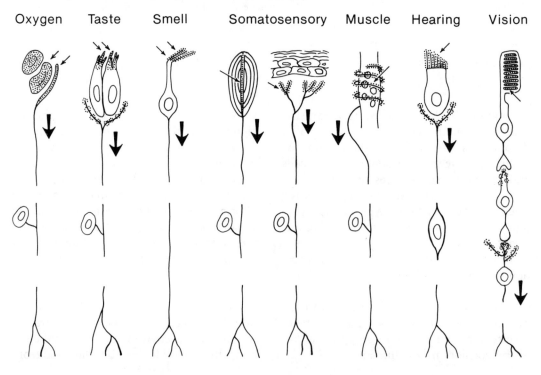

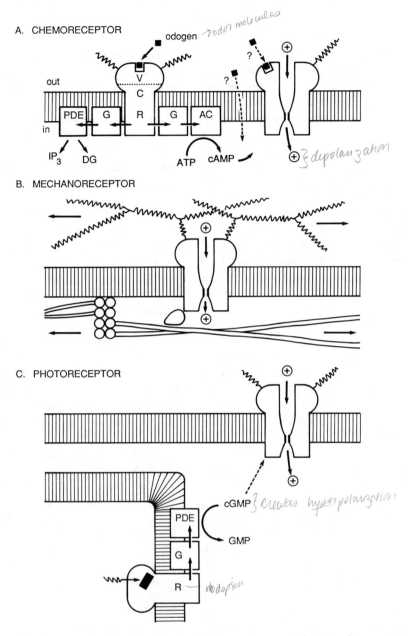

A. CHEMORECEPTOR

odogen → *Dodor molecules*

out

PDE | G | R | G | AC

in

IP₃   DG   ATP   cAMP

⊕ ↗ *depolarization*

B. MECHANORECEPTOR

C. PHOTORECEPTOR

cGMP ↗ *reduces hyperpolarization*

GMP

PDE

G

R — *rhodopsin*

Fig. 10.2 Three basic types of sensory receptors. **A.** Chemoreceptor. The stimulus consists of odor molecules (odogens). These activate receptor molecule (R), which may have variable (V) and constant (C) regions analogous to antibody molecules in the immune system. Receptor molecule activates a G protein (G) which activates adenylate cyclase (AC) to synthesize cAMP, which acts as a second messenger to increase channel conductance, depolarizing the receptor membrane and giving rise to the receptor potential. Odor molecules may also bind directly to an ion channel protein; lipid-soluble molecules may diffuse across the membrane to act on cytosolic receptors. **B.** Mechanoreceptor. The stimulus consists of stretch or tension (arrows). This pulls on carbohydrate chains anchored in the extracellular space, and/or membrane cytoskeleton, exerting stress on the molecular conformation of channel proteins and changing their conductance; the changed inflow of ions produces the receptor potential. **C.** Photoreceptor. The stimulus consists of photons (zig-zag arrow) which stimulate rhodopsin (R), activating a G protein (transducin), which in turn activates a phosphodiesterase (PDE). The PDE hydrolyzes cGMP, reducing its activation of Na⁺ channels. The shutting off of this "dark current" produces a hyperpolarizing receptor potential (see text and Chap. 6). (A based on Lancet, 1986)

Chemoreceptors. In the vertebrate, recent studies suggest that a 95-kdalton membrane protein is specifically found in the cilia of the olfactory receptor neuron. It is hypothesized that the initial step in olfactory transduction occurs when an odor molecule binds to this protein. The receptor neurons have high levels of adenylate cyclase activity, and there is increasing evidence that transduction of some olfactory molecules involves activation of this second messenger system (see Fig. 10.2A). The cAMP may act directly on a channel protein to change its conductance and produce thereby a receptor potential, in analogy with the action of cGMP in photoreceptors (see below).

Mechanoreceptors. Of the three main receptor types, least is known about the molecular mechanisms of mechanoreceptors. The common denominator for this group is mechanical movement of the sensory membrane. The key questions are exactly which molecular components move, and how this movement is transduced into a change in conductivity of channel proteins. Since the membrane itself is fluid due to its phospholipid composition, it is unlikely by itself to be the site of mechanical stress or distention. The most likely sites are the membrane cytoskeleton on the inside of the membrane, and the extracellular matrix on the outside. A pull on either or both of these relatively more rigid systems would be transmitted as a mechanical stress on the proteins within the membrane. This would lead directly or indirectly to a change in molecular conformation and change in conductivity of a channel protein (see Fig. 10.2B).

Photoreceptors. The universal mechanism for photoreception involves the transduction of light energy, in the form of photons, into a change in chemical bond energy in a molecular complex called rhodopsin (see Chap. 16). Rhodopsin is embedded in disc membranes within the photoreceptor. A great deal of work has shown that light

stimulation of this receptor activates a second messenger cascade, through a G protein and a phosphodiesterase (PDE) that hydrolyzes cGMP. In the dark, cGMP levels are therefore raised, and the cGMP binds to a channel protein that allows a dark current, carried by Na^+ and Ca^{2+}, to flow into the cell. Light stimulation, by activating PDE, lowers the concentration of cGMP, causing the conductance channel to close. Transduction of a light stimulus thus causes the membrane current to be turned off, rather than turned on as in the case of the other two sensory responses.

The similarity between the second messenger systems in olfactory reception and photoreception is summarized in Fig. 10.3. The reader should review Chap. 8 to compare these steps in sensory transduction with the corresponding steps involving second messenger systems in the actions of neurotransmitters and hormones. The mechanisms of mechanoreception are the most speculative, and the scheme in Fig. 10.3 allows for several possible sequences of steps; we will discuss a mechanism involving the extracellular matrix in hair cells in the vestibular (Chap. 14) and auditory (Chap. 15) systems. The pathways of Fig. 10.3 thus provide a framework for discussing the different adaptations found across the range of receptors covered in the ensuing chapters.

Receptor Potential

It is evident from Fig. 10.3 that in all sensory receptors, the common result of transduction is to produce a change in conductance of a membrane channel. The resulting change in membrane current produces a change in membrane potential, called the *receptor potential,* also sometimes called the *generator potential.*

The receptor potential shares similarities with a synaptic potential. The reader should review at this point the discussion of the receptor potential in a model receptor neuron, the crustacean stretch receptor cell, in Chap. 7. The main point to recall is that,

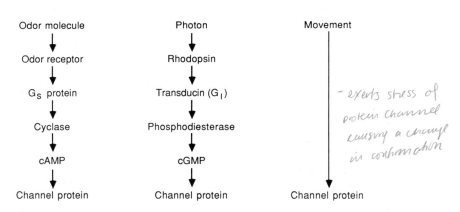

ODORECEPTION   PHOTORECEPTION   MECHANORECEPTION

(handwritten annotation: - exerts stress of protein channel causing a change in conformation)

Fig. 10.3 Summary of stages involved in the three basic types of sensory transduction.

like a synaptic potential, the receptor potential does not give rise directly to an impulse discharge. The site of receptor potential generation and the site of impulse generation are usually separated. In the stretch receptor cell, and in many other sensory receptors, the separation is some distance through the dendritic branches and axon. In other cases, the sites may be on different cells, requiring one or more synaptic relays in between (see Oxygen, Taste, Hearing, and Vision in Fig. 10.1).

Electrotonic Potential

As we have already discussed in Chap. 7, the spread of a receptor potential, like that of a synaptic potential, is accomplished by means of *electrotonic potentials*. The diagrams in Fig. 7.12 remind us of this fact. In the case of the stretch receptor cell, stretch increases the inward positive current across the nerve terminal membrane, setting up the receptor potential in the terminals. This spreads by electrotonic currents through the cell to the site of impulse initiation in the axon. In the case of the vertebrate photoreceptor, the action of the photon on the disc membrane leads to blockade of the dark current, and the resulting membrane potential change spreads electrotonically through the cell to the site of synaptic output at the receptor terminal. For the different receptor cells depicted in

Fig. 10.1, the reader may assess the importance of electrotonic current spread between the sites of transduction (stippled) and the sites of impulse generation (thick arrows). For further details on these mechanisms, the reader may refer to Chap. 7, and Chaps. 11–16 which follow.

Impulse Generation

The final step at the receptor level is the encoding of the electrotonically transmitted receptor response into an *impulse discharge* in the afferent nerve fiber that carries the information to the rest of the nervous system. This process has been studied in the crustacean stretch receptor cell and the vertebrate muscle spindle, and the results are very similar (Fig. 10.4). The stimulus in both cases is a stretch applied to the muscle. An important distinction is between the *dynamic* (phasic) period of the stimulation, when the stretch is increasing, and the *static* (tonic) period, when it is maintained constant. If impulses are blocked artificially (as by tetrodotoxin) in order to observe the receptor events, it is seen that the receptor potential rises to a peak at the end of dynamic stretch, and then falls to a lower, slowly declining level during static stretch. When the impulse discharge is recorded, the impulse frequency also rises sharply during dynamic stretch, and declines to a lower level during static stretch.

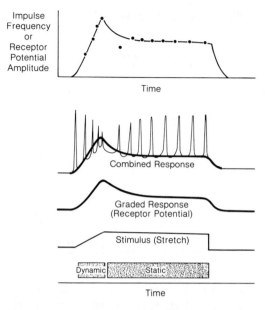

Fig. 10.4 Stimulus encoding in the crustacean stretch receptor and the frog muscle spindle. Diagrams show the relations between an applied stretch (containing dynamic and static phases), the graded receptor potential, the impulse discharge, and the impulse frequency. (After Ottoson and Shepherd, 1971)

The close correlation between receptor potential and impulse frequency can be seen in the graph at the top of Fig. 10.4.

An important point is that the receptor potential is graded smoothly and continuously in amplitude in relation to the intensity of the stimulus. Sensory reception thus involves the transformation, or mapping, from a continuously varying domain of sensory stimuli into a neural domain of all-or-nothing impulses. One can view it as converting from analog signals to digital signals. As we noted in Chap. 7, this is also what takes place during transmission at many types of synapses. The impulse discharge can function in this way, because the intervals between impulses (hence the impulse frequency) vary continuously in relation to the underlying depolarization level of the receptor potential and its rate of change.

From results such as these it is concluded that the impulse discharge faithfully en-codes the parameters of the applied stimulus. However, we can see that it does more than this; in the case of the stretch receptor and muscle spindle, it tends to heighten the response when the stimulus is increasing. This property is termed *dynamic sensitivity*. Receptors vary in how rapidly the response declines from the dynamic peak during the ensuing static stimulation. The decline is termed *adaptation*. Receptors that must signal slow and prolonged changes are *slowly adapting,* or *tonic* receptors; those that signal brief changes are termed *rapidly adapting* or *phasic* receptors. Our ability to maintain positions of our muscles over long periods of time depends on the slowly adapting properties of our muscle receptors, whereas the rapid fading of our appreciation of a pressure stimulus is due to the rapid adaptation of pressure receptors (Pacinian corpuscles). Adaptation may also be a property of the transmission of signals through sensory pathways (see below).

In summary, we have seen that there are four main steps (transduction, receptor potential generation, electrotonic spread, impulse generation) in the transfer of information from the domain of the sensory stimulus to the domain of the impulse discharge. We have also seen how the receptor determines the basic properties of the sensory response. Thus, *specificity* resides in the molecular mechanisms of the sensitive membrane. *Intensity* is mapped from graded receptor potentials into an impulse frequency code. *Adaptation* determines the profile of the response in relation to the dimension of time; there is often a tendency to heighten the sensitivity to stimulus change. The distribution of the whole population of receptors determines the *spatial organization* of the incoming information, as we shall soon discuss.

Sensory Circuits

The stimulus has been converted into a frequency code and the impulses are on their way to the central nervous system.

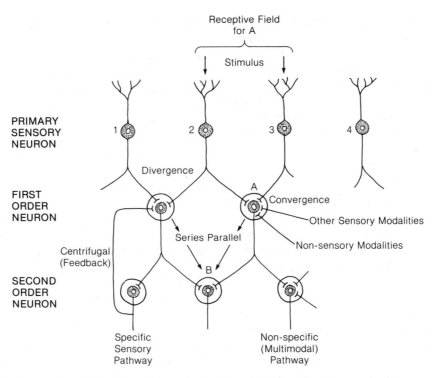

Fig. 10.5 Some common aspects of the organization of sensory circuits.

Within the central nervous system, sensory information characteristically is relayed through a series of centers. In each center there is opportunity for processing of the signals and integration with other types of information. A *sensory pathway* thus consists of a series of modality-specific neurons connected by synapses. All the circuits within and related to this pathway constitute a *sensory system.*

Basic Principles

The circuits of different sensory systems share some common properties, as illustrated in Fig. 10.5. The axons of primary sensory nerves divide to supply more than one neuron; this is referred to as *divergence* A neuron in turn is contacted by more than one axon; this is termed *convergence.* These features apply to connections both within and between different centers; thus, incoming axons diverge to more than one center, and different sources converge onto a given center. The chains of connections mean that a pathway consists of connections in *series,* in which there is obviously a temporal *sequence* of events. However, because of the divergence and convergence of connections at successive levels, there are connections in *parallel,* so the different forms of information can be transferred and combined at the same time.

Parallel processing is thus inherent in sensory pathways, and in neural systems in general. This fact has been recognized in recent years by computer scientists engaged in building the next generation of more powerful computers. It is likely that some of the principles discussed here will find their way into these computers.

Some central pathways are primarily concerned with transmitting the input from one type of receptor; these are termed *specific sensory pathways.* Other pathways, by divergence of their fibers and convergence with other inputs, become increasingly *multimodal,* or *nonspecific.* Finally, *centrifugal* connections provide for *feedback* of information from one level to the next. In general, specific sensory pathways provide for precise transmission of sensory information, while nonspecific pathways provide for sensory integration and adjustments in behavioral status of the whole organism. Both can be seen to be necessary for the analytic and synthetic functions of the organism.

Receptive Fields

An important concept in sensory physiology is the *receptive field*. For any neuron in a sensory pathway, the receptive field consists of *all the sensory receptors that can influence its activity*. Thus, cell A in Fig. 10.5 has a receptive field consisting of the two receptors (2 and 3) which connect to it. Cell B, at the second level in this system, has a receptive field consisting of receptors 1, 2, and 3. The connections to a cell may be excitatory or inhibitory, and they may be mediated by interneurons at a given level as well as relay neurons connecting levels. As we will see in the following chapters, the properties of receptive fields generally reflect the increasing degree of information processing and feature extraction that occurs in neurons at successively higher levels in sensory pathways.

Microcircuit and Local Circuit Organization

Within any center in the nervous system, the types of neurons and synaptic connections have many forms. However, as noted in Chap. 3, the microcircuits of a center are usually built up by patterns of connection between three elements: input fibers, output cells, and intrinsic neurons. These principles of organization are demonstrated very clearly in the centers of many sensory pathways.

Two examples are illustrated in Fig. 10.6. Part A is a schematic diagram of the neurons in the vertebrate retina, and their main patterns of synaptic interconnection. There are input elements (the receptors) and output neurons (the ganglion cells). There are interneurons for straight-through transmission (the bipolar cells), and there are interneurons for horizontal interactions. The horizontal connections are organized at two levels, the first (horizontal cells) at the level of receptor input, and the second (amacrine cells) at the level of ganglion cell output. The amacrine cells take part in a variety of reciprocal and serial synaptic connections, that correspond to the complexity of processing which occurs at this level (see Chap. 16).

Fig. 10.6   Comparison between simplified basic circuit diagrams of the vertebrate retina and olfactory bulb. (After Shepherd, 1978)

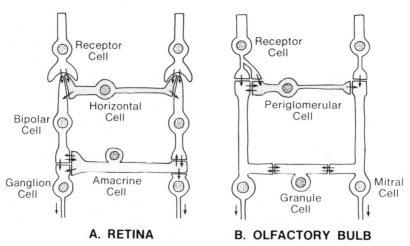

A. RETINA   B. OLFACTORY BULB

Figure 10.6B is a similar diagram of the neurons and connections in the vertebrate olfactory bulb. Here, too, are input elements (the olfactory receptors) and output neurons (the mitral cells). In this case the straight-through pathway is provided by the primary dendrite of the mitral cell. Horizontal connections are organized at two levels. The first, through periglomerular short-axon cells, is at the level of receptor input; the second, through granule cells, is at the level of mitral cell output. The granule and mitral cells interact through reciprocal synapses.

From this comparison it can be seen that, although the retina and olfactory bulb process two very different types of sensory information, their microcircuit and local circuit organization have many points in common. In both cases there is provision for straight-through transfer of signals to the output neuron, and local processing of signals through the interneurons. Recall in addition that olfactory and visual receptors bear certain similarities in their sensory transduction mechanisms (see above). Clearly, there are common principles underlying the functional organization of these two systems.

Lateral Inhibition

We have mentioned that in addition to transmitting faithfully certain aspects of the stimulus, receptors also enhance some aspects. This appears also to be a function of the intrinsic synaptic circuits at successive levels in a sensory pathway. The best known example of this is the lateral inhibition that enhances spatial contrast in the visual system. This was first revealed by Keffer Hartline and his colleagues at Rockefeller University in their studies of the compound eye of the horseshoe crab, *Limulus*. Let us consider this important model system in some detail.

The compound eye of *Limulus* consists of some 800 receptor units, called ommatidia. Each *ommatidium* has at its surface a corneal lens. Behind it are 10–15 receptor

(*retinula*) cells arranged in a circle (Fig. 10.7). At the center of the receptor group is the dendrite of a cell whose cell body is deeper and placed to one side, which has given it the name *eccentric cell*. This is a modified receptor cell: it has few microvilli, but a long thick axon, and is the principal projection neuron from the ommatidium (see Fig. 10.7).

Intracellular recordings have shown that the photoreceptors are electrically coupled to the eccentric cell dendrite. By this means, the output from the eccentric cell represents the summation of inputs to all the photoreceptors. The electrical synapses are rectifying; they pass current from the receptors to the eccentric cell dendrites, but not in the opposite direction. This prevents the electrical activity of the eccentric cell from interfering with the responses of the photoreceptor.

At rest, the eccentric cell shows background activity consisting of occasional, small depolarizing waves, first called "Yeandle bumps" after their discoverer. These represent photoreceptor responses to single photons, transmitted to the eccentric cell through the electrical synapses. With light stimulation, these quantal events fuse into a graded receptor potential which depolarizes the membrane. Note that this differs from the response of vertebrate photoreceptors; this difference will be discussed further in Chap. 16.

The receptor potential gives rise to action potentials, which encode the intensity and time course of the stimulation, and transmit this information to the central nervous system. The impulses arise in the axon at a distance from the cell body. The mechanism of electrotonic spread of receptor potential into the axon is similar to that discussed for the crayfish stretch receptor in Chap. 7. The axon gives rise to a number of collaterals which form a plexus beneath the ommatidia. Within this plexus, the collaterals are interconnected by reciprocal and serial synapses. These form the circuits which mediate the lateral inhibitory interactions (see Fig. 10.7).

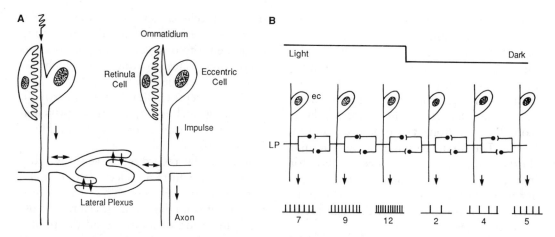

Fig. 10.7 Functional organization of lateral eye of *Limulus*. **A.** Synaptic organization, showing site of light transduction in ommatidium, impulse conduction in eccentric cell axon, and lateral interactions through dendrodendritic synapses in the lateral plexus. **B.** Pattern of activity in population of eccentric cells (ec) in response to light–dark edge stimulus (above). The impulse discharges recorded from the axons at the sites indicated by the arrows are shown below, with the numbers of spikes per unit time (arbitrary) as indicated. The enhancement of response on the light side of the edge and depression on the dark side are due to the inhibitory interactions mediated by the synaptic connections in the lateral plexus (LP). See also Fig. 10.8. (A, B based on Fahrenbach, 1985; Shepherd, 1986)

Fig. 10.8 Enhancement of spatial contrast in *Limulus* eye. **A.** Surface of *Limulus* eye, with superimposed rectangular stimulus pattern; pattern is divided into lighter (left) and darker (right) regions. Pattern is centered on test ommatidium (×). Arrows show directions in which the test pattern was displaced, to produce lower curve in graph in B. **B.** Recordings of spike frequency in axon from test ommatidium in A. *Lower curve:* responses to rectangular test pattern in A. *Upper curve:* responses to small spot of light, at high and low intensities corresponding to those of test pattern (see insert). The differences between the two curves illustrate that lateral inhibition enhances the response on the light side of an edge (because there is less inhibition from the more darkly lit neighbors to the right), and depresses the response on the dark side of an edge (because there is more inhibition from the brightly lit neighbors to the left). (From Ratliff, 1965)

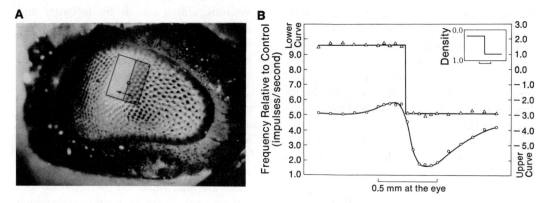

To analyze the way in which the whole ensemble of eccentric cells encodes information about a spatial pattern over the eye, Hartline and his colleagues first used small spots of light that could excite only one or a few eccentric cells. The responses faithfully reflected the relative intensities of the spot, as when changing from a high to a low intensity; this is shown by the square step in the graph of Fig. 10.8B. They then repeated the experiment, using a test pattern containing a region of light and dark (Fig. 10.8A). Under these conditions, the impulse discharges of the eccentric cells near the light–dark boundary were modified so that they did *not* faithfully reflect the real luminosity of the stimulus; the eccentric cells on the light side of the border fired faster, whereas those on the dark side fired slower, than expected. There is thus an enhancement of contrast in the activity of the eccentric cells near the border.

The reason for this enhancement lies in the extensive inhibitory interconnections between the eccentric cells through their collateral branches within the plexus lying just below the eye. With relatively even illumination of the eye, the branches mediate relatively similar levels of inhibition onto each other. With a sharp border of contrast, however, the eccentric cell on the light edge receives less inhibition from its neighbor on the dark edge, and fires faster; conversely, this feeds more inhibition onto the darkly lit neighbor, whose already low level of impulse discharge is suppressed even more. This mechanism is illustrated by the diagram of Fig. 10.7B, and the envelope of firing intensities recorded experimentally is shown in Fig. 10.8B.

The classical studies of *Limulus* emphasized the importance of lateral inhibition for contrast enhancement and feature extraction, but recent work suggests that it also has other functions. In invertebrates, lateral inhibition appears to aid in image reconstruction by contributing to compensation for blurring of the image due to dispersion of light as it passes through the lens. Another function is as a gain control. *Limulus*, for example, responds to intensi-ties over 11 log units. In order to cover this enormously wide range, and still have mechanisms that enhance sensitivity at low levels near threshold, there must be a reduction of sensitivity (that is, a gain compression) as the intensity of stimulation increases. One mechanism for achieving this kind of gain compression is through feedback inhibition (see Chap. 16).

Sensory Perception

The end effect of stimulating a sensory system is to produce a behavioral response of the organism. In studies of animals, the only end effect we can measure is an observable reflex response. In human experience, however, we know that a reflex response may or may not be obligatory; in most cases, what is produced is an internal representation, a conscious image, of the stimulus, and we then proceed to act on that. The process of producing an internal image we call *perception*. It involves our recognition that stimulation has occurred, and our ability to discriminate various aspects of the stimulus.

The study of the quantitative relations between stimulus and perception constitutes the field of *psychophysics*. One of the aims of sensory neurobiology is to understand the neural mechanisms underlying these relations. The ultimate aim is to identify the *building blocks of perception*—the functional mechanisms used to construct our perceptual representation of the world about us.

Let us briefly review the main aspects of a stimulus that contribute to sensory perception as an introduction to the following chapters.

Detection

The simplest aspect of a perception is the ability to detect whether a stimulus has occurred. The level of intensity is called the *behavior threshold*. We have seen previously that each receptor has its characteristic threshold for responding to some minimum amount of its specific stimulus. As a general rule, several receptor responses must summate in order for transmission to occur in the sensory pathway. This was first shown in a classic study of the visual system by S. Hecht, S. Shlaer, and M. H. Pirenne in 1942. They calculated that a single photon is adequate for stimulating a single photoreceptor in the human retina, but the simultaneous activation of about seven receptors is necessary to perceive that stimulation has occurred. The behavioral threshold is therefore somewhat higher than the individual receptor threshold. In some systems, however, the thresholds may be very similar (see Chap. 12).

Magnitude Estimation

The next important property of a stimulus is how much of it there is. Primitive visual receptors of invertebrates, and the eyes of primitive vertebrates, are examples of receptors that are concerned mostly with this property. More advanced sensory systems are exquisitely tuned to registering stimulus magnitude over a wide range of intensities, in addition to other sensory qualities.

The study of magnitude estimations involves varying the stimulus in a quantitative manner and determining the physiological, behavioral, or perceptual response along some quantitative scale. This was first attempted and formalized by Ernst Weber (1834) and Gustav Fechner (1860) in Germany, and was the foundation stone of psychophysics as a science.

As is well known, these studies suggested that the response varies with the stimulus according to an exponential relation. This "law" was widely believed until around 1960, when S. S. Stevens at Harvard obtained evidence that in many systems the relation can better be described by a power law. The beginning student does not have to be concerned about the relative merits of these laws. Over limited magnitude ranges, both are reasonable approximations, as illustrated by the graphs in Fig. 10.9. What is important is that in most

Fig. 10.9 Hypothetical relations between stimulus and response. Stimulus intensity is plotted on the abscissa, response intensity on the ordinate. Logarithmic relation (according to Fechner) is plotted on linear (**A**) and logarithmic (**B**) scales. Exponential relation (according to Stevens) is plotted on linear (**C**) and logarithmic (**D**) scales. The curves may be very similar, as shown in E. (From Somjen, 1972)

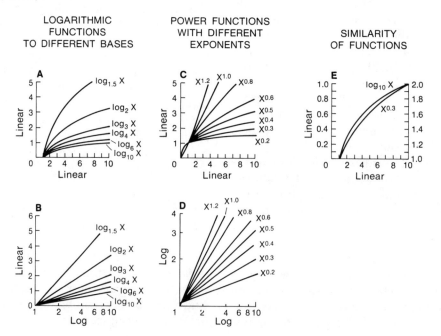

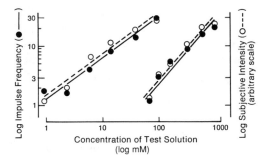

Fig. 10.10 Stimulus–response relations in a sensory system. Graph plots subjective intensity of taste sensation and frequency of impulse discharge in chorda tympani nerve in response to stimulation of the tongue with citric acid and glucose. Recordings were made in humans undergoing middle ear surgery, which exposes the chorda tympani nerve. (Modified from Borg et al., 1967)

sensory systems the psychological perception varies in strength with the intensity of stimulation in a quantitative manner.

In an attempt to get physiological evidence for this relation, neurobiologists have made recordings at various levels in several of the sensory pathways. Thus, as shown in Fig. 10.10, the concentration of a taste substance on the tongue was varied while recordings were made from the nerves from the tongue. The results showed that the magnitude of stimulation, of nerve response, and of perceptual estimation were all closely correlated. This experiment could be carried out in humans because of the accessibility of the nerve from the tongue for recording as it passes through the chamber of the middle ear. Another approach has been to study the behavioral responses and physiological recordings in primates, as a model for humans. In the somatosensory system, behavioral responses are closely correlated with the impulse discharge of neurons at successive levels, as we shall see in Chap. 12.

Spatial Discrimination

In sensory systems, natural stimulation of the receptors occurs in some spatial pattern. The ability to identify the site or pattern of stimulation is termed *spatial dis-*

crimination. This applies to the visual and somatosensory system, and also to the auditory system, in which different sounds affect different parts of the receptor population. A common way to study the somatosensory system for this quality is to test for *two-point discrimination,* to see how close together two points on the skin can be stimulated and still be perceived as two points rather than one. The comparable tests in the visual system are with two points of light (a measure of *visual acuity*), and with two tones in the auditory system.

The general finding is that at low intensities of stimulation, discrimination is poor, and is not much in evidence until some level of intensity above threshold. This is taken to indicate that weak stimulation mainly activates straight-through pathways in sensory systems, to enhance detection, and that only with increased intensities do horizontal interactions, such as those indicated in the diagrams of Figs. 10.5 and 10.6 come into play, to enhance spatial discrimination. This region, between threshold and discrimination, is called the *atonal area* in the auditory system; it is the region between the point at which we say "yes, I hear something" and "yes, I hear a different tone." The student can verify the phenomenon by weak and strong stimulation with two pencil points on his or her skin. That will also demonstrate that two-point discrimination varies widely in different parts of the body surface, as will be described further in Chap. 12.

Feature Abstraction

Natural stimulation does not usually consist of spots of light or points jabbing into the skin. Rather, it involves complex interplays of several stimulus properties. The strategy in studying the components that contribute to perception of a natural stimulus is to begin with spots of light, or a simple grating, in the case of the visual system, for example, and then change to increasingly more complex stimuli, such as moving spots and edges with different orientations, as we reach higher levels in the cerebral cortex. The results imply that a unit of perception involves a set of neurons and their connections that is tuned to a coordinated set of several stimulus properties, such as, in this case, light, movement, shape, orientation, and size. The set of properties may be said to constitute a feature, and the mechanisms whereby a neuron or circuit is tuned to this feature in preference to others is called *feature abstraction* or feature extraction. In the somatosensory system, the comparable process relates to the way we feel the texture of a surface by moving our hands over it ("active touch"), or the way we feel the texture of food with our tongues, which makes important contributions to the overall perception of palatability of food.

Both two-point discrimination and feature extraction, as they relate to spatial features, involve mechanisms of lateral inhibition and other types of interactions within sensory pathways. As we have seen, they enhance contrast between stimulated and unstimulated regions, and enhance changing stimuli over stationary ones. Analysis of these mechanisms has been one of the main achievements of sensory neurobiologists, as we will see in succeeding chapters.

Quality Discrimination

As pointed out previously, a given sensory modality characteristically contains several submodalities or qualities, and the discrimination of these as distinctly different is one of the main attributes of sensory systems. In general, the discrimination of qualities is regarded as being of two types, either analytic or synthetic. Consider a stimulus containing a mixture of two submodalities. In *analytic* discrimination, each submodality retains its individual character. Thus, in the taste modality, there are four basic qualities—sweet, salt, sour, and bitter. When we taste a mixture of, say, sugar and salt, the individual qualities can still be discerned; they do not merge to form a new sensation. The perception is analytic; it can be analyzed into its components. In contrast, in the perception of color, there are

primary colors—red, yellow, green—which when mixed together yield most other colors. The other colors are, in effect, *synthesized* from the primary colors, and have their own qualities, distinct from those of the primaries.

Pattern Recognition

In studying sensory mechanisms, we do experiments to analyze the system into its components, and then infer the process whereby the system uses those mechanisms to build up its behavioral response or conscious perception. In some cases, sensory systems may actually operate in that way, building up a perception from individual discriminations. However, one of the most vivid of mental experiences is the ability to take in a scene around us and instantly recognize a familiar pattern, or an unfamiliar one, or one that has some special significance. This is a capability that is prevalent throughout the Animal Kingdom. The actions of specific visual objects in releasing innate behavior patterns in many lower animals are vivid examples of this capability, as we shall discuss in Section III.

This property of sensory perceptions was first recognized by the Gestalt psychologists in the early part of this century. Gestalt means form, or shape, but as used by these workers it means the patterns we perceive and recognize as unitary wholes. As Edwin Boring (1950) put it:

In perceiving a melody you get the melodic form, not a string of notes, a unitary whole that is something more than the total list of its parts or even the serial pattern of them. This is the way experience comes to man, put up in significant structured forms . . .

This idea is sometimes thought to be opposed to the concept that perceptions are built up out of neural units, such as we have been discussing, but in fact there is no inconsistency. They are different aspects of the same problem, much as a table is made up of atoms, yet looks like a table.

Fig. 10.11 In this figure, the black areas appear as faces, the white area as the outline of an urn. Our perception alternates between these two interpretations. This illustrates that we perceive patterns as consistent wholes, each distinct from the other. It also illustrates that perception involves making a "decision" about what is the figure ("signal") and what is the background ("noise"). Finally, it shows that perception is not just a passive reception of individual sensory signals, but rather involves an active interpretation by the brain of the meaning of the stimulus patterns it receives. (Figure and legend from Gregory, 1966)

The important point is that many of our sensory experiences consist of complex patterns, either in space or in time, and we tend to perceive them as wholes more than in terms of their individual parts. This implies that such perceptions involve very large populations of neurons and very extensive sets of circuits. A related point is that although two patterns may be very similar, we can perceive them as distinctly different. The traditional example of this is the ability we all have to recognize our own grandmother in a crowd. Thus, although patterns may be similar, or may grade into each other, our perceptions are separate, distinct, discontinuous entities. This is illustrated in Fig. 10.11, just one of the many examples of this property in the visual system.

These considerations indicate that perceptions involve extensive sets of neurons and circuits, and that these sets, though overlapping, nonetheless mediate distinct responses. The analysis of individual neural components is the starting point, but we will obviously need information from many approaches, both experimental and theoretical, before a final understanding is reached.

11

Chemical Senses

From an evolutionary point of view it is convenient to start our study of sensory systems with the chemical senses. The first organisms to emerge from the primordial brine defined themselves as organisms by the degree to which they could sustain their own metabolism, and this required the ability to sense the appropriate nutritive constituents in their environment. The chemical senses are thus among our most primitive; on the other hand, they provide us (as well as our animal cousins) with some of our most powerful experiences. If you think about it, the ability of cells to "sense," or respond, to specific chemicals runs as a thread though much of the study of neurobiology: the responses to chemical neurotransmitters and hormones, the development of neural connections, and the sensory responses of chemoreceptors all depend on properties that at the molecular level are on the same continuum. In this respect, no other class of sensory receptors better illustrates the study of nerve cells as a part of molecular and cell biology.

The chemical senses may be divided into four categories: common chemical, internal receptors, taste, and smell. The *common chemical sense* includes all those cells that are sensitive to specific molecules or other chemical substances and which respond in ways that are communicated as signals to the nervous system. *Internal receptors* are a subclass of the above-mentioned receptors, which are specialized for monitoring various aspects of the chemical composition of the body that are vital for life. *Taste* and *smell* are familiar to everyone as distinct chemical modalities: taste, for sensing substances within our mouths; smell, for sensing airborne substances originating both in the outside environment and also from ingested foodstuffs.

Common Chemical Sense

Similar in many respects to those primordial inhabitants of Precambrian time are the present-day prokaryotes, the bacteria. Although at first glance they seem far removed from the subject of sensory receptors, they in fact express a number of properties of interest for our study.

Many bacteria show the property of *chemotaxis* (*chemo* = chemical, *taxis* = orientation). They have flagella by which they move about, swimming toward favorable environments and away from unfavorable ones. They do this by a process known as "tumbling," as illustrated in Fig.

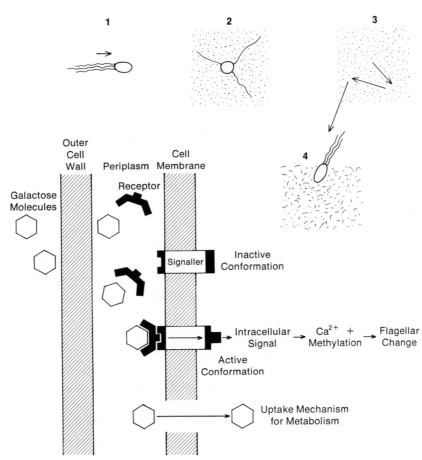

Fig. 11.1 Chemoreception in bacteria. Series 1–4 demonstrates chemotaxis. Bacterium swims with flagella together up a favorable nutrient gradient (**1**), "tumbles" when sensing an unfavorable environment (**2**), moves randomly (**3**), and finally senses a favorable gradient and swims up it (**4**). The molecular mechanism of chemical sensing is illustrated below. (After Koshland, 1980)

11.1. A favorable environment is one containing nutrients such as sugars and amino acids that are needed for metabolism so that the organism can survive; an unfavorable environment is one bereft of nutriment, or containing toxic or other harmful substances. The organism senses the favorable nutrient molecules by means of receptor molecules located just outside the cell membrane, or incorporated within it. The sensing mechanism is illustrated schematically in Fig. 11.1. Some molecules bind to the external receptors which then bind to membrane receptors; others bind directly to the membrane receptors. The binding induces a conformational change in the receptor protein which acts as a signal to initiate a second messenger system that leads to appropriate motor control of the flagella (see Fig. 11.1).

The sensory response has several properties that are shared with sensory responses in the nervous system. These include graded *specificity* (aspartate acts best on aspartate receptors, but also partially on other receptors), *summation* (responses to two or more different types of molecules are additive); and *adaptation* (there is a declining response to a maintained level of stimulation). Adaptation resets the motor activity to a baseline value, so that the bacterium can respond optimally over a wide range of stimulating concentrations; it thus resembles gain compression in the *Limulus* eye (Chap. 10). Adaptation also functions as a kind of short-term memory (see Chap. 29).

This system has been especially favorable for molecular analysis. Gene cloning has yielded the amino acid sequences of a number of the receptor peptides as well as several of the second messenger intermediates. Biochemical studies have shown that sensory adaptation is correlated with methylation of specific amino acid residues within the cytoplasmic domain of the receptor peptide (see Fig. 11.1). Genetic manipulation has produced receptor proteins lacking methylation sites; the flagella are still driven but the response does not adapt, showing that the single receptor protein has multiple roles for information processing within the cell. Thus, bacteria provide interesting insights into the nature of chemical receptor mechanisms and their genetic control.

Internal Chemoreceptors

Internal receptors for chemical substances in invertebrates have been studied relatively little. One example is the osphradial organ of molluscs. This organ is located under the mantle, and is believed to be involved in sensing the composition of water that circulates through the mantle cavity. Since the water enters directly from the outside, the osphradial organ is not really an internal organ, but its function is important for maintaining the composition of the internal fluids of the animal.

Internal receptors for a variety of substances have been identified in vertebrates (see Table 10.1, Chap. 10). We will have more to say about the common chemical sense when we discuss pain receptors (Chap. 12), and we will later study glucose receptors, and receptors for circulating toxins (Chap. 26). Here, we take as an example the *carotid body*, a sensory organ found in most vertebrate animals, which senses the

level of oxygenation of the circulating blood, and whose responses contribute to the reflexes which maintain blood oxygen at proper levels.

As shown in Fig. 11.2A, the carotid body is a small organ located between the internal and external carotid arteries which carry the blood supply to the head. Recordings from the fibers of cranial nerve IX (the glossopharyngeal) that connect the carotid body to the brainstem show a resting level of impulse discharge, as in Fig. 11.2B when the animal is breathing normal atmospheric air and the blood is normally oxygenated. When the oxygen tension decreases, under conditions of anoxia, the impulse discharge increases in frequency, as shown in the diagram.

The cellular organization of the carotid body is summarized in Fig. 11.2C. The IX nerve fibers, which arise from cells in the petrosal ganglion (a homologue of dorsal root ganglia), end within the carotid body in large terminals. Also within the carotid body are many *glomus cells*. These have few dendrites, and no axons. However, they have most of the fine structural characteristics of neurons, and they take part in synaptic connections with the large nerve terminals, and with each other. Most of these connections are arranged in pairs so that two synapses with opposite orientations are side by side, a type known as *reciprocal synapses*, discussed in Chap. 4.

It has been speculated that the carotid body functions in the following manner: lowering oxygen tension depolarizes the nerve terminal and makes it more excitable. This increases synaptic input to the glomus cells. The glomus cells feed back inhibition onto the nerve terminals, to control and modify the rate of impulse discharge. The glomus cells may be sensitive themselves to changing oxygen tension. They contain dopamine, stored in large dense-core vesicles (see diagram), which may also contribute to modulation of the afferent signals generated in the nerve terminals. Within the brainstem, the sensory input activates neu-

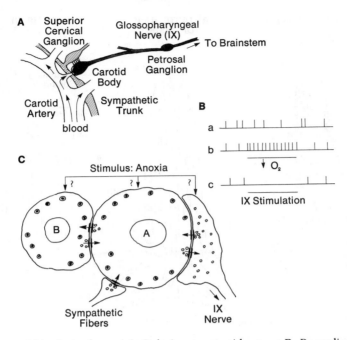

Fig. 11.2 The carotid body in the rat. **A.** Relation to carotid artery. **B.** Recordings from IX nerve, at rest (a), and when O_2 tension in blood is lowered (b). Electrical stimulation of IX nerve reduces sensory activity in the nerve (c), presumably by activating inhibitory reciprocal synapses between glomus cells (A, B in diagram C) and IX nerve terminals. **C.** Basic circuit diagram of synaptic organization of carotid body. (From Shepherd, 1979; C modified from McDonald and Mitchell, 1975)

rons in respiratory centers, to increase the rate of respiration and restore the normal level of oxygenation of the blood.

INVERTEBRATES

The Taste System

Cells that are preferentially sensitive to molecules in food materials may be designated as *taste receptor cells,* and the sensory modality is called taste, or *gustation.* Cells specialized for this purpose may be found almost anywhere on the body surface, for example, on antennae (in snails), tentacles (octopus), or legs (arthropods). A common location is near the mouth, where they can function to test for acceptance of nutritious food or rejection of toxic substances. A common arrangement consists

of a group of cells, each with a long distal process that reaches out to a pore opening in a pit at the body surface. Such an arrangement is seen in nematode worms, in a chemical sense organ called an *amphid.* These are paired organs near the mouth; there is often a similar pair of organs at the tail end of the worm. As seen in Fig. 11.3A, the distal processes of the cells are modified cilia. Substances enter the surface pore and stimulate the cilia at their tips.

There must be something effective about this arrangement, because chemoreceptors in insects are organized along similar, though more specialized, lines. The characteristic structure housing the receptors in these species is called a *sensillum.* This consists of a modification of the cuticle into the form of peg, pit, plate, socket, or hair. The hair has been most studied. As shown in Fig. 11.3B, the receptor cell bodies are at the base of

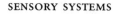

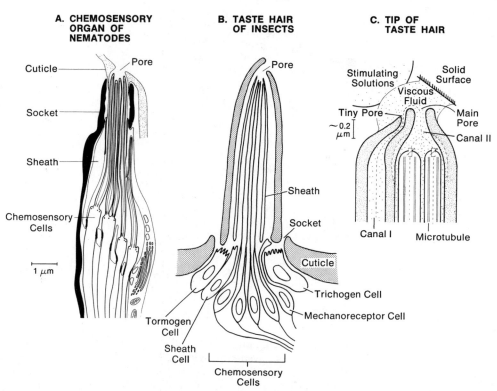

A. CHEMOSENSORY ORGAN OF NEMATODES

Cuticle
Pore
Socket
Sheath
Chemosensory Cells
1 μm

B. TASTE HAIR OF INSECTS

Pore
Sheath
Socket
Cuticle
Trichogen Cell
Mechanoreceptor Cell
Tormogen Cell
Sheath Cell
Chemosensory Cells

C. TIP OF TASTE HAIR

Stimulating Solutions
Solid Surface
Viscous Fluid
Tiny Pore
~0.2 μm
Main Pore
Canal II
Canal I
Microtubule

Fig. 11.3 A. The chemoreceptor organ (amphid) of a nematode worm. Note sensory neurons terminating in cilia. (From Ward, 1977) **B.** A labellar taste hair (sensillum) of a blowfly. **C.** Tip of hair at high magnification. Dashed lines: paths for electric current flow induced by chemical stimulation of tips of cilia. (After Hansen, 1978)

the hair, and their distal processes enter the hair and extend to its tip. The processes are regarded as dendrites, though they are actually cilia (like those of the nematode), containing a 9 + 2 array of microtubules. At the tip there is a pore opening, which is covered with a tiny drop of a viscous fluid (see Fig. 11.3C). Stimulus molecules diffuse in this fluid through the pore and contact the dendritic tips. Here the molecules are believed to bind to receptor proteins, which then bring about a change in membrane conductivity—this is the step of *sensory transduction*. Little is known as yet about these mechanisms at the molecular level.

The physiology of taste receptors has been studied intensively in the blowfly *(Phormia regina)*. Vincent Dethier of the University of Massachusetts has summarized a lifetime of work on this animal in

his book *The Hungry Fly*. Figure 11.4A shows a blowfly mounted on the shaft of a capillary micropipette, with the tip inserted into the proboscis for recording from receptor cell axons over long periods of time. Figures 11.4B and C are enlarged diagrams of the two most common locations of taste sensory hairs, the tip (labellum) of the proboscis, and the distal segments (tarsi) of the legs. For short-term recordings, a microelectrode can be inserted into the base of the hair, to record directly from the receptor cells; alternatively, a micropipette containing solutions of substances can be placed with its tip enclosing a hair, for both stimulation and recording.

With these methods it has been found that each of four sensory cells in the hair is preferentially sensitive to a particular type of stimulating molecule. The four taste

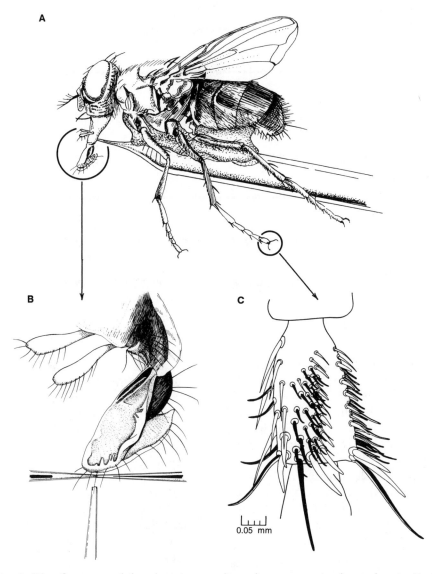

Fig. 11.4 **A.** Blowfly mounted for chronic recordings from nerves in the proboscis. **B.** Close-up view of labellum, with electrode arrangement for recording from single hair. **C.** Close-up view of chemosensory hairs on one tarsal segment. (From Dethier, 1976)

receptor cell types are water, sugar, and two types of salt receptor, based on sensitivity to the cation or the anion. The final cell type is a mechanoreceptor. Sample recordings from a hair are shown in Fig. 11.5, using a setup similar to that depicted in Fig. 11.4B.

When we say that a cell is preferentially sensitive to a given compound, we mean that it responds with the lowest threshold and the most vigorous activity in comparison with other compounds. However, there is usually, in addition, some responsiveness to other compounds. Also, there may be inhibitory interactions between the responses to two compounds; these interactions may occur at the receptor membrane sites, or they may occur between the cilia or cell bodies within the hair. These properties are seen in the responses to pure

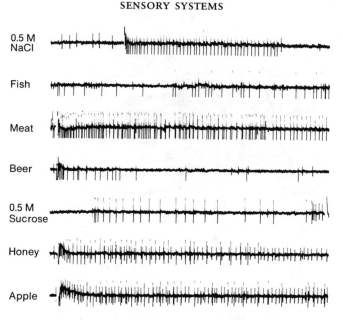

Fig. 11.5   Receptor responses of a single labellar hair to different substances. (From Dethier, 1976)

stimuli such as sugar or salt. When the stimuli are natural food substances, the cells within a single hair shown even more complicated combinations of responsiveness. Thus, results such as those in Fig. 11.5 have shown that sometimes the response of a hair is dominated by one cell (for example, a salt receptor response to beer), but more often more than one cell contributes significantly to the response. These different response patterns occur, Dethier has concluded,

> because each (natural) substance . . . is chemically complex, and because each receptor cell of the hair has a characteristic action spectrum rather than a unitary specificity. If the central nervous system is capable of analysing these patterns, there is contained within them sufficient information to characterize each substance as different.

We will have more to say about the neural code for different substances when we discuss vertebrate taste receptors later in this chapter.

The physiological evidence for different sensory receptors and for the encoding of taste information has been supported by studies of the behavioral responses of the fly. In these studies, the investigator determines the degree of acceptance or rejection of a substance, as judged by the amount of extension (acceptance) or retraction (rejection) of the proboscis. This is a very sensitive method for determining behavioral threshold; stimulation of only a single hair with a highly concentrated sugar solution will elicit the behavioral response of proboscis extension. Feeding behavior can be studied quantitatively with this method, and in Chap. 26 we will learn how the effectiveness of food stimuli is dependent on the state of hunger of the animal.

The Olfactory System

Many molecules of biological importance arise from sources at a distance from the organism. The sources may be plants, predators, prey, or other members of the same species (conspecifics). As we discussed in Chap. 4, molecules that transmit signals between conspecifics are called *pheromones*. Edward Wilson (1975), in his book *Sociobiology*, notes that

> pheromones . . . were probably the first signals put to use in the evolution of life . . . With

the emergence of . . . (higher) metazoan phyla, it was possible to create more sophisticated auditory and visual systems equipped to handle as much information as the chemoreceptors of single-celled organisms. Occasionally these new forms of communication have overridden the original chemical systems, but pheromones remain the fundamental signals for most kinds of organisms.

The evolutionary relation between pheromones and neurotransmitters was discussed in Chap. 4.

The receptors for pheromones and other distant stimulating molecules are called *olfactory receptors,* and the sensory modality is called smell, or *olfaction.* Nearly all organisms have olfactory receptors. In marine animals the stimulating molecules are transmitted through water, whereas in terrestrial animals the transmitting medium is

the air. The transmitting medium places certain requirements on the types of molecules that can be transmitted. Thus for aquatic organisms the molecules are generally soluble in water, such as acids and proteins, whereas in terrestrial organisms the molecules may be either lipid soluble or water soluble. Pheromone molecules range from 5 to 20 carbon atoms, and from 100 to 300 in molecular weight. The increasing complexity of larger molecules imparts higher information-carrying capacity, but the molecules cannot be too large or they will not be adequately volatile in the air.

The olfactory sense reaches its highest development, among the invertebrates, in the social insects. On the output side, these animals are, in Wilson's phrase, "walking batteries of exocrine glands." Figure 11.6

Fig. 11.6   Diagram of the body of a honeybee, showing the locations of different exocrine glands whose secretions are involved in social organization. The glands and their secretions and functions are listed. (From Wilson, 1975)

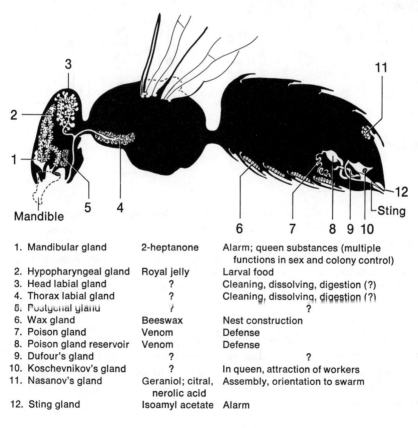

1. Mandibular gland	2-heptanone	Alarm; queen substances (multiple functions in sex and colony control)
2. Hypopharyngeal gland	Royal jelly	Larval food
3. Head labial gland	?	Cleaning, dissolving, digestion (?)
4. Thorax labial gland	?	Cleaning, dissolving, digestion (?)
5. Postgenal gland	?	?
6. Wax gland	Beeswax	Nest construction
7. Poison gland	Venom	Defense
8. Poison gland reservoir	Venom	Defense
9. Dufour's gland	?	?
10. Koschevnikov's gland	?	In queen, attraction of workers
11. Nasanov's gland	Geraniol; citral, nerolic acid	Assembly, orientation to swarm
12. Sting gland	Isoamyl acetate	Alarm

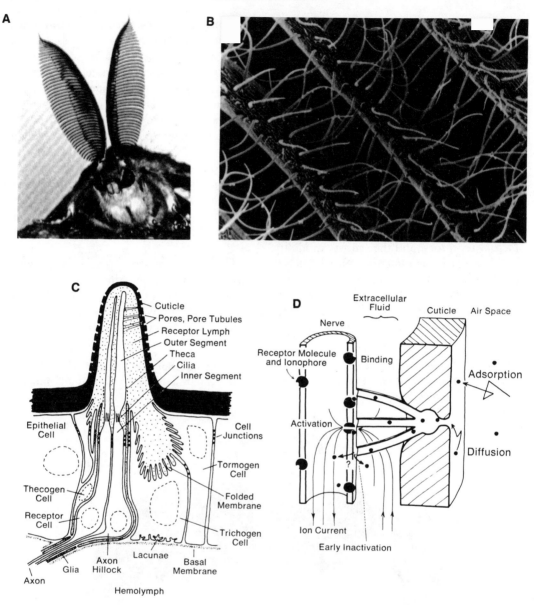

Fig. 11.7 **A.** Male gypsy moth, showing the two large antennae. The length of the antennae is about 8 mm. **B.** Scanning electron micrograph showing main branches (diameter, 50 μm) giving rise to many sensory hairs. Spacing of branches and hairs has been shown to be critical for optimal capture of odorant molecules. (From Schneider et al., 1977) **C.** Schematic diagram of an olfactory sensillum. (From Kaissling and Thorson, 1979) **D.** Schematic representation of transduction processes in a pheromone receptor cell of the silkmoth. (Courtesy of K.-E. Kaissling and J. Boeckh)

shows a schematic diagram of a honeybee and locations of these glands, including those that emit pheromones.

On the receptor side, most olfactory receptors are located in the *antennae,* which

are paired, unbranching or branching appendages arising from the head of the insect. The antennae of the gypsy moth are shown in the photograph of Fig. 11.7. The total number of receptors in both antennae ranges from 40,000 to 200,000 in different insects.

Receptor Mechanisms

Like the insect taste receptors, the olfactory receptor cells are organized within *sensilla,* or hairs (see Fig. 11.7). The basic structure is similar to that of the taste hair. However, the sensory cells within a hair may be one or several, and each cell characteristically has several peripheral dendrites (cilia). Olfactory hairs differ also in their surface pore systems. In some cases, there are many tiny pores (up to 15,000 per hair). Each pore opens inward into an enlargement (called a kettle) from which arise several tubules which communicate with the inner sheath space and receptor cell dendrites (see Fig. 11.7). There is evidence that odorous molecules are first absorbed onto an outer cuticle layer and then diffuse through it to the pore, where they diffuse inward through the kettle-tubule system to reach receptor dendrites.

The best-studied of the olfactory stimulating molecules are the sex attractants that female moths emit to attract males. The first one, identified in 1959, was that of the silk moth *Bombyx mori,* and was named *bombykol* (a bit easier to remember than the chemical name, *trans*-10, cis-12-hexadecadien-1-ol!). This is a 16-carbon, double unsaturated alcohol (see Fig. 11.8A). A number of sex attractants of other insect species have since been isolated and synthesized, and most of them are of a similar order of complexity.

The sex pheromones are legendary for their extremely high potency. It has been estimated that a single molecule is sufficient to elicit a detectable response in a receptor cell (see below), and 200 molecules, eliciting a discharge of 200 impulses per second, are sufficient to elicit the behavioral response of the male. Thus, olfactory stimulation by pheromones occurs near the theoretical limit of resolution, a situation that we will see also applies to auditory and visual reception; taste stimulation, by contrast, requires much higher stimulus concentrations.

The mechanism of transduction of the molecular stimulus into a receptor response has been studied with high-gain electrophysiological recordings from single olfactory hairs. With very weak stimulation (Fig. 11.8B), small, steplike negative deflections of the baseline can be seen preceding large spike responses. Karl-Ernst Kaissling and John Thorson in Germany have suggested that these deflections are *unitary receptor potentials* that represent the opening of single ion channels. With stronger stimulation (Fig. 11.8C), the unitary potentials of the several cells in the hair summate to give a graded receptor potential, called an *electro-antennogram.* It is presumed that the receptor potentials are coupled to action potentials by electrotonic spread of current through the dendrites, as we have discussed previously (Chaps. 7 and 10).

When tested with different odors, a given insect olfactory receptor will respond to a certain number, which constitutes its *response spectrum.* When the responses to a wide range of olfactory stimuli are analyzed, it is found that the receptors tend to fall into several categories with respect to their response spectra. According to Jürgen Boeckh of Regensburg, these may be summarized as follows (Fig. 11.9). The first category is the *pheromone odor specialist,* which is narrowly tuned to a given pheromone molecule. This may be thought of as a receptor for a "labeled line." Cells responding to one pheromone (e.g., bombykol) have identical narrow turning curves (see Narrow Specialists, Within Group Spectrum I in Fig. 11.9A), and those responding to another pheromone (e.g., bombykal) have identically distinct curves (see Within Group Spectrum II in Fig. 11.9A).

Second is the *group specialist.* A cell in this category responds to a group of compounds. Good examples are the esters or alcohols that make up the odors of meats, fruits, and other natural foodstuffs. Some cells have identical response spectra for a series of alcohols; others, for a series of

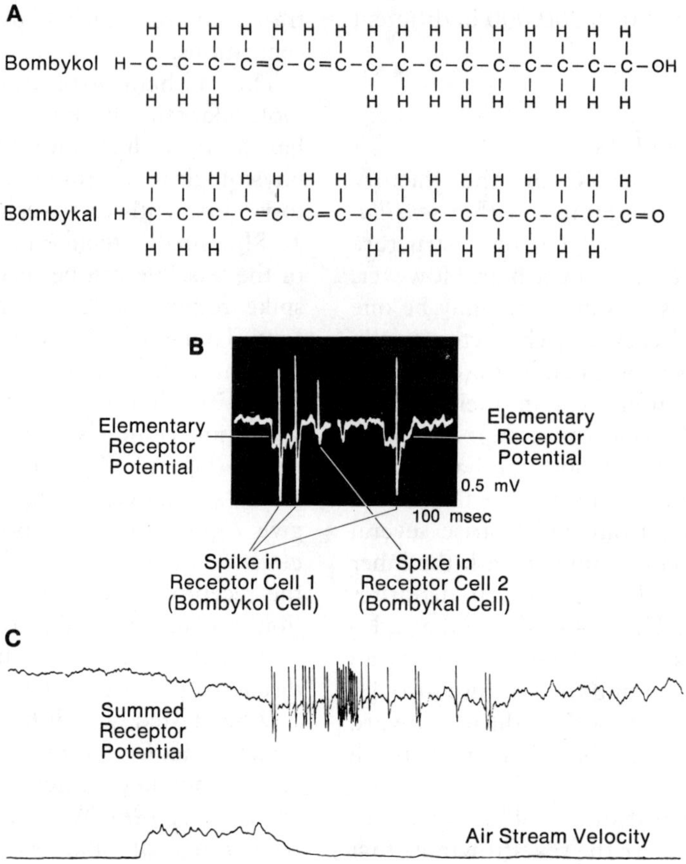

A

Bombykol

$$H-\underset{\underset{H}{|}}{\overset{\overset{H}{|}}{C}}-\underset{\underset{H}{|}}{\overset{\overset{H}{|}}{C}}-\underset{\underset{H}{|}}{\overset{\overset{H}{|}}{C}}-\overset{\overset{H}{|}}{C}=\overset{\overset{H}{|}}{C}-\overset{\overset{H}{|}}{C}=\overset{\overset{H}{|}}{C}-\cdots$$

Bombykal

B

Elementary Receptor Potential — Elementary Receptor Potential

0.5 mV

100 msec

Spike in Receptor Cell 1 (Bombykol Cell)   Spike in Receptor Cell 2 (Bombykal Cell)

C

Summed Receptor Potential

Air Stream Velocity

Fig. 11.8 Transduction of a pheromone-stimulating molecule. **A.** Molecular structure of bombykol and bombykal. Bombykol elicits fluttering in male moths, which initiates their search for females. Bombykal, acting through different receptors, suppresses fluttering. **B.** Receptor events in a single hair of a male gypsy moth antenna elicited by weak stimulation with bombykol. **C.** Receptor events elicited by strong stimulation with bombykol. (From Kaissling and Thorson, 1979).

esters (see Fig. 11.9B). Third is the *group generalist*. These cells also respond to only one group of compounds, but the response spectra for the cells are all different from each other (see Fig. 11.9C). The final category is called *broad generalist*. A cell in this category has a response spectrum that spans different types of compounds, and each cell is different from all others.

Our present understanding of the functional significance of these response categories is that they enable different odors to elicit different types of behavior. The *narrow specialists* function as labeled lines for

elliciting mating and other stereotyped behaviors that are essential for the survival of the species. The *group specialists* function as more broadly tuned, overlapping labeled lines that mediate behavior, such as certain feeding patterns, essential for the survival of the individual. The *group generalists* and *broad generalists,* by contrast, have spectra that overlap broadly. Although it has been difficult to understand how these overlapping spectra can provide a basis for the ability of an insect (and ourselves) to discriminate individual odor molecules, it may be speculated that they

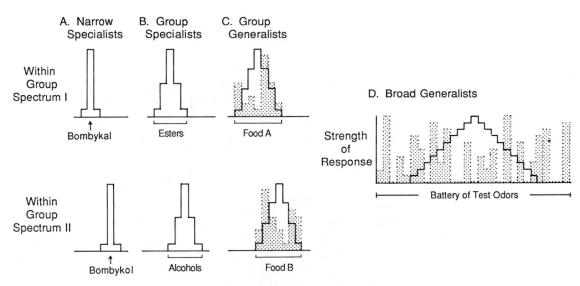

Fig. 11.9 Basic response categories of olfactory receptor neurons in insects. This figure summarizes results from different species. Each graph illustrates the different strengths of response (impulses per second) of a single receptor neuron to a series of test odors. **A.** Narrow specialists (found in moths and roaches). These neurons respond mainly to one type of pheromone molecule or closely related molecules; there is little overlap with other phermones (compare groups I and II). **B.** Group specialists (found in locust and cockroach). These neurons respond to a specific group of compounds, present especially in foods, such as esters or alcohols. The spectra are identical within a group; there may be considerable overlap between groups. **C.** Group generalists (found in honeybee). These neurons also respond to a specific group of molecules, but each spectrum is different. **D.** Broad generalists (found in some moths). These neurons respond in different degrees to a variety of compounds from different groups; each spectrum is different from the rest. (Based on J. Boeckh and V. Boeckh, personal communication)

perform a function analogous to the color spectra of cones in the retina. First, by overlapping, they provide the necessary means for distinguishing between odor identity and odor intensity. Second, they provide a basis for higher-order processing involving "opponent-odor" mechanisms, in analogy with opponent color mechanisms in the visual system (see Chap. 16). Here, as elsewhere, comparisons with the visual system provide insights that cut across different systems, and suggest principles that can be tested in future experiments.

Central Olfactory Pathways

The information encoded in the receptor cells is transmitted to the antennal lobe of the deutocerebrum of the insect brain. The interesting finding here is that the receptor axons terminate in small round regions known as *glomeruli* (see Fig. 11.10.). We noted in Chap. 4 the importance of modularization as a basis for the organization of neurons into functional circuits, and the glomerulus is one of the clearest examples of this principle.

We are only just beginning to learn about the significance of glomeruli for olfactory processing. One of the most important leads is the finding that there is a distinctive glomerulus, found only in the male, that is involved in transmitting information about the female sex attractant pheromone. We will discuss this further in Chap. 27. Another interesting fact is that olfactory transmission also takes place through glomeruli in the vertebrate olfactory system, and that glomeruli for specific types of molecules

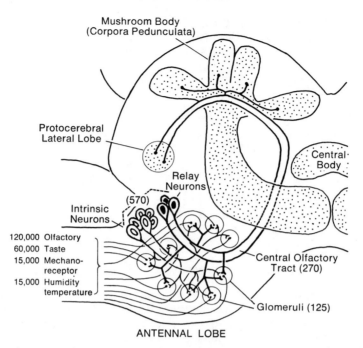

Fig. 11.10 The central olfactory pathway in the insect (cockroach). At the left are indicated the numbers of olfactory and other receptors that project from the antenna to the antennal lobe, where the axons terminate in glomeruli. The numbers of glomeruli, relay and intrinsic neurons, and output axons are indicated in parentheses. The output axons form the central olfactory tract, which projects to the highest centers in the brain, the mushroom bodies and the lateral lobe. (From Boeckh et al., 1975)

have been found there as well (see below, and Chap. 27). Thus, encoding information about odor molecules requires segregating and combining the information in modules. We will return to this question later in the chapter in discussing the vertebrates. Other aspects of the central olfactory pathway in insects are discussed in the legend to Fig. 11.10.

VERTEBRATES

The Taste System

Taste Receptors

In aquatic vertebrates, as in many invertebrates, taste receptors are not always limited to the mouth. For example, in some species of bottom-dwelling fish, there are fingerlike projections from the anterior (pectoral) fins that point downward, and carry taste receptors at their tips. This arrangement seems well designed to detect foodstuffs in the muddy bottom where these species live.

In vertebrates, taste receptors are characteristically found on the tongue, and to some extent at the back of the mouth and pharynx. At the cellular level, taste receptor cells are grouped together in *taste buds*. Taste buds are found in *papillae,*which are blunt pegs on the surface of the tongue. There are several types of papillae, and these have different distributions on the tongue surface, as shown in Fig. 11.11A,B.

The cell types within the taste bud are as follows. Types 1 and 2 (see Fig. 11.11C) are *supporting cells;* they have microvilli at their tips, and appear to secrete substances into the lumen of the taste bud. Type 3 is believed to be the *sensory receptor cell;* it

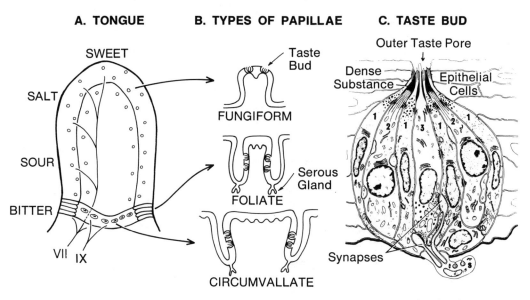

A. TONGUE   **B. TYPES OF PAPILLAE**   **C. TASTE BUD**

Fig. 11.11 A. Distribution of taste buds, innervation pattern, and lowest threshold regions for different tastes in the human tongue. **B.** Main types of taste papillae, containing taste buds. **C.** Fine structure of a taste bud. See text for explanation. (From Murray, 1973)

has peglike extensions into the lumen that are probably the sites of sensory transduction. The fourth type of cell is the *basal cell*. Radioactive labeling studies indicate that basal cells arise by inward migration of surrounding epithelial cells. The basal cells, in turn, differentiate into new sensory receptor cells. This process continues throughout adult life, because the receptor cells have lifetimes of only about 10 days. Thus, there is continual turnover of sensory cells in the taste buds. We will see that a similar process occurs in vertebrate olfactory receptors (next section). It is not known how the sensory specificity of a taste bud is maintained in the face of this continual replacement of the sensory elements.

Taste Qualities: Membrane Mechanisms

When we eat natural foods, our taste sensations are complicated mixtures of qualities. However, when humans are tested with pure chemical compounds, the taste sensations can all be grouped into four distinct qualities. These are *sweet, salt, sour,* and *bitter*. These qualties were first recognized

in a systematic way early in this century, and have dominated thinking about taste mechanisms ever since. When small droplets of different solutions are placed on the tongue, it is found that the taste qualities are preferentially (though not exclusively) elicited from different areas, as indicated in Fig. 11.11A.

Many studies have been directed at elucidating the molecular basis of the interaction between the taste molecule and the receptor cell membrane. Electrophysiological data are limited (see Fig. 11.12A,B); most come from *psychophysics*. As discussed in the previous chapter, this is the field in which the quantitative relations between sensory stimuli and sensory perceptions are analyzed, in order to gain insight into the physical nature of the stimulus and the psychological nature of the sensation. These studies may be summarized as follows, in relation to Fig. 11.12C. The *salt* taste is produced in its purest form by NaCl, and also to varying degrees by other inorganic salts and mixtures of various compounds. It has been postulated that the action of the cation (+) on the receptor

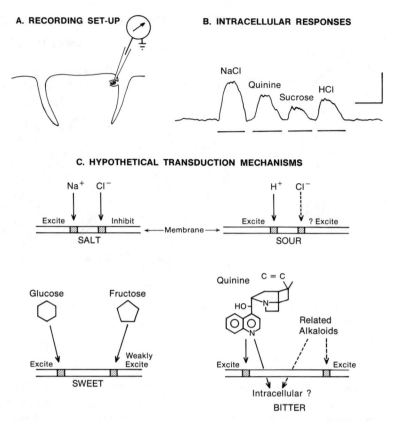

Fig. 11.12 Intracellular analysis of taste cells, showing recording setup (**A**) and typical responses (**B**). This is a "NaCl best" cell that shows sensitivity as well to the other three taste modalities. Horizontal scale, 10 secs; vertical scale, 10 mV. (From Kimura and Beidler, in Bartoshuk, 1978) **C.** Simplified models of hypothetical transducer mechanisms in the membranes of taste bud cells for reception of the four taste modalities. (Based on Beidler, 1980 and Bartoshuk, 1978) For further discussion of these mechanisms, see Teeter et al (1987).

membranes is excitatory, whereas the anion $(-)$ is inhibitory. The *sour* taste is produced by acids. The sourness may be due to the action of the hydrogen ion in the case of inorganic acids, but it may also depend on the action of the anion of organic acids. The *sweet* taste is believed to depend on the stereochemical configuration of glucose and related organic molecules, and the closeness of their fit to a membrane receptor molecule. The *bitter* taste is characteristically elicited by poisonous or toxic plant substances like quinine. The mechanism of action is unknown; it may occur at the surface membrane, or within the cell (see Fig. 11.12C).

Sensory Processing

The taste sensory cells have no axons; information is transmitted from them through synapses onto the terminals of sensory fibers within the taste bud (see Fig. 11.11C). The fibers arise from ganglion cells of cranial nerves VII (facial nerve) and IX (glossopharyngeal nerve) (see Fig. 11.11A). Most of the fibers from the anterior part of the tongue run in the chorda tympani, a branch of VII.

The fact that we distinguish four basic tastes and that they can be preferentially elicited from different areas of the tongue, suggests that each area might be the basis

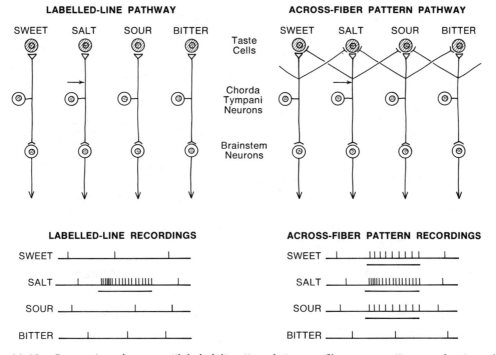

Fig. 11.13 Comparison between "labeled lines" and "across-fiber patterns" as mechanisms for processing information about taste. (Based on Pfaffman et al., 1976)

for a *"labeled line"* carrying information about its specific submodality to the brain. This situation is depicted in Fig. 11.13A. However, the first unit recordings from single fibers in the chorda tympani by Carl Pfaffman, then at Brown University, in 1941, showed that this could not be the case. A single fiber might respond best to one stimulation, but it also characteristically showed varying degrees of response to other types of stimuli. This implies that a given fiber receives synapses within the taste bud from several receptor cells with differing response specificities. Pfaffman et al. (1976) suggested that "in such a system, sensory quality does not depend simply on . . . activation of some particular fiber group alone, but on the pattern of others active." This became known as the *"across-fiber pattern"* theory of taste quality; it is depicted in Fig. 11.13B.

In recent years there has been much debate among workers in the field of taste as to the relative merits of the labeled line vs. the across-fiber pattern theory. As usual in such cases, there are elements of the truth in both theories. Specific receptor cells (Fig. 11.12B) and chorda tympani fibers each have their "best" stimulus, but at each level there is graded responsiveness to other stimulus types. Taste information thus appears to be encoded by means of interactions between many elements of different specificities; in other words, elements that have overlapping response spectra. If this is what is meant by "across-fiber patterns," it is the same principle that underlies the encoding of visual information, and possibly of odor information by generalist receptors, as discussed above.

Taste Pathways

The fibers carrying taste information make their synapses centrally in the medulla, in a thin line of cells called the *nucelus of the solitary tract* (see Fig. 11.14). These cells

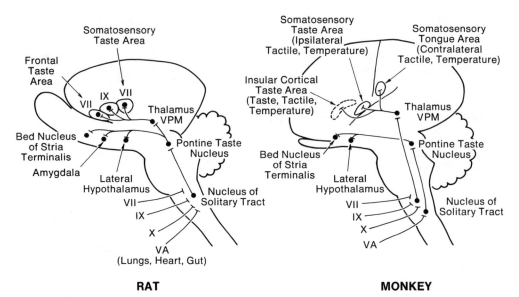

Fig. 11.14 Taste pathways in the central nervous system of the rat and monkey. VA: visceral afferents; VPM: ventral posterior medial nucleus of the thalamus. (Based on Norgren, 1980, and personal communication)

give rise to ascending pathways which differ in different species. The best known examples are the rat and the monkey, which are summarized in the diagrams of Fig. 11.14. Note, in the rat, the relay in the pons, the bifurcating connections from there to the basal forebrain and the thalamocortical projections. In contrast, in the monkey, the specific taste pathway connects only to the thalamocortial system. The pathways to somatosensory cortex presumably mediate the conscious perceptions of taste quality, whereas the pathways to hypothalamus, amygdala, and insula carry taste information to the limbic system. These pathways may be important for the affective qualities of taste stimulation, and they might also play a role in affective and memory processes that underlie learned taste aversions in feeding behavior, as we will discuss further in Chap 29.

The Olfactory System

A Comment on Noses

Although we think that we smell with our noses, this is a little like saying that we hear with our ear lobes. In fact, the part of the nose we can see from the outside serves only to take in and channel the air containing odorous molecules; the actual sensing is done by receptors lying deep within the nasal cavity. Thus, in analogy with the ear, there is an *outer nose* (as seen from the outside), a *middle nose* (the nasal cavity), and an *inner nose* (the olfactory sensory organ).

In a lower vertebrate like a fish or frog, the nasal cavity may be a relatively simple sac, and the stream of water or air passes directly over the receptor sheet (see Fig. 11.15A). In mammals, the situation is more complicated. The keenest sniffers, like opossums, rabbits, or dogs, have wondrously complex nasal cavities (Fig. 11.15B). In these species, the inhaled air first passes through a kind of "air conditioner," that consists of many folds of mucus membrane that warm and humidify it. The air then passes into the pharynx, but it also gives rise to eddy currents that circulate through a complex system of turbinates, at the back of the nasal cavity, which are lined with the olfactory receptor neurons. There is as

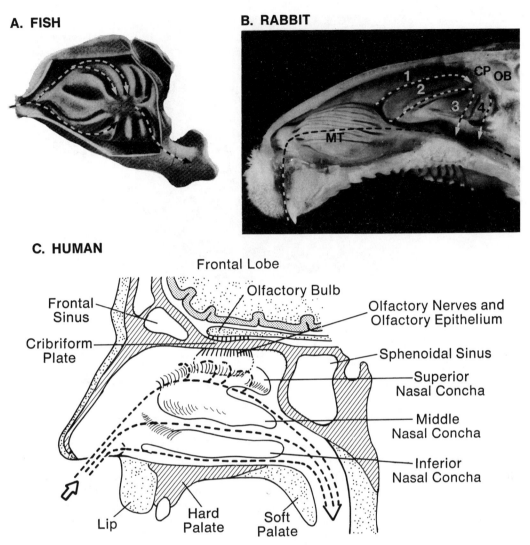

A. FISH

B. RABBIT

C. HUMAN

Fig. 11.15 Comparison of the olfactory organs in several vertebrates. **A.** Fish. Dashed line indicates pathway for flow of water over the folds of the receptor sheet. **B.** Rabbit. Dashed lines indicate air flow. MT, maxillary turbinates, where the incoming air is warmed and humidified; (1–4), nasal turbinates, containing the receptor sheet; CP, cribriform plate, the bone through which the olfactory nerves pass; OB, olfactory bulb, where the olfactory axons terminate. (Photograph courtesy of L. B. Haberly) **C.** Human. Dashed lines indicate air flow over the turbinates, and eddy currents over the olfactory epithelium in the dorsal recess of the nasal cavity.

yet no idea of precisely how the air is drawn through these turbinates to reach all the receptors. In the human (Fig. 11.15C), the turbinates are relatively simple, and the olfactory receptor neurons are confined to a patch of membrane in the most dorsal recess of the nasal cavity.

Olfactory Receptors

As noted in Chap. 9 (Fig. 9.14), the olfactory receptor neurons lie in a thin sheet. The mature cell has a long thin dendrite that terminates in a small knob at the surface (see Fig. 11.16). This knob gives rise

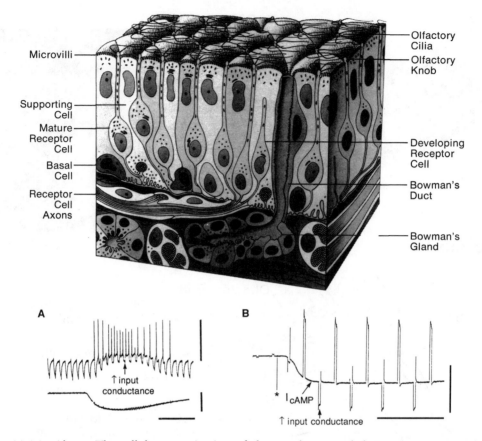

Fig. 11.16 *Above:* The cellular organization of the vertebrate epithelium. (From Warwick and Williams, 1973) *Below:* **A.** The response of an olfactory receptor neuron in the salamander to a puff of odor (camphor). The intracellular response consists of a slow depolarizing receptor potential giving rise to a burst of spikes (upper trace). Repeated brief injections of hyperpolarizing current produced smaller downward voltage deflections during the response, showing that the response was associated with an increased input conductance. The summed extracellular voltage response recorded from the epithelial surface is shown in the lower trace. Calibrations: voltage scale, 40 mV for upper trace, 5 mV for lower trace; time scale, 1 sec. **B.** Whole-cell patch-clamp recording from a salamander receptor neuron, showing the action of cAMP. The tip of a recording electrode containing cAMP was sealed onto the membrane of a freshly dissociated neuron. When the membrane under the tip was ruptured by suction (asterisk), cAMP diffused into the cell, eliciting a large inward depolarizing current (slow downward shift of trace), accompanied by an increase in membrane conductance (shown by larger responses to brief voltage pulses compared with before rupture; these responses increase, rather than decrease as in A, because the cell is under voltage clamp). Calibrations: current scale, 5 nA; time scale, 5 sec. (A from Trotier and MacLeod, 1986; B from D. Trotier, personal communication)

to several cilia, which may be up to 200 μm in length, but are only 0.1–0.2 μm in diameter. The cilia contain microtubules arranged in the 9 pairs + 2 pattern typical of cilia elsewhere in the body. When observed under the microscope at high power,

the cilia can be seen to be waving, slowly but asynchronously, in contrast to the coordinated, rapid beating of respiratory cilia. The cilia lie in a thin layer of mucus which is secreted by supporting cells and by Bowman's glands (see diagram, Fig. 11.16). The

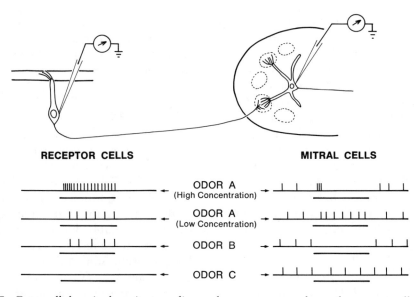

Fig. 11.17 Extracellular single-unit recordings of responses to odors of receptor cells (left) and mitral cells (right) in the salamander, showing different types of responses and different temporal patterns of activity. (After Kauer, 1974, and Getchell and Shepherd, 1978)

generation of new olfactory receptor neurons from basal cells has been described in Chap. 9.

Olfactory molecules stimulate the receptors by first being absorbed into the mucus, diffusing to the cilia (and perhaps olfactory knob), and binding to receptor molecules in the membrane. The mechanism of transduction and its linkage to a second messenger system has been discussed in Chap. 10 (see Fig. 10.2). Intracellular and whole-cell patch recordings have shown that transduction causes an increase in membrane conductance (see Fig. 11.16A), opening channels to inward cation flow that gives rise to the depolarizing receptor potential. Whole-cell patch recordings, as in B, support the biochemical evidence that cAMP acts as a second messenger in linking some olfactory receptor molecules (odoreceptors) to the conductance channels. Recent experiments by Tadashi Nakamura and Geoff Gold (1987) at Yale have shown that cAMP (and cGMP) acts directly on the channel, without a phosphorylation step, reminiscent of the direct action of cGMP on membrane channels in photoreceptors.

The single-channel events underlying the olfactory receptor responses are only just beginning to be revealed.

The receptor potential spreads from the cilia through the dendrite to the cell body by essentially the same process of electrotonic spread that we discussed in the crustacean stretch receptor cell (Chap. 7). In the cell body the depolarization triggers action potentials, which are conducted in the axon to the first relay station, the olfactory bulb.

In response to stimulation with a battery of odors, a given receptor cell characteristically shows a broad spectrum of sensitivity. As shown in Fig. 11.17 (left), it may respond briskly to odor A, weakly to odor B, and not at all to odor C. A cell may be sensitive in this way, in varying degrees, to 10 or 12 different odors. These responses thus fall into the category of "odor generalist" previously described for insect olfactory receptors. Odor "specialists" have not been seen, though the presence of receptors narrowly tuned to mammalian pheromones seems likely.

Several studies have shown that olfactory

receptors respond to prolonged or repeated stimulation with a slowly adapting, prolonged discharge of impulses (see Fig. 11.17). This is in contrast of course to our behavioral experience that odor sensations fade rapidly. Thus, when entering a closed, stifled room with an unpleasant odor, we are initially disgusted, but after a minute or two may cease to be aware of the odor unless we inhale more deeply. It appears that this adaptation is not due to fading of the receptor response, but rather is a property of inhibitory interactions in central neural circuits in the olfactory pathway.

The Olfactory Bulb

In the olfactory bulb, the olfactory axons terminate in rounded regions of neuropil called glomeruli. These are a constant feature of the bulb throughout the vertebrates, and are similar to the glomeruli in the insect olfactory pathway. The synaptic organization of the olfactory bulb has been discussed previously (Chaps. 4, 7, and 10). The olfactory axons make synapses within the glomeruli onto the dendrites of mitral and tufted cells, which are the output neurons of the olfactory bulb.

Odor Responses

In single-unit recordings, mitral cells show a range of responsiveness to different odors; in some studies it appears that the range is narrower than in the receptors, implying a higher specificity of response. On the other hand, the mitral cells display a greater variety of response patterns. There are three basic patterns. As shown in Fig. 11.17 (right) a cell may respond with excitation: a slow, prolonged discharge at threshold, changing to a brief burst followed by suppression at higher concentrations. Or a cell may respond with suppression throughout the stimulation period, and at all concentrations. Or a cell may not be affected at all by a given odor. One interpretation has been that the suppression is due to inhibition mediated by the dendrodendritic synapses of granule cells onto mitral cells. These extensive connections in effect lay down a curtain of inhibition within the bulb, which the excitatory responses punch through, as it were, carrying specific information about a given odor and its concentration.

Spatial Patterns

The spatial distribution of these odor-induced patterns of activity has been revealed by the 2-deoxyglucose (2DG) method of Sokoloff (1977). As already discussed in Chap. 8, odor stimulation elicits different degrees of activity in different glomeruli. This is presumably due to different degrees of activity in the receptors converging onto the glomeruli. Stimulation with one odor, such as amyl acetate (which has a fruity smell) activates glomeruli in certain regions of the olfactory bulb of a rat. Stimulation with a different odor, such as camphor, activates glomeruli in regions which overlap those of amyl acetate, but nonetheless have a different distribution. The maps for these two odors are illustrated in Fig. 11.18. These results, together with those from studies using electrophysiological recordings and anatomical tracing, have suggested that the spatial distribution of activity in the olfactory bulb may carry part of the neural code for different odors. Since we do not locate odors in our environment the way we locate visual or tactile stimuli, it appears that space can be used for encoding other aspects of the stimulus, such as the stereochemical configurations of the odor molecules or specific binding properties. These studies thus give insight into how the nervous system maps nonspatial stimulus parameters into neural space. Within these maps, individual glomeruli may transmit information about specific odor stimuli (see below). We will discuss an example of this for the case of the pheromone that mediates suckling by infant rats in Chap. 26.

Plasticity

The sense of smell is important in controlling early behavior in many species. During this early period, the system displays a re-

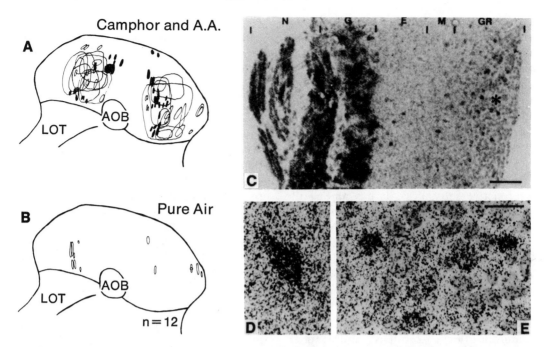

Fig. 11.18 Spatial patterns of activity in the rat olfactory bulb. **A.** Map of the glomerular sheet, showing distribution of 2-deoxyglucose foci in 21 animals exposed to amyl acetate odor (open circles) and 6 animals exposed to camphor odor (filled circles). **B.** In 12 control animals exposed only to pure air, few foci were observed. A.A., amyl acetate; AOB, accessory olfactory bulb; LOT, lateral olfactory tract. **C.** High-resolution study of the cellular uptake of 2DG in the olfactory bulb of the salamander exposed to the odor of amyl acetate. Autoradiograph shows dense uptake in the olfactory nerve (N) and glomerular (G) layers, and uptake in scattered cells in the external plexiform (E), mitral (M), and granule (GR) layers. The methods included preparation of the tissue by freeze-substitution, [^{14}C]2DG autogradiography, and cutting into 2-μm-thick sections. Bar is 125 μm. **D.** Higher magnification, showing a labeled mitral cell body. **E.** Same, several labeled granule cell bodies (from the area marked by the asterisk in C). Bar is 25 μm. These results show that it is possible to obtain 2DG labeling of both the projection neurons (mitral cells) and interneurons (granule cells) in a central region of the brain. (A,B from Stewart et al., 1979; C–E from Lancet et al., 1982)

markable degree of plasticity. Evidence for this plasticity has come to light from studies of rat pups. In one study, Patricia Pedersen and Eliott Blass (1982) at Johns Hopkins wished to know whether an artificial odorous substance could substitute for the normal pheromone that mediates suckling of rat pups. They injected citral (a lemony substance) into the amniotic fluid to expose the fetuses to this substance, delivered the pups by cesarian section, and found indeed that the presence of citral on the mother's nipples was required for suckling to occur. This showed that the olfactory system can adapt to different molecular stimuli for eliciting this crucial behavior.

The neural basis of this type of plasticity has been analyzed by Michael Leon and his colleagues at Irvine. They exposed rat pups to a specific chemical odor for 10 minutes a day during the first 19 days of life, and then examined the 2-deoxyglucose patterns induced in the olfactory bulb by this odor. A distinct focus was seen in the autoradiograms, which was correlated with a recognizable glomerulus not present in control animals (Leon et al., 1987). It appears that repeated stimulation enhances the response, and may induce a morphological rearrangement of the receptor axon terminals in the olfactory bulb. The results are of further interest for supporting the idea that a glomerulus may operate as a functional unit in processing odor information, in analogy with cortical barrels (Chap. 12) or columns (Chap. 16).

Neurotransmitters

The olfactory bulb is a rich repository of neuroactive substances. It has among the highest levels of taurine (an amino acid), carnosine (a dipeptide), thyroid hormone releasing hormone (a tripeptide), and opiate receptors in the entire brain. It is also the recipient of many centrifugal fibers from the brain. These arise from the olfactory cortical areas, the basal forebrain (horizontal limb of the diagonal band), and the midbrain (locus ceruleus and raphe). Through these fibers the olfactory bulb is modulated by central limbic centers, so that a given odorous substance has a different meaning depending on the behavioral state of the animal. Thus, the aromas of food are perceived quite differently, depending on whether we are hungry or sated. Through these centrifugal connections, the bulbar microcircuits are an integral part of central limbic circuits as they mediate nonolfactory functions as well. These multiple controls of olfactory bulb synapses and circuits presumably reflect the sensitiveness of olfactory functions to different developmental and behavioral states, as well as the pervasive influence of olfactory inputs on the life of the animal. This appears to be as true for the lives of most vertebrate species as for invertebrates, and we shall see ample evidence of this when we discuss feeding (Chap. 26) and mating (Chap. 27).

Olfactory Cortex

From the olfactory bulb the mitral and tufted cells send their axons to the olfactory cortex. As shown in Fig. 11.19, there is a parallel pathway, from the vomeronasal organ to the accessory olfactory bulb, and from there to a specific cortical site in the amygdala. The vomeronasal organ is a narrow tube lined with olfactory receptors, that is well developed in certain reptiles and mammals. It appears that the receptors are tuned to specific kinds of substances in these species. For example, in snakes, scents of prey are detected by flicking the tongue into the air and drawing it back over the inlet of the organ at the base of the nose. In hamsters, the vomeronasal organ mediates part of the response of a male to the vaginal odor emanating from a receptive female, and is thus an important link in reproductive behavior (see Chap. 27).

The olfactory cortex is divided into five main areas. Each has distinct connections and different functions, which we will briefly describe. The *anterior olfactory nucleus* is an integrative center connecting the two bulbs through the anterior commissure. The *piriform cortex* is the main area involved in olfactory discrimination. The *olfactory tubercle* is also the recipient of ascending dopaminergic fibers from the midbrain (Chap. 26); it has been implicated in various functions of the limbic system (Chap.

Fig. 11.19 Schematic diagram of the mammalian olfactory system. This view shows the three levels of the system, proceeding from the olfactory epithelium at the top, through the olfactory bulb, to the olfactory cortex (bottom). There is an attempt to emphasize the different subsystems as they are seen at each level. Abbreviations: AMYG, amygdala; AOB, accessory olfactory bulb; AON, anterior olfactory nucleus; epl, external plexiform layer; gc, granule cell; gcl, granule cell layer; glom, glomerular layer; MD thalamus, medial dorsal nucleus of the thalamus; MGC, modified glomerular complex; mc, mitral cell; ml, mitral layer; NHLDB, nucleus of the horizontal limb of the diagonal band; on, olfactory nerve layer; orn, olfactory receptor neuron; OT, olfactory tubercle; PC, piriform cortex; pg, periglomerular cell; SO, septal organ; tc, tufted cell; TEC, transitional entorhinal cortex; VNO, vomeronasal organ. (From Shepherd et al., 1987)

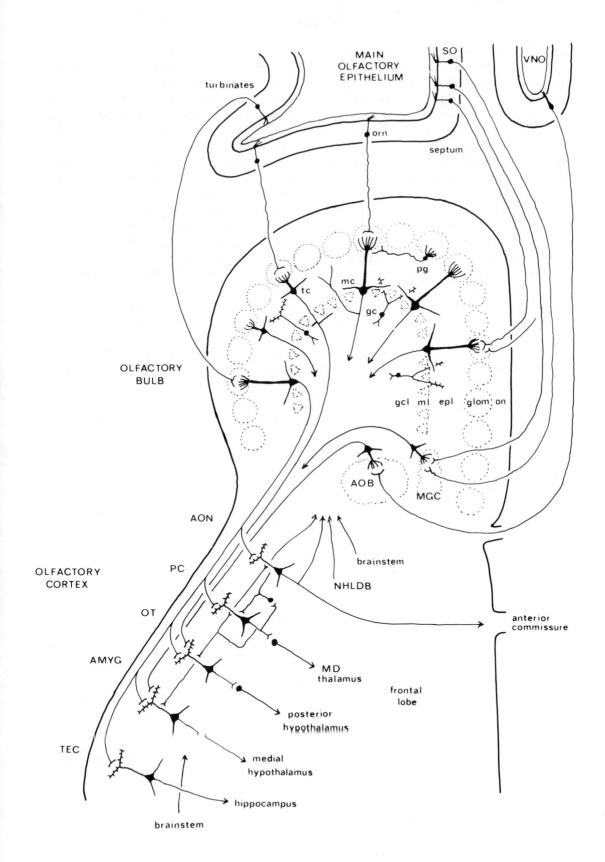

245

28). It has been hypothesized that malfunction of the olfactory tubercle (the anterior perforated substance in the human brain) may contribute to certain kinds of schizophrenia. The *corticomedial* parts of the *amygdala* receive inputs from both the main and accessory olfactory bulbs. Finally, a part of *entorhinal cortex* receives olfactory input, and projects to the hippocampus.

Some of the central projections of the cortical areas are indicated in the diagram. The piriform cortex projects to the mediodorsal thalamus, which in turn projects to the frontal lobe. This presumably is the circuit for conscious olfactory perception and discrimination. The amygdala, in contrast, projects mainly to the hypothalamus. Through those connections the amygdala is more concerned with the emotional and motivational aspects of odor stimuli (see Chap. 28).

Despite the varying connections and functions of these different cortical regions, they are all constructed on the same general plan. The reader may review in Chap. 4 how synaptic circuits are built of triads of neuronal elements: input, principal, and intrinsic. As shown in Fig. 11.19, in olfactory cortex the afferent input is to the distal dendrites of pyramidal neurons. In addition to their output axon, pyramidal neurons give rise to two types of intrinsic circuit: recurrent excitation through long association fibers, and recurrent inhibition through activation of inhibitory interneurons. This is a basic circuit for initial cortical processing of olfactory information, which is adapted in each of the subregions for differing specific functions. In Chap. 30, we will see how this basic circuit underlies the organization of other parts of the cerebral cortex.

12

The Somatic Senses

Every organism has an external skin or other covering that encloses its body and separates it from the environment. Through this covering, the animal receives information about the presence of objects, other organisms, or physical changes in its environment. The Greek word for body is *soma*, and the sensory modalities that are signaled by receptors in and near the body surface are referred to collectively as the *somatic senses*.

Before identifying the different components of the somatic senses, it is well to be reminded that the body covering in which receptors are embedded is not a simple structure. Table 12.1 lists some of the functions of the covering (integument) in different animals. It can be seen that the integument has a complex structure which provides for multiple functions. Sensory reception is only one among many special functions. Thus, the sensory receptors in any given animal have structures which reflect the particular functional adaptations of the integument in that species.

Because of the enormous variations in the structure and function of the integument in different species, it is not always easy to assign particular receptor cells to distinct categories. By the same token, it is

Table 12.1 Functions of the integument

Protection against:
  physical harm
  chemical damage
  infection
  water gain or loss
  excessive sunlight
  heat gain or loss
Camouflage (pigmentation)
Structures for:
  locomotion (cilia, feathers)
  aggression and defense (claws, horns, antlers)
  social displays
Exchange of substances:
  respiration of O_2 and CO_2
  excretion of metabolites
Glandular excretions
Special sensory structures

hazardous to assume too readily that a particular sensory modality is exactly equivalent in widely separated species. These considerations make it difficult to apply the terms "modality," "submodality," and "quality" in a consistent fashion. Despite such misgivings, however, it is common to consider that the somatic senses are comprised of four main modalities. These were summarized in Table 10.1. Perhaps the most basic and primitive is the *noxious* sense, the reception of stimuli that are harmful or signal potential harm to the organism. A second modality is the ability to sense the ambient *temperature*. A third category may be referred to as *crude touch;* this includes *light touch* and *pressure,* which are distinct in some organisms and mixed in others. Finally, there is the fine *tactile* sense, the ability to make precise surface discriminations in space and time.

These sensory modalities can also be grouped according to the nature of the stimulus energy. Thus, stimuli that affect the body may be classed as chemical (some kinds of noxious stimuli), radiant (temperature, sometimes noxious), and mechanical (some noxious stimuli, crude touch, and tactile). Chemical stimuli require chemical transduction by *chemoreceptor* mechanisms in the sensory membrane; temperature is transduced by *temperature receptors;* and the various kinds of mechanical stimuli are transduced by *mechanoreceptors.* The molecular bases of the transduction mechanisms have already been discussed in Chap. 10.

Regardless of how one classifies the sensory modalities, the receptors share some basic properties, even across different phyla. We will consider examples of each type among the invertebrates and vertebrates. Our focus will be on the properties of the receptor cells, and the organization of the sensory pathways.

INVERTEBRATES

The comments above regarding the complexity of the integument apply with special force to the invertebrates. Because of the small size of many invertebrate species, respiratory and excretory functions can take place through the integument, rather than requiring special internal organ systems. Also, because of their small size, the ratio of external surface area to internal volume is relatively high. While this helps in the exchange of substances, it also magnifies other problems, such as maintaining constant water balance in a changing environ-

ment. Small terrestrial organisms, for example, are at great risk of desiccation during periods of hot weather and drought. Special properties of the integument are therefore crucial for the survival of many organisms.

These considerations help us to understand the nature of the integument in which we find the sensory receptors. For the reasons mentioned above, invertebrates (above the sponges) characteristically have a tough outer covering, called a *cuticle.* In worms and molluscs, the cuticle is soft; in arthropods it forms a hard exoskeleton. We will consider briefly some receptors found within these two types of cuticle.

Leech Sensory Neurons

A useful preparation for studying the physiology of sensory neurons is the medicinal leech, *Hirudo medicinalis.* This was the organism used by medieval doctors for bloodletting, to rid the body of excess or unhealthy blood, a practice which continued through the eighteenth century, much to the detriment of George Washington and many others. (This is also the little creature that caused Humphrey Bogart and Katharine Hepburn such distress in the film *The African Queen!*)

The central nervous system of the leech consists of a ventral chain of 21 segmental ganglia, plus a head "brain" and a smaller tail ganglion. The nerve fibers that join the ganglia to each other form *connectives,* and those that run between the ganglia and the periphery form *roots.* The connectives are analogous to the spinal tracts of the vertebrate spinal cord, and the roots are analogous to the dorsal and ventral roots, though not separated into sensory and motor divisions, as in the vertebrate.

The leech exhibits most of the characteristics that make invertebrate nervous systems so attractive for neurobiological research. The ganglion is less than 1 mm thick, and is transparent, so that its cells can be observed under the microscope during an experiment. One can carry out in-

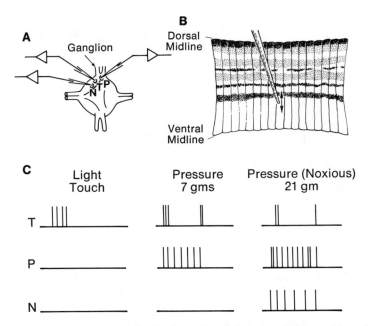

Fig. 12.1 Somatosensory neurons of the leech. **A.** A single segmental ganglion, showing location of noxious (N), touch (T), and pressure (P) neuron cell bodies. **B.** Piece of skin with nerves attached to the ganglion. The probe was used to stimulate the sensory endings by touch or pressure. **C.** Characteristic responses of T, P, and N cells to different types and intensities of stimuli applied to the skin. See text. (Modified from Kuffler et al., 1984)

tracellular recording and stimulating experiments in the intact animal, or in the isolated ganglion. Each ganglion contains about 350 cells. Under the microscope, individual cell bodies can be observed, and many of the larger ones can be identified by their distinctive size, shape, and position in the ganglion (see Fig. 12.1A). Using this preparation, John Nicholls and his collaborators have been able to investigate many basic properties involved in nervous signaling, such as the correlation of neuronal branching patterns with synaptic properties, the effects of prolonged activity on ionic conductances and electrogenic membrane pumps, and the roles of neuroglial cells during nervous activity. In the leech, the sensory cell bodies are in the segmental ganglia (equivalent to the vertebrate spinal cord). This contrasts with their position in peripheral ganglia in other invertebrates, and in dorsal root ganglia in vertebrates. By probing the skin with different types of natural stimuli while recording from cells

in the ganglia, it has been possible to identify specific cells for three cutaneous sensory modalities: touch, pressure, and noxious. The results of these experiments are summarized in Fig. 12.1C. The *touch* (T) cells are extremely sensitive (have a *low threshold*) to light touch, whether by a small probe, such as a whisker, or eddy currents in the bathing medium. The response to a simple maintained stimulus is a brief burst of impulses; this is, in other words, a *rapidly adapting* response. A prolonged discharge can be sustained by a stimulus continually *moving* within the receptive field.

With a stronger maintained stimulus such as a pressure indentation of the skin (Pressure 7 g in Fig. 12.1C), the T cell fires faster, and there may be an off discharge as well. In addition, the *pressure* (P) cell begins to respond; we say, therefore, that it has a *higher threshold* for stimulation than the T cell. The P cell gives a maintained, slowly adapting discharge, that is

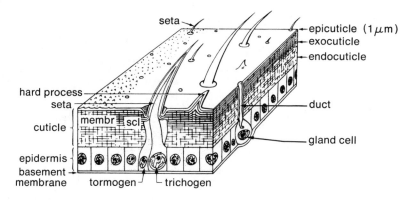

Fig. 12.2   Diagram of the integument of an insect, showing the most common type of sensory hair (seta). (From Richards, in Barrington, 1979)

graded in *frequency* with the strength of stimulation (see Pressure 21 g). At the highest stimulation intensities, a third type of cell begins to respond. This cell responds best to noxious stimuli, like crushing or stabbing, that cause tissue damage, and is therefore termed a *nociceptor* (N) cell.

It can be seen that these responses display many of the basic properties of sensory receptors we discussed in Chap. 10. It is particularly interesting that the three modalities of touch, pressure, and nociception are closely comparable to the somatosensory modalities in the vertebrate. Each type of sensory cell makes specific connections onto motoneurons, to establish pathways for reflex responses, as we will discuss in Chap. 19.

Arthropod Sensory Receptors

The importance of the body covering is beautifully exemplified by the insects, as attested to in the following quotation from David Smith (1968):

> The development of a cuticle resisting desiccation and the acquisition of a tracheal system for respiration of atmospheric oxygen opened up the terrestrial environment to the insects, an evolutionary opportunity that they exploited to the full.

Biochemically, the key constituent of the cuticle of the insect (and other arthropods) is *chitin.* This is a polysaccharide containing acetylglucosamine residues bonded together to form long, unbranched molecules of high molecular weight. It shares some structural properties with cellulose. Although found in the integuments of many species, it is absent from the cuticle of annelids; apparently, this represented a significant step in the evolution of the annelid–arthropod line. It is also absent from the deuterostome line, leading from echinoderms to chordates. Chitin is thus an important biochemical marker in evolution.

Chitin is bound together with protein and lipids to form the *endocuticle,* as shown in Fig. 12.2. In most insects the protein component is sclerotinized to impart the rigidity necessary for the exoskeleton. As we discussed earlier, this requires suitable adaptations of sensory receptors, so that they can detect mechanical and other forms of stimuli through the hard outer coating. The simplest and most common type of structure for achieving this is the sensillum trichodeum, or *sensory hair.* This type of hair is a simplified version of the sensory hairs that we studied in the insect taste and olfactory systems (Chap. 11). As shown in Fig. 12.2, each mechanoreceptive sensillum consists of a hair (seta) set in a flexible socket. The whole sensillum comprises four cells. The trichogen cell secretes the material for forming the hair during development. The tormogen cell forms the socket. A single sensory cell innervates the sensillum; its distal terminals contact the junction of the base of the hair and the socket. A fourth cell encloses the other three.

Sensory hairs are scattered widely over the body surface. Any force that displaces the hair, such as *touch, air movement,* or *changes in pressure,* causes stimulation of the sensory cell. The sensory cells in the cuticle of the body surface send their fibers to their corresponding segmental ganglion in the nerve cord. The central sensory connections have not yet been worked out.

It will be recalled (see Chap. 11) that each sensory hair in the taste sensilla of the insect has a mechanoreceptor as one of its five sensory cells. There are also mechanoreceptor cells and hairs among the olfactory hairs on the insect antennae. These cells send their axons to the glomeruli of the antennal lobe, along with the other sensory axons. Thus, the glomeruli function as relay stations for more than one kind of sensory modality (see Fig. 11.10). From the antennal lobe, the mechanoreceptor inputs make connections with motor centers, for mediating immediate motor reflexes, or with higher integrative centers, such as the mushroom bodies (see Chaps. 11, and 24, 30). Unfortunately, little is known as yet about these central circuits of the insect somatosensory system.

VERTEBRATES

Vertebrates differ from invertebrates in that they do not have cuticles and most do not molt, but in other respects their integument is similar in that it can take on a variety of structures and perform many different functions. The structural adaptations include a toughening of the surface to form scales, as in fish, or plates, as in turtles. The integument also may give rise to auxiliary structures such as feathers, as in birds, and hair, as in mammals—structures that are crucial for the motor abilities of a species, or its ability to withstand extremes of climate and temperature. There are also special adaptations, such as hoofs and claws, for particular kinds of locomotion or manipulation.

There are many fascinating adaptations of the skin senses to these specialized integumentary organs. However, our concern here will be with the reception of stimuli over the whole body surface. By far the greatest amount of information about the general somatosensory system in vertebrates has been obtained in the mammal, much of it in primates and humans. This is partly because the mammalian skin is a relatively general, unspecialized covering. Being soft, it is easy to dissect and experiment upon. An important advantage is that in humans one can stimulate different receptors selectively and test the sensory perception that is aroused. Let us therefore focus our attention on the mammalian skin in general, and the special properties of the human skin where information is available.

The human skin is a complex and fascinating structure. As we all recognize, there are two main types of skin. One type, found on our palms and fingertips, is called *glabrous,* or hairless, skin. The other type, found over most of the rest of our body, is called *hairy* skin. Of course, hair on humans varies widely in amount, from a little to a lot, and in the kind of hair, from peach fuzz to coarse. These variations do not affect the division of skin into these two general classes.

The structures of glabrous and hairy skin are shown in the diagrams of Figs. 12.3 and 12.4. First, we see that both types of skin are divided into two main layers, the epidermis and the dermis. The *epidermis* is the true outer skin, being derived from the ectodermal germ layer of the embryo. It also gives rise to the various specialized structures (hair, feathers, claws, and glands) that become especially prominent in higher vertebrates. The epidermis is composed of a *stratum germinativum,* where cells undergo continual mitosis and migrate toward the surface. As they reach the surface, they undergo degenerative changes, so that at

GLABROUS (HAIRLESS) SKIN

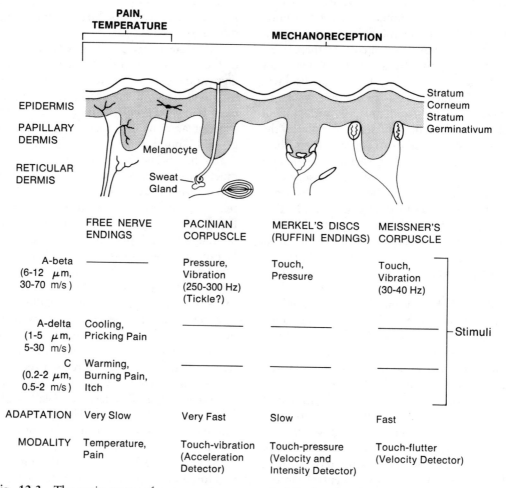

Fig. 12.3 The main types of sensory receptors and their functional properties in the glabrous (hairless) skin of the human. Above, diagrams showing the structure and location of each type. Below are listed the specific best stimuli, correlated with the type of sensory nerve fiber innervating the receptor (medium-thick myelinated A-beta fibers, thin myelinated A-delta fibers, and thin unmyelinated C fibers; for further information on fiber types, see Table 13.2).

the surface they form a layer of dead, flattened cells, the *stratum corneum*. This is rich in *keratin*, a very stable fibrous protein, resistant to water, most chemicals, and enzymatic digestion. Keratin is to the vertebrates what chitin is to the invertebrates. Also present in the epidermis are *melanocytes*, which contain melanin, derived metabolically from tyrosine. Melanin is responsible for the pigmentation of the

skin, and protects the skin and deeper layers from ultraviolet light.

Beneath the epidermis is the *dermis*. This is actually derived from the mesoderm, and becomes connected to the epidermis during embryonic development. The dermis is the layer that provides for the thick, bony scales that are so characteristic of lower vertebrates like fish. It is only in higher vertebrates that the dermis has evolved a soft,

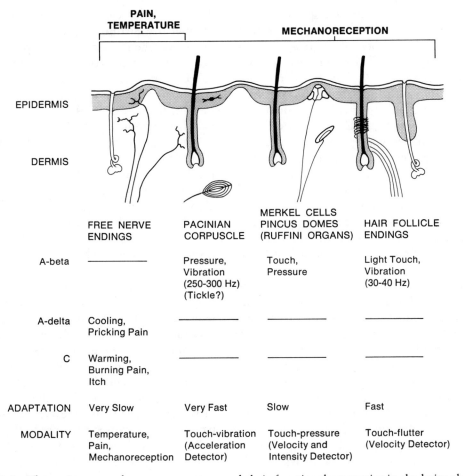

Fig. 12.4 The main types of sensory receptors and their functional properties in the hairy skin of the human. Compare with Fig. 12.3.

flexible structure, due to a thick, tightly interwoven layer of *connective tissue.* The layer is rich in collagen fibers, and also contains elastic fibers and, in deeper parts, fat cells. These components not only permit the freedom of movement so characteristic of mammals, but also are important for other functions such as protection, insulation, and temperature regulation.

Sensory Receptors

We are now in a position to identify the sensory elements within the skin. By way of brief history, this work began with the earliest microscopic studies of the skin in the middle of the nineteenth century. By around 1900, a number of specific, small end organs, each attached to a sensory nerve fiber, had been identified. The main interest of the physiologists of the time was in correlating each end organ with a specific sensation. To do this, the skin was stimulated with very small probes: a fine hair or bristle; a pin; a thin wire, heated or cooled. The results showed that sensitivity is not uniform over the skin surface; instead, there appeared to be a mosaic of sensitive "spots." There were "touch spots," "warm spots," "pain spots," and so forth.

Furthermore, a given spot seemed to be sensitive to only one modality. These results implied that a sensitive spot is the site of a specific sensory end organ for that modality. A number of correlations between sensory modality and sensory end organ were suggested; thus, free nerve endings for pain, Ruffini organs for warmth, Krause's end bulbs for cold, Pacinian corpuscles for pressure, Meissner's corpuscles and hair follicle endings for touch. These correlations seemed to be a logical realization of the doctrine of specific nerve energies set forth by Muller in the 1830s, as we discussed in Chap. 10.

Our modern correlations differ in certain details, and are not as strict as originally envisioned. Nonetheless, the idea that nerve endings, especially the specialized end organs, have a *preferential* sensitivity for certain types of stimuli, is widely accepted, and is a useful framework for our beginning study. Let us therefore consider each of the main types of sensory ending. We will start with free nerve endings, and move toward the more differentiated organs. Although this reverses the sequence in which they are usually described, it is more in line with the evolutionary development from simple to complex, and leads naturally to the description of central pathways later in the chapter.

Free Nerve Endings

The simplest type of sensory receptor in the skin is the free nerve ending. This is just what its name implies: a nerve fiber divides into branches and terminates in naked, unmyelinated endings in the dermis and deeper layers of the epidermis. The modes of termination are similar in glabrous and hairy skin, as indicated in Figs. 12.3 and 12.4.

Free nerve endings respond to mechanical stimuli, heating, cooling, or noxious stimuli. Some endings respond to only one modality; others respond to two or three modalities—these are called *polymodal* receptors. The endings arise from thin fibers,

either thinly myelinated axons *(A-delta* [Aδ] *fibers)* or unmyelinated axons *(C fibers).* The sensations evoked in these two types of fiber are distinctive. When we touch a hot stove, the immediate sharp pain *(sticking pain)* is mediated by the Aδ fibers; the subsequent constant aching *(burning pain)* is mediated by the C fibers. A correlation of pain fiber discharges with pain perception is shown in Fig. 12.5.

Temperature reception is also apportioned to different fibers in primates, *cooling* being sensed mainly by the Aδ fibers and *warming* being sensed by the C fibers. Cooling and warming receptors are actually defined by the fact that they have peak sensitivities that are cooler and warmer, respectively, than the body temperature. As shown in Fig. 12.6, each may fire faster or slower with increases or decreases in temperature, depending on where in the whole temperature range the change is taking place. Presumably, the overlapping ranges of warming and cooling receptors are part of the mechanism for enhancing the ability to discriminate small changes in temperature near body temperature; in this range, an increased response in one type is accompanied by a decreased response in the other.

At very high temperatures many thermoreceptors also signal *sticking pain,* a sensation akin to that produced by jabbing pins into the skin. Some C fibers respond to release of substances, such as bradykinin, from the capillary circulation, and mediate the sensation of *itching.* This may be regarded as part of the common chemical sense. Some fibers are responsive to various kinds of mechanical stimulation; among these, some Aδ fibers mediate *tickling* sensations. The free nerve endings thus provide for a rich variety of polymodal sensory reception. All of these fibers are slowly adapting; they continue to discharge impulses as long as the stimulus is present. This seems a necessary property for signaling the relatively slow changes that take place in the modalities of pain and temperature, and for signaling the organism to

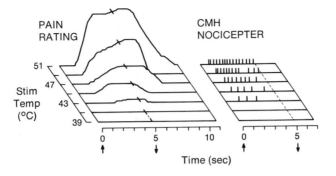

Fig. 12.5 Magnitude ratings of pain by a human subject (left) and evoked activity in a nociceptor fiber in the monkey (right) during heat stimulation of the skin. *Left:* Intensity of pain as judged by a subject during the heat stimulations of 39–51°C delivered in steps of 2°C to the volar forearm. Each horizontal line represents the passage of time during one trial. The base temperature was 38°C. Stimulus on and off are indicated by arrows. The vertical axis represents the magnitude of pain as rated continuously throughout testing. Pain threshold, in this case, was 43°C, the minimal stimulus temperature that elicited a rating of pain. *Right:* Responses of a C-fiber mechanoheat (CMH) nociceptor to the same heat stimuli delivered to the hairy skin of an anesthetized monkey. Each vertical mark represents a single nerve impulse. Response threshold, in this case, was 43°C, the minimal stimulus temperature that evoked a response. (From LaMotte et al., 1982)

remove the noxious stimulus or adjust itself to the ambient temperature.

Pacinian Corpuscle

The other sensory receptors in the skin are associated with special end organs, and all are endings of medium-sized myelinated fibers, the A-beta (Aβ) type (6–12 μm in diameter). For convenience we start with the Pacinian corpuscle, one of the largest of the end organs, situated deepest in the dermis. The Pacinian corpuscle has a widespread distribution, in the connective tissue

Fig. 12.6 Graphs of impulse firing frequencies in relation to applied temperature for "cold" and "warm" receptors. (Modified from Kenshalo, 1976, in Schmidt, 1978)

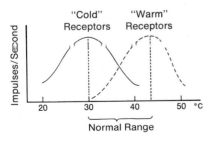

of muscles, the periosteum of bones, and the mesentery of the abdomen. It is relatively easy to isolate single corpuscles from the mesentery, and much of our information about Pacinian corpuscles, and indeed about many basic properties of sensory receptors in general, has come from these studies.

The Pacinian corpuscle is composed, like an onion, of concentric layers of cellular membranes alternating with fluid-filled spaces. The picture that has emerged from electron microscopic studies is the naked ending of the nerve fiber surrounded by an inner core of incomplete shells of cell processes and collagen fibers. Making up the bulk of the corpuscle are outer complete lamellae.

The Pacinian corpuscle has been studied physiologically by pressing on it with a carefully controlled probe while recording the response from the nerve where it exits from the corpuscle. If impulse activity is blocked selectively with such agents as local anesthetics or tetrodotoxin, we can record the receptor potential as it spreads into the nerve fiber. As shown in Fig. 12.7A,

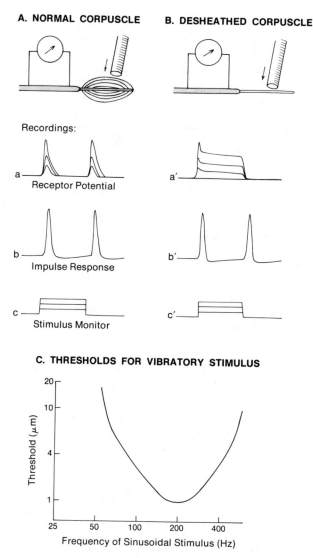

A. NORMAL CORPUSCLE

B. DESHEATHED CORPUSCLE

Recordings:

a — Receptor Potential

a′

b — Impulse Response

b′

c — Stimulus Monitor

c′

C. THRESHOLDS FOR VIBRATORY STIMULUS

Threshold (μm)

Frequency of Sinusoidal Stimulus (Hz)

Fig. 12.7 Experimental analysis of transduction in the Pacinian corpuscle. **A.** Diagram showing probe for stimulating the intact corpuscle, and recording from the nerve. Below, recordings of the receptor potential and impulse discharge. **B.** Repeat of experiment after removal of lamellae. **C.** Sensitivity of Pacinian corpuscle to vibratory stimulation at different frequencies. (A,B based on Loewenstein, 1971; C modified from Schmidt, 1978)

the receptor response takes the form of a very brief potential wave at the onset of the pressure pulse, and a similar brief wave at the termination. There is no response during the stationary plateau of the applied stimulus. This is therefore an extremely rapidly adapting receptor response. Each wave gives rise to a single impulse in the nerve fiber.

How does this type of response arise? In the isolated Pacinian corpuscle preparation, it was possible for Werner Loewenstein and his colleagues (1971), then at Columbia University, to dissect away very carefully the onion-skin lamellae, so that the stimulus could be applied directly to the naked nerve ending. When this was done, the receptor potential produced by a step pulse was a slowly adapting response (see Fig. 12.7B). This showed that the lamellae act as a filter, to absorb slow changes impressed upon them, while still passing on rapid changes to the nerve endings. Interestingly, the nerve fiber, at the first node of Ranvier, still responds with a single impulse despite the maintained receptor potential, a very nice matching of receptor and nerve properties.

The Pacinian corpuscle is thus constructed to signal rapid changes in *touch-pressure;* this is presumably why our sensation of a steady pressure applied to the skin soon fades away. This organ is well suited for signaling rapid vibratory stimuli; as indicated in Fig. 12.7C, the maximum sensitivity is in the range of 200–300 Hz. This form of stimulation may be important in our tactile perception of objects and textures. Note the extremely high sensitivity of the corpuscle; less than a $1 - \mu m$ displacement at its surface is sufficient to give a threshold response. We have previously discussed the molecular nature of the mechanotransduction mechanism in the membrane in Chap. 10.

Tactile End Organs

Most of the other end organs are located superficially in the skin, near the junction between the dermis and epidermis. These are specialized to be sensitive to different types of tactile stimuli.

A systematic study has been carried out in humans to identify different receptor types and relate them to sensory perception. This has been based on a method developed by Åke Vallbo in Sweden for inserting a fine tungsten microelectrode through the skin to record impulse discharges from nerves innervating the galbrous skin of the hand (see Fig. 12.8). Using this method, called microneurography, Vallbo and Roland Johansson have been able to study different types of responses in the awake human and relate them to psychophysical functions.

Two of the basic response properties of any receptor are its size of receptive field

and its rate of adapation. With regard to adaptation, the tactile receptors in the glabrous skin of the hand fall into two groups, fast or slowly adapting. The rapidly adapting type includes the Meissner corpuscle and the Pacinian corpuscle (refer to Figs. 12.3 and 12.8). Within this type, the adaptation shows interesting differences. The Meissner corpuscle is not quite as rapidly adapting as the Pacinian corpuscle, and therefore has a lower range for signaling vibratory frequency. In addition, the threshold for activation of the Meissner corpuscle is much higher than the threshold of the Pacinian corpuscle.

The slowly adapting type of response arises in Merkel's discs and Ruffini endings (Fig. 12.3). Here also there are differences. Both receptors respond to a steady indentation of the skin with a sustained discharge, but the Merkel's disc shows an overshoot during the initial phasic part of the indentation. It can thus provide information about changes in stimulus intensity as well as steady-state values (Fig. 12.8).

In addition to rates of adaptation, receptors also differ in receptive field sizes (Fig. 12.8). The receptive fields in the hand have been mapped with light tactile stimuli, and the results for the fast-adapting receptors are summarized in Fig. 12.9. The presumed Meissner's corpuscles have very small receptive fields, as shown in the diagram above and the graph below. This small diameter is part of the basis for our ability to make fine spatial discriminations with our fingertips (see below).

In contrast to FA I receptors, FA II receptors have very broad receptive fields. As can be seen in Fig. 12.9B, these fields can cover all of a finger or a large part of the palm. The graph in B shows that the field is almost flat, in comparison with the sharp boundaries of the FA I receptors over this same distance.

Pacinian and Meissner corpuscles thus provide an interesting comparison. The Pacinian corpuscle has an extremely low threshold, high temporal resolution, and low spatial resolution; by contrast, the

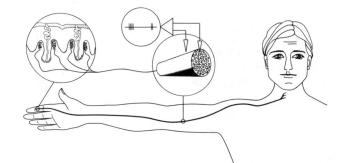

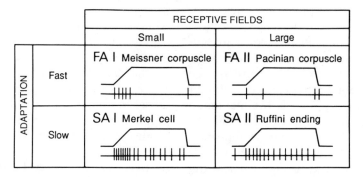

		RECEPTIVE FIELDS	
		Small	Large
ADAPTATION	Fast	FA I Meissner corpuscle	FA II Pacinian corpuscle
	Slow	SA I Merkel cell	SA II Ruffini ending

Fig. 12.8 Different types of mechanoreceptors, as determined by experiments in humans. *Above:* Experimental setup, in which mechanical stimuli are delivered to the palmar (glabrous) skin of the hand while recordings of impulse responses in single axons are made using thin microelectrodes inserted through the skin into the median nerve bundle. *Below:* Summary of the four main functional types of response, on the basis of adaptation and receptive field size, and their correlation with receptor type. FA, fast adapting; SA, slowly adapting. For each type is shown the stimulus monitor (ramp and hold) and the impulse discharge. Each receptor type is illustrated in Fig. 12.4. (Modified from Vallbo and Johansson, 1984)

Fig. 12.9 Comparison of receptors with narrow (**A**) and broad (**B**) receptive fields. The two broad fields shown in B have their centers of highest sensitivity at the sites marked by the dots. In the graphs, threshold (T) is plotted in multiples of the lowest threshold at the center; the absolute thresholds, in micrometers (μm) of skin indentation, are indicated on ordinates on the right. (From Vallbo and Johansson, 1984)

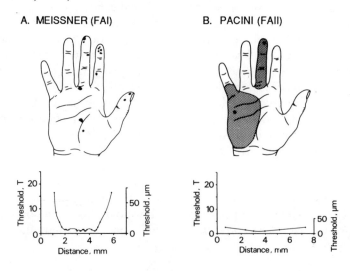

258

Meissner corpuscle has a higher threshold, lower temporal resolution, but higher spatial resolution. Similar differences have been found between the two types of slowly adapting (SA) receptors: the SA I receptors have small receptive fields, whereas the SA II receptors have very broad receptive fields

How do these receptor properties relate to the attributes of sensory perception, as tested in these same human subjects? Let us consider three main attributes discussed previously in Chap. 10: threshold, intensity of sensation, and spatial discrimination.

Threshold. The threshold for perceptual detection has been determined and compared with the threshold for eliciting an impulse response. For many years, there had been a debate about this comparison. Psychophysicists believed that the behavioral threshold was higher than the single receptor threshold, indicating that several receptor responses had to summate in central pathways and overcome "noise" in higher centers in order to give a perceptual response. Neurophysiologists, on the other hand, believed that the behavioral detection threshold was set only by the peripheral receptor threshold. Surprisingly, it turned out that both were right. In the regions of highest sensitivity, such as the digits, a single impulse elicited in a sensory nerve can indeed reach consciousness. In regions of lower sensitivity, such as the palm, the behavioral threshold is higher. It appears, therefore, that the most direct pathway to consciousness is reserved for specialized areas of highest sensitivity. (See the discussion of this issue in the visual system in Chap. 10, under *Detection.*)

Intensity of Sensation. In Chap. 10, we saw that there is generally a close correlation between the intensity of sensory stimulation and the magnitude of the perceived sensation, and we learned that this can be described by a simple power law, such that equal ratios between stimulus intensities are correlated with equal ratios between perceived intensities (see Fig. 10.9). The question then arises, similar to the question

regarding thresholds, as to whether the intensity of the sensory perception is set by the receptor response.

This was directly tested in the neurographic studies in humans by comparing the stimulus—response functions of the nerve responses with the magnitude estimation functions in the same subjects. Typical results are shown in Fig. 12.10A, for the case of three SA units with small receptive fields at three different sites on the hand. In the graphs, the nerve response functions (N) and the psychophysical response functions (P) are plotted. In all cases, the N response functions rose rapidly and then leveled off; this implied an average exponent in the power law of around 0.7 (see Chap. 10, Fig. 10.9). By contrast, the P response function began slowly and increased in slope, implying an average exponent of around 1.0.

These results suggest that the magnitude of a sensation is not determined solely by the rate of impulse discharge in the afferent fibers. As summarized by Vallbo and Johansson (1984):

. . . it appears that the central nervous system plays a major role in shaping the psychophysical functions. Moreover, different subjects seem to experience relative intensities in a different way probably because the intrinsic properties of their brains differ.

Later in this chapter we will see how the sensory pathways and the microcircuits within them can contribute to shaping the incoming information.

Spatial Resolution. As mentioned above, the size of receptive fields is related to our ability to make spatial discriminations. This ability is tested in humans by two-point discrimination, measured as the distance between two points that can just be perceived as separate. If you carry out this test yourself with two pencil points, you will find that this ability varies widely, from about 2 mm on the fingertips, to 30 mm on the arm, to 70 mm on the back.

Is the fineness of two-point discrimination set solely by the size of the receptive

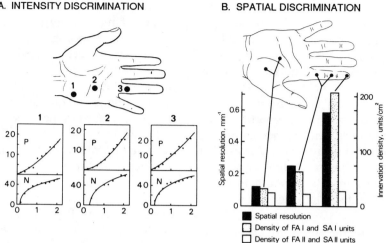

Fig. 12.10 Psychophysical studies comparing neural responses and perception. **A.** Intensity discrimination was measured for three SA receptors whose receptive field centers are at the sites indicated (1–3). For each receptor are plotted the increase in neural firing frequency (N) and perceptual intensity (P) for increasing stimulus intensity. The ordinate scales are in arbitrary units of magnitude estimation (P) and impulse firing frequency (N). Note that the P curve is not a simple function of the N curve. **B.** Spatial discrimination. Two-point discrimination tests were carried out in three skin regions, as shown above. The highest spatial resolution was found in the fingertip, and the lowest in the palm. The graph shows that the spatial resolution is correlated with density of receptors with small receptive fields (FA I and SA I receptors). (From Vallbo and Johansson, 1984)

field? This hypothesis was tested by first determining the behavioral thresholds at different sites on the hand. As expected, this showed the highest resolution near the fingertip, with lower resolution in the rest of the finger, and lowest resolution on the palm (Fig. 12.10B). One might anticipate that this would be correlated with corresponding sizes of receptive fields of the receptors in those areas, but we have already seen in Fig. 12.9 that small receptive fields have similar sizes everywhere on the hand (receptors with large receptive fields do not need to be considered, since they could not mediate fine discrimination in any case). How then does one achieve increasing spatial resolution without decreasing receptive field size?

The answer lies in the densities of the receptors. As shown in Fig. 12.10B, the density of small field receptors varies widely, and is closely correlated with the two-point discrimination thresholds. (By contrast, the density of large receptive field receptors is

constant.) The high density ensures that a restricted stimulus, such as a fine point, will have maximum chance of stimulating one or more receptors.

Active Touch

A vibrating probe is a very effective stimulus for Meissner's corpuscles, at 30–50 Hz, as illustrated in Fig. 12.7C. In life, this kind of receptor is probably most often activated by our fingers moving over rough or irregular objects. If two points on an object are 2 mm apart, and our finger moves past them at a rate of 80 mm/sec, the second point will excite a given site on the finger at a frequency of 40/sec—just right for a Meissner corpuscle. Although as physiologists and neurologists we tend to apply a given stimulus at a single site to study receptor responses or sensations, in natural behavior the fingers and hand take an active part by moving over and exploring surfaces in order to give rise to our sensory perceptions. This is called *active touch.* The tactile sense arising in the distal extremities thus illustrates vividly the close interrelationship that exists between sensory and motor systems. We will return to the subject of active touch in discussing movement of the hand in Chap. 22.

Spinal Cord Circuits

The information transduced by the sensory receptors is transmitted by impulse codes in the sensory nerves to the spinal cord. Within the spinal cord the information has two destinations. First, it is involved in local reflexes at the *spinal cord* level. Especially important in this regard are the circuits for withdrawing a limb from a painful stimulus, the so-called *flexor reflex.* We will study these circuits in Chap. 19. The second destination is the *ascending pathways* that relay the information to higher brain centers.

Dorsal Horn Microcircuits

Some of the basic aspects of organization of the dorsal horn are summarized in Fig. 12.11. The sensory fibers terminate within the dorsal horn, which is the sensory region of the spinal cord. The dorsal horn is arranged in layers (I–V), as indicated in Fig. 12.11B. The fine, unmyelinated fibers (C fibers) terminate mostly in the superficial layers (substantia gelatinosa). The Aδ fibers terminate in the most superficial layer, called the *marginal zone.* The large myelinated fibers (Aβ) sweep around the dorsal horn, giving off collaterals which ascend in the posterior columns, and then terminate as climbing fibers on the dendrites of cells in *layers III and IV.*

When we describe the entire somatosensory pathway (see below), the dorsal horn will be represented by a single relay site, but as Fig. 12.11B indicates, this is not a single site but rather a complicated set of microcircuits. The main point to realize is that through these connections, processing of somatosensory information begins at this first relay station.

Some of these microcircuits can be traced in the diagram of Fig. 12.11B and its inset. First, there are connections for straight-through transmission of each specific modality (e.g., large myelinated fibers to projection cell [PC] neuron). As shown in the inset, these include not only axodendritic synapses (for forward transmission), but also dendroaxonic synapses (for immediate feedback excitation or inhibition) and dendrodendritic synapses (for lateral interactions between responding cells). Second, there are connections that mediate interactions between modalities (e.g., INT in Fig. 12.11B, which mediates interactions between responses to the medial division and lateral division inputs). Third, there are connections from descending axons that provide for modulation of incoming sensory information by higher brain centers; these include especially the brainstem noradrenergic and serotonergic systems (see Chap. 24).

Theories of Pain

Among the interactions that can take place between modalities, one of the most interesting and one with important applications to humans, is that between tactile sensations and pain. It is a common observation that pain often can be relieved by gently stimulating around the hurt area, such as light brushing, massage, or tickling. It seems therefore as if the tactile pathway can have an inhibitory action on the pain pathway.

In a celebrated theory published in 1965, Melzack and Patrick Wall, then at the Massachusetts Institute of Technology, suggested a specific circuit within the dorsal horn that could account for this action. As shown in Fig. 12.11C, they began with the experimental finding that pain fibers excite relay cells. In addition, they postulated that pain fibers inhibit an interneuron in the substantia gelatinosa that normally inhibits the terminals of the pain fibers onto the relay cells. This *decrease* in presynaptic inhibition (which is called disinhibition) further enhances the transmission of pain inputs to the relay cells. Thus, the more active the pain fibers are, the more the excitability

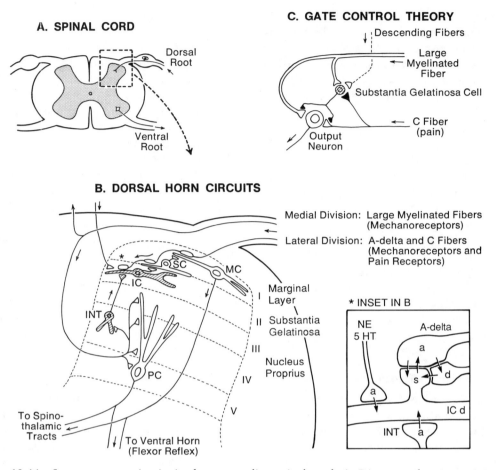

Fig. 12.11 Somatosensory circuits in the mammalian spinal cord. **A.** Diagram of cross section of spinal cord. **B.** Some of the main neuron types and synaptic connections that have been identified in the dorsal horn. I–V, laminae of the dorsal horn; MC, marginal cell; SC, stalked cell; IC, islet cell; INT, interneuron; PC, projection cell. The large myelinated fibers are believed to be glutamatergic; pain fibers contain substance P, somatostatin, vasoactive intestinal peptide, or possibly cholecystokinin; descending fibers contain norepinephrine or serotonin. (Based in part on Carol La-Motte, personal communication; Gobel et al., 1980) *Inset in B:* Synaptic organization of microcircuits in the marginal layer (site marked by asterisk in B). Abbreviations: a, axon; d, dendrite; s, spine; INT, interneuron; IC, islet cell; NE, norepinephrine; 5HT, serotonin. (Based on Gobel et al., 1980) **C.** Simplified diagram illustrating "gate-control theory" of Melzack and Wall (1965). Postulated excitatory terminals shown by open profiles, inhibitory by shaded profiles.

of the relay cells is enhanced, a kind of positive feedback effect that might underlie the powerful nature of pain sensations. When large mechanoreceptive tactile fibers are stimulated, they excite the relay cells, but they also *excite* the interneurons, bringing about an *increase* in presynaptic inhibition. This not only causes the excitatory effect of a given tactile input to be brief, but it also provides a general dampening of transmission of pain inputs. Transmission through the dorsal horn is thus seen to depend on the activity of the dorsal horn interneurons, which is the outcome of their own intrinsic resting activity, the tactile and pain inputs, and control by descending fibers from the brain. The interneurons thus can act as "switches" or "gates," to enhance or depress pain transmission, and the theory thus was called the *gate control theory of pain.*

This theory had an invigorating effect on the whole field of pain research. Some points seem doubtful (for example, the presence of both excitatory and inhibitory terminals arising from the same C fiber). Some points have been modified or expanded; in fact, new information is accumulating so rapidly that the actual status of the theory is unclear; it is undoubtedly incorrect in certain details. However, the idea of proposing a specific neuronal circuit for pain mechanisms was a significant step forward, and this goal continues to be a stimulus for many experiments on neuronal mechanisms in the dorsal horn and its equivalent, the caudal nucleus of the trigeminal nerve, in the brainstem.

Ascending Pathways

Sensory information reaches the rest of the brain by two main pathways. Since these rise from lower centers to higher centers, they are called ascending pathways. The oldest, phylogenetically, is made up of fibers that arise from dorsal horn cells, cross the midline, and form a tract in the anterolateral part of the white matter of the spinal cord. These fibers ascend all the way through the spinal cord and brainstem, and terminate in the thalamus (see Fig. 12.12). They are thus referred to as the *spinothalamic* tract. These fibers mediate mainly *pain* and *temperature* sensation, but there are also fibers that convey some *tactile* and *joint* information. Along the way in the brainstem they give off numerous collaterals to the reticular formation. The reticular neurons, in turn, form a system of polysynaptic ascending connections, which eventually also feeds into the thalamus. These neurons are part of the *ascending reticular system,* which is involved in *arousal* and *consciousness* (see Chap. 25).

The phylogenetically newer ascending pathway is made up of collaterals of large, myelinated sensory axons. As shown in Figs. 12.11 and 12.12, these collaterals gather in the posterior, or dorsal, part of the white matter of the cord, and form the *posterior columns,* or *dorsal columns.* As part of the somatosensory pathway, this system first can be delineated along the phylogenetic scale in reptiles. These fibers ascend only as far as the lower margin of the brainstem, where they terminate and make synapses in the *dorsal column nuclei.* From there, fibers sweep across the midline to form the *medial lemniscus,* and ascend to terminate in the thalamus. This pathway is often referred to as the *lemniscal system;* it is mainly concerned with conveying the most precise and complex information about touch and pressure. Lemniscal fibers give off collaterals to the reticular formation, and thus also contribute to arousal mechanisms.

Somatosensory Cortex

The ascending fibers in the somatosensory pathways terminate in the thalamus, where they make synapses with relay cells that project to the cerebral cortex. The thalamus is thus the gateway to the cortex, and it serves this function for all pathways ascending from the spinal cord and brainstem. The somatosensory fibers terminate in the group of cells called the *ventral posterior nucleus* (VP), the lemniscal and spinothalamic fibers in the lateral part (VPL), and the fibers from the trigeminal nucleus, relaying inputs from the face, in the medial part (VPM). In subprimate mammals, like cats, the whole group of cells is referred to as the ventrobasal complex (VBC).

Much of the work on the somatosensory cortex has been concerned with three main questions. First, what is the topographical representation of the body surface? Second, how many cortical areas are there, and how specific are they? Third, what is the intrinsic organization within an area of cortex; what are the basic functional units? These questions are also relevant to the other parts of the cerebral cortex that we will study.

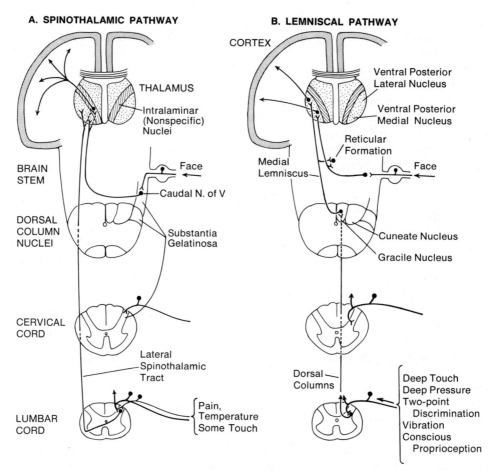

Fig. 12.12 Ascending pathways of the somatosensory system. (Modified from Carpenter, 1976, and Brodal, 1981)

Topographical Representation

Within the ventroposterior nucleus of the thalamus, the fibers terminate in an orderly geometrical arrangement that preserves the relations of the body surface. This arrangement is called *somatotopy*, or *topographical representation;* it is as if the body surface were projected onto the nucleus. This arrangement, in turn, is preserved in the projection of the relay cells onto the cortex. The area within which those fibers terminate defines the somatosensory cortex.

Within this cortex, the relations of the body surface are preserved, but the relative areas are modified. This was established by Wilder Penfield and his colleagues at Mon-

treal in their studies, from the 1930s to the 1950s, of patients undergoing neurosurgical operations. With punctate electrical stimulation, Penfield elicited descriptions from the patients of the tactile sensations (numbness, tingling, pressure) and their apparent sites on the body surface. From this emerged the well-known drawing called a "homunculus" depicted in Fig. 12.13, with its characteristic distortions, particularly the large areas given over to the the lips, face, and hands. The area of cortex varies with the acuity of perception, and the large cortical areas reflect the high sensitivity and fine discrimination possible in these parts of the body (a direct measure of this is

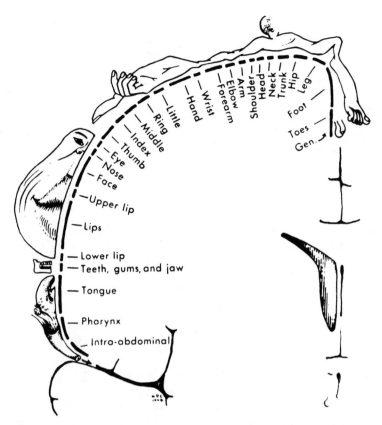

Fig. 12.13 The somatosensory "homunculus," representing the body surface as projected onto the postcentral gyrus of the human cerebral cortex. (From Penfield and Rasmussen, 1952)

provided by the two-point discriminations in Fig. 12.10).

Two particularly striking examples of the precision of cortical representation deserve mention. If you have ever observed a raccoon eating food, you know that it has remarkable forepaws, which though lacking an opposable thumb, are nonetheless capable of wonderfully dextrous manipulations resembling those of human hands. In the raccoon, the part of the somatosensory cortex representing the forepaw is greatly developed. It has been possible to identify five individual, small gyri (folds), one for each finger, and another five gyri for each of the volar pads of the paw. A summary of the maps obtained is shown in Fig. 12.14. The elaborate nature of this respresentation is taken to reflect the acute

tactile sensitivity of the raccoon hand. This sensitivity is expressed both in responses to passive stimulation, and by "active touch" during the dextrous movements of the forepaw (see Chap. 22).

A second example concerns the vibrissae (whiskers) of the snout of rodents; these function as sensitive detectors of the environment around the snout. The vibrissae project through VPM in the thalamus. Thomas Woolsey and Henrik van der Loos at Johns Hopkins discovered in 1970 a regular series of five rows of cell groups with hollow interiors, looking much like the cell clusters surrounding olfactory glomeruli in the olfactory bulb. They called each cluster a *"barrel,"* and showed that each barrel represents a vibrissa on the animal's snout (Fig. 12.15).

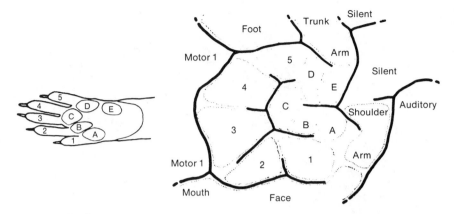

Fig. 12.14 Somatosensory cortex of the raccoon. There is a fold (gyrus) for each finger (1–5) and each palm area (volar pad: A–E) of the paw. (From Welker and Seidenstein, 1959)

When a vibrissa is removed early in life, anatomical studies show that the corresponding barrel disappears from the row. When a vibrissa is stimulated continuously, a single, dense focus of 2-deoxyglucose uptake can be demonstrated in the corresponding barrel. The fibers that innervate a vibrissa are tuned to several different submodalities, and these are transmitted to the barrel for that vibrissa. A barrel is thus a *morphological unit,* and it is also a *functional unit* within which *multisensory integration* takes place.

Cortical Areas

The maps for somatosensory cortex were soon shown to apply in their general outline to many species of mammals. In addition, these studies showed that there is a second, smaller area where the body surface is represented. The main area was called S I (primary somatosensory cortex, and the second area S II (secondary somatosensory cortex). With the methods available, it appeared that S I was the only region that receives the thalamic input. The belief therefore arose that *serial processing* takes place at the cortical level, beginning with analytical mechanisms in primary cortex, and proceeding to more integrative mechanisms in secondary cortex. The final

step was believed to occur in neighboring regions called *association cortex,* which appeared to lack topographical representations of the body surface, and therefore could be concerned with the synthetic mechanisms that seem to be necessary for perception to occur. This traditional view is depicted in Fig. 12.16A.

This tidy sequence has not been borne out by recent experiments. Instead, it has been found that there are not one but several subdivisions of the thalamus that relay somatosensory information, and these each have their specific inputs to one or more of several somatosensory areas. Furthermore, with more refined microelectrode recording techniques, it has been found that each cortical area is selective in the submodalities it processes. This new evidence is summarized in Fig. 12.16B.

These results have emphasized the importance of *parallel processing* of different aspects of somatosensory stimuli at the cortical level. They have indicated that there is much more detailed mapping present in the cortex, particularly in parts believed to be "associational," than previously suspected. This has required rethinking the question of where and how our unified perceptions are formed. We will examine similar evidence as it relates to other sensory systems in the following chapters, and

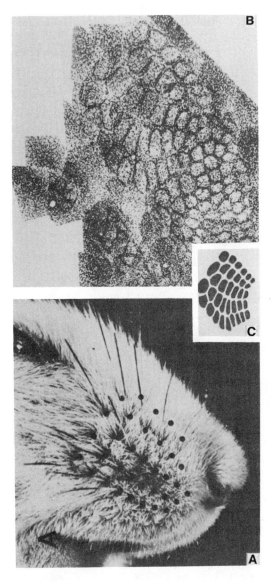

Fig. 12.15 **A.** Snout of a mouse; the vibrissae (whiskers) are marked by dots. **B.** Section across the somatosensory cortex receiving input from the snout. Note the rings of cells ("barrels," or glomeruli), each corresponding to a vibrissa (the barrel map is summarized in C). (From Woolsey and van der Loos, 1970)

return to this question in our final discussion of the cortex in Chap. 30.

Cortical Columns

In the early years of studying the cortex with the new microeletrode recording methods that had become available during the 1950s, Vernon Mountcastle at Johns Hopkins University carried out an analysis of cell responses in the somatosensory cortex of the cat to various types of stimuli. He found that when his electrode penetrated the cortex perpendicular to the surface, all the units he encountered tended to respond to the same sensory submodality (for example, light touch, or joint movement), but when he made an oblique electrode track, he encountered a series of units with different submodalities. From this he deduced that the cortex contains columns of cells with similar functional properties. Figure 12.17 illustrates some typical results from one of the early experiments on the monkey, performed in collaboration with T. P. S. Powell of Oxford, in which functionally characterized units were localized anatomically.

The concept of the column as a basic functional unit has turned out to be widely applicable in the cortex. The characterization of columnar organization has been one of the dominating forces in studies of sensory areas, motor areas, and even association areas, as we shall see in subsequent chapters. From this and related work, it is beginning to appear that the cortical column expresses a fundamental tendency of nerve cells and circuits to be organized in more or less discontinuous groups, or modules. We have already seen a clear example of this in the olfactory glomeruli, as well as in the somatosensory barrels. A point of some interest is that olfactory glomeruli and somatosensory barrels have dimensions of 100–300 μm, which is similar to the widths of several hundred micrometers for columns in the rest of the somatosensory cortex. Thus the smallest unit of anatomical representation in the cortex yet identified—the barrel—appears to be equivalent in size to the basic functional unit, the column. Other work has similarly revealed fine-grained representations that approach the dimensions of single columns.

Is the cortical column a building block

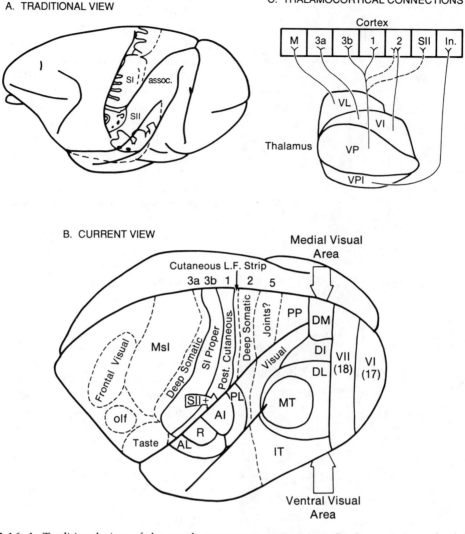

Fig. 12.16 A. Traditional view of the monkey somatosensory cortex. **B.** Current view of subdivisions of monkey somatosensory cortex, together with cortical areas for other sensory modalities. **C.** The main thalamocortical connections of the somatosensory system. AI, primary auditory; AL, anterior lateral auditory field; DI, dorsointermediate visual area; DL, dorsolateral visual area; DM, dorsomedial visual area; IT, inferior temporal; MsI, motor-sensory area I; MT, middle temporal visual area; PL, posterior lateral auditory field; PP, posterior parietal visual area; R, rostral auditory field; SI, primary somatosensory; SII, secondary somatosensory; VI, primary visual; VII, secondary visual; VI, ventralis intermedius nucleus; VL, ventralis lateralis nucleus; VP, ventroposterior nucleus; VPI, ventroposterioinferior nucleus. (From Merzenich and Kaas, 1980)

268

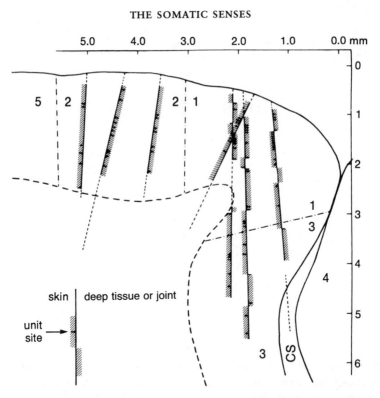

Fig. 12.17 Classical study showing columnar organization of monkey somatosensory cortex. Cross section containing electrode tracks, showing sites of unit recordings (short horizontal bars) and modality of units (shading on left for units activated by stimulation of the skin, on right for units activated by stimulation of joint, periosteum, or deep tissue; see inset). Numbers refer to cortical areas. CS, cortical sulcus. (From Powell and Mountcastle, 1959)

of perception? This was an obvious possibility from the moment of its discovery. Mountcastle early stressed that events within the column probably are involved in only the initial steps in cortical processing of sensory information. This view has been supported by studies of other areas, too, such as visual cortex. Thus, the discoveries of columns, of fine details in somatotopy, and the multiple representations of the body surface are basic steps along the way to perception, but there is still a way to go, as we will discuss in Chap. 30.

13

Muscle Sense and Kinesthesia

The tactile systems studied in the previous chapter tell us about the world around us. What about the world within? How do we know *when* we move our muscles; how do we know *how much* to move our muscles, limbs, and joints? The precise control of movements has a high priority in the behavior of most organisms, and increasingly so in higher animals. Two examples requiring this precision are shown in Fig. 13.1. Different kinds of motor behavior will be discussed in later chapters; the examples in the figure illustrate that motor control is the outcome of a complex interplay between genetics, motivation, training (especially in humans), and sensory factors. Sensory information is needed to help control posture and sequences of movements, and make adjustments to changes in the environment.

Information about movement is signaled by several different types of receptors. The receptors are located at almost every possible site in the musculoskeletal system at which movement can take place. As indicated in Fig. 13.2, the main sites are in the muscles, tendons, and joints. In addition, tactile receptors are also involved when movements are associated with movement of the skin.

It should be obvious that the central nervous system wants as much information as possible about ongoing movements. An important principle is that it does not entrust that task to just one information channel, but spreads the task among as many complementary kinds of channels as it can. As usual, this makes the subject more interesting, but makes definitions of terms more difficult. Table 13.1 lists some of the common terms and classifications, which deserve a brief discussion.

Muscle sense usually means the sensory information arising in the muscles and tendons. *Proprioception* is a term introduced by Sherrington to refer to all sensory inputs from the musculoskeletal system, which therefore includes inputs from joint receptors. Neither muscle sense nor proprioception necessarily implies conscious perception, and both can therefore be applied to invertebrates as well as all levels of vertebrates. *Kinesthesia* is the sense of the position and movement of the limbs. Contributing to this are skin receptors as well as proprioceptors. This sense includes conscious sensations—what Charles Bell, in the early nineteenth century, referred to as our "sixth sense"—and therefore applies primarily to higher vertebrates, especially

Fig. 13.1 Examples of motor behavior requiring precise sensorimotor coordination. *Left:* A male three-spined stickleback fish assumes a characteristic threat posture toward its own reflection in a mirror. According to Tinbergen, "this activity is innate, dependent on internal (motivational) and external (sensory) factors. It has an intimidating effect on other males. . . . Historically, it is displacement sanddigging, changed by ritualization." (From Tinbergen, 1951) *Right:* A ballerina, Jane Brayton, executing an arabesque. Ballet is a typical higher human activitiy, in which sensory factors, motivation, and innate capacities are molded by instruction, practice, and individual expression. (Photograph by Curt Meinel, courtesy of Ruth and Robert Brayton)

Fig. 13.2 Sites of sensory receptors for muscle sense and kinesthesia, as illustrated by the knee joint.

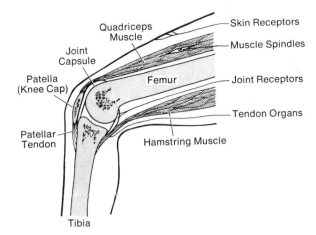

Table 13.1 Different sensory modalities related to movement, and their respective sensory receptors

Muscle sense	Proprioception	Kinesthesia	Functions
muscle receptors	muscle receptors	muscle receptors	Sensations of position and movement
tendon receptors	tendon receptors	tendon receptors	
	joint receptors	joint receptors	
		skin receptors	Sensation of force and weight
		central efferents	Sense of effort

humans. Kinesthesia also includes our sensations of effort, of force, and of weight; contributing to these sensations are signals in descending pathways within the central nervous system (see Chap. 21).

In this chapter we will focus on the proprioceptors in the musculoskeletal system. We will discuss briefly their central pathways and, in humans, their possible contributions to conscious sensations.

INVERTEBRATES

Proprioceptors are present in many invertebrate species, and are especially important in arthropods. In concert with the development of specialized muscle groups

to control the body segments and long, articulated appendages was the development of various kinds of specialized sensory receptors. Among the simplest of these is the stretch receptor cell of the crayfish. We have discussed the spread of electrotonic potentials in this cell in Chap. 7, and the basic properties of the sensory response in Chap. 10. Here this cell will further be used as a model for the control of excitability of muscle receptors.

Crayfish Abdominal Stretch Receptor

The long abdomen of the crayfish is composed of a number of segments (see Fig. 13.3). The dorsal cuticular plates of each segment are hinged on each other so that

Fig. 13.3 The stretch receptor cell of the lobster, showing relation to muscles and segments of the abdomen. MRO, muscle receptor organ; RM 1, 2, receptor muscles (compare with Fig. 7.11). (A, B from Florey, in Bullock, 1976; C, D from Alexandrowicz, 1951)

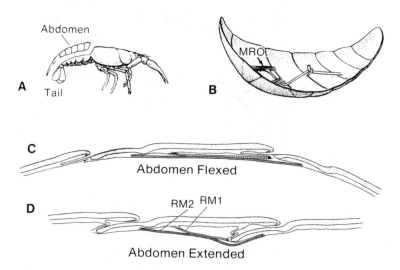

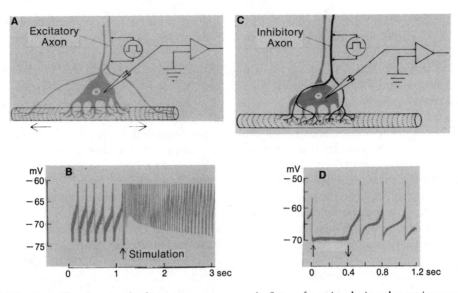

Fig. 13.4 Centrifugal control of sensory responses. **A.** Setup for stimulating the excitatory motor axon to the receptor muscle. **B.** During the receptor response to a maintained stretch, stimulation (at arrow) of the motor nerve produces contraction of the receptor muscle, further stretching the receptor cell membrane and increasing the receptor response. **C.** Setup for stimulating the inhibitory motor axon to the receptor cell dendrites. **D.** High-frequency electrical shock (150/sec) to the inhibitory axon (between arrows) inhibits the ongoing receptor response to a maintained stretch. (Adapted from Kuffler and Eyzaguirre, in Kuffler et al., 1984)

when the segmental muscles contract, the abdomen is flexed. The abdomen can thus be flipped like a tail, which is the method a crayfish uses for a quick retreat from danger (this escape response is described in Chap. 20). The muscles contain two types of fibers, the regular muscle fibers, that move the plates when they contract, and modified muscle fibers that contain the terminals of the sensory cells. The modified fibers contribute little to the movement of the plates, but indicate to the sensory cells the state of tension or lengthening of the muscle. The modified muscle fibers occur in two types of bundles, depending on whether they are slow fibers (slow summation of contraction) or rapid fibers (individual contractions). There are correspondingly slowly adapting and rapidly adapting types of receptor cells (see Figs. 7.11 and 13.3).

Each muscle bundle receives a motor innervation in the form of collaterals from the motoneuron axons to the main muscle fibers. Thus, whenever the motoneurons send impulses in their axons to signal the main muscles to contract, they also produce contractions of the sensory muscle fibers (Fig. 13.4A,B). Now, the question arises: what is the reason for having the sensory muscle fibers contract at the same time as the main muscle fiber? The answer is that if the sensory fibers did not contract, they would fall slack as the rest of the muscle contracted and shortened. By contracting at the same time, they, in effect, adjust themselves to the new length of the main muscle, and can therefore signal any departure from that length, such as occurs if an obstacle is encountered. The increase in sensitivity produced by motor stimulation is shown in Fig. 13.4B.

Each sensory cell also receives an inhibitory axon. Stimulation of this axon produces an inhibitory postsynaptic potential (IPSP) in the sensory cell, as we saw in Chap. 7, and the effect of the IPSP in depressing and interrupting an impulse discharge in the receptor cell is shown in Fig. 13.4C,D. The inhibitory axons arise from cells in the segmental ganglion. Because they carry impulses *away from* the central nervous system and its higher centers, they are referred to as *centrifugal fibers*.

It can now be seen that the stretch receptor cell, even though it is located in the periphery among the muscles it innervates, is under exquisite control by the central nervous system. The nervous system can either increase or decrease the sensitivity of this receptor. It is interesting that the output in the motoneurons themselves, in fact, functions as part of the centrifugal control, through the collaterals to the sensory muscle fibers. This control over the *reception* of stimuli in the body is a common feature in the organization of the invertebrates. In the vertebrates, in contrast, centrifugal control of sensory input reaches only to the site of the first synaptic relay in the spinal cord. This is taken to reflect the *encephalization* of nervous control, and the shifting of nervous integration to higher centers, an important feature in the evolution of higher organisms. A similar progression can be seen in motor systems (Chap. 17).

Crab Thoracico-coxal Receptor

A stretch receptor that fulfills the same sensory function as the abdominal receptor, but achieves it by different properties, is the stretch receptor at the base of each leg, called the *thoracico-coxal receptor*. As shown in Fig. 13.5, the cell body of this receptor is located in the segmental ganglion; it sends a long process to the periphery, to terminate among the muscles that control the joint between the limb and the thorax. As shown in Fig. 13.5, a brief stretch to the muscle sets up a receptor potential that resembles that seen in the abdominal receptors. The remarkable difference between the two cases is that the receptor potential is the entire signal in this receptor; there are no impulses. This was described in 1968 by S. H. Ripley, Brian Bush, and Alan Roberts at Bristol, and was one of the first demonstrations of nonimpulse transmission in neurons (see Chap. 7). The receptor potential spreads passively through the axon by electrotonic means (see b–e in Fig. 13.5), and synaptic output is caused by graded depolarization of the presynaptic branches, as we have previously discussed (Chap. 7). The effectiveness of transmission is shown by recording the reflex motor response in the motoneuron axons (a in Fig. 13.5).

We see here a very nice demonstration of how the same function (signaling of stretch) can be mediated by two cells that have very different structures, and use two different properties—graded electrotonic spread and all-or-nothing impulses—to transmit the signals. Thus, although transmission takes place in the analog and digital modes, respectively, in the two cases, the overall functions are nonetheless similar. The fact that nerve cells with different structures and different properties may carry out similar functions is an important principle in the organization of nervous systems.

VERTEBRATES

Evolution of Muscle Receptors

Specialized muscle receptors are rather late to appear in vertebrate evolution. There are apparently no sensory nerve endings within the body musculature of fish. In some speices of fish there are sensory fibers, including free nerve endings and corpuscle-like organs, within the connective tissue surrounding the muscles to the fins (Fig. 13.6A). These fibers signal extension and compression produced in the connective tissue by lengthening and contraction of the muscles that control the bending of the fins. A simple type of muscle spindle, consisting of a single modified muscle fiber innervated by a sensory axon, has been recently reported in a jaw-closing muscle in salmon.

Fins, of course, were the evolutionary

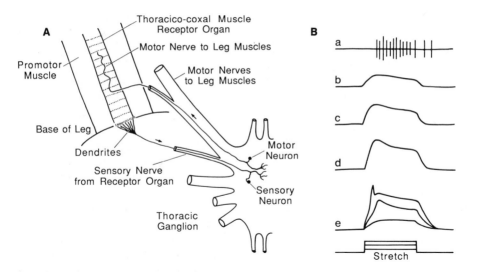

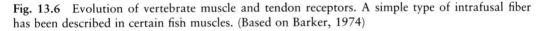

Fig. 13.5 A. Reflex circuit comprising the thoracico-coxal muscle receptor and the motor neuron of the crab. **B.** Intracellular recordings from sensory neuron. When stretch is applied to a muscle, the receptor cell responds with graded potentials (b–d, different amplitude of graded response), which are sufficient for synaptic transmission and impulse response of the motor neuron (a) (recorded extracellularly from the motor nerve). Under some conditions a small graded "spike" may be present (e), which appears to be due to a small number of voltage-sensitive sodium channels in the receptor cell membrane. This spike may aid in signaling very rapid muscle stretches. (Based on Bush, 1981)

Fig. 13.6 Evolution of vertebrate muscle and tendon receptors. A simple type of intrafusal fiber has been described in certain fish muscles. (Based on Barker, 1974)

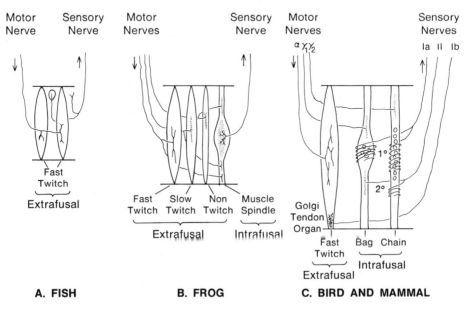

forerunner of the limbs of terrestrial animals. The amphibians are the first animals in the phylogenetic scale to possess muscle spindles; it is believed that they evolved here to provide the sensory input required for the limb muscles to oppose the force of gravity and maintain posture. Within the muscles are modified muscle fibers, gathered in small bundles and surrounded by a capsule. Their widened midregions reminded early histologists of the spindle used in spinning wool, and they were therefore named *muscle spindles*. There is a single sensory fiber innervating each muscle spindle (Fig. 13.6B). Each spindle also receives a motor innervation via collaterals from motor axons to the muscles. In the frog, the limb muscles characteristically are composed of different types of muscle fibers with different speeds of contraction. There are fast-twitch, slow-twitch, and nontwitch fibers, with corresponding motor nerve axons to each type of fiber, and corresponding axon collaterals to the muscle spindles (see Fig. 13.6B). The fibers that make up the main mass of the muscle and do all the work are called *extrafusal fibers,* and the modified muscle fibers within the spindle are called *intrafusal fibers* (these names being derived from the fusiform appearance of the spindle). The basic similarities in the arrangements of motor and sensory innervation of the frog spindle and the crayfish stretch receptor may be seen by comparing Fig. 13.6B with Fig. 13.4.

Further steps in evolution are seen in birds and mammals. In these species, several differences are evident, as illustrated in Fig. 13.6C. The first difference is that there are two types of intrafusal fibers. One type has a collection of nuclei within a saclike central portion, and is called a *nuclear bag fiber*. The other type contains a chain of nuclei, and is called a *nuclear chain fiber*. In the central portion, each type receives the spiral ending of a large sensory nerve fiber. The ending is called a *primary ending*. It arises from a group Ia axon, the largest of all the peripheral nerve fibers.

Table 13.2 summarizes the diameters and conduction velocities for the Ia fibers and for other types in peripheral nerves.

Near its central portion, the nuclear chain fiber receives smaller spiral terminals. This is called a *secondary ending*. It arises from a group II axon. There may also be a small twig from a group II axon that supplies secondary endings to the nuclear bag fibers.

A second difference is that, rather than the motor innervation being derived from the motor nerves to the extrafusal muscles, the intrafusal muscles receive their own motor axons. These have small diameters, and are called *gamma (γ) fibers* to distinguish them from the large *alpha (α) fibers* to the extrafusal muscles. Another name for them is *fusimotor fiber*. The γ fibers to bag and chain fibers are distinct from each other.

A third difference is that a new type of sensory organ makes its appearance. This was first described by Golgi in the late nineteenth century, and is therefore named the *Golgi tendon organ*. As indicated in the diagram of Fig. 13.6C, this organ is embedded in the tendon at the end of the muscle. It is innervated by a group Ib axon, only slightly smaller in diameter than the Ia axons.

Nearly all muscles in the mammalian body contain muscle receptors organized along the lines just described. This is rather remarkable, considering how radically such muscles as those in the legs, fingers, tongue, esophagus, and eye differ from each other. Acording to David Barker of England, who has carried out many detailed studies of muscle receptor anatomy, muscle spindles are present in highest densities in the hand, foot, and neck, where they are believed to be important in controlling *fine movements*, and also in certain leg muscles (such as the soleus) which are important for *maintaining posture*. In contrast, spindles are fewest in shoulder and thigh muscles, and in muscles (such as gastrocnemius) involved in initiating gross movements. Spindles are also present in high density in the

Table 13.2 The fiber spectrum of the peripheral nerves in the mammal

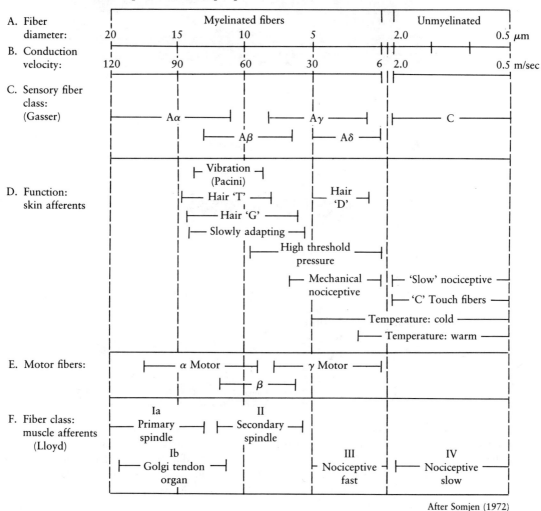

After Somjen (1972)

extraocular muscles of the eye in most mammals (such as primates, horses, pigs, etc.). In these muscles, the muscle fibers are divided into subclasses, and the spindles receive some of their motor innervation from motoneuron axon collaterals. The situation thus appears intermediate between the frog and the common mammalian pattern. Muscle spindles have been reported absent from the extraocular muscles in several species (such as rat, cat, and dog). There is as yet no explanation for this puzzling difference.

In summary, muscle receptors are neural sensors that, once appearing in evolution, have been strongly conserved. Like other types of neural modules (e.g., the rhabdomere of the insect eye; the cortical column in the mammalian brain: see Chap. 16), they have been adapted to a variety of functions; these include differential sensing of dynamic and static changes in muscles, and control of different types of motor reflex responses. Let us next consider the physiological properties of muscle receptors, as exemplified by the frog and the mammal.

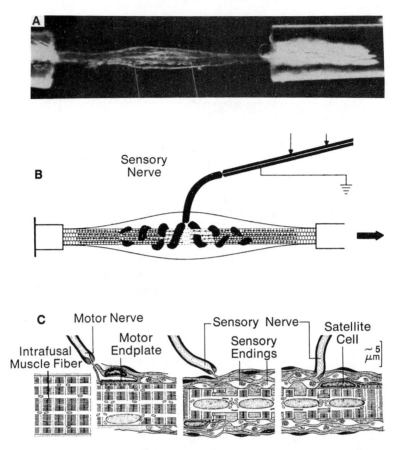

Fig. 13.7 The muscle spindle of the frog. **A.** Darkfield photomicrograph of a spindle mounted between two nylon rods (thickness, 300 μm). The two thin lines indicate the central sensory region. **B.** Diagram of a spindle mounted as in **A**, showing the recording setup. **C.** Diagram of the fine structure of the spindle, showing the relation of motor and sensory terminals to the intrafusal muscle nerve fiber. (A,B from Ottoson and Shepherd; C from Karlsson et al.; for complete references, see Ottoson and Shepherd, 1971)

Frog Muscle Spindle

The frog muscle spindle, like the Pacinian corpuscle, has played an important part in the development of our knowledge about sensory receptor mechanisms. It was the first receptor from which single unit recordings, from the sensory axons, were made; this was accomplished by Yngve Zotterman and Edgar Adrian at Cambridge University in 1926. Its response properties were analyzed in a quantitative manner by Brian Matthews in Cambridge in the 1930s. It was the first receptor from which a receptor potential was recorded; this was

obtained by Bernard Katz in London in 1950.

A careful analysis of the frog spindle was carried out by David Ottoson and his colleagues in Stockholm. With fine forceps Ottoson dissected out a single spindle with its single afferent axon and mounted it between two nylon threads in a recording chamber. The setup is shown in Fig. 13.7. Below the setup are schematic diagrams of the ultrastructure of different regions of the spindle: the muscle; a transition zone; and the central, main sensory zone. In the central zone the regular striations of the mus-

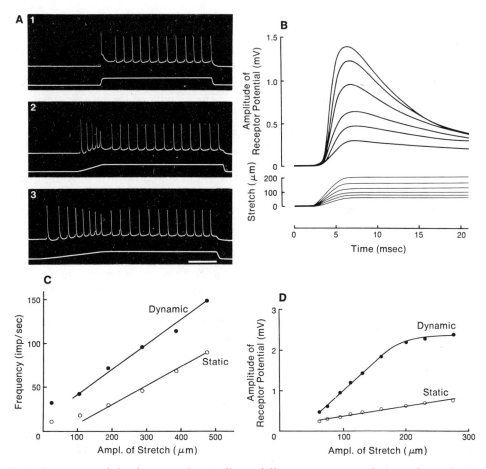

Fig. 13.8 Responses of the frog muscle spindle to different amounts and rates of stretch. **A.** Impulse response to stretches of decreasing rate of extension (1–3), to the same steady extension. Note higher impulse frequencies during dynamic stretching in (2) and (3). (1) 130 mm/sec; (2) 13 mm/sec; (3) 5 mm/sec. Time bar, 50 msec. **B.** Receptor potential recorded from the sensory nerve after blocking impulses with local anesthetic in the bathing medium. Note dynamic peaks followed by decline toward static plateau. **C.** Comparison between impulse firing frequencies at the dynamic peak and the static plateau of the response. Dynamic stretch rate was 2.6 mm/sec; static plateau frequencies were measured 200 msec after the dynamic peak. **D.** Comparison between amplitudes of the dynamic and static receptor potentials for rapidly applied stretches to different static levels. (From Ottoson and Shepherd, 1971)

cle are partially replaced by connective and reticular tissue, within which are embedded the sensory terminals. The terminals consist of bulbous varicosities several microns in diameter, alternating with thin linking processes only a few tenths of a micrometer in diameter. It is believed that sensory transduction occurs in the membrane of the bulbs, by mechanically gated channels as was discussed in Chap. 10.

With the setup shown in Fig. 13.7, stretch is applied very close to the sensory endings, and the receptor properties can be studied with great accuracy. Examples of typical recordings are shown in Fig. 13.8. Note the extremely regular nature of the impulse discharge shown in A, even when the stretch is applied very slowly. The receptor potential shown in B is finely graded in rate of rise and amplitude in correlation with the applied stretch. The greater sensitivity of the spindle during the dynamic phase of the applied stretch is seen in the recordings in A and B, and is plotted in the graphs of C and D. These studies leave little doubt of the ability of the spindle to signal the rate of change and the steady amplitude of an applied stretch with exquisite precision.

Mammalian Muscle Receptors

As we have seen, mammalian muscle receptors are characterized by differentiation into spindles and tendon organs, and the spindle fibers are further differentiated into bag and chain fibers, each with primary and secondary sensory endings, and separate γ motor supply. This makes for a rather complicated situation, which permits different combinations of sensory signaling under different states of muscle activity. A number of these combinations have been studied, mostly using the muscles of the hindlimb of the cat (for example, the soleus). Many workers have contributed to this study, and the diagrams in Fig. 13.9 summarize much of this work. Since there are so many permutations of sensory and motor activity, the student should examine this figure slowly—one diagram at a time!

The simplest situation is stretch applied to a passive muscle. As shown in Fig. 13.9A, the primary spindle endings give a brisk response, especially to dynamic stretch, while the secondary endings give a slowly adapting response with little dynamic sensitivity. From this it has been concluded that the primary endings are the main channel through which information about changing stretch of a muscle is communicated, and secondary endings are more specialized for transmitting information about position. Tendon organs show a high threshold and low sensitivity to passive stretch, and thus contribute little information under these conditions.

In the normal animal, there is ongoing activity in the γ motor fibers, and the effects of this activity on responses to passive stretch are shown in Fig. 13.9B. In general, there is increased background firing of the

sensory fibers, due to the background contractions of the intrafusal muscle fibers, and an increased sensitivity to an applied stretch. There is no effect of the intrafusal contractions on tendon organs, however.

The activity of the muscle receptors during active contraction of a muscle is shown in Fig. 13.9C,D. During a brief muscle twitch (C), both primary and sensory endings of muscle spindles show a "pause"—an interruption in their ongoing discharge. Tendon organs, in contrast, give a high-frequency burst of impulses during the contraction. In a brief paper in 1928, Pi-Suñer and John Fulton, then at Harvard, speculated that this difference arises because the tendon organ is in series with the contracting muscle, whereas the spindles are in parallel. Because of this arrangement, the tendon organ is subjected to increased tension, while the spindle tends to fall slack. Note the high sensitivity of the tendon organ to active contraction, which stands in contrast to its low sensitivity to passive stretch.

Finally, we consider the case of active contraction with γ innervation intact, as in the normal cat (Fig. 13.9D). As in part B of the figure, the background discharge is increased, but, in addition, the sensory endings continue to give rise to impulses during the twitch, so that there is no pause. This role of the γ fibers was first indicated by the work of Lars Leksell in Stockholm in 1945, and was established in a classical series of papers by Carlton Hunt and Stephen Kuffler at Johns Hopkins in the 1950s. By this means, the muscle spindle remains under tension during a muscle contraction, and can thus signal changes in load when they occur. The separate γ innervation of the bag and chain fibers (see D) allows the dynamic and static responsiveness of the sensory endings to be controlled independently, thereby adding to the precision of the sensory signals.

In summary, different types of motor activity give rise to different patterns of sensory signals from the muscles, as is necessary if the central nervous system is to receive accurate information about the on-

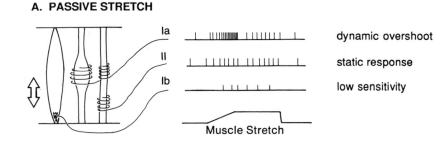

A. PASSIVE STRETCH

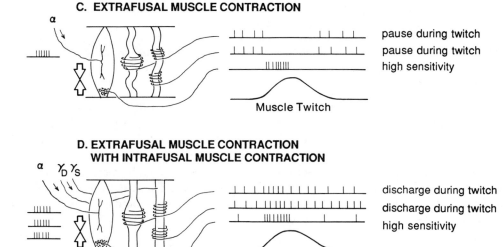

Ia — dynamic overshoot

II — static response

Ib — low sensitivity

Muscle Stretch

B. PASSIVE STRETCH WITH INTRAFUSAL MUSCLE CONTRACTION

γ γ

increased background
and response

increased background
and response

low sensitivity

Muscle Stretch

C. EXTRAFUSAL MUSCLE CONTRACTION

α

pause during twitch

pause during twitch

high sensitivity

Muscle Twitch

**D. EXTRAFUSAL MUSCLE CONTRACTION
WITH INTRAFUSAL MUSCLE CONTRACTION**

α   γ_D γ_S

discharge during twitch

discharge during twitch

high sensitivity

Muscle Twitch

Fig. 13.9 Responses of mammalian muscle spindles and tendon organs under different conditions of muscle stretch, muscle contraction, and centrifugal (gamma) control. **A.** Passive stretch alone causes a dynamic response in Ia spindle endings, a mostly static response in II endings, and little response in Ib (tendon organ) endings. **B.** Stimulation of γ axons (left) increases the background activity of both types of spindle endings and their responses to stretch, but has little effect on tendon organ responses. **C.** When impulses in the nerves of a motoneuron (left) cause the muscle to contract and shorten (see muscle twitch), the muscle spindles become slack, while the tendon organs are activated. **D.** Stimulation of the dynamic (D) and static (S) γ axons (left) causes the corresponding intrafusal fibers to contact, so that they are not slack during a muscle twitch, and can continue to signal the amount of stretch. α, axon of alpha motoneuron; γ, axon of gamma motoneuron [dynamic (D) and static (S)]. (Based on Pi-Suñer and Fulton; Leksell, Hunt, and Kuffler; Matthews, Gordon, and others; references in Kuffler et al., 1984)

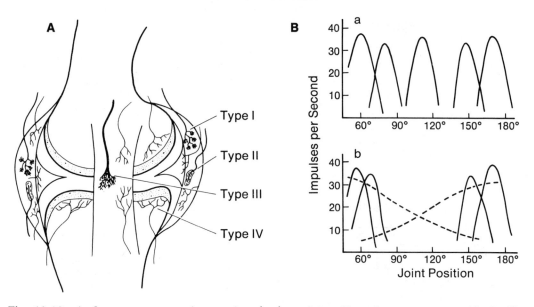

Fig. 13.10   A. Sensory receptors innervating the knee joint. Type 1 receptors resemble Ruffini endings in the skin. Type II receptors have the form of flattened Pacinian corpuscles. Type III receptors resemble Golgi tendon organs. Type IV receptors are unmyelinated nerve endings, resembling pain fiber terminals. (From Brodal, 1981) B. Tuning curves of joint receptor nerves for different joint positions in the cat. a. Population of fibers covering most of the range of joint position. (From Skoglund, 1973) b. Population of fibers covering only extremes of the range of joint position. Dashed lines show recordings from primary endings of muscle spindles in antagonistic muscles around the ankle joint. Muscle receptors may contribute to sensation of joint position through this activity, which Burgess et al. have termed an opponent frequency code. (Based on Burgess et al., 1982)

going actions of the muscles. The central nervous system itself contributes to setting the sensitivity of the spindle receptors by ongoing biasing through the γ motor system. The way that these motor and sensory fiber systems are integrated into the neural machinery for muscle control will be explained in the discussion of motor systems in Chap. 19.

Joint Receptors

Joints are typically encased in tough connective tissue capsules and extensions of ligaments of muscles. Embedded in the joint capsules are several kinds of sensory receptor. Each appears to be a modified version of a corresponding receptor in the skin. They have been classified as follows (see Fig. 13.10). The type I receptor consists of small corpuscles around the branches of thin, myelinated fibers. These receptors resemble Ruffini end organs in the skin. They respond to stretch with slowly adapting discharges. The type II receptor is a large corpuscle supplied by a medium-thick myelinated fiber. These receptors resemble Pacinian corpuscles, and like them, are rapidly adapting. The type III receptor consists of a large, dense arborization of a large, myelinated fiber. They are found in ligaments near the capsule, and resemble a Golgi tendon organ. They have high thresholds and are slowly adapting. Type IV receptors are free nerve endings of fine, unmyelinated fibers, resembling those in the skin.

This rich innervation suggests that sensory information from the joints might contribute to position sense. The early experiments provided evidence that type I receptors are tuned to respond over narrow angles within the range of joint movement (Fig. 13.10). It was proposed that these slowly adapting discharges signal joint position, whereas the rapidly adapting type II receptors are acceleration detectors. This suggested a beautifully tuned system for signaling joint position, and seemed all the more persuasive in view of other behavioral evidence that muscle receptors did not seem to contribute to position sense.

In recent years, however, the relative significance of the roles played by joint and by muscle afferents has been reversed. Reinvestigation of the slowly adapting fibers indicates that most of these fire impulses only at the extremes of joint movement, but rarely over the middle range, where signals in the normal physiological range of joint position and movement are needed (see Fig. 13.10). On the other hand, there has been increasing evidence for the contribution of muscle receptors to kinesthesia. We will return to these questions when we discuss cortical mechanisms below.

Ascending Pathways

We have seen that information from muscles and joints is carried to the spinal cord in an array of different axons, ranging from the largest myelinated axons (type I and II from muscle receptors) to the several types of fibers from joint receptors. The array of fibers is similar from both the hindlimb and forelimb, but in the spinal cord the connections and ascending pathways are different.

The fibers from the *hindlimb* bifurcate within the cord. One branch terminates within the cord, to take part in segmental reflex circuits (Chap. 19) or to connect to cells of a nucleus called Clarke's column, which projects to the cerebellum via the spinocerebellar pathway (Chap. 21). These fibers also give off collaterals to a nucleus with the somewhat mysterious name of "nucleus Z," which in turn relays through the medial lemniscus to the thalamus. These connections are summarized in Fig. 13.11.

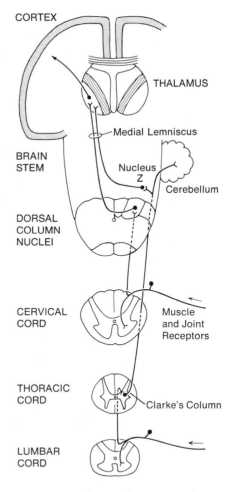

Fig. 13.11 Ascending pathways carrying sensory information from muscles and joints. Compare with somatosensory pathways shown in Fig. 12.12. (Adapted from Carpenter, 1976, and Brodal, 1981)

The fibers from the *forelimb* also bifurcate on entering the cord, but their destinations are simpler. One branch takes part in local reflex circuits, whereas the other ascends to the dorsal column nuclei at the anterior end of the cord. This ascending pathway, through the medial lemniscus to the thalamus, is thus similar to that for cutaneous afferents, as discussed in the previous chapter.

The different central connections presumably reflect the different functions of hindlimbs and forelimbs. The spinocerebellar pathway, for example, provides for integration of muscle and joint information with cerebellar mechanisms that are essential for sensorimotor coordination and maintenance of muscle tone and posture. This is particularly relevant to the functions of the hindlimbs in standing posture and in locomotion. In contrast, the forelimbs are closely related to the neck and head; their direct connections to lemniscal pathways presumably reflect the more discriminative functions, including manipulation by the paw or hand, of the forelimb. The separation of these two pathways may therefore reflect functional specialization that was important in the evolution of primates.

The Cortex and Kinesthesia

The ascending pathways carrying muscle and joint information enter the medial lemniscus and terminate in the VP nucleus of the thalamus, as indicated in Fig. 13.11. The fibers terminate topographically, similar to the cutaneous fiber terminations. From here, muscle and joint information is relayed to the cortex. These submodalities have their own specific areas in the cortex, which are closely related to the multiple representations of the somatosensory system. At this point, the reader should refer to Fig. 12.16B. The main cortical representation for muscles is area 3a, which receives input relayed especially from Ia fibers from muscle spindles. There is a representation of some muscle afferents in area 5 of the parietal lobe, and of various deep tissues in area 2 (see Fig. 12.16B).

These cortical representations are all recent findings, made possible by application of modern techniques such as horseradish peroxidase (HRP) tracing and unit recordings in unrestrained animals. They have brought about a revision in our thinking about perception of movement. As mentioned above, the traditional view had been that muscle afferent pathways do not reach the cortex, and that our perceptions of joint position and the movements of our joints and muscles are mediated only by joint receptors. Proprioceptors were supposed to take part only in subcortical and subconscious muscle reflexes. This seemed to receive support from behavioral studies in humans, in which finger joints were infiltrated with local anesthetic, producing loss of position sense.

Fig. 13.12   A. Site of recording from a single pyramidal neuron in the primary motor area (MI) of an awake, behaving monkey. Also shown are primary (SI) and secondary (SII) somatosensory areas. (From Woolsey, in Henneman, 1980b; see also Fig. 21.11) **B.** Response of this neuron to flexion of the joint at the base of the middle finger (metacarpophalangeal (MC-P) joint) is shown in (B). The neuron did not respond to other types of movement, as shown in: (C) flexion of proximal interphalangeal joint (P-IP), (D) ulnar (lateral) deviation of MC-P joint, and (E) radial (medial) deviation of MC-P joint. (From Lemon and Porter, 1976)

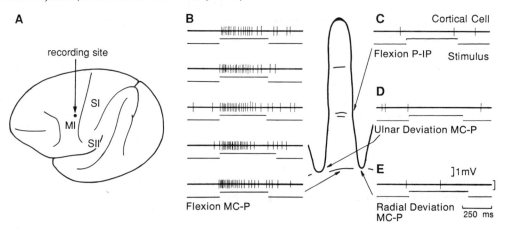

This conception began to topple with the finding that relatively few joint receptors are tuned to the physiological range of mid-joint ankle position, as mentioned above (Fig. 13.10B). Then, in 1972, G. M. Goodwin, Ian McCloskey, and Peter Matthews at Oxford carried out careful behavioral studies which showed that, with local anesthesia of all cutaneous afferents from the arm, position sense of the fingers still persisted. This showed that muscle afferents have access to mechanisms of perception, and it implied that there must be projections of the muscle afferent pathways to the cortex for this to occur. Recent work, as we have seen above, has confirmed the presence of these connections.

Muscle and joint afferents not only have access to somatosensory cortex, they also are relayed to the motor cortex. This is illustrated in Fig. 13.12, which shows results from an experiment in an unanesthetized monkey by Robert Porter and Roger Lemon in Australia. The recording is from an identified projection neuron (a pyramidal cell) in motor cortex (MsI, Fig. 12.16B). The neuron, as can been seen, responds briskly to movement at a single joint of the finger. Results such as this extend the specific parallel and serial pathways underlying perception to include sensory mechanisms within motor areas as well. We shall discuss how this may relate to kinesthesia and "sense of effort" in Chap. 21.

14

The Sense of Balance

All animals exist in a physical environment, and must therefore be able to orient appropriately within it in order to carry out their functions. In a few species, simple contact with the environment is sufficient. This is true, for example, for a sessile animal like the tapeworm which lives its life attached to the gut wall. However, active organisms are always changing in their relations to the environment, and therefore require constant monitoring of those relations. In general, the more active they are, the more important it is to obtain precise information about different aspects of position and movement. This information is the basis for maintaining the *balance,* or *equilibrium,* of the animal, either in anticipation of motor tasks that involve changes in body position or movement, or through reflexes induced by disturbances from the environment.

The different kinds of sensory information that are used in maintaining balance are indicated in Fig. 14.1. Proprioceptive inputs are a constant source of information about the relative positions and movements of different parts of the body. Cutaneous inputs also contribute. Visual information is important, as anyone can discover by seeing how long it is possible to stand on

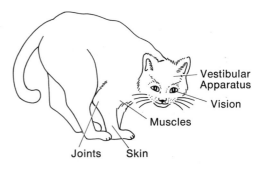

Fig. 14.1 Sensory modalities that contribute to maintaining balance.

one foot with eyes closed! However, these inputs from other sensory systems are usually not enough, and most organisms have therefore evolved sense organs (vestibular apparatus in Fig. 14.1) that are specially adapted for this function.

In general, these special organs fall into two categories. One is the *statocyst*. This characteristically takes the form of a fluid-filled pocket that has, in its wall, a patch (called a *macula*) of sensory cells (see Fig. 14.2). The cells have fine hairs which support, at their tips, some dense crystals glued together with a jellylike material. When the statocyst is tilted, the heavy crystals weigh on the hairs, making them bend (see figure),

286

A. STATOCYST - MACULA

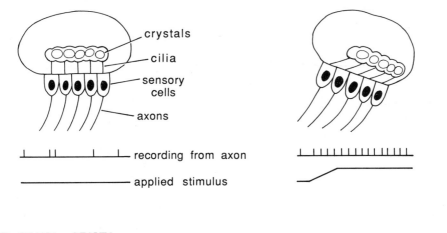

B. CANAL - CRISTA

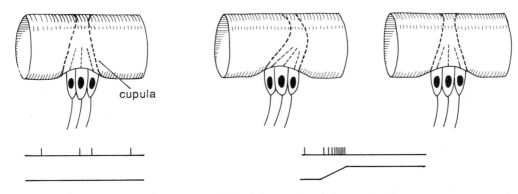

Fig. 14.2 The main type of organs specialized for sensing balance. **A.** The statocyst, or macula, for sensing the force of gravity and linear acceleration. **B.** The canal, with crista, for sensing angular acceleration of movement.

which leads to an increased discharge of impulses in the sensory fibers. This arrangement is sensitive to velocity. Since the mechanism is sensitive to the force of gravity, the statocyst is a *gravireceptor*. Gravity is a universal force on all organisms, and it is not surprising that nearly all active organisms should have gravireceptors. The statocyst must be an effective organ for this purpose, because, with the conspicuous exception of the insects, most animals have gravireceptors constructed along the general lines shown in Fig. 14.2.

The other type of organ contributing to the sense of balance is the *canal*. As shown in Fig. 14.2, it is fluid-filled canal with a patch of sensory cells in the wall. These cells also have hairs, which project into the lumen, and are embedded in a structure called the *cupula,* a jellylike matrix composed of glycoprotein, which stretches across the lumen of the canal. The patch of cells forms a raised protuberance which is called a *crista*. When the head rotates, the fluid in the affected canal is displaced, which causes a shearing force on the hairs projecting into the cupula, and this is converted into a burst of impulses. As long as the body movement is changing (either accelerating or decelerating) the cupula will be displaced, but when constant velocity is attained, the fluid of the canal moves at the same rate as the body, and the cupula returns to its original position. Thus, the canal type of organ is specially adapted to detect angular *acceleration*. There are a few examples of this type of organ in invertebrates (e.g., lobster, octopus) but they are a constant feature of the vertebrates, where they are called the *semicircular canals*.

Although the principles expressed in Fig. 14.2 are intuitively clear, the details of the functioning of the organs of balance are exceedingly complicated. This is partly because we are not accustomed to thinking in terms of the properties of movement. It is relatively easy to think about *static* responses of statocysts to the force of gravity. The relations of mechanical forces to constant *velocity* are more difficult to grasp. Properties related to *acceleration* are more difficult, involving as they do concepts of mathematical differentiation, phase lag, and the like. This study is becoming increasingly sophisticated, and interested students will find appropriate references in the legends to the figures. For the remainder of the chapter we will concentrate on the peripheral receptors and their functional circuits within the central nervous system.

INVERTEBRATES

Statocysts were identified in invertebrates by morphologists during the nineteenth century, but they were first mistaken as organs of hearing. Their function as gravity receptors was demonstrated in a classic and oft-told study of Kreidl in Austria in 1893. Kreidl kept an acquarium of shrimp in his laboratory, and was studying their statocysts, which by good fortune (for biologists) open to the outside. Each statocyst contains, as its *statoliths,* grains of sand. Now it happens that each time the shrimp molts, it sheds its statoliths and takes in new grains of sand. Kreidl replaced the sand of the aquarium with iron filings, and showed that with a strong magnet he could make the shrimp assume different orientations that were the result of the magnetic and gravitational fields. It could therefore be concluded that the normal stimulus for the statocyst is gravity.

Receptor Mechanisms

The statocyst and its gravireceptive function have been demonstrated throughout

Fig. 14.3 Statocyst in a medusa, shown in a horizontal (A) and a tilted (B) position. (From Singla, in Alexander, 1979)

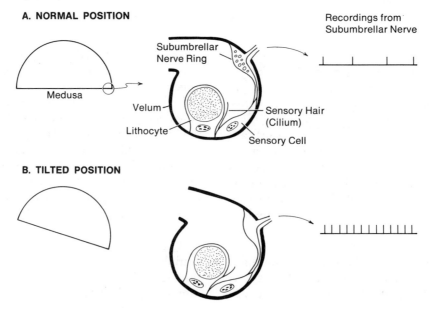

the invertebrate classes (except for insects). As a matter of fact, the first multicellular sense organs to appear along the phylogenetic scale are the statocyst (for balance) and the ocellus (for vision).

Coelenterates

Statocysts are found in coelenterates, as in the medusa, where they are located in the rim of the bell. As shown in Fig. 14.3, the *statolith* is contained within the cell *(lithocyte)* that secretes it. Next to it is a sensory cell with a cilium that, in the normal resting position of the medusa, does not touch the lithocyte. When the medusa tilts, the weight of the statolith presses the lithocyte against the cilium, causing it to bend. This is believed to cause distortion of the sensory cell membrane, setting up a receptor potential by gating of membrane channel conductances. This generates impulses, which are conducted into the subumbrellar nerve ring and induce reflexes that tend to right the organism. It is somewhat sobering to realize that all the basic elements of the sensory and motor systems for sensing and maintaining balance are present so near the lowest rung on the evolutionary ladder!

Molluscs

The nature of the transduction process has been analyzed in the statocyst of the mollusc *Hermissenda.* In this slug, the statocysts are located near the eyes and optic ganglia. A view of the inside of a statocyst, with its group of *statoconia,* is shown in the scanning electron micrograph of Fig. 14.4. Some of the hairs arising from the sensory cells lining the wall can also be seen. Intracellular recordings from single receptor cells during rotation of the experimental preparation have been performed by Daniel Alkon and his colleagues at Woods Hole. With increasing amounts of centrifugal force, there is an increase in the noise level in the recordings (see Fig. 14.4). These voltage fluctuations are believed to be produced by a shot-noise process of random conductance increases in channels in the hair cell membrane. The fluctuations sum

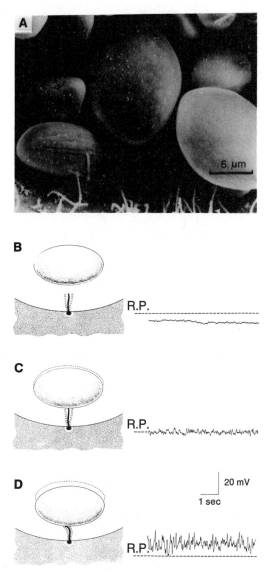

Fig. 14.4 A. Scanning electron micrograph of the statocyst of the mollusc *Hermissenda,* showing statoconia contacting cilia. B–D. Model of statoconia in different relations with cilia. *Right:* Recordings from hair cells, showing increasing depolarization and voltage noise with increasing force of statoconia against cilia, produced by rotating the animal at faster rates. (From Grossman et al., 1979)

to produce the slow depolarizing receptor potential, from which arise impulses at increasing frequencies as the centrifugal force increases. A model of the interactions be-

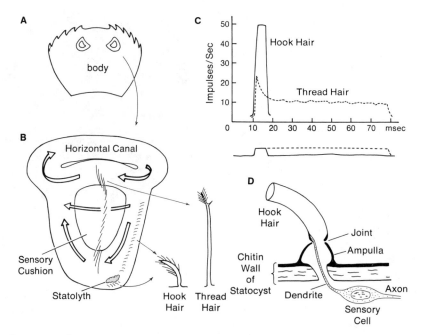

Fig. 14.5 Statocyst of crustacea. **A.** Positions of statocysts in the body. **B.** Structure of the lobster statocyst, showing difference between hook and thread hairs. **C.** Differing response properties of hook and thread hairs to bending. **D.** Details of base of hook hair and its relation to sensory cell. (Adapted from Cohen, in Markl, 1974)

tween statoconium and hair cell that could produce these properties is illustrated in Fig. 14.4B–D.

Crustacea

A more complex type of statocyst is found in crustaceans. In the lobster, for example, there is a large statocyst which lies against the antennal nerve that runs from the antenna to the supraesophageal ganglion. The statolith consists of a mass of sand grains stuck together. The hairs that project from the sensory cells into the cavity are of several distinct types (see Fig. 14.5B,D). Depending on their appearance, they are referred to as *hook* hairs and *thread* hairs. Some of these hook hairs are in contact with the statoconia, while others end freely. The thread hairs end freely in one part of the statocyst. In general, the hairs are quite long, up to 800 μm in length.

Recordings have been made from the axons of the sensory cells under different conditions of movement. Beginning with the studies of Melvin Cohen in Oregon in

the 1950s, it has been possible to characterize the contributions of the different types of cell. Receptor cells with hook hairs that contact the statolith show slowly adapting responses to bending of the hair (see Fig. 14.5C). Since the statolith and the cyst wall are three-dimensional structures (see diagram in B), the spatial pattern of responses from all the sensory cells in contact with the statolith provides a three-dimensional representation to the animal of its position in space relative to gravity. In contrast to the hook hairs, the thread hairs give a phasic-tonic response to an imposed bending (see Fig. 14.5C). Since these hairs end freely, they are normally stimulated by movement of the fluid within the cavity caused by rotation of the animal; that is, they are responsive to angular acceleration. Thus, the differing properties of the hairs, and their relations to the statolith and the movement of fluid, enable the statocyst to signal both position of the body relative to gravity and amount of angular acceleration (rotation) of the body.

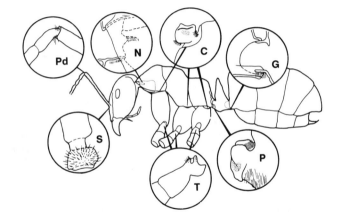

Fig. 14.6 Hair plates at different joints in a worker ant. Pd, joint between first and second antennal segments; N, neck joint; C, coxal joint; G, gaster joint; P, petiole joint; T, joint between trochanter and coxa; S, joint between head and antenna. (From Markl, 1974)

The signals from these types of receptors are necessary in animals that move quickly. The information is used to bring about reflexes of body musculature to maintain equilibrium. Included in these reflexes are compensatory eye movements that enable the animal to maintain a constant orientation of its eyes despite changes in the position of the body. Among other invertebrates, the octopus also has statocysts with similar properties and functional significance. These properties all have counterparts, developed to an even higher degree, in the vertebrates.

The Special Case of Insects

Before leaving the invertebrates, we should briefly discuss the insects. As already mentioned, insects lack statocysts; one can imagine that these animals need to travel light, and statoliths are too much baggage to carry around. However, the sense of balance is of extreme importance to insects, and this information is provided by an elaborate system of proprioceptors. This system is based on the same fundamental mechanism of the hair cell. As shown in Fig. 14.6, these specialized hair sensilla form *hair plates*, which are present at a number of joints. The hair cells have been found to be extremely sensitive to very small mechanical displacements. The downward pull of gravity on the appendages sets up a differentiated pattern of tonic inputs from the whole set of hair plates, and this provides the gravitational reference for orienting the muscular activities of the animal. In a sense, the whole exoskeleton of the insect performs the function of a statolith in providing the hard material that stimulates the hairs; in both cases, gravity is signaled by the entire spatial pattern of tonically firing receptor cells.

Insects also have a mechanism for detecting rotation. In flying insects such as *Diptera*, this is provided by the *halteres*. These are two dumbbell-shaped appendages that are modified hind wings. When the insect is flying, they oscillate rapidly up and down. Changes in direction of flight involve rotation about the axes of the animal, and this is communicated as torques and strains which stimulate certain hair sensilla in the base of the haltere. The haltere thus provides information about angular acceleration in a fashion that in some respects resembles the way that a gyroscope is used for stabilization in aircraft and submarines.

VERTEBRATES

The fundamental nature of the statocyst as a gravity detector is reflected in the fact that a comparable structure, called an *oto-*

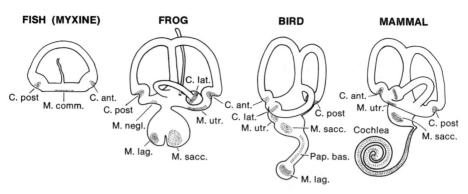

Fig. 14.7 Evolution of the labyrinth in vertebrates. C. ant., anterior crista; C. lat., lateral crista; C. post., posterior crista; M. comm., macula communis; M. lag., macula lagenae; M. negl., macula neglecta; M. sacc., macula sacculi; M. utr., macula utriculi; Pap. bas., papilla basilaris. (From Wersäll and Bagger-Sjöbäck, 1974)

lith organ, is present in all vertebrates. Attached to it are one or more canals for detecting rotation, which, because of their form, are called *semicircular canals*. The otolith organ and semicircular canals from the *vestibular organ*. In the course of evolution the otolith organ gives rise to an outpocketing which becomes the organ of hearing, the *cochlea*. Together this makes for a very complicated geometry, which the early morphologists (perhaps in bewilderment) dubbed a labyrinth; since it is all enclosed in membranes, the whole structure is called the *membranous labyrinth*.

The key steps in the evolution of the labyrinth are illustrated in Fig. 14.7. These diagrams also indicate the sites of the sensory receptor cells. The otolith organ is divided into two sacs, utricle and saccule, and the receptor cells are grouped in a macula in each sac. Similarly, each semicircular canal has an enlargement *(ampulla)*, within which the sensory cells are grouped in a crista.

Structure of the Receptors

The sensory elements of the vestibular organ were diagramed in Fig. 14.2, and are illustrated in greater detail in Fig. 14.8. Here, again, one finds testimony to the effectiveness of extremely small structures as sites for sensory transduction. Each hair

cell gives rise to a simple cilium, called a *kinocilium*. This is a true cilium, containing a ring of nine pairs of tubules. In addition, each cell gives rise to a number of *stereocilia*. These are thin extensions of the cell cytoplasm, enclosed in a three-layered plasma membrane; they are a form of microvillus, rather than a true cilium. These are always shorter than the kinocilium, and grade down in height with distance from it (see Fig. 14.8).

The features thus far described are common to hair cells of both the maculae of the otolith organ and the cristae of the semicircular canals. The accessory structures of the hairs, of course, are quite different. In the maculae, there is a covering of *otoliths*. These are largely composed of calcium carbonate crystals, called *otoconia*, which are glued together by a jellylike matrix to form a thick *otoconial membrane* (see Fig. 14.9). In the cristae, on the other hand, the hairs project into a dome of jelly (the cupula) that reaches across and fastens to the other side of the ampulla (see Fig. 14.9).

Because of the placement of the kinocilium to one side of the group of stereocilia, the whole group of hairs has an orientation in the direction of the kinocilium. Each collection of receptors has a characteristic orientation. As shown in Fig. 14.9, in the maculi sacculi the hair cells point away

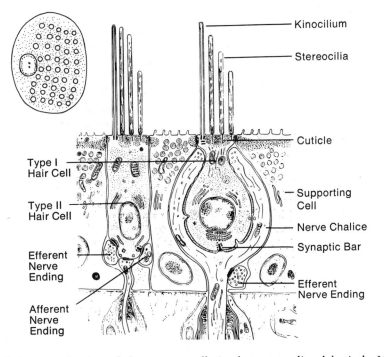

Kinocilium

Stereocilia

Cuticle

Type I
Hair Cell

Supporting
Cell

Type II
Hair Cell

Nerve Chalice

Synaptic Bar

Efferent
Nerve
Ending

Efferent
Nerve Ending

Afferent
Nerve
Ending

Fig. 14.8 Cellular organization of the sensory cells in the mammalian labyrinth. Note the two types of cell, depending on the size of the afferent terminal. Inset shows relation of single kinocilium to rows of stereocilia. (From Wersäll and Bagger-Sjöbäck, 1974)

from each other on either side of the midline. In the maculi utriculi, the hair cells radiate outward toward a perimeter, where the polarization changes in the opposite direction. As a consequence, movements of the head which cause movements of the otolithic membrane and cupula of the cristae do not simply produce a massive and similar discharge in all the sensory receptors. The situation is nicely summarized in

the following quotation from Otto Loewenstein (1974):

In his theoretical exposition of labyrinth function, Mygind . . . compared a macula to the curved palm of a hand holding an irregularly shaped heavy object . . . We are aware of a changing pattern of contact with the complex contours of the object and localize these accurately as the object rolls in the palm . . . In this situation the tactile sense, depending chiefly on

Fig. 14.9 Functional organization of the labyrinth. A. Macula, showing covering layer of otolithic membrane. B. Different orientations of hairs within the macula. (A from Spoendlin; B from Lindeman, in Wilson and Melvill-Jones, 1979)

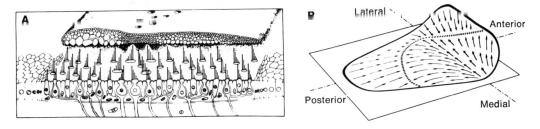

Lateral

Anterior

Posterior

Medial

an apparently random network of . . . nerve endings, performs a feat of pattern recognition which the orderly arrangement of polarized sensors in a macula is bound to surpass. The difference is that we become aware of tactile sensation but remain ignorant of labyrinthine afference.

Transduction Mechanisms

The hair cells are excited by bending of the hairs in the direction of increasing stereocilia length, toward the kinocilium, and inhibited by movement in the opposite direction. The site where the mechanical stimulus of hair bending is transduced into the electrical change in the membrane potential has been the subject of much speculation. The kinocilium can be ruled out, because it is present only during early development in mammals, and can be removed by microdissection in amphibians without effect on receptor potentials (see Fig. 14.10A–C). Attention has therefore focused on the stereocilia.

A. J. Hudspeth, David Corey, and their colleagues have considered several possible mechanisms in the stereocilia (see Fig. 14.10D):

1. The stereocilia are packed with an array of longitudinally oriented actin filaments. One possibility is that this cytoskeletal array releases a second messenger molecule when stressed, which acts on channel proteins in the cilia membrane to generate the sensory response, in analogy with photoreceptors (Chap. 16) and olfactory receptors (Chap. 11). However, the enzymatic reactions involved would be too slow to account for the response, which occurs within several microseconds of the application of a mechanical stimulus.
2. The actin array might pull the channel proteins in the membrane directly to set up the sensory response. A difficulty with this explanation is that it does not account for the directionality of the response.
3. The cilia bend mostly at the narrow process, called the ciliary anchor, that connects them to the hair cell, where there is an elaborate cuticular plate composed of contractile proteins (see Fig. 14.10D). This seems unlikely to be the site of sensory transduction, however, because electrophysiological recordings in the medium surrounding the hair cells indicate that the site of inward current flow during the sensory response is at the tips of the cilia, not their bases.

A clue to the transduction mechanism has come from electron microscopic studies, showing that there are thin filaments connecting the tip of a cilium to the side of its taller neighbor. Using this information, the mechanism as presently conceived is illustrated in Fig. 14.10D. Movement of the cilium in the direction of increasing height ① pulls on the filaments connecting to the ciliary tips ②. This causes a mechanical distortion of a channel protein selective for K^+, allowing K^+ to enter the tip, passing down the electrochemical gradient due to the high concentration of K^+ in the endolymph surrounding the cilia ③. This current spreads into the cell and outward across the membrane ④, setting up the depolarizing receptor potential (the circuit diagram of Fig. 7.9 may be consulted as a precise representation of these current flows, with substitution of K^+ for Na^+ in that diagram). The outward K^+ current in ④ is also passive, down the normal electrochemical gradient between high intracellular K^+ and low extracellular K^+ in the perilymph.

This mechanism thus accounts for most of the properties of sensory transduction in vestibular hair cells. Movement in the opposite direction, toward shorter cilia, would not have this effect, thus providing for the directionality of the response. The extracellular filaments represent an example of the role of the extracellular matrix in mechanoreceptor responses (Chap. 10). In

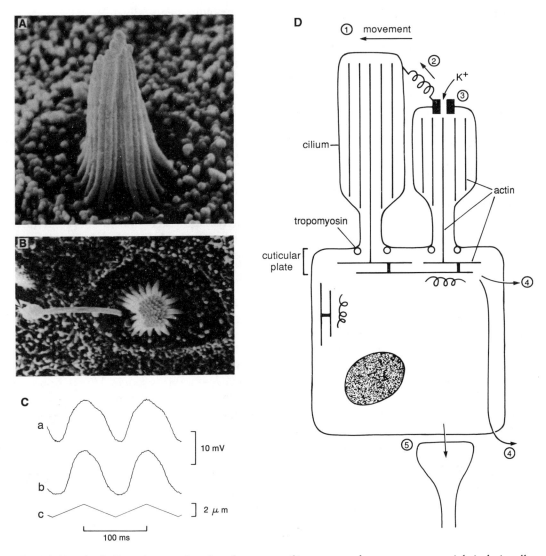

Fig. 14.10 A–C. Experiments showing that stereocilia generate the receptor potentials in hair cells. A. Scanning electron micrograph showing a group of sterocilia on a single hair cell after removal of the single kinocilium. B. View from above, showing how the kinocilium (to the left) was deflected and removed. C. Similar receptor potentials obtained from a normal hair cell (a) and from a hair cell with kinocilium deflected as in B (b). Recordings were by an intracellular electrode. Stimulation was a series of deflections applied to the hair bundle by a vibrating probe (c). (From Hudspeth and Jacobs, 1979) D. Mechanism of transduction in the vestibular hair cell. Movement ① in the direction of increasing cilia height stretches thin interciliary strands ②. This causes an increase in membrane conductance to K^+ ③, which moves into the cilium down its concentration gradient (extracellular K^+ concentration is very high in the endolymph). The resulting depolarization spreads into the cell ④, and triggers transmitter release at the hair cell synapse onto vestibular nerve sensory terminals ⑤. (Based on Hudspeth, 1985)

the next chapter (Chap. 15), we will see how this mechanism is adapted for reception of sound stimuli in the inner ear.

Unlike the invertebrate hair cell, which itself gives rise to an axon, the vertebrate hair cell has no axon, and the graded receptor response therefore activates chemical synapses onto the terminals of sensory fibers. Transmission at this synapse is blocked by the usual method of increasing Mg^{2+} and decreasing Ca^{2+}. As indicated in Fig. 14.8, some hair cells (type II) contact small sensory terminals, whereas others (type I) are embraced by large terminals. The significance of this difference is not understood.

Sensory Signaling

During natural behavior, the transduction mechanisms described above are activated by normal movements of the head. Electrophysiological studies have elucidated the relation between head movements and the neural responses transmitted in the nerves from the semicircular canals. This has required elaborate rotating animal holders, complete with recording instruments. Typical results obtained by Cesar Fernandez and Jay Goldberg (1976) at Chicago are illustrated in Fig. 14.11. Note first the high resting rate of impulse activity in these fibers, in the range of 80 spikes/sec; this

high "set point" means that inhibition as well as excitation can be accurately signaled. During slow, constant, angular acceleration (sloped part of monitor trace), the impulse frequency rises to a relatively steady level. This is believed to reflect the press of the displaced endolymph against the cupula of the crista. The amplitude of the displacement (which is transduced into the receptor potential of the hair cell) is determined by the balance between the inertial force of the fluid and the elastic restoring force of the cupula. When constant velocity is reached, the discharge returns (with an undershoot) to the resting level. Mathematically, one says that this response represents an integration of the angular acceleration to give a signal proportional to the angular velocity of the head. In doing this, the vestibular mechanism is performing a precise mathematical operation using mechanical and electrical components, as would an analog computer. When deceleration occurs, this is signaled in the opposite direction, by reduction of the impulse frequency below resting level.

Central Vestibular Pathways

The axons that transmit the hair cell responses to the central nervous system form part of the eighth cranial nerve. There are surprisingly few of these fibers—only about

Fig. 14.11   Responses recorded in single sensory nerve fibers from the semicircular canals to stimulation by rotation (angular acceleration) of the whole animal (squirrel monkey). (From Fernandez and Goldberg, 1976)

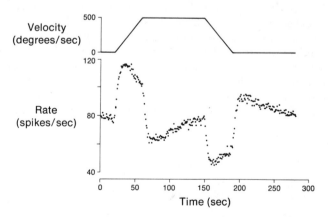

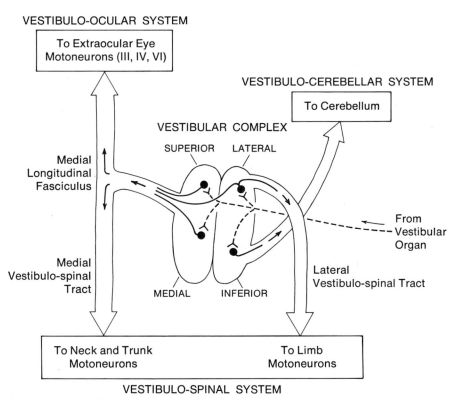

Fig. 14.12 Divisions of the vestibular nucleus, and their output connections to different parts of the brain. (Modified from Carpenter, 1976)

20,000 on each side in most mammalian species, including humans. They enter the brainstem and terminate in several large cell groups, which are called the *vestibular nuclei*. From here there are three main projection systems, as indicated in Fig. 14.12. We will discuss each of these.

Vestibulospinal System

Fibers that project to the spinal cord form the vestibulospinal pathway. There are two divisions, medial and lateral. The medial tract consists of fibers that arise from cells in most of the vestibular nuclei, and gather in the midline to form the *medial longitudinal fasciculus*. The descending fibers terminate in anterior segments of the spinal cord, where they connect to motoneurons that control the axial muscles of the neck and trunk. In contrast, fibers to motoneurons that control limb muscles arise from

the lateral vestibular nucleus, and descend in the lateral tract. Although these vestibular pathways mediate reflex mechanisms that belong in Section III, we will discuss them here because they are essential for understanding the sensory functions of the central vestibular pathways.

A basic approach to analyzing vestibular control of body muscles has been to deliver single electrical shocks to the vestibular nerve or vestibular nuclei and record from single spinal neurons. This tells the neurophysiologist whether a synaptic action is excitatory or inhibitory, and whether the action is monosynaptic or mediated through interneurons. Much of this work has been carried out by Victor Wilson and his colleagues at Rockefeller University. A summary of recent studies using these methods is shown in Fig. 14.13. The important points to be made in connection with this diagram are as follows:

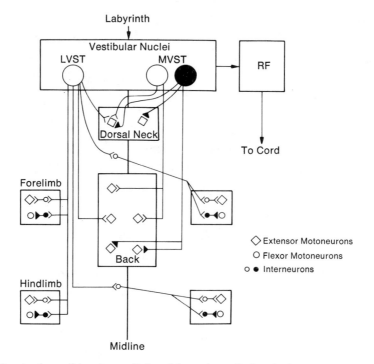

Fig. 14.13 Circuits formed by the medial and lateral vestibulospinal tracts. Open profiles indicate excitatory neurons, closed profiles indicate inhibitory neurons. Abbreviations: LSVT, lateral vestibulospinal tract; MVST, medial vestibulospinal tract; RF, reticular formation. For explanation, see text. (From Wilson and Melvill-Jones, 1979)

1. The macula projects mainly, but not exclusively, to the lateral tract, and the cristae of the canals to the medial tract.
2. The lateral tract is mainly concerned with controlling limb motoneurons, while the medial tract is exclusively concerned with controlling neck and trunk muscles.
3. Lateral tract fibers are exclusively excitatory, while the medial tract contains both excitatory and inhibitory fibers.
4. Within the spinal cord, lateral tract fibers control motoneurons to the limbs through excitatory or inhibitory interneurons; in other words, the pathway is disynaptic. Medial tract fibers, by contrast, make direct monosynaptic excitatory or inhibitory connections onto neck and trunk motoneurons.

The pathways indicated in Fig. 14.13 provide an extensive system through which the vestibular input can make precise adjustments in body musculature to maintain orientation in space. If we recall the analogy between the vestibular receptor sheet and the palm of the hand, the central system depicted in Fig. 14.13 can be thought of as the internal neural representation of the palm, allowing the body muscles to "feel" the changes occurring in the receptors and adjust their states of contraction accordingly.

Figure 14.13 makes a distinction between the muscles of the head (dorsal neck) and the body, and this is important in understanding vestibular reflexes. The main point is that the head, which contains the vestibular apparatus, is connected to the neck, the neck to the trunk, and the trunk to the limbs. Neck reflexes are thus the link between movements of the head and the rest of the body. These reflexes were first studied in a systematic way by Rudolf

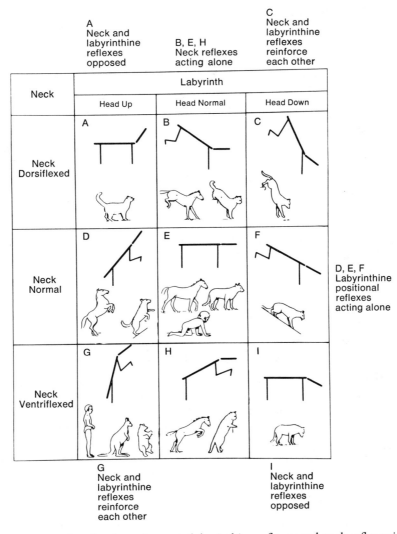

Fig. 14.14 Diagrams showing how the static labyrinthine reflexes and neck reflexes interact in the control of the limbs under different conditions of body posture. (Front Roberts, in Wilson and Melvill-Jones, 1979)

Magnus of the Netherlands in the early part of this century. Modern studies have led to the concept of these reflexes as servosystems for stabilizing the head in space. The neck reflexes act as a closed-loop, negative feedback system; since the neck muscles are attached to the head, their responses to labyrinth stimulation tend to restore the head to its normal position and reduce the stimulation. These reflexes are generally obligatory, and unconscious, which is consistent with the direct synaptic pathways shown in Fig. 14.13. In contrast, body and limb muscles have variable relations to head position, through the linkage of the neck. This may be why the vestibulospinal system has both excitatory and inhibitory fibers, and the synaptic linkages are through both excitatory and inhibitory interneurons (see Fig. 14.13). The interacting effects of labyrinthine and neck reflexes on the limbs are summarized in Fig. 14.14.

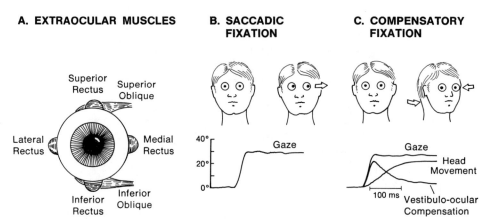

Fig. 14.15 Organization of the extraocular muscles. **A.** Arrangement of the six muscles around the right eyeball. **B.** Jumping saccadic movement, brought about through activity of the descending motor system. **C.** Compensatory eye movements, to maintain visual fixation after movement of the head; this is brought about by the vestibulo-ocular reflex. (Based in part on Morasso et al., in Wilson and Melvill-Jones, 1979)

Vestibulo-ocular System

The vestibular system plays a central role in controlling the eyes. This is necessary in order to maintain a stable image of the visual field on the retina despite movements of the body. The importance of a stable image is vividly exhibited in the way a bird walks with its head appearing to move with exaggerated jerks. In fact, film analysis of these movements has shown that the head is actually held almost perfectly still relative to the surrounding space, while the body moves along smoothly beneath it! This enables the animal to maintain maximal visual sensitivity to movement in its visual field while moving about itself. The stabilization is believed to be brought about by the neck reflexes mentioned above. Presumably, similar though more fluid mechanisms are present in mammals.

Movements of the eyes are controlled by a set of six extraocular muscles; their arrangement is indicated in the diagram of Fig. 14.15A. Coordinated movements of both eyes together are called *conjugate movements;* it is obvious that this requires fine coordination of both sets of extraocular muscles.

We can obtain a grasp of the principles involved in this coordination by considering, in a simplified fashion, movements only in the horizontal plane. Consider that we fix our gaze on a point, and then shift our gaze to another point to the left, without moving our head. A recording of this mechanical shift of our eyes would look like the trace in Fig. 14.15B. In the horizontal plane, this movement is brought about by contraction of the lateral rectus muscle and relaxation of the medial rectus muscle of the left eye, and the opposite activation of muscles in the right eye. This type of jumping *(saccadic)* eye movements with the head held still is characteristic of activities like reading or examination of near objects. These movements are controlled by fibers descending from the frontal eye fields of the cerebral cortex to the extraocular motoneurons, and do not involve the vestibular system.

Now consider the case in which the gaze of the eyes is directed to a new point in the visual field and the head moves in order to maintain the point at the center of the visual field, with the eyes in their normal centered positions. In this case, the gaze can remain fixed in the new position only be means of compensatory eye movements

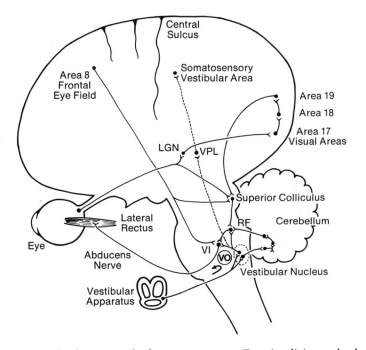

Fig. 14.16 Circuits involved in control of eye movements. For simplicity, only the control of the lateral rectus muscle is illustrated. Similar connections are involved in control of the other extraocular muscles. VI, trochlear nucleus giving rise to the abducens nerve; RF, reticular formation; LGN, lateral geniculate nucleus; VPL, ventroposterior lateral nucleus of thalamus; VO, vestibuloocular reflex. (Adapted from Robinson, Gouras, Schmidt, Ito, and other sources)

which are in the opposite direction to the rotation of the head. The relative movements of eye and head are indicated in the traces of Fig. 14.15C.

Compensatory eye movements are brought about by the *vestibulo-ocular reflex.* For movements in the horizontal plane, the circuit that connects the input from the horizontal canals to the motoneurons controlling the medial and lateral rectus muscles is shown in Fig. 14.16. This circuit operates without benefit of visual or other sensory feedback; in systems terminology, one says it is an *open-loop reflex,* in contrast to the closed-loop neck reflexes described previously.

The circuit shown in Fig. 14.16 constitutes a disynaptic pathway from vestibular afferents to extraocular motoneurons. This pathway is supplemented by polysnaptic connections through the *reticular formation,* as is also true for the vestibulospinal

system. The disynaptic pathway is consistent with the rapid transmission necessary in controlling eye movements.

One might suppose that a pathway of this kind would be "hard-wired" and immutable. However, much evidence indicates that the connections in this system have an extraordinary degree of plasticity. For example, after removal of one labyrinth, the ability of monkeys to perform a complicated locomotor task is completely lost and then slowly recovers; the recovery presumably depends on the establishment of new or more effective synaptic connections. More dramatically, when people wear spectacles with prisms that invert the visual field, they are initially disoriented and helpless, but gradually learn to move about in a near-normal fashion. This has implied a considerable rearrangement of the synaptic circuits involved in vestibular reflexes. Microelectrode studies of single neuron activity carried out in several laboratories have documented plastic changes in the synaptic connections of the central vestibular pathways after ablations of different components of the system (cf. Ito, 1985).

Vestibulocerebellar System

The importance of the vestibular system for sensorimotor coordination is further shown by the close relations of vestibular pathways to the cerebellum (see Fig. 14.16). We will discuss these relations and functions further in Chap. 21.

Vestibular Cortex

A small number of fibers ascend from the vestibular nuclei to terminate in a small part of the ventral posterior nucleus of the thalamus. From here there is a projection to a small region of cortex within the face area of somatosensory cortex (see Fig. 14.16; also 12.17). It is attractive to suppose that this vestibular area of cortex is involved in conscious perceptions of balance and movement arising from vestibular inputs. Other studies have suggested that other areas of cortex also receive vestibular thalamic inputs, including the somatosensory arm area and the temporal lobe, depending on the species of animal investigated. In addition to these sensory areas, there is a well-known area of the frontal lobe which contains cells that control the voluntary eye movements mentioned above. This is called the frontal eye field; electrical stimulation of this area causes conjugate eye movements to the opposite side. Figure 14.16 summarizes these cortical sensory and motor areas in the human.

The Vestibular System and Weightlessness

We live in the space age. The most dramatic sensory effect of space travel is the effect of weightlessness on the sense of balance. Dr. Joseph Kerwin, who was aboard Skylab 2 in 1973 as the first U.S. physician astronaut in space, describes the experience in the following words (1977):

. . . I would say there was no vestibular sense of the upright whatsoever. I certainly had no idea of where the Earth was at any time unless I happened to be looking at it. I had no idea of the relationship between one compartment of the spacecraft or another in terms of a feeling for "up or down" . . . What one thinks is up, is up. After a few days of getting used to this, one plays with it all the time . . . It's a marvellous feeling of power over space—over the space around one. Closing one's eyes made everything go away. And now one's body is like a planet all to itself, and one really doesn't know where the outside world is.

As the above quotation indicates, the astronauts adapted quickly, over the course of a few days, to the condition of weightlessness, and found the experience (apart from episodes of motion sickness) rather pleasant and intriguing. This adaptability is remarkable if one considers that the vestibular system and the other systems contributing to balance evolved over millions of years without ever having been exposed to these conditions.

Some indication of the neural processes of adaptation that take place during flight is seen in the behavior of the astronauts after return to earth. In a simple experiment carried out by J. L. Homick and his colleagues (1977), the astronauts were tested on their ability to stand, one foot in front of the other, on narrow rails of different widths, from ¾ in. to 2¼ in. (1.9–5.7 cm), as well as on the floor. In a typical result, the pilot of Skylab 3 showed a deficit on the day after splashdown in his ability to stand on relatively narrow rails with eyes open, with recovery to normal on subsequent testing days. Even with the thickest rail, there was a long-lasting deficit in the ability to maintain standing balance with the eyes closed; in fact, on the day after splashdown, he could barely stand on the floor with eyes closed, but improved to normal on the subsequent test.

These data give clear evidence that postural mechanisms are affected by prolonged periods (8–10 weeks) of weightlessness.

Probably several systems contribute to these results. First, the leg muscles undergo a degree of disuse atrophy during flight, which probably affects the ability to stand in the immediate recovery period. Second, muscle tendon reflexes (see Chap. 19) are hyperactive; this could cause incoordination of the muscles used in standing. Finally, it has been postulated that a "pattern center" in the central nervous system undergoes a process of habituation during flight, and that this process must be reversed on return to earth. This pattern center integrates inputs from the vestibular organ, the muscle and tendon receptors (Chap. 13), and the tactile receptors in the skin and deep tissues (Chap. 12). It represents the distributed system for the maintenance of standing posture. The ability of this entire system to adapt between the conditions of normal gravity and zero gravity is in accord with the remarkable degrees of plasticity that are present in nervous circuits in general, and have already been demonstrated in parts of the vestibular system, as mentioned above in connection with the vestibulo-ocular system. It may be hoped that there will be opportunities to test this hypothesis, through experiments on animals as well as humans, in further space flights in the future.

15

Hearing

The senses we have considered thus far are widespread throughout the Animal Kingdom. Information about molecules and chemicals, the physical environment, muscular states, and spatial orientation may be considered obligatory for any multicellular organism that carries on an active life. We now consider a type of information that is less widespread. Audition—the sense of hearing—is largely limited to the insects and the vertebrates. This, of course, does not mean it is any less important; on the contrary, those species that have this sense use it with great effectiveness in various ways—for example, to escape predators, find mates, and communicate socially. And in humans, there can be little doubt that hearing has been the key to development of language and, through it, much of our culture.

The Nature of Sound

A good approach to our discussion of this modality is to begin with some definitions. Audition in its broadest interpretation is the sense of sound. Generally speaking, sound consists of waves of compression of air or water. Sound waves are produced by a wide variety of natural phenomena, in-

cluding many kinds of animal movements—the beating of wings, for example, or the clatter of hooves. These sounds are important; indeed, they may be matters of life or death, e.g., a warning of an approaching predator. However, audition is usually of more specific interest as the reception of sounds made explicitly by one member of a species to communicate to another; it is here that the full potentialities of the auditory sense are realized.

Animals have developed many mechanisms for producing sounds for communication (see Chap. 23). The sounds vary in their frequency over a wide range, as illustrated for a number of different animals in Fig. 15.1. Some species have relatively narrow ranges (some crickets, frogs, birds). Some ranges extend to extremely low frequencies (fish, whales and dolphins, humans). The lowest frequencies, in fact, involve vibrations that act as stimuli for various kinds of mechanoreceptors in the body, as well as auditory receptors. On the other hand, some species are able to sense extremely high frequencies, as high as 100 kHz (various mammals and insects). It is interesting to compare the wavelength at this frequency (a few millimeters) with that at the extremely low frequencies (almost

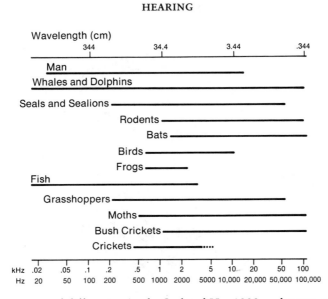

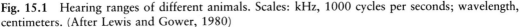

Fig. 15.1 Hearing ranges of different animals. Scales: kHz, 1000 cycles per seconds; wavelength, centimeters. (After Lewis and Gower, 1980)

10 m). Finally, some species have very broad ranges (especially whales and dolphins, and humans). Within these different ranges, the receptors and circuits of many species are tuned to certain frequencies of special importance for their behavior, as we shall see.

Modern studies of audition employ sophisticated instruments and rigorous mathematical methodologies, and many of the results are expressed in terms of decibels, power spectra, Bode plots, and other concepts that are difficult for the beginning student to grasp. We will therefore focus our attention on the structures and properties of different kinds of auditory receptors, and the central nervous circuits for processing auditory information.

INVERTEBRATES

Most invertebrates are sensitive to low-frequency vibrations emanating from their environment. In general, these vibrations are due to sounds, like a clap of thunder, or the tread of an animal, which signal danger, and produce generalized startle or escape reactions. Such vibrations produce physical displacements which are sensed in

most animals by mechanoreceptors of the somatosensory and proprioceptive systems, without further specializations.

Auditory Receptors

Insects have developed special receptors for low-frequency sounds. One type of such a receptor is the *thread hair*. An example is the hair sensillum located on small appendages called *cerci*. Another type of receptor is found in *Johnston's organ*. This is located at the base of an antenna, and consists of a cavity spanned by one or more elongated sensory processes called *chordotonal sensilla*. Thread hairs and Johnston's organs are sensitive to sounds up to about 2 kHz (in other words, up to a medium-pitched hum; see Fig. 15.1).

Reception of high-pitched, true "auditory" sounds is found only in certain insects. The receptors are contained in *tympanic organs*. These function like the ears of vertebrates, except that they are markedly different in structure and functional properties. Also, insect ears may be located in many different places on the body: on the thorax (moths), abdomen (beetles), or legs (crickets). The tympanal organ is actually

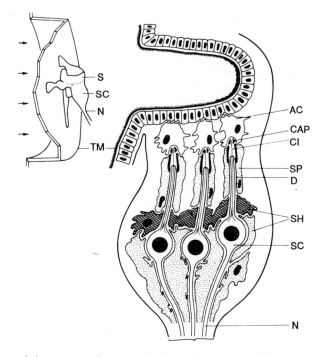

Fig. 15.2 Structure of the tympanal organ. **A.** Overall structure. The tympanic membrane (TM) oscillates when impinged upon by sound waves (arrows); this is detected by sensory cells (SC), whose cilia are embedded in the sclerite (S), and which give rise to the tympanal nerve (N) that connects to the nerve cord. **B.** Fine structure. AC, attachment cell; CAP, cap cell; CI, cilium; SP, scolopale cell; D, dendrite; SH, sheath cell. (From Boeckh, 1980)

a modification of an inlet of the tracheal system used for respiration. It consists of a thin membrane of cuticle, called a *tympanum,* drawn over an air cavity to make a kind of drum head. Sound waves produce vibrations of the membrane, and these are sensed by chordotonal sensilla attached at one end to the drum (see Fig. 15.2). There may be only one chordotonal sensillum, or there may be as many as 1000 sensilla. Regardless of how many there are, each contains a bipolar sensory neuron with a cilium at one end; the cilium attaches to the underside of the tympanum through a complicated joint. Variations in the structure of this joint and in the resonant properties of the tympanic membrane confer different frequency-tuning characteristics on the tympanal organs of different species.

Tuning Curves

A standard way of analyzing auditory receptors is to record from single cells and determine the stimulus intensity necessary to give a threshold response at different frequencies of pure tones. This yields what is called a *tuning curve.* Figure 15.3 shows typical results obtained in recordings from single fibers of receptor cells in crickets. Two classes of response are found in this animal. One class (low frequency: LF) has a low threshold at a relatively low-frequency (around 5 Hz), and much higher thresholds to surrounding frequencies. Such cells are said to have a *best frequency* or *characteristic frequency* around 5 kHz, and to be *sharply tuned,* or have *narrow bands.* The frequency of the song that crickets use to call to each other has a frequency of about 5 kHz, so these receptors appear to be adapted for the purpose of hearing this song.

The nature of this song, and the motor mechanisms for producing it, will be discussed in Chap. 23. The song consists of sound bursts *(chirps)* repeated at different

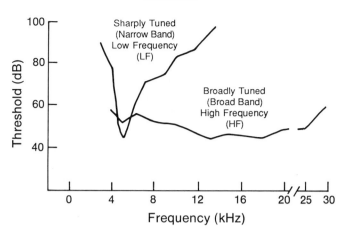

Fig. 15.3 Tuning curves for single auditory nerve fibers in the cricket. (After Markovich, in Elsner and Popov, 1978)

intervals. Thus, the main variable in information transmission is the amplitude modulation of the signal. The tympanal receptors are slowly adapting, which ensures accurate reception and encoding of the changes in signal amplitude and duration.

Several other properties of the receptors are also important. One is that the receptor response varies with the logarithm of the stimulus intensity. Another is that different receptors have different thresholds at their best frequencies. These two properties provide the basis for *intensity discrimination,* and with it, the ability to determine the distance of a calling cricket. Finally, the construction of the tympanal organ (see Fig. 15.2) imparts a directionality to signal reception, so that the cricket has the means for *sound localization.* Thus, the properties of the tympanal organ and its receptors provide the mechanisms for discriminating most of the characteristics of the auditory signal from a conspecific individual: frequency, amplitude, intensity, and localization.

The second main class of tympanic auditory receptors is broadly tuned over a wide band that covers high frequencies (HF; see Fig. 15.3). In crickets the frequencies reach beyond the human range, up to 30 kHz, and in other insects they may go even higher (see Fig. 15.1). These high frequencies are part of the courtship call between crickets (see below). In addition, they cover the range of sounds emitted by various predators (for example, bats). The receptors do not have to be sharply tuned for these information purposes; hence, their broad band and relatively low threshold (high sensitivity). It appears that these receptors are specially adapted for detecting the sounds of natural predators and alerting the organism so that it can perform appropriate escape maneuvers.

Central Auditory Pathways

The auditory receptor cells in insects give rise to axons which connect directly to the central nervous system. Recent studies of these connections, and the central auditory pathways arising from them, illustrate in a beautiful way the effective use of single-neuron recording and staining techniques. The results will be discussed in relation to the diagrams of Figs. 15.4 and 15.5.

The axons of relatively low-frequency (LF) receptors (those tuned to 5 kHz) enter their segmental ganglion and terminate in a circumscribed region called the *auditory neuropil* (Fig. 15.4A). Some neurons in the ganglion receive and integrate these inputs from both sides of the body, and therefore play a role in sound localization. Other neurons receive the inputs and, through

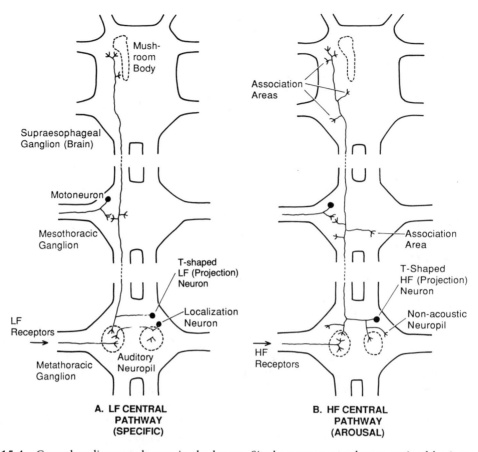

Fig. 15.4 Central auditory pathways in the locust. Single neurons are shown, stained by intracellular dye injection, and identified physiologically as low-frequency (LF) cells for specific auditory discrimination (**A**), and high-frequency (HF) cells for arousal (**B**). The LF tympanal fibers project to caudal and frontal regions of the neuropil in the metathoracic ganglion, whereas the HF fibers project only to the frontal neuropil. The projection sites within the auditory neuropil are tonotopically organized (Römer, 1983). The diagram is much simplified: the prothoracic and subesophageal ganglia, between the mesothoracic ganglion and the brain, are not shown; tympanal fibers and central neurons have other connections which are not included for the sake of simplicity.

ascending axons, transmit the signals to other ganglia and to the brain. These neurons have similar LF tuning properties to those of LF hair cells (see Fig. 15.5A); these LF *relay cells* therefore mediate specific information about the conspecific calling sound. Appropriate to this task, the responses of these neurons reflect very accurately the characteristics of the "chirps" as transmitted by the LF hair cells. The ascending axons of these cells make monosynaptic connections onto motoneurons, to bring about immediate motor orientation

to the calling song. In the brain, the axons distribute terminals in the vicinity of the mushroom bodies, the highest integrative centers in the insect nervous system.

The axons of high-frequency (HF) hair cells also terminate, but more widely, in the segmental auditory neuropil (see Fig. 15.4B). There they make connections onto *HF relay neurons*. These neurons receive bilateral inputs, and their ascending axons make more widespread connections in the neuropil of other ganglia and of the brain. The HF neurons have broad tuning curves

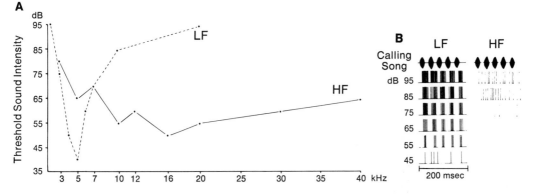

Fig. 15.5 **A.** Tuning curves for single low-frequency (LF) and high-frequency (HF) auditory cells in the central nervous system of the cricket. **B.** Different response properties of LF and HF cells in response to the conspecific calling song. (From Rheinlander et al., in Elsner and Popov, 1978)

over the higher frequency range, similar to HF hair cells (see Fig. 15.5A), and are therefore tuned to mediate information about sounds of predators. They also are tuned to the high-frequency sounds that are part of the courtship call of the cricket. The widespread connections of the HF relay neurons provide for generalized arousal and escape reactions of the animal in response to the high-pitched sounds of predators. The courtship call, in contrast, consists of alternating low-frequency "chirps" and high-frequency "ticks"; this specific sequence causes arousal of the female without eliciting the escape reactions (see Fig. 15.5B), and leads to mating (see Chap. 27).

The central auditory pathways thus illustrate a division between specific pathways for sensory discrimination and more widespread pathways for arousal, a division that is also present in vertebrates. Also, the temporal sequence of sensory signals in these pathways is critical in calling forth different behavioral responses, another important principle in the organization of central nervous systems. In the next chapter, we will further discuss common principles involved in the processing of bilateral sensory input in the insect auditory pathway and the visual pathway of the leech.

VERTEBRATES

Lateral Line Organs and Electroreception

The sense of hearing in the vertebrates has an interesting and rather complicated phylogenetic history (see Table 15.1) that is closely related to the development of the

Table 15.1 Evolution of organs for electroreception and hearing in the vertebrates

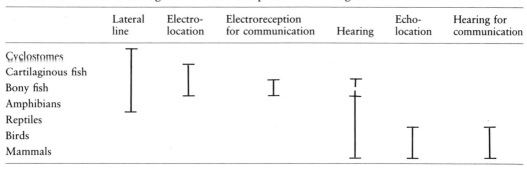

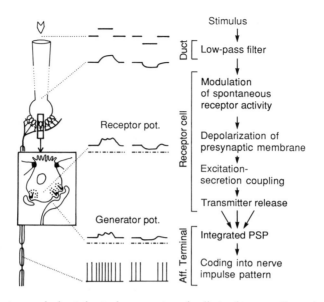

Fig. 15.6 Organization and physiological properties of cells in the ampullary electroreceptor organ of the marine catfish, *Plotosus*. (After Obara, in Viancour, 1979)

vestibular apparatus. Both senses are commonly regarded as adaptations of the *lateral line organ*. Lateral line organs are found in all aquatic vertebrates, from primitive cyclostomes like the lamprey up through the amphibia. They consist of either pits *(ampullae)* or tubes along the sides of the body, head, or snout of the animal. At the base of the pit, or at intervals along the tubes, are tight clusters of cells, called *neuromasts*. The cells are a type of hair cell, with the hairs embedded in a gelatinous mass that projects into the fluid-filled pit or tube.

The specific stimulus for the hair cells varies in different species. In some it is *mechanical vibrations* set up by the turbulence of the water around the fish. In others it may be changes in *hydrostatic pressure*. The receptors in some species are also very sensitive to *temperature*, or to the *salinity* (saltiness) of the water. Finally, in certain species of fish, these receptors are sensitive to *electrical signals*.

Although electroreception is not found in higher vertebrates, it is a fascinating sensory capability that deserves mention here. The most sensitive electroreceptors are in pits called *ampullae of Lorenzini*, which are distributed on the head and snout of certain species of fish. The threshold for eliciting a response in an individual receptor can be as low as 1 μV/cm (that is, an electric field with a gradient of 1μV for each centimeter of distance). The threshold for a behavioral response is 10–100 times higher. The electric fields may be set up by electric organ discharge in the same fish; nearby objects produce distortions of the field, which are sensed by the electroreceptors. Alternatively, the electroreceptors may sense the fields set up by the electric organ discharges of other fish.

The mechanism of electroreception is summarized in Fig. 15.6. The stimuli applied by the experimenter are steps of voltage. Within the ampulla these steps become rounded, as a result of the membrane capacitance of the cells lining the walls. In this way the ampulla acts as a low-pass filter (it reduces the high-frequency step while letting the steady voltage pass through; this is just the opposite of the action of a Pacinian corpuscle on a pressure step; Chap. 12). The stimulus is transduced into a receptor potential in the hair cell. This alters the release of neurotransmitter at synapses onto nerve terminals. The postsynaptic potentials in the terminal encode the receptor response as modulations in the ongoing spontaneous activity of the nerve.

Note that the hair cell has no axon and transmits only graded potentials; this is a basic characteristic of the vertebrate hair cell, whether vestibular or auditory. The synaptic linkage provides for more complex processing at this peripheral level than is the case for invertebrate hair cells. Note also (bottom, Fig. 15.6) the high rate of resting impulse discharge in the nerve; this means that inhibitory as well as excitatory changes are faithfully encoded. This high set point is a common property of many cells in the vestibular and auditory pathways and the associated cerebellar system. In some species the resting frequency is incredibly constant, which enhances the ability of the nerve to transmit extremely small signals and have them detected by centers in the central nervous system.

The sequence of events illustrated in Fig. 15.6 applies to ampullary electroreceptors in teleost (bony) fish. The details of the sequence vary in other species, and in other types of receptor organs. Thus, in the ampullary electroreceptors of elasmobranch (cartilaginous) fish, the polarities of electric signals giving depolarizing and hyperpolarizing receptor potentials are the opposite of those shown in the figure. Tuberous electroreceptor organs, found in some electric fish, are generally less sensitive than ampullary receptors, and show lower resting discharge rates and differences in the way electric signals are encoded into impulse discharges.

The Ear of Mammals

Hearing reaches its highest development in birds and mammals; in fact, the organ of hearing in these animals is one of the most complex of all sensory organs. We will describe this organ and the central auditory pathways in the mammal, with brief mention of lower forms.

The organ of hearing—the ear—has three main parts (see Fig. 15.7). The *outer ear* aids in the collection of sound and funnels it through the external ear canal to the tympanic membrane. The *middle ear* contains a system of small bones—hammer, anvil, and stirrup—that conveys the vibrations of the tympanic membrane to the inner ear. The *inner ear* consists of a fluid-filled bag, the *cochlea*, which developed as an outpouching from the vestibular labyrinth (see Fig. 14.7). Through the middle of the cochlea stretches the *basilar membrane*, containing the hair cells which are the auditory sensory receptors.

In order for sound to stimulate the hair cells, it must first be transmitted mechanically to the inner ear, and then stimulate the hair cells in an appropriate manner. The first step requires changing the sound waves from vibrations in air to vibrations of the perilymph. This is achieved through the intermediary movements of the middle ear bones. Since air is highly compressible but perilymph is incompressible, the bones must provide for a matching of the forces in the two media, a process called *impedance matching*. They do this by absorbing energy from the large area of the tympanic membrane and concentrating it in the small area of stirrup where it fits against an opening (the *oval window*) in the bone onto the membrane surrounding the cochlea (Fig. 15.7B).

The Basilar Membrane

The next step is to induce appropriate vibrations in the basilar membrane that contains the hair cells. The cochlea in humans is a coiled structure; we can understand its function best if we imagine it straightened out, as in Fig. 15.7C. We then see that the the cochlea tapers in size like a cone toward a tip, so that there is a *base*, at the oval window, and an *apex*, at the tip. In contrast, the basilar membrane is *narrower* at the base, and *widens* at the apex. The student has to remember, therefore, that the basilar membrane gets wider as the cochlea gets narrower.

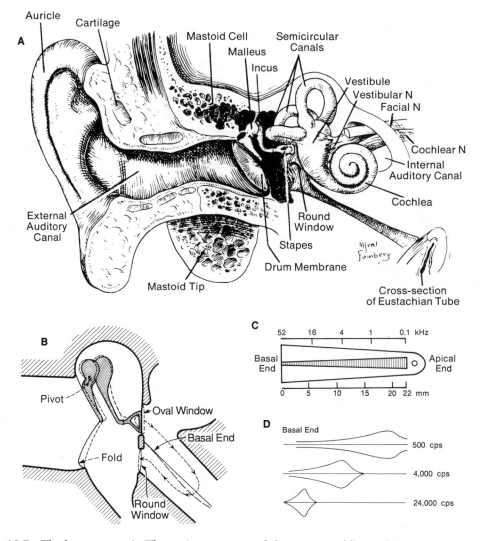

Fig. 15.7 The human ear. **A.** The main structures of the outer, middle, and inner ear. **B.** Transmission of sound vibrations through the middle ear to the inner ear (cochlea). **C.** Diagram of the cochlear partition and the basilar membrane (above), and the traveling waves and their external envelopes induced by sound at different frequencies. (A,B from Davis and Silverman, 1970. C,D based on von Békésy, 1960)

When the early anatomists first examined the basilar membrane under the microscope, they observed cross-striations that reminded them of the strings of a piano. They imagined that the short strings would resonate in response to high notes, and the long strings to low notes. Helmholtz, the great physiologist and physicist of the late nineteenth century, formulated these ideas as the *resonance theory of hearing*, which states that different frequencies of sound are encoded by their precise position along the basilar membrane. This attractive theory fell victim, however, at least in part, to a stubborn fact. A string will not vibrate unless it is under tension; when George von Békésy (1960) tested this by making tiny slits in the basilar membrane of cochleas obtained from human cadavers, he found that the edges of the slit did not pull apart, as they would if the membrane were under tension.

By direct observation, von Békésy found that vibratory movement is transmitted as a *traveling wave* along the basilar membrane from the round window to the apex. As shown in Fig. 15.7D, the wave has its largest amplitude at a specific site along the membrane, depending on the frequency. Thus, although the wave itself travels, the envelope of the wave is stationary for a given frequency. The peak displacements for high frequencies are toward the base (where the basilar membrance is narrowest) and for low frequencies are toward the apex, just as Helmholtz postulated, but the envelope of the traveling wave is broader than he envisaged.

These experiments appeared to lend support to Helmholtz's theory, but in fact they posed a difficult problem which only recently appears to be on its way to a solution. The problem was that the envelope of the traveling wave, as measured in the human cadavers, is relatively broad, which contrasts with psychophysical data, as well as with common experience, which demonstrates that we are very good at hearing tones, that is, the ear is sharply tuned for different sound frequencies. To deal with this, Békésy proposed that sharpening occurs by means of lateral inhibition in the neural connections of the auditory pathway (see below). However, this was proved inadequate when recordings from single auditory nerve fibers gave clear evidence of sharp tuning already at this peripheral level. This discrepancy, between the auditory nerve recordings and the traveling wave envelope, is illustrated in Fig. 15.8.

This discrepancy has been resolved by experiments in which movements of the basilar membrane could be observed directly in the living animal by use by sensitive instruments to detect responses to small stimuli. These showed that the movements of the basilar membrane closely parallel the frequency selectivity of the neural discharge (Fig. 15.8). There are thus properties of living cells within the cochlea which, added

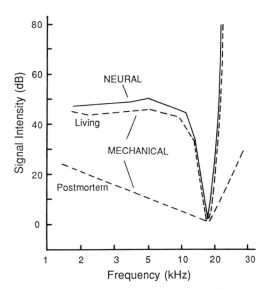

Fig. 15.8 Mechanical and neural responses in the cochlea to sound stimuli. The mechanical displacements of the basilar membrane in human cadavers shown by the lower dashed line (postmortem), as measured by von Békésy (1960). Displacements of the basilar membrane as measured in the living animal in situ are shown by the upper dashed line. Recordings of the impulse response in the auditory nerve in the living animal are shown by the solid line (Sellick et al., 1982). Ordinate: sound pressure stimulus level required to produce a given displacement or impulse frequency; abscissa: frequency of tone stimulus. (Based on Dallos, 1985)

to the traveling wave, produce frequency selectivity of the hair cell responses. In order to gain insight into these properties, we must next consider transducer mechanisms in the hair cells.

Hair Cell Transducer Mechanisms

How are movements of the basilar membrane transduced into electrical responses of the hair cells? As indicated in Fig. 15.9A, the hair cells rest on the basilar membrane, with their raised tips covered by a thin flap of tissue called the tectorial membrane. The key fact about hair cells is that there are two types, depending on their relation to the organ of Corti (see Fig. 15.9A). Herein lies much of the mystery about sound reception in the cochlea: why are there two

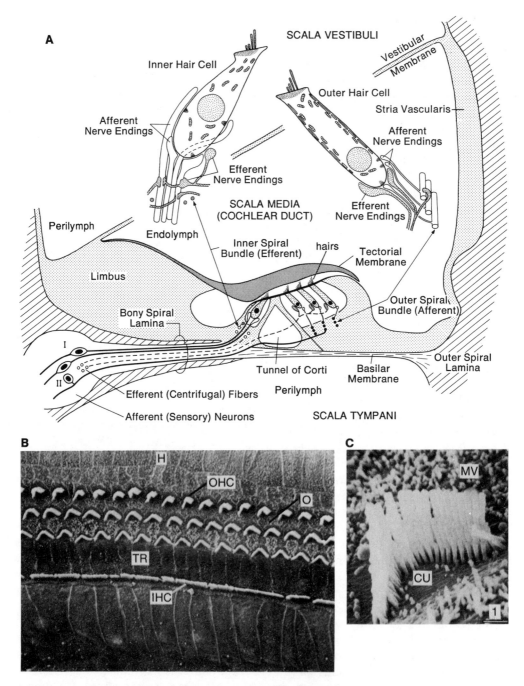

Fig. 15.9 **A.** Cellular organization of the cochlea (organ of Corti) of the guinea pig. Enlarged diagrams (see arrows) summarize the fine structure of the inner and outer hair cells. **B.** Scanning electron micrograph, looking down on hair cells, showing differences in arrangements of the inner (IHC) and outer (OHC) hair cells and their stereocilia. H, Henson's cell; TR, tunnel rod. **C.** Scanning electron micrograph of stereocilia of an outer hair cell. MV, microvilli (stereocilia); CU, cuticular plate. (From Smith, in Eagles, 1975; A redrawn from Smith in Brodal, 1981)

314

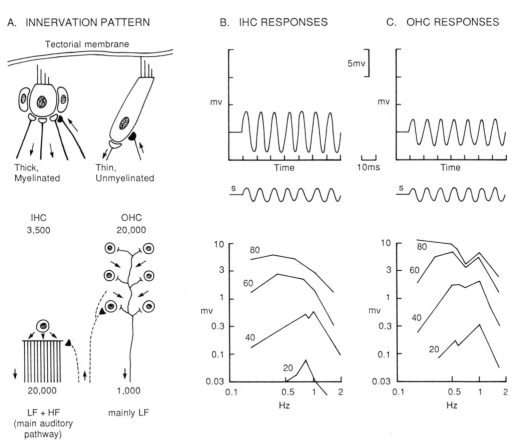

Fig. 15.10 Comparison of the organization and properties of inner hair cells (IHC) and outer hair cells (OHC). **A.** Innervation pattern. In the lower diagrams, the numbers of hair cells are given above and the numbers of auditory nerve fibers below. LF, low-frequency fibers; HF, high-frequency fibers. **B.** IHC response properties. *Above:* intracellular responses to tone stimulus (s). *Below:* response magnitude (as above) for different stimulus frequencies (abscissa) and at different stimulus intensities (20–80 dB). **C.** OHC response properties. (A based on Spoendlin, 1969; B,C based on Dallos, 1985)

types, and what is the specific function of each?

Outer hair cells are by far the most numerous type, numbering about 20,000, arranged in three rows. Their hairs are arranged in a characteristic V-shape, as seen from above (Fig. 15.9B,C). *Inner hair cells* number about 3,500, and are aligned in a single row (Fig. 15.9B). As in the case of the vestibular organ, the hair cells transmit their sensory responses by means of synapses onto the terminal dendritic knobs of second-order cells, the sensory neurons, which transmit the response as an impulse

discharge to the central nervous system. The puzzle here is that the ratio of dendritic fibers connecting to the two hair cell types is the reverse of the ratio of the number of hair cells: some 20,000 nerve fibers connect only to the 3,500 inner hair cells, whereas only 1,000 or so connect to the much more numerous outer hair cells. There is thus convergence of many nerve fibers onto a single inner hair cell, in contrast to divergence from one fiber onto many outer hair cells. These relations are depicted schematically in Fig. 15.10. The great preponderance of fibers to the inner hair cells means that these are the main sites of auditory transduction; the fibers connecting to them are the main auditory pathway and the main sources of single-unit recordings in studies of neural responses (e.g., Fig. 15.8).

Intracellular recordings have shown that sound stimuli produce responses in which the oscillations of the membrane potential closely parallel the applied mechanical oscillations. An example of a typical inner hair cell (IHC) response is shown in Fig. 15.10B. When the entire frequency range is swept at different sound intensities, a family of tuning curves is generated, as shown at the bottom of Fig. 15.10B. For a given cell, there is a best frequency, shown as a peak in the tuning curve. Outer hair cells (OHC) have qualitatively similar response properties, but there are quantitative differences; as shown in Fig. 15.10C, the receptor potentials are somewhat smaller in amplitude, and their tuning is not as sharp.

The generation of the receptor potentials is presumed to be due to a sequence of mechanoelectric coupling events that is similar to those in vestibular hair cells: these transduction steps are indicated by steps ① through ④ in Fig. 15.11A. In addition, single-channel analysis has indicated the presence of three additional steps: the depolarization spreading from the cilia activates an inward voltage-dependent Ca^{2+} current ⑤; the increase in free Ca^{2+} in turn activates a Ca^{2+}-dependent outward K^+ current ⑥, followed by slower activation of a Ca^{2+} pump ⑦. The interplay of inward depolarizing Ca^{2+} and outward repolarizing K^+ produces an oscillating membrane potential, which gives the hair cell an electrical resonance.

Active Processes in Hair Cells. The ability of the hair cell to generate an oscillating membrane potential is of interest for two reasons. First, this property can add to the sensory response of the cell; by increasing the response at the best frequency, it can be an electrical mechanism for sharpening the tuning curve within the hair cell. Sec-

ond, this property can provide the means for the hair cell to produce a mechanical output. The possibility that hair cells might function in this mode was first suggested by the finding that following a brief weak "click" delivered to the ear, there was a weak brief vibration of the eardrum, called a "Kemp echo" after its discoverer (Kemp, 1978). This and subsequent experiments have indicated that the echo is due to output from the hair cells, and is closely related to the properties that generate the frequency selectivity of the basilar membrane and hair cells. Dramatic evidence for this property is the recent finding that the stereocilia can undergo spontaneous beating movements, associated with oscillatory changes in the membrane potential (Fig. 15.11B).

The present scheme which attempts to relate these properties, and at the same time provide an explanation for the difference between inner and outer hair cells, is shown in Fig. 15.11A. In addition to the molecular mechanisms for sensory transduction (steps ①–④), it is envisaged that outer hair cells have the mechanisms (steps ⑤–⑦) for generating an oscillating membrane potential. This activates the actin assemblies of the cuticular plate and cilia to produce a corresponding oscillation of the ciliary bundle. The cilia of the outer (but not the inner) hair cells are attached to the tectorial membrane. This adds to any sensory-induced movements of the tectorial membrane, increasing the mechanical sensory input to the inner hair cells. The large number of outer hair cells thus is important for their output function; the result of this output is to increase the sensory response of the main sensory pathway through the inner hair cells. The student should review the diagrams of Figs. 15.9 and 15.10 to understand these relationships.

Centrifugal Fibers

In addition to afferent fibers, the auditory nerve also contains efferent (centrifugal) fibers, which arise from cells in the brainstem. These fibers make synapses mainly

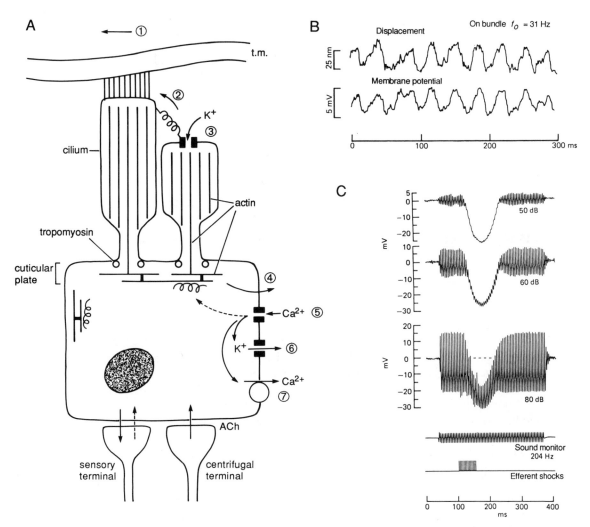

Fig. 15.11 Sensory and motor properties of the outer hair cell, and their centrifugal control. **A.** Molecular and cellular organization of the outer hair cell. The sequence of events in sensory transduction is indicated by the numbers: ① movement of tectorial membrane (t.m.); ② stretch of ciliary connecting strands, which changes conductance of membrane channels in cilia tip; ③ inflow of K^+ due to high concentration of extracellular K^+ in the perilymph; ④ depolarization spreads to the body of the hair cell; ⑤ depolarization activates a Ca^{2+} conductance channel; ⑥ Ca^{2+} activates a K^+ conductance channel; ⑦ the Ca^{2+} gradient is restored by a pump. The motor function is due to interplay of the Ca^{2+} and K^+ conductances, which amplifies the oscillations of membrane potential; these electrical changes are coupled to activation of actin, which moves the cilia and the tectorial membrane to which they are attached, producing a resonant amplification of the tectorial membrane, and thereby a sharper tuning of both inner and outer hair cells. (Based on Hudspeth, 1985; Dallos, 1985) **B.** Motor function of the hair cell, as exemplified by spontaneous mechanical (above) and electrical (below) oscillations. These recordings were made in hair cells of the turtle cochlea (From Crawford and Fettiplace, 1985) **C.** Inhibitory effect of centrifugal fibers on intracellularly recorded sensory responses. Centrifugal fibers were excited electrically while sound stimuli at 204 Hz were delivered at three intensity levels (50–80 dB). Experiments were carried out in the turtle. (From Art et al., 1984)

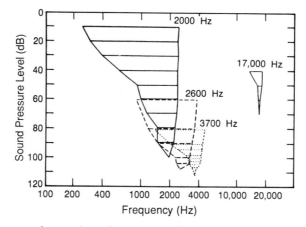

Fig. 15.12 Tuning curves for single auditory nerve fibers in the cat. (From Galambos and Davis, 1943)

onto the dendritic knobs of the afferent fibers connecting to inner hair cells, but they make synapses directly onto outer hair cells (see Figs. 15.9A, 15.10, and 15.11A). For many years, it has been known that stimulation of these fibers suppresses sensory responses in the auditory nerves. This was taken to be an example of descending control of sensory systems. It was believed to protect the hair cells from overstimulation, but beyond this the mechanism and its functional significance were unknown.

Our understanding of these problems has been helped considerably by the intracellular analyses of hair cells. These have shown that the centrifugal fibers inhibit hair cells by hyperpolarizing the hair cell membrane, as shown in Fig. 15.11C. The transmitter at these synapses is ACh. These actions are believed to be relatively specific for outer hair cells, which, it will be recalled, centrifugal fibers contact directly (cf. Figs. 15.9A, 15.10, and 15.11A). In view of the recent studies discussed previously, the significance of this inhibitory input is clear; by reducing the motor *output* of the outer hair cells, it reduces the movement of the tectorial and basilar membranes and the sensory response of the inner hair cells. The original interpretation that these fibers provide a protection against overstimulation is therefore supported by this evidence.

Auditory Nerve Fibers

Since vertebrate hair cells lack axons, the auditory signals are transmitted to the central nervous system, as we have already noted, by a second-order neuron. This is a bipolar ganglion cell, with its cell body in the cochlea. The peripheral fiber of this cell receives the synapses of the hair cells. There are only about 25,000 auditory nerve fibers in mammals, including humans. It is sobering to think that human language, and so much of our society and culture, depends on these fibers. It recalls the words of Winston Churchill: "Seldom has so much been owed by so many to so few."

Single-unit recordings from individual auditory nerve fibers provided some of the earliest and most essential information about the encoding of auditory signals. Hallowell Davis and David Galambos in the 1940s first showed that each fiber has a characteristic tuning curve (see Fig. 15.12). As already mentioned, it is now known that the hair cells themselves have similar tuning curves (Fig. 15.10), so the synaptic coupling between hair cells and nerve fibers provides for faithful transmission of sound stimuli. An important result of the single-fiber recordings was also the finding that the nerve impulses fired in synchrony with low-frequency vibrations, but only up to about 1 kHz (1000/sec). The fibers cannot fire above this frequency because the refractory period associated with each impulse lasts about 1 msec.

These results proved that auditory frequency could not be encoded solely by the frequency of impulse firing. Rather, frequency is encoded primarily by position along the basilar membrane, referred to as *tonotopic organization*. Impulse frequency may contribute to coding at low frequencies, but in general it is primarily involved in coding stimulus *intensity*. It may be noted that in the absence of stimulation, the auditory fibers show considerable spontaneous activity. This means that hair cells, synapses, and auditory fibers are primed to respond to threshold stimuli and small changes in stimulation, just as in most other sensory systems.

Brainstem Auditory Pathways

Since the auditory nerve contains so few fibers, it might be wondered if the auditory input would simply get submerged when it enters the central nervous system. Our acute sense of hearing tells us that this is not so, and a consideration of the synaptic organization at the first central relay shows how this comes about.

Cochlear Nucleus

There are two specializations that ensure that auditory acuity is preserved despite the small number of input channels. The first is that each auditory nerve fiber, on entering the brainstem and reaching the collection of cells known as the *cochlear nucleus*, divides into a large number of terminal branches. Within the nucleus, the branches form a rigid geometrical array. In this way, each fiber projects to several terminal regions in an orderly fashion. In addition, the tonotopic sequence along the basilar membrane is projected by the array of auditory fibers onto the separate regions of the cochlear nucleus. Thus, the single cochlea is mapped into *multiple representations* within the cochlear nucleus.

The second specialization is seen in the types of synapses and cells in the different parts of the nucleus. The main parts have large and distinctive relay neurons, each of which receives a distinctive type of synaptic terminal. Two examples are shown in Fig. 15.13. The significance of these specializations is twofold: they provide for a very secure coupling of input to output, and they provide the morphological basis for different kinds of input–output processing of the auditory signals.

The nature of the processing that takes place at these different relay sites has been revealed by single-cell recordings. A useful scheme of classification was introduced in 1966 by Ross Pfeiffer, on the basis of the type of response to a pure-tone stimulus. Figure 15.14 shows the main response types, together with diagrams of the cells and simplified circuits which may account for the response properties. The legend of this figure may be consulted for details. The important general conclusion from these data is that the bifurcations of the primary axons and their synaptic connections with different types of relay cell provide the basis for the conversion of the single response envelope in the primary axons into different output patterns. The different synaptic microcircuits create, in effect, new classes of responses, each class representing an abstraction of one particular feature of the input. For example, the simple ON response is ideally suited to transmitting high-frequency stimulation. The "primary-like" response obviously preserves the envelope of the auditory input signal. The "pauser" and "buildup" types provide for a differentiation of the onset and ensuing phases of a tone, similar to the dynamic and static phases of responses we have noted in other sensory systems.

Ascending Pathways

The organization depicted in Fig. 15.14 provides a means by which different properties of the auditory stimulus are given their own private (or semiprivate) channels. This is an expression of the same general

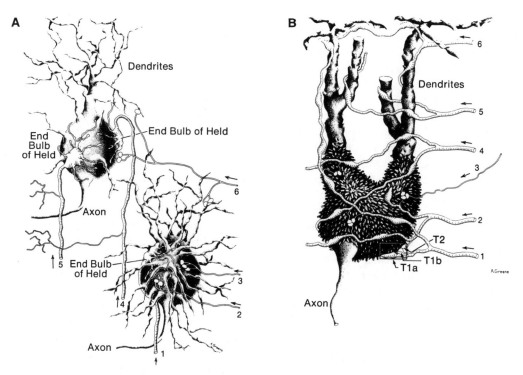

Fig. 15.13   A. Synaptic connections onto a "bushy" neuron in the anterior ventral cochlear nucleus of cat. Numbers indicate types of auditory nerve axons: (1), (4), and (5) are thick axons making large terminals (end bulbs of Held) on a bushy cell body; (2), (3), and (6) are thin axons making small boutons on cell body [and dendrites (6)]. **B.** Synaptic connections onto an octopus cell in the posterior ventral cochlear nucleus of the cat. Axon types: (1), (2), and (4) are thick axons making large, mostly en passant (in passage) contacts with cell body of octopus cell; (3) is a thin axon making small bouton on cell body; (5) and (6) are thick axons making large en passant contacts on octopus cell dendrites [see also ascending branch of (1)]. Heterogeneity of terminals from a single axon is shown by large terminal (T1a) and small terminals (T1b and T2) from single thick axons (1) and (2). (From D. K. Morest, in Eagles, 1975)

principle found in other sensory systems, which we may summarize as follows:

Different functional properties are processed and transmitted in parallel pathways. Each channel has its unique set of microcircuits, mediating a set of functions extracted from the input.

There are extraordinarily rich and complex relations between each part of the cochlear nucleus and various brainstem centers (see Fig. 15.15). However, if we keep in mind the principle of parallel pathways, some of the relations can be seen to be logical. The spherical and globular cells make ipsilateral and contralateral connections to a cell group known as the *olivary nuclear complex,* a center that is essential for the binaural localization of sounds in space. The octopus cells project to cells within the same complex which, in turn, project through the olivocochlear bundle back to the cochlea, to provide for centrifugal control of the hair cells, as previously mentioned. Cells of the dorsal cochlear nucleus do not share these close relations with lower brainstem centers; instead, their outputs are destined for higher centers, in the midbrain (inferior colliculus) and thalamus. It may be noted that the general

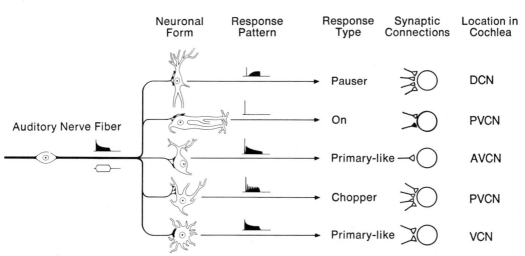

Fig. 15.14 Correlation of synaptic connections and neuron types with response properties in the cochlear nucleus. Responses to a tone burst (50 msec duration) are displayed as poststimulus time histograms. Some postulated circuit connections are indicated to the right (open terminals are excitatory, filled terminals are inhibitory). Abbreviations: AVCN, anterior ventral cochlear nucleus (end bulbs of Held); DCN, dorsal cochlear nucleus (pyramidal-fusiform cell); PVCN, posterior ventral cochlear nucleus (On: octopus cell; Chopper: globular-bushy cell); VCN, ventral cochlear nucleus (multipolar stellate cell). (Adapted from Kiang, in Eagles, 1975)

organization of these pathways, with some information processed at lower levels and some at higher levels, is similar to that in the insect auditory system discussed previously.

Auditory Cortex

The main thalamic relay nucleus for auditory information is the medial geniculate nucleus (MGN). As in the somatosensory and visual systems, the projection area of the thalamic relay cells onto the cortex defines the primary auditory cortex.

Cortical Areas

Traditionally, it has been thought that there is a single area of primary cortex, but here, as in the other systems, recent work has provided evidence for multiple divisions within both thalamic relay nucleus and cortex, and parallel pathways connecting them. For example, HRP injections were made by Irving Diamond and his colleagues at Duke

University into different areas, and the labeled cells in the thalamus were identified. As summarized in Fig. 15.16, these studies showed that, in the cat, the most specific thalamic projection is from a ventral subdivision of the MGN to primary auditory cortex. In contrast, the magnocellular subdivision projects not only to the primary cortex, but to a number of surrounding cortical areas as well. Several other subdivisions have multiple, but more specific, projections. Diamond has suggested that the multiple and diffuse projections are phylogenetically older and the single specific system projection is more recent, in analogy with the presumed phylogeny of the two ascending pathways in the somatosensory system (Chap. 12).

Multiple auditory areas are also found in primates (these were depicted in the diagram of sensory cortical areas in Fig. 12.16). The auditory areas in humans are localized on the dorsal aspect of the temporal lobe (see Fig. 30.1). We will discuss their relations to other cortical regions, including

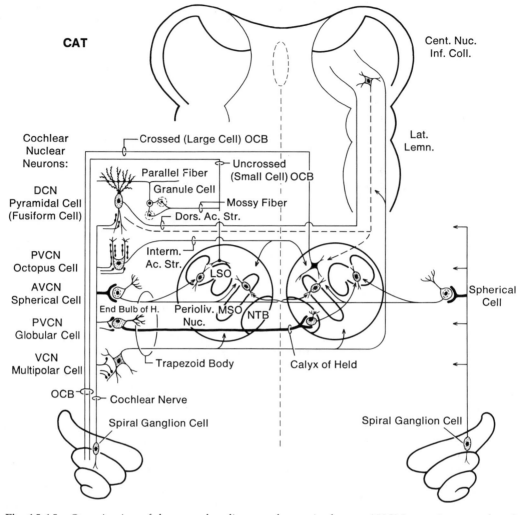

Fig. 15.15 Organization of the central auditory pathways in the cat. AVCN, anterior ventral cochlear nucleus; Cent. Nuc. Inf. Coll., central nucleus of inferior colliculus; Dors. Ac. Str., dorsal accessory stria; DCN, dorsal cochlear nucleus; End Bulb of H., end bulb of Held; Interm. Ac. Str., intermediate accessory stria; Lat. Lemn., lateral lemniscus; LSO, lateral superior olive; MSO, medial superior olive; NTB, nucleus of trapezoid body; OCB, olivocochlear bundle; Perioliv. Nuc., periolivary nucleus; PVCN, posterior ventral cochlear nucleus; VCN, ventral cochlear nucleus. (From Moore and Osen, 1979)

the language and speech areas, in Chapter 30.

Tonotopic Representation

The discovery of a topographical representation within the primary somatosensory cortex suggested that there might be a corresponding representation in auditory cortex of the cochlea *(cochleotopy)* or of the localization of tones along the cochlea *(ton-otopy)*. The first evidence for this was obtained in experiments on dogs by Archie Tunturi in Oregon in 1944. This fit very well with other evidence showing precise tonotopy in lower centers like the inferior colliculus and medial geniculate nucleus. However, subsequent workers had difficulty in replicating the results in the cortex, and for many years the matter was unresolved. One of the problems appears to

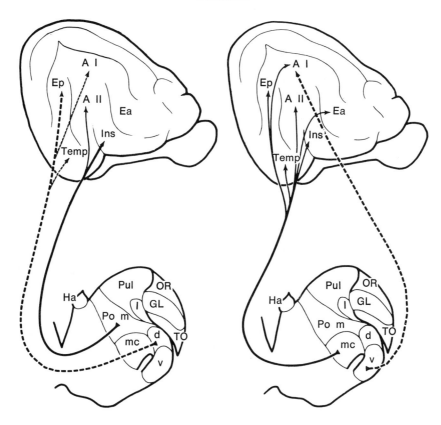

Fig. 15.16 Projections of different parts of the auditory thalamus (medial geniculate nucleus) to the cerebral cortex of the cat. A I, auditory area I; A II, auditory area II; Ea, anterior ectosylvian gyrus; Ep, posterior ectosylvian gyrus; GL, dorsal lateral geniculate body; d, dorsal division of the medial geniculate body; mc, magnocellular division of the medial geniculate body; v, ventral division of the medial geniculate body; Ha, habenula; I, inferior division of the pulvinar complex; Ins., insular area; OR, optic radiations; Po m, medial division of the posterior nuclear group; Pul., pulvinar complex; Temp, temporal field; TO, optic tract. (From Diamond, 1979)

have been that tonotopic organization is more evident in anesthetized than in unanesthetized animals. In 1975, Michael Merzenich and his colleagues in San Francisco clearly demonstrated tonotopic organization in the auditory cortex of anesthetized cats. A typical map is shown in Fig. 15.17 (cat).

These results have been followed up and confirmed in other species. In most mammals there is an area in primary auditory cortex that has a large and detailed map; this is called A I. There are additional representations in several other areas. There are also some areas receiving thalamic input, as discussed above, which are not organized tontopically; for example, A II in the figure.

The regular progression of frequency bands in the tonotopic representation of animals like cats and humans reflects the broad spectrum of sounds to which we are responsive. What about an animal like the bat, which uses special vocal signals as a kind of radar for echolocation? Let us discuss one example, the mustache bat. The echolocating sound emitted by this animal is an almost pure tone of 61 kHz (far above the hearing range of humans; see Fig. 15.1). The specializations of the bat for sensing

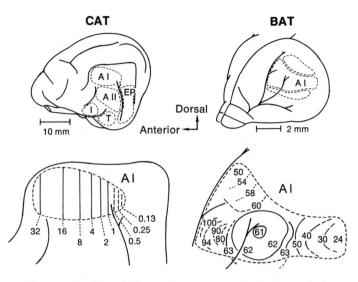

Fig. 15.17 Tonotopic organization of the auditory cortex in the cat and the mustache bat *Pteronotus*. Note the regular tonotopic representation in the cat, and the distortion of this regularity by the large representation of 61–62 kHz in the bat (the frequency of the echolocating signal in this species). EP, posterior ectosylvian gyrus; I, insula; T, temporal field. Frequency bands in cortical maps are indicated in kHz. (Based on data from Woolsey, Merzenich et al., and Suga; in Suga, 1978)

Fig. 15.18 Relation of tonotopic bands to binaural bands in cat auditory cortex. In this schematized view, isofrequency bands are at right angles to binaural bands (EE: neurons excited by both ears; EI: neurons excited by stimulation in contralateral ear and inhibited by ipsilateral ear). The combination of a binaural band and an isofrequency band forms a hyperband, or hypercolumn. AI, primary auditory area; AAF, anterior auditory field. Frequencies indicated in kHz. (Based on Middlebrooks et al., in Merzenich and Kaas, 1980)

A. COCHLEAR REP. in TWO CAT AUDITORY FIELDS (AAF and AI)

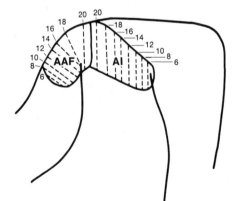

B. BINAURAL BANDS within AI

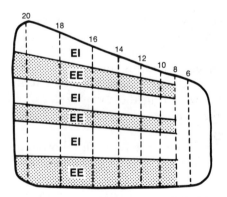

this signal begin in the periphery, where auditory nerve fibers with relatively broad tuning curves may be found across the whole frequency spectrum, but those with best frequencies of 61 kHz have extremely narrow tuning curves. In the cortex, there is a tonotopic organization within A I, but it is distorted by an extremely large representation for 61 kHz (see Fig. 15.17 (bat)). One can consider this as analogous to the large thumb area in somatosensory cortex (Fig. 12.13), or the large area for the fovea in visual cortex (Chap. 16), all places where the highest acuity occurs. The acuity in this auditory area is used to detect Doppler shifts between the emitted sound and the echo, to tell the bat whether a moth or other prey is approaching or receding.

Functional Units

In view of the difficulty in demonstrating the tonotopic organization of auditory cortex, it is perhaps not surprising that there has been less clear evidence for columnar functional organization than in the somatosensory or visual systems. However, in penetrations perpendicular to the surface, an electrode characteristically records units in different layers that respond to the same frequency, which would appear to represent the same principle of functional organization as in the other systems. The isofrequency bands, of course, are in the form of slabs, not columns. In addition, recent experiments indicate that, when tested with tones in either ear, cortical cells show either summation of excitation from both ears (EE), or excitation by the contralateral ear and inhibition by the ipsilateral ear (EI). The EE and EI responsive cells are organized into slabs which cut across the isofrequency bands at right angles, as shown in Fig. 15.18. This overlay of slabs with different functional properties is also present in the visual cortex, as we shall see.

16

Vision

The earth is bathed in a constant flow of energy from the sun and the rest of the universe. This energy is in the form of electromagnetic radiation that has both the properties of waves and of particles, called photons. The radiation all travels at the speed of light (300,000 km/sec), but it has different wavelengths, as indicated in Fig. 16.1. Radiation with short wavelengths (and correspondingly high frequencies) has high energies that disrupt molecular bonds. Although they played a role in early chemical evolution of this planet (see Chap. 2), they are deleterious to life as we know it. Fortunately, these waves are absorbed by the protective blanket of ozone in the atmosphere, or else life as we know it would not be possible. Radiation with long wavelengths has very low energy, for which there are few known receptors in living organisms. However, there is a narrow band of wavelengths with not too much energy nor too little, and this we call *light*. Given the crucial role that this radiation plays in sustaining life on this planet, it is not surprising that plants and animals have developed special mechanisms for sensing it, and for using these signals to control a variety of behavioral actions.

The simplest kind of sensitivity to light is the ability to perceive different *intensities* of diffuse illumination. This ability is present in many plants and most animals. We can refer to it as the basic property of *photosensitivity*. This property is found in single-cell animals, in the skin of many simple organisms, as well as in specialized visual organs. Sensitivity to different levels of light underlies the daily rhythms of activity that govern the lives of most animals (see Chap. 25).

Most complex organisms have evolved mechanisms for sensing changes in illumination that are more rapid in time and more localized in space. These abilities constitute what we call the sense of *vision*. A remarkable feature of light is the large number of submodalities, which means that there are correspondingly a number of different functions that vision may subserve. As summarized in Table 16.1, the simplest function, beyond the sensing of intensity, is the ability to detect *motion* in the visual field; this capacity is widespread among animals, attesting to its usefulness in detecting both predators and prey. This function requires that the receptors be arranged in a sheet in order to portray the movement across the visual field. Discrimination of the *form* of objects, so they can be recog-

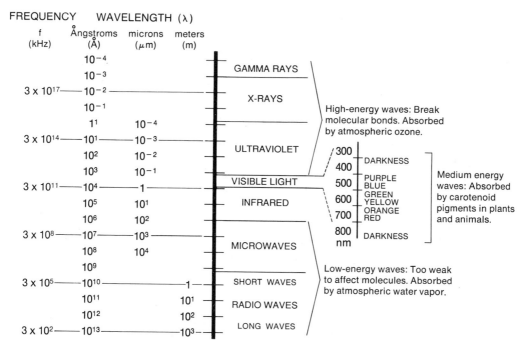

Fig. 16.1 The electromagnetic spectrum. (Modified from Gordon, 1972)

nized and manipulated, requires focusing of the visual image, and the development of a number of accessory structures for accomplishing this. Some animals can discriminate the *polarization* of diffuse light, and use it for orientation and navigation. Since most animals are organized bilaterally, the two images from the eyes need to be combined, and this is used in some animals for *depth perception*. Finally, a few species have mechanisms for discriminating different wavelengths within the visible spectrum, so that they can perceive *colors*.

Thus, it is readily apparent that parallel processing is a basic principle in the organization of the visual system, as it is in the other sensory systems. The subsystems mentioned above act in parallel; each subsystem consists of neural elements which also act in parallel, as we shall see.

The neuronal mechanisms underlying these functions have received a great deal of attention from neurobiologists, for several reasons. First, although other senses, such as the olfactory, play the dominant role in providing the cues that initiate feed-

Table 16.1 Submodalities of vision

Function	Mediated by
Photosensitivity (diffuse light)	Photosensitive molecule (rhodopsin) in microvilli/cilia
Form discrimination (spatial localization)	Sheet of photoreceptors (continuous or cartridges) plus focusing mechanism
Movement discrimination	Sheet of photoreceptors
Binocular vision and depth perception	Fusion of images (extraocular muscles, etc.)
Polarized light	Cellular organization and orientation
Color vision	Different photopigments

ing and mating behavior in most animals, vision is often crucial in carrying out the behavior. Second, vision becomes increasingly important in the higher invertebrates and vertebrates, particularly insects and mammals. Third, vision is overwhelmingly important in the life of humans; the more we learn about vision, the more we learn about ourselves, and also, hopefully, the more we learn about ways to prevent or cure the diseases that can cause blindness. Finally, light is a stimulus that can be controlled easily and accurately, which gives the experimenter a great advantage in analyzing neural mechanisms. The work in the visual system thus not only has given us insight into vision, but also has provided some of the best models for the functional organization of nervous systems.

We will begin by noting some basic properties of photoreception, and then discuss examples of visual systems among invertebrates and vertebrates that have been particularly well studied.

Mechanisms of Photoreception

In a number of places in this book we learn about a particular mechanism that is so effective that it has been adapted for use across a wide range of different cells and organisms. Such, for example, is the nature of the Krebs cycle for energy metabolism, the actin–myosin complex for muscle contraction, and the synapse for neuronal communication. The same applies to photoreception. We have noted that radiation in the narrow band of visible light has energy just sufficient to be absorbed by molecules but not so much that it disrupts them. What is needed is a molecule that will convert light energy into a maximum possible amount of chemical free energy. The molecules that do this most efficiently belong to the class called *carotenoids,* of which vitamin A is a member.

As explained by George Wald, who received a Nobel Prize for his studies of photopigments, these molecules include parts with straight chains that can readily undergo geometrical isomerization. One particular molecule is 11-*cis*-retinal, which has its long-chain part bent and twisted in a very unstable configuration. When a photon of light is absorbed, there is a change, through several intermediate forms, to the more stable 11-*trans* isomer, with a release of free energy. This energy can then be used within the cell as the signal for photoreception.

The 11-*cis*-retinal is normally bound to a colorless protein called opsin, to make a molecule called *rhodopsin* (see Fig. 16.2); this, in one variation or another, is the nearly universal molecular mediator of photoreception in animals. The effect of light, in addition to isomerization, leads to splitting of the retinal and opsin. This causes loss of color of the molecule, an effect called *bleaching.* Reconstitution of rhodopsin occurs by enzymatic resynthesis, requiring biochemical energy in the form of high-energy phosphate bonds (ATP).

The whole rhodopsin molecule has a molecular weight of 28,000. It is associated with the plasmalemma of the photorecep-

---

Fig. 16.2   **A.** The amino acid sequence and secondary folding structure of bovine opsin. The receptor consists of a single polypeptide of 348 amino acids. The amino acids are represented here by their one-letter symbols. The folding structure is interpreted from analysis of hydropathic (intramembrane) and hydrophilic domains, supported by other studies. The seven transmembrane segments proceed from left to right in the diagram. There is almost 50% homology between bovine and *Drosophila* opsin. The cytoplasmic loops (on the C-terminus side) are believed to be sites of interaction with the G protein, transducin. **B.** The rhodopsin molecule as viewed from the cytoplasmic surface, showing the seven transmembrane segments and associated loops. Black arrows indicate potential phosphorylation sites (serine and threonines) on the cytoplasmic side. The 11-*cis*-retinal chromophore nestles in the interior of the opsin, covalently attached as a Schiff base to lysine residue 296 (segment 7). (From Baehr and Applebury, 1986)

A

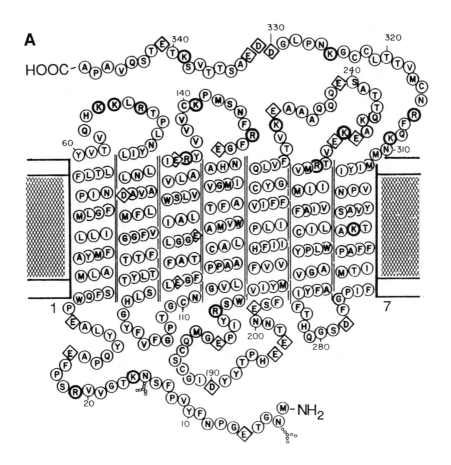

B

329

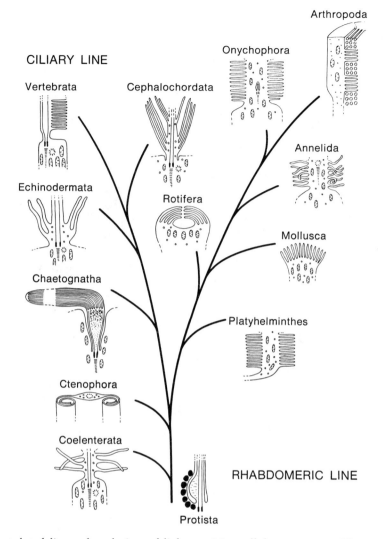

Fig. 16.3 Postulated lines of evolution of light-sensitive cellular structures. There are two main lines, one utilizing modified cilia, the other the elaboration of the rhabdome. (From Eakin, 1965)

tor cell. A schematic representation of the molecule, and the way it spans the membrane and projects beyond both inner and outer surfaces of the membrane, is shown in Fig. 16.2. In the disc membranes of vertebrate photoreceptors it has been estimated that the rhodopsin molecules constitute up to 80% of the protein of the membrane, which indicates how specialized photoreceptors are for capturing photons.

In photoreception we find a second expression of a universal mechanism; in most species, the rhodopsin is contained in fine hairlike processes. In some cases these are cilia, or modifications of cilia; in other cases they are microvilli, or modifications thereof. Richard Eakin of the University of California at Berkeley reviewed the varieties of these structures in different species, and suggested that there are two main lines in the evolution of photoreceptors. As summarized in Fig. 16.3, there is a line through flatworms–annelids–arthropods which uses the microvillus, arranged in a rhabdome, as the site of rhodopsin and photoreception, and a line through coelenterates–echinoderms–chordates which uses modified cilia at these sites. Although there are exceptions in these lines (as always in biology), the schema is a useful way of summarizing the diversity across species, and it also serves to highlight the importance of hairlike processes as sites of sensory transduction. Eakin suggested that membranes of cilia or microvilli "provide a planoarrangement of the molecules of photopigment for the most effective absorption of photons of light."

INVERTEBRATES

Types of Eyes

The simplest organ specialized for sensing light is a group of cells in a shallow surface pit. This is called an *ocellus* (see Fig. 16.4A). It is present in the coelenterates, and is thus, together with the neuromast, one of the first special sense organs to appear in phylogeny. Its main function is sensing light intensity. It apparently does this quite effectively, for ocelli are present in many invertebrate organisms, including the social insects.

In order for an eye to mediate true vision, it must have a way of forming an image.

There are three main ways to do this, and the invertebrates have tried all of them. The simplest uses the principle of the pinhole camera, in which the image is formed by narrow rays passing from the object through the pinhole. The eye of the mollusc *Nautilus* is constructed on this principle (see Fig. 16.4B). Because of the small pinhole, the eye can work effectively only in bright light.

A much more efficient way to form an image is to funnel the light through multiple channels. If the channels are arranged so that they point out at different angles, a large visual field will be projected onto a small sheet of receptors, thus producing a magnification effect. By virtue of many separate channels, called *ommatidia*, this is referred to as a *compound eye* (see Fig. 16.4C). It is the characteristic eye of arthropods. As noted by A. Knowles and J. A. Dartnall (1977), the great advantages of this type of eye are that:

(1) its great depth of focus makes it sensitive to movement at any distance; (2) the relatively short path length for light entering the ommatidium minimizes the loss of UV radiation, and this, coupled with freedom from the chromatic aberration of lens systems, allows it to operate over a very wide range of wavelengths, and (3) the receptor cells can be arranged to make the eye sensitive to the plane of polarization of light.

Fig. 16.4 Different types of eyes in invertebrates. (Adapted from Knowles and Dartnall, 1977)

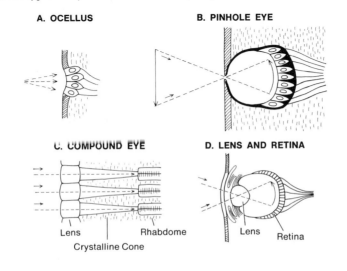

A. OCELLUS

B. PINHOLE EYE

C. COMPOUND EYE

Lens   Rhabdome

Crystalline Cone

D. LENS AND RETINA

Lens   Retina

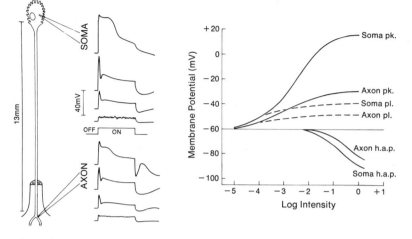

Fig. 16.5 *Left:* Diagram of medial photoreceptor of the barnacle *Balanus*. *Middle:* Intracellular receptor potentials at four different light intensities, recorded in the soma (above) and axon terminals (below). *Right:* Intensity–response relations plotted from recordings such as those shown, for the dynamic peak (pk.) of the response, the static plateau (pl.), and the afterhyperpolarization (h.a.p.). (From Hudspeth, Poo, and Stuart, in Laughlin, 1981)

In order to achieve its advantages, the compound eye sacrifices resolving power, which, by contrast, is maximized in the *refracting eye*. In the refracting eye, the image is formed by refraction of the light rays through a lens. The image formed is brought into focus on a receptor sheet, called the *retina*. This, of course, is similar to the lens system and film of a modern camera. The refracting eye is found in certain molluscs, such as the octopus, and is characteristic of all vertebrates (see Fig. 16.4D).

The ocellus and the compound eye have been studied intensively by neurobiologists; let us briefly consider examples of these two types.

The Ocellus

The ocelli of the barnacle have most of the advantages that neurobiologists seek in a simple invertebrate system: few cells (3–5), large cell bodies (30–100 μm in diameter), and easy accessibility. Their only known function is to sense the shadow of a passing object and mediate a protective "shadow reflex." Stimulation of one of these pho-

toreceptors with a step of light produces a receptor potential that is graded with the light intensity, as shown in Fig. 16.5. The response is depolarizing, and the inward current that brings about this change in the membrane potential is carried by both Na^+ and Ca^{2+}. As can be seen in Fig. 16.5, the response has a complicated time course, with an early phasic overshoot followed by adaptation to a slowly declining static phase. This adaptation is due to several factors, including reduction of the inward Na^+ current by the rise in intracellular Ca^{2+}, and changes in the membrane properties due to a voltage-dependent K^+ conductance. Thus, although the response is "nonspiking," it is nonetheless shaped by several mechanisms that include voltage-dependent processes. Studies of this simple receptor permit the conclusion that, as expressed by Simon Laughlin of Canberra in 1981, "the neural membrane is a multicomponent system capable of great functional plasticity," This is in line with comments in Chap. 7, and we will see further evidence of the generality of this statement in Chap. 29.

The ocellar cell has an axon, with a diameter of 10–20 μm and a length of up to 10 mm or so, that connects to the supraesophageal ganglion. The axon does not conduct action potentials: the receptor potential spreads passively through the axon to the axon terminals, as indicated in Fig. 16.5. Note the similarity with non-impulse transmission in the thoracico-coxal receptor axon (Fig. 13.5), and the photoreceptor axon in the insect ommatidium (see below). Because of the large diameter of the axon, there is only moderate decrement of the passively spreading potential. There appears to be partial compensation for this decrement by virtue of voltage-dependent Ca^{2+} channels in the terminals. In the presence of tetraethylammonium (TEA), which blocks outward current through K^+ channels, the terminals generate a Ca^{2+} action potential. By this means, even a small signal can give rise to a significant increase in intracellular Ca^{2+} in the terminal, which in turn can enhance release of neurotransmitter from the terminal. This may serve as a model for gain control and amplification at other synapses in the nervous system.

Central Ocellar Pathways

In the leech, there are five pairs of ocellar-like eyes in the head, and the photoreceptor mechanisms are similar to those in the barnacle. The photoreceptor axons generate impulses, however, and project to central ganglia. Here they excite an ipsilateral *lateral visual* (LV) neuron through electrical synapses, and inhibit the contralateral LV neuron through one or more inhibitory interneurons. The LV neurons in turn project to higher centers (sub- and supraesophageal ganglia). According to Eric Peterson (1983):

There are remarkable parallels between the LV cells and other neurons that process bilateral sensory input, most notably the auditory ganglion cells of crickets (which) receive direct excitatory input from the receptors of the ipsilateral tympanum and indirect inhibitory input from the receptors of the contralateral tympanum, exactly paralleling the input pattern of the LV cells.

By enhancing bilateral differences in sound intensity, this circuit is believed to mediate sound localization to aid crickets in finding mates (see Fig. 15.4A for similar circuit in locusts). Its function in the visual system could be to provide the leech with a coarse bilateral representation of its surroundings that is used for phototaxis (orientation towards light) and to keep the body upright during swimming. The fact that the same type of circuit is found in different sensory systems extends the general principles underlying sensory organization discussed previously in Chap. 10.

The Compound Eye

Limulus

The horseshoe crab, *Limulus*, has several eyes, including a pair of dorsal ocelli and a ventral eye. Like other arthropods, of which it is an ancient member, it has a pair of compound eyes. Their simple structure and accessibility made them the first simple system for studying visual mechanisms. The use of this preparation by Hartline and his colleagues for elucidating the basic principle of lateral inhibition has been discussed in Chap. 10. Here we will discuss the insect as a well-studied example of visual mechanisms in animals with compound eyes.

Insects

The most highly developed compound eyes are found in fast-moving arthropods such as insects. The insect eye has been intensively studied, and we will draw on several examples for our discussion.

The large eyes of an insect like the common housefly are familiar to anyone who has taken a close look after swinging a flyswatter (see Fig. 16.6A,B). Each eye consists of a mosaic of some 10,000 individual ommatidia. The ommatidium is more highly developed than in the case of *Limulus*. An ommatidium comprises eight receptor cells, each an identifiable cell with a characteristic morphology and placement. Each cell gives rise along its length to thousands of microvilli that form a *rhabdomere*. The

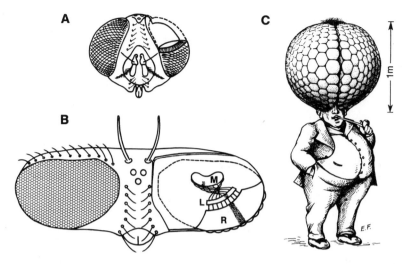

Fig. 16.6 **A.** Anterior view of head of a fly, showing large, compound eyes. **B.** Dorsal view; on the right, the cutaway shows the relations between the retina (R) of the compound eye and the next stages in the visual pathway: the lamina (L) and medulla (M). Stippling indicates one ommatidium and its projection to lamina and medulla. **C.** Relatively poor resolving power of compound eye is shown by this representation of a man with compound eyes which have a resolving power equivalent to that of the human eye. Each facet pictured on the man actually represents 10,000 facets. (A,B from Meinertzhagen, 1977, C from Kirshfeld, in Land, 1981)

corneal lens focuses incoming light such that it is funneled through the rhabdomere, where photoreception takes place. Unlike the case in *Limulus*, the insect photoreceptors themselves have long axons, which project to the first site of synaptic transmission and integration in the optic lamina (L in Fig. 16.6B) just beneath the eye. The limited resolving power of this eye is illustrated by the humorous cartoon in Fig. 16.6C.

Intracellular recordings have been made from the photoreceptors, their terminals in the lamina, and the relay cells in the lamina; Fig. 16.7 summarizes these findings. It can be seen that the receptor potential recorded from the retinula cell body consists of a graded depolarization, as in other invertebrate photoreceptors. The response to weak stimulation (upper trace) is "noisy." The small deflections are believed to reflect both photon quantum bumps and transducer noise due to molecular fluctuations in conductance channels. Note at high intensities (bottom trace) the complicated response envelope, presumably reflecting

complex membrane conductances, as discussed above for ocellar cells. There are numerous electrical synapses between the photoreceptors; they function to enhance the signal-to-noise ratio (by lowering the input resistance and thereby lowering the noisiness of individual receptors) and increase photon capture (by increasing the number of photoreceptors feeding into a given second-order cell).

Transmission of the receptor potential through the axon to the axon terminals is by passive electrotonic spread; as in the other examples we have considered, there is little evidence for spike activity in these axons under normal conditions (see recordings under retinula axon in Fig. 16.7). In the optic lamina, the terminals make multiple synapses onto the relay neurons, called large monopolar cells (LMC). As can be seen in the figure, these cells respond to input from the photoreceptors with a hyperpolarization. The response is mediated by a neurotransmitter, possibly acetylcholine. There are several factors in the presynaptic terminal which work together to

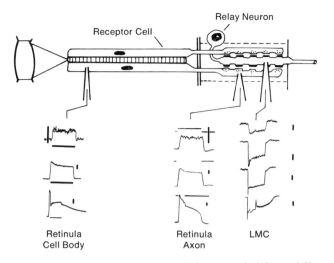

Fig. 16.7 Graded receptor potentials in response to light, recorded from different locations in the eye of the dragonfly. LMC, large monopolar cell (relay neuron). Stimuli last 500 msec; voltage calibrations (vertical bars) are 10 mV. (From Laughlin, 1981)

enhance transmitter release at low signal intensities. These include the fact that the synapses are continually active in the dark; that they have no threshold for transmitter release; that at background illumination they are in the most sensitive part of their operating range; and that there are multiple synapses from individual terminals. These properties have already been discussed in relation to other invertebrate photoreceptors, and we will see that they are shared by vertebrate receptors as well.

Central Visual Pathways

Figure 16.7 shows the essential synaptic connections for straight-through transmission of visual information, but it does not indicate the circuit connections through which the information from all the ommatidia interact to provide for movement discrimination and pattern recognition.

The main centers in the visual pathway are indicated in Fig. 16.8. As can be seen, there is a sequence from the *lamina* through the *medulla* to a bipartite structure, *lobula* and *lobula plate,* and from these to the *protocerebrum* of the brain. Studies of the neurons within and connecting these centers began with the first use of the Golgi method in the late nineteenth century, and

culminated in an exhaustive analysis by Nicholas Strausfeld in Heidelberg in the 1970s. Fig. 16.8 gives a summary view of some of the circuits and organizational units identified in this analysis. The sequence of steps that occurs as information is transmitted through the lamina and medullar to the lobula and lobula plate, from there to be combined with other sensory information to effect appropriate motor orientation to visual stimuli, is indicated in the diagram and discussed in the legend of Fig. 16.8. These steps involve most of the principles of sensory processing we discussed in Chap. 10: divergence, convergence, lateral interactions, functional segregation, and topographical ordering.

This overall scheme has been extended in several more specific directions by recent work. The synaptic connections within the lamina have been analyzed under the electron microscope, aided by single-cell staining and identification. From this work the simple relay connections depicted in Fig. 16.7 have been fleshed out with circuits for local processing through a variety of interneurons, much as in the vertebrate retina. Physiologists have pieced together circuits that mediate specific types of visual behavior. Perhaps the best understood at present

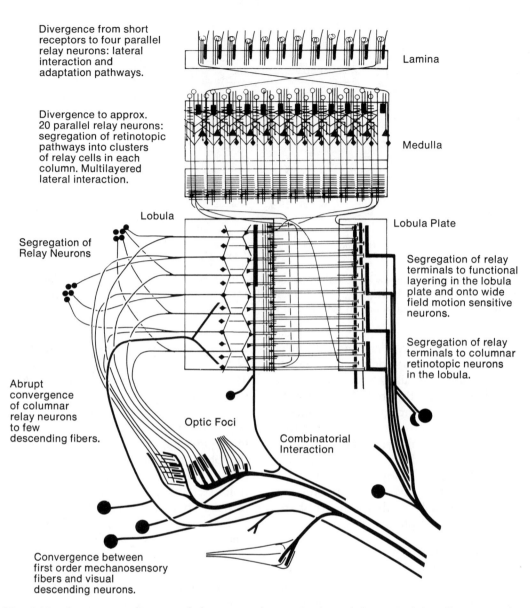

Divergence from short receptors to four parallel relay neurons: lateral interaction and adaptation pathways.

Lamina

Divergence to approx. 20 parallel relay neurons: segregation of retinotopic pathways into clusters of relay cells in each column. Multilayered lateral interaction.

Medulla

Lobula

Lobula Plate

Segregation of Relay Neurons

Segregation of relay terminals to functional layering in the lobula plate and onto wide field motion sensitive neurons.

Segregation of relay terminals to columnar retinotopic neurons in the lobula.

Abrupt convergence of columnar relay neurons to few descending fibers.

Optic Foci

Combinatorial Interaction

Convergence between first order mechanosensory fibers and visual descending neurons.

Fig. 16.8 A summary diagram of the neuronal organization of the optic lobe, illustrating the sequence of processing and the output to the lateral protocerebrum. Note the following organizational principles. The system is massively parallel at all levels. The neural elements are not diffusely parallel, but rather segregated into parallel clusters, which form multicellular functional units (the same principle that is expressed by olfactory glomeruli (see Chap. 11); somatosensory barrels (Chap. 12), and cortical columns (Chaps. 12 and 16). There are lateral interactions between the clusters within a given region. There are multiple layers for these interactions. There is divergence and convergence of projections from one level to the next, providing for combinatorial mixing of information between the parallel channels. (From Strausfeld and Nässel, 1981)

is the *movement detector system* in the locust. This circuit is tuned to respond optimally to rapid movements of small objects in the visual field, and elicit an escape jumping reaction. The elements of this circuit have been identified all the way from the peripheral visual system through the brain down to the thoracic motoneurons that elicit the jumping. The part of the circuit that feeds into the giant movement detector in the lobula is shown in Fig. 16.9. One sees here the way that the properties of sensory processing, mentioned previously, are utilized in a circuit for a specific behavioral function. The hierarchical nature of such a circuit, and its relation to motor control, will be discussed in Chap. 21.

VERTEBRATES

The importance of vision in vertebrate life is paralleled by the attention given by neurobiologists to this subject. Studies of vertebrate visual systems, in all their aspects, may well exceed those for any other part of the nervous system. Some of these aspects, such as the optics of the eye, are subjects for special study. From a cellular point of view, we wish to concentrate on cellular properties and synaptic circuits, in order to understand the principles that underlie visual processing. We will compare these principles with those in invertebrates, and also assess the insights they may give us into the neural basis of visual perception.

The Retina

The vertebrate eye works on the principle of the refracted image, as already mentioned. The photoreceptors, together with the neurons involved in the first two levels of synaptic processing, are arranged in a thin sheet called the *retina* at the back of the eye, where the image is formed (see Fig. 16.4).

Photoreceptors

The receptors are arranged along the outer (posterior) surface of the retina. This is different from the situation in the compound eyes of invertebrates, where the light has direct access to the photoreceptor membranes, and it is also different from the squid eye, which, though also working on refractive principles, has the photoreceptors arranged on the inner surface. The explanation offered is that this peculiar arrangement is due to the embryological origins of the retina as an outpouching from the brain. There is in any case little loss of light in reaching the receptors, because the retina is transparent.

The receptors are of two types, *rods* and *cones* (Fig. 16.10). In both types the *outer segments* are modified cilia. They contain stacks of *disc membranes,* which are formed by inpouchings of the plasma membrane. The disc membranes contain the photopigment molecules: rhodopsin in rods, and related molecules sensitive to red, green, and blue wavelengths in cones. The receptors continually shed disc membranes from their distal tips and synthesize new membranes proximally. The location of the receptors against the outer surface of the retina facilitates the removal of the discarded membranes. The cones of reptiles and birds contain oil droplets of different colors in their inner segments, a filtering mechanism that contributes to color vision; this is an additional use of the outward placement of the receptors mentioned above.

The Second Messenger Mechanism. The mechanism of transduction of photons into the electrical response of the photoreceptor has been discussed in Chap. 10, where we saw that a second messenger is the link between the activation of rhodopsin in the disc membrane and the closing of Na^+ channels in the plasma membrane of the outer segment.

The identity of this second messenger has been the focus of intense interest. Around

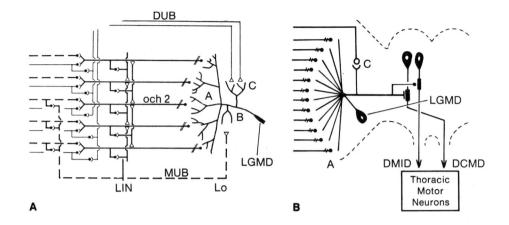

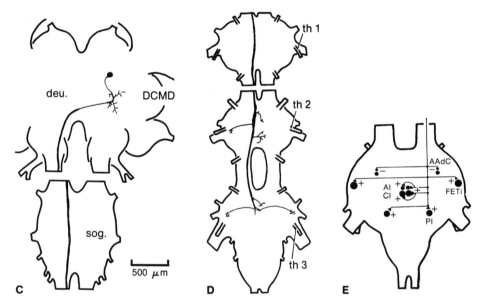

Fig. 16.9 The central visual pathway in the locust mediating movement detection. **A.** Convergence of parallel array of axons from medulla (see Fig. 16.8 above) onto the dendritic tree of the lobula giant movement detector cell (LGMD). **B.** Projection of LGMD cell within the brain (deutocerebrum) to two types of descending neurons: descending ipsilateral movement detector (DMID) and descending contralateral movement detector (DCMD). **C.** Trajectory of the axon of a DCMD neuron from the deutocerebrum (deu.) through the subesophageal ganglion (sog). **D.** Termination of the DCMD axon in the second (th 2) and third (th 3) thoracic ganglia. **E.** Synaptic connections of the DCMD axon terminals with th 3 on different types of motoneurons that control the muscles subserving the motor response of the locust. Excitatory synapses (+), inhibitory synapses (−). Other abbreviations: AAdC, anterior coxal adductor motoneuron; AI, anterior inhibitory flexor tibiae motoneuron; CI, common inhibitory motoneuron; DUB, dorsal uncrossed bundle; FETi, fast extensor tibiae motoneuron; LIN, lateral inhibitory network; Lo, lobula; MUB, medial uncrossed bundle; och 2, second optic chiasm; PI, posterior inhibitory flexor tibiae motoneuron. (Based on Rowell et al. and others, in Strausfeld and Nässel, 1981)

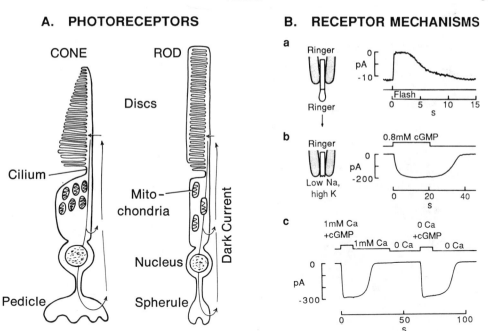

Fig. 16.10 **A.** Diagrams of vertebrate cone and rod photoreceptors, showing main cellular features and pathways for flow of dark current. **B.** Experiments providing evidence that the second messenger for phototransduction is cGMP. (a) Single rods from the toad retina are inserted in electrode tip and placed in a Ringer solution in the dark. A flash of light on the rod produces complete suppression of the inward "dark" current, as shown in the recording on the right. (b) The inner segment and part of the outer segment are then broken off, leaving the interior of the remaining outer segment exposed to the bath; the bath is changed to a low Na, high K solution, approximating the intracellular medium. Addition of 0.6 mM cGMP to the bath results in a large inward current. (c) Changing the concentration of Ca^{2+} in the bath had no effect on the cGMP response, showing that Ca^{2+} is not essential as a second messenger for the responses. Current is given in picoamperes (pA; 10^{-12} A); time in seconds. (From Yau and Nakatani, 1985)

1970, evidence was brought forward by William Hagins and his collaborators at the National Institutes of Health that this second messenger was Ca^{2+} released by rhodopsin isomerization, and soon equally suggestive evidence was obtained by William Miller and his colleagues at Yale that the second messenger was cGMP. In the intervening years, the battle has swayed back and forth, until recent experiments have resolved the question. Persuasive evidence has been obtained in favor of cGMP, from experiments such as that illustrated in Fig. 16.10B.

In this experimental technique, pioneered by Dennis Baylor, K.-Y. Yau their colleagues at Stanford (1979a), single photoreceptors are teased out from small pieces of toad retina and gently sucked up in a recording electrode. With this technique (see also Fig. 16.11), the responses to light stimuli can be recorded while the rod is exposed to different conditions in the bathing medium. In the dark, the rod showed a large inward current that was transiently suppressed by a flash of light (Fig. 16.10B,a), in a manner similar to the normal receptor potential response to a light stimulus. The rest of the rod was then broken off, leaving the intracellular compartment of the outer segment open to a bathing medium of intracellular composition; application of cGMP then produced a large inward current (b). The conclusion is that in the nor-

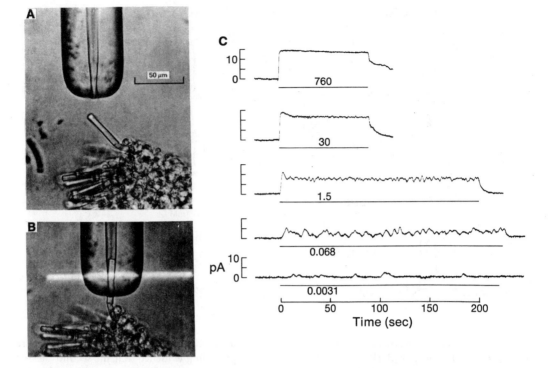

Fig. 16.11   Recordings of responses from single isolated rod photoreceptors of the toad. **A.** Suction electrode approaching the outer segment of a receptor protruding from a piece of retina. **B.** Outer segment is sucked up into electrode. Light bar is shone on small parts of the outer segment, while membrane current, proportional to longitudinal current flowing along the outer segment, is recorded by the electrode. **C.** Receptor responses, showing quantal events at low illumination (bottom), merging to a smooth graded response at higher illumination (upper traces). Note that these are recordings of membrane current (in pA: 10^{-12} A); the upward deflections signal the current flows associated with the membrane hyperpolarization that is characteristic of vertebrate photoreceptors. Intensity of light stimulation in photons μm^{-2} sec^{-1}. (From Baylor et al., 1979a,b)

mal rod, cGMP acts to open Na^+ channels in the membrane (this produces the resting "dark current" recorded in a); isomerization of rhodopsin by photon capture activates the transducin–phosphodiesterase system (see Fig. 10.2C) which hydrolyzes cGMP, reducing its concentration and causing the Na^+ channels to close. This shuts off the dark current, producing the receptor potential. Experiments on outer segment patches have shown that cGMP does not phosphorylate the Na^+ channels, but acts directly on the channel proteins. Changing the concentration of Ca^{2+} in the bath has little effect on the cGMP response (c). Although Ca^{2+} is likely to contribute in some way to the light response, there is little evidence at present for its role as a second messenger. One suggestion is that Ca^{2+} gradually opens the Na^+ channels during continued visual stimulation, and this may play a role in visual adaptation.

Quantal Responses. The smallest response of the photoreceptor is the reduction in cGMP molecules caused by one photon, referred to as the *quantal response.* Quantal responses have been recorded by Baylor and his colleagues (1979b), using this same elegant technique. Figure 16.11 shows how the rods are teased apart and drawn into the pipette (A) and stimulated with small bars of light (B). The resulting response of the rod, due to the closing of Na^+ channels, changes the amount of current flowing across the membrane, as discussed previously. This current has to flow electrotonically along the rod to complete the electrical circuit. The tight seal of the electrode tip against the rod places a high resistance in this longitudinal current path, which generates voltages that can be recorded by the electrode.

Use of this method with very weak illumination made it possible to record small voltage fluctuations, as shown in Fig. 16.11C (bottom trace). Each fluctuation is a quantal event, due to the photoisomerization of a single rhodopsin molecule by a single photon. There is a quantal current of 1 pA (10^{-12} amperes), and also a corresponding conductance change very similar to that of a single acetylcholine-sensitive channel in the neuromuscular junction. The photoreceptor quantal response has a rounded shape and a duration of a few seconds. It is believed that this represents the action of cGMP on a number of channel sites. Patch recordings have shown that the light-sensitive channel has a unitary conductance of only 3 fS (3 femtosiemens, or 3×10^{-15} fS), one of the lowest values known for any membrane channel.

With stronger illumination, the quantal events merge, and the response becomes a smoothly graded waveform (Fig. 16.11C). Note the similarities (except for the polarity) of these responses to those of the invertebrate receptors discussed previously.

Comparisons Between Invertebrates and Vertebrates. The fact that vertebrate receptors normally respond to light only with graded potentials, added to the evidence in invertebrates, indicates that this is a near-universal property of animal photoreceptors. This similarity is all the more striking in view of the fact that the response to illumination in the invertebrates is depolarization, and in the vertebrates is hyperpolarization. Given the similar graded nature of the responses, it is perhaps not surprising that many of the properties we discussed in invertebrate receptors also appear

to apply to vertebrates. These include voltage-sensitive channels for Ca^+ and K^+, normally masked by other conductances; high sensitivity to small signals in the presynaptic terminal, enhanced by voltage-dependent conductances; and multiple synaptic contacts onto second-order neurons. These and other properties are summarized and compared in Fig. 16.12.

Retinal Circuits

The basic organization of the retina has already been discussed in Chap. 10. It may be recalled that there are five main cell types—receptors, bipolar cells, horizontal cells, amacrine cells, and ganglion cells—and that these are arranged in a kind of lattice-array that provides for straight through transmission as well as lateral interactions. The connections between the cells include some of the specialized synaptic types that were discussed in Chap. 4.

The first systematic intracellular recordings from all the cell types were obtained by Frank Werblin and John Dowling, then at Johns Hopkins, in 1968. These experiments were carried out in the retina of *Necturus,* the mudpuppy. The cell bodies in this retina are large, making inviting targets for the probing microelectrode. A summary of the results is shown in Fig. 16.13. The diagram is arranged to show, on the left, the responses of each cell to a spot of light and, on the right, to a surround.

There are three main points to take away from this diagram. First, in addition to the receptors, the horizontal cells and bipolar cells show only graded responses to stimulation. These have thus far provided the clearest examples of nonspiking neurons in the vertebrate nervous system. Amacrine cells show mostly graded potentials also, though they do generate a few small spikes, which may help to boost transmission through their long dendritic processes. Only the ganglion cells generate large action potentials, which is consistent with their role as the output neurons of the retina.

Second, there are marked differences be-

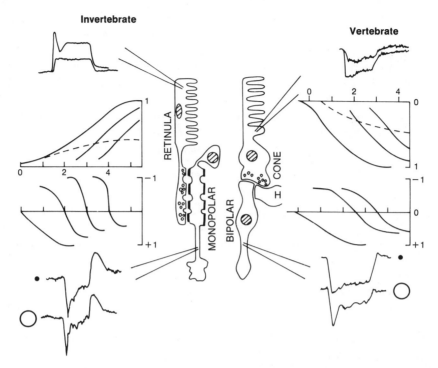

Fig. 16.12   The similarities between the responses and intensity/response functions of the receptors and first-order interneurons of invertebrate and vertebrate retinas. Despite the difference in response polarity, the graded potentials of the receptors (insect retinula cells and vertebrate cones) both exhibit a broad dynamic range, a relatively small range shift with light adaptation, and a standing background signal (---). The relay neurons (monopolar and bipolar cells) also respond with graded potentials, but have a narrow dynamic range that is shifted in step with background intensity so that there is little representation of the standing background intensity level. Comparisons between the responses to a point source (•) and a broad stimulus (O) show that both interneurons are subject to lateral inhibition. (Figure and legend from Laughlin, 1981, based on data from Laughlin and Hardie, and Normann and Werblin)

tween the responses in the center and the surround. The bipolar cell potentials are of opposite polarities, and ganglion cells (G_1) show excitation at the center and inhibition in the surround. This expresses the fundamental property of center–surround antagonism in the organization of receptive fields of ganglion cells. Since the receptors show only a graded reduction of their responses in the surround, these results demonstrate that the center–surround antagonism is the result of processing by the synaptic circuits in the retina, principally those through the laterally oriented elements, the horizontal and amacrine cells.

Third, the ganglion cell (G_2) depicted in

Fig. 16.13 shows transient responses at ON and OFF of the stimulus. This type of response is especially tuned to transmitting information about moving stimuli. This property can be seen to be due to synaptic circuits, principally through complex interactions of the amacrine cells.

Different species differ in the amount of synaptic processing that takes place in their retinas. One of the most complex retinas in this respect is that of the frog or toad. As shown in the pioneering studies of H. R. Maturana, Jerome Lettvin, and their colleagues at M.I.T. in 1960, frog ganglion cells may be tuned to one of several features of a visual stimulus, including a stationary

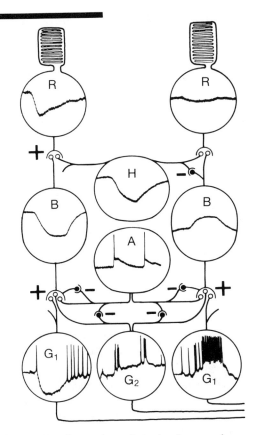

Fig. 16.13 Synaptic actions in the vertebrate retina, as recorded intracellularly from neurons in *Necturus* (mudpuppy). *Left:* Responses recorded at the center of a spot of light (bar above). *Right:* Responses in the surround. R, receptor; B, bipolar cell; H, horizontal cell; A, amacrine cell; $G_{1,2}$, ganglion cells. (From Dowling, 1979)

interactions with other circuits can take place. We will return to this theme when we discuss the visual cortex.

Ganglion Cell Types

In the mammal, the ganglion cells are differentiated into several distinct morphological types, each with special functional properties. The main distinction is between the majority of cells (X cells) located mostly near the fovea where they are responsible for high-acuity vision, and a minority of cells (Y cells) located in the periphery where they subserve motion detection. This demonstrates how differnt submodalities of vision are mediated in parallel by different subsets of neurons. These and other properties of ganglion cells are summarized in Table 16.2. We will see that these properties continue to be transmitted in separate channels as far as the visual cortex.

Color Vision

Color vision is limited in most mammals, reflecting the fact that the early mammals were probably nocturnal animals. Color vision reemerged mainly in the line leading to primates, in association with the adoption of diurnal habits. As Timothy Goldsmith of Yale has pointed out (1980), our color vision system has been reconstructed, in an evolutionary sense, from a less capable retina. It therefore lacks the specializations, such as oil droplets and sensitivity to ultraviolet light, that make the avian retina the supreme instrument for both day and night vision.

Cone Mechanisms. The rhodopsin present in rods has different sensitivities to different wavelengths of light, giving a spectral sensitivity curve as shown by the dashed line in Fig. 16.14A. Despite this varying sensitivity, a rod receptor containing only rhodopsin, or a cone receptor containing only one pigment such as green (G in Fig. 16.14A), cannot signal a specific wavelength (color), because it cannot distinguish between wavelengths in ascending and descending limbs of the curve that produce

edge, a convex edge, a moving edge, or a dimming or brightening of illumination. Some cells are so narrowly tuned that they seem to function virtually as "bug detectors"! An interesting note is that complex retinas are found in some mammals (such as rabbits) as well as in lower vertebrates, so there is not a consistent phylogenetic progression. The fact that higher mammals, like cats and primates, have relatively simple retinas is taken as an expression of encephalization of nervous control; that is, the tendency for complex processing to be shifted from peripheral to central sites, where

Table 16.2 Summary of different morphological types of retinal ganglion cells and their functional properties, in the cat

	X	Y	W
Morphology			
ganglion cell size	medium	large	varied
number	many; most near fovea	few; most in periphery	few
axons	medium conduction rate	fast conduction rate	varied conduction rate
projection sites	lateral geniculate nucleus	lateral geniculate nucleus and superior colliculus (and medial interlaminar nucleus)	lateral geniculate nucleus and superior colliculus
Function			
spatial summation	linear	nonlinear	mixed
movement sensitivity	+	+ + +	±
directional selectivity	no	no	yes (a few cells)
center–surround antagonism	yes	yes	±
color coded	yes (in primates)	no	?

equal responses, and it cannot distinguish color from brightness; that is, a smaller response in the receptor could be due to lower place in the spectral sensitivity curve (compare objects 1 and 2 in Fig. 16.14A) or to less light, and the central nervous system receiving these signals could not tell the difference.

This ambiguity is overcome partly by the presence of two types, and completely by the presence of three types, of cone receptors, each type having a visual pigment with a different spectral sensitivity curve. These three curves peak in the blue, green, and red regions. The key fact about these curves is that they overlap. Because of this, a particular wavelength of light gives a unique combination of degrees of activation of the three cone populations. Thus, as shown in Fig. 16.14B, the light reflected by object 1 at 450 nm produces a small response in G cones, a large response in B cones, and none at all in R cones. By contrast, object 2, reflecting light at 600 nm, produces a different pattern of responses (see Fig. 16.14B). Because the patterns are unique for different wavelengths, by comparing the information coming from the three sets of receptors the central nervous

system can distinguish which wavelength is being signaled, no matter what the level of brightness. This mechanism, comparing overlapping spectra across elements acting in parallel, is a basic model for discrimination in other sensory systems (see taste and olfaction, Chap. 11; audition, Chap. 15).

Color Coding. From these considerations it can be seen that perception of color depends on comparisons between information arising in different cone systems. How is this information incorporated into the receptive field organization of retinal cells?

As we learned above (Fig. 16.13), a basic principle of retinal ganglion cell organization is center–surround antagonism. As was first shown by Steven Kuffler at Johns Hopkins in 1953, a cell may be excited or inhibited by a small spot centered over a group of receptors feeding into it, but oppositely by an annulus activating surrounding receptors. These antagonistic effects are due to synaptic interactions within the retinal circuits (Fig. 16.13.). The example of an on-center cell is shown in Fig. 16.15A. When the stimulus is broad-band (white)

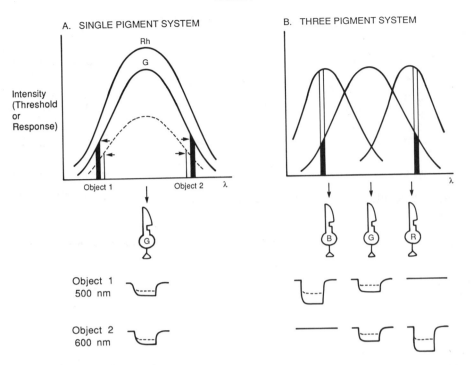

Fig. 16.14   Color-coding mechanisms at the photoreceptor level, illustrating the necessity for more than one visual pigment. **A.** A single pigment (G, for maximum sensitivity in green) gives a receptor different sensitivities to different wavelengths (λ), but the receptor could not distinguish between objects reflecting wavelengths of 450 nm and 600 nm (which have identical sensitivities). If the luminosity is decreased (dashed line), the receptor could not distinguish between the change in luminosity and a change in wavelength (arrows). Sample recordings in the G receptor under these conditions are shown below. **B.** A three-pigment system can distinguish wavelength independently of intensity. The pigments must have overlapping spectra. The two objects stimulate the three photoreceptors (B, blue; R, red) in different amounts. Each object stimulates the receptors to different degrees, so that the color code for each object is unique, and maintained despite a reduction in luminosity (dashed lines in recordings). (Modified from Gouras, 1985)

light, this center–surround organization enables the ganglion cells to signal borders between regions of differing brightness.

The first step in building a system to code for color is to organize the connections to the ganglion cells in such a way that the receptive field center response is due to one type of cone and the surround response is due to another. This property is illustrated in Fig. 16.15B, where a ganglion cell is excited by a red center spot (1) and inhibited by a green surround (2). This is called a single-opponent color ganglion cell (for the other types, see figure legend). This type of receptive field organization transmits information about both brightness and color. Because of this, there is ambiguity about the specific information contained in the ganglion cell response.

In the primate, single-opponent color contrast receptive field organization is found in retinal ganglion cells and maintained in the thalamic relay neurons to which they project, so that brightness and color information is still ambiguous when it reaches the visual cortex. The mechanism for extracting specific color information is found in cortical cells with double-opponent color receptive fields. In the example shown in Fig. 16.15C, the cell has a red-on, green-

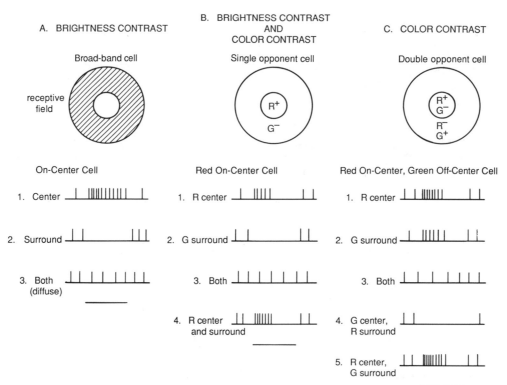

Fig. 16.15 Color-coding mechanisms in neurons of the visual pathway. **A.** Ganglion cell coding for brightness contrast, not color. The receptive field is shown, with a center spot and surround annulus. The example of an on-center cell is illustrated, with typical recordings below. **B.** Ganglion cell or thalamic relay cell, coding for brightness and color contrast. The case of a red on-center, green off-surround cell is illustrated. This is termed a single-opponent color cell. This cell would have difficulty distinguishing between red spots with different sizes and luminosities (cf. 1 and 4). **C.** Cortical cell with double-opponent color receptive field. This cell gives its maximal response to a red spot on a green surround (5) and is suppressed by a green spot on a red surround (4). A cell could have this receptive field by receiving excitatory connections from a single opponent R^+ center, G^- surround cell (as in B), or inhibitory connections from a G^+ center, R^- surround cell, in its center, and the reverse type of connections in the surround. (Modified from Gouras, 1985)

off center (1) and a red-off, green-on surround (2). Maximal excitation occurs with a red center and a green surround. This receptive field organization thus has a color-opponent mechanism *within* the center and the surround, and a color-contrast mechanism *between* the center and the surround. It is believed that the color-opponent mechanism provides for mixing effects that give rise to the different hues when wavelengths are mixed, whereas the contrast mechanism accounts for the color constancy which is independent of the strength of illumination.

Further details regarding these mecha-

nisms will be found in the legend to Fig. 16.15, and in the ensuing discussion of the central visual pathway.

Central Visual Pathways

The ganglion cell axons run along the inner surface of the retina and gather together to form the optic nerve. This is the second cranial nerve. By embryonic origin it is a part of the central nervous system. In lower vertebrates, the main projection of the optic nerve is to the optic tectum of the midbrain. The retina is mapped in an orderly, *retinotopic* manner onto the optic tectum, as discussed in Chap. 9. Single-unit studies have shown that in the frog or toad, tectal cells are exquisitely tuned to detect particular types of movements and spatial patterns that allow them to discriminate prey (such as a worm or fly), which elicits prey-catching behavior, or predator, which elicits escape reactions.

In mammals, the optic nerve also projects to the lateral geniculate nucleus (LGN) in the thalamus (Fig. 16.16). The input to the superior colliculus, the homologue of the optic tectum, still mediates midbrain reflexes important in prey and predator behavior. Most of this input is carried by the Y axons (see Table 16.2), which arise from ganglion cells in the peripheral parts of the retina, and are tuned to detecting movements in the peripheral visual field. By contrast, the input to the LGN is carried in both X and Y axons. The X axons arise mostly from ganglion cells near the *fovea*, the center of the visual field, where visual acuity is highest.

In addition to the visual projections to the midbrain and thalamus, there is a projection to the hypothalamus. This is important in the control of circadian rhythms, as will be discussed in Chap. 25.

In lower vertebrates, the two optic nerves cross (decussate) and supply the tectum and thalamus on the opposite side. In most of these animals the eyes are set on the side of the head, and there is little overlap of the two visual fields. In most mammals, however, the eyes are set forward in the head, and the two visual fields partially overlap. Associated with this is usually only a partial decussation of the optic nerve fibers. The situation in the human is depicted in Fig. 16.16. As can be seen, the ipsilateral fibers are those that arise from the outer (temporal) half of the retina, which receives stimuli from the inner (nasal) half of the visual field.

In the LGN, the inputs from the two eyes are kept separated from each other in a series of layers before being relayed to the visual cortex. Figure 16.17 shows how this

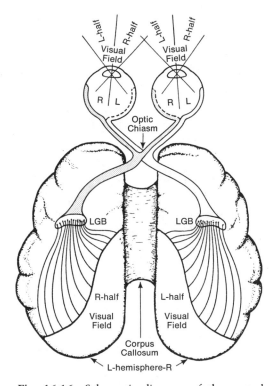

Fig. 16.16 Schematic diagram of the central visual pathway in the human. Note the projections of the visual fields onto the retinae, the partial decussation of the optic tracts, and the orderly projection from the lateral geniculate body (LG13) in the thalamus to the primary visual cortex in the occipital lobe. (From Popper and Eccles, 1977)

comes about. The LGN in primates consists of six layers. Ipsilateral retinal input is transmitted through layers 2, 3, and 5, whereas contralateral input is transmitted through layers 1, 4, and 6. Together, the six layers transmit a complete representation of the contralateral (i.e., temporal) visual hemifield, as is illustrated in Fig. 16.17. The lamination of the LGN appears to be necessary, for reasons not fully understood, to keep channels of information from the retina separate before they are combined in the cortex. A further example of this principle is that layers 1 and 2 contain large cells (magnocellular) and transmit mainly inputs from Y cells, whereas layers 3–6 have small cells (parvocellular), and

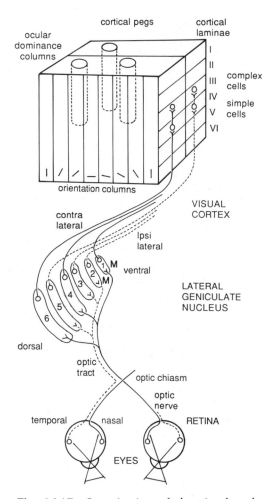

Fig. 16.17 Organization of the visual pathway. Anatomy of the pathway, beginning with the retina (below); the nasal and temporal parts of the optic nerve decussate in the optic chiasm, and connect to different laminae of the lateral geniculate nucleus in the thalamus as shown (uncrossed fibers project to layers 2, 3, and 5, whereas crossed fibers project to layers 1, 4, and 6). The thalamic relay cells project in turn to the primary visual cortex (above), with segregation of projections from ipsilateral and contralateral eyes to form ocular dominance columns (500 μm diameter). Cortical cells responding to different edge orientations of a light stimulus are organized into narrower columns (50 μm). A cortical unit containing both types of column is sometimes called a hypercolumn. A third type of column is the cortical peg, which stains richly for cytochrome oxidase; it is concerned with the processing of color information (see text).

transmit inputs mainly from X cells. The Y cell axons have large terminal ramifications correlated with their wide fields for movement detection, whereas the X cell axons have small terminal fields correlated with their role in mediating high visual acuity.

Visual Cortex

Figure 16.16 indicates that in humans the LGN projects to the occipital lobe of the cerebral cortex. This projection defines the primary visual cortex, called visual I (VI) by physiologists and area 17 by anatomists. As in other sensory systems, the visual pathway retains a precise topographical order, in which the map of the retina, and hence of the visual field, is projected onto the cortex. The fovea, where acuity is highest, occupies a large part of the cortical representation, similar to the way that regions of highest acuity dominate the maps in other sensory cortical areas (see for example the large areas for face and thumb in the somatosensory homunculus in Chap. 12).

Cortical Processing

The discovery by Stephen Kuffler in 1953 of the center–surround organization of ganglion cells not only was the basis for our understanding of the retina, but also provided the key to unlocking the mysteries of the cortex, which until then had seemed too complex to yield to single-unit analysis. Armed with this tool, David Hubel and Torsten Wiesel, in Kuffler's laboratory, took the first step centrally by recording from single cells in the LGN. They found little difference from the properties of ganglion cells. Emboldened, they tackled the visual cortex. By careful control of the visual stimuli, they were able to elucidate a logical sequence of processing of visual signals, and suggest some simple ways the cortex could be organized to accomplish this. Their work called forth an enormous outpouring of papers, which have extended and modified the original findings and concepts in many ways. For a generation the Hubel and Wiesel approach was the touchstone for virtually all work in the field. It not only focused speculations on the visual mechanisms underlying perception, but also has been an inspiration to those working in other parts of the nervous system as well, in showing that a complicated system can be made to be understandable. This was recognized by the awarding of the Nobel Prize in 1981.

The basic findings of Hubel and Wiesel begin with the fact that, in the primary visual cortex, the terminals of LGN input fibers are the only elements with center–surround antagonism. The simplest properties of cortical cells are responsiveness to a bar or edge of light, with a particular orientation, in a particular position in the visual field. Cells with these properties are called *simple cells*. More complicated are responses to a bar or edge, with a specific orientation, but placed anywhere in the visual field. Cells with this property, of signaling orientation independently of position, are called *complex cells*. Responses to bars of specific length and width are another type, initially called *hypercomplex;* some workers consider these to be variations of the other two types. In addition to these properties, cells can be classified as to whether they are driven by one eye or the other *(ocular dominance)* and by their sensitivity to movement.

With the same technique of making vertical electrode penetrations used by Mountcastle in somatosensory cortex (see Chap. 12), Hubel and Wiesel found that cells encountered in a single microelectrode penetration all tend to be driven by one eye or the other. This suggested that cells are organized in alternating *ocular dominance* columns. Similarly, it was found that all the cells in a penetration tend to be tuned to the same orientation of an edge or bar. These are called *orientation columns.*

A schematic diagram showing how, in an idealized manner, the two types of columns combine to form a *hypercolumn,* is depicted in the top diagram of Fig. 16.17. Each orientation column is actually a thin slab or wall, about 50 μm $\times$ 500 μm, which receives input mainly from one eye. An ocular dominance column is actually a larger slab or wall, 500 μm wide and extending through an indefinitely long repeated sequence of orientation columns. A hypercolumn is a pair of ocular dominance columns, containing all the input from both eyes in all possible orientations. A hypercolumn also contains other types of organizational units for other aspects of the visual stimulus; for example, as shown in Fig. 16.17, cells processing color information are grouped in columns called cortical pegs. The cells in these pegs have the types of single- and double-opponent color receptive fields illustrated previously in Fig. 16.15 (see also next section).

A Synthesis of Intracortical Mechanisms A synthesis of some of the main mechanisms reviewed above is provided by Fig. 16.18, which summarizes an experiment carried out by Charles Michael at Yale on the visual cortex of the monkey. Michael was interested in analyzing the series of steps involved in processing color. He found color columns, consisting of cells that are excited only by monochromatic (that is, a particular narrow wavelength band) light. Within this column, cells display in addition the several types of properties described by Hubel and Wiesel.

Figure 16.18 shows the results of an electrode penetration through such a color column. The vertical line in the center shows the locations of the 15 cells encountered in this penetration. The simplest type of response had a concentric center–surround receptive field. As shown by the example of cell 10, these were double-opponent color cells with green-on, red-off centers and the opposite surrounds. The remaining 11 cells encountered in the penetration all had similar orientation sensitivity to a bar stimulus, as shown by the short slanting lines. Also encountered in layer IV were two simple (S) cells which also had a double-opponent organization, with green-on, red-off center rectangle and the opposite flanking regions

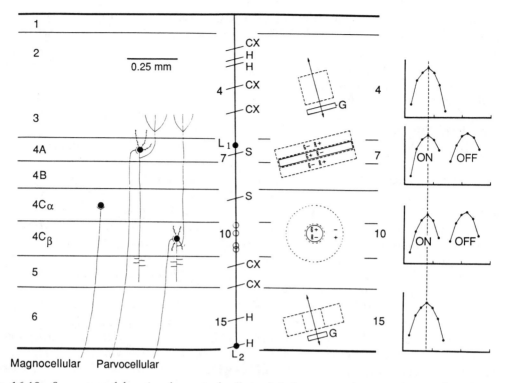

Fig. 16.18 Summary of functional types of cells and their presumed connections within the primary visual cortex of the monkey. *Center:* vertical line represents the electrode track, located by two lesion sites (L_1, L_2). Fifteen cells are shown by location along the track, together with their orientation selectivity and receptive field type (O, concentric; S, simple; CX, complex; H, hypercomplex). *Right:* Examples of receptive field types are shown for cells 4, 7, 10, and 15. G, green light; R, red light *Far right:* Spectral sensitivity curves for these cells are shown (ordinate: logarithm of reciprocal of threshold intensity; abscissa: spectral range, 400–700 nm). *Left:* Schematic drawing depicts main connections of magnocellular (luminance) and parvocellular (color) LGN axons onto stellate cells, and their presumed projections, according to Lund and Boothe. *Far left:* cortical layers 1–6. See text. (From Michael, 1985)

(see cell 7). Cell 4 is an example of a complex (CX) cell, responding to a moving green bar, and cell 15 is an example of a hypercomplex (CH) cell, also responding to a green bar which, however, consisted of a central activating region and two antagonistic flanks. On the far right are spectral sensitivity curves, showing that these cells had similar sensitivities for "on" and "off," as expected within a color column.

The intracortical connections that could mediate these properties are indicated in the left of the figure. Nearly all opponent color cells in the monkey LGN are found in the parvocellular layers, which project

mainly to sublamina 4A and to a lesser extent $4C_\beta$. It is tempting to speculate that the concentric and simple cells in this experiment were stellate cells located in these layers. The complex and hypercomplex cells were located in more superficial and deeper layers, activated perhaps by convergent connections from the stellate cells. By contrast, axons from the magnocellular laminae of the LGN, transmitting only luminance (light–dark) information, terminate mainly in sublamina $4C_\alpha$, and thus form a separate channel for processing in the cortex.

The evidence from these types of experiments thus supports the idea that there are parallel pathways in the cortex for processing different types of visual information, but that within each type there is serial processing through a series of intra-cortical steps. Thus, as indicated in the figure, there appear to be at least two parallel channels in the color pathways. Similarly, there are multiple channels for processing luminance input.

Anatomists have in fact found that LGN axons connect onto both simple and complex types of cells. Physiologists have found that LGN cells relaying X inputs connect to simple cells, whereas Y inputs connect to complex cells (review Table 16.2 for the properties of X and Y cells). Thus, there appear to be parallel connections to simple and complex cells, as summarized in Fig. 16.19. Thus, rather than parallel vs. serial, the processing of information within a cortical functional unit involves both types of connections. How they interact to give rise to the functional properties of cortical neurons is under active study at present. We will discuss further the synaptic organization of cortical neurons in Chap. 30.

Fig. 16.19 Circuit diagrams of synaptic organization of visual cortex, showing serial and parallel connections of inputs from thalamus, and multiple output pathways originating from cells in different layers.

COLUMN FOR SERIAL AND PARALLEL PROCESSING

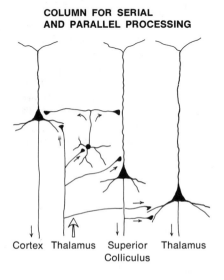

Cortex   Thalamus   Superior   Thalamus
                     Colliculus

Visual Cortical Areas

In the traditional view, the only precise retinotopic map was contained in area 17, and the surrounding bands of cortex (areas 18 and 19) were given over to nontopographical "association" functions. As in the auditory and somatosensory systems, recent studies indicate that there are more representations of the peripheral fields than previously suspected. According to David van Essen (1985) at least 15 specific visual areas have been identified in the monkey. These have been recognized by a variety of methods: cell lamination; synaptic connections; topographic representation; physiological properties of single neurons; behavioral effects of ablations. Some of these regions represent sequential processing of the visual input arriving from the lateral geniculate nucleus. Some of these in addition derive their functional specialization from parallel pathways, involving especially connections with the superior colliculus and a region of the thalamus called the pulvinar, which is especially large in primates and humans.

The significance of these different areas is that they provide for abstraction, enhancement, and mixing of specific visual submodalities. As earlier emphasized in Table 16.1, vision is not one sense but many, and the different cortical areas give expression of this. Deyoe and van Essen (1987) have summarized some of the best understood areas and their submodalities in the diagram of Fig. 16.20. We see, first, that color information arrives from parvocellular LGN and is processed through V1 and V2 to V4. Stimulus orientation, however, arrives in V1 from both parvo and magnocellular LGN, and is processed through V1 and V2 to V4. Stimulus orientation, however, arrives in V1 from both parvo and magnocellular LGN, and is processed through V2 and V3 to V4 and a region referred to as MT. A similar sequence applies to binocular disparity information. Information about direction of movement, by contrast, arrives in V1 from magnocel-

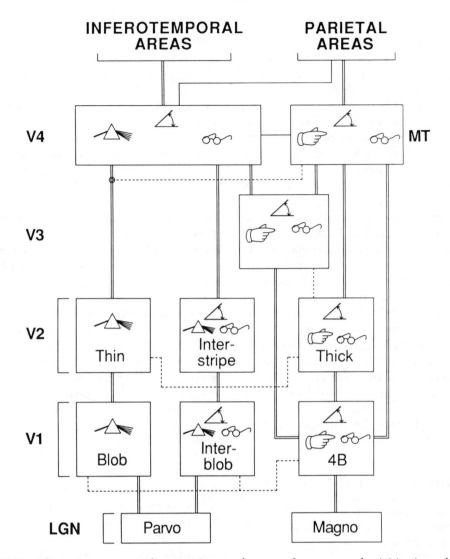

Fig. 16.20 The major anatomical connections and neuronal response selectivities in early visual areas of the macaque monkey. Icons are placed in each compartment to symbolize a high incidence of cells showing selectivity for stimulus wavelength (prisms), orientation (angle symbols), direction (pointing hands), or binocular disparity (spectacles). The lateral geniculate nucleus (LGN) is indicated with its parvocellular and magnocellular subdivisions. Subdivisions of cortical area V1 include layer 4B plus the dark "blobs" and pale "interblobs" of the superficial layers revealed by cytochrome oxidase histochemistry. The same technique reveals a tripartite subdivision of area V2, including a set of thick and thin dark stripes and an interposed set of pale "interstripes." Double-line connections denote robust pathways; single line connections denote weaker pathways; dashed lines denote pathways only tentatively identified. Higher level processing in inferotemporal and parietal cortical areas is discussed in Chap. 30. (From Deyoe and van Essen, 1987)

lular LGN, and is transferred directly, and also through V2, to MT above.

It can be seen that, in general, a given area is not specialized for a single function. It may have cells preponderantly tuned to a given submodality, such as color in V4 or motion in MT, but other submodalities are integrated with that information as well. Thus, each area provides for a unique combination of specific submodalities. This parallel array of abstracted information is then fed into the higher visual centers. As indicated in Fig. 16.20, the two main streams for this information are into the inferotemporal and parietal regions, where complex processing related to the qualities and the spatial relations of objects in visual space is carried out. We will discuss these mechanisms of higher level vision in Chapter 30.

III
Motor Systems

17

Introduction: The Nature of Motor Function

Animal experience begins with information about the world that flows in through sensory organs and sensory pathways, as discussed in the previous section. However, the behavior of an animal depends on how it combines that information with its internal states and drives in order to do something. Doing something requires motor organs and the nervous circuits to control them, which together form what is called *motor systems*.

Motor systems bring about movement, and the importance of movement has always been apparent to students of animal life. The early Greek philosophers recognized that the ability to move is the essence of being alive. Furthermore, the ability of an organism to move itself about and perform actions on its environment, under control of a nervous system, is one of the crucial features that distinguishes animals from plants. In the evolution of animal life, different motor abilities have been among the chief agents for the diversity of adaptations that characterize different species. Motor abilities have been no less important in human evolution. The making of fire, development of tools, invention of the wheel, and use of weapons for hunting and implements for farming—all involved the elaboration and extension of the human motor apparatus. Finally, the capacities for speech, writing, and artistic expression are all motor activities.

The study of this amazing array of activities is a fascinating one for neurobiologists. In one respect, the study is easy, because motor actions are observable and can be measured. To get much farther than this, however, is very difficult. One of the main problems has been to identify basic units of nervous organization relative to motor function. When reflexes were recognized in the course of the nineteenth century, it was hoped that the reflex arc might serve as a basic functional unit. This has been true to some extent, as we shall see in Chap. 19. However, modern studies are leading toward a wider view in which motor organization shares many of the basic principles that characterize the general organization of nerve circuits throughout the nervous system.

A related problem in approaching motor systems is that they may seem quite different from the sensory systems discussed in the preceding section. After all, information flows *into* the organism (through *afferent* pathways) in sensory systems, whereas it flows *out* of the organism (through *effer-*

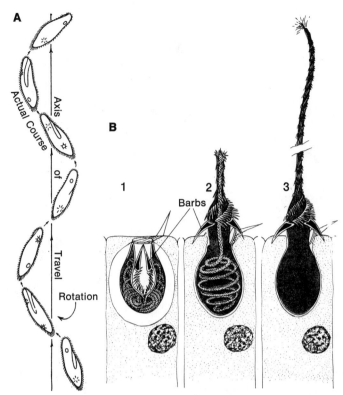

Fig. 17.1 Specialized motor structures of primitive animals. **A.** Locomotion of *Paramecium* by ciliary beating. The animal progresses in a spiral manner because of the asymmetry of the body. **B.** The nematocyst of *Hydra*. This single-cell organelle is discharged in the manner shown. Different nematocysts are specialized for attachment and for stinging (killing or defense). (A from Storer, 1943; B from Wells, 1968)

ent pathways) in motor systems. Furthermore, the peripheral motor organs—glands and muscles—appear to be radically different from the receptors that receive sensory stimuli. However, at the *cellular* level, glands and muscles represent logical variations on the basic cellular plan discussed in Chap. 3. The *junctions* between these motor organs and the nerve fibers that innervate them are similar in principle to synapses between neurons, and between neurons and receptors (Chaps. 2 and 4, and Section II). Finally, motor pathways are organized into *circuits* along many of the same general principles as are sensory pathways.

These similarities mean that we can approach the study of motor systems using the same logical approach to basic mechanisms that was applied to sensory systems.

The basic mechanisms operate at similar levels: the peripheral *organs,* the *neural circuits,* and the *behavior* of the whole organism.

Effector Organs

In sensory systems there are different types of sensory receptors. Similarly, in motor systems there are different types of motor organs. Because their actions have effects, we also refer to them as *effectors* or *effector organs.*

In very primitive animals, effectors may be present in rather special forms. Thus, the motor activity of the single-cell *Paramecium* involves the beating of *cilia,* which propels it in the manner shown in Fig. 17.1A. Motile cilia are, of course, present

Table 17.1 Types of motor organs

	Examples	
	Invertebrate	Vertebrate
Glands		
Endocrine	neuroendocrine cells	neuroendocrine cells
		hypothalamus
	neurohemal organs	pituitary gland
	endocrine organs	endocrine organs
Exocrine		
internal	goblet cells (mucus)	goblet cells (mucus)
	digestive glands	digestive glands
	salivary glands (enzymes, silk, jelly)	–
external (integument)	slime-secreting cells	sweat, sebaceous glands
	adhesive-secreting cells	–
	pheromone-secreting cells	pheromone-secreting cells
	toxin-secreting cells	toxin-secreting cells
	ink glands	–
	chromatophores	chromatophores
Muscles		
Smooth muscle	(rare)	visceral (involuntary)
Striated muscle		
cardiac	–	heart
skeletal	gut, trunk, appendages	trunk and appendages
Modified muscle	–	electroplaque organ
Cilia	numerous small organisms	lining of various organs
Self-contained organs	nematocysts	–

on many types of cells throughout the invertebrates, but in general they are not under nervous control. In the coelenterate *Hydra*, one of the main effector organs is the *nematocyst* (arising from the cnidoblast; hence, the class name, *Cnidaria*). The nematocyst is released on contact by an appropriate foreign organism. The local sensory stimulus is sufficient to trigger discharge (see Fig. 17.1B), without intervention of the nerve net of the *Hydra*. This has the advantage of an immediate response, but the disadvantage is that the discharge cannot be incorporated by nervous control into integrated and purposive acts of the whole organism.

Among higher metazoans the two main types of effector organs are *glands* and *muscles*. Corresponding to these are the two main types of effector (motor) actions, *glandular secretion* and *muscle contraction*. It has been said (somewhat irrever-

ently) that the only things an animal can do are squeeze a muscle and squirt a juice! It is true that glands and muscles are the characteristic effector organs of most invertebrates and vertebrates. However, as Table 17.1 shows, this simple statement hides a wealth of diversity. To begin with, glands are divided into two main classes (endocrine and exocrine). Within these two classes is an enormous variety of specialized types; Table 17.1 lists only a few examples. Similarly, muscles are divided into two main types, smooth and striated, and these are deployed in many different ways. Finally, there are other types of effectors; these include, for example, the electroplaque organ, composed of modified muscle cells, which we discussed in Chap. 2. Thus, as Table 17.1 illustrates, animals can send shocks, spin silk, change color, and do a number of things not adequately accounted for by the traditional functions of simple glandular secretion or muscular contraction.

With this perspective on effector organs, let us consider briefly the functional properties of glands and muscles.

Glands

The cellular basis for the secretory activity of gland cells has been described in Chap. 3. It will be recalled that in secretory cells the transitional endoplasmic reticulum of the cytoplasm is grouped in stacks, called the Golgi complex, where the specific proteins are stored, and packaged into secretory granules. The granules are released when the cell receives its appropriate stimulus. The features vary considerably, depending on the particular type of secretory activity. For example, secretory granules may not be demonstrable in the electron microscope in some cells, particularly those that continuously secrete small amounts. On the other hand, granules tend to be more prominent in cells that store the secretions and release them intermittently in massive amounts. Secretory cells exhibit variations in fine structure, reflecting these differences in function.

Types of Glands

As previously noted, there are two main classes of glands.

Endocrine. These glands manufacture hormones which are secreted into the bloodstream and act on distant cells and organs within the body. Some consist of nerve cells and their processes that, in addition to their "neuronal" properties, such as synaptic actions or impulse generation, are also modified to secrete hormones. Such cells are termed variously *neurosecretory* or *neuroendocrine* cells. They appear to have arisen very early in animal evolution. For example, some cells in the nerve net of *Hydra* contain large neurosecretory granules. It is believed that these granules contain hormones that are secreted during growth, budding, and regeneration of branches, and are involved in activating or controlling those processes. An example of an invertebrate neurosecretory cell is shown in Fig. 17.2A.

Neurosecretion is a good mechanism for mediating hormonal effects, particularly in small animals, because fibers can extend from the central nervous system to make close contacts with target organs. In large animals, however, this process becomes unwieldy. Some neuroendocrine cells are therefore grouped in peripheral ganglia, and act on their target organs by discharging their hormones into the bloodstream or other body fluid. These ganglia, in invertebrates, are referred to as *neurohemal* organs. This mode of action, to be most effective, requires a well-developed circulatory system, which seems to be why neurohemal cells and organs have arisen later in evolution. They are prominent mainly in annelids and arthropods. In vertebrates, counterparts of the neurohemal organ are found in the hypothalamus, posterior pituitary, and adrenal medulla (see Chap. 24). An example of a neurosecretory cell of the hypothalamus is shown in Fig. 17.2B.

In higher metazoans there are, throughout the body, specific cells grouped in glands that do not depend on direct innervation for their control. Secretions of these cells are controlled by blood-borne factors arising from distant nerve cells, from other glands, or from target organs. Such cells may be grouped in special endocrine organs, like the thyroid or adrenal cortex, or be found within other organs, such as the kidney or gonads. Although a full account of the endocrine system falls outside the scope of this book, we will often refer to the various endocrine organs in the context of their ultimate neural control through the hypothalamus and pituitary gland.

Exocrine. In contrast to endocrine cells is the *exocrine* type of secretory cell. Characteristically these cells are grouped together to form a gland, and the substance is carried away in a duct. Glands of this type perform a variety of functions in the

A. PLANARIA

Neurosecretory
Granules

B. RAT

Neurosecretory
Granules

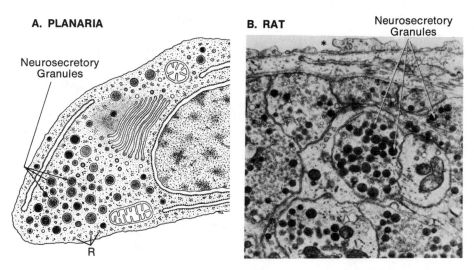

Fig. 17.2 Neurosecretory cells. **A.** Neurosecretory cell of a worm *(Planaria)*. Note variety of vesicle sizes and contents, including large neurosecretory granules. R, ribosomes. **B.** Neurohypophysis (posterior lobe) of the rat pituitary gland. Note nerve terminals containing large dense-core neurosecretory granules and small clear vesicles; note also fenestrated capillary wall, permitting passage of secreted materials into bloodstream (asterisk). (A from Lentz, 1968; B from P. Orkand and S. L. Palay, in Bloom and Fawcett, 1975)

body. Some are involved in nonnervous functions, such as the digestive glands of the gastrointestinal system. Most, however, are under some degree of nervous control. This control is exerted through the autonomic nervous system, which we will consider in the next chapter.

We generally think of the glands of the body as involved mostly in housekeeping chores, helping to maintain the constancy of the internal environment *(milieu interieur)* and enabling it to respond to stress. These are indeed important functions. However, as indicated in Table 17.1, many glands are parts of the motor apparatus through which the animal operates on the external world. The neural control of these glands characteristically involves sensory recognition of the appropriate releasing stimuli and precise timing of secretion within a sequence of behavioral acts.

Excitation–Secretion Coupling

In glands under neural control, stimulation occurs by means of a neurotransmitter liberated from the terminals of the motor axon. The neurotransmitter generally brings about a depolarization of the gland cell, similar to the endplate potential in a muscle. The depolarization gives rise to an action potential in some gland cells, as was pointed out in Chap 6; in others the electrical response consists only of the graded postsynaptic potential.

What is the linkage between this depolarization and the release of secretory substances? This linkage has been termed *excitation–secretion coupling* as mentioned previously, in analogy with excitation–contraction coupling in muscle. In the gland cell, the coupling usually involves the following sequence: depolarization of the membrane; activation of second messenger systems; rise in intracellular Ca^{2+}; movement of superficial granules to plasmalemma; fusion of vesicle membrane and plasmalemma and release of secretory substances. The sequence is similar to the steps controlling release of neurotransmitter at a chemical synapse. In fact, it seems very likely that the basic mechanism of excitation–secretion coupling became

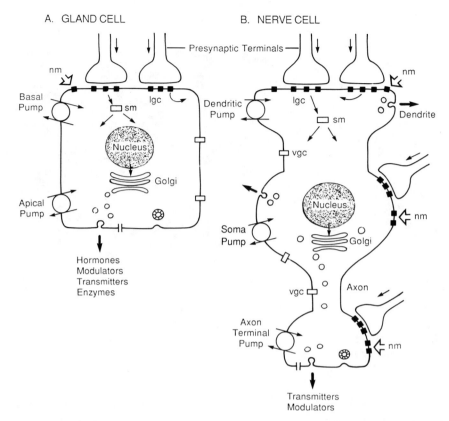

Fig. 17.3 Comparison between cellular organization of a gland cell and a neuron. Note that the gland cell is polarized, with a basal (receptive) and apical (effector) region. The neuron is also polarized, from dendrite to axon, but receptive and effector sites may be distributed widely over the surface. Most of the cellular elements are common to the two types. Abbreviations: nm, neuromodulator; sm, second messenger; lgc, ligand-gated channels; vgc, voltage-gated channels.

adapted in evolution for synaptic transmission. The similarities between excitation–secretion mechanisms in a prototypical gland cell and nerve cell are summarized in Fig. 17.3.

Skeletal Muscle

Like gland cells, muscle cells owe their properties to specializations of their cytostructure. Also like gland cells, these structures are part of the basic equipment of all cells, but developed to a higher degree. In the case of muscle, the properties reside in two filamentous proteins, *actin* and *myosin.* These proteins are widely distributed in body cells, and subserve a variety of functions related to cell movements, such as

formation of pseudopodia and the cell movements that occur during development (Chap. 9). In muscle, these proteins and their mechanism of interaction have become specialized for the specific tasks of producing movement, not just of individual cells, but of whole organs.

We know most about these proteins and their mechanisms in *skeletal muscles,* those that move bones and joints. Skeletal muscle is also called *striated,* or *striped,* muscle, because under the light microscope the individual muscle fibers have a banded appearance. The bands reflect the division of each fiber into a series of *sarcomeres,* which are the contractile units of the fiber. Each sarcomere is composed of a set of myofilaments; the myofilaments are actin or

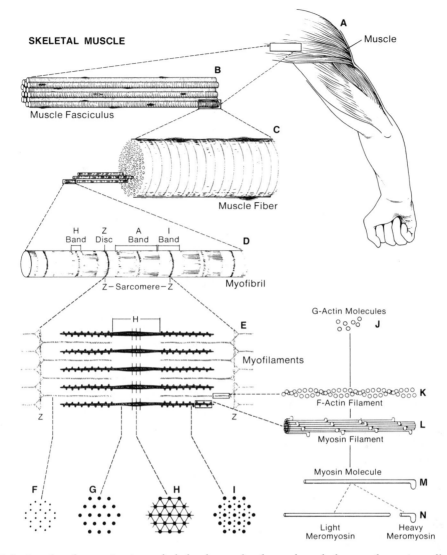

SKELETAL MUSCLE

Fig. 17.4 Levels of organization of skeletal muscle, from the whole muscle to its cellular and molecular constituents. (From Bloom and Fawcett, 1975)

myosin, organized in a precise overlapping array. These features are depicted in Fig. 17.4.

Sliding-Filament Model

The explanation for how the overlapping actin and myosin molecules bring about contraction is embodied in the *sliding-filament model*. This was first conceived in 1954 by two independent groups of workers, Hugh Huxley and Jean Hanson in London, and Andrew Huxley and Robert Nied-

ergerke in Cambridge, England. Their work was initially based on observations in the light microscope, and has since been confirmed and greatly elaborated by many studies.

The essence of the model is illustrated in Fig. 17.4. It had previously been speculated that contraction might come about by a shortening or crumpling of the individual filaments, but this was replaced by the idea that the actin (K) and myosin (L) filaments slide along between each other. This sliding

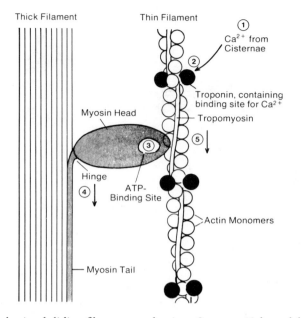

Fig. 17.5   Molecular basis of sliding filament mechanism. See text. (Adapted from Huxley, in Lehninger, 1975)

brings about changes in the widths of some of the bands (D), without changing the lengths of the filaments themselves.

The molecular mechanism which has been postulated to cause the sliding of the actin filaments past the myosin filaments is illustrated in Fig. 17.5. Actin filaments contain tropomyosin and troponin, in addition to actin. In the relaxed state, tropomyosin inhibits the myosin attachment sites on the G-actin filaments. Also, in the relaxed state, free Ca^{2+} is very low around the filaments. Muscle activation begins with release of Ca^{2+} ①, which binds to the troponin. This induces a conformational change in the troponin ②, which exposes the myosin binding sites of the B-actin subunits. The attachment of myosin ③ forms a *force-generating complex*. This induces a conformation change in the heavy meromyosin head, and a consequent rotation at the hinge between the head and the rest of the myosin molecule ④. The rotation generates the *power stroke* that causes the actin to be displaced ⑤.

The energy for these movements is supplied by ATP. The myosin heads have binding sites for ATP. It is believed that the ATP may be bound in the form of ADP + P with the energy of the phosphate bond transferred in some way to the myosin head to hold it in the *energized* conformation (Fig. 17.5). At the end of the power stroke, the myosin head assumes its *deenergized* form when the ADP + P are released; they are replaced by new ATP, which causes the myosin head to return to its energized conformation.

Excitation–Contraction Coupling

There remains to account for the initial release of Ca^{2+} that sets this molecular machinery in motion. The full sequence of these events is depicted in Fig. 17.6. In some muscles, usually smaller and more slowly contracting fibers, the graded endplate potential (EPP) ② may be the only electrical response. In large and rapidly contracting muscles, an action potential ③ is set up by the EPP. The action potential propagates along the muscle membrane in essentially the same manner as the action potential in a nerve. The depolarization spreads rapidly into the interior of the mus-

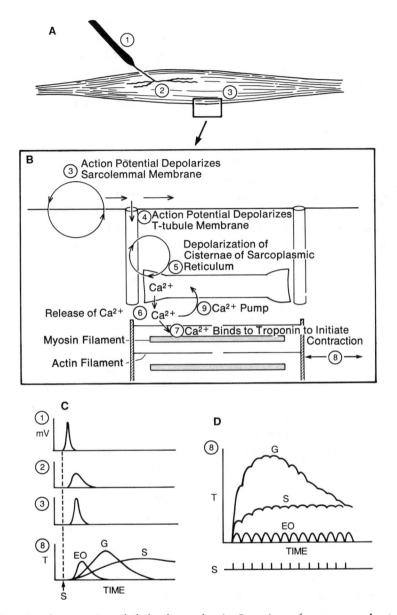

Fig. 17.6 Functional properties of skeletal muscle. **A.** Overview of neuromuscular unit. Steps in excitation–contraction coupling begin with nerve impulse ①, which activates neuromuscular junction to release ACh and set up endplate potential (EPP) ②. This triggers the muscle action potential ③. **B.** Further steps in muscle include depolarization of T-tubules ④, depolarization of sarcoplasmic reticulum ⑤, release of Ca^{2+} ⑥, binding of Ca^{2+} to troponin ⑦, to initiate contraction ⑧, and pumping of Ca^{2+} into sarcoplasmic reticulum ⑨. There is recent evidence that the inositol-lipid system may be involved in step ⑥. **C.** Time sequence at different steps: nerve impulse ①, EPP ②, muscle impulse ③, and muscle contractions ⑧. In ⑧, examples are shown of muscle tensions (T) developed by a single twitch in three types of muscle: extraocular muscle (EO), gastrocnemius (G), and soleus (S). Time of initial stimulus (s) to nerve is shown by vertical dashed line. **D.** Muscle contractions in response to tetanic stimulation (s) in the three types of muscle. See text.

cle fiber through a special membrane system called the *T-tubule system* ④. The T-tubules are in close apposition (30nm) to the membrane of the sarcoplasmic reticulum. Depolarization of the tubules brings about depolarization of the cisternae ⑤, which causes release of free calcium ⑥ into the sarcoplasm surrounding the muscle myofilaments. The Ca^{2+} binds to troponin ⑦ and initiates the contractile events ⑧ depicted in Fig. 17.5. The Ca^{2+} is restored to the cisternae by a very active *Ca pump* ⑨.

The whole sequence of events shown in Fig. 17.6 brings about a transformation from the electrical signal in the muscle membrane to a mechanical change in the myofilaments. This sequence is referred to as *excitation–contraction coupling*. It is analogous to the sequence of *excitation–secretion coupling* that takes place in gland cells.

Muscle Properties

In contrast to these rapid events, the mechanical movements of the sliding filaments are slower. The tensions produced in different types of muscle are shown in (⑧) in Fig. 17.6. Note that the peak latencies (times to reach the peaks) vary by a factor of 10 in these examples, reflecting different functions of the muscles.

Extraocular muscles are specialized for fine, rapid movements, without generating great tensions (see diagram). Muscles of the trunk and limbs are generally of two types: fast and slow. *Fast muscles* are specialized for fast contractions that generate large tensions. These are the muscles used in running short distances, such as the 100-meter dash. A well-trained sprinter will scarcely take a breath over this short distance; during this short time, energy to the muscle is supplied by anaerobic glycolysis within the muscle, and the muscle is accordingly poor in vascularization and mitochondria, and looks pale to the naked eye. *Slow muscles,* by contrast, are specialized to contract slowly and generate more modest tensions, but over long periods of time. These are the muscles used in running

longer distances, like the mile or the marathon. Over these longer times, oxygen must be continually supplied to the muscle so that ATP can be generated by the Krebs cycle, and the muscle fiber is accordingly richly vascularized and contains many mitochondria, and looks red. The gastrocnemius (G) is a mixed fast and slow muscle, whereas the soleus (S) is a slow muscle (Fig. 17.6C, ⑧).

Summation

When muscles are brought into play, it is usually not by a single nerve impulse but by a train of impulses. The individual muscle twitches, being slower than the nerve impulses, start to build up on top of each other as the impulse frequency increases, until they fuse into a relatively smooth plateau (see EO, G, and S in Fig. 17.6C). This maintained contractile state is called a muscle tetanus. For the reasons discussed above, red muscles are better able to sustain tetanic contractions than are pale muscles (see diagram). Muscles can show complex grading of their tetanic contractions with different frequencies; we will discuss an example in invertebrates below.

Two important principles emerge from these properties of muscles. First, brief nerve impulses give rise to prolonged muscle responses. Thus, a single brief neural event can serve to trigger a longer-lasting mechanical event in another cell. This could apply to actin—myosin interactions in nerve cells as well as in muscle cells, and it applies also to secretory events in nerve cells as well as in gland cells (see above). Second, during the long-lasting mechanical responses in a skeletal muscle, repeated neural inputs find the muscle fiber at different stages of contraction and relaxation. The summation that occurs is therefore complex, and very frequency-dependent. High-frequency tetanic stimulation, summed over many fibers in a muscle, is the basis for the generation of maximal muscle power. Medium-frequency contractions, providing for complex summation among subgroups of fibers with similar properties at different frequencies, are the basis for movements requiring precision. These two principles underlie much of the diversity of motor behavior which we will encounter in the ensuing chapters.

Smooth Muscle

For the student of the nervous system, smooth muscle cells are of particular interest, because they share many contractile properties with neurons and thus give insight into these properties of neurons. Knowledge is limited, however, because of inherent difficulties in working with smooth muscle: the cells tend to be small and thin; they form syncytial networks, often intertwined within other complex structures (like the gut or blood vessels); they characteristically undergo spontaneous contractions, which make a very unstable target for a probing microelectrode.

Membrane Properties

In order to circumvent the difficulties of working on smooth muscle, investigators have developed preparations of isolated muscle cells for physiological analysis. A single smooth muscle cell from the stomach wall is shown in Fig. 17.7A. In the middle panel (b), a pulse of ACh was ejected from the micropipette, causing contraction of the cell. ACh causes a slow depolarization of the cell, giving rise to a discharge of impulses, as shown in Fig. 17.7B. What is the mechanism of this response?

The response begins with the binding of ACh to muscarinic receptors in the membrane. These are distributed widely over the cell membrane; there is not a well-defined endplate, as in the case of skeletal muscle. The slow depolarization is characteristic of the slow excitatory responses to ACh mediated by muscarinic receptors. For many years it has been believed that this slow depolarization is due to a simple increase in membrane conductance for cations (Na, Ca, K) in a relatively nonspecific manner. Recent experiments with patch recordings have indeed confirmed that this mechanism is present; ACh evokes a depolarization of the membrane that is associated with an overall increase in input conductance; under voltage clamp, this response to ACh is associated with an inward current, due to Na and Ca. However, ACh

Fig. 17.7 Contractile properties of smooth muscle. **A.** Video images of an isolated gastric smooth muscle cell: (left) in normal Ringer's; (middle) 15 seconds after pressure ejection of ACh from pipette tip at lower right; note vigorous contraction; (right) recovery after 4 minutes. **B.** Electrical response of another cell to the cholinergic agonist muscarine. The trace shows intracellular recording of slow burst of Ca^{2+} action potentials which generate the muscle contraction (cf. Fig. 17.8). (From Sims et al., 1986)

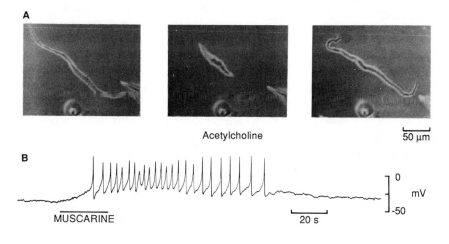

A

Acetylcholine   50 μm

B

MUSCARINE   20 s   0 / mV / -50

has other actions through muscarinic receptors as well. One is to suppress spontaneous Ca^{2+}-activated K^+ channels; another is to close K^+ channels, thus turning off an M current (cf. Chap. 8). The M channels can also be modulated by peptides such as substance P and LHRH. The slow depolarization activates voltage-dependent Ca^{2+} channels, which generate the impulse discharge. This influx of Ca^{2+} then contributes to excitation–contraction coupling.

Excitation–Contraction Coupling

The mechanism of excitation–contraction coupling differs in certain respects from that in skeletal muscle. Since there is no endplate, there is no endplate potential (see Fig. 17.8). The muscarinic receptors are coupled to second messenger systems in the membrane ③. One of the main systems is the inositol phospholipids ④ discussed previously in Chap. 8. Activation of the second messenger system has two effects. One is to change the conductance of channel proteins in the membrane, leading to depolarization of the membrane and entry of Ca^{2+} ⑤, as discussed above. The second is to produce an increase in internal free Ca^{2+} through the second messenger ④. The rise in free Ca^{2+} from both these sources activates calcium/calmodulin (Ca/CaM), which is similar to troponin C in skeletal muscle ⑦. Ca/CaM activates the enzyme myosin light-chain kinase, which phosphorylates the regulatory subunit of the myosin head, so that it binds actin ⑧, and brings about contraction.

Slow Contractile Properties

Like skeletal muscle, smooth muscle contains actin and, in smaller amounts, myosin, but they are not organized into repeating sarcomere units (see Fig. 17.8). The contractile mechanism itself is believed to involve sliding of the actin past the myosin, essentially as in the sliding-filament model. Other types of filaments are also present in smooth muscle, which may provide for additional force generation, as well as attachment to the cell wall.

By virtue of these adaptations, smooth muscle shows special contractile properties. The contractions, compared with those of skeletal muscle, are slow and sustained, lasting for seconds or minutes (or even hours or days) instead of 10–100 msec as in the case of vertebrate skeletal muscle. An example is shown in Fig. 17.7. These slow contractile properties are important for a wide range of functions, such as maintaining the tonus of blood vessel walls. The rate of sliding of the actin and myosin filaments is 100–1000 times slower than that of skeletal muscle, although the force of contraction reached is nearly as great. The rate of energy consumption due to ATP hydrolysis is 5–10 times lower to reach the same force, so the slow contractions can be maintained for long periods of time with minimal energy demands or fatigue. Thus, smooth and skeletal muscle can be seen to be each beautifully adapted for distinctly different motor tasks.

Rhythmic Activity

The electrical activity underlying the excitation of smooth muscles varies considerably. Some smooth muscles, such as those in the gut, undergo spontaneous contractions. These are due to periodic slow depolarizing waves which generate action potentials in the fibers. The effect of nerve stimulation is to modify and coordinate this spontaneous rhythm. The rhythm is due to both inward Na^+ and Ca^{2+} currents, that generate the slow depolarizations and the spikes, and outward K^+ currents, including K^+ currents activated by Ca^{2+}, that repolarize the membrane and control the slow rate of impulse firing. Some smooth muscles are active only when stimulated by their autonomic nerve supply. Throughout the Animal Kingdom, smooth muscles are particularly sensitive to modulation by neuropeptides. This is an important property shared with neurons; many of the neuropeptides were in fact first identified by their actions in smooth muscles of

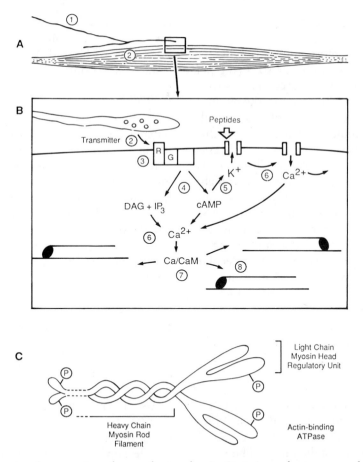

Fig. 17.8 Functional properties of smooth muscle. **A.** Overview of neuromuscular unit. Steps in excitation–contraction coupling begin with nerve impulse ①, which activates diffuse release of transmitter ②. **B.** Further steps in muscle include activation of a receptor ③, which stimulates or inhibits a second messenger system (inositol-lipid or cAMP system: ④). This may cause closing of M-type K^+ channels ⑤, which leads to membrane depolarization and generation of a Ca^{2+} action potential ⑥ (A. Marty, personal communication). Alternatively, the second messengers may cause an increase in free Ca^{2+} in the cytosol, activating Ca/CaM ⑦ contractile apparatus ⑧. **C.** Molecular conformation of myosin, consisting of heavy and light chains, and actin-binding sites.

the gut. We will discuss further the way these molecular properties, combined with the actions of synaptic circuits, generate smooth muscle rhythms, in the next chapter.

In summary, smooth muscles carry out slow motor functions that may be precise or powerful, and neuronal circuits that control them must be organized to control these functions. At the molecular level the interactions of actin and myosin in smooth muscle cells serve as a valuable model for understanding the contractile properties of neurons, especially with regard to the motility of axonal growth cones (Chap. 9), cell migration during early development (Chap. 9), axonal regeneration and sprouting in response to injury (Chap. 9), and synaptic plasticity underlying these processes and memory (Chap. 29). We may conclude that, just as the neuron can be viewed as a modified secretory cell (Fig. 17.3), so can it also, with equal validity, be viewed as a modified smooth muscle cell.

Invertebrate Muscle

In invertebrates, most muscles, whether skeletal or visceral, are of the striated type. The organization of the sarcomeres is similar to that in vertebrates, and the sliding-filament model seems to apply in general. There are a number of variations on this basic plan, however, reflecting the diverse ways that muscle is employed. This extends from the extremely rapidly contracting flight muscles of insects to the very slowly contracting "catch" muscles of molluscs. The adaptations to this range of functions involve such differences as the ratios of actin to myosin filaments, details of molecular composition of the actin and myosin, and the distribution of T-tubules and mitochondria (see below).

Diversity of Muscles, Junctions, and Nerves

From the foregoing discussion it can be appreciated that muscle fibers vary considerably in their structure and their functional properties. The same may be said of the junctions between the muscle fibers and their motor nerves. The neuromuscular junctions of skeletal muscles have a specialized structure, as we discussed in Chap. 2; in contrast, the motor nerves to smooth muscles terminate in free nerve endings among the fibers, with little evidence of special contacts.

All these differences mean that there is actually a rich variety of combinations of properties that the peripheral motor apparatus can have. The variety is largest in invertebrates, consistent with the fact that invertebrates have more complexity of neural control in the periphery, in contrast to vertebrates with their tendency toward central control. A particularly good preparation for demonstrating these properties is found in the limb muscles of crustaceans. Work on the neural control of these muscles began with the pioneering experiments of Kees Wiersma and Graham Hoyle, and has been carried forward by many workers in differ-

ent disciplines. We will summarize some of the principles that have emerged, drawing on studies of Harold Atwood and his colleagues in Toronto.

Muscle Properties

A single muscle may contain fibers with different structures and properties. As shown in Fig. 17.9 (top), the opener muscle of the crab *Chionoecetes* contains fibers that are long, intermediate, or short, according to the lengths of their sarcomeres; these types vary in the lengths of their myofilaments and the distribution of the T-tubule system. Associated with this structural diversity are differences in the electrical properties of the muscle membrane (Fig. 17.9, middle). The fibers with long sarcomeres show mostly graded responses to electrical stimulation. Fibers with intermediate-length sarcomeres respond with partially regenerative depolarizations. Only the fibers with short sarcomeres generate large, brief action potentials.

Also illustrated are three types of mechanical properties, varying from slow to rapid development of tension when the muscle contracts. In these muscles, therefore, there is a close correlation of structural, electrical, and mechanical properties. In other muscles, however, there may be diversity of function without apparent structural differences. These studies indicate that the muscles themselves provide the basis for considerable diversity of functional properties.

Innervation Pattern

The neuromuscular junction is the second site of functional diversity. The vertebrate muscle fiber receives its excitatory input from the branch of a single motoneuron, but invertebrate fibers may be innervated by more than one nerve fiber (*polyneuronal innervation*). The innervation pattern of the opener muscle of the crab is outlined in Fig. 17.10. There is a large-diameter, fast-conducting axon, and a small-diameter, slowly conducting axon. The former mainly innervates the fast-acting, more ex-

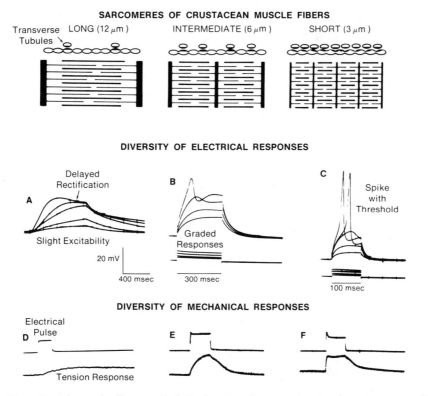

Fig. 17.9 Diversity of muscle fibers and their functional properties, in the opener muscle of the crab, *Chionoecetes,* and lobster muscle fibers (E,F). Three types of muscle, with long, intermediate, and short sarcomeres. *Middle* (A-C): different electrical responses of the three muscle cell types to step pulse of depolarizing current. *Bottom* (D-F): correspondingly different mechanical responses of the three muscle cell types to a step pulse. Note contrast between graded excitability and slow tension of the long-sarcomere fibers, and action potential generation and rapid twitch of the short-sarcomere fibers. (From Atwood, 1977)

citable muscle fibers, whereas the latter tends to innervate the more slowly acting, less excitable fibers.

Functional Patterns

Repetitive nerve stimulation of the fast axon sets up, initially, a large EPP that gives rise to an action potential. As stimulation continues, the EPP decreases in amplitude, and the action potential fails. As discussed above, the repetitive stimulation is called *tetanization,* and the decrease of the response is called *depression*. In contrast, repetitive stimulation of the slow axon first elicits only a small, slow, graded potential response. However, as tetanization proceeds, the response begins to increase in size, and

may even give rise to an action potential (see Fig. 17.10). This increase in response is called *facilitation*.

These results are mainly due to differences in the mobilization and release of the neurotransmitter glutamate at the neuromuscular junction. They demonstrate that the functions of these synapses are exquisitely dependent on the duration and pattern of nerve stimulation. This property of "*use dependence*" is an expression of synaptic plasticity, one that is believed to be important in the synaptic mechanisms underlying memory and learning (Chap. 29).

In addition to these excitatory axons, there is also an inhibitory axon that supplies all the muscle fibers in the opener

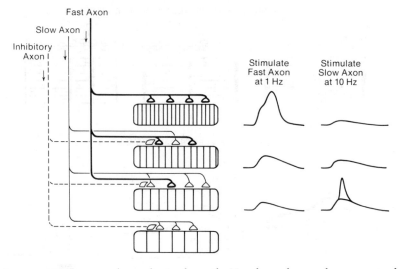

Fig. 17.10 Innervation pattern of muscles in the crab. Use-dependence of neuromuscular junctions at fast and slow muscles. On the right are shown representative recordings of the electrical responses recorded intracellularly in a muscle fiber during electrical stimulation of the fast axon at 1 Hz and the slow axon at 10 Hz. (After Atwood, 1973)

muscle. The terminals of this axon have been shown to make two kinds of inhibitory synapses (Fig. 17.11). One is onto the muscle itself; by this means, the axon produces an inhibitory *post*synaptic potential (IPSP) in the muscle fiber. The other is onto an excitatory terminal; by this means, an IPSP is produced in the terminal. We say

that this causes *pre*synaptic inhibition of the muscle fiber. The inhibitory transmitter is γ-aminobutyric acid (GABA), which causes an increase in Cl⁻ conductance of the postsynaptic membrane.

We thus can see that the excitatory and inhibitory nerve terminals actually form, together with the muscle endplate, a kind

Fig. 17.11 Synaptic organization of nerve terminals on crustacean muscle. Main paths for rapid excitation and inhibition of muscle are shown on the right, together with microcircuits for presynaptic control. Main paths for modulation of muscle excitability are shown on the left. These modulatory effects include (1) muscle contraction, as in the maintenance of different postures (see Chap. 20); (2) increase in input conductance (R_l), which increases the amplitude of the endplate potential; (3) elicitation of small endplate potentials; (4) lowering of the threshold for generation of Ca^{2+} spikes. Abbreviations: PROCT, proctolin; OCT, octopamine; EXC, excitation; INH (inh), inhibition. (Based on Atwood, 1977; Kravitz et al., 1985)

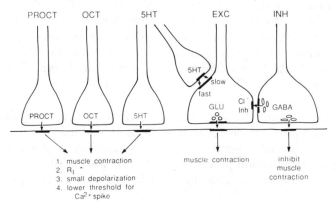

of local circuit, which is organized along principles very similar to those that we outlined for synaptic circuits in neural centers in Chap. 4. This peripheral microcircuit provides for local control of input–output transmission at the final relay from the nerves to the muscle. It is as if the organism wants to fine-tune its motor output, out to the last possible step of neural control. Neuromodulators also contribute to this control; the actions of serotonin (5HT), octopamine, and proctolin are indicated in the diagram. The behavioral actions of 5HT and octopamine will be discussed in Chap. 19.

Motor Units

Thus far our focus has been on each muscle cell as an individual unit. However, to be useful in generating movements, cells must be brought together in functional groups, and provided with appropriate nervous control. As indicated in Fig. 17.4, the simplest arrangement of muscle fibers is in a fasciculus, and many fasciculi together make up a given muscle.

The lowest level of nervous control of muscles is concerned with the connections of the motoneurons to the muscle cells. A motoneuron, along with the population of muscle fibers it innervates, is called a *motor unit*. In many invertebrate muscles, a single fiber may receive endplates from more than one motoneuron, and multiple innervation also occurs during early development of vertebrate muscle. However, in the adult, the rule is that a muscle fiber receives an endplate from only one motoneuron.

Because of this rule, the size of a motor unit is determined by the extensiveness of branching of the motoneuron axon. This in turn is matched to the particular functional demands in a given muscle. Motor unit size varies widely, in accord with the range of functions of different muscles in the body. At one extreme are very small muscles involved in controlling very fine movements. This is exemplified by the extraocular muscles to the eye (Chap. 14; Fig.

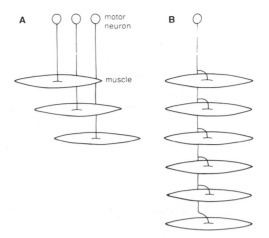

Fig. 17.12 The organization of motor units. A. Each motoneuron innervates only one muscle; this is the smallest possible motor unit size. B. A larger motor unit with an innervation ratio of 6.

14.15). In these muscles, the motor unit may approach the limit of a single muscle cell for each motoneuron (Fig. 17.12A). At the other extreme are muscles that are large, and whose functions are to generate large forces (such as the gastrocnemius), or sustained contractions (such as the soleus). These properties have been discussed above (Fig. 17.6). For these kinds of muscles, the innervation ratios may be several hundred, even up to 1000 (Fig. 17.12B).

The Motor Hierarchy

How then are the motor units controlled? That is a central question of motor systems, and the subject of the remaining chapters in this section. The essence of these systems is that they are organized in a hierarchical fashion. In fact, they illustrate, better than any other part of the nervous system, the principle of hierarchical organization that was introduced in Chap. 1.

The concept that motor control is embedded in successively higher levels of organization was recognized at an early stage by students of animal behavior. A schema which expresses this is shown in Fig. 17.13. It relates specifically to the re-

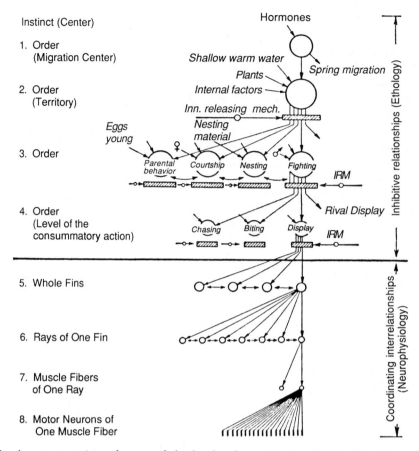

Fig. 17.13 A representation of some of the levels of organization involved in the generation of motor behavior. See text. (After Tinbergen, 1951)

productive behavior of the male stickleback fish, but it should be regarded as a framework for motor behavior in general. Beginning at the bottom are the muscle fibers and motor units ⑧. Above this are several levels (⑦ to ⑤) building up to the coordinated movement of a whole fin. Above this are the levels (① to ④) of increasingly larger components of behavior that involve the whole animal. For example, one goes from biting ④, to fighting ③, to territorial behavior ②, to migration ①. Although nerve circuits are not explicitly included in this diagram, they are implied for the mechanisms controlling the lower levels of organization and generating the behaviors at the higher levels.

The important aspect of the higher levels is that a particular behavior is characterist-

ically elicited by a particular stimulus, called an innate releasing mechanism (IRM). As an example, Fig. 17.14 shows a simple shape that was used as a visual stimulus to test for escape responses in turkeys. When the pattern was moved to the left, it elicited avoidance by the turkeys, because the shape and orientation (short neck, long tail) mim-

Fig. 17.14 A simple pattern elicits quite different motor responses in a test animal, depending on the direction of movement. See text.

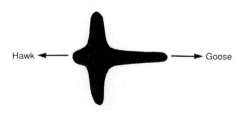

icked a hawklike bird of prey. By contrast, when the pattern was moved in the other direction, it elicited little or no response, because it had gooselike features (long neck, short tail) which were not threatening.

This kind of result has an interesting connection with properties of sensory systems. Recall from our discussion in Chap. 10 that perception involves recognition of a pattern as a whole, called a gestalt; in the example of Fig. 10.11, the illustration tends to be perceived as a face or a vase, but not both. Similarly, for the turkey, the shape in Fig. 17.14 tends to be seen as predator or innocuous neighbor, and the entire motor pattern appropriate for one or the other gestalt is played out. This illustrates why our study must proceed step by step to the higher levels of circuit organization in motor systems and central systems in order to achieve an understanding of motor behavior.

18

Autonomic Functions

Despite all the variations in body form, one can usually divide the animal body into two parts: a *visceral* part containing the internal organs, and a *somatic* part consisting of the musculoskeletal apparatus. The first is concerned with maintaining the internal environment and carrying out functions within the body, the second with moving the animal about and mediating interactions with the external environment. In some simple species the division between the two is so clear that it seems as if there are two animals, the muscular animal moving about with a visceral animal on its back (see Fig. 18.1, top). In the vertebrates, a similar principle is at work, with visceral and somatic body parts clearly distinguishable (Fig. 18.1, bottom).

The nerves that supply the internal organs constitute the autonomic nervous system. "Autonomic" indicates that most of the nervous control is believed to be "autonomous." What does this term mean? One meaning is that this control is automatic and involuntary, in contrast with voluntary, willed control over skeletal muscles. Another meaning is that this functions as an independent, "autonomous" system, with a self-contained hierarchy of functional units and internal state generators.

These distinctions are useful, but they are not hard and fast. For example, autonomic nerves control the blood supply to muscles and skin, although they are contained in the somatic part of the body. In the opposite direction, activity of skeletal muscles requires the autonomic nervous system to divert blood from gut to muscles. So the line between autonomic and voluntary nervous control, between involuntary and voluntary actions, is crossed in both directions, and there is accordingly a higher level of central control which coordinates these two great systems (see Chap. 24).

As commonly defined, the autonomic nervous system consists only of the nerves carrying motor impulses to the internal organs; by this definition, it is exclusively peripheral and motor. While it is useful to be able to define this component, a larger view of the nervous mechanisms involved in regulating the body requires a much broader perspective. This would take account of the sensory information from the internal organs, the effects of a great many peptides and hormones, and the circuits in the central nervous system that control the peripheral ganglia and nerves.

This chapter will deal mainly with the motor ganglia of the autonomic system,

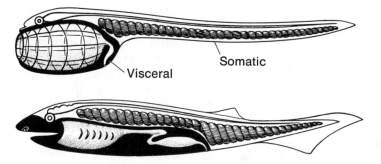

Fig. 18.1   Organization of the vertebrate body. *Above:* Hypothetical primitive chordate. *Below:* Representative lower vertebrate, such as the fish. Note the divisions into somatic and visceral (shaded) body parts. (After Romer and Parsons, 1977)

comparing the organization of ganglia in the invertebrates and vertebrates. Since there are many types of ganglia, our focus will be on the nerves that control the salivary gland and the heart. In both invertebrates and vertebrates, these nerves have provided particularly clear examples of the principles involved in the functional organization of the autonomic nervous system. We will note nerves and ganglia covered in other chapters and some central circuits involved in autonomic controls, in anticipation of further treatments in Chaps. 27 and 28.

INVERTEBRATES

The basic plan for invertebrates consists of a ganglion containing output cells that innervate a particular visceral organ or organs. The ganglion, in turn, receives input fibers from other ganglia, which in many cases are part of the central nervous system, or "brain." Actual systems include more complicated networks of fibers and ganglia, building on this simple scheme.

Let us now consider a specific example of autonomic innervation of the salivary gland, and two examples of the heart.

Salivary Gland

Salivary glands are found widely in invertebrates, where they function, much as in vertebrates, to secrete a fluid containing enzymes which aid in the initial breakdown and digestion of food entering the oral cavity. An example of this type of organ is the salivary gland of gastropods.

As shown in Fig. 18.2, the gland cells receive their innervation through fibers of an identified neuron (no. 4) in the buccal ganglion. Intracellular electrodes can be introduced into both a Cell 4 neuron and a gland cell to study the response properties of the gland cells. Depolarizing current injected into the Cell 4 neuron elicits single action potentials (Fig. 18.2B,c). In the acinar gland cells, the response, after a delay for impulse conduction and synaptic transmission, consists of single, discrete EPSPs, which, if large enough, give rise to an action potential (Fig. 18.2,B,b). The action potential is presumably responsible for an influx of Ca^{2+} that is involved in "excitation–secretion coupling." We have previously noted that many types of gland cells are excitable, and the *Ariolimax* salivary cell nicely demonstrates this property.

Another interesting property of these cells is that they are electrically coupled to each other. Intracellular experiments show that there may be coupling coefficients between neighboring cells as high as 0.8 (i.e., 80% of a signal in one cell can be recorded in another cell). By this means, action potentials set up in one part of the acinar cell population rapidly propagate to other cells. This provides for both rapid spread and synchronization of the activities of all cells.

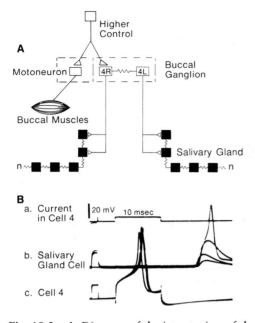

Fig. 18.2 A. Diagram of the innervation of the salivary gland in the snail *Helisoma*. Chemical synapses shown by open terminals, electrical synapses by sawtooth lines. **B.** Electrophysiological recordings in the slug *Ariolimax*. (a) Monitor of depolarizing current injected into neuron; (b) intracellular response of salivary gland acinar cell; (c) response of buccal ganglion neuron into which current was injected. (From Kater, 1977)

The outputs to the right and left halves of the gland are synchronized by means of electrical coupling between the Cell 4 neurons.

Figure 18.2 also indicates that the activity of the acinar cells is coordinated with the ingestion of food. This takes place through coordination of the Cell 4 neurons with motoneurons of the buccal ganglion during the feeding cycle. In this hierarchy, the Cell 4 neurons occupy a position that is similar to that of the autonomic ganglion cells in the vertebrate (see below).

Cardiac Activity

Cardiac muscle activity characteristically involves rhythmic contractions, and these rhythms can be generated by two general types of mechanisms. The rhythmic nature can reflect properties of the muscles themselves *(myogenic rhythm)*, or it can be imposed by nervous activity *(neurogenic rhythm)*. These two types of mechanisms are basic to rhythmical behavior in most animals, as we will see in later chapters.

The rhythmic contractions of heart muscle may have either a myogenic or neurogenic basis, or a combination of the two. The usual way to demonstrate this experimentally is to cut the nerves to the heart (see Fig. 18.3). If the heart stops beating, the rhythm is neurogenic. An example is the lobster, in which the rhythm is generated by interaction between nine neurons that form the cardiac ganglion. If the heart continues to beat at the same rate with the nerves cut, the rhythm is myogenic; an example is the heartbeat in *Aplysia*. If the heart continues to beat but at a lower rate, this can arise because the neurons fire rhythmically at a faster rate, and the heart normally becomes entrained to this higher rate (we will take up further examples of the entrainment of oscillatory systems in Chap. 25, Biorhythms). Alternatively, a myogenic rhythm can be influenced by tonic nerve fibers which are modulatory in function.

The beating of the heart of the leech, *Hirudo medicinalis,* is an interesting example to study because it is controlled by both a myogenic rhythm and a neural oscillator. In addition, both are subject to neuromodulation. We have already encountered the leech in studying the somatosensory system (Chap. 12). The circulatory system consists of four main vessels which run the length of the worm: one dorsal, one ventral, and one on each side (lateral). Together, the two lateral vessels constitute the heart. Muscle cells arranged in spirals within the walls of these vessels contract rhythmically, driving blood through the great vessels.

The lateral hearts are innervated by two types of neuron. One type, called HE motor neurons, is found bilaterally in numbers 3–18 of the 21 ganglia in the leech (see Fig.

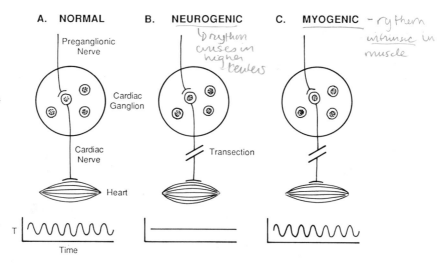

Fig. 18.3 Test for source of rhythmic heart beat. **A.** Normal neural pathway to the heart. **B.** Cardiac nerve transection causes heart to stop beating; rhythm therefore arises in neurons in the cardiac ganglion (or higher centers). **C.** Transection has no effect; rhythm therefore is intrinsic to the heart muscle cells. T, tension in heart muscle.

18.4A). Each HE motor neuron sends its axon through an ipsilateral root to establish neuromuscular junctions with the muscle cells within that segment of the heart. The other type, called HA neurons, are found only as a bilateral pair in ganglia 5 and 6. The HA neuron of ganglion 5 sends its axon contralaterally to muscles in anterior segments; the HA neuron of ganglion 6 sends its axon contralaterally to muscles in posterior segments. Although these nerves form neuromuscular junctions on the muscles, impulses in the nerves do not give rise to recordable endplate potentials in the muscles.

The activity of the HE neurons is closely correlated with the beating of the heart. The HE neurons fire intense bursts for 2–3 seconds, which are followed by periods of inhibition; the intense bursts are closely correlated with the onset of each heartbeat [Fig. 18.4B; HE(R,5)]. An HA neuron fires more slowly, alternating with briefer periods of inhibition. The HE neurons entrain the myogenic rhythm to their neurogenic rhythm by driving the muscle cells. The HA neurons contribute a modulatory influence on the entrained rhythm.

How does the neurogenic rhythm of the HE and HA cells arise? Experiments have shown that it is due to a cyclic pattern of inhibition that terminates each excitatory burst (see Fig. 18.4B). This is due to a network of eight paired HN interneurons located in ganglia 1–7. The HN neurons are interconnected by inhibitory synapses; a combination of intrinsic bursting properties and reciprocal inhibitory connections between HN neurons produces the cyclic inhibition of the HE and HA neurons.

The HN network is a type of *central pattern generator,* such as we will study in subsequent chapters. The heart rate must be adjusted to meet the changing behavioral states of the animal, which means that the central pattern generator must be appropriately adjusted: this process is called *modulation.* Vigorous swimming movements, as well as stimulation of 1, P, or N sensory cells (see Chap. 12), cause acceleration of the central pattern generator, and consequently the heart rate which it entrains.

The myogenic rhythm can also be directly modulated by activity in the HA cells. Experimentally, it has been found

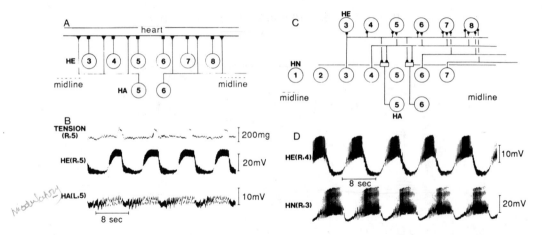

Fig. 18.4 Heartbeat system of the leech. **A.** Two types of neurons innervate the heart: HE moto-neurons are excitatory, HA motoneurons are modulatory. **B.** Recordings of rhythmic firing of HE and HA motoneurons, and resulting rhythmic beating of the heart. **C.** Interneurons (HN) have inhibitory connections onto HE motoneurons (see ③ in diagram), and onto HA neurons (see ④ in diagram); rectangles indicate spike initiation site separate from cell soma. **D.** Alternating burst activity of HE and HN cells, due to inhibitory network in C. See text. (From Calabrese and Arbas, 1985)

that when the HA cell is depolarized with injected current, the resulting tonic firing of the HA cell is correlated with an increase in the strength and duration of each heart beat. It is postulated that since HA cells do not set up detectable synaptic potentials in the cardiac muscle cells, the action may take the form of modulation of a voltage-dependent conductance (to affect the heart rate), or modulation of excitation–contraction coupling (to affect contraction strength). Cardioaccelatory peptides are widespread in invertebrates; one of these, FMRFamide (Phe-Met-Arg-Phe-NH$_2$), has been localized to the HA neurons by im-munocytochemistry, and has been shown to mimic the effects of HA neuron stimu-lation on the heart.

In summary, the circuit diagram in Fig. 18.4 illustrates several important princi-ples. It can be seen that there is a *hierarchy of control*, through successive sets of neu-rons and their connections. The connec-tions of each HE motoneuron are directed to a specific target. The connections of the HA interneurons, however, go to sets of

motoneurons. In this way, the action of a single neuron may bring about a coordi-nated sequence of motor activity involving one or several segments. One traditionally refers to a cell with this property as a *command neuron,* and the motor sequence elicited is referred to as a *fixed-action pat-tern.* We shall have more to say about these and related principles of motor control in succeeding chapters.

VERTEBRATES

The discovery that the nerves to the viscera constitute a distinct system was made by anatomists from observations in humans. Thomas Willis in 1664 first described the two chains of ganglia running on either side of the vertebral column. Willis also made the important distinction between nerves that subserve voluntary (somatic) and involuntary (visceral) functions. It was not until 1732 (how slow progress can be!) that Winslow, in France, described the many nerves that connect the chain to the internal organs, and speculated that these nerves bring the organs into "sympathetic" relation with each other.

Modern studies of these nerves began with Gaskell and Langley in England, around 1900; the contributions made by their early work toward laying the foundation for our concepts of the chemical nature of synaptic transmission were noted in Chap. 8. The terms that are now generally used date from that time. The nerves to the internal organs constitute the *autonomic nervous system*. The system has two main divisions: the *sympathetic* nervous system (originally termed the orthosympathetic by Langley) and the *parasympathetic.* This is shown for the human in Fig. 18.5. The basic organization of these two systems appears to be similar in most vertebrate species.

In the parasympathetic division, the peripheral ganglia are located in the organs that their cells innervate. The ganglia receive their neural inputs from fibers arising from cells in certain nuclei of the brainstem and sacral spinal cord. By virtue of their positions relative to the ganglia, fibers innervating a ganglion are called *preganglionic,* and those arising from it are *postganglionic.*

Sympathetic ganglia, in contrast, are arranged in a cord along the vertebral column (see Fig. 18.6) or in the mesentery of the gut. Their cells have long, postganglionic fibers which branch and innervate the internal organs. The cells, in turn, are innervated by preganglionic fibers of cells located in the intermediolateral column of the thoracolumbar portions of the spinal cord. It can thus be seen that in both divisions of the autonomic nervous system, there is, in addition to the centrally located motoneuron within the spinal cord, a peripherally located motoneuron within a ganglion.

A special subdivision of the sympathetic system is located in the interior (medulla) of the adrenal gland. Here cells known as *chromaffin* cells are packed together. These cells contain vesicles filled with catechol-amines (mostly epinephrine). Like sympathetic ganglia, the adrenal receives its innervation from motor cells of the intermediolateral column of the spinal cord. The chromaffin cells themselves lack axons; upon stimulation, they discharge their epinephrine into the bloodstream. Through this mechanism, the sympathetic nervous system can mediate hormonal-type actions on various organs throughout the body.

Recently, the chromaffin cells have taken on a new significance for neurobiology through the experiments on brain transplants. Since the synthetic chain for epinephrine passes through dopamine, these cells have been transplanted into the neostriatum (see Fig. 9.17B) in the hope of inducing them to synthesize and release dopamine, and thereby replace the dopamine that has been lost through the degeneration of dopaminergic cells in Parkinson's disease. Animal experiments have showed that these experiments are feasible, and the first operations on human patients have given encouraging results in producing relief of the motor incapacities of these patients.

The main functions of the parasympathetic and sympathetic nerves are summarized in Table 18.1.

Several general conclusions about the relations between the two divisions can be drawn from the table. First, either system may be stimulatory or inhibitory to a given organ. Second, when an organ is innervated by both systems, they are usually (but not always) opposed to each other in their actions. Third, some organs are predominantly or exclusively controlled by one system or the other.

The different patterns of innervation of the two divisions depicted in Fig. 18.5 are important to understand in assessing the contrasting actions of the two divisions on the behavior of the organism. The ganglion cells in the sympathetic system have wide fields of peripheral innervation, and this means that their activity tends to have widespread effects and evoke mass re-

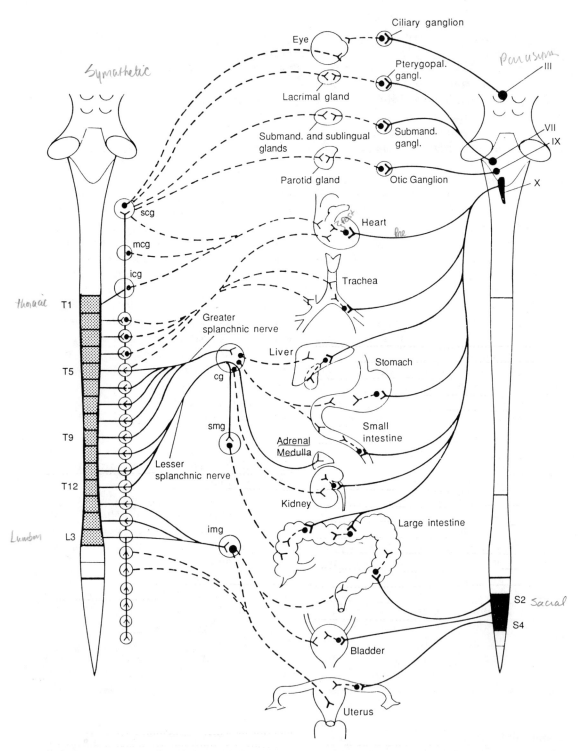

Fig. 18.5 Organization of the autonomic system. The sympathetic system is shown on the left, the parasympathetic system on the right. Abbreviations for the names of <u>sympathetic ganglia</u> are as follows (from top to bottom): scg, superior cervical ganglion; mcg, middle cervical ganglion; icg,

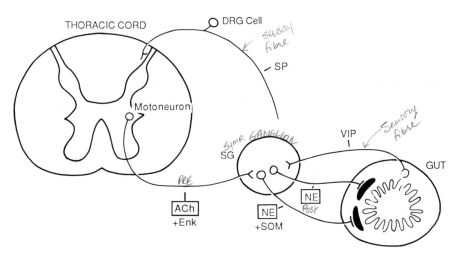

Fig. 18.6 Localization of neurotransmitters and neuropeptides in neurons of the sympathetic nervous system. Abbreviations: DRG, dorsal root ganglion; SP, substance P; SG, sympathetic ganglion; ACh, acetylcholine; Enk, enkephalin; NE, norepinephine; VIP, vasoactive intestinal peptide; SOM, somatostatin. (Modified from Hökfelt et al., 1980)

sponses. Traditionally, it has been believed that the overall effect of the sympathetic system is to decrease activity in the visceral organs and stimulate the heart and somatic muscles, and that these effects prepare the whole organism for "fight-or-flight" behavior. In contrast, the ganglion cells of the parasympathetic system, being located in their target organs, have narrow fields of innervation. It has been generally thought that their effects are thereby local, and related to facilitating the activities of their respective organs. While the patterns of innervation in the two systems are indeed clearly different, and while it is true that sympathetic activity has more global effects, Table 18.1 makes it clear that there are exceptions to the traditional generalizations about the functions of the systems.

We will discuss further the relation of autonomic activity to behavior below and in Chaps. 24–28. For the remainder of this chapter, we will consider the organization within a ganglion, and examples of mechanisms involved in the control of the three types of effector cells: glands, smooth muscle, and cardiac muscle.

Sympathetic Ganglion

The traditional view of the autonomic nervous system represented in the diagram of Fig. 18.5 has been greatly extended by recent studies of transmitter substances, and the synaptic organization within a ganglion.

Transmitters and Modulators

A simple rule for autonomic neurotransmitters was laid down by the classical workers. In both divisions, the preganglionic motoneurons use acetylcholine (ACh); the postganglionic cells also use ACh in the parasympathetic system, but

inferior cervical ganglion; cg, celiac ganglion; smg, superior mesenteric ganglion; img, inferior mesenteric ganglion. T1–T12, segments of thoracic spinal cord; L3, third lumbar spinal segment; S2, S4, sacral spinal cord segments. III–X, cranial nerves. The diagram represents the human, but applies generally to vertebrate species. (Modified from Heimer, 1983)

Table 18.1   Effects of autonomic nervous activity on different body organs

Organ	Effect of sympathetic stimulation	Effect of parasympathetic stimulation
Eye:		
Pupil	dilated	contracted
Ciliary muscle	none	excited
Glands:		
Nasal	vasoconstriction	stimulation of thin, copious secretion
Lacrimal		containing many enzymes
Parotid		
Submaxillary		
Gastric		
Pancreatic		
Sweat glands	copious sweating (cholinergic)	–
Apocrine glands	thick, odoriferous secretion	–
Heart:		
Muscle	increased rate	slowed rate
	increased force of contraction	decreased force of atrial contraction
Coronaries	vasodilated	constricted
Lungs:		
Bronchi	dilated	constricted
Blood vessels	mildly constricted	–
Gut:		
Lumen	decreased peristalsis and tone	increased peristalsis and tone
Sphincter	increased tone	decreased tone
Liver	glucose released	–
Gallbladder and bile ducts	inhibited	excited
Kidney	decreased output	–
Ureter	inhibited	excited
Bladder:		
Detrusor	inhibited	excited
Trigone	excited	inhibited
Penis	ejaculation	erection
Systemic blood vessels:		
Abdominal	constricted	–
Muscle	constricted (adrenergic)	–
	dilated (cholinergic)	
Skin	constricted (adrenergic)	dilated
	dilated (cholinergic)	
Blood:		
Coagulation	increased	–
Glucose	increased	–
Basal metabolism	increased up to 100%	–
Adrenal cortical secretion	increased	–
Mental activity	increased	–
Piloerector muscles	excited	–
Skeletal muscle	increased glycogenolysis	–
	increased strength	

From Guyton (1976)

norepinephrine (NE) in the sympathetic system. Figure 18.6 summarizes this pattern of localization in the sympathetic innervation of the gut.

When neuroactive peptides began to be identified, it was soon found that they were present in the autonomic nervous system. Some of the clearest evidence for colocalization of neuropeptides with classical transmitters has come from these studies.

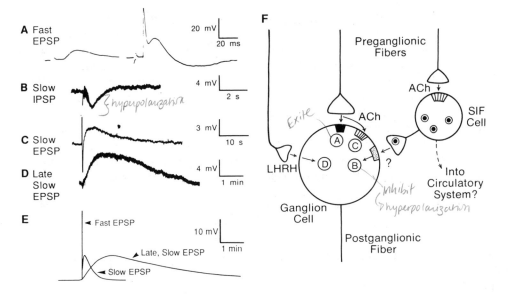

Fig. 18.7 Synaptic actions on ganglion cells in the sympathetic ganglion of the frog. **A–D.** Intracellular recordings from ganglion cells, showing different types of responses to electrical stimulation of preganglionic fibers; note the increasingly slower oscilloscope traces from A to D. (From Jan et al., 1979) **E.** Comparison of the responses in A, C, and D on the same time base and with the same amplification, to emphasize the contrasting time courses of these responses. (From Jones and Adams, 1987) **F.** Summary diagram of the synaptic organization of the sympathetic ganglion, showing sites of generation of different types of response in A–D. (Modified from Libet, in Shepherd, 1979) Abbreviations: LHRH, luteinizing hormone releasing hormone; SIF, small intensely fluorescing.

Thus, as indicated in Fig. 18.6 in the sympathetic division, enkephalin (Enk) is found in cholinergic preganglionic nerves, and somatostatin (SOM) is found in many postganglionic noradrenergic nerves. In addition to motor fibers, peptides are also present in the sensory fibers; vasoactive intestinal peptide (VIP) has been found in sensory neurons in the gut, and substance P (SP) in dorsal root ganglion cells (see Fig. 18.6).

Synaptic Organization

What are the actions of transmitters and neuropeptides in the autonomic pathways? Diagrams such as those of Figs. 18.5 and 18.6 give the impression that a sympathetic ganglion is the site of a simple relay from pre- to postganglionic nerve. However, we have already seen that neuromodulators may have complex effects on synaptic transmission (see Chap. 8, Fig. 8.11). Studies of synaptic organization have shown

that in fact the ganglion is a complex integration system, in which the different transmitters and neuropeptides act on specific receptors with distinct properties for controlling the transmission of information to the target organs.

The sympathetic ganglion of the frog has served as a valuable model for elucidating these principles.

As shown in Fig. 18.7, stimulation of the preganglionic fibers gives rise to a sequence of synaptic effects in a ganglion cell. The briefest action (A, in Fig. 18.7) is a *fast EPSP*, lasting 10–20 msec. It is mediated by ACh, liberated from the nerve endings and acting on nicotinic receptors (receptors that are blocked by the substance nicotine; see circuit diagram in F). The mechanism underlying this response is believed to be similar to that at the neuromuscular junction, involving an increased conductance to cations (Na^+, Ca^{2+}, and K^+).

The next component of the response (B in Fig. 18.7) is a *slow IPSP*, lasting several hundred milliseconds. This appears to be mediated by a conductance-decrease synapse, which hyperpolarizes the membrane by turning off Na^+ conductance (see Chap. 7). A number of studies have been carried out to identify the transmitter for this synaptic action. One possibility has been that the nerves excite an interneuron, and that this interneuron inhibits the ganglion cells by releasing a catecholamine, either dopamine or norepinephrine. Anatomical studies have shown that many ganglia contain small cells, packed with large dense-core vesicles. Since these cells fluoresce when treated with the paraformaldehyde technique, they are called *small intensely fluorescing* cells, or SIF cells. It has been proposed that the slow IPSP response of the ganglion cell involves activation of an adenylate cyclase and a second messenger system, as described in Chap. 8. However, a slow IPSP is seen in some ganglia that lack SIF cells, so other mechanisms must be considered as well.

The third response component is a *slow EPSP*, lasting several seconds (C in the figure). This is mediated by ACh acting on muscarinic receptors (receptors sensitive to blocking by the substance muscarine). Forest Weight and J. Votava showed in 1970 that this is due to a decrease in a resting K conductance; when the K conductance falls, the membrane depolarizes toward the Na equilibrium potential, according to the mechanism discussed in Chap. 7. Paul Adams and his colleagues termed this resting K current the M current and have characterized its voltage-dependent properties (see Fig. 7.10). It is an important type of K current (cf. Chap. 7) that is present in many types of cells (see smooth muscle cells in previous chapter, and gland cells below).

The final response component (D) is a *very slow EPSP*, lasting several minutes. In 1979, an elegant analysis by Lily Yeh Jan, Yuh Nung Jan, and Stephen Kuffler of Harvard implicated the polypeptide luteinizing hormone releasing hormone (LHRH) (see

Chap. 8) in mediating this response. Several procedures could be carried out in this simple system, such as microionophoresis of LHRH and its analogues, and radioimmunoassay for presence of LHRH in the ganglion, which thus satisfied several of the criteria deemed necessary for positive identification of a neurotransmitter or neuromodulator (Table 8.3 in Chap. 8). Suppression of the M current is also the mechanism for this response, as shown in Fig. 7.10.

Receptors for Different Durations, Operations, and Strengths

Why are multiple transmitters and receptors needed in this pathway? Better insight into this question is obtained by replotting the responses of Fig. 18.7A–D on a common time scale, as in E. This brings out more clearly that each receptor function is distinctive in at least three ways: duration, actions, and strength. In *duration*, each synaptic potential has its distinctive time course, though there is also overlap (cf. also Fig. 8.14). In *action*, the synaptic responses are depolarizing or hyperpolarizing, excitatory or inhibitory. Other operations would include biasing actions (cf. Chap. 7), second-messenger metabolic effects (Chap. 8), or the setting of a behavioral state (Chap. 24). In *strength*, the responses vary in amplitude. At one extreme, the fast EPSP has a large amplitude, presumably with the function of generating an impulse response; at the other extreme, the late slow EPSP has a small amplitude, as would be suitable for modulating the frequency of the impulse discharge.

These considerations suggest the principle that the complexity of information processing in a neural system is likely to depend on how rich a repertoire of molecular receptor functions it has for generating responses with different durations, actions, and strengths. This helps to answer the question, why are there so many transmitters and modulators in the nervous system? The answer is that they are needed to enable a neural center to provide for different functional operations, coordinated over different time periods, and adjusted for different strengths.

Seen in this light, the sympathetic ganglion is a local circuit system (see diagram in Fig. 18.7). It is much more complex than the simple relay as traditionally conceived, but it probably is not as complex as some regions of the central nervous system, which have to deal with spatial processing and exquisite temporal discrimination as well. As a model system, it demonstrates admirably how circuits integrate multiple inputs by distinctive mechanisms covering a range of durations, actions, and strengths. These principles are likely to be important for the contribution of the sympathetic system to the behavior of the organism.

Target Organs

Let us move on from the site of the ganglion cell body, and examine the synaptic mechanisms whereby the ganglion cell exerts control over its target organ. We will consider the three main types of target in the autonomic nervous system: glands, smooth muscle, cardiac muscle.

Glands

As indicated in Table 18.1, a number of glands are under autonomic control. Glands in the walls of the intestinal tract are the *tubular* type, which take the form of pits or tubules. They contain cells that secrete either mucus, to lubricate the gut wall, or enzymes, to aid in digestion.

The other main type of gland is the *acinar* type, which consists of collections of cells which discharge their contents into central ducts. This characterizes more complex glands, such as the salivary glands, pancreas, and liver.

Secretion may be stimulated in several ways: by local chemical cues from the ingested food; by nervous reflexes elicited by local chemical, tactile, or mechanical cues; by central nervous activity; or by circulating hormones. The relative importance of these mechanisms varies for different glands.

The cellular mechanisms of glandular se-

cretion in vertebrates are similar to those in invertebrates. One of the earliest and best studied examples in vertebrates is the salivary gland. You should compare the following description with the account of the invertebrate salivary gland above (Fig. 18.2). The salivary gland is of interest because it can be activated by both parasympathetic and sympathetic nerve stimulation, by local application of their respective neurotransmitters, ACh and NE, and by substance P. The molecular mechanisms activated by these transmitters are summarized in the diagram of Fig. 18.8. Sympathetic stimulation activates a β-receptor, which, through cAMP, stimulates the cell to exocytose salivary enzymes; however, it also activates an α receptor which turns off Ca^{2+}-activated exocytosis of both enzymes and fluid carrier. Parasympathetic stimulation, on the other hand (as when we see a tasty morsel we are about to eat), leads to activation of a muscarinic receptor, leading to an increase of intracellular free Ca^{2+}. This is believed to be mediated by the inositol triphosphate (IP_3) second-messenger system (see Chap. 8). The mobilized calcium promotes release of both salivary enzyme and fluid, resulting in copious secretion. Substance P can also stimulate or potentiate secretion by a similar mechanism. Stimulation of the cell is terminated by a Ca^{2+}-activated K^+ conductance (see diagram and legend for further details).

The salivary gland was in fact one of the first organs in which evidence for the involvement of phosphatidylinositols in cell responses was obtained. Note that the salivary gland cell is oriented, with a receptor (basal) surface and an effector (luminal) surface. It corresponds closely to the model of excitation–secretion coupling of gland cells introduced in Chap. 17 (Fig. 17.3).

Smooth Muscle

As mentioned earlier (Chap. 17), motor nerves do not connect to smooth muscle cells by means of distinct neuromuscular junctions. Instead, the nerve fibers ramify (branch) and terminate within the muscle in free

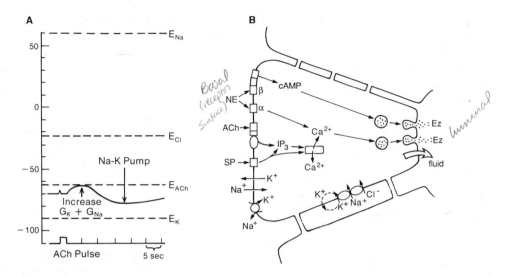

Fig. 18.8 Salivary gland acinar cells. Excitation–secretion coupling in the mammalian-salilvary gland cell. **A.** Intracellular response to an ionophoretically applied pulse of acetylcholine (ACh). Equilibrium potentials *(E)* for different ions and for the ACh response (due to both Na and K) are indicated. **B.** Schematic diagram of gland cell, summarizing molecular mechanisms of excitation–secretion coupling. Note the polarity of the cell: basal excitation, luminal secretion. Abbreviations: NE, norepinephrine; ACh, acetylcholine; SP, substance P; IP$_3$, inositol triphosphate; Ez, secreted enzymes. (Based on Petersen and Maruyama, 1984; Marty et al., 1986)

nerve endings. The effect of the nerve on the muscles depends on their physical proximity. The muscle fibers that receive nerve contacts respond to release of transmitter by graded postsynaptic potentials; in many cases, the fibers do not generate action potentials. Neighboring fibers are depolarized by spread of these responses through electrical synapses. Activation of more distant fibers is believed to require spread of action potentials through electrical synapses; in addition, there may be activation or modulation by transmitter diffusing from distant terminals. Note that this grading of the response of muscle fibers to nerve stimulation resembles the spread of electrotonic currents in gland cells of *Helisoma*, mentioned above.

The smooth muscle of the gut undergoes *myogenic* spontaneous contractions. These contractions are slow, lasting several seconds, and are associated with slow depolarization of the muscle membrane giving rise to impulse discharges (see Fig. 18.9).

Slow contractions induced by ACh are associated with modulation of an M current, influx of Ca^{2+}, and release of internal Ca^{2+} through second messenger systems, as discussed in Chap. 17. The slow contractions that occur spontaneously require a pacemaker mechanism, involving a relatively slowly inactivating channel which depolarizes the membrane and sets up a discharge of impulses. The increase in Ca^{2+} influx leads to activation of the Ca^{2+}-activated K$^+$ channels which repolarize the membrane and terminate the contractile wave. The steady pacemaker depolarization then initiates a new cycle.

This example demonstrates how rhythmic cell activity can arise from the interplay of membrane conductances and second messengers. Variations on this basic mechanism underlie the generation of rhythmic activity throughout the nervous system. In this case, ACh speeds up the rhythms and makes them stronger, through increasing the membrane depolarization; norepineph-

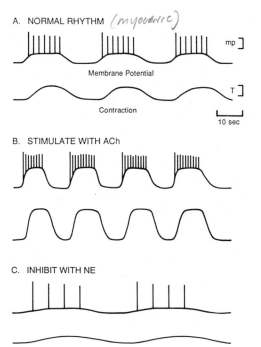

A. NORMAL RHYTHM *(myogenic)*

mp

Membrane Potential

T

Contraction

10 sec

B. STIMULATE WITH ACh

C. INHIBIT WITH NE

Fig. 18.9 Rhythms of contraction of smooth muscle in the gut. **A.** Normal rhythm. Membrane potential (mp) scale is 20 mV; tension (T) scale is in arbitrary units. **B.** Acetylcholine (ACh) stimulates stronger and more rapid contractions. **C.** Norepinephrine (NE) makes contractions weaker and slower. (After Golenhofen, in Schmidt and Thewes, 1983)

rine, by contrast, opposes this action, making the rhythm slower and weaker.

The neural systems which modulate smooth muscle rhythmic contractions in the gut are contained in two ganglia within the gut wall, named Meissner's and Auerbach's plexuses. From a combination of morphological, neurochemical, and electrophysiological studies, a picture of the organization of Auerbach's plexus has emerged, which is summarized in Fig. 18.10. As can be seen, the circuit has its own source of *neurogenic* rhythm, in the "burst-type oscillators" that fire periodic bursts of impulses. These drive bursting follower cells that have inhibitory noradrenergic synapses on the muscles. Tonically discharging interneurons, activated by stretch of the muscles, have inhibitory synapses on the follower cells; through these connections, they can release the circular muscles of the gut from inhibition. By sequential activation of mechanoreceptors and interneurons, a peristaltic contractile wave moves along the gut wall, as from left-to-right in the figure. The slow and smoothly graded nature of the contractions arises from the diffuse spread of neurotransmitter to the muscle, the modulatory action of neuro-

Fig. 18.10 Neuronal circuit that mediates inhibitory control of intestinal circular muscles. Nerve cells have excitatory (+) or inhibitory (−) connections. Muscle cells are interconnected by electrical synapses. Neuronal interactions, as described in text, cause peristaltic wave of contraction of the circular muscles to move from left to right. (From Wood, 1975)

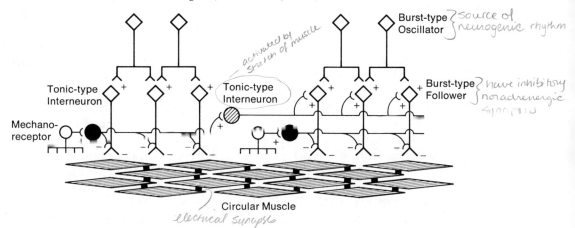

peptides present in the gut wall, and the electrical synapses that couple the muscles together in a functional syncytium. In 1975, J. D. Wood of the University of Kansas characterized this neural circuit as "a simple integrative system analogous to ganglia . . . of invertebrate animals," that functions to coordinate and program the various patterns of mobility of the gut. He has suggested that it shares common integrative properties with many centers in the central nervous system. This circuit may be compared with that for control of the heartbeat in the leech (Fig. 18.4, above). It can be seen that both systems involve a hierarchy of neural control, combined with intrinsic rhythmic properties of the muscles; both systems are under multiple controls by different transmitters and modulators.

Heart

The vertebrate heart is *myogenic,* that is, it continues to contract in the absence of innervation. In this it resembles the molluscan heart, but differs from the arthropod heart (see earlier). Although the heart thus can beat in isolation, it nonetheless has extensive innervation, from both parasympathetic and sympathetic nerves. This is part of the nervous control of the cardiovascular system that is essential for providing the flexibility that is necessary to adapt the organism's motor performance to ongoing needs. This combined neurogenic and myogenic control resembles the way that the heartbeat of the leech is governed (Fig. 18.4, above).

Sequence of Activation. Rhythmic activity arises in the heart in the sinus node (see Fig. 18.11A,B). Since activity here leads the activity in other parts of the heart, it is called the "pacemaker." The impulses spread through the cardiac muscles of the atrium to a second pacemaker site, in the atrioventricular (AV) node. From here arise *Purkinje fibers,* which course together in a bundle and then distribute themselves throughout the ventricular walls. The Purkinje fibers are large, contain few myofi-

brils, and are closely coupled electrically. By these specializations, they conduct impulses at 2–4 m/sec, some six times faster than normal cardiac fibers.

Action Potential Mechanisms. The action potential takes on characteristic forms in the different types of cardiac fiber (see Fig. 18.11B), and these forms reflect the differing ionic conductances involved. Analysis of these conductances has benefited greatly from the Hodgkin-Huxley model of the action potential in nerve. Beginning in 1960, Dennis Noble in England adapted the Hodgkin-Huxley equations to the specific properties of the different cardiac impulses, so that we now have quantitatively precise models incorporating information about different ionic conductances.

Let us begin with the sinoatrial (SA) node, because it serves as the pacemaker for the others. The upper trace in Fig. 18.12A shows the voltage recordings of the rhythmical firing generated by the model for the SA node. The currents in the lower trace allow us to understand the time course of each impulse, and the factors that control the frequency of firing. The rapid upstroke of the impulse is determined by a rapid inward Ca current (I_{Ca}). The slow decline from the impulse peak is the outcome of the interplay between persisting I_{NaCa} and turning on of I_K. I_K brings the membrane to a hyperpolarized level, which turns on a hyperpolarization-activated nonspecific cation current (I_f), carried by both Na and K ions. This inward current, combined with the waning I_K, underlies the slow depolarization which leads to the next impulse firing when threshold for the regenerative I_{Ca} is reached.

The mechanism for rhythmic firing of Purkinje fibers is illustrated in Fig. 18.12B. There are several interesting differences. The impulse has a more rapid upstroke to a sharper peak, due to a very fast inward calcium current (I_{Ca}). This is followed by a maintained depolarization, called a plateau, which is due to the balance between a slow inward current (I_{NaCa}), the onset of

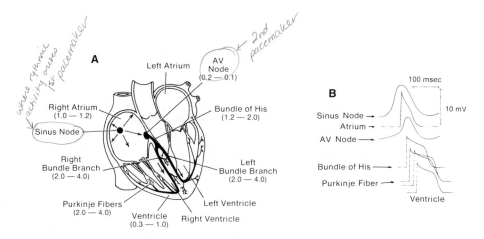

where rhythmic activity arises / *pacemaker*

← 2nd pacemaker

Fig. 18.11 **A.** The conducting system of the human heart. The electrical impulses begin in the sinus node, and are conducted to the AV node, through the bundle of His, to the branches and finally the Purkinje fibers which connect to the cardiac muscle fibers. Conduction velocities (meters per second) are indicated by numbers in parenthesis. **B.** Intracellular recordings of action potentials at different sites. (From Shepherd and Vanhoutte, 1979)

Fig. 18.12 Rhythmic impulse activity in cardiac cells. **A.** Sinoatrial node. A computational model has generated the rhythmic action potentials (above) and the underlying changes in membrane currents which cause them (below). Abbreviations: i_{Ca}, calcium current; i_K, delayed potassium; i_{NaCa}, Na^+-Ca^{2+} exchange current; i_f, hyperpolarizing-activated current. **B.** Purkinje fibers. Top trace shows rhythmic action potentials generated by the computational model. Bottom trace shows changes in membrane currents. Abbreviations as in A. Not shown are additional currents that are also present, including the anomalous (inward) rectifying K current. (From Noble, 1985)

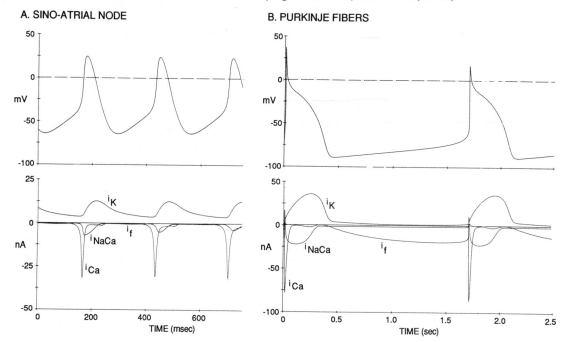

the delayed rectifier-like K current (I_K), and the turning off of a K current by the depolarizing impulse (I_{IR}, not shown). The impulse is terminated by a hyperpolarization which, as in the SA node, activates a hyperpolarization-activated nonspecific cation current (I_f). The depolarizing effect of this current is opposed by I_{IR}, however, resulting in a slower rhythm than in the SA node.

The heart therefore provides two carefully worked out examples of how the interplay of voltage-gated channels brings about generation of rhythmical activity. Some of the channels, such as I_{Ca} and I_K, have their counterparts in neuronal membranes, and Chap. 6 should be consulted for further comparisons. Some of the mechanisms appear different from nerve: for example, Ca^{2+}-activated K^+ channels, which appear so prominently in neurons, appear to have a lesser role in cardiac rhythms.

Control of Calcium Channels. It is evident from this analysis that Ca conductances play a key role in the generation of cardiac action potentials. This was recognized many years ago, before the role of Ca in neurons was suspected. Thus, heart cells have served as models for Ca mechanisms; it was here that neurochemical modulation of a voltage-gated channel and the role of cAMP in that modulation were first recognized. As Richard Tsien (1987) of Yale has observed, "Heart cells have provided a Rosetta stone for neuromodulation."

The importance of Ca is reflected by the fact that many neurotransmitters and neurohormones converge in its control. This is summarized in Fig. 18.13, where it can be seen that the common convergence point is adenylate cyclase. The sympathetic neurotransmitters (E and NE) stimulate adenylate cyclase through a G_s protein, whereas ACh mediates parasympathetic suppression through a G_i protein. The effects of cAMP are mediated by phosphorylation of the Ca channel or a closely associated protein.

By regulating Ca current, an exquisite control over many dynamic properties of heart muscle is achieved. As was apparent in Fig. 18.12, initiation of action potentials depends on Ca, and this in turn determines the rate of the heartbeat. Thus, the enhanced Ca current due to sympathetic stimulation increases the heart rate, and also increases the strength of ventricular muscle contraction (reviewed in Tsien, 1987).

Innervation and Synaptic Control. The nervous pathways that provide for modulation of the heart are shown in Fig. 18.14. The sympathetic innervation comes from postganglionic fibers of the sympathetic chain. When stimulated, these fibers release NE from their terminals; the NE acts on β_1 receptors on the cardiac cells. As discussed above, this results in increases in heart rate, impulse conduction, and contractility.

The parasympathetic innervation of the heart comes from *preganglionic* fibers arising in the motor nucleus of the vagus, situated in the brainstem. The vagus is the source of most parasympathetic fibers to the viscera. As shown also in Fig. 18.5, the cardiac fibers, being preganglionic, do not innervate the heart cells directly, but instead terminate on ganglia located in the heart. The ganglia contain interneurons, and there are interactions between interneurons and ganglion cells. The ganglia thus appear to be complex integrative centers, like sympathetic ganglia. The studies of Kuffler and his colleagues showed that the vagal fibers have *excitatory* cholinergic synapses on the cells of the ganglion which, in turn, have *inhibitory* cholinergic synapses on the cells of the heart. Acetylcholine inhibits the heart by decreasing Ca^{2+} permeability, thereby slowing the action potential and slowing the heart rate.

These details of synaptic organization are of interest for two reasons. First, they illustrate rather nicely how a transmitter (ACh) can have an excitatory action at one synapse and an inhibitory action at another. Second, they should be kept in mind

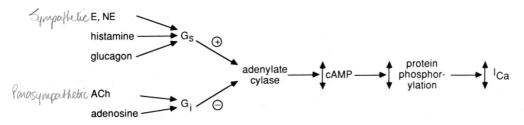

Fig. 18.13 Convergence of excitatory (+) and inhibitory (−) neurotransmitters and neurohormones on Ca channels in cardiac muscle. Abbreviations: E, epinephrine; NE, norepinephrine; ACh, acetylcholine; G_s and G_i, stimulatory and inhibitory G-binding proteins; I_{Ca}, calcium current. (From Tsien, 1987)

Fig. 18.14 The autonomic innervation of the heart. The right (R) and left (L) vagi mediate parasympathetic control; sympathetic control is mediated through the sympathetic (Symp.) nerves. SA, sinoatrial node; AV, atrioventricular node; ACh, acteylcholine; NE, norepinephrine (noradrenaline). (Adapted from Shepherd and Vanhoutte, 1979)

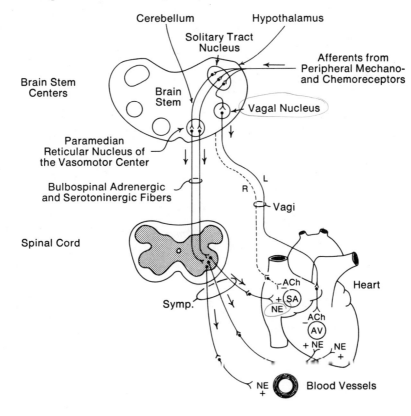

when one encounters the common statement that "the vagus inhibits the heart." The vagus, as we have just seen, actually *excites* the cardiac ganglion, which then inhibits the heart. Furthermore, under natural conditions the ganglion is likely to mediate more subtle modulations of cardiac activity, through its local circuit interactions, than the simple inhibition revealed by strong electrical stimulation of the vagus. Thus, knowledge of synaptic organization gives us a much richer understanding of the peripheral neural mechanisms involved in controlling visceral functions.

Brainstem Centers. The sympathetic motoneurons of the spinal cord are under control of descending catecholaminergic and serotonergic fibers originating in the vasomotor center of the brainstem. The "vasomotor center" is, in fact, a collection of different nuclei, that include the motor nucleus of the vagus and the nucleus of the solitary tract (see Fig. 18.14), which receives sensory inputs from mechanoreceptors in the walls of blood vessels and chemoreceptors such as the carotid body. This level of organization, in the brainstem, is analogous to the central ganglia controlling the cardiac ganglia in invertebrates. The brainstem nuclei, in turn, are affected by higher nervous centers, especially the cerebellum, hypothalamus, and the limbic system.

19

Reflexes and
d Motor Responses

One of the primary objectives in the study of motor systems is to identify the *elementary units of motor behavior*. There are two main concepts that have dominated thinking about this problem. One is the idea that the simplest unit of behavior is the *reflex*, and that complex behavior is built up by a chaining together of reflexes. The other idea is that much of behavior (particularly in invertebrates and lower vertebrates) involves stereotyped sequences of actions that are either generated within the organism or triggered by appropriate environmental stimuli. These are usually referred to as *fixed-action patterns*. Figure 19.1 and Table 19.1 summarize the main features of these types of behavioral units.

This chapter first gives a brief historical background of these two concepts and then presents examples in the invertebrates and the vertebrates. The relevance of the fixed action pattern concept for more complex types of behavior will be discussed in later chapters.

Reflexes: A Brief History

The fact that there are immediate motor responses to sensory stimulation was apparent through the ages, and implicit in the

writings of many scholars. However, the term "reflex" actually did not appear in the language until the eighteenth century. It comes as a surprise, for example, to realize that Shakespeare could dramatize so much of the human condition without using the word. Georg Prochaska of Vienna

Fig. 19.1 Comparison between a reflex and a fixed-action pattern. *On the left,* there is a simple motor response (for example, a knee jerk). *On the right,* there is a coordinated sequence of motor acts, such as the tail flip of a startled fish. We will discuss both of these examples in this chapter.

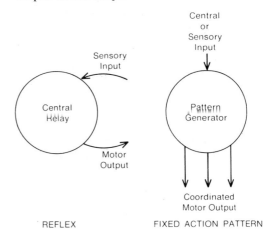

395

Table 19.1 Main features of reflexes and fixed-action patterns

Reflex	Fixed-action pattern
1. A simple motor action, stereotyped and repeatable.	1. A complex motor act, involving a specific temporal sequence of component acts.
2. Elicited by a sensory stimulus, the strength of the motor action being graded with the intensity of the stimulus.	2. Generated internally, or elicited by a sensory stimulus. The stimulus acts as a trigger, causing release of the coordinated motor act. The action may be all-or-nothing or graded in intensity, and it may be contingent on the type of sensory stimulus or internal state, but it maintains its basic pattern.

was one of the first to use the term in 1784 when he wrote:

The reflexion of sensorial into motor impressions . . . takes place in the sensorium commune (common sensory center) . . . This reflexion may take place either with consciousness or without . . .

Our present use of the term dates from the earliest experimental investigations of the role of the spinal cord in mediating muscle responses to sensory stimuli. Among the important studies were those of Charles Bell in England and François Magendie in France, who first established in the 1820s that sensory fibers are contained in the dorsal roots, and motor fibers in the ventral roots, of the spinal cord. Bell stated it clearly: "Between the brain and the muscle there is a circle of nerves; one nerve conveys the influence of the brain to the muscle, another gives the sense of the condition of the muscle to the brain." The action may be all-or-nothing or graded in intensity, and it may be contingent on the type of sensory stimulus or internal state, but it maintains its basic pattern.

Marshall Hall (1790–1857) vigorously advocated the notion that spinal reflex movements are distinct from voluntary movement, dependent on the spinal cord but unconscious and independent of the rest of the brain. Hall and many other workers in the course of the nineteenth century identified and categorized a number of types of reflexes. Much of this work, however, was clouded by wrangling about whether reflexes were conscious or not, and the prevailing reticular theory of the neuron misled many people in thinking about the nervous pathways involved.

It was at this stage, around 1890, that Charles Sherrington came onto the scene. We have already seen (Chap. 4) how his work led to the concept of the synapse. With regard to reflexes, his work was built on two essential foundations: he carried out a careful anatomical analysis of the nerves to different muscles, and he then used this knowledge to analyze quantitatively the reflex properties of specific nerves and muscle groups. This painstaking work was the means for obtaining the first clear view of the reflex as a combined structural and functional entity, and it established the reflex arc as a subject for further anatomical and physiological analysis by many twentieth-century workers. In addition, Sherrington emphasized the importance of the reflex as an elementary *unit of behavior*, and thus laid one of the cornerstones for the modern studies of animal behavior (see Sherrington, 1906).

Fixed-Action Patterns: A Brief History

There are, in general, two ways to study the behavior of an organism. One is to bring the animal into the laboratory and devise various kinds of instruments and procedures to test its abilities. This type of approach began around 1900, and gave rise to the fields of *behaviorism* and *animal psychology*. We shall discuss these fields and their methods further in Section IV.

The other approach is for the investigator to go out in the field and observe the animal in its daily life. This, of course, is as old as humankind itself, but it became a science only in the late nineteenth century. Charles Darwin's other great book, *On The Expression of Emotions in Man and Animals* (1872), in which he attempted to demonstrate similarities in instinctual behavior between animals and humans, is often regarded as the starting point for the systematic study of naturally observed behavior. This led to the modern field of *ethology*.

How can observations of natural behavior provide evidence for basic units of behavior? A number of workers in the early part of this century contributed to this study by their careful observations of animals in the field. This culminated in 1950 with the suggestion of Konrad Lorenz that much of the repertoire of individual motor actions and motor responses of animals can be described as *fixed-action patterns*. These are acts that are instinctual, stereotyped, and characteristic of a given species. Table 19.1 summarizes some of their attributes. Since they are coordinated and purposeful, they occur at a higher level in the hierarchy of motor organization which we discussed in Chap. 17 (see Fig. 17.12). They are in turn only part of a larger behavioral unit that includes at least three components: first, the "drive" to search for a certain stimulus context; second, the selective response to it—its "innate recognition"; and third, the discharge of an equally innate motor activity coping with the situation (von Holst, in Lorenz, 1981). The innate motor activity is thus fixed only in a relative sense. It can be selectively activated by different stimuli under different conditions of internal state or motivational drive. It

can vary in intensity, from the slightest intentional gesture to a full-blown all-or-nothing action, such as a startle response. In fact, one of the main themes to arise from recent work is the conditional nature of most motor acts. For this reason, many workers prefer other terms, such as "response," "complex reflex," "motor pattern," or "behavior." In general, these all have in common that they describe a complete and purposeful pattern of motor response to some initiating input.

Apart from their importance for behaviorists and ethologists, the reflex and the fixed-action pattern have been useful tools in guiding the experiments of neurobiologists on the cellular mechanisms of motor systems. This has been particularly true in invertebrates, where it has been possible to isolate and study relatively simple nervous components that correspond rather closely to the circuits for specific reflexes and even simple fixed-action patterns. To the extent that reflexes and fixed-action patterns are innate, they have also been attractive for genetic experiments; for example, mutations can produce selective loss of parts of a circuit, and these parts can be correlated with the behavioral deficits produced.

In the remainder of this chapter, we will discuss several of the best-known examples of reflexes and fixed-action patterns. First, we consider skin reflexes and startle responses in invertebrates. We then consider startle responses in the vertebrate, and finish with an overview of the reflex organization of the vertebrate spinal cord.

INVERTEBRATES

The Leech: Skin Reflexes

The neurons involved in receiving stimuli in the skin of the leech and transmitting the information to the central nervous ganglia were described in Chap. 12. It will be recalled that touch, pressure, and noxious modalities have identifiable cell bodies and given locations (see Fig. 19.2). One main

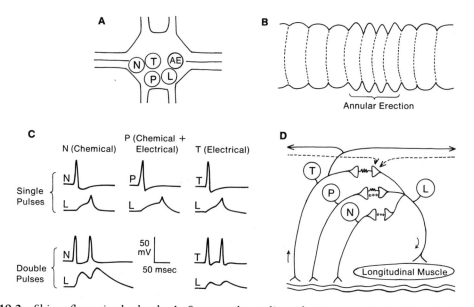

Fig. 19.2   Skin reflexes in the leech. **A.** Segmental ganglion, showing positions of touch (T), pressure (P), and noxious (N) sensory neuron cell bodies, and two motoneurons, the longitudinal (L) and annulus erector (AE). **B.** Stimulating the L motoneuron shortens the segment. **C.** Intracellular recordings from different combinations of sensory and motor neurons, to show chemical and electrical transmission, and summation of responses. **D.** Circuit diagram summarizing the pathways for the skin reflexes. Chemical synapses are indicated by small circles, electrical synapses by zig-zag lines. (Based on studies of Nicholls and collaborators, in Kuffler et al., 1984)

type of motoneuron is the L type, which innervates the longitudinal muscles. When these contract, they shorten the segment. The other main type is the AE motoneuron, which innervates the annulus erector muscles. When these contract, they pucker the segment into a sharp ridge.

When touch, pressure, or noxious stimuli are applied to the skin of the intact animal, contractions are elicited in the segmental muscles. One therefore has a simple reflex pathway, and we can deduce right away that it has the three components of a classical reflex arc: a sensory inflow pathway, a central relay site, and a motor outflow pathway. The key questions for the neurobiologist are: what kinds of connections are made between the sensory and motor cells, and what are their functional properties?

Work from the laboratory of John Nicholls, of Stanford and Basel, has provided

answers to these questions. Let us consider the case of the L cell. Intracellular electrodes were introduced into a sensory cell body and a motoneuron cell body in the same ganglion. When the sensory cell was directly stimulated by an electrical pulse through the intracellular electrode, an impulse was elicited in that cell, and also a response in the L cell. The L cell response consisted of a synaptic depolarization leading up to a small spike (see Fig. 19.2). When the latencies and other properties of the responses were analyzed for the responses elicited by the three types of sensory cell, it was found that the T cell is coupled to the L cell by an electrical synapse, the N cell by a chemical synapse, and the P cell by a combination of electrical and chemical synapses. It was further found that the chemical synapses are readily modifiable, giving a much facilitated response to a second pulse, whereas the electrical synaptic response was relatively invariant (see Fig. 19.2).

In addition to these short-term effects, there are long-term changes in the reflex pathways brought about by sustained or repeated natural stimulation of the skin. This is seen as a hyperpolarization of the sensory cells that may last for seconds or minutes after stimulation has ceased. Nicholls and his colleagues have shown that the hyperpolarization may be due either to an electrogenic sodium pump, activated by the influx of Na^+ during the impulse discharge, or to a prolonged Ca^{2+}-dependent increase in K^+ permeability. The pump mechanism predominates in T cells, the K^+ permeability mechanism in N cells, and both are present in P cells. The hyperpolarizations induced in these cells raise the thresholds for impulse generation and affect synaptic integration, but the significance of these effects for the reflex behavior of the organism is not yet understood.

The diagram in Figure 19.2 summarizes the circuits for the reflex arcs from T, P, and N cells through L cells. Since the connections are direct, without intervention of an interneuron, we say that these are *monosynaptic pathways,* and *monosynaptic reflexes.* Note that the cells in these pathways make connections with other central neurons, and in turn receive connections from other neurons; these are the means for coordinating the reflexes with other nervous activity.

Skin reflexes are virtually universal, providing the means whereby organisms withdraw from unfamiliar or harmful stimuli. It is of interest that in the leech the pathway for reflex withdrawal from a noxious stimulus is monosynaptic; the corresponding pathway in vertebrates is polysnaptic (see below).

Crayfish Escape Response

A common type of behavior in many invertebrates is a quick escape movement. This is elicited by a sensory stimulus, and consists of a sudden synchronous contraction of special fast muscles that moves the animal away from the site of danger. Animals as diverse as the earthworm, crayfish, and squid all show this type of behavior (and also some vertebrates; see below). In most cases it has been found that a giant axon is a part of the nervous pathway. This is logical, because, as we learned in Chap. 6, the larger a fiber, the faster the conduction rate of the impulses—and the essence of an escape movement is speed.

The escape response is produced by the discharge of only a single impulse in the successive components of the nervous pathway. In the case of the leech reflexes, the motor responses could be seen as small pieces of larger behavioral patterns. In the case of the escape response, the motor action is an entire purposeful behavioral act in itself. There are, in fact, two pairs of giant fibers in the crayfish: medial and lateral. The medial giant fiber connects to all segments, and the resulting muscle contractions propel the animal backwards. The lateral giant fiber lacks connections in the most posterior ganglia; this tends to produce an upward movement of the animal. These connections and their correlated behaviors are shown in Fig. 19.3.

The escape response happens so quickly that there is not time for feedback information to guide or adjust the movement. Thus, there is no role for feedback information from muscle receptors, for example. It is a movement that, once triggered by peripheral stimuli, is completely under *central control.*

The ability of a single neuron or fiber, such as the giant fiber, to trigger an entire behavioral act implies that it occupies some special position in the hierarchy of motor control. From this has emerged the concept of the *command* neuron or fiber, and the idea that such a neuron or fiber has some kind of executive power to initiate or control a specific coordinated motor act. We shall discuss this concept further in Chap. 21.

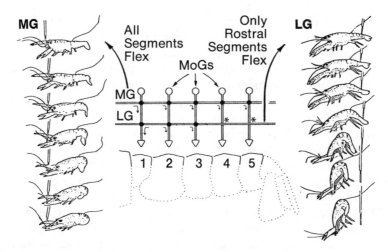

Fig. 19.3 Flexion responses of the crayfish. *On the left,* an electrical shock delivered to the medial giant fiber (MG) elicits postsynaptic responses in motoneurons (MoG) in all segmental ganglia (G₁– G₅). *On the right,* a shock to the lateral giant (LG) fiber elicits responses in motoneurons only in segmental ganglia G₁–G₃. The differences in behavioral responses are shown in the sketches of frames from high-speed cinematography; the tail flip mediated by the medial giants moves the animal backward, that by the lateral giants moves the animal upward. Large dots indicate sites of electrical synapses from giant fibers onto motor giants. These synapses are lacking at sites marked by asterisks. (From Wine and Krasne, 1981)

Neural Circuit

The neural circuit mediating the escape response has been worked out in detail in the crayfish, and the components and the sequence of events can be summarized in relation to the diagram of Fig. 19.4. Abrupt mechanical stimulation of the integument excites the hair cells (tactile afferents, TA) to discharge an impulse, which activates electrical synapses on a giant fiber (lateral giant command cell, LG) and chemical synapses on an interneuron (transient sensory interneuron, T); the interneuron, in turn, also has electrical synapses on the giant fiber. Although the hair cell thus has a direct connection to the giant fiber, the route through the interneuron is actually much more powerful. The impulse set up in the giant fiber excites segmental motoneurons (motor giants, MoG) in rapid sequence as it passes through successive segmental ganglia; this occurs by means of electrical synapses. These, in fact, were the first electrical synapses to be identified, and their mechanism has been described in Chap.

9. The excited motoneurons then activate their respective muscles to contract.

This response is similar to the reflexes of the leech that were discussed above, in that a sensory stimulation activates a nervous pathway which leads to an immediate motor act. It differs, however, in several important respects. Instead of one synaptic relay, it involves at least three synaptic links; we say, therefore, that it is a *polysynaptic* reflex. It has a relatively high threshold for sensory activation because it is a specialized movement which is appropriate only under specific environmental conditions. When activated in this way, it therefore has the character of an *all-or-nothing response,* in contrast to the reflexes we discussed above in the leech, whose magnitude is *graded* with the intensity of the stimulation.

The simple circuit in Fig. 19.4 represents only a beginning in understanding the principles underlying this escape response. We will discuss briefly several of the mechanisms that need to be added to this circuit.

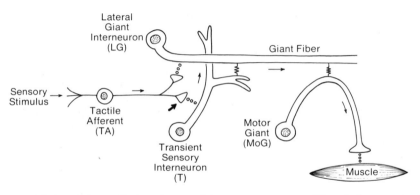

Fig. 19.4 Simplified circuit mediating the crayfish escape response. Chemical synapses shown by dots, electrical synapses by zig-zag lines. Short thick arrow indicates site of habituation. (From Wine and Krasne, 1981)

First, the reflex *habituates* with repeated stimulation. If a crayfish is tapped at intervals of one minute, the escape response disappears within 10 minutes. Most of this is accounted for by decreased release of neurotransmitter from the sensory afferent terminals onto the thick sensory interneurons (arrow in Fig. 19.4). We will discuss mechanisms of habituation more fully in Chap. 29.

Second, the simple circuit of Fig. 19.4 is a part of much more extensive circuits mediating control of the escape response and related motor behavior. The LG neuron not only excites the motoneurons that cause the tail flip, but also mediates feedback inhibition. This inhibition is massive and widespread, and affects synaptic sites at virtually every level in the hierarchy of motor control. This so-called *command-derived inhibition* has several functions; for example, it can set the threshold for subsequent elicitation of the response, and protect against the onset of habituation.

Third, the fact that the tail flip can be elicited by a single impulse in the lateral giant interneuron (LG in Fig. 19.4) has implied that the LG–MoG pathway is the sole pathway for the tail flip. However, recent studies have shown that there is a set of nongiant motoneurons, called fast flexor motoneurons (FF). These differ in innervating smaller groups within the flexor musculature of each segment. The giant and nongiant motoneurons are the final output sites of two parallel, linked pathways, each of which exerts different kinds of motor control (see Fig. 19.5). The giant system is specialized exclusively for producing rapid tail flips. The nongiant system, according to Krasne and Wine (1984), is specialized for "finesse of control." Synchronous stimulation of premotor neurons within this system can also elicit tail flips, though not so rapid nor so vigorous; the main function of these neurons, however, is to provide for finer motor control. Stimulation of the giant system also activates the nongiant system (through a segmental giant interneuron, SG; see Fig. 19.5) which appears to reinforce the giant-mediated tail flip. There is no connection in the reverse direction, which is reasonable, because it would be inappropriate for the nongiants to recruit the giants in their finer mechanisms of control.

Finally, recent work gives testimony to the pervasive effects of diffuse *arousal systems*, that set and modulate the level of activity in specific neural circuits. Thus, a hungry crayfish is highly aroused; its escape threshold is high, and it will fight for food until it acquires it, at which time the escape threshold abruptly lowers.

The escape response is thus not a simple reflex. It possesses many of the defining properties of a fixed-action pattern. It also exhibits many of the functional properties

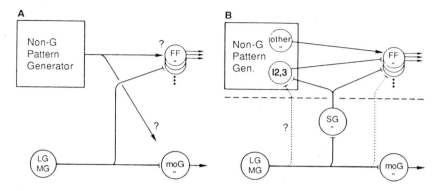

Fig. 19.5 Summary diagram of circuits controlling the tail flip. Precision tail movements are mediated by the nongiant pattern generator neurons (labeled Non-G Pattern Gen. I2.3, and other) which make excitatory chemical synapses (arrow) and electrical synapses (bar) on fast flexor motoneurons (FF). The most rapid tail flips, on the other hand, are mediated by the medial and lateral giant axons (MG and LG) which make electrical synapses on the gaint motoneurons (moG). They also can activate the nongiant system, either indirectly, through activation of a segmental giant interneuron (SG), or possibly directly (dotted line). Midline is indicated by dashed line. Multiple neurons are indicated by ditto marks. See text. (From Krasne and Wine, 1984)

that are characteristic of more complex motor and central systems. Finally, it illustrates the very important principle that each synapse within a neural circuit it not just a simple relay, but rather is a site at which *multiple controls* are present. These controls enable the circuit to operate in different modes, depending on the history of use of the circuit, and the behavioral state of the organism.

Neuromodulation in the Lobster

Another approach to the analysis of stereotyped motor patterns is to analyze how they may be mediated by the actions of specific types of neurotransmitters or neuromodulators. Ed Kravitz and his colleagues (see Kravitz et al., 1985) at Harvard carried out a series of experiments on the effects of biogenic amines in the lobster which nicely complement the experiments described above in the closely related crayfish. The basic behavioral finding was that after a systemic injection of serotonin, lobsters assume a doubled-up, flexed posture, resembling their posture when they are

startled or incited to fight. After injection of octopamine, on the other hand, the animals lie flat, with legs extended—a submissive posture such as is normally seen in a mating female.

If these substances can have these effects when injected, it suggests the hypothesis that they are released endogenously to mediate natural behavior. In order to identify the cells that might do this, serotonin (5HT) was conjugated to a large molecule (albumin); antibodies were prepared to it, and the location was visualized by a fluorescent marker. Some 100 cells throughout the nervous system were seen; each ganglion contained at least one of these cells, such as the pair shown in Fig. 19.6. It therefore appears that these 5HT-containing cells contribute to mediation of the flexed posture. This is an excellent illustration of a correlation between a specific molecule, a specific cell type, and a specific behavior, one of the goals of neurobiology, as we discussed in Chap. 1. The next steps in the analysis are to localize the serotonin more precisely by use of monoclonal antibodies, to analyze transcription and translation of the enzymes that synthesize 5HT, and to

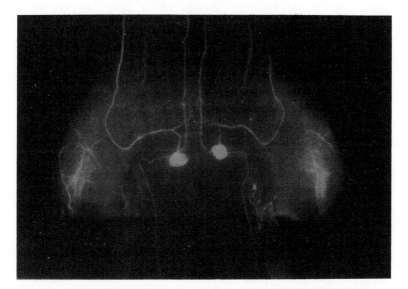

Fig. 19.6 Identification of the nerve cell type that contains serotonin in the lobster. The photomicrograph shows the T5 thoracic ganglion, with immunocytochemical staining for serotonin. The two paired cell bodies are located near the midline; their processes arborize within the ganglion, and extend to neighboring ganglia. (From Kravitz et al., 1985)

characterize the molecular receptors for 5HT.

In further work, it was shown that the contrasting postures are not due to different actions of the two amines on the extensor and flexor muscles: Both amines cause long-lasting contractures when applied directly to the muscles. This effect has been interpreted as a priming action of the amines on the muscles. Where, then, do the different actions occur?

The answer to this question emerged from experiments in which intracellular recordings were made of responses of motoneurons to the two amines (Fig. 19.7). It was found that excitatory motoneurons to flexor muscles were excited by 5HT and inhibited by octopamine; by contrast, excitatory motoneurons to extensor muscles were excited by octopamine and inhibited by 5HT. The differential actions of the amines on the motoneurons were thus in accord with the behavioral findings. It was interesting that the action of an amine on the inhibitory motoneuron to a muscle was the opposite of its action on the excitatory motoneuron

(thus 5HT *inhibited* inhibitory motoneurons to flexors), so that the effects were synergistic.

The interpretation of these experiments was that the amines have two sites and modes of action. In the periphery, they prime the muscles to contract more vigorously in response to the excitation by glutamate at the neuromuscular junction. In central ganglia, they have specific synaptic actions. The central actions of 5HT synapses result in activation of the central motor program for flexion; octopamine synapses activate the central motor program for extension. Kravitz et al. (1985) concluded that "amines are interacting with the 'command neuron' circuitry in some way to trigger the readout of central motor programs for flexion and extension."

VERTEBRATES

The studies of invertebrates illustrate the advantages of being able to work on systems composed of large, identifiable cells

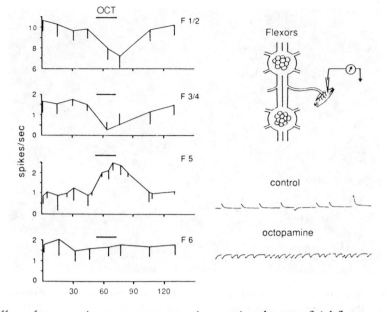

Fig. 19.7   Effect of octopamine on motoneurons innervating the superficial flexor muscles. *At upper right*, experimental setup is shown. *At lower right* are shown sample intracellular recordings of excitatory (upward deflections) and inhibitory (downward deflections) junctional potentials in a muscle fiber. Octopamine caused an increased frequency of inhibitory potentials. *On the left* are shown impulse firing rates of motoneurons following application of octopamine (OCT) $(3 \times 10^{-5}$ M); F5 is an inhibitory motoneuron; all others are excitatory. Octopamine inhibited impulse firing in flexor motoneurons F1/2 and F 3/4, but enhanced firing in F-5. Vertical bars indicate ± 1 SD. (From Kravitz et al., 1983)

and fibers. In the vertebrates, similar advantages are offered by Mauthner cells.

Mauthner Cells

These cells are present in the medulla oblongata of many species of fish and amphibians. When the fish is exposed to a sudden vibratory stimulus (such as a tap on the aquarium), it responds with a quick flip of the tail that displaces the animal sideways (see Fig. 19.8). It is thus essentially similar to an escape response; another term is a *startle response.*

The Mauthner cell is the key element in the startle response. Because of its large size, it has been possible to study it carefully. As indicated in Fig. 19.9, there is a single Mauthner cell on each side, situated at the level where the eighth nerve enters, carrying input from the auditory and vestibular nerves. The eighth nerve fibers make

direct electrical synapses on the distal parts of the lateral Mauthner cell dendrites by means of large club endings. Some eighth nerve fibers make synapses on vestibular nucleus neurons, which then make excitatory chemical synapses on the lateral dendrite. There is thus both a monosynaptic and disynaptic pathway from the eighth nerve fibers to the Mauthner cell. Note the close similarity of this arrangement to that in the afferent connections to the giant fiber in the crayfish escape response circuit (see Fig. 19.4 above).

Another set of connections mediates feedback control of the Mauthner cell. After the Mauthner fires its impulse, the impulse not only travels down the axon to excite the tail motoneurons, but also invades axon collaterals to excite interneurons. Through polysynaptic pathways, two kinds of interneurons are ultimately excited that feed back onto the Mauthner cell. One type has

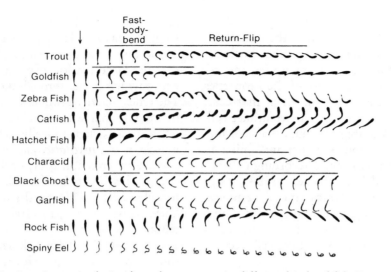

Fig. 19.8 Moving picture analysis of startle responses in different kinds of fish. Frames were taken at 5-msec intervals. Stimulus was a tap of a mallet on the aquarium, delivered at time indicated by arrow. (From Eaton et al., 1977)

chemical inhibitory synapses on the lateral dendrite. The other has axon terminals which wind around the axon hillock and initial segment of the Mauthner cell. This region is encased in a thick wrapping of glial membranes, which form an *axon cap*. The terminals make electrical synapses on the initial segment, and the axon cap increases the effectiveness of their inhibitory action by limiting the spread of extracellular current. (This mechanism was explained more fully in Chap. 7; see Fig. 7.1.)

At a *cellular* level, the Mauthner cell illustrates the importance of dendrites in integrating different types of synaptic inputs. It also exemplifies the strategic siting

Fig. 19.9 Synaptic organization of the Mauthner cell. Electrical synapses are shown by zig-zag connections, chemical synapses by small circles. Compare this circuit for a startle reflex in a vertebrate with that in Fig. 19.4, for an invertebrate. (After Furmkawa, in Kuffler et al., 1984)

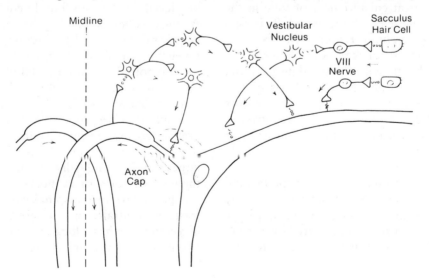

of a specific type of synapse to control the axonal output of the cell at the initial segment. At a *behavioral* level, the startle response resembles the crayfish escape response in showing many of the properties of a fixed-action pattern. As in that case, there are in addition to the Mauthner cell, other non-Mauthner circuits that can mediate rapid responses which are similar in their pattern. However, according to Robert Eaton and John Hackett (1984), it appears that for a typical initial response, such as that of the trout and goldfish shown in Fig. 19.8, the short-latency fast starts are mediated by the Mauthner cell circuits.

Motoneurons and Spinal Reflexes

The best known examples of reflexes, and the ones most characteristic of vertebrates, are those mediated by the spinal cord. Our knowledge about them has progressed in several stages over the past 100 years or so, being dependent on the experimental techniques available.

Sherrington's first studies, as we have mentioned, involved a correlation of anatomical tracing of sensory and muscle nerves with meticulous observations of different reflex behaviors. He introduced methods for cutting across the brainstem of a cat at the level of the midbrain (between the superior and inferior colliculi), which produced a great enhancement of tone in the extensor muscles of the limbs. This was termed *decerebrate rigidity*. The extensor muscles are the ones responsible for maintaining the animal in a standing position. In order to study the reflex basis of this activity, Sherrington and his collaborators in 1924 began to analyze the responses to passive stretch of an extensor muscle (for example, the quadriceps femoris of the thigh, which attaches to the knee cap.)

Figure 19.10 illustrates the experimental setup and results. Stretch of the muscle by only a few millimeters gives rise to a large increase in tension, as measured by a strain gauge. If the muscle nerve is cut, the tension

developed is small, because it results only from the passive elastic properties inherent in the muscle and its tendon. This shows that the large tension depends on a reflex pathway that passes through the spinal cord. The reflex activity produces contractions of the muscle that was stretched. Because the reflex feeds back specifically to the stretched muscle, it is a *myotatic reflex;* because it is elicited by stretch, it is also called a *stretch reflex.* This is the familiar "knee-jerk" reflex elicited by a tap on the tendon of the knee. Most muscles, invertebrate and vertebrate, show this type of reflex, though extensor muscles that work against gravity show it the best. Although the feedback to the muscle stretched is excitatory, there is, in addition, an inhibitory effect on muscles with antagonistic actions at a joint; thus, when a knee-flexor is stretched, some of the tension in the knee-extensor melts away (see Fig. 19.10). This illustrates the principle of *reciprocal innervation* of the muscles to a joint.

The next step was to analyze the nervous pathways involved in these and other types of reflex activity. David Lloyd at Rockefeller University began these studies around 1940. The experiments required laborious dissection of individual peripheral nerves combined with removal of the laminae of the vertebral bones (laminectomy) to expose the spinal cord so that electrodes could be placed on the dorsal and ventral roots. A single volley could then be set up in a peripheral nerve, and the response of motoneurons could be recorded in terms of the compound action potential of their axons in the ventral root. Representative results are shown in Fig. 19.11. Stimulation of a muscle nerve produces a short-latency, brief volley in the ventral root. This shows that the input from muscles is carried over large, rapidly conducting axons, and that there is only one, or at most two or three synaptic relays in the spinal cord. In contrast, the ventral root response to a volley in a skin nerve has a long latency, and lasts a long time. This suggests the involvement,

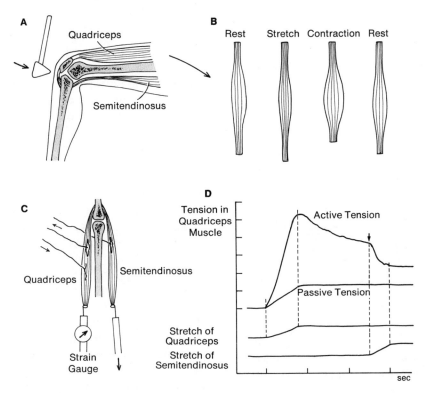

Fig. 19.10 **A.** Testing for the stretch reflex by tapping the patellar tendon of the quadriceps muscle. **B.** Different conditions of a muscle. **C.** Experimental setup for analyzing the stretch reflex in the cat. **D.** Tension of quadriceps muscle in response to stretch, before (active) and after (passive) cutting the motor nerve. Arrow indicates onset of reciprocal inhibition of quadriceps motoneurons produced by stretch of the semitendinosus muscle, an antagonist. (Based on Liddell and Sherrington, in Henneman, 1980a)

in skin reflexes, of slower-conducting fibers, polysnaptic pathways, and prolonged activity in the neurons in these pathways. Note that this polysynaptic pathway for skin reflexes in the vertebrate spinal cord contrasts with the monosynaptic pathways in the leech (Fig. 19.2, above). The polysynaptic pathways may provide for more complex processing of the input information from the skin.

The most definitive analysis of the neural reflex circuits has been with the use of intracellular recordings. We have already discussed the properties of synaptic excitation and inhibition in motoneurons, and the mechanisms of integration (see Chap. 7). A key question has been the number and type of synaptic connections within the

spinal cord for each of the main types of reflexes elicited by inputs in specific sensory afferent fibers (see Chap. 12). The first evidence from intracellular recordings, obtained by John Eccles and his collaborators in the 1950s, has been largely confirmed and much extended by subsequent studies. As shown in Fig. 19.12, inputs over the different types of muscle nerves are set up by either brief muscle stretch or a shock to a nerve. Motoneuron responses are recorded and synaptic relays estimated from delay times. From such measurements it has been concluded that group Ia afferents make monosynaptic excitatory synapses onto their own motoneurons and disynaptic inhibitory synapses onto antagonist motoneurons. Group II afferents, by compar-

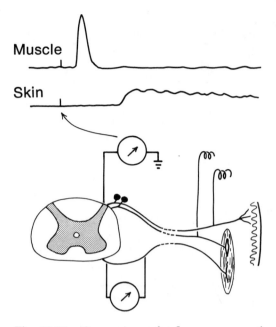

Fig. 19.11 Comparison of reflex responses of motoneurons to electrical stimulation of a muscle nerve (gastrocnemius) and a skin nerve (sural) in the cat. (After Lloyd, in Henneman, 1980a)

ison, make mostly disynaptic excitatory synapses onto their own motoneurons (see Fig. 19.12). (The terminology of peripheral nerve groups was covered in Chap. 12; see Table 12.2.)

We can briefly summarize the main types of reflex circuits that have been identified by this kind of analysis at the segmental level, using the simplified diagrams in Fig.

19.13. The circuits are categorized in terms of their main type of sensory input. The top three are muscle reflexes, and the bottom one is a skin reflex. The reader may review the main types of sensory fibers in Chaps. 12 and 13. Let us briefly review each circuit here; the role of each in relation to locomotion and larger patterns of motor behavior will be discussed in subsequent chapters.

Stretch Reflex

As we discussed above, the largest-diameter sensory nerves, the Ia fibers from muscle spindles, make monosynaptic excitatory synapses on their own motoneurons, and disynaptic inhibitory synapses onto antagonist motoneurons. This is the main pathway for the stretch reflex. Figure 19.13 shows that this reflex is present for both extensors and flexors. Classically, the prominence of the stretch reflex in antigravity extensor muscles was presumed to provide the reflex basis for maintenance of upright posture. The way this comes about is as follows. Begin with a standing posture, and let your knees start to bend. This begins to stretch your quadriceps (the large thigh muscle that extends the knee; see Fig. 19.10, above). This stretches the muscle spindles in the quadriceps, setting up a barrage of impulses in their axons. As can be traced in the circuit of Fig. 19.13A, this will lead to excitation of the extensor motoneurons, causing the extensor muscle to

Fig. 19.12 Experimental demonstration of monosynaptic and disynaptic connections onto motoneurons of the cat. See text. (Based on Eccles, 1957, and Watt et al., 1976)

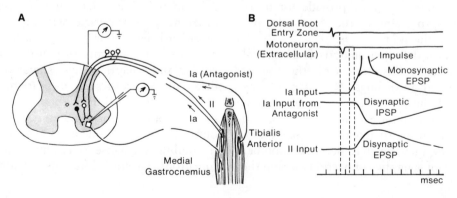

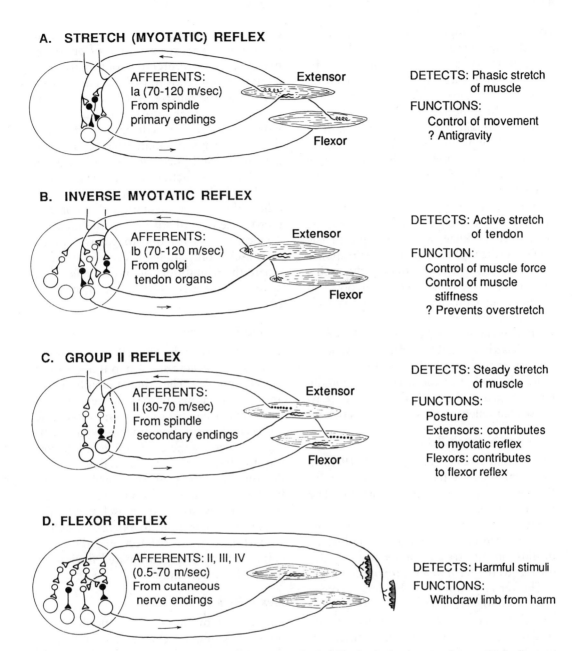

A. STRETCH (MYOTATIC) REFLEX

AFFERENTS:
Ia (70-120 m/sec)
From spindle
primary endings

Extensor

Flexor

DETECTS: Phasic stretch
of muscle
FUNCTIONS:
Control of movement
? Antigravity

B. INVERSE MYOTATIC REFLEX

AFFERENTS:
Ib (70-120 m/sec)
From golgi
tendon organs

Extensor

Flexor

DETECTS: Active stretch
of tendon
FUNCTION:
Control of muscle force
Control of muscle
stiffness
? Prevents overstretch

C. GROUP II REFLEX

AFFERENTS:
II (30-70 m/sec)
From spindle
secondary endings

Extensor

Flexor

DETECTS: Steady stretch
of muscle
FUNCTIONS:
Posture
Extensors: contributes
to myotatic reflex
Flexors: contributes
to flexor reflex

D. FLEXOR REFLEX

AFFERENTS: II, III, IV
(0.5-70 m/sec)
From cutaneous
nerve endings

DETECTS: Harmful stimuli
FUNCTIONS:
Withdraw limb from harm

Fig. 19.13 Neural circuits for the main types of spinal reflexes in the vertebrate. Each diagram shows only the minimum circuit elements involved in a reflex; for the sake of simplicity, additional interneuronal pathways contributing to modulation and control of the reflex are not shown. The spinal cord is on the left, and a flexor and extensor muscle are on the right. Within the spinal cord are flexor (F) and extensor (E) motoneurons; excitatory terminals of afferent fibers and interneuron are shown as unfilled (open) profiles, while inhibitory cells and connections are shown as filled (black) profiles. The dashed line in C indicates a weak action. See text. (Based in part on Matthews, 1972, 1982)

contract and oppose the gravity-induced stretch, thereby tending to return the body to its upright posture. At the same time, by means of reciprocal inhibition through inhibitory interneurons, the flexor motoneurons will be inhibited, further allowing the extension to take place. In addition to these segmental loops, the extensor motoneurons are under considerable excitatory control from descending fibers from higher centers (see later).

It may thus be appreciated that when we test for the stretch reflex by tapping the tendon at the knee, we are using a phasic stimulus (the tap) to elicit a phasic response (the knee jerk), whereas mainly this reflex circuit mediates tonic activity involved in maintaining a posture. In fact, the Ia endings are especially sensitive to the rate of change of small stretches, as was shown by Peter Matthews at Oxford using small vibratory stimuli applied to a muscle. This work showed that the secondary spindle endings (group II fibers) also contribute to the stretch reflex, as we shall discuss below.

Tension Feedback Reflex

The second circuit shown in Fig. 19.13 is that established by the large-diameter group Ib fibers from Golgi tendon organs. The connections onto motoneurons are all disynaptic. The effects on the motoneurons from a given muscle tend to be the reverse of those in the stretch reflex pathway, giving rise to the term *inverse myotatic reflex*.

The sensory input for this reflex comes from the Golgi tendon organs. As we discussed in Chap. 12, tendon organs are particularly sensitive to tension aroused by muscle contraction. When a muscle contracts, it exerts tension on the tendon organs, sending a barrage of impulses in the large Ib afferents. Within the spinal cord, the afferents activate inhibitory interneurons onto homonymous motoneurons (motoneurons to the same muscle), and excitatory interneurons onto antagonist muscles (see Fig. 19.13B).

By virtue of the synaptic organization, the effect of a muscle contraction is to decrease the amount of contraction of that muscle but increase excitation of opposing muscles. One interpretation of this arrangement is that it tends to maintain a constant tension in the muscle. Another interpretation is that the inhibitory interneuron provides a switch for reducing contraction; thus, cutaneous and joint afferents also can activate Ib inhibitory interneurons, and can switch off contraction if a limb encounters an obstacle. When combined with the stretch reflex, the inverse myotatic reflex contributes to the overall stiffness of the muscles. Tendon organs respond to passive stretch of muscles only at high levels of stretch, where their inhibitory action is believed to have a protective function against overstretch.

Group II Reflexes

The third circuit in Fig. 19.13 is that involving the medium-size group II fibers from muscle spindles. These make mainly disynaptic connections onto motoneurons. In some experiments a weak monosynaptic connection onto homonymous motoneurons (shown by the dashed line in C), similar to that in the stretch reflex, can be demonstrated. Regardless of sensory input, disynaptic excitatory connections are directed mainly to flexor muscles, and the inhibitory connections to extensor muscles. By virtue of these connections, these circuits contribute to coordinated flexion reflexes of a whole limb.

Flexor Reflex

Stimulation of the skin or muscles by a noxious stimulus characteristically produces withdrawal of the affected limb. This is termed the *flexor reflex*. It can be mediated by a wide range of receptors and fibers, which are often referred to collectively as *flexor reflex afferents (FRA)*.

The bottom diagram in Fig. 19.13 indicates that these fibers make polysynaptic connections which are excitatory to flexors and inhibitory to extensors. In addition, these fibers make widespread connections throughout the spinal cord which have the opposite effect: excitation of extensors and inhibition of flexors. Thus, while the hindlimb is being withdrawn, the other limbs are being extended, for maintaining posture and participating in locomotion. Or, in more picturesque terms, the hindlimb is removed from danger, while the other three legs run away! This is another demonstration of the fact that reflexes do not take place in isolation. Here, as in the other examples of Fig. 19.13, the reflex circuit not only plays back upon the stimulated limb, but also calls forth appropriate and coordinated actions of the other limbs.

20

Locomotion

The ability to move about can be regarded as the most important characteristic of animal life. We generally refer to this overall ability as locomotion. Locomotion can be defined, in precise terms, as *the ability of an organism to move in space in purposeful ways under its own power, by efficient mechanisms suitable for the purposes of the movement.* In this chapter we will be concerned with the main types of locomotor activity in invertebrates and vertebrates, and the types of nervous organization that control these activities.

Down through the ages, people have made careful observations of the movements of their fellow humans and of the animals about them, but naked-eye observations of rapid movements could be little more than fleeting impressions; of the most rapid movements, such as the wing movements of a hummingbird, there was only ignorance. Of course, ignorance is the fertilizer for the flowers of debate, and by the nineteenth century there were heated controversies about such matters as the exact positions of a horse's legs during trotting or galloping, or how a cat held upside down can right itself as it falls. (Some scholars were able to prove that the latter is theoretically impossible!)

Accurate knowledge of locomotor activity awaited the application of photographic techniques in the late nineteenth century. The pioneers in this were Emil Marey in Paris and Eadweard Muybridge in the United States. Muybridge set up a battery of 24 still cameras side-by-side along a track, and triggered them in sequence while an animal walked or ran by. Examples of his results are shown in Fig. 20.1. These studies cleared up the old controversies about galloping horses and the like, and provided a wealth of information about the locomotor patterns of a wide variety of animals, including humans.

Evolution of Locomotor Structures and Functions

In order to understand the neural systems that control a locomotor pattern like that shown in Fig. 20.1, we need to backtrack briefly at this point and recall the phylogeny of invertebrates and vertebrates, for much of the basis for the evolution of different body forms is to be found in the adaptations for different types of locomotor activity.

The simplest types of locomotion are found in unicellular or small multicellular

412

Fig. 20.1 Sequences of still photographs of a galloping horse. This proved for the first time that during a gallop there is a time when all four hooves are in the air. (Obtained by Eadweard Muybridge in 1887, and republished in 1957)

organisms, which move about mainly by means of *pseudopodia* or *cilia,* aided often by *secretions* of slime. These mechanisms are in fact, exploited in higher organisms in many cellular functions, as we saw in Chap. 3. However, as mechanisms for moving the body through the environment they are effective only for very small organisms (cf. Fig. 17.1). Several additional specializations accompanied the development of larger and more complex organisms. A key one was the ability to develop significant amounts of *force* through muscular contractions. This depended on the development of a *skeleton,* a hydrostatic type in worms and molluscs, and a rigid type in arthropods and vertebrates. A second adaptation was the ability to carry out different *specialized functions* (for example, walking, grasping, feeding, etc.); this is greatly enhanced by the *metameric* body form, with its potential for specialization of different segments. A third specialization was the development of *appendages,* adapted for locomotion, and for many different types of locomotion. These specializations of body structure and function, and their significance for the main types of locomotor activity, are summarized in Table 20.1.

Some Common Principles in Nervous Control of Locomotion

The modern study of locomotion depends on a variety of methods. In addition to cinematographic recording of movement patterns, measurements are made of joint positions and angles, and the forces generated. The activity in individual muscles can be recorded by means of fine electrodes inserted into the muscles; the recordings are made on an *electromyograph* (EMG). Underlying any study, of course, is a thorough knowledge of the anatomy of the bones and muscles involved in the movements of interest.

Elements of Control

Whatever the pattern of locomotor activity, it is ultimately due to a pattern of nervous activity. In the analysis of nervous mechanisms there have been several areas of interest. The first efforts, directed at *muscle reflexes,* originated in the studies of Sherrington and co-workers. One of the main concepts that came out of these studies is the idea that locomotion involves a modulation of postural reflexes. A second area, to which Sherrington also contributed, con-

Table 20.1 Relations of structural specializations to modes of locomotion

Modes of locomotion	Adaptations of body structure	Significance for locomotion
swimming, creeping	hydrostatic skeleton (coelenterates)	transmission of pressure into force
swimming, creeping	coelom (annelid worms, molluscs)	more efficient transmission of pressure into force
swimming, creeping, burrowing	metamerism (annelid worms, arthropods)	1. more effective deployment of force 2. opportunity for specialization of segments 3. coordination of segments by specialized nervous system
swimming, walking, running, flying	jointed skeleton with appendages (arthropods, vertebrates)	1. extreme localization of force 2. amplification of force through limbs acting as levers 3. reduction and specialization of appendages, sometimes for multiple functions 4. more complex nervous controls

cerns the ability of the spinal cord to generate *intrinsic rhythms*. This concept owes its origin, in the early part of this century, particularly to Graham Brown in England, who studied cats with transected spinal cords. A third area of research is concerned with the control of the spinal cord by *higher motor centers*. Many workers have contributed to this area, as we shall see in the next chapter.

At one time or another there have been claims for the predominant influence of each of these main types of mechanisms for the control of movement. One of the important developments in motor studies in recent years has been the synthesis of all these mechanisms into a general framework for nervous control. This synthesis is summarized in Fig. 20.2. The first element in this framework is the *central pattern generator* in lower centers in the spinal cord (or the relevant ganglia in the case of invertebrates). This contains the essential neural mechanisms for generating coordinated rhythmic outputs of the motoneurons. The central pattern generator is activated and controlled by descending fibers from the second key element, *higher motor centers*. There is commonly a succession of higher centers, which form the hierarchy of

motor control as we discussed in Chap. 17 (Fig. 17.12). Third, there are *feedback circuits*, which feed back information from the *muscles* (proprioceptor reflexes); from the external *environment* through other sensory pathways; and, within the nervous system itself, from lower to higher *centers* (central feedback). This internal feedback

Fig. 20.2 The main neural components common to most motor systems.

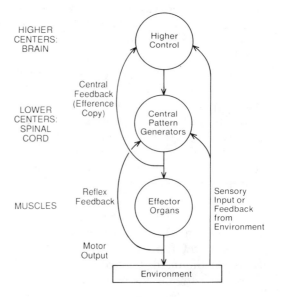

constitutes a copy of the output which informs the higher center how faithfully the output followed the descending instructions, and how much difference there is between that output and the output needed to reach some behavioral goal of the organism. It is called by several names, including *corollary discharge* (because it is a corollary of the primary output discharges), *efference copy* (because it is a copy of the efferent [output] signal), or *reafference* (because it is an internal afferent ["sensory"] signal).

Despite the variety of body forms and types of locomotive activity in different species, these main components are present to some extent in the nervous systems of most higher organisms. Randy Gallistel of Philadelphia has synthesized this view of a hierarchy of motor control in *The Organization of Action* (Gallistel, 1980), which presents a persuasive case that most of the main types of motor behavior can be accounted for by motor hierarchies containing three elementary units of action: the *reflex*, the *oscillator*, and the *servomechanism*. These are all represented in the diagram of Fig. 20.2. We have dealt with the reflex in the preceding chapter, and turn now to the oscillator.

Central Pattern Generators

The generation of repeating or oscillatory patterns of muscle activity is one of the main functions of motor systems. In recent years, it has been recognized that this property rests within nerve circuits that form what is called a *central pattern generator*. This type of circuit, which may be local or distributed, has emerged from studies of both invertebrates and vertebrates. It is one of the key organizing principles for present-day concepts of mechanisms of locomotion, though it has yet to be adequately incorporated into the traditional view of mechanisms underlying human locomotion, which draws more on studies of reflexes (Chap. 19) and upper motoneuron influences (Chap. 21).

The view emerging from recent studies is that, despite the diversity of body structure and locomotion patterning in the animal world, the basic types of neural circuits for generating rhythmic motor output are actually quite limited. Three of the main types that have been proposed are illustrated in Fig. 20.3.

Half-Center Model. The first model (A) was proposed by Graham Brown to account for the alternating activation of flexor and extensor muscles of the limb of the cat during walking. Each pool of motoneurons for flexor (F) or extensor (E) muscles is activated by a corresponding "half-center," or pool, of interneurons. Another set of neurons (D) provides for a steady excitatory drive to these interneurons. Between each pool of interneurons are inhibitory connections which ensure that, when one pool is active, the other is suppressed. Graham Brown hypothesized that, as activity in the first pool progressed, a process of fatigue would build up in the inhibitory connections between the two half-centers, thereby switching activity from one half-center to the other. In more modern terms, the process of fatigue can be replaced by any process bringing about self-inhibition of the active cells. The application of this model to the cat has received support from the more recent studies of Anders Lundberg and his colleagues in Sweden.

Closed-Loop Model. A second, and related, type of model (B) conceives of the interneurons as organized in a "closed-loop" of inhibitory connections. There are corresponding pools of motoneurons activated, or inhibited, in sequence. Because of the fractionation of the pools of interneurons and motoneurons, there can be a finer differentiation in the activation of different muscles. This seems to be a more accurate description of the slightly different activation patterns of individual muscles during many locomotor acts. George Szeckely of Hungary proposed this model for the salamander in 1968, and it has been applied

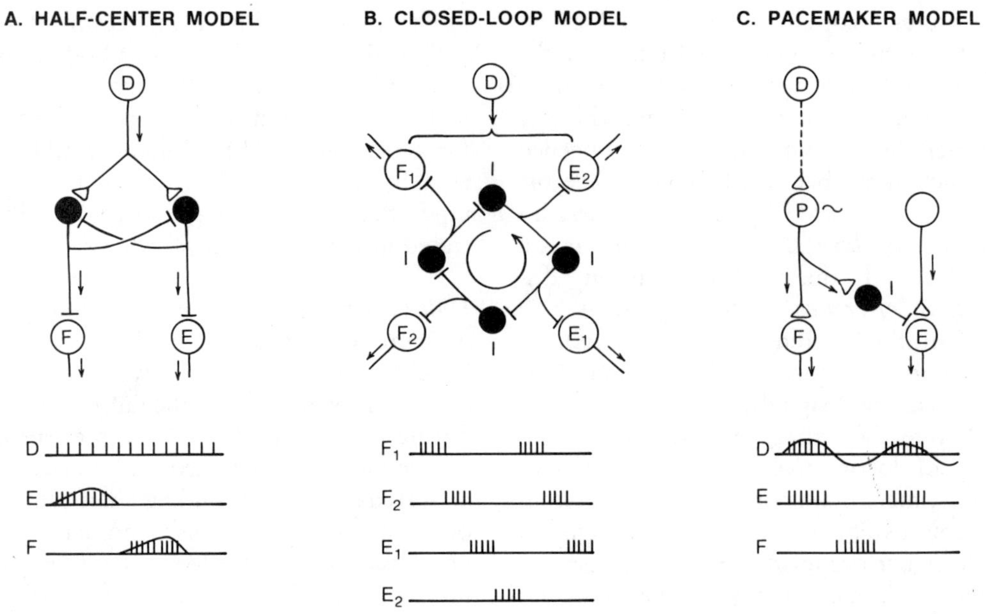

A. HALF-CENTER MODEL   **B. CLOSED-LOOP MODEL**   **C. PACEMAKER MODEL**

Fig. 20.3 Basic types of rhythm generators. **A–C.** Simplified diagrams of minimum number of neurons and connections for each type. Abbreviations for types of neurons: D, driver; E, extensor motoneuron; F, flexor motoneuron; P, pacemaker; I, interneuron. Neurons with excitatory actions are shown by open profiles; inhibitory, by filled profiles. Sequences of spike firing or graded potentials are shown in idealized recordings below. (For sources, see text)

also by the Russian school of Shik and Orlovsky in the cat. Another example is the model of Gunther Stent and his colleagues (1979) for swimming in the leech.

Pacemaker Model. In the models of Fig. 20.3A and B, rhythms result from neuronal circuit organization. In contrast, in the model of C a rhythm arises as a membrane property of a *pacemaker* cell or group of cells. This cell undergoes rhythmic excitation by intrinsic membrane mechanisms, involving the interplay of ionic currents. As discussed in Chap. 7, a common mechanism involves voltage-gated calcium channels; slow depolarization due to the entry of Ca^{2+} generates repetitive impulse firing, which is terminated by the hyperpolarizing action of calcium-sensitive K channels. In the model of Fig. 20.3C, the pacemaker cell drives flexor motoneurons directly, and brings about concurrent inhibition of extensor motoneurons through inhibitory interneurons.

INVERTEBRATES

With these principles in mind, let us examine locomotor systems in invertebrates. We will take three examples that illustrate the nervous organization involved in control of swimming, walking, and flying.

Swimming

Swimming generally takes place by means of undulatory (wavelike) movements of the whole body. This type of mechanism is very widespread in the animal world, and characterizes, for example, the whiplike movements of the tail of a sperm, and the locomotion of animals as diverse as worms, molluscs, fish, and snakes. Swimming is closely related to *creeping* and *burrowing*. They all involve coordinated sequences of muscle contractions, and their effectiveness (in terms of increased *speed* or *force* of movement) is enhanced by the development of a hydrostatic coelom, metameres, and a

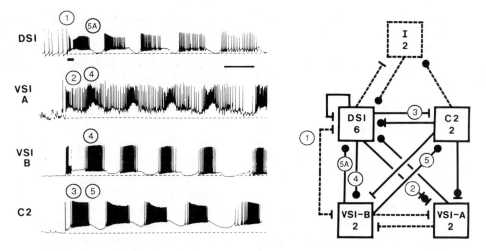

Fig. 20.4 The swimming generator in *Tritonia*. *Left:* Intracellular recordings of the firing patterns in the main types of neurons, induced by an initial brief period of electrical stimulation ① of the dorsal swim interneuron (DSI). The other neuron types are ventral swim interneurons (VSI, class A and B) and cerebral cells (C2). Numbers ② through ⑤ indicate the sequence of impulse firing patterns. Time bar, 5 seconds. *Right:* diagram of connections deduced for generating the firing patterns. T-bars represent excitatory synapses; filled circles, inhibitory synapses. Note that some connections are mixed or sequential (e.g., connection ② is excitatory–inhibitory–excitatory). Dashed lines show postulated pathways. I2, unidentified neurons. (From Getting and Dekin, 1985)

more complex organization of muscles and nervous system.

Tritonia is a sea slug that swims by making a series of alternating dorsal and ventral flexions of its body. The mechanisms that generate these movements have been studied intensively by Peter Getting and his colleagues at Iowa, and as a result this has become a useful model system.

The swimming movements are produced by alternating contractions of dorsal and ventral flexor muscles. These are activated by dorsal flexion neurons (DFN) and ventral flexion neurons (VFN), respectively. Their alternating pattern of impulse discharge can be set up even when the ganglia containing the DFNs and VFNs are dissected out of the organism and placed in a recording chamber, showing that the rhythm is due to a central pattern generator located within these ganglia.

The swimming generator has been localized to several groups of premotor interneurons. The main groups are dorsal swim interneurons (DSI) which activate the dor-

sal flexion neurons, and ventral swim interneurons (VSI) which activate the ventral flexion neurons. These two groups are interconnected with each other and with a third group of cerebral (C2) cells and a fourth group of interneurons (I). The basic circuit for these connections is shown in Fig. 20.4B.

The swimming generator arises out of the membrane properties, molecular receptors, and synaptic organization of these four types of neurons. This information has come from intracellular recordings combined with intracellular current injection to test resetting of the rhythms. The way the circuit works is illustrated in Fig. 20.4A,B. Swimming is initiated by sensory stimuli which feed into DSI and cause it to begin to fire a burst of impulses ①. DSI inhibits VSI ②, and at the same time excites C2 ③. C2 has excitatory synapses on VSI; however, the initial response of VSI neurons is delayed because of inhibition. This is due to an initial inhibitory action of the neurotransmitter followed by excitation in some neurons (VSI-A), or to initial activation of a fast transient I_A potassium current, which then inactivates so that excitation can proceed (VSI-B). The delays are important for the circuit to oscillate. VSI then fires ④, during which there is inhibition by VSI of C2 ⑤ and DSI (5A). Since this means that VSI no longer receives excitatory input from C2, its firing declines; DSI is therefore released from inhibition, and is ready to fire again to initiate a new cycle.

The principles of organization of this central pattern generator can be summarized as follows. First, the rhythm is neurogenic, and arises out of interactions between interneurons; the motoneurons are simply driven by the interneurons. Second, the oscillations are a network property, due to a combination of synaptic connections and membrane conductance channels, both ligand and voltage-gated. Third, the network is heavily dependent on inhibitory connections; in this respect, it resembles the type illustrated in Fig. 20.3B above, but it is better to consider it as a mixed excitatory–inhibitory type. Fourth, the generation of this rhythm is dependent particularly on complex postsynaptic potentials (PSPs) that include multiple components for excitation and inhibition, acting through different membrane conductances over different time scales.

From this analysis, it was concluded that the *Tritonia* swim generator cannot be described by a simple division into a pattern generator and a "command" neuron or system that turns it on and off. For example, the C2 and DSI neurons function both as command neurons (in initiating the rhythm) and as part of the pattern generator itself. Getting and Dekin (1985) therefore suggest that

. . . the command function appears to be an emergent property of the network as a whole. It is not a function of a single cell, but a process that emerges as a consequence of multiple synaptic interactions within the network . . .

The same network can function in the two modes by virtue of the multifunction synapses, with different actions over different time scales, as explained above. We will return to the question of command neurons within the context of motor hierarchies in the next chapter.

Walking

An essential aspect of the mechanism of swimming is that it involves the whole body. Terrestrial animals, moving through the less resistive medium of the air, can achieve greater efficiency by developing appendages (legs) that are specialized for the purpose. As summarized in Table 20.1, appendages evolved in conjunction with the advantages of a rigid, jointed skeleton and associated musculature. The problem for the body is thus changed, from alternating contractions of the axial musculature in the case of swimming, to alternating contractions of appendage musculature and coordination between the different appendages. The coordinated movements of the appendages are referred to as *stepping* or *striding*. Depending on the rate of movement, locomotion by this means takes the form of *walking* or *running*.

Walking is a very effective and adaptable means of locomotion, as shown by the many forms it takes among the thousands of species in the phylum Arthropoda. In general, the fewer the legs, the more efficient the locomotion, at least as far as speed is concerned. Part of the reason for this is illustrated in Fig. 20.5, which compares an animal with many legs (a centipede) with one with few legs (a crayfish). The centipede can actually move rather quickly (about 0.4 m/sec, or better than 1 ft/sec), and does so by means of relatively long legs, with slightly differing lengths. However, with so many legs, there is a tremendous problem of coordination, and there are severe restrictions on individual leg movements, in order that the centipede doesn't continually trip over itself. In contrast, rapid locomotion is achieved in the crayfish (and many other arthropods) by means of only a few pairs of legs. In those animals with only three pairs, it is often the case that the front

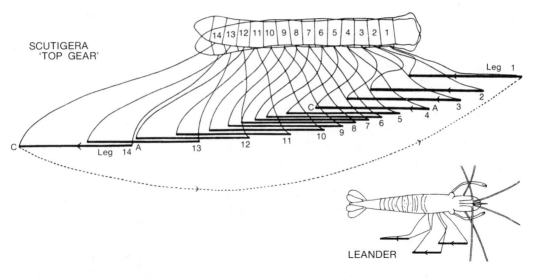

Fig. 20.5 Comparison of locomotor appendages (legs) of the fastest centipede *(Scutigera)* and a crayfish *(Leander)*. Heavy lines indicate the movement of the "foot" relative to the body during one step forward. (From Manton, in Barrington, 1979)

legs are specialized for *traction* or *attachment,* the middle ones for *support,* and the rear ones for *propulsion.* An additional advantage of fewer legs is that it permits other appendages to be specialized for other functions, such as grasping prey (claws) or rapid escape maneuvers (tail).

Among the species that have been studied, the *cockroach* provides some particularly interesting examples of the neural

mechanisms that are involved (see Fig. 20.6). The central rhythm generator is composed of a group of cells which undergo oscillations of their membrane potential. Keir Pearson and Charles Fourtner in Alberta showed that some of these are nonspiking cells, which synaptically drive the motoneurons that innervate flexor muscles of the leg. At the same time, the extensor motoneurons are inhibited through an in-

Fig. 20.6 Rhythm generator for stepping in the cockroach. Diagram shows neural circuit controlling one leg. Characteristic activity patterns recorded from burst-generator interneuron and from flexor and extensor motoneurons are shown at right. (Modified from Pearson, 1976)

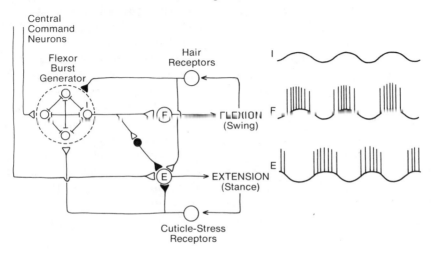

hibitory interneuron. Both the flexor-burst generator cells and the extensor motoneuron pool are under tonic excitatory drive from higher command fibers, and the result is that extensor excitation can occur only "out-of-phase" with flexor excitation. This assures an orderly alternation of contractions in the flexor and extensor muscles of the leg, and is the basis of stepping. This arrangement of connections to the flexors and extensors thus has similarities to the pacemaker model of Fig. 20.3C. However, nothing is known at present about the details of the network that generates the flexor burst.

Flying

The extraordinary utility of the articulated appendage is well-illustrated in the ability of many insects to fly. A characteristic of invertebrates is that the appendages for this purpose—the wings—have developed independently of the legs for walking. This means that flying insects retain their mobility and other motor capabilities on surfaces. Also it means that the wing is not a modified walking leg, but rather is designed solely for the purpose of flying. This is believed to account for the great variety of wing structures and flight mechanisms of insects, as compared with birds (see below).

Flight involves the generation of *lift* (to counteract gravity) and *thrust* (to move forward against the resistance of the air). Both of these depend on the aerodynamics of the wing structure, and the *orientation, force,* and *frequency* of the wing beat. These three factors, in turn, are the outcome of the properties of the peripheral muscles and skeleton, and the signals that come from the nervous system.

In assessing the relative importance of all these factors, a basic distinction is first made between *synchronous* and *asynchronous* flight mechanisms (see Fig. 20.7). In the synchronous type, each impulse in a motoneuron gives rise to a contraction of a muscle and a beat of the wing. The mus-

cles attach to the wing itself (*direct* muscles). The wing beat frequency is commonly in the range of 10–30 per second. This type is characteristic of most flying insects.

The asynchronous mechanism is found only in a few insect orders: Hemiptera (bugs), Coleoptera (beetles), Hymenoptera (bees and wasps), and Diptera (flies and mosquitoes). As indicated in Fig. 20.7, in this mechanism there is not a one-to-one relation between nerve impulse firing and the wing beat. Instead, the nerve impulses set up a tonic contraction state in thoracic (*indirect*) muscles. The contractions of these muscles put tension on the articulation of the base of the wing with the thorax, and a special property of this joint allows it to snap back and forth ("click" mechanism) at a high frequency. Thus, any unpatterned nerve discharge with sufficiently high frequency to set up the tonic state will generate the wing beats. This mechanism is well-suited for generating very high wing-beat frequencies. The frequencies for the housefly and honey bee, for example, are in the range of 200 beats per second, and those for the mosquito are as high as 1000 beats per second (only 1 msec between beats)!

The asynchronous mechanism thus depends on special properties of the thoracic muscles and wing joints. This is economical for the nervous system, which is freed of the burden of providing precise timing at high frequencies, with the attendant demands on nervous controls and energy metabolism. The spike intervals are so brief, in fact, that the nerve fibers could not fire fast enough to drive the muscles one-for-one, because of the duration of the refractory period (it may be recalled that a similar problem arises with the encoding of information about high-frequency tones in the auditory nerve, in Chap. 15). For the synchronous mechanism, on the other hand, there is close coupling between nerve firing and muscle contractions. For this mechanism, similar principles for the generation of rhythmic activity apply as in the other forms of locomotion we have considered.

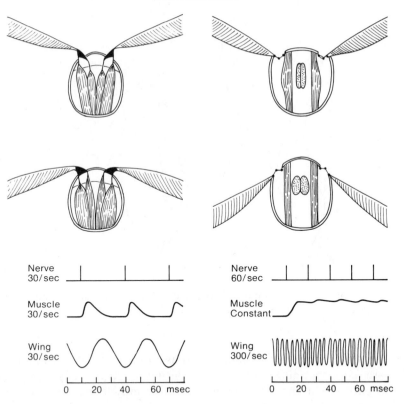

Fig. 20.7 Comparison between two types of flight muscle in insects. *Left:* Synchronous flight muscle, with direct connection of muscles to wing, as in the damselfly. *Right:* Asynchronous flight muscle, with indirect relation to wing, as in the wasp. *Below:* Characteristic activity in motor nerves (impulses), flight muscles (mechanical tension), and wing (movements). (After Smith, 1965, in part)

VERTEBRATES

Despite the differences in body structure, vertebrates engage in the same basic types of locomotion as invertebrates (see Table 20.1). Let us briefly consider some of the principles involved, with particular emphasis on walking in the mammal.

Swimming

As already mentioned, the undulatory motions of swimming in fish or slithering in snakes are similar to those of worms. Higher speeds are achieved by increasing the frequency of the alternating contractions of muscle groups that underlie the body undulations. The waves persist after deafferentation of the spinal cord when most of the dorsal roots are cut. After a high spinal transection, interrupting all descending fibers, most fish show no spontaneous movements, but during tonic sensory stimulation (such as a pinch of the tail), wavelike contractions of the body appear. From such experiments it has been concluded that a central rhythm generator is present in the spinal cord, which in many species requires tonic input for its expression.

Walking

Apart from the snakes, terrestrial vertebrates have particularly exploited the locomotory abilities of the leg in their invasion of the land. The evolution of legs from fins follows a logical sequence. In lower fish the function of the fins is mainly to

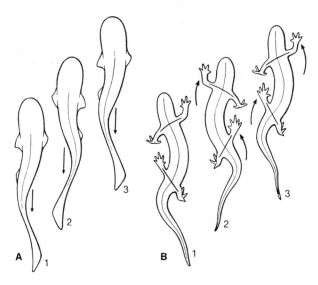

Fig. 20.8 Comparison between swimming movements of a fish (**A**) and primitive walking movements of a salamander (**B**). (From Romer and Parsons, 1977)

provide *stabilization,* but in higher (bony) fish the fins are more specialized and contribute to *propulsion.* In the transitional forms (Crossopterygia) the pectoral and pelvic fins are more elaborate, and have the appearance of being the basis for the fore- and hindlimbs of tetrapods.

The primitive walking movements of amphibians reflect rather strongly the basic swimming movements of fish. This is illustrated in Fig. 20.8. Note in B how the limbs have attachment points on either side of the pectoral (anterior) and pelvic (posterior) girdles. Forward movement is achieved by extension, placing, and thrust of the limbs, in coordination with the swimming movements of the body.

The diagrams of Fig. 20.8B might seem to imply that limb movements and their neural control in amphibians are relatively simple, but experimental investigations have shown that they are actually rather complicated. George Szekely inserted fine recording wires into individual muscles of the forelimb of the newt, and recorded the EMG activity during normal walking. The results are illustrated in Fig. 20.9. Alternating bursts of activity are present, but it can be seen that each of these eight muscles

has a rather complicated pattern of activity during the stepping cycle, and no two muscles or muscle groups have the same pattern. Also, contraction of two or more muscles is common at any given point in the cycle. These patterns are found to persist even after deafferentation by transection of the dorsal roots, showing that they are due to a central rhythm generator in the spinal cord. The half-center model, with similar activity patterns in extensors and flexors (see Fig. 20.3A), is too simple to account for the individualized activity patterns, and Szekely therefore proposed a network of inhibitory connections to account for the findings. This model has been presented in Fig. 20.3B.

Amphibians and reptiles are constructed so that the limbs are attached laterally to the trunk, whereas in birds and mammals the legs support the body from underneath. The lateral placement has the advantage of a low center of gravity and a more stable equilibrium. The vertical placement, however, is regarded as more efficient for the purposes of locomotion. In general this is so; nonetheless, some reptiles are capable of moving very swiftly indeed. Outstanding in this regard are the lizards. The little

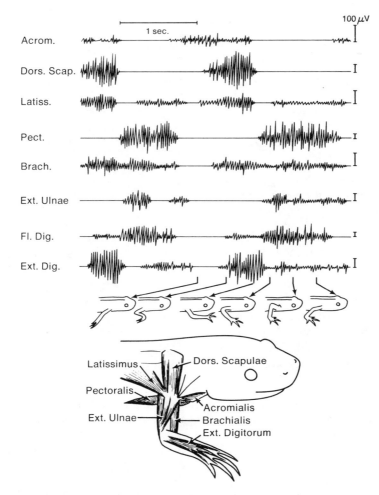

Fig. 20.9   Patterns of muscle activity during walking in the newt. *Above:* Activity of eight forelimb muscles, recorded in the electromyograph (EMG) in the freely moving animal. *Middle:* Movement of limbs during locomotion. *Below:* Positions of forelimb muscles. (From Szekely, 1968)

basilisk lizard can skitter along at rates up to 7 m per second (about 10 miles per hour). It does this by tucking in its fore-limbs and running on its hindlimbs, with the heavy tail helping to maintain balance (see Fig. 20.10). The lizard thus runs with a *bipedal* gait. Several other animals, be-sides humans, have developed a bipedal gait (for example, kangaroos), which illus-trates the principle of convergent evolution.

Control of Locomotion of the Cat

Because of its convenient size and general-ized body form, the domestic cat has been a favorite subject for studies of neural mechanisms of locomotion in higher ver-tebrates. The patterns of movements of the feet during normal locomotion of the cat are illustrated in Fig. 20.11. The stepping sequence is: left hind leg, left front leg, right hind leg, and right front leg. Watch your cat the next time you have a chance, and see if you can identify this sequence—without the help of a photographic analy-sis! It has been found that this is the basic pattern for most vertebrate species, as well as for fast moving invertebrates like the cockroach (see figure). The reason for this prevalence is that the pattern seems to pro-

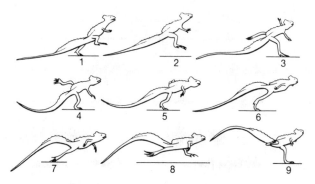

Fig. 20.10 Running of the basilisk lizard. (From Gray, 1968)

vide for the best *stability*, which becomes increasingly important in the longer-legged animals.

Gaits and Step Cycles

As the cat moves forward at increasing speeds, the steps are faster, but the same progression is maintained. However, different combinations of legs are on or off the ground at the same time as the speed increases, and these combinations are expressed as different *gaits*. The cat has several gaits, for moving to higher speeds, just as a car has several gears; these are illustrated in Fig. 20.11. For comparison, the cockroach has just one fast-moving gait. The cat can change relatively smoothly from one gait to the next (*gait conversion*),

Fig. 20.11 Comparison of the stepping movements of the cockroach and the cat for different gaits characteristic of the two species. Open bars, foot lifted; closed bars, foot planted. (Adapted from Pearson, 1976)

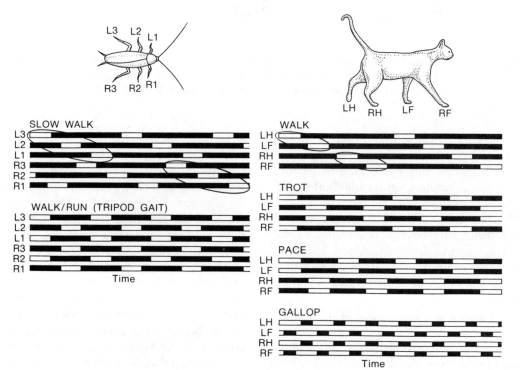

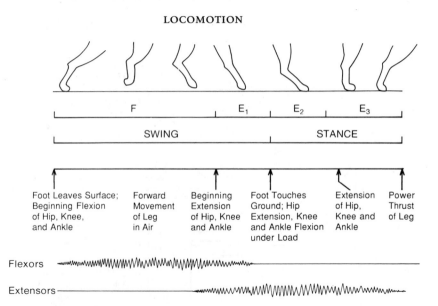

Fig. 20.12 The step cycle, showing phases of leg flexion (F) and extension (E) and their relation to the swing and stance. *Bottom:* Electromyograph (EMG) recordings. (Adapted from Wetzel and Stuart, 1976)

whereas the cockroach shifts more abruptly from the one to the other.

A closer analysis of the movement of one leg through a step cycle is illustrated in Fig. 20.12. As we have seen, a step consists of two phases, swing and stance. During the *swing* phase, the leg is lifted and brought forward, mainly by action of the leg flexor muscles (F). At the end of the swing phase (E_1), the extensors become active, and the combined activity of flexors and extensors stiffens the leg as it is planted. During the *stance* phase, extensor activity becomes dominant (E_2, E_3), providing the force that thrusts the animal forward. These phases of muscle activity seem to be quite general, and apply to our own bipedal steps as well as to quadrupeds.

If we examine again the different gaits as depicted in Fig. 20.11, we see that the total time for a step cycle decreases as the speed goes up, but the decrease is almost entirely taken in the stance phase; the duration of the swing phase stays relatively constant. Thus, speed of locomotion comes about mainly by faster and quicker thrust. There is presumably an economy in having the swing phase be relatively stereotyped, so that the central motor circuits can change gaits by controlling muscle activity mainly during the stance phase.

Spinal Stepping

The different gaits and how they are controlled brings us back to the questions originally posed by Muybridge and his photographs. We have seen how Graham Brown's studies led to the idea of "half-centers" in the spinal cord, with intrinsic rhythmic activity controlling flexor and extensor motoneuron pools. Further analysis awaited more refined methods, in which there could be experimental control of locomotor behavior under well-defined conditions. This was first achieved by the Russian physiologists, Shik, Severin, and Orlovsky, in Moscow. The experimental setup is illustrated in Fig. 20.13. The cat may have a transection at one of several levels in the neuraxis: in the brainstem (for example, a transection between the superior and inferior colliculi, producing a decerebrate animal), between brainstem and rostral spinal cord (high spinal transection), and at various levels in the spinal cord. The animal is held rigidly in a holder, and its paws are

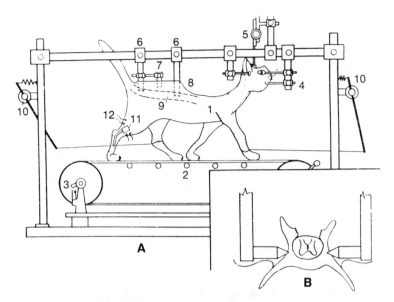

Fig. 20.13 Experimental setup for studying neuronal activity during treadmill walking in the decerebrate cat. **A.** General view. **B.** Inset showing rigid holding of vertebrae. Numbers identify the following components: 1, cat; 2, treadmill; 3, belt tachometer; 4, stereotaxic head holder; 5, electrode holder; 6, clamps to hold spine; 7, electrodes for recording unitary activity; 8, skin flap forming oil bath; 9, spinal cord; 10, detectors of longitudinal displacement of limbs; 11, joint angle detectors, 12, implanted electrodes in muscle. (From Severin et al., in Wetzel and Stuart, 1976)

placed on a treadmill. Stepping movements of the paws can be initiated by various procedures, such as movement of the treadmill, electrical stimulation of different parts of the brainstem below the transection, or by injection of substances into the bloodstream.

Studies of this preparation have been pursued especially vigorously by Sten Grillner and his colleagues in Stockholm. They

have showed that with a high spinal transection, a cat can still generate alternating and coordinated movements of all four limbs. Even with a lower, midthoracic transection, the hindlimbs can display walking movements, and change to approximately simultaneous galloping movements when the speed of the treadmill is increased. Examples of recordings from the muscles of the knee, ankle, toe, and hip are shown in

Fig. 20.14 Pattern of muscle activity in the hindlimb of a decerebrate cat placed on a moving treadmill. **A.** Control electromyograph (EMG) recordings from the knee extensor (E) quadriceps (Q) muscle, the ankle extensor lateral gastrocnemius (LG), the toe dorsiflexor extensor (EDB), and the hip flexor (F) iliopsoas (Ip). **B.** Recordings from the same muscles after bilateral transection of the dorsal roots to the hindlimbs. (Adapted from Grillner and Zangger, 1984)

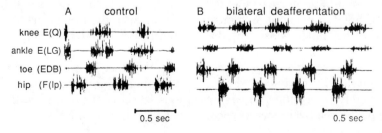

Fig. 20.14A, for the case of a high midbrain transection. The coordinated pattern of discharge reflects the normal sequence of activation of these muscles during walking. This basic pattern persists in some animals even after deafferentation (shown in B), although it is not as stable and can readily break down.

The conclusion from these and related studies is that locomotion depends on "a central network that generates essential features of the motor pattern and sensory feedback signals that form an integral and crucial part of the control system" (Grillner, 1985). A third element is the descending control from higher brain centers, which includes the mechanism of efference copy (see next chapter). We thus have accounted for the three fundamental units of motor action mentioned at the beginning of this chapter.

In conclusion, the examples we have studied share common principles of organization that are adapted for widely different types of low-motor activity. It expresses beautifully the importance of understanding the nature of nervous system function at the circuit level. As Meldrum Robertson and Keir Pearson (1985) have eloquently phrased it:

. . . motor patterns are produced by nearly universal neuronal processes . . . the overall circuits are unique only in the way that well-described components are assembled. This is heartening for those in search of general principles of neuronal organization.

21

Motor Hierarchies

The four preceding chapters have introduced the major elements of the motor apparatus: the glands and muscles themselves, the motoneurons that innervate them, the simplest neural networks for generating rhythms and fixed action patterns to drive the motoneurons, and the simplest reflex pathways involving sensory inputs. For the most part, all of this neural machinery is at the segmental level of the nerve cord in invertebrates, and the spinal cord and brainstem in vertebrates.

The next step is to ask, what are the neural mechanisms for operating this segmental apparatus, so that it serves the whole organism in purposeful ways? The two parts of this question actually relate to different higher levels within the hierarchy of motor organization referred to in preceding chapters. At the first level are the descending pathways by which the segmental apparatus is controlled. That is the subject of this chapter. Above this are levels of organization that operate within the context of the whole organism. For example, is a given movement voluntary or involuntary, purposive or automatic? What is the adaptive value of a given type of movement for the individual and for the species? These questions are dealt with in the final section of the book, which elaborates the central systems. However, it is important even while dealing with lower levels of organization to realize that the most profound students of motor function, such as Charles Sherrington, have always regarded individual motor mechanisms from a perspective of their significance for the behavior of the whole organism. This demonstrates precisely the point made at the very outset of this book (Chap. 1), that "Nothing in neurobiology makes sense except in the light of behavior."

The conceptual framework of the motor hierarchy has been fundamental both for analysis of motor control in animal experiments and for the diagnosis of neurological diseases of the motor system in human patients. For more than a century, clinical neurologists have used this framework to distinguish between the *lower motor neuron,* in the spinal cord, and the *upper motor neuron,* which includes all the centers in the brainstem and motor cortex that project to the spinal cord. Our concern with the immediate descending control of the segmental apparatus is therefore with these different types of upper motor neurons.

The same general framework applies to

motor control in invertebrates, where the ganglia of the nerve cord are equivalent to the spinal segments, and fibers from higher centers are equivalent to the descending fibers in the vertebrate. An important difference is that in the invertebrate these are characteristically giant neurons and fibers, or other kinds of individually identifiable neurons. The fact that a single such neuron or fiber can be selectively stimulated to produce a motor response has given rise to the concept of the "command neuron." This concept has been a mixed blessing; it has stimulated much of the research on invertebrate motor systems, but its validity as a concept for understanding motor control has been heatedly debated. Since one cannot study invertebrate motor systems without understanding this debate, we will begin with a brief history of the development of this concept, and attempt to outline a broader definition consistent with recent research. We will then consider how decisions are made within motor control circuits, as revealed by experiments in invertebrates. We will then be in a position to study the mechanisms of descending motor control in the vertebrate.

Command Neurons: A Brief History

This concept arose from the work of C. A. G. "Kees" Wiersma, at California Institute of Technology, on motor systems in the crayfish. Beginning in the 1940s, this work was focused on the giant fiber system that controls the escape response, and also the circuit that controls the rhythmic beating of small abdominal appendages called phyllopodia, or *swimmerets*. Wiersma realized that large, identifiable fibers in the connectives to the segmental ganglia can be selectively stimulated and their individual effects on the motor output determined. In 1964, he and Kazuo Ikeda showed that the endogenous bursting of the segmental motoneurons that innervate the swimmeret muscles can be turned on and off by stimulation of specific interneurons in more rostral ganglia and connectives. They intro-

duced the term "command fiber" for the fibers they stimulated. The details of the swimmeret system were worked out subsequently by Paul Stein at Washington University in St. Louis and by Donald Kennedy and his colleagues at Stanford. A summary of the circuit is shown in Fig. 21.1.

Problems of Definition

The terms *command fiber* and *command neuron* quickly found application to a variety of systems. Very soon, however, controversy arose over the definition of these terms. A suggestion, by David Bentley and Mazakazi Konishi (1978), was as follows:

Fig. 21.1 **A.** Rhythm generator circuits for control of swimmerets in the crayfish. Two neighboring hemiganglia are shown, connected by a coordinating fiber. In each hemiganglion, there is an oscillator neuron that receives its input from a nonrhythmic command fiber. (From Stein, in Wetzel and Stuart, 1976) **B.** Movements of swimmerets. The most anterior appendage, at right, is completing the power stroke, while the others are in successive phases of their return strokes, in the direction shown by the arrows. Movement of water is indicated by the large heavy arrow. (From Davis, in Kennedy, 1976)

A

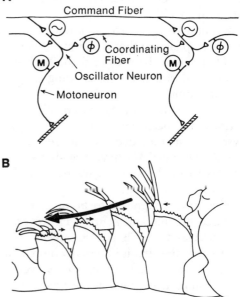

B

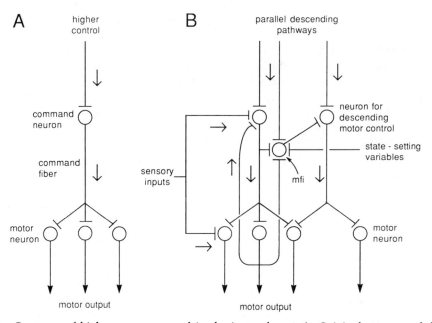

Fig. 21.2 Concepts of higher motor control in the invertebrate. **A.** Original concept of the command neuron or fiber. **B.** More complex types of circuit connections revealed by recent work. mfi, multifunction interneuron. See text.

Command (neurons) can be defined as interneurons whose activation alone suffices to elicit a recognizable fragment of behavior through excitation and/or inhibition of a constellation of motoneurons.

This simple definition is represented by the diagram in Fig. 21.2A. Similarly, Kupfermann and Weiss (1978), in a much quoted essay, emphasized that a command neuron or fiber should be proven to be both necessary and sufficient for eliciting a given motor output.

The problem with these and other definitions has been that the more a given system is investigated, the more complicated it becomes. We have already seen this in several of the systems we have studied thus far. For example, the escape response of the crayfish appears to be mediated by a classical command neuron. However, as we discussed in Chap. 19, recent work shows that the circuit is actually quite complicated. It includes nongiant as well as giant components; feedback as well as feedforward pathways; interneurons with complex excitatory and inhibitory actions; and sensory input at several levels. In addition, virtually every type of synaptic junction in the circuit is under control of state-setting variables, such as the state of arousal, adaptation, or fatigue; we saw an example of how dramatic these variables can be in the effects of serotonin and octopamine in eliciting completely different postures in the crayfish. Motor control is thus much more complex than originally envisaged, and an expanded circuit, such as that in Fig. 21.2B, is needed to reflect the actual situation.

Another example of the problem of defining a command neuron is the swimming circuit for *Tritonia*. As we learned in the previous chapter, the central pattern generator (CPG) consists of three types of neuron: cerebral (C2) cells, and the dorsal and ventral swimming interneurons (DSI and VSI). By the criteria mentioned above, C2 and DSI are also command neurons, because they are both necessary and sufficient for the initiation and maintenance of the swimming rhythm (refer to Fig. 20.4B). Since these two function both as central pattern generators and as command neurons, they must be regarded as multifunctional neurons. In addition, there is a group of interneurons (I2) which coordinate C2 and DSI (see Fig. 20.4B), and represent a higher level in the hierarchy of control.

Toward New Concepts of Motor Control in Invertebrates

From these considerations, it is obvious that the simple concept of the command neuron is no longer tenable in its original form. Individual types of neurons can have more than one function and can take part in more than one level of motor control. The motor hierarchy does not involve a rigid delegation of certain functions to certain neurons, but rather is a conceptual framework for understanding the fundamental operations involved in motor control.

Notwithstanding these new developments, it remains true that under controlled experimental conditions we can stimulate single elements in many invertebrate nervous systems to elicit specific patterns of motor outputs. One therefore is faced with the practical problem of designating these elements with an appropriate term. Since the term "command neuron" is so closely associated with its original, restricted, meaning, one needs a more general, noncommital term, free of this historical reference. For our purposes, we may consider this as equivalent to the *upper motor neuron* in the vertebrate; alternative terms in the invertebrate might be *neuron mediating descending motor control*, or, more simply, *motor control neuron*.

In addition to rethinking definitions, workers have sought new ways of characterizing the nature of the higher levels of motor control in invertebrates. At an early stage, W. Jackson Davis in California proposed (1976) that different neurons could perform command functions at different times in a motor sequence. This is in line with the view of the swimming generator in *Tritonia* discussed above. More recently,

in a study of descending fibers that control walking in the locust, Jenny Kien (1983) at Regensburg found no neurons that fit the definition of command neurons; that is, no single neurons were found whose stimulation was both necessary and sufficient to elicit walking. In fact, she found that microstimulation of many sites in the head ganglia and connectives could elicit walking. From these results, Kien (1983) suggested that

walking is normally initiated by many fibers acting in consensus, and the type of walking produced normally depends on which combination or pattern of "recommendations" to the walking generators is active. This pattern of activity across a large number of labelled input lines has been called the "across-fibre pattern" (Erickson) . . . The concept that it is this pattern that contains the information that is used . . . has been well applied to sensory systems. . . . Motor systems in insects may function in a similar way to sensory systems.

We discussed the "across-fiber pattern" concept of information processing in the taste pathway in Chap. 11. The important rule that this expresses for motor systems is that motor commands issue from ensembles of neurons; experimentally one can sometimes elicit a motor action from a single neuron, but in general, populations of neurons form parallel lines for descending control, so that the motor apparatus can be adjusted to perform tasks appropriate for the behavioral state and the sensory environment on a moment-to-moment basis.

This is a rule that applies to both invertebrates and vertebrates. In invertebrates, one can pick out and stimulate individual elements that transmit an identifiable component of a whole motor task. In vertebrates, the whole task is distributed within complex circuits involving many small units. It is interesting that the work in vertebrates has benefitted from a more accurate characterization of the specific types of control involved in escape responses and locomotion that are similar to those in invertebrates, while work in invertebrates has benefited from the realization that the circuits there have additional degrees of complexity that are shared with the vertebrates. In this way, despite the problems of terminology, we are moving toward a unified view of higher motor control within the general framework of a motor hierarchy.

Decision Making

How does the nervous system decide to activate a given neuron or set of neurons, with its associated behavior pattern, rather than another? In some cases, the activity is obligatory and ongoing (such as the heartbeat), and the problem is simply to modulate it appropriately in relation to different activity levels. In other cases, however, particularly those involving locomotion, there has to be some kind of *decision-making* function that selects one behavior (such as a tail flip or a jump) rather than another (such as walking or feeding).

An example is the giant-fiber escape system. We have already noted that this reflex pathway has a relatively high threshold for activation. Thus, the threshold alone can serve the decision-making function; if sensory stimulation is below threshold, there is no tail flip; above threshold, there is a tail flip. However, the threshold itself is affected by a number of factors, such as whether, in the case of the crayfish, the animal is in or out of the water, or whether it has been injured. Sensory pathways are indeed very important in activating or modulating motor pathways; potentially, this may occur at all levels, from motoneurons up to command neurons, and also may involve the cells that control the command neurons.

Several systems have been analyzed in which the decision-making mechanism is more complicated. One example is the movement detector-jump system in the locust. The visual detector part of the system has already been described in Chap. 16. On the motor side, the motor program for the jump actually has three distinct stages. First is flexion of the leg; second is cocon-traction of extensor and flexor muscles; third, there is sudden relaxation of the flexors, giving rise to the jump. Thus, rather than a single neuron or gate, there is a sequence of gates; at each stage, the decision to proceed depends on the presence of several factors, including the intensity of specific sensory stimulation, the coincidence of other sensory stimuli, the state of arousal, and activity in other motor systems. These results show that under natural conditions a given behavior is not mediated by a single command neuron, but rather by a network of such cells providing for multiple state-dependent gates.

Motor Hierarchies in Vertebrates: A Brief History

Historically, the idea that motor systems in vertebrates are organized in hierarchical fashion has a long and distinguished lineage. The idea was formulated in the latter part of the nineteenth century by the great English neurologist, John Hughlings Jackson (1835–1911). Jackson, the son of a farmer, had a limited education and medical training. His genius lay in the meticulousness of his observations of patients with neurological diseases, combined with a philosophical cast of mind which enabled him to recognize the principles implied by the observations. One of his main studies was of epileptic seizures, particularly those that involve restricted parts of the body musculature. This type is now known, in his honor, as Jacksonian seizures. A tragic footnote is that his profound insights into this disease drew on his wife, who suffered from these seizures and died at an early age from cerebral thrombosis.

Jackson's study of the motor derangements associated with seizures convinced him that there are successive levels for motor control in the nervous system. In evolution, he deduced, there has been a progression from automatic toward purposive movements, and this is reflected in the nervous system in the control of automatic movements by lower levels and purposive movements by higher levels. He reasoned that the higher levels normally exert control over the lower levels, and that this control can be either excitatory or inhibitory. When upper-level function is interrupted or destroyed by disease, lower centers are "released" from higher control, and the result may be hyperactivity (such as exaggerated reflexes) if the normal descending control was inhibitory. Although knowledge of anatomy was limited in Jackson's time, he postulated that the lowest level for motor control is in the spinal cord and brainstem, the next (middle) level is in the cerebral cortex along the central (Rolandic) fissure, and the highest level is in the frontal lobe.

Motor Organization

These concepts have influenced all subsequent workers, and today they still provide a useful evolutionary framework for thinking about the organization of motor systems. A recent update of this framework is depicted in the schema of Fig. 21.3. The reader may wish to compare this with the diagrams of Figs. 19.1 and 20.2, which were mainly concerned with representing the lowest, segmental level of organization in the spinal cord. Figure 21.3 shows the immediate control of the spinal apparatus by specific motor regions of the brainstem and cerebral cortex, representing Jackson's "middle level" of control. These regions, in turn, are under the combined control of several areas, including the cerebellum and the basal ganglia (rather than exclusively the prefrontal cortex, as Jackson thought).

Several additional points may be made in reference to Fig. 21.3. One is that motor control is not, in fact, strictly hierarchical. The hierarchical sequence descending from "projection areas" to "segmental motor programs" to "motoneurons" is bypassed by some direct pathways from the projection areas to the motoneurons. In other words, there are parallel pathways as well as serial ones. This recalls the studies of sensory systems, in which recent findings have emphasized the presence of both serial and parallel pathways. Thus, it appears that in both sensory and motor systems, greater adaptability and processing power are obtained by building in both types of pathways.

A second point is that there are feedback connections from every level of the motor system. Some of this feedback is from sensory pathways, conveying information from the periphery, information that alerts the animal, or tells it the effect of its motor actions on the environment. The sensory pathways themselves are under the influence of the motor outflow. In addition, the motor pathways not only carry information to the motoneurons, but also send a copy of that information back to the higher levels. As discussed in Chap. 20, this internal feedback referred to as *reafference, corollary discharge,* or *afference copy.* Through it, higher levels are kept informed of what lower levels are doing. It seems to express a principle of good management, that presidents and admirals should not put their trust entirely in their vice-presidents and colonels, but should see for themselves what is actually happening in the offices, factories, and battlefields. We have already discussed reafference as a type of circuit

Fig. 21.3 Hierarchical organization of motor control. (Modified from Phillips and Porter, 1977)

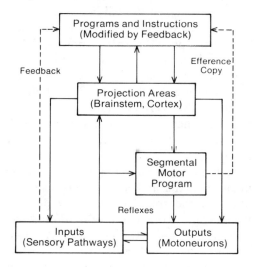

component which, together with the reflex and the rhythm generator, forms one of the three fundamental units of action for the organization of motor control systems (Chap. 20).

A final point is that this schema for the vertebrate brain is general enough to be applicable to the invertebrate nervous system as well. Thus, motor control neurons of invertebrates are at a level equivalent to the projection areas of vertebrates, and the highest level in both cases contains the *"programing instructions."*

Brainstem Centers

It will be helpful to keep Fig. 21.3 in mind as our discussion moves to higher control of motor function in the vertebrate nervous system. First, the projection areas that constitute the middle level will be identified. These include the regions that are sources of descending fibers that terminate in the spinal cord. The main regions are shown in Fig. 21.4.

Reticular Nucleus

The reticular system is distributed diffusely through the brainstem. As we learned in the discussion of sensory systems (Chaps. 10–16), it receives collaterals from sensory projection pathways, and has as one of its functions the mediation of states of arousal. This involves fibers that ascend toward the thalamus, and descend toward the spinal cord. The functions of the reticular system, considered as part of central systems, are discussed in Chaps. 24 and 26.

The descending fibers are the ones directly involved in motor control. In fish and amphibians, a few cells in the reticular substance of the medulla are differentiated into *giant cells,* with large dendrites, and a long axon which descends into the spinal cord to make synaptic connections with segmental interneurons and motoneurons. These are known as *Mueller cells* (6–8 cells in lamprey, for example) or *Mauthner cells* (a single pair, as in many teleost fish, and amphibians).

From a phylogenetic viewpoint, the sig-

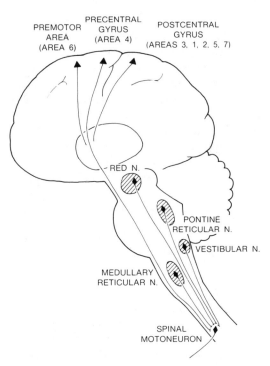

Fig. 21.4 Principal regions of the human brain involved in immediate motor control through descending fibers to motoneurons.

nificance of these large, reticular neurons appears to be mainly in relation to control of the *tail.* In most vertebrates the tail is an important motor organ. It serves as an organ of locomotion, and it is also used in maintaining balance (as in fish swimming or lizards running: see Fig. 20.9). Part of the importance of the tail lies in the power it can generate; this is why it is so important in escape and startle responses. As we discussed in Chap. 19, the Mauthner cell, with its giant axon, provides a fast pathway for initiating quick and powerful movements of the body and tail, and we noted that its function in this respect is closely analogous to that of giant fiber systems in invertebrates.

In higher vertebrates, reticular neurons in the medulla and in the pons also send fibers to the spinal cord. Some of these fibers come from giant cells, though the cells are not uniquely identifiable. A variety of studies have indicated that the reticulospinal neurons constitute the main brainstem system for immediate control of the segmental spinal apparatus as it is employed in standing and stepping. We will discuss more details of this control below.

Vestibular Nucleus

The vestibular nuclear complex is closely associated with the reticular nuclei. This nucleus receives the afferents from the vestibular canals (Chap. 14) and also fibers from the cerebellum, and in turn provides one of the main inputs to the Mauthner cell in lower vertebrates (Chap. 19). Of the four main parts of the vestibular complex (see Fig. 14.12) in the mammal, the *lateral nucleus* is the main source of fibers to the spinal cord. The lateral nucleus contains *giant cells*, named *Deiters cells* after the early German histologist who first described them in 1865; the nucleus is accordingly referred to as *Deiters nucleus*.

The *vestibulospinal tract*, composed of fibers from the giant cells as well as other cells of the lateral nucleus, descends the length of the spinal cord. The lateral nucleus is organized somatotopically, and this order is maintained in the projections to different levels of the cord. Electrical stimulation of the lateral nucleus produces polysynaptic EPSPs in *extensor* motoneurons of the limbs. This has suggested that, through the vestibulospinal tract, the cerebellum exerts a facilitatory control over muscle tone in the extensor limb muscles involved in standing.

It may be noted that the *medial vestibular nucleus* sends fibers to the upper part of the spinal cord by way of the *medial longitudinal fasciculus*. The role of these fibers in the control of eye movements has been discussed in Chap. 14. The *inferior* and *medial vestibular nuclei* project fibers to the cerebellum (see below). Through all these connections the signals from the vestibular canals are widely dispersed throughout the brainstem and spinal cord.

Red Nucleus

The red nucleus is a prominent structure in reptiles, birds, and mammals. It has a slightly pinkish color in fresh specimens, hence its name. Part of the nucleus contains *giant cells;* these, as well as cells of other sizes, project their axons to brainstem centers and to the spinal cord. In higher mammals, including humans, which are fewer giant cells, and the spinal tract is less prominent; other pathways become more important, especially the corticospinal tract (see below).

Electrical stimulation of the red nucleus in the cat causes *flexion* of the limbs. Intracellular recordings have shown that such stimulation produces polysynaptic EPSPs in flexor motoneurons, and polysynaptic IPSPs in extensor motoneurons to the limbs. The excitatory effect may be mediated through segmental interneurons, or by activation of γ motoneurons and the γ loop (Chap. 13). The facilitative effect of the red nucleus on limb flexion thus contrasts with the facilitative effect of the vestibular nucleus on limb extension.

The Control of Walking

The significance of the three brainstem centers discussed above for the control of walking has been assessed by G. N. Orlovsky of Russia, who used the preparation of the cat depicted in Fig. 20.13. Some of his results are summarized in Fig. 21.5. Chief among the three centers in the control of walking is the reticular formation. In unit recordings, the reticulospinal cells increase their discharge in order to facilitate flexor motoneurons, as is necessary to bring the foot up and forward during the swing phase of stepping. After removal of the cerebellum, the spontaneous activity of reticulospinal neurons falls precipitously, associated with a loss of muscle tone and loss of coordination of the limbs (see A in Fig. 21.5). From these results it has been concluded that the maintained discharge of reticulospinal neurons is involved in "switching on" the stepping generator, and the modulated discharge facilitates flexor activity in the swing phase.

By contrast, vestibulospinal neurons (B in Fig. 21.5) show peak firing that phase-leads the onset of the stance phase, thereby

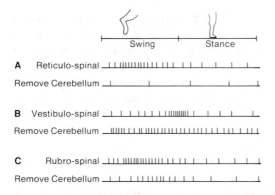

Fig. 21.5 Single-cell activity in brainstem motor centers in relation to stepping. See text for explanation. (Based on Orlovsky, in Wetzel and Stuart, 1976)

facilitating extensor motoneurons as the limb is extended to support the body against gravity. Finally, the activity of rubrospinal neurons (C) resembles that of reticulospinal neurons in facilitating flexor motoneurons during the swing phase. Neither the vestibular nor the red nucleus is essential for stepping; their roles thus appear supportive in relation to the reticular formation.

From these and related studies it has been concluded that brainstem centers control the spinal rhythm generator by two mechanisms: a *generalized activation* by means of ongoing spontaneous discharge, and *modulated discharges* that facilitate specific phases of the stepping cycle. The level of activation appropriate for switching on the generator depends exquisitely on the cerebellum, while modulation is due to sensory feedback from the limbs relayed through the cerebellum. As expressed by Mary Wetzel and Douglas Stuart (1976) of Arizona:

. . . afferent modulation of efferent output by way of the cerebellum provides for selection from a larger array of corrective signals than if the modulation was achieved by directly ascending tracts, such as the spinoreticular and spinovestibular systems. The cerebellum's importance is becoming evident in the building of large-scale neural ensemble activity from stepping signals that arrive from many different parts of the nervous system.

Cerebellum

It is obvious from the foregoing remarks that a key center for sensorimotor control at the level of the brainstem is the cerebellum. The cerebellum lacks direct connection to the spinal cord, and thus stands higher in the motor hierarchy than the middle level, as indicated in Fig. 21.3. However, it is so intimately involved in brainstem mechanisms that it is appropriate to consider it here.

The cerebellum is an outgrowth of the pons. It arises early in vertebrate phylogeny. In brains of different vertebrate classes, the cerebellum varies from a mere nubbin in some species to a large, much convoluted structure in others. It is often stated that the cerebellum increases in size during phylogeny, but there are numerous exceptions to this generalization. Most notable is the enormous expansion in certain species of electric fish, which contrasts with the generally small size in most amphibians and reptiles. The large size of the cerebellum in mammals is believed to be related to several important functional roles. Three roles have traditionally been identified; they involve control of (1) *muscle tone;* (2) *balance;* and (3) *sensorimotor coordination.* Let us consider the organization of the cerebellum in terms of its input and output connections, and see how they relate to these functions.

Like Caesar's Gaul, the cerebellum is divided into three parts, which reflects its phylogenetic history. First is the *archicerebellum,* consisting of the small flocculonodular lobe. Next is the *paleocerebellum,* consisting of the anterior lobe. Third is the *neocerebellum,* formed by the great expansion of the lateral hemisphere.

Inputs to the Cerebellum

The *inputs* to the cerebellum are specific for these three parts. As shown in Fig. 21.6A, *vestibular* fibers make connections to the flocculonodular node. Fibers from the *spinal cord* ascend in the spinocerebellar tract and terminate mainly in the anterior lobe. The ventral portion of this tract

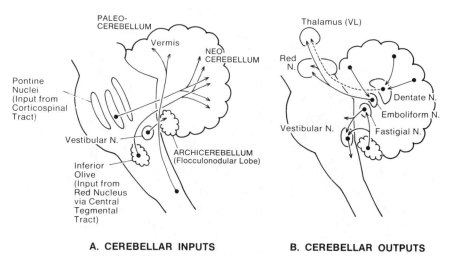

Fig. 21.6 Main input (A) and output (B) pathways of the mammalian cerebellum.

is presently as early as fish, but the dorsal tract is present first in reptiles. These fibers carry information from muscle receptors. Finally, input to the neocerebellum comes mainly from large masses of cells in the *pons,* and from the *inferior olivary nucleus* in the medulla.

Outputs from the Cerebellum

The *output* fibers from the cerebellar cortex project to the midbrain in fish and urodele amphibians; the midbrain in these animals is one of the main centers for sensorimotor coordination. In higher vertebrates, however, the output from the cortex goes to a set of *deep cerebellar nuclei* (which may represent specializations of the more primitive midbrain center).

The relations between cortex and deep nuclei are somewhat more complicated than the simple tripartite division mentioned above. Thus, as shown in Fig. 21.6B, the *fastigial* nucleus receives fibers from the midline vermal zone of the cortex, and projects in turn to the lateral vestibular nucleus; there is also a direct connection to this nucleus as well. The *emboliform* nucleus receives fibers from a strip of cortex next to the midline; it projects in turn to the red nucleus, and also has some terminals in the ventrolateral nucleus of the

thalamus. The *dentate* nucleus is by far the largest of the deep nuclei, reflecting the fact that it receives the output fibers of the large cerebellar hemisphere. The dentate nucleus projects some fibers to the red nucleus, but in higher mammals most of them go to the ventrolateral nucleus of the thalamus.

The connections to the vestibular nucleus account for the powerful control exerted by the cerebellum on mechanisms of balance. The connections to the red nucleus and reticular nucleus mediate control over reflexes and muscle tone, through the projections of these nuclei to the spinal cord. The role of the lateral cerebellar hemisphere→dentate→ventrolateral thalamus circuit in sensorimotor coordination is more subtle; it is expressed through the cerebral cortex, as we will see below.

Microcircuits of the Cerebellar Cortex

We have identified the main cerebellar pathways, and the overall effects they mediate, but what actual operations are carried out within the cerebellum itself? For this we must consider the microanatomy and microphysiology of the cerebellar cortex. When we do, we find that this is one of the most astonishing pieces of cellular machinery in the animal body. It consists of a convoluted sheet, divided into a deep

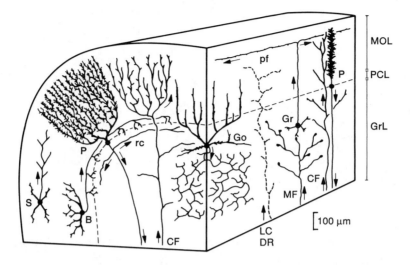

Fig. 21.7 Neuronal organization of the cerebellar cortex. Inputs: mossy fibers (MF) and climbing fibers (CF), parallel fibers (pf), fibers from locus ceruleus (LC), and raphe nucleus (DR). Principal neuron: Purkinje cell (P), with receurrent collateral (rc). Intrinsic neurons: granule cell (Gr); stellate cell (S); basket cell (B); Golgi cell (Go). Histological layers are shown at the right: molecular layer (MOL), Purkinje cell body layer (PCL), granule layer (GrL). (Modified from Shepherd, 1979)

and a superficial layer. The deep (granule) layer is packed with tiny *"granule"* cells; the best estimates put their numbers at 10–100 billion, which is more than all the other cells in the nervous system combined! The granule cell axons ascend to the superficial (molecular) layer and bifurcate into two *"parallel fibers"* which run for several millimeters in opposite directions. The molecular layer also contains the large *Purkinje cells,* of which there are about 7 million. Each has a widely branching dendritic tree, that is flattened into a two-dimensional plane and oriented at right angles to the parallel fibers. These relations are diagramed in Fig. 21.7. The Purkinje cell dendrites are covered with *spines,* which are the sites of synapses from the parallel fibers as they pass through successive Purkinje cell dendritic arbors. The Purkinje cell axons carry the output of the cerebellar cortex to the deep cerebellar nuclei.

There are three main types of fiber that carry inputs to this neuronal machinery. One type is the *mossy fiber,* which arises from the pontine nuclei, as well as several other sites, and terminates on granule cell dendrites in large endings that, to some early anatomists, seemed to have a "mossy" appearance. This input is relayed through the granule cells to the Purkinje cells, and in so doing is subjected to considerable convergence and divergence, due to branching of the parallel fibers and overlap of their connections. The second type is the *climbing fiber,* which arises mainly from the inferior olivary nucleus. This fiber ends in an extensive arborization which literally climbs over the Purkinje cell dendritic tree and makes synapses onto it. This input thus has a one-to-one, direct relation to the Purkinje cell. A third type of fiber ramifies widely throughout the cortex; these have been identified as norepinephrine- and serotonin-containing fibers arising from the brain stem (see Chap. 24).

Basic Circuit of Cerebellar Cortex

The basic circuit put together from anatomical and physiological studies is summarized in Fig. 21.8. We will focus on four essential features of this circuit. First, the direct input pathway, through the climbing fibers, and the indirect pathway, through

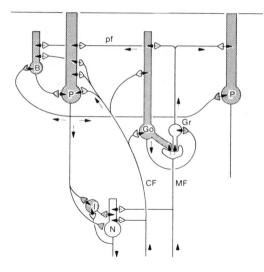

Fig. 21.8 Basic circuit diagram for the mammalian cerebellum. Note deep cerebellar nuclear cells: principal neuron (N) and intrinsic neuron (I). Other abbreviations in Fig. 21.7. (Modified from Shepherd, 1979)

the mossy fiber→granule cell→parallel fiber relay, are both excitatory. Second, all other connections, by the various types of interneurons present (Golgi, basket, stellate), are inhibitory. This means that the responses of cerebellar cortical neurons to their excitatory inputs are brief, being rapidly terminated by inhibition. Third, the connections of Purkinje cell axons onto their target neurons in the deep nuclei are also inhibitory. This was surprising when first discovered, and it means that one of the basic input–output operations of the cerebellar cortex is to convert its excitatory inputs into inhibitory outputs. Fourth, the deep nuclei, as shown in Fig. 21.8, also receive inputs from the climbing and mossy fibers. The cerebellar cortex can therefore be regarded as a highly sophisticated interneuronal system, mediating feed forward inhibition to control the input–output operations of the deep nuclei. Finally, both deep cerebellar neurons and Purkinje cells have high rates of resting discharge (50–100 impulses per second). One function of this high rate is to act as a high *set point,* so that the cerebellum will be maximally

sensitive to both decreases and increases in firing rate caused by changes in input activity.

Motor Cortex: A Brief History

A crucial component of the middle level of motor control is the *motor cortex.* The identification of the motor part of the cerebral cortex is one of the most dramatic chapters in the history of neurophysiology. During the American Civil War in the early 1860s, Weir Mitchell, a Philadelphia neurologist, noted that one side of the brain appeared to be related to the opposite side of the body. In the Prusso-Danish War of 1864, the German physician Theodor Fritsch observed, in dressing a head wound, that irritation of the brain caused twitching in the opposite side of the body. He took this information to Eduard Hitzig, then in medical practice in Berlin, and they set about to test this finding experimentally. According to the legend (Haymaker, 1953):

At that time there were no laboratories available for work on warm-blooded animals, and as a consequence Hitzig and Fritsch did their first studies on dogs in Hitzig's home, operating on Frau Hitzig's dressing table.

This was one of the great discoveries in neurobiology, for it demonstrated both the *electrical excitability of the brain* and the *localization of motor function* in the cerebral cortex. The importance of the finding of localization was not lost on David Ferrier of London, who proceeded in the 1870s to map very thoroughly the excitable cortex in a variety of mammals, including monkeys. One of his aims was "to put to experimental proof of the views entertained by Dr. Hughlings Jackson. Ferrier found that the most excitable area for eliciting movements in the monkey is a strip of cortex on the precentral gyrus, the gyrus of Rolandi (where Jackson had expected it to be). He showed an orderly progression of focal areas along the gyrus for eliciting movements of the leg, hand, and face. This was dramatic confirmation indeed of Jackson's postulate that there must be an orderly sequence of discharging foci in the cortex to explain the "march of spasm" of the muscles that is so characteristic of focal epileptic convulsions (the kind now known as Jacksonian seizures).

Studies of localization of the motor cortex were extended to the great apes by Sherrington in the early 1900s, and finally to humans by Wilder Penfield, a student of Sherrington's, in the 1930s. Penfield, with his colleagues at the Montreal Neurological Institute, focally stimulated the cortex of patients during neurosurgical operations. They found, as had many workers before them in other species, a great deal of overlap between the areas for different parts of the body (see Fig. 21.9A). The areas for the hand and face had the lowest thresholds and widest fields (A and B). Penfield and his colleagues summarized their findings in a homunculus, as shown in Fig. 21.9C. This is the motor counterpart to the sensory map of the body surface previously shown in Chap. 12.

These findings left little doubt that the precentral gyrus (cytoarchitectonic area 4 of Brodmann) is the cortical region most closely involved in immediate control of motoneurons in the spinal cord. This control is mediated by the *corticospinal tract,* which provides a direct connection between the cortex and the spinal cord. Because its fibers are funneled through the pyramids on the ventral surface of the medulla in the brainstem, it is also called the *pyramidal tract.* The traditional view, that this tract mediates voluntary control of movement, seemed to many to be almost self-evident. However, this view concealed several difficult problems that have required many years of work to resolve, and have led to a much expanded view of "motor cortex."

The Organization of Motor Cortex

The first question to be asked is, which cells give rise to the fibers in the pyramidal tract? The fibers arise from pyramidal-shaped neurons in cortical layer V, which is an obvious source of terminological confusion; it must be kept in mind that the pyramidal tract derives its name from the fact that it passes through the medullary pyramids, not because its fibers arise from pyramidal shaped neurons! The layer V cells include some giant neurons, called Betz cells after their discoverer (see Fig. 21.10). For many years it was thought that all corticospinal fibers arise from Betz cells, but now it is known that only about 3% of the tract fibers can be accounted for on this basis. Betz cells are found mainly in the leg area, and thus their large size appears to be correlated with the greater length of axon they send to caudal parts of the spinal cord. Nonetheless, it is of interest that, like the brainstem centers, the motor cortex of the middle level of the motor hierarchy exerts some of its control through giant neurons.

The second question is, does the corticospinal tract arise only from area 4? Both anatomical and physiological studies have shown that area 6 (just anterior to area 4) and the postcentral gyrus (3, 1, and 2 of the somatosensory area) also contribute fibers. Thus, as shown in Fig. 21.4, the corticospinal tract arises from extensive areas of cortex. Movements elicited from area 6 (also called the premotor area) and areas 3, 1, and 2 by electrical stimulation are less precise and have higher electrical thresholds than those elicited from the motor strip in area 4. There is thus *multiple representation* of the motor map in the cerebral cortex (Fig. 21.11).

The third question is, does the corticospinal tract mediate direct (monosynaptic) control of motoneurons? Phylogenetic comparisons provide a useful perspective on this question (see Fig. 21.12). In lower mammals, such as the rabbit, the corticospinal tract barely reaches the anterior segments of the spinal cord, so that further connections within the cord have to be by propriospinal interneurons. In mammals like the cat, the tract reaches most of the cord,

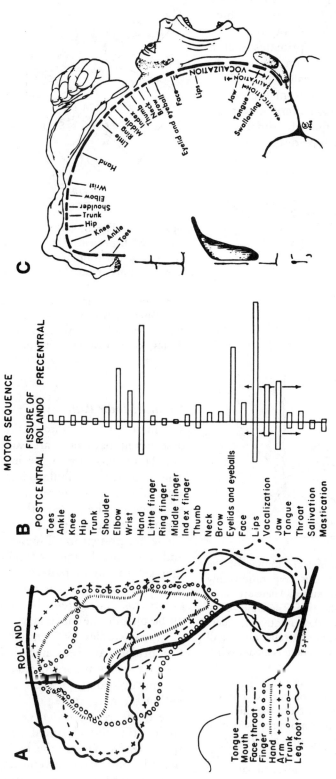

Fig. 21.9 A. Lateral view of the surface of the human brain, in the region of the Rolandic sulcus. Outlines show areas from which electrical stimulation elicited movements in different body parts, in the series of patients explored by Penfield and Boldrey in 1937. Anterior surface is to the left. B. The relative proportions of movements elicited by stimulation anterior and posterior to the central (Rolandic) sulcus in the series of patients of Penfield and Rasmussen, 1950. C. The motor homunculus of Penfield and Rasmussen. (From Phillips and Porter, 1977)

but the fibers make synaptic connections only onto segmental interneurons, which provide a polysynaptic pathway onto motoneurons. It is only in primates that a monosynaptic pathway from the tract fibers to spinal motoneurons exists.

This direct connection from the cortex to spinal motoneurons is very important for the motor capacities of primates, including humans, as will be discussed in the next chapter.

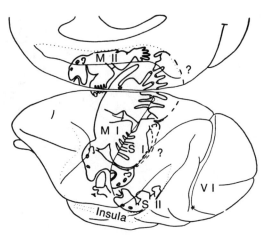

Fig. 21.11 The motor areas of the monkey cortex. M I, precentral motor area (equivalent to areas 4 and 6 of the human cortex); M II, supplementary motor area; S I, primary somatic sensory area. All these areas send fibers to the pyramidal tract as well as extrapyramidal centers. Also shown are the secondary somatic area (S II) and primary visual area (V I). (From Woolsey, in Henneman, 1980b)

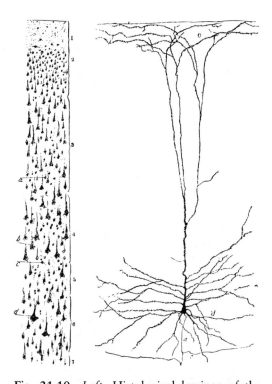

Fig. 21.10 *Left:* Histological laminae of the human motor cortex. In this preparation only the cell bodies have been stained. There are seven laminae in Cajal's classification. The laminae are identified on the basis of their relative numbers of large cell bodies (pyramidal cells) and small cell bodies (pyramidal or granule (stellate) cells). The significance of the laminae will be discussed further below (cf. Fig. 21.13). *Right:* Single Betz cell of the motor cortex, impregnated by the Golgi method. Note the thick apical dendrite which divides into three ascending branches that ramify at the cortical surface, the many shorter basal dendrites, and the axon (a) which arises from the cell body and gives off two horizontal axon collaterals. (From Cajal, 1911)

Parallel Motor Pathways

The main types of motor centers and their descending pathways are summarized in Fig. 21.13. First are the brainstem centers. The reticular, vestibular, and red nuclei were discussed as representative of these, to which can be added others such as the superior colliculus and its tectospinal tract. These are present in all higher vertebrates, and constitute the middle-level mechanisms that set the main patterns of control of motor behavior. This is referred to as the *extrapyramidal system*, because the fibers all lie outside the medullary pyramids.

Recent studies by Henricus Kuypers at Cambridge have indicated that the brainstem pathways are organized into two main groups, according to where they terminate within the gray matter of the spinal cord. One is the *ventromedial* group, which includes the reticulospinal and vestibulospinal tracts. This is the basic system for overall control of movements, pertaining to "maintenance of erect posture, to integrated movements of body and limbs such

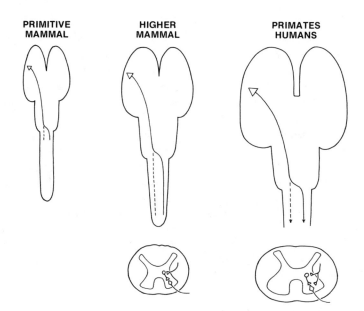

Fig. 21.12 Comparison of pyramidal tract pathways and terminations in the spinal cord of a primitive mammal (opossum), a higher mammal (cat), and a primate. Dashed lines indicate small uncrossed portion of the tract.

Fig. 21.13 Summary view of descending pathways, showing multiple projections and different laminar locations of cortical output neurons. Note that superficial cortical lamainae (II, III) project to other cortical areas, whereas deep cortical laminae (V, VI) give rise to descending projections, both pyramidal and extrapyramidal. Lamina IV (granule layer) is poorly developed in most parts of primary and secondary motor cortex. (Based in part on Jones, 1981)

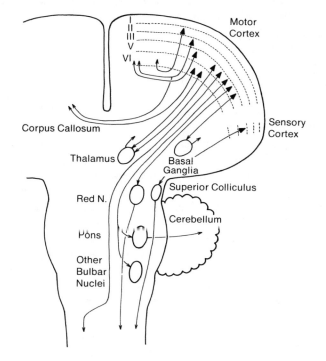

as orienting movements, to synergistic movements of the individual limbs and to directing the course of progression" (Kuypers, 1985). This is in accord with our above discussion. The other is the *lateral* group, which includes the rubrospinal tract. This supplements the ventromedial control, but especially adds the ability for fine control of the distal extremities. A lesion, for example, of the red nucleus has little effect on overall motor control (which by contrast is severely affected by vestibulospinal lesion), but impairs the ability of a monkey to use its hand and fingers. The corticospinal tract is a part of the lateral group, and adds further refinement to independent movement of the fingers, as we shall see in the next chapter.

The motor cortex, which gives rise to the corticospinal tract, may be regarded to some extent as a component of the middle level of control because of its direct connections to the spinal cord. However, it is also at a higher anatomical level, and also assumes a higher-level function relative to the brainstem. The corticospinal fibers not only project directly to the spinal cord, but also give off collaterals to the brainstem centers. In addition to these inputs, there are fibers from other cortical cells which terminate only in the brainstem, and do not proceed further. Many of these connections have been established by making horseradish peroxidase (HRP) injections into subcortical nuclei and identifying the labeled cells in the cortex. These studies, in addition, have shown that the fibers to these nuclei arise from neurons in layer V. By contrast, motor cortical cells projecting to other areas of cortex arise from several layers. This is summarized in Fig. 21.13.

Traditionally it has been believed that the corticobulbar cells are found in the premotor and postcentral areas, as mentioned above. Recent experiments, however, have shown that the origin of these fibers is much more extensive. For example, when HRP injections are made into the superior colliculus, retrogradely labeled cells are found in the visual and auditory cortex,

as well as somatosensory. The cells are pyramidal-shaped cells in layer V, the same as the motor cells of the motor cortex. The superior colliculus, in turn, has direct connections to the spinal cord through its tectospinal tract, as well as indirect connections through other brainstem connections.

These findings suggest several important points regarding the organization of motor control. First, the pyramidal and extrapyramidal systems provide to some extent separate and parallel pathways for the control of the spinal cord. Second, the two systems are interrelated by interconnections at all the main levels: cortex, brainstem, and spinal cord. Third, the extrapyramidal centers in the brainstem are influenced by connections from extensive areas of cortex. Together, these form what has been termed the *cortically originating extrapyramidal system,* to distinguish it from the *cortically originating pyramidal system.*

The Basal Ganglia

Now that we have identified the middle level of the motor hierarchy, we need to finish by discussing where the "Programs and Instructions" are found that represent the highest level in Fig. 21.3. One of the main regions is the basal ganglia of the forebrain.

Anatomy

The forebrain includes all of the nervous system above the diencephalon. It consists of two kinds of structure, the outer layer, called the cortex, and an inner mass, called the basal ganglia (*basal,* because they seem to be within the base of the cerebral hemispheres, and *ganglia* because this was the term applied by nineteenth-century histologists to large groups of neurons).

The positions of the basal ganglia are shown in Fig. 21.14. Of the several ganglia, the caudate is an elongated extension of the putamen; the two have a similar neuronal structure, and together are called the *striatum* (this term comes from the fact that there are bands of fibers passing through,

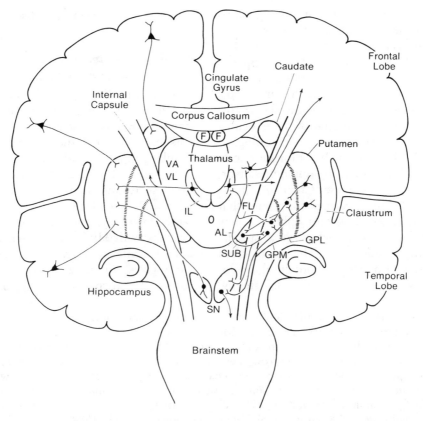

Fig. 21.14 Schematic frontal section of human brain, showing main connections and relations of the basal ganglia (shaded). Globus pallidus, lateral segment (GPL); medial segment (GPM). SUB, subthalamic nucleus; SN, substantia nigra; AL, ansa lenticularis; FL, fasciculus lenticularis. Thalamic nuclei: VA, ventral anterior; VL, ventral lateral; IL, intralaminar nucleus; F, fornix; O, cerebral aqueduct. Connections of caudate are similar to those shown for putamen. (Modified from Shepherd, 1979)

which produce a striated appearance). As indicated in the diagram, the striatum receives widespread inputs from the cerebral cortex; its output, in turn, is directed to another of the basal ganglia, the *globus pallidus,* and to the *substantia nigra.* The substantia nigra is actually located in the midbrain, but its main connections are with the striatum and globus pallidus, and it is therefore functionally linked with the basal ganglia. The output of the globus pallidus is directed to the thalamus, to the same nuclei which receive inputs from the cerebellum and project widely to the cerebral cortex. The output of the substantia nigra is directed both to the thalamus and back

to the striatum. These connections can all be traced in Fig. 21.14.

Until the 1960s, almost nothing was known about the functions of these large masses of cells; they were the great silent interior of the cerebral subcontinent. The only clues were that pathological changes were found in these regions in patients with certain striking movement disorders. Lesions in the putamen and globus pallidus were associated with slow writhing movements (athetosis). Degeneration of cells in the striatum was found in patients with Huntington's chorea, characterized by involuntary jerking movements. Lesions of a small region called the subthalamic nucleus were associated with violent flinging movements of the extremities (ballismus).

The most interesting correlation was the finding of degeneration of the dopaminergic input from the substantia nigra to the striatum in patients with Parkinson's disease. This was established in the 1960s, and was the first correlation of a neurotransmitter deficiency with a neurological disease. It provided the basis for the use of levodopa (L-dopa), a dopamine precursor, to treat these patients (see Chap. 24). It has also provided the precedent for hoping that other diseases, such as schizophrenia, may also be linked to a defect in a specific transmitter or substance. The use of brain transplants of dopamine-containing or dopamine-synthesizing cells to alleviate the symptoms of Parkinson's disease was discussed in Chap. 9.

Local Circuits and Microcircuits

All this work indicated that the basal ganglia are crucially involved in the control of movement and in sensorimotor coordination. Spurred by these findings, neuroscientists have directed their attention to the cellular properties and microcircuits within each region. Figure 21.15 illustrates some of these results. In the striatum, Stephen Kitai and his colleagues, then at Michigan State University, injected single projection neurons with HRP and shown that most have dendrites covered with spines (A). The axon gives off an enormous number of collateral branches, providing for multiple

Fig. 21.15 Synaptic organization and interactions in the basal ganglia. **A.** Caudate–putamen. *On the left,* the profuse dendritic tree of an HRP-filled neuron. *On the right,* the schematic diagram shows some posssible synaptic actions of dopaminergic fibers from the substantia nigra. Thick arrow, brief synaptic action; dotted arrow, slow synaptic action; other arrows, actions of dopamine on autoreceptors and on other synaptic terminals. **B.** Substantia nigra. *On the left,* two dopaminergic output neurons. *On the right,* some possible actions of dopamine, analogous to those in A. (HRP-filled neuron in A is from Kitai, 1981; diagrams are based on Aghajanian and Bunney, 1976; Nowycky and Roth, 1978; Groves et al., 1979; and Glowinski et al., 1984)

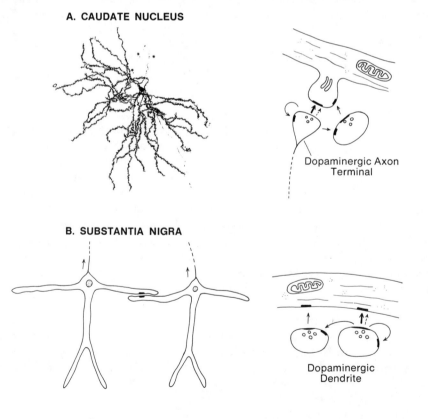

A. CAUDATE NUCLEUS

Dopaminergic Axon Terminal

B. SUBSTANTIA NIGRA

Dopaminergic Dendrite

local circuit connections to neighboring neurons.

On the input side, neuroanatomists have found that fibers from the cortex, thalamus, and substantia nigra make synapses onto the spines. Most of these synapses have a type I morphology (see Chap. 4), suggesting an excitatory action. However, the action of the input fibers has been a matter of keen debate. For the case of the dopaminergic fibers, some studies have suggested a rapid, brief excitatory action, while others have suggested a slower, inhibitory action. Biochemical studies have identified a dopamine-sensitive adenylate cyclase in the striatum, presumably activated by the dopaminergic fibers. In addition to its specific synaptic action, dopamine (DA) may act by diffusing from varicosities to postsynaptic sites, and it may also act on presynaptic terminals, as indicated in A in Fig. 21.15.

These studies indicate that a single type of fiber secreting a single transmitter can have several kinds of actions at several sites. This is in accord with similar results obtained under more precisely controlled conditions in invertebrate neurons. At each site, a specific combination of cellular properties is brought into play, to integrate information, transmit it to neighboring sites, and exert local feedback and modulatory control, actions that in addition may be use-dependent and lead to plastic changes.

Similar results have been obtained in the substantia nigra. Phillip Groves and his colleagues in San Diego have postulated that the output firing of the dopaminergic cells is controlled by feedback of DA, similar to the presynaptic control in the striatum. DA is contained within the dendrites of these cells. Its release from the dendrites has been shown by Jacques Glowinski and his colleagues (1984). They inserted a push–pull cannula into the substantia nigra, which allowed them to infuse various substances that activate the nigral neurons and then collect the released DA. During natural activity it is postulated that released DA may act on autoreceptors in the same dendrites, or diffuse to receptors on neighboring dendrites, or act at dendrodendritic synapses; such synapses have been identified in the electron microscope (see Fig. 21.15B).

Functional Organization for Control of Movement

To complete the picture of organization, we need to consider the basal ganglia as a system, and the way it relates to other systems. The basal ganglia feed into two thalamic nuclear groups, the ventral lateral–ventral anterior group, and the intralaminar group. These, in turn, project to the cortex, and thus complete a loop through cortical cells back onto the striatum, as shown in Fig. 21.16. This organization into closed loops is one of the outstanding characteristics of basal ganglia circuits, at all levels: it is seen in the several forms of feedback in microcircuits, in the reciprocal relations between striatum and substantia

Fig. 21.16 Distributed system formed by the loop circuits through basal ganglia, cortex, thalamus, and cerebellum. Putative transmitters: DA, dopamine; GABA, γ-aminobutyric acid; GLU, glutamate; SP, substance P; VA-VL, ventroanterior and ventrolateral.

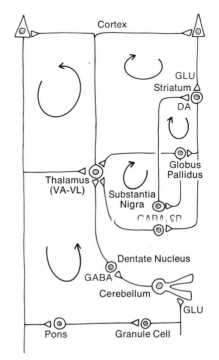

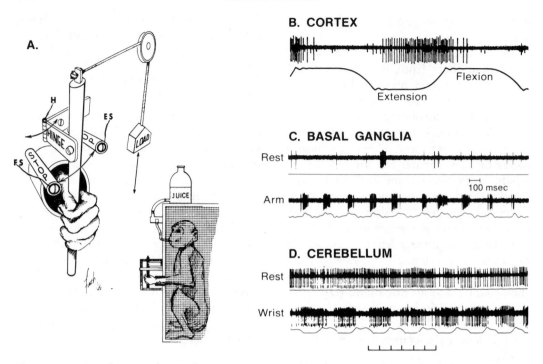

Fig. 21.17 Correlations of central neuron activity and movement in the awake, behaving monkey. **A.** Experimental setup for training a monkey to perform an extension or flexion of the wrist; it received a reward of fruit juice if the movement was performed within a brief specified period of time (400–700 msec). **B.** Activity of a single pyramidal tract neuron in the motor cortex in relation to movement. This unit was active prior to and during flexing of the wrist to a steady flexed position (but not during the maintained flexion). It increased its activity when flexion was performed against a flexion load (as in A), but was silent when flexion was performed against an extension load; this indicates that the motor cortex encodes force of movement as well as direction, displacement, and speed. **C.** Activity of a single neuron in the globus pallidus. The unit showed regular bursting in relation to push–pull movements of the arm, but not in relation to similar movements of the leg. Note the low rate of impulse firing at rest. **D.** Activity of a single Purkinje cell in the cerebellum. This cell showed regular bursting in relation to alternating extension and flexion of the wrist. Note the high rate of firing at rest, compared with the low rate of the basal ganglia cell in C. Time bar: 100-msec divisions. (A, B from Evarts, in Phillips and Porter, 1977; C from DeLong and Georgopoulos, 1981; D from Thach, in Brooks and Thach, 1981)

nigra, and in the loop through thalamus and cortex. In the thalamus, the input from the basal ganglia is integrated with input from the cerebellum. The cerebellum is embedded in its own loop, through thalamus to cortex and back through the pons (see above). The organization of these circuits into loops apparently confers the advantages of tight feedback at all levels in the control of movement. It appears, however, to have the disadvantage of uncontrollable oscillations when any part is dam-

aged, as in the disorders seen in neurological diseases.

The extensively related circuits shown in Fig. 21.16 involve many regions of the brain, and are a good example of a *distributed system* (see Chap. 24). In order to gain insight into how activity throughout this system is coordinated, single-unit recordings have been made in several of the regions, using the methods of Evarts (see next chapter). Figure 21.17 summarizes the results obtained from three regions—cortex, basal ganglia, and cerebellum—in relation to specific movements performed by awake monkeys. These experiments have shown that in both the cerebellum and the basal ganglia, single cells begin their discharges in advance of the onset of a volitional movement. Furthermore, cerebellar cells have been found to change their activity in advance of cortical cells during the state of "readiness" that precedes a motor act, as will be discussed in the next chapter.

From these results, the remarkable conclusion emerges that the distributed system that contains the highest motor programs includes centers (i.e., cerebellum and basal ganglia) that are anatomically at lower levels. This means that when we try to formulate concepts of motor control, we need to free ourselves of the idea that higher functions are lodged exclusively in the cortex. The cortex is the necessary instrument of higher function, but it is an instrument played by programs fashioned from the interactions between centers throughout the central nervous system. The multiple interconnections between centers both provide for the higher levels of abstraction underlying volition and purpose, and ensure that those functions emerge from the fabric of the organism as a whole. At this level, we pass from the motor hierarchy into the realm of central systems which are the subject of Part IV.

22

Manipulation

The success of an animal in thriving and procreating depends on more than simply moving about in its environment; what matters is its ability *to operate on the environment,* to extract from it the means of sustenance, to attack or defend itself, and to find mates and engage in cooperative behavior with others of its kind. These abilities usually depend on special motor organs suited for the purpose. In general, these organs, which an animal uses to operate on the environment, are complex, and require nervous control by more complex mechanisms than those mediating locomotion.

Some representative animals with their specialized motor organs are portrayed in Fig. 22.1. It can be seen that these organs generally take one of two forms: they are either modifications of the *limbs* (usually the forelimb), or they are modifications of the *head* (usually the face). The forelimb commonly has, as an elaboration of its distal part, an apparatus for *grasping,* that may take the form of *claws* or *hands.* The facial apparatus is characteristically elaborated in relation to the mouth, and consists mainly of a set of jaws, or a quite elongated and complicated *snout* or *proboscis.* These various organs can carry out a range of

operations, and it is difficult to find one word to characterize them all; somewhat arbitrarily we will class them all as one form or another of *manipulation,* to distinguish them from forms of locomotion.

The motor mechanisms we have considered in previous chapters have mainly involved repetitive events, such as the heartbeat or stepping, or single events, such as a tail flip. Specialized organs for manipulation involve more complex sequences of events. In addition, they involve higher levels of control in the motor hierarchy.

It can therefore be appreciated that the reductionist strategy of analyzing simple systems, which has been so successively applied to lower levels of motor control, has to be modified for the task of analyzing the more complex movements and the higher levels of control that are involved in manipulation. In general, the strategy must be to analyze a series of movements into its separate parts, and to identify the neural mechanisms at different levels in the hierarchy not only in relation to each part, but also in relation to the series as a whole. We will see that the neural mechanisms for manipulation incorporate principles for lower levels of motor control that we have already studied, as well as new principles

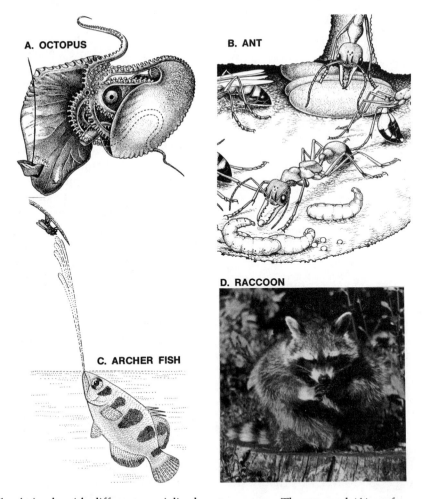

Fig. 22.1 Animals with different specialized motor organs. The octopod (A) performs manipulations with its tentacles, which are modified limbs, the ant (B) with its pincers, which are modified jaws (mandibles). The archer fish (C) "manipulates" water with its mouth and pharynx, in order to shoot droplets of water at airborne insects; this actually represents a form of tool use. The raccoon (D) performs dextrous manipulations of foodstuffs with its handlike forepaws. (A from Young, 1964; B from Wilson, 1975; C from Alcock, 1979)

involved in the initiation, maintenance, and termination of sequences of movements (sometimes called "motor programs") that arise at higher levels of control (see Fig. 21.3).

INVERTEBRATES

Invertebrates have evolved many kinds of organs for carrying out a variety of manipulative functions. As previously noted, the invertebrate has achieved its flexibility in this regard by virtue of the fact that the manipulative appendages evolved independently of the limbs for locomotion, and could therefore be individually adapted to their specific tasks. Table 22.1 gives at least a partial idea of the range of tasks carried out by limbs and facial organs.

Are lower species on the evolutionary scale capable of carrying out manipulative operations on their environment? One might think that such operations are possible only

Table 22.1   Various specialized motor operations

Limbs (legs, arms)	Face (proboscis, jaws)
grasping	grasping
pinching	pinching
tearing	tearing
clasping	clasping
holding	holding
squeezing	squeezing
crushing	crushing
exploring	exploring
feeling	feeling
	sucking
	grinding
	beating

with the evolution of complex organs in the higher invertebrates—the tentacles of the octopus, for example, or the pincers of the crayfish. It is true that these are among the best examples, but a moment's thought reminds us of the "arms" of coelenterates such as the *Medusa,* which function to entrap food and bring it to the mouth. This movement is controlled by the simplest kind of nervous organization, the *nerve net.* This type of manipulative function is even found in the plant world, as the Venus flytrap well exemplifies. However, the rigidly stereotyped nature of the reflex response of the flytrap to a stimulus reflects the limitation of not having a nervous system. Thus, it is not motor organs that are the key to the complexity of manipulative functions so much as the nervous mechanisms for controlling them.

Let us consider two types of manipulative organs that illustrate both the complexities and limitations of nervous control mechanisms in invertebrates.

Octopus Tentacles

The motor apparatus of the octopus consists of muscles controlling *gland cells* (chromatophores for protective color changes, and cells for discharging ink), *muscles for rapid movements* (jet propulsion and giant fiber systems), and muscles

for moving the arms, or *tentacles.* The tentacle is one of the most versatile manipulative organs devised by Nature. It is used to catch prey (either while the octopus is lurking quietly among the rocks and crannies of the seafloor or while swimming by jet propulsion); to convey the prey to the mouth; to explore the environment and test possible sources of food or danger by means of tactile and chemosensitive receptors in the arms; and to defend against predators.

Although one tends to think of the tentacle as being like an arm, it actually differs markedly from its vertebrate counterpart. The lack of bones and joints is an obvious difference; the advantage gained is that the muscle movements have great degrees of freedom, but the disadvantage is that this places heavy demands on their neural control mechanisms. The octopus has evolved a hierarchy of nervous centers for this purpose. At the lowest level are the motoneurons that innervate the muscles that move the individual suckers, and the muscles that move the arm. These motoneurons are located in ganglia within the arm. Chemosensory and tactile receptors in the skin and suckers, as well as muscle receptors, send their axons to these ganglia and establish connection with motoneurons and interneurons (see Fig. 22.2). By this means, reflex pathways for exploratory feeling or for withdrawal are present within the arm itself. A severed arm continues to show coordinated, purposeful movements such as conveying food in a mouthward direction, and, similarly, in animals whose brains have been removed, the tentacles still perform movements of grasping or withdrawal.

The tentacle thus contains its immediate motor control mechanism, and in this respect the nerve ganglia of the tentacle are analogous to the axial nerve cords of annelids and arthropods, and the spinal cords of vertebrates. It is as if the octopus has attached to it eight wormlike appendages, each with its self-contained motor ganglia for carrying out simple movements. There is thus a *decentralization* of motor control.

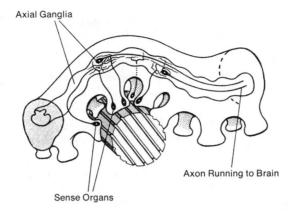

Fig. 22.2 Diagram of part of an arm of an octopus touching a plastic cylinder. The pathways from the receptors are inferred from physiological and degeneration experiments. The diagram illustrates an experiment in which the octopus was tested for its ability to discriminate between rods with different numbers of grooves. (After Wells and Wells, in Barrington, 1979)

The degree of this decentralization is dramatically reflected by the fact that, of the total of about ½ million nerve cells in the octopus nervous system, over half of them (300,000) are found within the ganglia of the tentacles.

Some limitations of this degree of decentralization in the motor control hierarchy have been revealed in behavioral tests. The experiment illustrated in Fig. 22.2 showed that the octopus can distinguish between different amounts of roughness of the surface of a cylinder, but is poor at distinguishing patterns or shapes. Other experiments showed an inability to learn to discriminate between objects with different weights. These limitations appear to be due to the fact that sensory information is largely confined to local reflex pathways within the arm; it is not made sufficiently available to the rest of the nervous system to serve as a basis for more sophisticated spatial discriminations, or learning. Martin Wells, of England, who carried out these studies, has suggested that all of this is a consequence of the completely flexible nature of the cephalopod body and tentacles, and the enormous amounts of sensory information about limb positions that this generates. It is more economical of nervous tissue to monitor this sensory information through peripheral circuits, but this limits the learning capacity that can be obtained only through central associative pathways. Thus, the tentacle as a manipulative organ attains its extraordinary flexibility at the expense of limitation in discrimination abilities, and the inability of the organism to learn new manipulations.

The ganglia in the arms are connected to a region of the brain called the *subesophageal* ganglia, which can be regarded as *intermediate* motor centers. The lobes and cords within the brain are complicated; many connections between the different lobes have been identified, and a summary is shown in Fig. 22.3. According to the studies of J. Z. Young and Brian Boycott in London, above the intermediate centers are *higher* motor centers, located in the *supraesophageal* ganglia. Above this, as indicated in the figure, are the *optic* and associated lobes, which function as *sensory* analyzers and *memory* stores, and the *frontal, vertical, and subfrontal* lobes, which are the main substrate for *motivation* and *reward* systems.

Proboscis of the Fly

One of the main functions of manipulative organs is to obtain food. The problem is

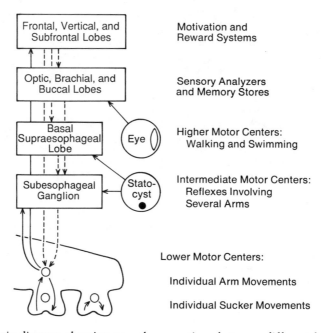

Frontal, Vertical, and
Subfrontal Lobes

Motivation and
Reward Systems

Optic, Brachial, and
Buccal Lobes

Sensory Analyzers
and Memory Stores

Basal
Supraesophageal
Lobe

Eye

Higher Motor Centers:
Walking and Swimming

Subesophageal
Ganglion

Stato-
cyst

Intermediate Motor Centers:
Reflexes Involving
Several Arms

Lower Motor Centers:

Individual Arm Movements

Individual Sucker Movements

Fig. 22.3   Schematic diagram showing neural connections between different lobes, and their relation to the hierarchical organization of motor control and learning in the octopus. (Adapted from Wells, 1968)

to get food to the mouth, and there are two general strategies for doing this. One is to bring the food to the mouth: this is the function performed by the octopus tentacles. The other strategy is to bring the mouth to the food. A sophisticated organ for doing this is the proboscis of the fly.

A schematic view of the proboscis and its relation to the head and thorax is shown in Fig. 22.4A. The distal end of the proboscis is modified into an enlargement called the *labellum*. As the diagram indicates, the mouth is situated in the labellum. We may note in passing that this means the situation is quite different from the proboscis of the elephant, in which the trunk is a modification of the nose: the elephant's trunk thus represents the other strategy, of conveying food to the mouth (Fig. 22.4B).

The proboscis of the fly is far more than a simple extension from the head. As shown in Fig. 22.5A, it contains a complex and delicate system of muscles and joints. There are, in general, two main types of movement, extension and retraction. *Extension*

occurs in response to stimulation by food substances of taste receptors in the labellum (see Chap. 11). The proximal part, the *rostrum,* is extended by the pumping of air into its air sacs. The intermediate part, the *haustellum,* is extended by coordinated contractions in a set of five pairs of muscle. *Retraction,* on the other hand, can occur slowly by elastic recoil, or rapidly by contractions in another set of five pairs of muscle. Some of these muscles and their relations to skeletal elements are indicated in the diagram.

The labellum is a complex organ in its own right. The diagram in Fig. 22.5B shows its rich innervation. The sensory fibers come from chemoreceptors in the labellar hairs and skin, tactile receptors, and muscle proprioceptors; there are also motor fibers to the intrinsic muscles. Unlike the octopus tentacle, the sensory receptors do not establish reflex connections within the proboscis; the fibers make these connections in the subesophageal ganglia of the brain (see Fig. 22.4), where the motoneurons are

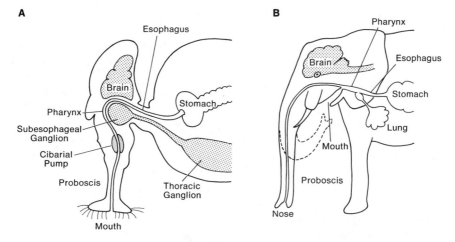

Fig. 22.4 Comparison between the proboscis of the fly (A) and elephant (B). (A modified from Dethier, 1976)

Fig. 22.5 Proboscis of the fly. **A.** Front view of the head, showing the structure and some of the muscles of the proboscis. **B.** The nerve supply to the aboral region of the labellum; open circles show positions of hairs. **C.** Diagrammatic view of a cross section of the labellum in a position to take up surface fluids by cupping and filtering. See text for explanation. (From Dethier, 1976)

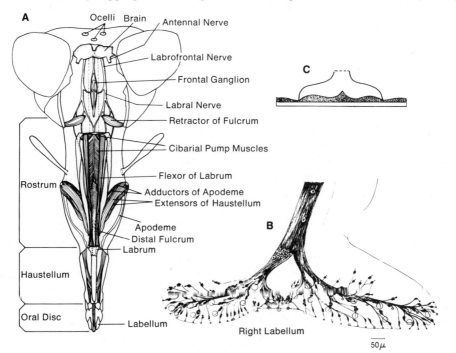

455

located. There is thus centralization, or encephalization, of reflex and motor control of the proboscis.

The key properties of the labellum are that it is *flexible,* and that it is under close nervous control. The *flexibility* allows it to adapt to a variety of surfaces (see Fig. 22.5C). Thus, it can be set to *filter* particulate suspensions through the teeth surrounding the mouth; *scrape* solid food matter from the surface, with the teeth everted; or *suck* up fluids with the mouth completely everted. These may be regarded as the manipulative functions of the proboscis, and they are obviously essential to the effectiveness of the fly in being able to feed and survive in so many different habitats. Once inside the mouth and moistened with saliva, the food is conveyed by the pumping action of an internal organ called the *cibarium* to the stomach (see Chap. 26).

The coordination of all these delicate adjustments of the labellum with the extension and retraction of the proboscis and the pumping of the cibarium is the province of the nervous system. The coordination is the outcome of the different information arriving by means of sensory receptors, and control by motor commands from the brain. The extraordinary sensitivity of this sensorimotor apparatus has already been noted (Chap. 11). Stimulation of a single sensory receptor cell in a hair of the labellum is sufficient to elicit extension of the proboscis (Fig. 22.6A). This involves much more than a simple muscle twitch; as Dethier has pointed out (1976), the information must pass from the axon of the single receptor to the subesophageal ganglion, and active interneurons there that control motoneurons to five sets of ipsilateral extensor muscle and five sets of contralateral muscles. Peter Getting at the University of California carried out experiments on the neural basis of this behavior in which he stimulated single sugar-sensitive receptor cells in the labellum and recorded the activity of their axons and of the axon to an extensor muscle. Figure 22.6B shows the impulse discharge when two receptors are stimulated

individually (upper two pairs of traces) and simultaneously (bottom pair). The upper pairs of traces show the ability of the single receptor to elicit responses in the motoneurons, and the bottom records show that the inputs from receptors can summate to elicit stronger motor responses.

These experiments represent a first step in correlating the motor behavior of the proboscis with dynamic properties of the sensorimotor central circuits. We shall have more to say about feeding behavior of the fly in Chap. 26.

VERTEBRATES

The Hand

In our discussion of locomotion, we noted the change that occurred when vertebrate animal life became adapted from aquatic to terrestrial environments. Some of these changes involved a relatively direct adaptation of preexisting structures and functions. Two pairs of limbs were elaborated, the forelimbs from the pectoral girdle and fins, the hindlimbs from the pelvic girdle and fins. The segmental neural apparatus was adapted for generating rhythmic alternating activity in the limbs, coordinated with the undulatory movements of the trunk; higher centers were elaborated for descending control.

These adaptations can be summarized by the principle that "Form ever follows function," a statement made by the architect Louis Sullivan many years ago to express his belief that buildings should have forms that facilitate their functional uses. This statement can serve as well to express the principle that underlies the relation between structure and function in the evolution of the nervous system. Many of these modifications of structure reflect the economical tendency in phylogeny toward adaptation of a preexisting structure to different functions in a new environment, rather than development of an entirely new structure. Some changes, however, have been

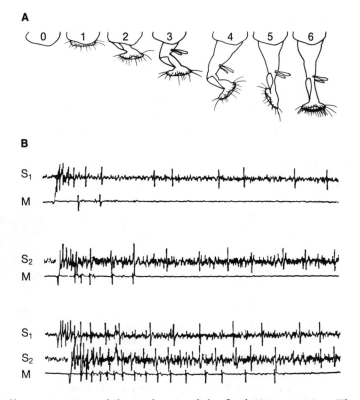

Fig. 22.6   A. Different positions of the proboscis of the fly during extension. These positions are used by investigators to quantify the motor response to sensory stimulation, and the effects of different behavioral states (hunger vs. satiety) on the feeding behavior of the fly. **B.** Sucrose stimulation of two individual hairs, S_1 and S_2 (upper traces), and the effect on activity of a single motor fiber to the proboscis (M). Separate stimulation of S_1 and S_2 in upper pairs of traces. Concentration of sucrose was 100 mM; fly had been starved for three days. Time bar: 100 msec. (From Getting, in Dethier, 1976)

more radical, and among these were the development of elongated *limbs,* and the development of complicated distal appendages. These changes are illustrated in the diagrams of the skeletal elements in Fig. 22.7. Our interest here is in the forelimbs, because they gave rise to the *arm* and the *hand,* which were crucial in the evolution of the primates. The hand is one of the most effective and adaptable appendages to emerge along the phylogenetic scale, and its manipulative abilities were crucial to the evolution of primates. The nervous mechanisms involved in the control of the primate hand are the subject of the rest of this chapter.

The control of the hand is not simply a matter of controlling the distal digits. For most functions, many major muscle groups are brought into play. First are the muscles of the trunk that insert on the humerus, and move the whole arm at the shoulder joint. Second are the muscles that arise from the humerus and insert on the radius and ulna; these move the lower arm and the elbow. Third are the muscles that arise from the lower humerus and insert in the hand; these flex or extend the whole hand or the individual digits. Fourth are the intrinsic muscles of the hand that spread or close the fingers; of those, the muscles that enable the thumb to oppose the fingers are especially important. Although individual functions can be assigned to individual

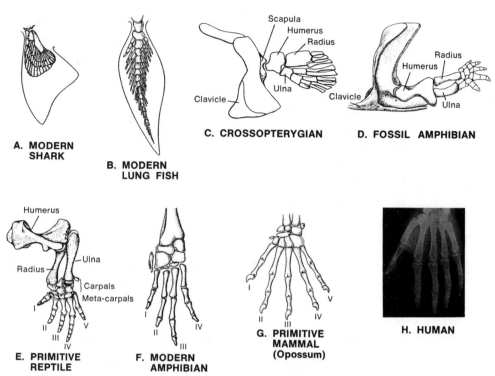

Fig. 22.7 Evolution of the bony structure of the forelimbs. (A–G from Romer and Parsons, 1977; H from Warwick and Williams, 1973)

muscles (for example, the abductor policus moves the thumb toward the fingers), *a given muscle always functions as a part of the whole ensemble of muscles.* It can be readily appreciated, for example, that swinging a hammer or a tennis racquet involves coordinated activity of all of the muscle groups mentioned above.

One of the main manipulative functions of the hand is *prehension,* that is, the ability to *grasp.* One sees this as a primitive reflex in a human baby; a finger placed in the baby's hand is always immediately enclosed by warm tiny fingers. One sees it revealed also in disease in the adult; a stroke commonly damages motor cells or fibers in the cortex, resulting in "release" or reflexes from their normal descending inhibitory control. Stretch reflexes become hyperexcitable, and more primitive reflexes such as the grasp reflex may be revealed. As previously noted, Jackson's study of these release phenomena was important for

the development of his concepts of motor hierarchies.

In our normal, everyday activities we tend to take it for granted that the manipulative positions of the hand are infinitely variable. However, to some extent they all involve some degree of either power or precision. A *power grip,* for example, is used by a monkey when it swings from one branch to another, or by us when we swing a tool or weapon, or lift a heavy object. A *precision grip,* in contrast, is used by a raccoon when it is cleaning and eating its food, or when a monkey picks up seeds or grooms its mate, or when we are writing with a pencil. Most manipulations involve degrees of both power and precision (Fig. 22.8). And most express the principle stated above, that any given movement depends on the coordinated action of an ensemble of muscles. For example, we know from our own experience that a power grip requires not only flexion of the digits but also

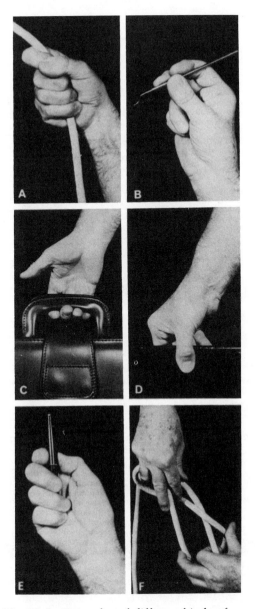

Fig. 22.8 Examples of different kinds of manipulative functions of the human hand. **A.** Power grip. **B.** Precision grip. **C.** Power (hook) grip. **D.** Power (pinch) grip. **E.** Combined power and precision grip. **F.** Complex posture and manipulation. (From Warwick and Williams, 1973)

extension of the hand itself (remember the childhood trick of making someone drop an object by pressing down their hand?); thus, it is the synergy of finger flexion plus wrist extension that gives the greatest power.

Similarly, threading a needle involves a delicate counterpoise between extensor and flexor muscles at every level of the hand, arm, shoulder, and indeed the whole body.

Neural Mechanisms

The axial and proximal limb muscles that contribute to movements of the hand are the same as those that take part in maintaining posture and providing for locomotion. We therefore turn our attention to the muscles of the distal forearm and hand, and the neural mechanisms that relate to their control.

Properties of the Corticospinal Tract. The neural mechanisms that are used in the fine control of the hand are summarized in Table 22.2. We have already discussed some of them in the previous chapter, such as the importance of the direct connection between the cortex and the spinal cord through the corticospinal tract. The physiological properties of this connection have been studied extensively in the monkey by Charles Phillips and his colleagues at Oxford. They have recorded intracellularly in the cervical region of the cord from motoneurons that send their axons into the median nerve of the forearm and thence to muscles controlling the hand (see Fig. 22.9). These motoneurons respond to stimulation of the peripheral Ia fibers from the muscle spindles with monosynaptic EPSPs, which remain about the same amplitude during a

Table 22.2 Neural mechanisms for fine motor control of the hand

Cortical
1. Large cortical representation of movements of hand and individual digits
2. Low threshold for cortical activation
3. Complex intracortical organization
4. Transcortical sensory feedback loops

Spinal
1. Strong corticospinal projection to spinal cord
2. Convergence of many fibers onto motoneurons
3. Monosynaptic connections to motoneurons
4. Facilitation of repetitive synaptic potentials

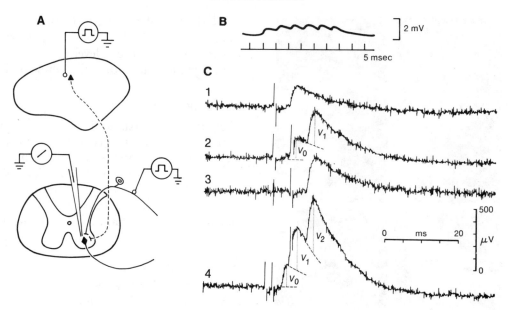

Fig. 22.9 **A.** Experimental setup for intracellular recording of responses of motoneurons to stimulation of input pathways in the baboon. **B.** Nonsummating EPSPs elicited by a train of six volleys in Ia afferents. **C.** Facilitating EPSPs elicited by 1, 2, and 3 shocks to the hand area of the motor cortex. Each trace is the average of 156 repetitions. The trace in 3 was obtained by subtracting 1 from 2, showing the facilitation of the second response compared with the first. (From Muir and Porter, in Phillips and Porter, 1977)

repetitive train (Fig. 22.9B). They also respond to cortical stimulation with a monosynaptic EPSP to cortical stimulation; however, with repetitive stimulation the EPSPs quickly undergo a marked *facilitation* of their amplitude (Fig. 22.9C,2,4).

This property of facilitation is not unique to the corticospinal synapses; it is also seen with stimulation of the rubrospinal pathway, for example, or with activation of polysynaptic pathways through segmental interneurons. This means that when any of these inputs is activated, the higher the frequency and the longer the burst, the more potent that input becomes in commanding the motoneurons. Also, as Phillips and Porter observed in their definitive monograph on *Corticospinal Neurones* (1977), this enables the corticospinal tract "to adjust, by alteration in frequency, the power of its excitatory action on targets." It is interesting to recall that a similar dependence of muscle activity on impulse frequency occurs in crustaceans, but in the

periphery at the neuromuscular junction (see Fig. 17.10).

Cortical Organization. What of the neural mechanisms at the cortical level? The maps of cortical representation (Fig. 21.9) are the starting point for investigation at this level. One of the most interesting questions is whether the intracortical circuits at a given site are organized on the basis of *modules* similar to those of the glomeruli, barrels, and columns of sensory cortex (see Chaps. 11, 12, and 16). A motor cortex module has been extremely difficult to define; to begin with, there is no highly ordered thalamic input, which imparts to sensory cortex much of its modular structure. The technique of *intracortical microstimulation* has given insight into this problem. This technique, introduced in the 1960s by Hiroshi Asanuma of the Rockefeller University, involves very selective stimulation of corticospinal neurons through a microelectrode introduced into the cortex. The

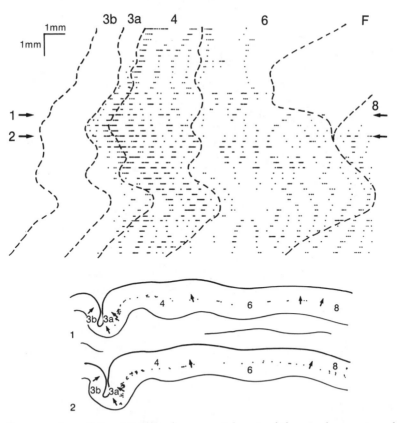

Fig. 22.10 Cross sections (below) and surface map (above) of the monkey cortex, showing clustering of corticospinal neurons as revaled by injection of HRP into the red nucleus. Arrow to left of map indicates location of the cross sections. Arrows in cross sections below indicate boundaries of different numbered areas. HRP injections into other subcortical motor centers, including the spinal cord, give similar results. (From Jones and Wise, 1977)

results have provided evidence that corticospinal neurons activated along a given electrode track through the cortex tend to be related to the same muscle, and to receive inputs from the corresponding part of the limb. This has suggested that there is a radial organization within the cortex for input–output function related to the same muscle. It is possible that this provides the basis for columnar modules. In fact, anatomical studies have shown that, after HRP injections into lower motor centers, the retrogradely labeled output cells in the cortex are grouped in clusters (see Fig. 22.10). However, the physiological studies to date indicate that the modular organization is less distinct than its sensory counterpart; there is variation in the sizes

of modules, and overlap of neighboring modules. This probably reflects the point we stressed at the outset of this section, that muscles are not controlled in isolation, but always as part of an ensemble of muscles with complementary or antagonistic actions.

Synthesis of Motor Circuits

A summary of the circuits that link the cortical and spinal levels in control of the hand is given in Fig. 22.11. Voluntary movements begin with central programs ① which activate, in appropriate pattern and sequence, the modules of the motor cortex. The corticospinal fibers ② activate the motoneurons to the muscles ③, by the mechanisms we have discussed. Through collat-

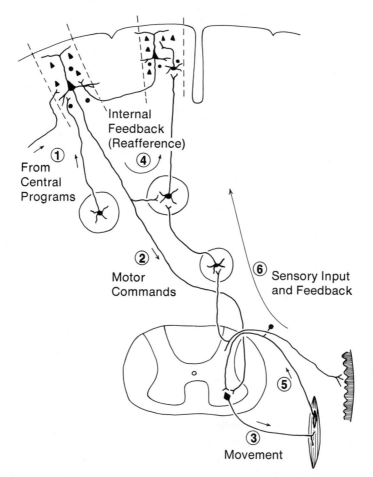

Fig. 22.11 Summary of some of the circuits and functions involved in voluntary control of movements of the hand. Most of these elements are similar in principle to those involved in control of locomotion, and are adapted for fine control of the hand, as discussed in the text.

erals, the corticospinal fibers also activate central sensory pathways and other ascending central systems ④ that feed back information to the cortex about the signals that have been sent; this is the "reafference," or "corollary discharge," mentioned previously (Chap. 21). Sensory input from the muscles ⑤ provides information about the state of contraction of the muscles and the extent of movement that has actually taken place. Some of this information reaches the motor cortex through direct connections from the somatosensory relay nuclei in the thalamus (see Chap. 12), while some is relayed from the somatosensory cortical areas. Connections between the somatosen-

sory and motor areas thus provide for a "transcortical reflex loop," that can function as part of a servomechanism by which the nervous system can assess errors in accuracy of movements and correct them.

More precise information about the relation between the organization at the cortical level and the organization at the spinal level has been obtained in studies of awake, behaving animals. These experiments have combined single-cell recordings and single-cell microstimulation within motor cortex with electromyographic (EMG) recordings from individual muscles. Using these methods, Eberhard Fetz and his colleagues at Washington (see Cheney et al., 1985) have

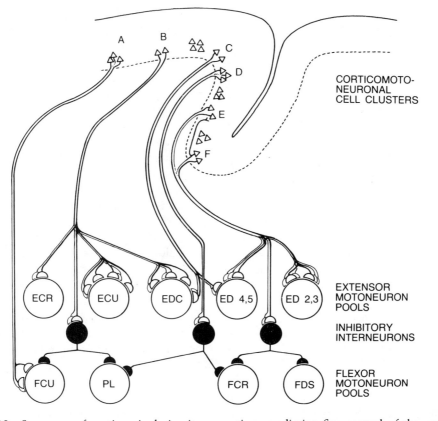

Fig. 22.12 Summary of corticospinal circuit connections mediating fine control of the wrist and fingers, as indicated by experiments in awake, behaving monkeys. A–F, clusters of pyramidal tract neurons in the motor cortex. Groups (pools) of motoneurons to different types of muscles: The six extensors were extensors carpi ulnaris (ECU), digitorum communis (EDC), digitorum 2 and 3 (ED2,3), digitorum 4 and 5 (ED4,5), carpi radialis longus (ECR-L), and carpi radialis brevis (ECR-B); the six flexors were flexors carpi radialis (FCR), digitorum profundus (FDP), carpi ulnaris (FCU), digitorum sublimis (FDS), palmaris longus (PL), and pronator teres (PT). Open profiles, excitatory actions; filled profiles, inhibitory actions. See text. (From Cheney et al., 1985)

studied the precise ways that cells in the cortex control fine movements of the wrist and fingers. The experimental setup is similar to that shown in Fig. 21.17 (see also below, Fig. 22.14). In one set of experiments, intracortical microstimulation of single pyramidal tract cells was used to elicit activation of individual flexor and extensor muscles of the wrist and fingers. These findings were then correlated with recordings from single cells during these same movements.

Three basic patterns of cortical cell influence on wrist flexor and extensor motorneurons were found. The hypothesized cir-

cuit connections mediating these influences are summarized in Fig. 22.12. One pattern is pure facilitation of agonist muscles (related muscles with the same physiological action, of extension or flexion). This is mediated by cell groups A and C in Fig. 22.12. The second pattern is facilitation of agonists with suppression of antagonists, which can be mediated by cell groups B, E, and F. The third pattern is pure suppression of agonists, such as can be mediated by cell group D. For each of these cell groups, the pathways can be traced in the figure to the connections with specific types of extensor and flexor motoneurons and inhibitory in-

terneurons that give rise to the corresponding physiological pattern.

This scheme is useful in relating the pathways for descending control of fine movements to the principles of organization we
have already studied, which relate to the
cortical and spinal levels. At the cortical
level, the pyramidal tract cells to the wrist
motoneurons are found in the wrist area
of the motor map within the motor strip
(Figs. 21.9 and 21.11). Within that area,
cells with a similar distribution of output
effects appear to be grouped into clusters.
These clusters reflect the columnar organization of cells revealed in the anatomical
studies (Fig. 22.10, above). At the spinal
level, Fig. 22.12 makes clear that the descending connections are incorporated into
the segmental circuits for motoneuron control. An expression of this is the fact that
reciprocal organization, which we have seen
underlies the segmental control of locomotion (Fig. 19.13), also underlies the descending control of fine movements. The
same circuit elements may be involved in
both kinds of control. It seems likely, for
example, that the inhibitory interneuron
mediating reciprocal inhibition from the
cortex (Fig. 22.12) is the same interneuron
mediating Ia inhibition from the muscle
spindles as a part of the stretch reflex (Fig.
19.13). Thus, the evolution of the higher
control of fine movements in our distal
extremities has arisen by adaptation of
preexisting circuits for locomotion.

Active Touch and Precision Grip

Figure 12.11 indicates the information that
flows in from other somatosensory receptors in the skin and tissues of the hand and
fingers (⑥). This flow contributes to control of motor performance, but it also has
an additional significance. As we discussed
in Chap. 12, the fingers have a high density
of sensory receptors. This is correlated with
their large cortical representation, which
parallels that for the muscles that move the
fingers. We employ this sensory capacity to
gather information about the environment,
such as the shapes of small objects or the
texture of surfaces. This use of the hand is
called *active touch* (see Chap. 12). It reminds us that the hand is a sense organ, as
well as a motor organ.

The diagrams in Figs. 22.11 and 22.12
indicate the direct, corticospinal pathway
to the spinal cord, but it should be emphasized that the corticospinal fibers have collaterals to all the brainstem motor nuclei
we have mentioned earlier in this chapter
(reticular, vestibular, red). These are involved in the control of all the axial and
proximal muscles during movements of the
hand. In addition, motor control involves
pathways through the cerebellum (in the
brainstem) and basal ganglia (in the telencephalon), as we discussed in the previous
chapters.

The way that sensory input from the
hand is used in control of hand movements
has been analyzed by Roland Johansson
and his collaborators in their studies of
precision gripping in humans. In these experiments, the subject grasped a small
weighted disc between thumb and forefin-
ger and, at a signal, raised it a couple of
centimeters, held it there, and then lowered
it to rest (see Fig. 22.13A). The surface on
the disc were covered with different materials; this gave them different degrees of
slipperiness, and required the subject to
adjust the amount of *grip force* to produce
a vertical lifting force (called *load force*)
that would raise the disc without slipping.

The force coordination related to three
different surface materials is shown in Fig.
22.13B. The load force required to raise
the weighted disc was the same for all
trials, as was the position to which it was
moved. However, the grip force was greatest for the smoothest material (silk), intermediate for suede, and lowest for the
roughest material (sandpaper). This meant
that the ratio of grip force to load force
was highest with silk and lowest with sandpaper. There was an initial period of high
ratio, followed by a period of lower ratio
while the disc was held maintained in the
raised position. The subject was then asked
to lower gradually the gripping force until
the disc slipped; this defined the slip ratio
(see arrowheads in Fig. 22.13B).

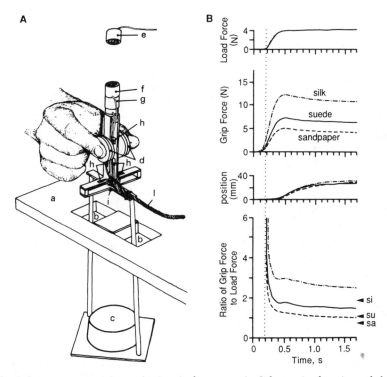

Fig. 22.13 Experiment on precision gripping in humans. **A.** Schematic drawing of the apparatus. a, table; b, holes in table; c, exchangeable weight shielded from the subject's view by the table; d, exchangeable discs; e and f, vertical position transducer with an ultrasonic receiver (e) and an ultrasonic transmitter (f); g, accelerometer; h, strain-gauge force transducers for measurement of grip force and load force (vertical lifting force); i, peg with a hemispherical tip on which the object rests while standing on the table; l, electric line. **B.** Force coordination during the initial part of lifting trials with three different surface structures (silk, suede, and sandpaper). From top, the graphs show load force, grip force, vertical position, and ratio between grip and load force as a function of time. Weight constant at 400 g. Vertical lines indicate the beginning of the loading phases. Force ratio not shown for the preload phase. Time scale with an arbitrary origin. *Top:* 16 sample trials superimposed (single subject). *Bottom:* Data averaged from a total of 120 trials by nine different subjects. Arrows indicate mean slip ratios for the three surface structures, respectively. (Figure and legend from Johansson and Westling, 1984)

These experiments demonstrated several principles in goal-directed manipulation involving precision gripping. First, sensory receptors provide exquisitely refined information about the frictional condition of the gripped surface. This comes not from a single type of receptor, but from the entire ensemble of receptors in the skin and connective tissue of the finger tips. Second, the motor system uses this information to generate a critical balance between force and load force that is adequate for raising and maintaining the lift under the different surface frictional conditions. This grip/load

ratio is set at a level above the slip ratio. Third, this grip/load force combination occurs automatically; according to Johansson and Westling (1984), this

. . . agrees with the notion that a particular pattern of afferent information might trigger release of a particular set of preprogrammed motor commands or update certain parameters of the currently executed motor programmes.

The authors speculate that these motor commands are mediated by the motor cortex and by the cerebellum, which is well-known to be involved in vestibular and

A

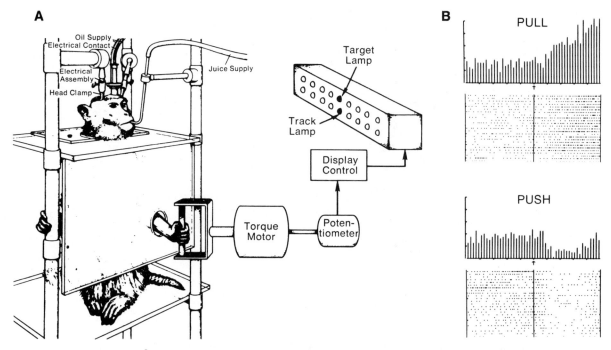

B

PULL

PUSH

Fig. 22.14   A. Experimental setup for recording from single cells in the monkey motor cortex during visual pursuit tracking. Movements of the handle produced shifts in the lighting of the lower (tracking) row of lamps. The task was to keep the tracking lamp aligned with changing positions of the target lamps. **B.** Discharge of a corticospinal neuron 1 sec before and 1 sec before and 1 sec after the appearance of a red light (signaling "get ready to pull") and a green light (signaling "get ready to push"). *Top:* Histograms of number of impulses in 40-msec bins. *Bottom:* Raster displays of occurrences of impulses in successive trials; see text. (From Tanji and Evarts, in Evarts, 1981)

postural reflexes (see Chap. 14), and in the initiation of certain movements (see Chap. 21). A final point is that force coordination in precision gripping is learned; the motor command level therefore contains in its circuit organization the memory for adjusting grip/load force to the appropriate frictional condition, and this memory is constantly updated for changes that occur in the surface or load.

Voluntary Movements

The motor cortex is partly at an intermediate level in the hierarchy of motor control as we have seen, but is, nonetheless, at the highest level to which we can trace pathways that can be labeled "motor." Above this, the inputs to the motor cortex come from central systems, to which the terms "motor" and "sensory" do no apply. It is these central systems that provide the "central programs" (see ① in Fig. 22.11) that control the motor cortex.

At present we are only beginning to understand the nature of these central motor programs. Part of the answer will come from more precise mapping of complex central circuits. But higher motor control in humans is not just more complex than in other animals; its essence lies more in the fact that what we do seems "voluntary," and is performed with "purpose." We cannot ethically study this dimension of motor control in humans at the cellular level with present techniques, but we can approach it through experiments on awake, behaving monkeys. The results of these experiments have given us insights unobtainable by other means.

This approach to the study of motor behavior was pioneered by Edward Evarts at the National Institutes of Health in the 1960s. A typical experimental setup is illustrated in Fig. 22.14. A monkey is first prepared for chronic recording by placement of a closed recording chamber over an opening in the skull. For the behavioral study, the animal sits under light restraint in a chair and performs a task. A microelectrode inserted into the motor cortex records the activity of a single cell in relation to performance of the task.

In the example of Fig. 22.14, the task was first to hold a handle in a given position for a few seconds. Then either a red or green lamp was lit. A red light meant "get ready to pull" on the handle, a green light meant "get ready to push." The handle was then displaced automatically and the task of the monkey was to give it either a pull or a push, depending on what the instruction had been. The results are shown in Fig. 22.14B. The impulse discharge of this neuron is displayed for the period of one second before and one second after the onset of the red or green light (arrow). As can be seen, the cell increased its discharge after the instruction to pull, but decreased it after the instruction to push. These changes in cell activity occurred in advance of the actual motor response to the displacement of the handle.

From these kinds of results Evarts (1981) concluded that the warning light "set up preparatory states for a particular direction of centrally programmed movement." This state is reflected in the specific activity of a single cortical cell. Remarkably, this motor activity is entirely internal, as far as the behavior is concerned; there is no overt motor movement during the warning period, and no EMG discharge in the muscles. Thus, the central motor program drives the cortical motor cells, but the motor output stays within the brain. States of readiness, such as this, can also be detected as "readiness potentials" in the electroencephalogram, recorded by gross electrodes on the scalp (see Chap. 25).

23

Communication
and Speech

Communication is an essential element of any level of organization. At the level of the cell, molecular signals and messengers are needed for accomplishing cellular functions. Similarly, the organization of individual organisms into functional groupings depends on their ability to send signals to each other. Many types of communication involve the whole organism, and draw on virtually all the motor mechanisms we have discussed thus far; for example, animals communicate with each other through different postures, different forms of walking, or by specific gestures. In contrast are the types of communication that depend on specific signals, such as pheromones or tactile stimulation.

In this chapter, we will consider a type of communication that depends on special organs designed specifically for that purpose. This is communication by *sound*. Since special organs are necessary for making sound, communication by this means is limited to larger or more complex organisms, similar to the case for manipulation. Communication by sound is particularly important in certain orders of insects, in birds, and in mammals. We have already discussed the sensory mechanisms for reception of sound signals in these organisms

in Chap. 15, where we also discussed briefly the importance of this mode of communication for humans.

In this chapter, we will consider the motor mechanisms for generating sound signals in insects, birds, and humans. Insect and bird song are both active fields of investigation. Many recent advances have been made in understanding neural mechanisms at all levels of the motor hierarchy, from muscles up to central programs; however, these results have received less general notice than work on locomotion.

With regard to vocalization in mammals, there has been surprisingly little interest shown by neurobiologists. Indeed, apart from the identification of the speech area of the human cortex, the subject of mammalian vocal mechanisms does not even exist as far as many textbooks are concerned. This is partly explained by the fact that the neural mechanisms seem to be too complex for successful experimental analysis, compared to those for insects and birds. However, vocalization and speech are much too important to humans to allow us to ignore them. In fact, we shall see that considerable information is available on some aspects of the mechanisms, and comparison with the studies of insects and birds provides some valuable perspectives on the properties that have been important for the evolution of speech as a mechanism for human communication.

Insect Song

Most rapid movements produce sounds, some of which may have a signaling value. Among higher invertebrates, crustacea and insects produce various kinds of noises. However, as specific signals these sounds are of limited value, because of their relatively coarse nature, and the fact that, as we discussed in Chap 15, many of these organisms appear to lack specialized auditory sensory cells. Among insects, however, certain species have specialized organs for producing and receiving specific types of sound. Best studied are crickets and grasshoppers (order Orthoptera) and cicadas (order Cicadidae). In these species the structures for producing sound are adapted from structures for locomotion. This contrasts with the evolution of flight, which in insects took place not by the adaptation of limbs to wings, but by the adding on of wings (see Chap. 20).

Sound Production

The general mechanism for producing sound in insects is by scraping two parts of the exoskeleton against each other. The technical term for this is *stridulation* (meaning to scrape). It is the mechanism that a violinist uses in drawing a bow over the strings of a violin. The mechanism in the cricket is illustrated in Fig. 23.1. Across the dorsum of each wing is a structure called an *elytron*, originally a vein that has been transformed into a row of teeth, like a file. Under the median edge of each wing is a ridge, called a *pectrum*. When one wing is drawn across the other, the pectrum of one wing scrapes the file of the other, as shown in Fig. 23.1A, and induces vibrations of the wing, which make sound.

The sound produced depends on the rate of movement and the resonant properties of the wing. In some crickets, the teeth are

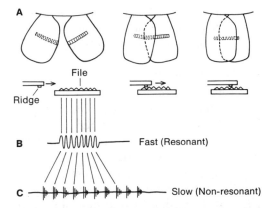

Fig. 23.1 Mechanism for producing sound in the cricket. **A.** Movement of the ridge (elytron) over the file (pectrum). **B.** Fast movement producing resonant sound. The oscillations of the wing are near the natural resonant frequency of the wing. **C.** Slow movement producing nonresonant sound. Each impact produces a burst of high-frequency oscillations of the wing.

small, the movement rapid, and the wing thin and flexible. In this case, each tooth impact produces an undamped oscillation, and the tooth impact rate during the wing excursion produces a sound at a frequency near the natural resonant frequency of the wing. This is called *resonant sound emission* (Fig. 23.1B). The frequency spectrum is narrow, in the range of 2–6 kHz for different species. In other crickets, the teeth are larger, the wing movement is slow, and the wing is relatively stiff. In this case each tooth impact produces a heavily dampened, rapidly decaying wave transient containing high-frequency oscillation. The slow wing excursion, with its slow tooth impact rate, produces a series of these individual complex wave forms. This is referred to as *nonresonant sound emission* (Fig. 23.1C).

Sounds produced by these two mechanisms thus differ in their frequency characteristics by virtue of both the resonant frequencies and the rates of wing beating. The main method for using these sounds to send information is by periodic interruptions of the wing beats, so that the sounds are sent in groups, called *chirps*. By this means, a cricket is able to signal several types of behavioral states. There is a general *calling* song, a song signifying hostility or *aggression,* and a *courtship* song.

Neural Mechanisms

What are the neural mechanisms for generating these distinct motor output patterns? These have been analyzed in electrophysiological studies at several levels of the motor hierarchy. As illustrated in Fig. 23.2A, recordings have been made from the muscles ①, motor nerves ②, and thoracic ganglion ③. Recordings from these sites have shown that activity in the nerves to the wing muscles is closely correlated with the chirps of the cricket song; an illustration of recordings from the muscles themselves is shown in Fig. 23.2B. These studies have shown that synchronous volleys of impulses alternate between the nerves to the antagonistic muscles that close and open the wing. These volleys in the motoneurons arise within the thoracic ganglion; their rhythmic alternating character is relatively unaffected if the ganglion is isolated from all proprioceptive input from the muscles, and all intersegmental or descending input from other ganglia or from higher levels. There is thus a stable motor pattern generator within the thoracic ganglion that is responsible for the wing movements that produce sound.

It thus appears that communication by sound utilizes the principle of a rhythm generator at the segmental level, which is the same as that involved in generating the rhythmic movements underlying locomotion. This, in fact, is no surprise when we realize that the muscles that move the cricket's wings to produce sound are the same ones that move the wings during flight. In both cases the wing beat is neurogenic (see Chap. 20). The main difference is that, during flight, the opener and closer muscles are changed in their orientation by other muscles so that they function as depressors and elevators of the wings.

Hierarchical Control

The hierarchical control of the song generator follows the same principles we have discussed for flight and other forms of locomotion. Stimulation of motor control fibers (command fibers) turns on chirping, and maintains it throughout the period of stimulation. Thus, as shown in Fig. 23.2C, maintained repetitive stimulation of command fibers gives rise to intermittent bursts of impulses in the motoneurons in the chirping generator. This illustrates the same principle underlying the mechanism by which a constant command generates alternating stepping movements (Chap. 20). The upper motor neurons giving rise to these fibers are themselves under control of higher centers in the insect's brain.

Insight into the higher mechanisms of song control has been gained by using electrical microstimulation at different sites in the brain to elicit different types of song. As shown in Fig. 23.3, repetitive stimulation at one site in the "mushroom bodies" elicited a "calling song" or a "rivalry song," dependent on the strength and frequency of the shocks. Stimulation at another site elicited either the calling song or a "courtship song." The mushroom bodies represent the highest level in the motor hierarchy; as shown in Fig. 23.3, their neurons interact with each other to form circuits that control lower centers in the brain, which in turn control the motoneurons in the segmental ganglia. The stimulation experiments show that the song programs are stored in these circuits and read out from them in a very stereotyped manner; there are obviously not the overlapping and flexible synaptic circuits that characterize higher control of many other types of motor output patterns, especially in vertebrates.

A schematic representation of the elements involved in higher control is shown in Fig. 23.4. The most important elements are sensory inputs, hormonal effects, and central feedback. In different species, singing is evoked by specific *sensory* cues such as a certain temperature of the air, or amount of light or dark, or the sight or song of another member of the species, or by tactile stimulation. Song production is also under close *hormonal* control; in most species only the males sing, and usually only when

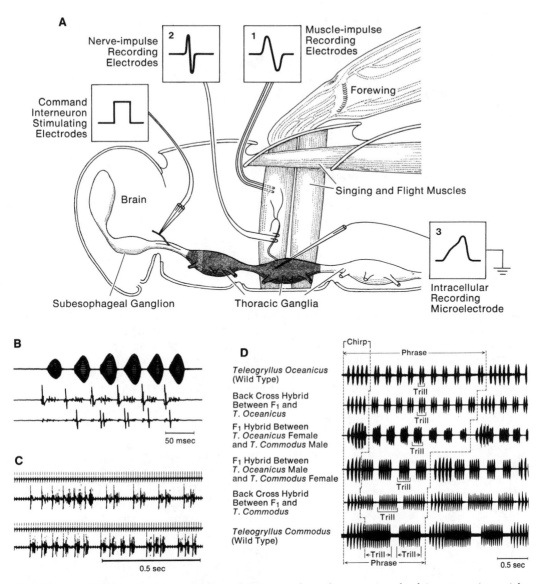

Fig. 23.2 **A.** Experimental setup for studying neural mechanisms involved in generating cricket song. **B.** Relation of chirp sounds in the cricket (top trace) to impulse activity in the wing-opening muscle (middle trace) and wing-closing muscle (bottom trace). **C.** Prolonged repetitive electrical stimulation of command interneuron fiber (upper trace) elicits intermittent chirping pattern of impulse discharge in motoneuron fibers to the muscles (lower trace). **D.** Song patterns of two wild cricket species (top and bottom traces), and of their hybrid offspring. (From Bentley and Hoy, 1974)

sexually mature, or when carrying a spermatophore prior to copulation.

Genetic Control

The distinctiveness of the songs for a given species, and their resistance to environmental effects, are strong indications of the importance of genetic factors in determin-

ing the song pattern. This has been investigated by making crosses between males of one species and females of another. The pioneering experiments by David Bentley and Ronald Hoy at Berkeley are illustrated in Fig. 23.2, presented earlier. The results show that each genotype is associated with a distinctive song, which differs from the

Brain Stimulation

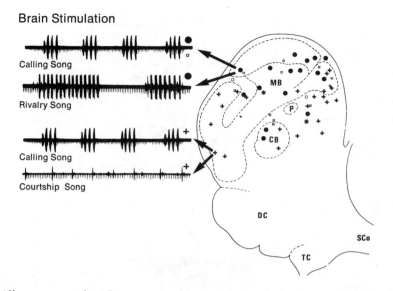

Calling Song

Rivalry Song

Calling Song

Courtship Song

Fig. 23.3 Different types of cricket song. In this experiment the brain was stimulated at different sites in and around the highest brain centers (mushroom bodies; MB); at a given site, one or more song patterns could be elicited by applying electrical shocks at different frequencies or intensities. Two such sites are illustrated in the diagram. Sites that elicited calling or rivalry song are shown by (●); calling or courtship (+); calling only (○); calling, courtship, or rivalry (*); song suppression (□). Abbreviations: P, pons; CB, central body; DC, deutocerebrum; TC, tritocerebrum; SCo, connective to subesophageal ganglion. (From Otto, in Elsner and Popov, 1978)

Fig. 23.4 Hierarchical control of song generation in the cricket.

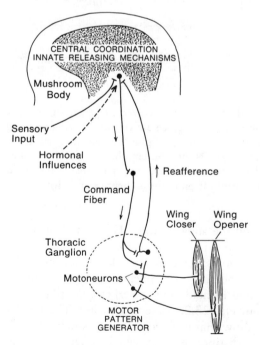

others in its intervals between pulses within a chirp or trill, and the intervals between chirps or trills. Further experiments have indicated that the intertrill interval is controlled by genes in the X chromosome. Because of the gradual way in which the characteristics of the song patterns change with different hybrid crosses, Bentley and Hoy concluded: "The genetic system that specifies the neuronal network accounting for cricket song is therefore a complex one, involving multiple chromosomes as well as multiple genes."

Why are cricket songs so stable, so genetically dominated? Part of the answer appears to lie in the fact that there is little overlap in generations of many singing species, so that the young have no opportunity to learn the song of their species from their parents (see Fig. 27.1).

This account gives only a brief introduction to the field insect song communication.

The stable nature of the song pattern makes this an important field for analyzing the neural basis of specific motor behavior; it is thus an important meeting place for neurobiologists and neuroethologists.

Birdsong

In vertebrates, locomotion, as we have seen, depends on the adaptation of four limbs to a variety of locomotory skills, and manipulative organs have evolved as adaptations of the limbs. In contrast to insects, in vertebrates, specific organs for communicating by sound have evolved independently of the organs for locomotion. This has freed them from the evolutionary pressures on the limbs for locomotion, which is a factor limiting the complexity of song production by insects.

In fish, primitive kinds of sound communication occur in some species by muscular thumping of the swim bladder. In terrestrial vertebrates, however, the key strategy has been to adapt the respiratory apparatus, by expelling air from the lungs through a constricted orifice in the respiratory tract. The production of sound by this means is referred to as *vocalization*. Some amphibians and reptiles communicate by vocalization, but it is in birds especially that we see a sophisticated use of acoustic signals comparable to that in the insects.

The Syrinx

In birds, the organ for producing sound is the *syrinx*. This is located at the site where the two bronchi arise from the trachea, and is, in fact, a modification of the walls of these structures. Note that the syrinx is distinct and quite separate from the larynx, which is also present, but in birds serves merely to regulate overall air flow. The mechanism of sound production by the syrinx is illustrated in Fig. 23.5. Within the syrinx, the bronchial walls are modified into thin *tympaniform* membranes, surrounded by air sacs. Contractions of muscles attached to the syrinx set the amount of tension on the membrane. As shown in Fig. 23.5B, when air is pressed out of the air sacs and tension is relatively slack, the tympaniform membrane bulges inward, and air flow through the bronchi sets the membranes into high-frequency oscillations.

With this relatively simple mechanism, birds are able to produce an astonishing range of songs. These serve a variety of functions, many of them similar to those

Fig. 23.5 Sound production by the syrinx in birds. **A.** The tracheolateralis muscles are contracted, while the sternotrachealis muscles are relaxed. Under this condition, the syringeal membranes are taut, and the bore from bronchi to trachea is maximally open; air flow through the syrinx generates low-frequency sounds or no sound. **B.** Tracheolateralis muscle relaxed and sternotrachealis contracted. The syringeal membranes bulge inward, and the bore leading from bronchi to trachea is maximally reduced; air flow through the syrinx generates high-frequency sounds. (From Hersch, in Nottebohm, 1975)

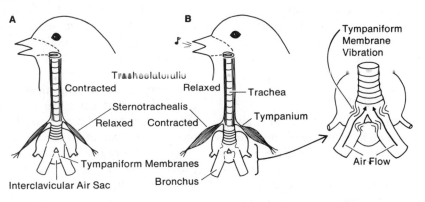

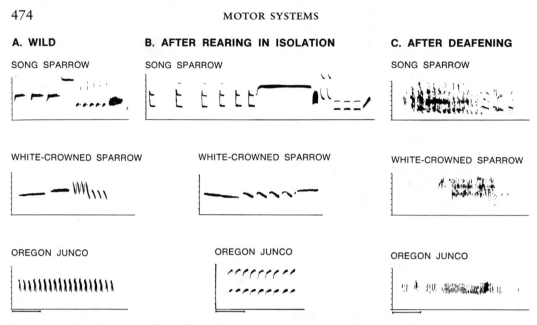

Fig. 23.6 Contributions of genetics and environment to the development of songs in three closely related members of the sparrow family. Each graph is a sonogram, with frequency on the ordinate and time on the abscissa. See text. (From several authors, in Marler, 1976)

in insects. Thus, there are sounds of alarm, distress, or warning. These are usually referred to as *calls*. They are usually simple in structure, and may be made by any member of the species. Contrasting with those are the elaborate vocalizations we refer to as *songs*. These are characteristically made only by males during the breeding season. The song identifies the singer and conveys information that he is defending his territory and is ready to mate. In many species, females also vocalize; these vocalizations include alarm calls and songs related to mating and nesting. In contrast to insect songs, bird songs have a rich tonal structure (as we all know from comparing the chirp of a cricket to the song of a robin), in which the different frequency components are important in conveying information.

Development of Birdsong

The songs of birds are distinct for a given species, and they have therefore been analyzed for the relative importance of genetics and environment in determining their pattern. We can surmise, to begin with, that, unlike insects, the generations overlap; par-

ents care for their young, and thus some degree of learning by the young is possible. The degree to which this takes place is illustrated in Fig. 23.6, which summarizes the result from several workers. In the wild (A of the figure), the songs of the three species are distinct. After rearing in isolation (B), the song of the song sparrow retains most of its structure; the songs of the other two lose some of their species-specific structure, through retaining some aspects of vocal control. However, when the young are deafened (C), their vocalizations as adults are coarse and scratchy, lacking in structure and species-specificity.

From these results it has been concluded that there is a sensitive period, between 10 and 15 days for the male white-crowned sparrow, during which auditory stimulation with the appropriate song pattern is necessary for the development of the ability to produce that song. This has suggested that sensory stimulation with the song pattern sets up an *auditory template* in the central auditory nerve circuits, that not only provides the means for *recognition* of the species-specific song pattern, but also for *generation* of the motor output for produc-

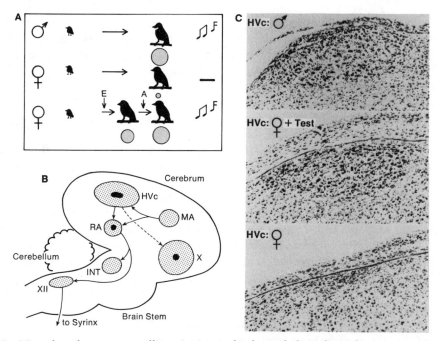

Fig. 23.7 Neural pathways controlling singing in birds, and their dependence on sex hormones. **A.** Diagrammatic representation of experiment with hormones in the finch. Normally, male finches sing but females do not (upper two rows). However, females treated at hatching with estradiol (E) and subsequently with androgens (A) as adults, are able to sing and show other male behavior. Relative size of the nucleus hyperstriatum ventrale (HVc) is shown by the shaded circles. **B.** The pathways for vocal control in the canary. Dots indicate sites of binding of systemically injected [³H]testosterone. Shading indicates areas more highly developed in males than in females (Area X is present only in the male.) Brain regions: INT, nucleus intercollicularis; MA, nucleus magnocellularis anterior (neostriatum); RA, nucleus robustus archistriatalis; XII, twelfth cranial nerve. **C.** Histological sections, showing the HVc in normal male (upper), hormone-treated female (middle), and normal female (lower). Note the much smaller size of the HVc cell group in the female. (A from Nottebohm, 1980; B from Miller, 1980; C from Gurney and Konishi, 1980)

ing the song itself. Since the sensitive period for auditory learning precedes by several weeks the time when the bird actually begins to sing, it is as if the bird sings from memory. As a young male bird begins to sing, it makes an ever closer match between its template and its performance. Thus, genetics, sensory stimulation, sensory feedback, and, probably, internal corollary feedback, all are necessary in the ontogeny of song.

Hormones and Birdsong Circuits

A final factor involved in the control of birdsong is the effect of hormones. As noted above, singing during courtship is characteristically done only by males (see Fig. 23.7A, top and middle). This ability in the male Zebra finch is dependent on the male sex hormones; castrated males do not sing, but singing can be reinstated by administration of androgens. Injections of androgens do not induce singing in females (A in Fig. 23.7A, bottom), but they do if the females were treated at birth with testosterone metabolites (dihydrotestosterone or estradiol; E in Fig. 23.7A, bottom). Even when reared in isolation, these females are able to produce a song that is very similar to that of the male.

Studies of the brain have begun to reveal the neural basis for these hormonal effects. Previous stimulation and ablation studies had permitted identification of several levels in the motor hierarchy: these include the vagal motoneurons to the syringial and chest muscles, located in the brainstem; a center in the midbrain; and several centers in the telencephalon (see Fig. 23.7B). Arthur Arnold, Fernando Nottebohm, and Donald Pfaff at Rockefeller University showed that nerve cells in several of these centers are able to bind injected and radioactively labeled testosterone or its metabolites (see Nottebohm, 1980). The cells in the male are larger than in the female; they are thus *sexually dimorphic*. Mark Gurney and Mazakazu Konishi (1980) have shown that the ability of hormone-treated females to sing is closely correlated with enlargement of brain centers in the song-producing pathways. The much smaller sizes of regions RA, HVc, and X in the female are indicated in the diagram of Fig. 23.7B. An example of the effects of hormones on one of the centers (HVc) is shown in Fig. 23.7C. These studies thus give evidence of the powerful ability of hormones to act as *organizers* of neuronal circuits (see Chaps. 8 and 27).

In addition to sexual dimorphisms, the vocal pathways in birds also demonstrate bilateral asymmetries. Each half of the syrinx is supplied by a right or left branch, respectively, of the twelfth (hypoglossal) cranial nerve. Nottebohm (1975) cut each branch separately, and found that cutting the left syringeal nerve branch severely affected the ability to sing, whereas cutting the right branch had very little effect. The basis for this difference is still not completely understood; it appears to be correlated with the fact that a greater portion of the air expired during singing comes through the left bronchus from the left lung. From this work emerged the concept of left hypoglossal dominance in song production. It is somewhat surprising to realize that at the time of its discovery, around 1970, it was the only asymmetry in neural function known in a vertebrate, other than humans. Among invertebrates, there are several well-known asymmetries, such as the pincer and crusher claws of lobsters,

and in recent years a number of behavioral asymmetries have been discovered in vertebrate species. We will return to this theme in discussing human speech (below and Chap. 30).

Mammalian Vocalization

Vocalization plays a prominent role in communication among members of most mammalian species. As in birds, this is correlated with a keen sense of hearing (Chap. 15). Some of this keenness is used to respond to intraspecies signals as indicated by the complexity of many of the sounds produced. In fact, the more this question has been investigated, the more complex appear the vocalizations, their neural control, and the behavior they mediate.

The purring of a cat involves precise timing between contractions of laryngeal muscles and the diaphragm (see Fig. 23.8A). It is also of interest that purring is largely under central control; the purring rhythm continues in the motoneuronal discharge despite deafferentation, or removal of the muscles.

Figure 23.8B illustrates sonograms of the song of the humpback whale. The entire song lasts 7–30 minutes; each whale sings its own song, which it repeats faithfully, as indicated in the figure. The ability to repeat a message of this complexity testifies to considerable powers of memory and motor readout. It has been said that this may be the most elaborate single behavioral display in any animal species.

These considerations indicate that a sophisticated apparatus for vocal communication has emerged in the course of mammalian evolution. Let us see how this apparatus has been adapted in humans for producing speech.

Human Speech

The Vocal Apparatus

Although we commonly think of speech as emanating from the larynx, our vocal ap-

A. CAT PURRING

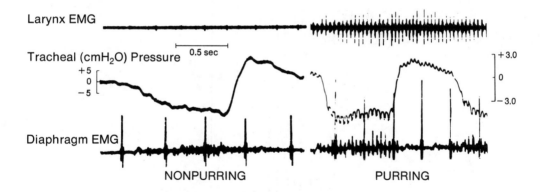

Larynx EMG

Tracheal (cmH$_2$O) Pressure

Diaphragm EMG

NONPURRING   PURRING

B. SONG OF THE HUMPBACK WHALE

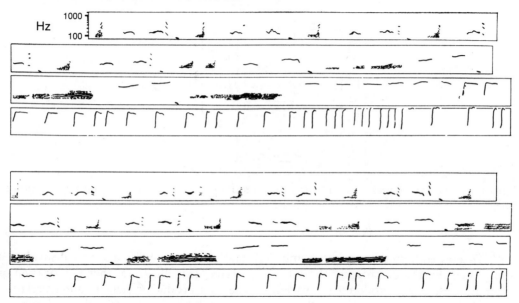

Hz

Fig. 23.8 Sound production in mammals. **A.** Purring of a cat. Upper trace electromyograph recordings from laryngeal muscles; middle trace: pressure in the respiratory tract; lower trace: electromyograph (EMG) recordings from the diaphragm. Note correlation between impulses in EMGs and oscillations in pressure during purring. **B.** Sonograms of the song of the humpback whale, obtained from an animal in the vicinity of Bermuda. Top four strips are from a song that lasted over 10 min; bottom four strips are from a subsequent repeat of the song by the same animal. (A from Remmers and Gautier, in Doty, 1976; B from Payne and McVay, in Wilson, 1975)

paratus is a good deal more complicated than that. Sound production is based on the principle of forced air. This requires three main components: a source of *pressure,* a set of *vibrating* elements, and a

system of *resonators* and *articulators.* As shown in Fig. 23.9, each of these is a carefully coordinated system of subcomponents. *Pressure* arises by taking air into the lungs (inhalation) and expelling it (expira-

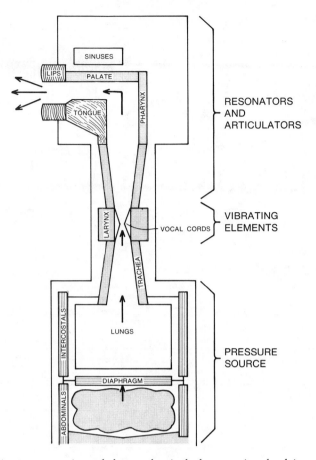

Fig. 23.9 Schematic representation of the mechanical elements involved in sound production in humans.

tion). This depends on the *respiratory* muscles, principally the diaphragm, the intercostal muscles, and the abdominal muscles. The *vibrating* elements are the *vocal cords* within the *larynx;* they are controlled by a complicated set of *laryngeal* muscles. The larynx converts the rush of air through the trachea into a buzzing sound with many frequency components. The *resonators* and *articulators* are composed of the structures of the *upper respiratory tract;* these include the pharynx, mouth, tongue, lips, sinuses, and related structures. These provide for resonance chambers and filters that transform the laryngeal buzz into sounds with specific qualities.

These same main components are present in birds and in other mammals, except

that in birds there is a syrinx instead of a larynx. This illustrates that the location of the buzz-producing element and its relation to the resonators is movable. Still another location is used when we play a musical instrument of the horn or wind family, such as a trumpet. When we blow a trumpet, we supply the pressure with our lungs; the buzz comes, not from the larynx, but from our lips pressed to the mouthpiece. The tone is formed by the resonant chambers within the tubes of the instrument.

The vibrating elements that generate the laryngeal buzz are the *vocal folds.* These are two folds of muscle tissue that have a tough ligament at their free edge and a mucous membrane cover (see Fig. 23.10). They are housed within the *thyroid* carti-

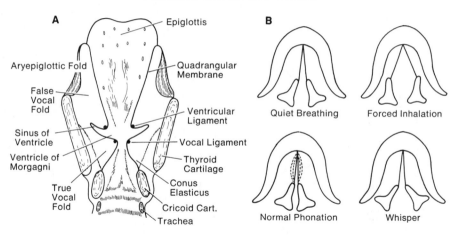

Fig. 23.10 **A.** Longitudinal section through the human larynx. **B.** Configurations of the glottis under different conditions. (From Zemlin, 1968)

lage, which forms a protective shield around them. The *cricoid* cartilage forms a ring around the base of the larynx; it supports the thyroid cartilage and provides surfaces of articulation for the *arytenoid* cartilages. These are two small triangular cartilages, each of which is attached at its apex to a laryngeal fold. The base has a complex articulation with the cricoid cartilage, which allows it to rock, rotate, or slide. These movements are brought about by contractions of the intrinsic laryngeal muscles. These include the *thyroarytenoid* (which constitutes the main mass of the vocal cords); *cricoarytenoid; interarytenoid;* and *cricothyroid.*

Production of Speech

The individual actions of each of these muscles are too complex to detail here; suffice it to say that they provide for delicate and precise adjustments in the length, tension, and separation of the vocal cords. Figure 23.10B indicates some of the positions of the vocal folds and the way they are brought about by movements of the arytenoid cartilages. The *pitch* of the laryngeal buzz is set by the length, tension, and separation of the folds; the folds then vibrate at that frequency. The buzz is *louder* if more pressure is applied, though the mus-

cles must counteract the pressure precisely in order to maintain pitch.

How is this buzz converted into intelligible vocal signals? This is the task of the resonators and articulators. Each of the structures of the upper respiratory tract plays an important role, as becomes apparent when any one of them is compromised. Thus, a stuffy nose markedly changes the quality of the voice. Also, just try to say anything at all while holding the tip of your tongue! In human speech the tongue is the most important of the organs of articulation. Its complex arrangements of muscle fibers make it a most versatile motor organ, and the high density of innervation is matched by the large representation of the tongue in the motor cortex (see Chap. 21). We should also note the importance of the tongue as an organ for manipulation and mastication of food in this regard.

All of these properties render the tongue well suited to the function of making finely graded adjustments in the configuration of the resonant chamber of the mouth. These configurations are most critical in the production of *vowel* sounds; in fact, each vowel sound is produced by a specific position of the tongue, and there is a systematic shift in these positions for the sequence of vowels (see Fig. 23.11). Consonants, by contrast, result from obstructing the air pas-

A. Midsagittal Section of the Vocal Tract

B. Magnitude of the Vocal Tract Transfer Function

C. Cross-sectional Area Function of the Vocal Tract

D. Idealized Vocal Tract Shapes

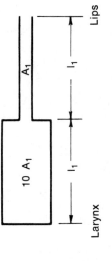

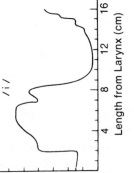

/i/

F1 = 300 F2 = 2300

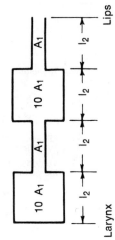

/i/

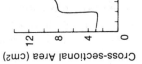

/i/

10 A₁   A₁   l₁   l₁   Larynx   Lips

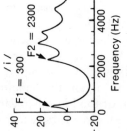

/a/

F1 = 750 F2 = 1200

/a/

A₁   10 A₁   l₁   l₁   Larynx   Lips

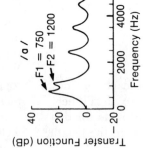

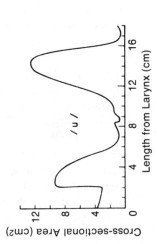

/a/

/u/

F1 = 350 F2 = 800

/u/

10 A₁   A₁   10 A₁   l₂   l₂   l₂   l₂   Larynx   Lips

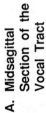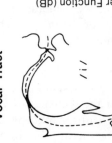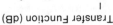

/u/

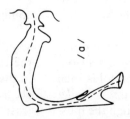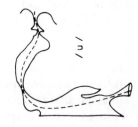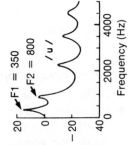

480

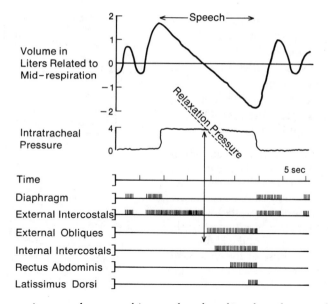

Fig. 23.12 In this experiment, a human subject took a deep breath and counted slowly from 1 to 32. The recordings show the changes in air volume in the lungs, intratracheal pressure, and impulse activity in different muscles. (From Draper et al., in Zemlin, 1968)

sage through the vocal tract, at the lips, teeth, hard palate, soft palate, or glottis. In English, these produce sounds that are called stops (t,p), fricatives (f,s), nasals (m), or glides (l). If you place your fingers on your face or neck while producing any of these sounds, it will become obvious that speech involves coordination of activity in most of the muscles in these regions.

Control of Pressure

We have concentrated on the muscular control of the vibrating elements and the resonators and articulators, but we must not give the impression that the pressure source acts merely as a crude bellows. In a classic study in 1959, M. H. Draper, P. Ladefoged, and David Whitteridge in Edinburgh investigated the activity of different respiratory muscles during vocalization. In addition to the EMGs of the muscles, recorded with needle electrodes, they monitored the volume of air in the lungs and the intratracheal pressure. Figure 23.12 shows the results in an experiment in which the subject took a deep breath and slowly counted to 32. It can be seen that there is a very precise sequence of activity in these widely different muscle groups during this period of phonation. The results show that

Fig. 23.11 Some principles in the production of human speech. **A.** Positions of the tongue for forming the vowel sounds "ee" (/i/), "ah" (/a/), and "oo" (/u/). There is evidence that these are basic phonemes present in all human languages, and that other vowel sounds are variations on these. **B.** Specific frequency patterns of the different vowel sounds. **C.** Cross-sectional areas of the supralaryngeal speech-producing spaces, from the larynx (0) through the phrarynx and mouth to the lips (16), for the three different vowel sounds. **D.** Simplified computer simulations of the supralaryngeal spaces in C. Note that the considerable length of the space means that the pharyngeal and oral segments can be independently manipulated by the tongue. This is crucial for the formation of the vowels, and hence for human speech. It has been shown that the pharyngeal space is diminished or absent in champanzees and Neanderthal man, as well as in the human newborn (see Chap. 26). (From Lieberman et al., 1972)

the diaphragm is relaxed through most of expiration and phonation, and that maintenance of the appropriate subglottic pressure is due to activity in the intercostal, abdominal, and latissimus dorsi muscles. Much the same sequence takes place during the singing of a single note. As Donald Proctor of Johns Hopkins has observed:

> . . . the production of a tone of any given intensity requires the appropriate subglottic pressure. This is accomplished by the exact blending of inspiratory and expiratory muscle effort with the elastic force associated with the lung volume at the time. This blending is largely produced through a balancing of the abdominal muscles against or with those of the chest wall across a relaxed diaphragm, occasionally supplemented by accessory expiratory muscles.

When the "appropriate subglottic pressure" is controlled by a trained and gifted singer, one of the transcendent artistic experiences of human life is produced, as illustrated in the following description of the great tenor, Enrico Caruso (Scala recording 825):

> . . . his voice floated on a deep and perfectly controlled column of air—something beautiful beyond description.

Birgit Nilsson (1984) has described the process as follows:

> I always want a very, very deep support for the breath. The whole body has to work . . . The key to producing the sound . . . lies in . . . "support from downstairs"—that is, from the muscular area just above the pubis.

Neural Circuits for Vocalization

This delicate balancing of activity in many body muscles suggests that the motoneurons to these muscles are under close control by descending motor pathways. In fact, it has been found that the intercostal motoneurons receive monosynaptic inputs from corticospinal fibers. These findings remind us that it is not only the muscles of the hand that are involved in fine motor performance; muscles as different as those of the tongue and chest and abdomen may accomplish equally delicate maneuvers.

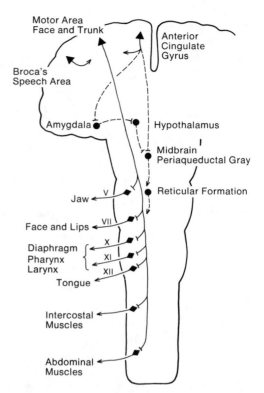

Fig. 23.13 Motor circuits and motor hierarchy involved in control of vocalization in humans. Pathways involved in precise motor control are shown by continuous lines; pathways involved in mediating emotional aspects of vocalization are shown by dashed lines. (Based in part on Jürgens and Ploog, 1981)

We can think of all the muscles of the abdomen, chest, larynx, head, and neck as being coordinated together to perform complex *manipulations of air* as it is expelled from the lungs. What are the nervous mechanisms involved in this coordination? We can begin by identifying the motoneurons involved (Fig. 23.13). For the muscles of the *pressure* apparatus, the motoneurons are located in the spinal cord: the motoneurons to the diaphragm are in cervical segments 3–5; those to the intercostals are in thoracic segments 2–5; and those to the abdominal muscles in thoracic segments 6–12. For the larynx, the intrinsic muscles are supplied by the vagus (X) and accessory (XI) nerves. The main branch to the larynx is the recurrent laryngeal nerve, which supplies all of the intrinsic muscles except the cricothyroid. This nerve is thus crucial to human speech; loss due to injury or infection leaves one able to speak only in a whisper. The *resonators* and *articulators* are controlled by nerves to the muscles of the pharynx (XI, X, VII), tongue (XII), and lips and face (VII). Other cranial nerves also contribute, as indicated in Fig. 23.13.

It can be seen that the motoneurons involved in vocalization constitute a complex array that is distributed along a considerable extent of the neuraxis, from the metencephalon (pons) to the lower thoracic levels of the spinal cord. The voluntary control over this array is mediated by descending fibers in the corticospinal tract.

These originate in the face, neck, and trunk areas of the motor cortex (see Fig. 22.9) and make either monosynaptic or polysynaptic connections onto the motoneurons. Thus, as in the case of movements of the hand, the "intermediate" level of motor hierarchy is in the motor cortex. The mechanism of vocalization control by the motor cortex is virtually unknown, though it seems likely that it involves circuits through the basal ganglia and cerebellum, as in the case of control of manipulation. The highest level of speech control in the human includes Broca's area; the nature of the relation between Broca's area and the motor cortex in the control of speech will be discussed in Chap. 30.

IV

Central Systems

24

Introduction: The Nature
of Central Systems

In previous sections of the book, discussions of specific sensory and motor systems have pursued pathways into the central nervous system and then, just when things were getting interesting, have broken off with the excuse that the story belongs to the province of "central systems." We have finally arrived at that point, and this last section will identify these systems, and will attempt to explain how they provide the neural substrates for behavior.

At the outset, it is well to be reminded that the analysis of sensory and motor systems has depended on the fact that they consist of localized circuits and pathways accessible to the investigator; they can be activated discretely, and they give a precise and quantifiable output. In central systems, most of these advantages are lost. The systems are deep within the central nervous system and thus relatively inaccessible to the investigator. The cells and circuits form systems that overlap and are difficult to localize, thus making selective activation difficult or impossible. The output from such systems may be too widespread to record or characterize adequately. To this is added the fact that, in the temporal domain, many of the actions of central systems last for days, months, or years. Small wonder, then, that although behaviors generated by central systems can be observed and classified, their neural substrates are extremely difficult to identify. It is, in fact, a testimonial to the power of modern methods in neurobiology that much of the experimental evidence for the molecular and cellular elements and the specific circuits of central systems has become available within the past generation or so.

The possibility of understanding the central neural substrates that govern behavior is exciting not only because it deepens our understanding of humans and of all animal life, but also because it holds the promise that we may be able to correct imbalances in behavioral functions or restore functions lost by disease. However, it is important to realize that making correlations between specific neural substrates and specific behaviors is one of the most difficult challenges in all of biology, and the history of endeavors in this area is a record of many deceptions and discouragements. Thus, any apparent correlation or claim must be regarded with healthy skepticism. This is all the more important in a book of this nature, in which accounts of many very complex subjects must necessarily be brief.

Definitions of Central Systems

Central systems may be defined as *cells and circuits that mediate functions necessary for the coordinated behavior of the whole organism.* The intent here is to distinguish central systems from specific sensory and motor pathways. As one proceeds more centrally, these pathways overlap with, and become incorporated in, central systems. Thus, higher levels of sensory processing clearly involve central systems involved in perception and cognition; it depends on how far centrally, through how many synaptic connections and circuits, one goes. Similarly, higher levels in the motor hierarchy involve central pattern generators and motor programs that are part of central as well as motor systems. The definition is therefore only a guide to help in identifying and characterizing systems that are less concerned with the specific tasks of sensory processing and motor control that we have discussed to this point, and more concerned with global aspects of behavior.

Central systems generally fall into two categories. One concerns systems that mediate interactions between the brain and the body. As indicated in Table 24.1 and Fig. 24.1, there are three main systems in this category. The *autonomic nervous system* was discussed in Chap. 18; it is usually regarded as a motor system, but it partially qualifies as a central system by its broad coordination of internal organ functions.

Table 24.1 Summary of central systems

Systems relating brain and body
  Autonomic nervous system
  Neuroendocrine system
  Neuroimmune system

Systems within the brain
  Diffuse transmitter systems
  Specific transmitter systems
  Distributed systems

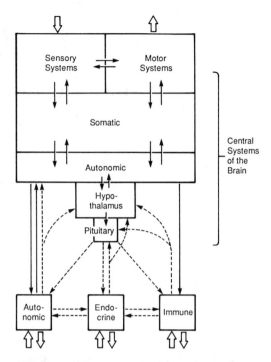

Fig. 24.1 Schematic diagram of the central systems of the brain (somatic and autonomic) and their relations to sensory and motor systems, other body systems, and the environment. Solid lines indicate neural connections, dashed lines indicate humoral communication, and open arrows indicate interactions with body or environment.

The *neuroendocrine system* is responsible for coordination between the nervous system and the various endocrine organs of the body. The *neuroimmune system* mediates interactions between the nervous system and the network of organs and cells that constitute the immune system.

The other main category of central systems involves neural circuits wholly within the brain. As indicated in Table 24.1, first there is a widely projecting system of cells that can be regarded as a counterpart of the *autonomic nervous system* within the brain. Second, there are more specific *transmitter-identified systems;* they include central as well as sensory and motor pathways. Finally, there are systems that include circuits embracing different regions, with different transmitters, which mediate com-

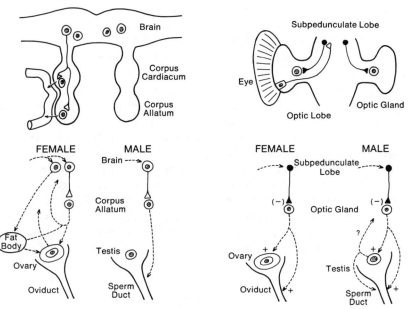

Fig. 24.2 Neuroendocrine systems for control of reproduction in the insect (A) and octopus (B). Diagrams above show the neural parts of the system; diagrams below show how they interact through circulating hormones with body organs, in both male and female. (Adapted from Gordon, 1972)

plex, higher brain functions; these are called *distributed systems.*

In this chapter, we will first discuss the neuroendocrine and neuroimmune systems. We will then summarize evidence for diffuse and specific transmitter-defined systems. The subsequent six chapters in this section will be mainly concerned with distributed circuits underlying important types of whole-organism behavior.

Neuroendocrine Circuits

As we have seen, hormones are used in a variety of ways in the body. Those peptides and hormones that are secreted by central neurons, under central nervous control, and with actions that affect the coordinated behavior of the entire organism, may be considered to be parts of central systems.

Invertebrates

Our previous discussions have emphasized the large role played by neurosecretory cells among invertebrates. The grouping of neurosecretory cells and terminals into neurohemal organs is a common finding in many phyla, notably annelids, arthropods, and molluscs.

Neuroendocrine cells control reproductive processes in the insect, as shown in Fig. 24.2A. The neural part of the circuit consists of the neuroendocrine cells and the central fibers that control them. These in turn are parts of larger circuits, in which there is transport in the circulation of the peptides and hormones released from the terminals, and the substances released from the target organs which act on each other and back on the central neurons. Thus, our concept of a central "circuit" needs to be broadened to include these blood-borne connections throughout the body. Together these circuits form the neuroendocrine system for control of reproduction. Note, in this case, the more elaborate actions and feedback controls in the female as compared with the male.

In the crayfish, (not shown in the figure) the neuroendocrine control of molting is mediated by a system that is attached to the eyestalk. The fact that the molting hormone in crustacea is a steroid molecule (β-ecdysone, or crustecdysone) closely related to the α-ecdysone of insects, indicates the close similarity between the two systems.

For comparison, the neuroendocrine control of sexual differentiation in the octopus is illustrated in Fig. 24.2B. Light stimulates a pathway that projects to neuroendocrine cells in the *subpedunculate lobe*. These cells project to the *optic gland*, which is attached to the eyestalk, and is normally inhibited by the neurosecretory cells; they are active therefore in the dark, when they secrete their hormone, which promotes sexual differentiation. Note in this case the more elaborate interactions in the male than in the female.

An important aspect of these interactions is their long time course. The latency of action of a hormone may be hours or days, and the processes may last days or weeks. Much of this time, as we have seen, is taken up by the cellular events induced by the hormone: the action on the genome, the activation of enzymes, the synthesis of protein, and the remodeling of the cell (see Chap. 8). This stands in contrast to the rapid transmission and processing of information that takes place in many nervous pathways, where the time scale of action is on the order of milliseconds and seconds. Some of the conversion from rapid to slow events takes place in the neuroendocrine cells themselves, as well as in related neurons; this conversion may depend on second messengers and protein phosphorylation, as discussed in Chap. 8. Neuroendocrine systems thus embrace a broad time scale of actions, and one of the challenges of current research is to understand how these actions are coordinated.

Vertebrates

Vertebrates also have a master neurohemal organ, the pituitary gland. It has been traced back in phylogeny to the tunicates, the earliest chordates, where it is believed to be represented by a ciliated pit organ. An interesting fact about this pit organ is that it seems to be sensitive to pheromonal signals from other tunicates; furthermore, these pheromones have a molecular structure similar to steroid sex hormones. These similarities have supported J. B. S. Haldane's suggestion that the hormonal system of internal messengers originated from the pheromonal system of external messengers.

The pituitary consists of an endocrine and a neural part. The endocrine part (anterior, or adenohypophysis) is derived embryologically from an outpouching of the pharynx, whereas the neural part (posterior pituitary, or neurohypophysis) is derived from an outpouching from the diencephalon. Both parts are under the control of the hypothalamus, but by different means. The *neurohypophysis* contains the terminals of axons from specific nerve cells in the hypothalamus (see Fig. 24.3). From these terminals are secreted two peptide hormones: *oxytocin,* which promotes contraction of smooth muscle in the uterus and mammary glands, and *vasopressin* (also called antidiuretic hormone, or ADH), which acts on kidney tubule membrane to promote retention of water, and on smooth muscle in arterioles of the body to raise blood pressure. We shall discuss these actions further in Chaps. 26 and 27. These hormones also have actions within the nervous system outside the hypothalamus (see below).

The *endocrine* pituitary system, from its sites of neural control in the hypothalamus to its actions in the body, is summarized in Fig. 24.3. The identification of the pituitary hormones and our understanding of their actions on target organs was largely achieved by 1950, and forms the body of classical endocrinology. The work of Geoffrey Harris and his colleagues in England thereafter showed that the anterior pituitary is controlled by the hypothalamus by means of factors transported in the hypophyseopor-

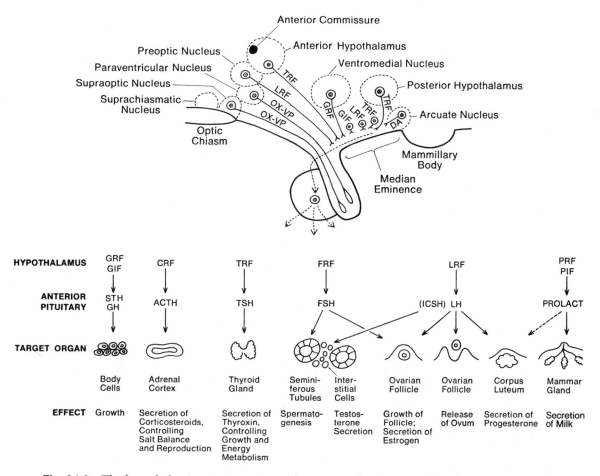

Fig. 24.3   The hypothalamic–pituitary system for neuroendocrine control in the mammal. ACTH, adrenocorticotropic hormone; CRF, corticotropin releasing factor; FRF, follicle-stimulating hormone releasing factor; FSH, follicle-stimulating hormone; GIF, growth hormone release inhibiting factor (somatostatin); GH, growth hormone; GRF, growth hormone releasing factor; ICSH, interstitial cell stimulating hormone; LH, luteinizing hormone; LRF, luteinizing hormone releasing factor (also called LHRH, luteinizing hormone releasing hormone); OX-VP, oxytocin-vasopressin; PIF, prolactin release inhibiting factor; PRF, prolactin releasing factor; STH, somatotropic hormone; TRF, thyroid hormone releasing factor; TSH, thyroid stimulating hormone. (Modified from Mountcastle, 1980)

tal system. As Harris wrote in his monograph *Neural Control of the Pituitary Gland* in 1955:

. . . it seems likely that nerve fibers in the hypothalamus liberate some humoral substance into the primary plexus of the vessels, and that this substance is carried by the vessels to affect anterior pituitary activity. . . . If the hypothalamus . . . regulates the rate of secretion of the anterior pituitary hormones, are there as many humoral mechanisms involved as there are hormones?

This set the stage for an eager search for these substances, in which biochemists prepared extracts of hypothalamic tissue and identified compounds which either promote or inhibit the release and synthesis of pituitary hormones. By 1973, three of these compounds—luteinizing hormone releasing hormone (LHRH), thyrotropin releasing hormone (TRH), and somatostatin, or somatotropin-release inhibiting factor (SRIF)—had been isolated and synthesized. These releasing factors are all peptides; their molecular structures are given in Chap. 8 (Fig. 8.10).

While this work was proceeding, other studies aimed at identifying the mechanisms for release of these factors. By electrical stimulation and local injections of hypothalamic extracts into hypothalamus, it was possible to localize the neuroendocrine cells producing the factors. More recently, these results have been extended by binding studies of receptor localization, and hybridization of cell DNA and RNA to the respective cDNA and mRNA probes to localize cells expressing genes for specific types of peptides.

Some of these sites are indicated in Fig. 24.3. The general pattern is that the cells in different regions all send axons to the median eminence, on the floor of the hypothalamus. The peptides are stored in the axon terminals, which rest on the vessels of the portal system. Discharge of the factors is controlled by neural activity within the cell, and by circulating hormones. The factors act quickly (within minutes) before being inactivated in the blood. The actions on pituitary cells are to stimulate immediate release, as well as to induce long-term synthesis of hormones. Like other peptide hormones, the releasing factors act on the pituitary cells through membrane receptors and second mesengers, as previously discussed in Chap. 8.

Since Harris's time, it has been clear that the nervous system is not only involved in controlling the pituitary, but is itself the target of actions of circulating hormones. This is illustrated in Fig. 24.4. If we take the case of the gonadotropins, these stimulate the production of sex hormones in the gonads (G), either testosterone or estrogen. These hormones induce the secondary sex characteristics of males and females, as well as stimulate the maturation of sperm

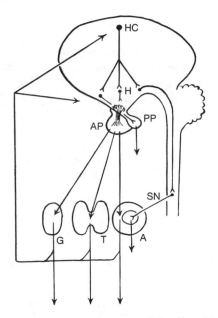

Fig. 24.4 Original diagram of Geoffrey Harris illustrating his postulate of the reciprocal relationship between the central nervous system and endocrine system. A, adrenal gland; AP, anterior pituitary; G, gonad; H, hypothalamus; HC, higher centers; PP, posterior pituitary; SN, splanchnic nerve; T, thyroid gland. (From Harris, 1955)

and eggs, receptively. The levels of circulating gonadotropins are controlled by several factors; primary among them are sensory stimuli to the nervous system, eventually reaching the hypothalamus, and negative feedback by the circulating hormones onto pituitary cells (AP) and central neurons (HC). Thus, although specific details are different, the principles of organization of the central neuroendocrine control system in the vertebrates are similar to those in the invertebrates.

This scheme for the pituitary system will be complete when we have identified all the central neural connections made by the neuroendocrine cells in the hypothalamus. Recordings have been made from single hypothalamic cells that project to the median eminence (as determined by antidromic backfiring) and thus presumably secrete releasing factors. These cells can

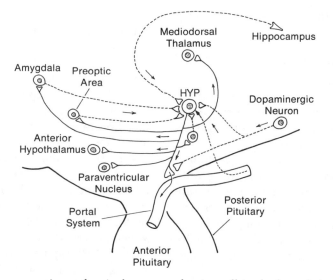

Fig. 24.5 Multiple connections of a single neuroendocrine cell in the hypothalamus. The cell and its output axon and branches are shown in continuous lines; inputs to the cell are shown in dashed lines. (After Renaud, 1977)

also be backfired from a number of other sites, including the thalamus, preoptic area, amygdala, anterior hypothalamic area, and periventricular nucleus (see Fig. 24.5). Synaptic inputs, on the other hand, have been identified by orthodromic firing; these inputs have been found to arise in the amygdala, preoptic area, and hippocampus. To complete the picture on the input side, the neuroendocrine cells receive copious innervation from dopamine-containing neurons (see below). The cells are also subject to feedback regulation by local circuits. Finally, they are regulated by levels of circulating hormones and other humoral factors.

The picture that emerges in Fig. 24.5 is of a neuroendocrine cell that is under extensive control by both neural and humoral mechanisms. Through the neural connections, inputs from many central regions, including the cerebral cortex and limbic systems, reach the hypothalamus. By this means, a variety of behavioral states, such as arousal, stress, and sexual maturation, all have their influence in setting the level of discharge of releasing factors and thus the control of pituitary function.

Neuroimmune Circuits

Traditionally, the immune system has been considered to be separate from the nervous system. To begin with, its anatomical location is widely dispersed in various glands, organs, circulating lymphocytes, and immunoglobulins, in contrast to the apparently "hard-wired" nerves and brain. Its function of protecting the body against invading substances and organisms seems markedly different from the function of the nervous system of processing information. The mechanisms of the immune response involve binding of antigen, proliferation of circulating lymphocytes, and secretion of antibody molecules, mechanisms that have no obvious counterpart in the nervous system.

This traditional view is now being replaced by a new concept, which recognizes that the two systems interact in a coordinated manner, and that the molecular and cellular mechanisms share many common principles. This new perspective is beginning to bring about revolutionary changes in our understanding of both systems. Let us summarize the evidence for how they interact, first at the systems level, and then at the molecular level.

Immunoregulatory Circuits

For many years, it has been known that psychological stress has a depressive influence on the immune system. In studies of people bereaved by the death of a spouse, or suffering severe depression, it has been shown that there is suppression of lymphocytic proliferation in response to an antigenic stimulus. Animal experiments support these findings; rats subjected to stressful situations, such as a restraining apparatus or tail shocks, also have reduced lymphocytic responses to antigen or mitogen injections.

What is the pathway by which psychological and behavioral states can affect the immune response? There is general agreement that the main pathway is through the hypothalamus (see Fig. 24.6). In some experiments, it has been shown that electrolytic lesions of the anterior hypothalamus in rats have a suppressive effect on the proliferation of lymphocytes in response to intravascular injection of a mitogen such as concanavalin A (Con A). By contrast, lesions in other brain regions, especially regions in the limbic system (see Chap. 28) such as the hippocampus which feed into the hypothalamus, lead to an increase in lymphocyte numbers.

Many experiments have documented that the hypothalamic control is exerted through the hypothalamic–pituitary–adrenocorticosteroid neuroendocrine axis. The earliest experiments showed that injections of cortisol have a suppressive effect on the immune response, implying that the influence of the brain was only suppressive and was exerted exclusively through corticosteroids. Recent experiments, however, suggest a more complicated mechanism, in which the hypothalamic–pituitary system is *immunoregulatory* rather than merely immunosuppressive, in line with the lesion experiments above. As indicated in Fig. 24.6, corticosteroids have been found to act mainly at the earliest stages of lymphocytic

proliferation, and to be stimulatory at low concentrations, changing to suppressive at high circulating levels. An interesting recent finding is that stress causes suppression of the immune response even in rats that are adrenalectomized and therefore secrete no corticosteroids; this has implied that pituitary hormones themselves, such as ACTH and endorphins, may participate in mediating the immunosuppressive effects.

How is the hypothalamic–pituitary pathway modulated? Proliferating lymphocytes secrete a variety of specific messenger molecules, collectively called lymphokines, which are crucial for coordination between B and T cell populations. Lymphokines, as well as thymokines secreted by thymus cells, have several sites of action in the brain immunoregulatory pathway: on lymphocytic corticosteroid receptors, and on cells in the pituitary body and hypothalamus. Other feedback pathways from circulating corticosteroids and ACTH contribute to the peripheral regulation of corticotropin releasing factor (CRF) secretion from the hypothalamus. Within the brain, several transmitter systems (5HT, ACh, NE, and DA) have inputs to hypothalamic cells and can be shown to affect the neuroimmune pathway; for example, lesions of 5HT neurons in the midbrain raphe nucleus (see below) lead to increased antibody titers in response to an immunologic challenge, whereas lesions of NE neurons in the locus ceruleus lead to decreases in lymphocyte counts. Finally, there are direct nervous connections to lymphoid organs through nerves of the autonomic nervous system. These various elements can be said to constitute circuits for neuroimmune control (see Fig. 24.6).

Although many of the component parts of these circuits have been identified, the way they work together to achieve integrated control is not yet clear. For example, it is known that levels of circulating corticosteroids rise and fall in close association with the time course of the antibody response (see Fig. 24.7). Also correlated with the antibody response is an increased firing

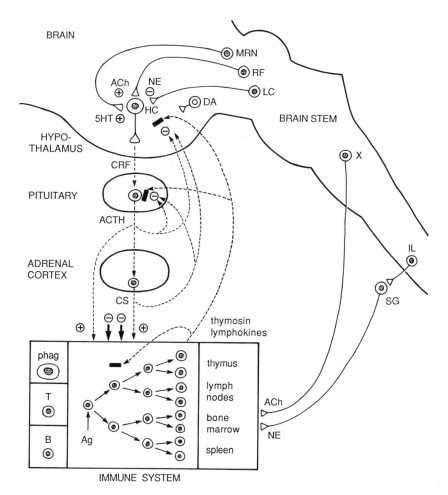

Fig. 24.6 Neuroimmune circuits. The brain regulates the immune system and the immune system modulates brain activity through interactions summarized in this diagram. A central point in the neural circuit is the hypothalamic cell (HC) secreting corticotropin releasing factor (CRF); as shown in the diagram, this cell is heavily regulated by neural inputs and by humoral factors. The hypothalamic–pituitary–adrenal cortical (HYPAC) axis is the main route of immunoregulation; there is also sympathetic and parasympathetic innervation of organs of the immune system, as shown. Within the immune system organs, phagocytic (phag.) and B and T lymphocytes proliferate in response to an antigenic (Ag) stimulus. The early stages of proliferation are facilitated (+) by low concentrations of corticosteroids (CS) and ACTH, but are suppressed by high concentrations (thick arrows), such as occur in behavioral states of high anxiety or stress. This is believed to be the basis of the immunosuppression that occurs in people suffering depression. The cells of the immune system secrete various substances (lymphokines, etc.), which not only regulate the immune response but also act to block the actions of other humoral substances at different levels in the HYPAC axis (see black bars). Various humoral feedback pathways in the HYPAC axis are also shown. Other abbreviations: IL, intermediolateral nucleus of the spinal cord; LC, locus ceruleus; MRN, median raphe nucleus; RF, reticular formation; SG, sympathetic ganglion; X, vagal nucleus (parasympathetic). (Based on Bulloch, 1985; Hall and Goldstein, 1985; Hall et al., 1985)

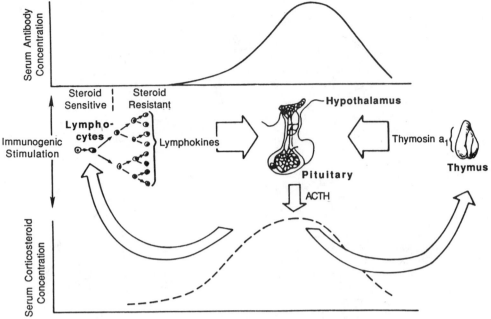

Fig. 24.7 Correlation between the time course of the antibody response of the immune system to an antigenic stimulus (above) and the corticosteroid response of the hypothalamic–pituitary–adrenal cortical axis (below). Between the graphs, mechanisms correlating the two systems are postulated. See text. Compare with Fig. 24.6. (From Hall et al., 1985)

frequency of hypothalamic cells; these may be the cells that release CRF to bring about the rise in corticosteroids. But what is the functional significance of these correlations? A possibility is that the corticosteroids would have their greatest suppressive effect on lymphocytes with low affinity for the antigen, thereby contributing a kind of lateral inhibition to help make the immune response more specific. There is clearly much work ahead to test these and other hypotheses.

Membrane Mechanisms

If there are influences of the nervous system on the immune system, there must be membrane mechanisms to mediate them. Research at the molecular level is providing abundant and fascinating evidence that this is the case. The plasma membranes of cells of the immune system appear to be loaded with receptors for a variety of different types of molecules. Best known are the lymphokines, which serve as lymphocyte growth factors and coordinate the proliferation of T and B cells.

Receptors are also present to mediate the influence of the adrenal cortical steroids, but the recent demonstration of receptors to ACTH and endorphins suggests that these provide the means for more direct regulation by the pituitary. In addition, an extraordinary variety of substances can affect the immune response, implying the presence of appropriate membrane receptors; some of these have been identified, as summarized in Fig. 24.8. The surprising finding has been that these are all receptors for neurotransmitters and neuropeptides common to the nervous system.

Stimulated by this array of receptors is an arsenal of secretory products. In addition to the lymphokines are ACTH and β-endorphin, as in pituitary cells, as well as several neuropeptides. It should be recalled that ACTH and β-endorphin are both de-

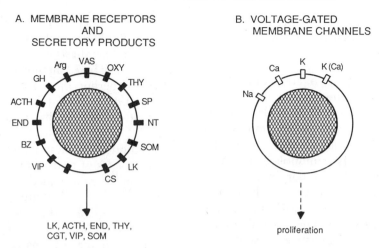

Fig. 24.8 Molecular properties of immune cells that are shared with nerve cells and are involved in neural–immune interactions. Abbreviations for membrane receptors in A: CS, corticosteroids; LK, lymphokines; SOM, somatostatin; NT, neurotensin; SP, substance P; THY, thymosine; OXY, oxytocin; VAS, vasopressin; Arg, arginine; GH, growth hormone; ACTH, adrenocorticotropic hormone, END, endorphins; BZ, benzodiazepines; VIP, vasoactive intestinal peptide. For secretory products in A: CGT, chorionic gonadotropin. The voltage-gated channels in B have been described in Chap. 6. (Based on Blalock and Smith, 1985; Cahalan et al., 1985)

rived from pro-opiomelanocortin (POMC) (cf. Chap. 8). These studies indicate that virus infections elicit not only the antibody response but also the secretion of various hormones and neuropeptides, which may act as lymphocyte growth factors as well as modulate cells at other levels in the hypothalamic–pituitary–immune circuit.

In addition to its many ligand-gated channels, the lymphocyte membrane contains a variety of voltage-gated channels. As indicated in Fig. 24.8B, these include channels for inward, depolarizing currents (Na^+, Ca^{2+}) and outward, hyperpolarizing currents [K^+, $K^+(Ca)$]. These have properties shared with neurons (see Chap. 6). Macrophages have in fact been shown to have the ability to generate impulses. A point of some interest is that mitogenesis in lymphocytes is accompanied by an increase in the numbers of K^+ channels (from 50 to 300 per cell in the rat). An increase in K^+ conductance might also accompany differentiation of olfactory receptor neurons (see Chap. 9). This could be a mechanism shared by cells undergoing mitosis in both the nervous and immune systems,

providing for control of membrane excitability during critical development periods.

The Immune System as a "Mobile Brain"

The idea that the immune system itself has brainlike properties has tantalized a number of workers in the field. The variety of studies summarized above has led to the suggestion (Blalock and Smith, 1985) that

cells of the immune system can apparently be controlled in a fashion similar to pituitary cells by a positive signal from the hypothalamus (corticotropin releasing factor) and a negative signal from the adrenal gland (a glucocorticoid hormone). Hence, 'stress' as defined by an increase in circulating glucocorticoid hormone levels can, depending on the stimulus, apparently have its ultimate origins not only in the central and peripheral nervous systems but also in the immune system itself. Such findings have led to the notion that a primary function of the immune system may be to serve as a sensory organ for stimuli such as bacteria, viruses, and tumors cells that are not recognized by central and peripheral nervous systems . . . leukocyte information then being transferred to the neuroendocrine system by peptide hormones and lymphokines . . . [thus,] certain cells of the immune system may serve as 'free-floating nerve cells'. Perhaps collectively, such cells represent a mobile brain.

Does the immune system constitute a "parallel brain?" Do the cells of the immune system form a network, as Niels Jerne has suggested, which has sensory, motor, and central functions equivalent to those in the nervous system? Is immunological "memory," for example, similar in any of its properties to neural memory? These questions signify that this field holds interest not only for new experimental findings, but also for conceptual advances as well.

Central Systems: Survey of Methods

In Chap. 8, the biochemistry and molecular actions of putative neurotransmitter substances were discussed. We now ask, where within the brain are the neurons that contain these substances?

Historically, the first step in answering this question was the technique for localizing monoamines introduced by Olavi Eränkö in the 1950s and refined by Falck and Hillarp in the 1960s. This technique consists of treating tissue sections with formaldehyde vapors or glyoxylic acid, which causes the monoamine compounds to fluoresce with colors characteristic for the three main types (NE, DA, and 5HT). The second step came in the 1970s with the ability to prepare antibodies to transmitter molecules. Thus, a molecule such as serotonin (5HT) is conjugated with bovine serum albumin and injected into a rabbit to produce rabbit antibodies to 5HT. This is applied to the tissue sections of interest, where the antibodies bind to the conjugated 5HT contained within cells. The sections are then treated with a fluorescence-labeled anti-rabbit antibody in order to visualize the cells containing the serotonin. We discussed examples of this technique in Chaps. 8 and 19. This technique is called immunocytochemistry. Its specificity has been greatly enhanced by the use of monoclonal antibodies.

The third step has been the ability to localize the DNA and mRNA involved in coding and synthesis of specific transmitter molecules. These methods, described in Chap. 2, permit the unequivocal identification of the cells containing the machinery for synthesis of specific transmitter molecules.

In addition to these methods for localization of sites of transmitter synthesis, there are complementary methods for localization of sites of transmitter receptors. The most widespread of these is ligand binding, combined with autoradiography. In this technique, tissue sections are treated with radioactively labeled molecules that bind to transmitter receptors. The sites of binding are visualized by coating the sections with a photographic emulsion so that the radioactivity makes a photographic imprint of the receptor sites, a technique called autoradiography (the section so to speak makes a radiograph of itself).

The power of this technique is two fold. First, the specific molecules used—transmitters, agonists or antagonists of transmitters, or other drugs—are employed in order to assess receptor function. Furthermore, if serial sections are made, the distribution of receptor sites may be determined throughout the entire brain; for this reason, the technique is also called *receptor mapping*.

Central State Circuits

Among the central neurons that have been shown to contain specific transmitters, there is a considerable range in the extensiveness of the branching patterns. Two transmitters in particular—norepinephrine (NE) and serotonin (5HT)—appear to be associated with neurons whose axons project widely throughout the central nervous system. This branching pattern appears to preclude functions involved in transmitting specific information about space or time, and favors the view that these neurons are more involved in slower and more global adjustments of the excitability state of neurons

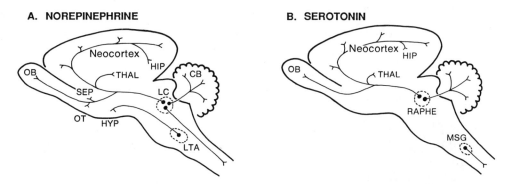

Fig. 24.9 Maps of the distribution of cell groups containing different neurotransmitters in the mammalian brain. A sagittal view of the rat brain is shown for this and succeeding figures. **A.** Distribution of norepinephrine-containing neurons and their axonal projections. **B.** Distribution of serotonin-containing neurons and their projections. These are discussed in the text under the category of central state circuits. Abbreviations for this and the following maps: AM, amygdala; AR, arcuate nucleus; ARC, arcuate nucleus; BN, basal nucleus; DB, diagonal band; DCN, deep cerebellar nuclei; DH, dorsal horn, DRG, dorsal root ganglion; EPN, endopeduncular nucleus; GP, globus pallidus; HAB, habenula; HIP, hippocampus; HYP, hypothalamus; LC, locus ceruleus; LTA, lateral tegmental area; MED, medulla; MSG, medullary serotonin group; NA, nucleus accumbens; OB, olfactory bulb; OT, olfactory tubercle; PC, pyriform cortex; PERI-V., periventricular gray; R, reticular nucleus; SC, superior colliculus; SEP, septum; SM, stria medullaris; SN, substantia nigra; STR, striatum; TH or THAL, thalamus; VTA, ventral tegmental area.

throughout the brain. In this respect, they appear to provide a central parallel to the actions of the peripheral autonomic nervous system.

Let us begin our consideration of central brain systems with these two types. The discussion of the location of neuronal pathways will be related to a standard lateral (parasagittal) view of the rat brain, which will permit ready comparisons between different systems. In this way, the student can have a single framework for the study of the comparative neurochemistry of brain circuits.

Norepinephrine

Norepinephrine (NE) or noradrenaline (NA) is synthesized from DA by the enzyme dopamine β-hydroxylase. NE is found especially in clusters of cells in the midbrain. One of these groups is called the locus ceruleus, and it is certainly one of the most extraordinary cell populations in the entire nervous system. There are only a few hundred neurons in the locus ceruleus, yet they send axons to almost every region in the central nervous system (see A in Fig. 24.9). In order to do this, each axon branches repeatedly. There are relatively few terminals within any region, but the NE branches and terminals achieve their effects by secreting NE diffusely onto synaptic terminals in the surrounding neuropil. As noted in Chap. 8, these actions are believed to be neuromodulatory in nature. Because of their widespread ramifications and diffuse action, the NE cells are well suited for setting levels of central neural activity underlying different behavioral states. As noted above, they may in this respect act somewhat like a central autonomic nervous system, to complement the peripheral autonomic system, and function in parallel with the adrenal medulla and its release of epinephrine into the bloodstream.

Complementing the locus ceruleus is a nearby cluster of NE cells in the lateral tegmental area (LTA). These projections overlap those of the locus ceruleus, but are directed mainly to the hypothalamus, where they are believed to participate in the regulation of releasing factors.

Epinephrine

We note that epinephrine (adrenaline) is synthesized from norepinephrine in the catecholamine pathway. It is an important hormone of the peripheral autonomic system, where it is liberated from the adrenal medulla and is crucial in preparing the body for action and stress (see Chap. 17). In the nervous system, it is present in a few clusters of cells in the lower brainstem (medulla), which project anteriorly as far as the diencephalon, and posteriorly to the spinal cord. Terminals are found particularly in the dorsal motor nucleus of the vagus (cranial nerve X) and the nuclei of the solitary tract (cranial nerves VII, IX, and X), where epinephrine may have a role in modulating motor control of the viscera and taste information from the tongue, respectively.

Serotonin

Serotonin, or 5-hydroxytryptamine (5HT), is a monoamine because it has a single terminal amine group, but it has a two-ring indole structure that differentiates it from the single-ring catecholamines. It is synthesized from the precursor tryptophan (see Fig. 8.6). Serotonin is present throughout the body, especially in blood platelets and the intestines. In the brain, it is found mainly in the midbrain, in clusters of cells called the raphe, and in the medulla. As shown in Fig. 24.9B, the fibers of these cells project widely to the forebrain, cerebellum, and spinal cord, in a pattern that resembles that of the NE fibers. Thus, like the NE system, the 5HT system appears to exert a widespread influence over arousal, sensory perception, emotion, and higher cognitive functions.

The first evidence for these effects came from experiments with the hallucinogenic agent lysergic acid diethylamide (LSD) in the 1950s. LSD was found to block 5HT receptors in muscle membranes, and it was suggested that the disastrous effects of LSD on mental states could therefore be attributed to blocking of 5HT receptors in the brain. Subsequent studies have shown that LSD depresses 5HT-containing neurons, and it has been suggested that this action may occur at receptors where raphe neurons receive synapses from each other by means of recurrent axon collaterals or dendrodendritic interactions. However, it has been impossible to incorporate this view into a view that accommodates conflicting evidence from lesion experiments and pharmacological experiments. Thus, rather than serving as a model for understanding the functions of a transmitter-defined pathway, the raphe pathway has served as a model of the difficulty of correlating central brain circuits with brain functions. Cooper, Bloom, and Roth (1987) stated this principle eloquently:

The student must realize that to track down all of the individual cellular actions of an extremely potent drug like LSD and fit these effects together in a jigsaw puzzlelike effort to solve the question of how LSD produces hallucinations is extremely difficult. Similar jigsaws lie just below the surface of every simple attempt to attribute the effects of a drug or the execution of a complex behavioral task like eating, sleeping, mating, and learning to a single family of neurotransmitters like 5-HT. While it is clearly possible to formulate hypothetical schemes by which divergent inhibitory systems like the 5-HT raphe cells can become an integral part of such diverse behavioral operations as pain suppression, sleeping, thermal regulation, and corticosteroid receptivity, a very wide chasm of unacquired data separates the concept from the documentary evidence needed to support it.

Specific Transmitter-Defined Systems

We turn now to transmitter-defined neurons that are relatively specific in their projections. This is a broad category, however, and it should be recognized that it ranges from neurons with relatively wide projections to several regions, to intrinsic neurons whose connections are contained entirely within a region, or one lamina of a region.

Neurotransmitters

Dopamine. Dopamine (DA) is the first neuroactive substance in the synthetic pathway for catecholamines (refer back to Fig. 8.6A). The locations of DA neurons are shown in Fig. 24.10. There are two main populations of projection neurons, located within the midbrain (mesencephalon). One consists of the output cells of the substantia nigra, which project to the caudate-putamen (striatum). In Parkinson's disease these cells degenerate, and the resulting loss of DA synapses in the striatum is believed to be a primary cause of the movement disorders, such as limitation of movement and the resting tremor of the hands, that are characteristic of this disease. The therapy of high doses of the compound L-dopa, the precursor of DA, is aimed at correcting this deficiency, and is successful in some, but unfortunately not all, patients. Neurosurgical operations to correct this deficiency by transplantation of dopamine-producing cells to the striatum have been discussed in Chap. 9.

The other main population of projection neurons is located in the ventral tegmental area (VTA) of the mesencephalon. These cells project to a number of sites in the forebrain, including the amygdala, olfactory tubercle, septal area, nucleus accumbens, and prefrontal cortex. Since these regions are part of what is called the limbic system, this is called the mesolimbic projection. The limbic structures served by this pathway are implicated in such functions as emotion and aggression (Chap. 29); the prefrontal cortex is crucial for some of our highest cognitive functions (Chap. 30). It is likely, therefore, that the mesolimbic pathway plays a role in coordinating these functions. There is also evidence that schizophrenia may be associated with derangements of DA metabolism and DA synaptic transmission, possibly within the mesolimbic pathway.

In addition to these projection tracts, there are also short-axon DA cells in several regions. In the hypothalamus, DA cells

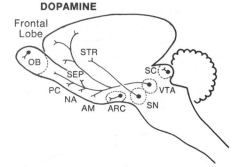

Fig. 24.10 Distribution of dopamine-containing neurons in the rat brain. For abbreviations, see legend to Fig. 24.9.

send axons to the median eminence, to modulate the output of releasing factors by neuroendocrine cells there (see above). Intrinsic DA cells in the retina, olfactory bulb, and optic tectum take part in local circuits in those structures. Finally, there is a system of DA cells around the fourth ventricle, extending within the core of the brainstem to the hypothalamus.

Acetylcholine. Acetylcholine (ACh) is quickly hydrolyzed and inactivated by the enzyme acetylcholinesterase. The presence of ACh is therefore sometimes inferred from the presence of this enzyme. However, this gives many false positive results, because the enzyme is widely distributed in the brain and the body, as if on guard to chew up any stray molecules of this transmitter. The better method is to identify the presence of the enzyme choline acetyltransferase, which synthesizes ACh. To this has recently been added other methods, such as the ability to identify ligand binding sites by different types of ACh receptors (recall Chap. 8).

The locations of ACh neurons are shown in Fig. 24.11. Among central systems, ACh is specific for two cell populations in the limbic system, the septal-hippocampal and habenulo-endopeduncular projection neurons, and a cell population in the caudate-putamen nucleus which is involved in motor coordination (see below). ACh acts on either nicotinic receptors (producing brief synaptic potentials) or muscarinic

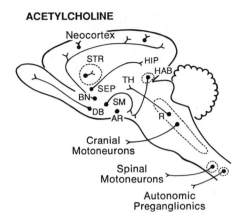

ACETYLCHOLINE

Fig. 24.11 Distribution of cholinergic cell groups and their projections in the rat brain. For abbreviations, see legend to Fig. 24.9.

receptors (producing slow synaptic potentials) (see Chaps. 8, 17, and 18). It produces EPSPs by both these actions on Renshaw interneurons in the spinal cord. In the hippocampus, it produces both slow excitatory and inhibitory responses on pyramidal cells (see Chaps. 7 and 29). In the caudate, it is believed to be the transmitter of short-axon cells and of axon collaterals that are involved in local circuits. Degeneration of these cells occurs in certain neurological diseases in which there are uncontrollable jerky movements (Huntington's chorea) and dementia.

In recent years, much of the interest in ACh in the human brain has been motivated by the apparent link between ACh and the type of senile dementia known as Alzheimer's disease. This disease is characterized by the presence of neurofibrillary tangles within the cell bodies of cortical neurons, and extracellular amyloid accumulations forming plaques in the cortical gray matter. In patients dying with Alzheimer's disease, there is also a reduction in the ACh-synthesizing enzyme, acetylcholine acetylase, and the hydrolyzing enzyme, acetylcholinesterase; this reduction has been traced to degeneration of cholinergic cells in the nucleus basalis (see Fig. 24.11). It has been attractive to postulate that Alzheimer's disease might belong to the same

category as Parkinson's disease in being due to the degeneration of a single type of transmitter-specific neuron. However, investigation of the pathology of this disease has necessarily been limited to study of brains of terminally ill patients, and there is much more work to be done on the factors that are responsible for the initial changes—genetic, viral, or otherwise—that lead to the derangements of brain functions.

Glutamate and Aspartate. We next consider some neurotransmitters that are amino acids. One of the main representatives of this type is glutamic acid, or glutamate, and its close relative, aspartate. These compounds are widespread constituents of intermediary metabolism in the body and the brain, and, as noted in Chap. 8, might seem to be unlikely candidates for the specific actions required at synapses. However, beginning with the studies of van Harreveld and Mendelson in 1959, glutamate has been established as the transmitter at the crustacean neuromuscular junction (see Chap. 17). Although experiments as definitive as these have not been carried out in the brain, there is considerable evidence that glutamate and/or aspartate, acting as transmitters, mediate brief, intense excitatory actions in several types of projection neuron in the brain. These neurons are shown in A of Fig. 24.12.

Of particular interest are the granule cells of the cerebellum. The granule cells are a type of short-axon projection neuron, linking the two layers of the cerebellum cortex. Because of their large numbers (10 to 100 billion, as noted in Chap. 21), we can say that there are more glutamatergic cells than all other cells combined in the nervous system! Other projection tracts using these substances include the olfactory bulb input to olfactory cortex, the entorhinal cortex input to the hippocampus and dentate fascia, and the cortical input to the caudate. At all these sites, glutamate and aspartate have excitatory actions. An intriguing note is that the mitral cells of the olfactory bulb

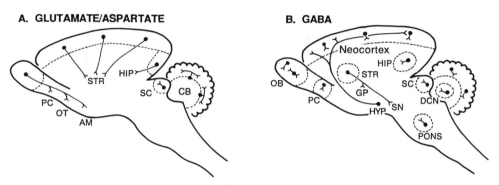

A. GLUTAMATE/ASPARTATE

B. GABA

Fig. 24.12 **A.** Distribution of neurons believed to use glutamate and/or aspartate as a neurotransmitter in the rat brain. **B.** Distribution of GABAergic neurons. For abbreviations, see legend to Fig. 24.9.

not only project to the olfactory cortex, but also take part in dendrodendritic synapses within the microcircuits of the olfactory bulb. According to Dale's Law (Chap. 8), one might expect the transmitter at the dendritic synapses also to be glutamate or aspartate, and there is in fact evidence to support this.

λ-Aminobutyric Acid (GABA). In mammals, GABA is found almost exclusively in the brain, where it is a constituent of intermediary metabolism. Its role as a neurotransmitter was first established in the crayfish, where it was shown to be the transmitter of the inhibitory axon to the stretch receptor cell (Chap. 7) and at the neuromuscular junction (Chap. 17). Localization of this neurotransmitter in the brain has been aided by immunocytochemical methods for identifying the synthesizing enzyme, glutamic acid decarboxylase (GAD) (see Chaps. 4 and 8).

GABAergic neurons are shown in B of Fig. 24.12. There are short projection tracts from striatum to substantia nigra and from cerebellar cortex to deep cerebellar nuclei. The only long projection pathway thus far known has been demonstrated by immunohistochemical staining for GAD (Vincent et al., 1983). It arises from cells in the posterior hypothalamus and projects diffusely to the cerebral cortex. This could "provide a direct pathway by which limbic,

emotional and visceral information can reach many regions of cortex." It appears that this pathway shares properties with the diffuse transmitter systems discussed above.

Apart from these, most GABAergic neurons are intrinsic neurons, in such regions as cortex, olfactory bulb, hippocampus, cerebellum, and retina. Within these regions, GABA is present in high concentrations, of the order of μmoles per gram of frozen tissue, which is about 1000 times the concentrations of the monoamines. This is in accord with the powerful and specific actions of the GABAergic neurons in these regions. The predominant action of GABA is inhibitory, by increasing Cl or K conductance, though other types of actions are beginning to come to light, too (see Chap. 8). These actions are exerted at both axonal and dendritic output synapses, and are usually directed at controlling the output neurons. The inhibitory actions are important for many functions, such as sensory processing, negative feedback, gating of rhythmic discharges, and timing and coordination of motor output. Drugs like picrotoxin and bicuculline, which block GABA receptors (see Chap. 8), cause seizures, which has suggested that dysfunctions of GABAergic interneurons in the cortex may be critical in the development of epilepsy.

Glycine. Traditionally, glycine has been localized mainly to the brainstem and spinal

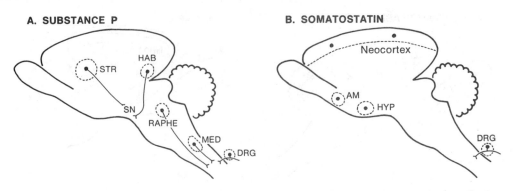

Fig. 24.13 **A.** Distribution of substance P-containing neurons in the rat brain. **B.** Distribution of somatostatin-containing neurons in the rat brain. For abbreviations, see legend to Fig. 24.9.

cord. In the spinal cord, it is believed to be an inhibitory transmitter of certain inter-neurons onto motoneurons. Classically, ionophoresis experiments have found little evidence for any action of glycine on neu-rons above the brainstem. However, the role of glycine in the brain is undergoing reevaluation in view of the recent evidence that glycine modulates glutamatergic syn-apses, and that it is present in the cerebro-spinal fluid at a concentration sufficient to bring about these modulatory effects (see Chap. 8).

Peptides

The above substances include those tradi-tionally associated with specific neuro-transmitter actions. We next consider sev-eral representatives of the neuropeptides.

Substance P. Substance P has the distinc-tion of being the first neuroactive peptide isolated from the brain. In 1931, Ulf von Euler of Sweden and John Gaddum of Eng-land showed that this compound, present in both brain and gut, has a stimulating effect on smooth muscle. Around 1970, Susan Leeman and her colleagues at Har-vard isolated a compound from the hypo-thalamus that stimulates the salivary gland, and named it a sialogog (sialo = saliva, gog = factor). When they synthesized this compound, it turned out to be identical to substance P isolated some 40 years previ-ously (see amino acid sequence in Fig. 8.10).

Substance P is found in several specific short projection tracts, as shown in A of Fig. 24.13. Its presence in the striatonigral pathway has suggested that it is a trans-mitter in these fibers, and is therefore im-portant in the motor functions of the basal ganglia (see Chap. 21). In the spinal cord, it is present in dorsal root ganglion cells. Although it is 200 times more potent than glutamate in depolarizing motoneurons when applied ionophoretically, its slow time course of action contrasts with the rapid discrete transmission of input signals in many dorsal root fibers. This is consistent with the idea that substance P has a slower modulatory action, but so far it has not been proven.

Somatostatin. This compound derives its name from its action in inhibiting the se-cretion of growth hormone (somatotropin) from pituitary cells. It is a tetradecapeptide (14 amino acids) (see Fig. 8.10). Like so many neuroactive peptides, it is found in autonomic fibers and other nonneural cells in the visceral organs (see Chap. 17). Within the nervous system, it is found in dorsal root ganglion cells, and, centrally, in cells of the hypothalamus, amygdala, and cere-bral cortex (see B in Fig. 24.13). When injected into the cerebral ventricles, it has a depressant effect on motor activity. Like several other peptides, it has a slow inhib-itory action when ionophoresed onto single neurons.

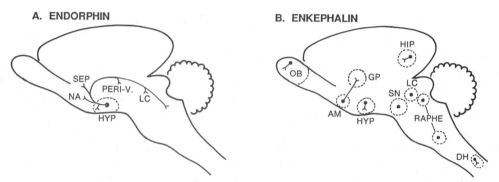

Fig. 24.14   **A.** Distribution of endorphin-containing neurons in the rat brain. **B.** Distribution of enkephalin-containing neurons in the rat brain. For abbreviations, see legend to Fig. 24.9.

Endorphins. Among the peptides generating the most interest in recent years are the endorphins and enkephalins. This work began in 1975 with the finding of Hans Kosterlitz and Robert Hughes in Scotland that extracts of brain contain a compound which competes with opiates in assay systems, and is blocked by opiate antagonists such as naloxone. The short-chain pentapeptides (5 amino acids) are called enkephalins, whereas the longer-chain compounds (16–31 amino acids) are called endorphins. Since the enkephalin chain is contained within the endorphin chain, the term *endorphin* may be used to refer to both in general. The synthesis of these compounds from the larger molecule β-lipotropin was discussed in Chap. 8, as were the receptor mechanisms.

Cells containing endorphins are located almost exclusively in the hypothalamus. As shown in Fig. 24.14A, their fibers project to different nuclei within the hypothalamus, and to several regions outside the hypothalamus, including the septal area and amygdala, and reach as far as the higher brainstem, where they innervate monoamine cells of the locus ceruleus and raphe nuclei. Most of the termination sites are in the core of the brain, around the ventricles.

From the moment of their discovery, it has seemed that the endorphins might act like opiate drugs, and thus function as an internal mechanism for opposing or modulating pain sensations. Part of the interest

in analyzing this mechanism lies in the hope of developing a more natural substitute for morphine that is free of addictive properties and side effects. In addition, there has been much speculation on the natural functions in which the endorphins may be involved. In their enthusiasm, people have implicated them in almost every behavior imaginable, from temperature regulation to our sense of self. It is becoming clear, however, that much more work is required to establish the precise contributions of endorphins to specific behaviors. The caution expressed by Cooper, Bloom, and Roth above applies precisely to this task.

Enkephalins. Enkephalin-containing neurons are widespread in the nervous system, with a distribution that is quite distinct from that of the endorphins. The main regions in which they are found are shown in Fig. 24.14B. In the peripheral nervous system, enkephalin is found in the adrenal medulla and in fibers that innervate the smooth muscle of the gut. In the central nervous system, enkephalins are characteristically found in intrinsic neurons; in this respect they resemble GABAergic interneurons. In these cells, the enkephalin is in a position to modulate the processing of information by local circuits. A prime example is the dorsal horn of the spinal cord, where it is believed that enkephalin neurons modulate the processing of input arriving over pain fibers (see Chap. 12). In addition, enkephalins are implicated in most of the functions ascribed to endorphins, as discussed above.

Closely related to the localization of endorphins and enkephalins has been the mapping of opiate-receptor binding sites. As discussed in Chap. 9, there are several types of opiate receptors, defined by binding of certain agonists and antagonists. The distribution of these receptors may be briefly summarized as follows (see Snyder, 1984; Cooper et al., 1987). The mu (μ) receptor preferentially binds morphine and its antagonist, naloxone; it is localized primarily in pain pathways in the brain, and is believed mainly to be responsible for the pain-killing and addicting properties of morphine. The delta (δ) receptor preferentially binds enkephalin; its localization in limbic parts of the brain may be related to influences on the emotions (see Chap. 28). The kappa (κ) receptor has a high affinity for dynorphin, which is believed to mediate more sedative actions at the cortical level. The sigma (σ) receptor binds a hallucinogenic drug, phencyclidine, and is especially localized in the hippocampus. The epsilon (ϵ) receptor binds β-endorphin; it is present in neurons at the base of the brain that receive β-endorphin-containing terminals from cells in the hypothalamus and mediate a variety of behavioral effects when β-endorphin is injected into an animal, including inability to move (akinesia) and prolonged avoidance reactions.

Transmitters Across Phyla

Our attention has been focused on vertebrates and it remains to comment on the distribution of neuroactive substances across different phyla.

With regard to neurotransmitters, it should already be apparent that there is a strong tendency toward conservation across the phyla. Thus, we have seen that glutamate is an excitatory transmitter and GABA is an inhibitory transmitter (Chap. 17); indeed, the earliest evidence for the identification of these substances as transmitters was obtained in invertebrates. Similarly, ACh is widespread as a neurotransmitter in many invertebrate species; in fact, many insecticides have as their primary mode of action a blocking of cholinergic synapses. Finally, we have noted the role of 5HT in modulating behavioral states of some invertebrates (see Chap. 20). One can conclude that there is a limited set of small molecules that have similar functions across many phyla.

The situation with regard to neuropeptides is more complicated. As Greenberg and Price (1983) have pointed out, invertebrate neuropeptides fall into two categories: those that are shared with vertebrates, and those that are unique to invertebrates. From a review of different phyla, they conclude that "each vertebrate peptide family is represented by one or more active structural homologues in all invertebrate animals." Unfortunately, little is known as yet about the physiological roles of these peptides in any phylum. In contrast, similar functions such as gonad stimulation, pigment dispersal, or glucose mobilization, on the evidence thus far, appear to be mediated by peptides that are different in invertebrates as compared with vertebrates. The conclusion is that peptides have diverse families with different modulatory functions within the different phyla, and that there is still much work to be done in identifying these families and characterizing their functions.

25

Biorhythms

Although motor activity is one of the cardinal features of animal life, animals are not ceaselessly in motion. Characteristically, periods of activity alternate with periods of inactivity. The inactivity can take many forms, such as simply sitting, lying, or standing still; sleeping; hibernating; or passing through stages of larval development. Underlying these periods are fluctuations in the secretions of glands, and fluctuations in many cellular functions, such as the synthesis of RNA, protein, and other molecules. Cyclical activities are thus basic characteristics of animal life, and we refer to them collectively by the term *biorhythms*.

Any cyclical activity can be defined in terms of its *period,* that is, the time it takes to complete one full cycle of activity. A cycle that lasts a day, such as the sequence of waking and sleeping, is said to have a period that is *circadian* (circa = approximately; die = day). Longer periods (less frequent) are called *infradian* (infra = less), whereas shorter periods (more frequent) are called *ultradian* (ultra = more). Some representatives of these types are listed in Table 25.1. These biorhythms almost always involve in some way, directly or indirectly, the nervous system, and many are directly under nervous control. We have, of course, already encountered ultradian rhythms in the discussion of impulse discharge, heart rate, and patterns of locomotion.

In this chapter, we will focus on circadian rhythms, and the cellular mechanisms that lead to their generation. We will attempt to gain an understanding of the baseline they provide for the centrally controlled behaviors to be discussed in the following chapters.

A Brief History

It might be thought that the obvious relations of many plant and animal activities to day and night would have invited close study even in ancient times. However, it appears that the facts were simply too familiar. It was not until 1729 that the French geologist de Mairan did the simple experiment of placing a plant under constant temperature and illumination, and observed that its normal daily period of fluctuations still persisted. This showed that periodic behavior could be a function of the organism itself. Although this finding aroused some interest, people still did not quite know what to make of it; there were

Table 25.1 Main categories of rhythmic activity, with some examples

Infradian (longer than one day)	Circadian (approx. one day)	Ultradian (shorter than one day)
menstrual cycle	waking–sleeping	feeding
seasonal variations	body temperature	respiration
lifetime	body electrolytes	heart rate
	various hormones	nerve impulse discharge

suspicions that the experiment might be affected by some undetectable rays or forces.

It was not until the 1930s that biologists began to make the connection between photoperiodicity (the changing illumination during the day) and bodily rhythms. A breakthrough came in 1950, in the work of two German biologists, Gustav Kramer and Karl von Frisch. Kramer showed that birds could use the sun as a compass by virtue of the fact that they have an "internal clock" which, in effect, tells them the time of day and how much to correct for the position (azimuth) of the sun in the sky. Von Frisch came to a similar conclusion for bees. A number of biologists then initiated the search for the cellular basis of the "internal clock," a search that has continued to the present. The importance of circadian rhythms has grown in parallel with the increasing understanding of their mechanisms, and the increasing realization of how pervasive they are in the life of the organism. As Colin Pittendrigh (1974), one of the early pioneers, put it:

. . . a circadian oscillation assumes a unique phase relationship to the 24-hour light/dark cycle that entrains it . . . . The functional significance of this is many-sided: It permits *initiation* of events in *anticipation* of the time at which their culmination most appropriately occurs, and it permits timing that cannot be entrusted to control by conditions for which the system has no adequate modality.

From the extensive work that has been carried out on circadian oscillations, we will focus on three examples: studies of simple cells and small systems in *Aplysia* and birds, and studies of multiple systems

controlling waking and sleeping in mammals, especially humans.

Circadian Rhythms in Invertebrates

In our earlier discussions of rhythmic behavior (for example, heart rate or locomotion), we saw that there are two basic types of mechanism: there can be a pacemaker cell, which imparts its rhythmic output to other cells, or there can be a rhythmic cell group or network, in which no one cell has an intrinsic rhythmic property, but in which there is a rhythmic output by virtue of the interconnections. The same two alternatives apply in the analysis of mechanisms of circadian oscillation.

A Circadian Pacemaker

The sea hare *Aplysia* has been a useful system for studying circadian mechanisms; it was introduced for this purpose by Felix Strumwasser of the California Institute of Technology in 1965. Like most animals, *Aplysia* shows a circadian rhythm of locomotor activity; in general, it is active during the day and inactive at night. Since we do not know whether an invertebrate animal like *Aplysia* ever "sleeps," in the same sense that we apply that term to mammals, it is best to refer to the inactive periods as periods of *rest*. We then say that there is a *basic rest–activity cycle* that characterizes the overall behavior of an animal through a 24-hour day. Some animals, like *Aplysia*, are active during the day, but of course many animals, particularly warm-blooded predators, are active at night.

An *Aplysia* that has been entrained to a

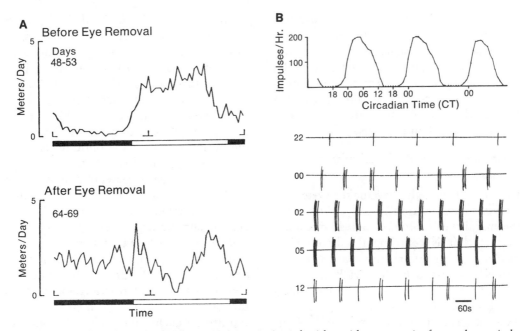

Fig. 25.1 A. The average locomotor activity (monitored with a video camera) of a sea hare, *Aply-sia*, before (top) and after (bottom) removal of both eyes. Each trace represents the average of six days' observations. The observations for the bottom trace began three days after eye removal. (From Strumwasser, 1974) **B.** Circadian rhythm in the frequency of extracellularly recorded action potentials of the optic nerve innervating an isolated eye. *Top:* Graph of discharge frequency (in impulses per hour), plotted against circadian time (CT). *Bottom:* Representative recordings, at times indicated. (From Jacklet, 1981)

normal dark–light cycle and is then exposed to constant illumination or constant dark still shows its basic rest–activity cycle for several days. This indicates that the circadian rhythm persists in the absence of inputs from the environment, or from other ganglia. The rhythm of the ganglion maintained under constant conditions is referred to as the *free-running rhythm*. The free-running period is not quite precisely 24 hours (hence the general term circadian); we say therefore that in the intact animal the rhythm is *entrained* by the 24-hour light–dark cycle.

This result indicates that the rest–activity cycle has a circadian generator somewhere within the nervous system. The generator is not the large bursting neuron, R15, in the abdominal ganglion; removal of the ganglia has no effect on the free-

running cycle. However, removal of both eyes does abolish the locomotor cycle, in both normal and maintained conditions (Fig. 25.1A). Correlated with this is the finding that the eye of an animal maintained in constant darkness shows a free-running rhythm in the amount of spontaneous impulse activity that can be recorded from the optic nerves. A similar rhythm can be recorded from the isolated eye (see Fig. 25.1B). These experiments have therefore indicated that the neuronal mechanisms that drive the circadian rhythm of locomotor activity in *Aplysia* are found within the eye itself.

The pacemaker neurons have been localized to a group of neurons at the base of the eye. These neurons are entrained through synaptic inputs from optic nerve collaterals. They are also modulated by centrifugal fibers from the brain; these fibers are serotonergic, and their effects on the pacemaker neurons are mediated through cAMP. The centrifugal fibers are part of a widespread serotonergic system for behavioral arousal of the animal, so they provide a means whereby the state of arousal can affect the circadian rhythms.

Centrifugal Control of a Circadian Rhythm

By contrast with the pacemaker system of *Aplysia* which is centrifugally modulated, the lateral eye of *Limulus* shows a circadian rhythm that is centrifugally driven. The mechanisms of this rhythm have been extensively analyzed by Robert Barlow and his colleagues at Syracuse. As background for this discussion the student should review the structure and function of the *Limulus* eye in Chaps. 10 and 16.

A flash of light delivered to the *Limulus* eye is transduced by the mechanisms discussed in Chaps. 10 and 16, leading to a discharge of impulses in the optic nerve. The intensity of the discharge is not a constant; it shows a circadian rhythm, being greater to the same flash during the night than during the day. The increase in impulse response is plotted in Fig. 25.2A. One might anticipate from this that there could be a similar variation in the spontaneous rate of impulse firing in the optic nerve. The rate does vary, but surprisingly, in the opposite direction, showing a decrease during the night.

The mechanism underlying this disparity was analyzed by use of intracellular recordings from the photoreceptors (retinula cells). As shown in Fig. 25.2B, during the day (6 P.M.), the membrane potential is noisy, as a result of frequent small deflections representing quantal responses to single photons, and there is a relatively small response to a light flash. At night (10 P.M.), the membrane becomes quiet (which accounts for the decrease in spontaneous impulse activity in A), and there is an increase in the depolarization by a light flash (which produces the increased responses in A).

Thus, during the night there is an increased sensitivity and an increased signal-to-noise ratio, which would be advantageous to this nocturnally active animal. Because the experiments are carried out at all times in constant darkness, the differences must be due to a circadian rhythm generated either within the eye or within the brain. Tying off the optic nerve eliminates the rhythm, so, in contrast to *Aplysia,* the rhythm must be generated in the brain.

The centrifugal input brings structural as well as functional changes in the *Limulus* eye. As summarized in Fig. 25.3, these included (1) movement of pigment cells to widen and shorten the lens aperture, accompanied by (2) outward movement of photoreceptors and rearrangement of the rhabdome. These changes increase photon capture by each ommatidium. In addition to increasing sensitivity and signal-to-noise ratio, efferent activity also reduces lateral inhibition by modulating the dendrodendritic synaptic interactions that take place between the neurites of neighboring eccentric cells (refer to diagram in Fig. 10.7). This contributes to increased sensitivity at the expense of contrast enhancement.

These experiments have shown that the circadian efferents exert their effects on retinular cells at the earliest stages of visual reception. The synaptic mechanisms that mediate these effects have been studied by use of microinjections of different neuroactive substances beneath the cornea of the eye. These experiments have suggested that octopamine, a biogenic amine that is common in invertebrates (see Chaps. 17 and 19), may be the transmitter for these centrifugal synapses; an injection of as little as 10 μmol octopamine can convert the daytime retina toward its nighttime structure and function. There is evidence that octopamine acts through cAMP, as summarized in the diagram and legend of Fig. 25.4.

Genetics of Circadian Clocks

Circadian pacemaker rhythms, such as those in the eye of *Aplysia,* can be reset or abolished by exposure of the cells to protein

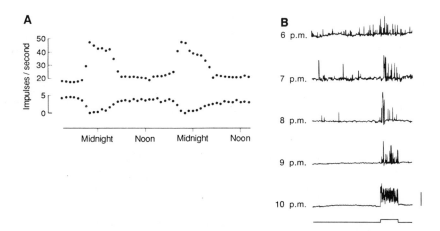

Fig. 25.2 Circadian rhythms in activity in the *Limulus* eye. **A.** Graphs of the impulse firing rate of optic nerve fibers. In the upper graph, each point gives the mean firing rate during a 6-second light flash delivered to the eye every hour, while the animal was maintained in the dark. In the lower graph, each point gives the mean rate of spontaneous firing during a 25-second interval in the dark each hour. **B.** Intracellular recordings from a *Limulus* retinula cell at different times indicated at left. In each trial, a 20-second recording period preceded the 5-second test flash. Calibration bar, 10 mV. (A from Barlow et al., 1984; B from Kaplan and Barlow, 1980)

Fig. 25.3 Structural changes that occur in the *Limulus* ommatidium as a result of the circadian clock. *On the left,* the structure during the day, when there is no activity impinging on the ommatidium via efferent fibers. *On the right,* a summary of the structure during the night, when activity in the efferent nerves from the circadian clock produces the changes indicated (see text). (From Barlow et al., 1984)

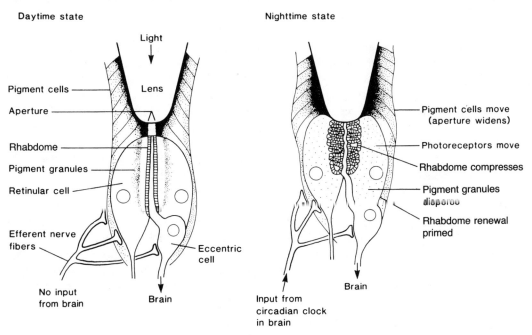

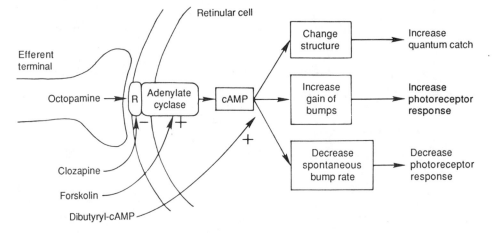

Fig. 25.4 Summary of neurochemical pathways involved in the effects produced by the circadian clock within the retinular cells of the *Limulus* ommatidium. Compare these changes with the electrophysiological recordings in Fig. 25.2 and the structural changes in Fig. 25.3 above. (From Barlow et al., 1984)

synthesis inhibitors. This has suggested that the daily synthesis of protein is a general requirement for circadian clocks (Jacklet, 1981).

Search for the genetic basis of this requirement has led to the study of certain *Drosophila* mutants with circadian defects (Konopka and Benzer, 1971). One mutant shows a shorter period of 19 hours (*per^s*), another a longer of 29 hours (*per^l*), and in a third circadian periodicity is abolished (*per^0*). All of these mutations map to a single *per* locus on the X chromosome. In addition to these circadian abnormalities, the mutants show defects in other behaviors: in *per^s*, the courtship song is briefer, whereas in *per^l* it is prolonged; the *per^l* mutants are difficult to condition behaviorally.

These results indicate that there are complex interdependencies between circadian clocks, rapid (infradian) endogenous rhythms, and learning abilities. That systems with overlapping functions should share products of overlapping gene families is entirely in accord with concepts regarding the molecular diversity of neurons discussed in Chap. 2.

Is the *per* gene unique to *Drosophila?* Michael Young and his colleagues (1984) at Rockefeller have identified certain limited *per* sequences in DNA from birds, mice, and humans. One possibility was that the sequences would code for an ion channel protein, but surprisingly, the amino acid sequences in the gene products are similar to those in proteoglycans. These are molecules with a protein moiety in the plasma membrane and a large carbohydrate moiety within the extracellular space (Chap. 3). This type of molecule is important in cell–cell adhesion and recognition. Experiments are presently aimed at characterizing the way in which these extracellular molecular interactions are related to the generation of circadian rhythms of electrical activity.

Circadian Rhythms in Vertebrates

As in invertebrates, the basic rest–activity cycles are closely linked to the day–night cycle in most vertebrates. Vertebrate animals also vary in whether they are active principally during the day or night, or at specific times such as dawn or dusk. This obviously reflects the strategy of a particular species in finding food or sexual mates with the greatest success, while minimizing the risks of being preyed upon. From this perspective it can be seen that the circadian

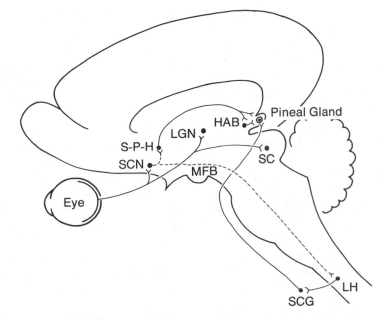

Fig. 25.5 Some pathways and related regions involved in the control of circadian rhythms in vertebrates. HAB, habenula; LGN, lateral geniculate nucleus; LH, lateral horn containing autonomic (sympathetic) motoneurons; MFB, medial forebrain bundle; SC, superior colliculus; SCG, superior cervical ganglion; SCN, suprachiasmatic nucleus; S-P-H, septal, preoptic, and hypothalamic regions.

clock or clocks within an organism are essential components of the apparatus for survival, and for carving out the ecological niche of the species. The niche may in fact be very narrow in a temporal sense, requiring very strict timing of specific activities during the day–night cycle. This is seen in the fact that many species have only a few hours a day for foraging for food, and it is also seen in the exquisite coordination in timing of male and female activities at specific hours of the day or night to bring about mating in many species.

The changing illumination that occurs during the day–night cycle is as important in entraining circadian rhythms in vertebrates as it is in invertebrates. In Chap. 16, the visual pathways involved in visual perception were discussed; here we will become acquainted with the pathways that mediate this other very important visual function. As far as is known, this function is an unconscious one; this reflects the fact that sensory information may have essen-

tial roles in nervous and body functions that are separate and distinct from their roles in perception, discrimination, and consciousness. Visually entrained circadian rhythms depend simply on levels of illumination rather than on the discrimination of any particular visual pattern.

The Suprachiasmatic Nucleus

The visual pathways that are involved in control of circadian rhythms in the vertebrate are shown in Fig. 25.5A. The key pathway is made up of a small bundle of fibers which emerges from the optic nerve and terminates in a small group of cells at the anterior border of the hypothalamus. In the 1960s Curt Richter of John Hopkins showed that the anterior hypothalamic region was essential for circadian rhythms in rats. Then, in the early 1970s, a small cell group in this region was identified by independent studies of Robert Moore and V. B. Eichler at Chicago, and F. K. Stephen and Irving Zucker at Oregon. Because of its position just over the optic chiasm, this cell group is called the *suprachiasmatic nucleus* (SCN). A number of studies since then, using autoradiographic tracing methods, have permitted the anatomical identification of this *retinohypothalamic tract,* made up of retinal ganglion cell axons that terminate in the suprachiasmatic nucleus.

Many studies have provided evidence for the functional properties of the SCN in relation to circadian rhythms. For example, ablation of the SCN bilaterally results in disruption of circadian rhythms of many nervous and bodily functions; some of them are summarized in Table 25.2. The term "disruption" is carefully chosen; in general, the free-running rhythms are not totally abolished, and some degree of visual entrainment may persist. This has suggested that the SCN is the principal center in an extensive system including several other cell groups with weaker circadian oscillators. These groups include the lateral hypothalamic nucleus, the retrochiasmatic area, and the ventromedial hypothalamic nucleus. The relations between these regions are reciprocal and complex (Moore, 1982); together, these interconnections form a distributed system as previously defined (Chaps. 1 and 24). This system is modulated by an extraordinary array of neuropeptides. Vasopressin, somatostatin, VIP, and enkephalin have been localized in SCN neurons by immunocytochemical methods. SCN rhythms are sensitive to microinjections of neuropeptide Y (reviewed in Jacklet, 1985).

Some of the clearest evidence for the

activity of the SCN has come from application of the 2-deoxyglucose (2DG) method (Chap. 8). William Schwartz and Harold Gainer at the National Institutes of Health injected [^{14}C]-2DG into rats during either the day or night, and examined the autoradiographs of sections through the brain. As shown in Fig. 25.6, the SCNs showed a marked circadian rhythm, with low levels of 2DG uptake indistinguishable from neighboring regions during the night (when the rats, being nocturnal animals, were most active), and high levels during the day (when the rats mostly slept). Since 2DG uptake is a tag for the glucose uptake needed for energy metabolism (Chap. 8), the changes in uptake presumably reflect widely differing levels of activity in the SCN during the day–night cycle.

Further work has shown that the SCN metabolic rhythm appears in the rat on the last day of gestation, before synaptic connections between the SCN neurons have been formed to any significant extent. The implications of these findings have been summarized by Robert Moore of Stony Brook (1982):

SCN neurons are produced as genetically determined, independent circadian oscillators which become coupled and interconnected during development. Initially they are entrained by maternal influences, but postnatally this function is taken over by development of the retinohypothalamic projection to the SCN. Within the SCN, what is initially an individual neuronal function becomes subsumed by groups of neurons functioning as interconnected networks or coupled oscillators.

Pineal Gland

In discussing visual control of circadian rhythms, we should also mention the *pineal gland*. It is, embryologically, an outpouching from the dorsal part of the diencephalon. In lower vertebrates (such as sharks, frogs, and lizards), it forms a third eye in the dorsal cranium, and functions to detect changes in levels of illumination. In birds, it may retain some photoreceptive properties. However, in birds and especially in

Table 25.2 Circadian rhythms disrupted by lesions of the suprachiasmatic nucleus in rats or hamsters

Locomotor activity (wheel running)
Drinking
Sleep–wake rhythms
Adrenal corticosteroid levels
Estrous periods and ovulation
Temperature
Pineal N-acetyltransferase

Adapted from Menaker et al. (1978)

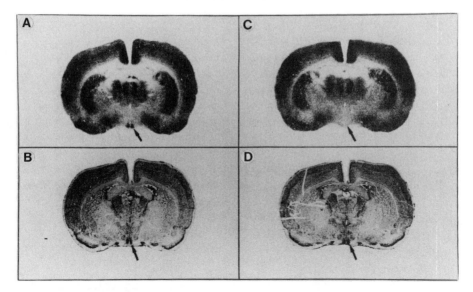

Fig. 25.6 Correlation of activity in the suprachiasmatic nuclei (SCN) with the day-night cycle in rats, with the use of the 2-deoxyglucose (2DG) method. **A.** Autoradiogram of [^{14}C]2DG patterns, showing localization of 2DG in the SCN during the day. **C.** Autoradiogram showing lack of 2DG localization in SCN at night. The circadian rhythm shown in A and C peristed even when the rats were maintained continuously in the dark. **B,D.** Histological sections used for obtaining the autoradiograms in A and C, stained with cresyl violet, to confirm the location of the SCN. (From Schwartz and Gainer, 1977)

mammals, it is more important as a gland that secretes a hormone called *melatonin.* Melatonin is one of the indole family, and arises from metabolism of serotonin (5-hydroxytryptamine). Synthesis of melatonin has a marked circadian rhythm, as shown in Fig. 25.7. The rate-limiting enzyme is N-acetyltransferase. In mammals (though not in birds), this enzyme is controlled by norepinephrine from the fibers of the sympathetic nervous system that innervate the pineal gland. The superior cervical ganglion, the source of the fibers, is believed to be influenced by fibers ultimately arising from the SCN, because lesions of either the SCN or the median forebrain bundle (containing fibers from the SCN) block the rhythm of N-acetyltransferase activity.

The norepinephrine is believed to act on a β-adrenergic receptor, which in turn activates adenyl cyclase to increase the concentration of cAMP, according to the se-

quence we discussed in Chap. 8. The linkage between the second messenger cAMP and the changes in N-acetyltransferase is not yet known.

Recent studies of pinealocytes (cultured cells prepared from the pineal gland) have shown that stimulation of N-acetyltransferase by NE (acting through a β-adrenoreceptor and cAMP) can be potentiated by stimulation of α_1-adrenoreceptors, acting through diacylglycerol and protein kinase C to enhance cAMP (and cGMP) production. This is an interesting example of a synergistic relation between the two types of second messenger systems, and indicates the complex biochemical control of this circadian rhythm (Sugden et al., 1985).

Multiple Circadian Oscillators

We thus see that many body functions have circadian rhythms, and that these are entrained by the daily light–dark cycle, acting through the visual pathway. The most im-

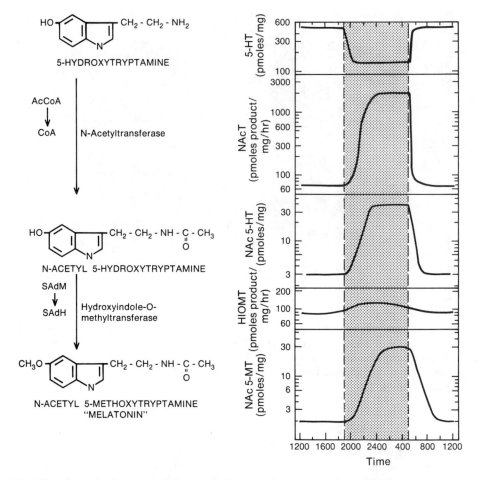

Fig. 25.7 Circadian rhythms in indole metabolism in the rat pineal gland. The pathway from 5-hydroxytryptamine (serotonin) to melatonin is shown at left. The variations in concentrations of metabolites and activities of enzymes are shown at right, in relation to dark (shaded) and light periods of the day. (From Klein, 1974)

portant center in this pathway is the SCN, but there are other centers that also contribute to maintaining and modulating the rhythms. From this and related work has emerged the concept that circadian systems are composed of *multiple oscillators,* each with properties to some extent specific and distinct from the others. The oscillators may not only have distinct properties but may also possess different intrinsic rhythms.

A classical experiment providing evidence for multiple oscillators in humans was carried out by Jurgen Aschoff in Germany in 1969. The subject lived in an isolated chamber, deprived of any time cues.

After several days he fell into a circadian sleep–wake cycle of approximately 33 hours, while his cycle of body temperature held to a period of approximately 25 hours. This suggested that these two functions are controlled by two oscillators with different free-running rhythms, that normally are both entrained to the 24-hour night–day cycle.

Recently this experiment has been repeated, by Zulley and Campbell, with Aschoff's assistance, using different measures of sleepiness and different ways of plotting the data. As shown in Fig. 25.8, this subject had indeed a 25-hour temperature rhythm (wave at top of graphs); the periods of sleep

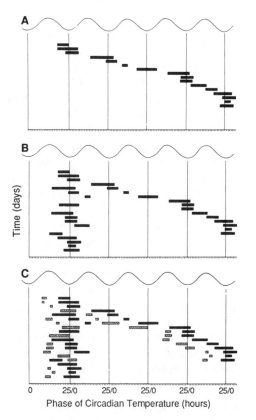

Fig. 25.8 Analysis of two circadian rhythms—body temperature and sleeping–waking—which are free-running in a human subject who lived under constant conditions. The oscillations in body temperature occurred over 25-hour periods, and are shown schematically at the top of each graph. **A.** Black bars show periods of sleep on successive days (moving from top to bottom). Note that the sleep rhythm lengthens to a period of around 30 hours. **B.** The same data are plotted a second time in relation to the first temperature cycle. **C.** Hatched bars show naps taken by subjects. Note that both sleep and naps tend to occur near temperature minima. (Based on Zulley and Campbell, in Mrosovsky, 1986)

were variable in their time of occurrence, but nonetheless tended (with occasional exceptions) to occur near times of low body temperature (A,B). In addition, some subjects take naps, and when these are included, they tend also to occur at times of body temperature minima (C). These experiments thus indicate that the relation

between different circadian oscillators may be stronger in some instances than heretofore recognized, and that new strategies of behavioral experiments will be needed to demonstrate the independent operation of individual circadian controls.

WAKING AND SLEEPING

The circadian rhythms we have discussed so far concern variations in bodily functions and locomotor activity that provide a kind of baseline for the organism during the 24-hour day. During the period of activity we say we are "awake" and "aroused"; during the period of rest we fall into a state we refer to as "sleep." Within the awake period our levels of activity and alertness vary widely, as any student sitting in a warm lecture room after eating a large lunch well knows! Similarly, sleep is a process that contains within it alternating periods of deep and light sleep, the light sleep correlated with dreaming and with a modified state of arousal. Our next task is to understand the neurobiological mechanisms which are responsible for the waking and sleeping states, and, within the sleeping state, for the periods of arousal and dreaming.

The Electroencephalogram

The study of sleep has drawn on many disciplines. An important starting point for modern studies was the discovery that different patterns of brain activity are related to different levels of consciousness.

A Brief History

Richard Caton of England had shown as early as 1875 that waves of electrical activity can be recorded from the surface of the brains of animals, but this finding lay unnoticed until the work of Hans Berger, of Germany, in the 1920s. Berger was a psychiatrist, and also served as Rector of the University of Jena. His main research interest was determining what he called the

Fig. 25.9 Illustration from Berger's original report, showing recording of electrical waves (electroencephalogram) above, time marker below. (From Berger, in Brazier, 1970)

physical basis of psychic functions. In pursuing this interest, he was led to place electrodes on the scalp of human subjects and attempt to record the electrical activity of the brain. Although the electrical activity of the heart had been recorded from skin electrodes for many years, Berger's report in 1929 that electrical waves could be recorded from the scalp (the first published recording, obtained from Berger's young son, is reproduced in Fig. 25.9), and his interpretation that they represented the activity of the brain, were greeted with incredulity and even derision.

The evidence for the nervous origin of "Berger's waves" included the demonstration that the regular rhythms present in a subject resting quietly with eyes closed are replaced by low-amplitude random waves when the subject opens his or her eyes. Within a few years disbelief gave way to acceptance as many leading neurophysiologists, including Edgar Adrian of Cambridge, confirmed and extended the findings. In analogy with the electrocardiogram (ECG) recorded from the heart, "Berger's waves" came to be called the electroencephalogram (EEG).

Some Definitions

These early studies established that the dominant rhythm in the resting subject is 8–13 cycles per second, and is most prominent when the recording leads are over the occipital lobe of the brain (where the primary visual cortex is located; see Chap. 16). This is called the *alpha rhythm*. The replacement of these waves during arousal was termed *alpha blocking*. It was surmised that the alpha rhythm is due to populations of brain cells acting periodically in *synchrony*, and that the low-voltage fast waves

during alpha blocking are due to *desynchronized* activity, as different cells become active in different ways during waking.

Subsequent work has enabled researchers to identify several types of EEG rhythms and correlate them with different levels of awakeness and sleep. Some characteristic patterns are shown in Fig. 25.10. Note that the largest-amplitude synchronous waves are present during deepest sleep. By EEG criteria, therefore, we refer to deep sleep as *S sleep* (for synchronous or slow-wave), and light sleep as *D sleep* (for desynchronous). A desynchronized EEG can also signify *arousal* or *waking*. Thus the EEG patterns are clues to fundamentally different levels of activity of the brain as they relate to waking and sleeping. Since observation of an animal is often not sufficient to characterize its levels of consciousness, the EEG has served as an overall monitor of brain states, especially in animals subjected to various experimental procedures.

Mechanism of the EEG

The cellular basis of the EEG has been the subject of intense study. The problem has two parts: how is the rhythm generated, and how do the potentials arise?

The Thalamic Rhythm Generator. The EEG rhythm is believed to arise mainly in the thalamus. The first comprehensive theory setting forth this concept was reported by S. Andersson of Sweden and Per Andersen of Norway in 1968. They suggested that the cortical cells are driven by cells of the thalamic nuclei, and that the rhythms arise as properties of synaptic circuits within the thalamus. These circuits provided for the gating of impulse output by means of inhibitory feedback through interneurons, in analogy with the generation of rhythmic motor output as a product of circuit properties (cf. Chap. 20).

Subsequent work has extended this concept in two ways: first, the thalamic circuits are recognized to include both the specific relay nuclei (such as the lateral geniculate nucleus) and the nonspecific reticular tha-

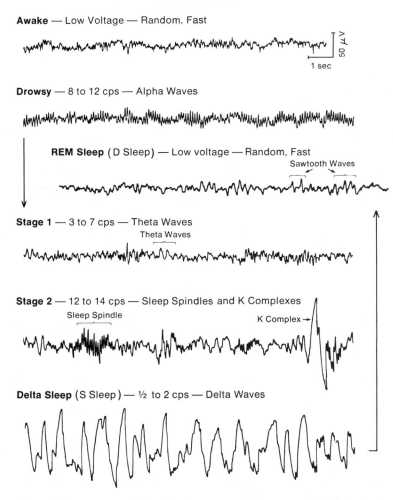

Fig. 25.10 Stages of sleep, as recorded in the electroencephalogram of the human. See text. (Modified from Hauri, 1977)

lamic nucleus. The latter receives three types of input: (1) that from the brainstem reticular system (see below); (2) collaterals of specific thalamocortical relay neurons; and (3) cortical pyramidal neurons. The intrinsic organization of the thalamic nuclei consists mainly of inhibitory dendrodendritic and axodendritic synapses; the output is directed solely at the specific relay nuclei, and is also inhibitory. Thus, the reticular neurons constitute a special system for inhibitory control of the thalamic relay neurons, and, through them, of thalamocortical circuits.

Second, the membrane properties of thalamic neurons have been revealed by electrophysiological analysis in in vitro slice.

preparations. Henrik Jahnsen and Rodolfo Llinás in New York have shown that the thalamic neurons have two modes of impulse firing. In one mode, the resting membrane potential is relatively hyperpolarized, and the cell fires in brief bursts at a rate of 6 per second. In the other mode, the resting membrane potential is relatively depolarized, and the cell fires at a rate of 8–12 per second, the range of the alpha rhythm. These two modes of firing depend on different ion channels being differentially activated at these membrane potential levels. The membrane potential in turn is controlled by the synaptic inputs. Our present understanding of the ionic and synaptic mechanisms is summarized in Fig. 25.11.

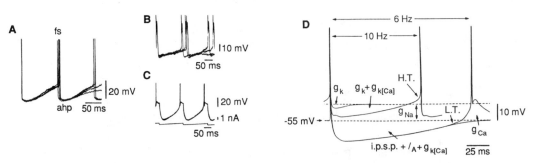

Fig. 25.11 Oscillatory properties of thalamic neurons. **A.** Recordings of 9- to 10-Hz oscillations. The fast Na$^+$ spike (fs) is followed by an afterhyperpolarization (ahp) generated by a voltage-sensitive K$^+$ conductance (g_K), and a Ca^{2+}-dependent K$^+$ conductance ($g_{K[Ca]}$). The membrane conductance is brought back to the threshold for the fast spike by the slow Na$^+$ conductance because the voltage-sensitive K$^+$ conductance is reduced after the preceding ahp. **B.** An oscillation of 6 Hz is produced as a rebound response following a short hyperpolarizing pulse (not shown). This oscillation was facilitated by the presence of 4-aminopyridine (4-AP) in the bath. **C.** An oscillation of 6 Hz was generated by ramp hyperpolarizing potentials; 6 Hz is the range frequency that the cells follow most readily. **D.** Summary diagram of oscillatory mechanisms in the thalamus. In addition to the 10-Hz oscillations generated solely by the membrane conductance as shown in A, slower oscillations (about 6 Hz) can occur (shown in B and C) by facilitating rebound excitation or by repeated hyperpolarizing potentials simulating IPSPs. The initial spike is followed by a marked hyperpolarization produced by a synaptic inhibiton or by voltage- and Ca-dependent conductances. The hyperpolarization deinactivates the transient K$^+$ current, I_A, which increases the duration of the ahp. This ahp deinactivates the low-threshold Ca^{2+} conductance, generating a rebound low-threshold spike (lts) which triggers the process once again. L.T. and H.T. are the thresholds for lts and fs, respectively. (Figure and legend reproduced from Jahnsen and Llinás, 1985)

These studies thus provide evidence for the membrane properties and circuit organization that generate the rhythmic input to the cortex. We will discuss below how this thalamic apparatus is activated and modulated by brainstem systems.

Generation of Cortical Potentials. The first interpretation of EEG potentials was that the waves represent the envelope of summed impulses of many cells in the region of the cortex beneath a recording electrode. However, beginning in the 1950s, evidence began to accumulate in favor of the importance of synaptic activity, and it is now clear that the waves represent mostly the contributions of summed synaptic potentials in the apical dendrites of the cortical cells.

How can the activity of cells within the brain give rise to electrical potentials detectable on the surface of the scalp? The explanation is somewhat similar to the interpretation of the electrocardiogram. The rhythmic contractions of the heart are brought about by a sequence of impulses in the muscle cells and conducting fibers (Chap. 18). Each impulse discharge is so powerful and so synchronous that it gives rise to electric current that flows not only through the heart itself, but also throughout the tissues of the body. A similar argument applies to the EEG waves, except that they are much smaller in amplitude (50 μV compared with 1 mV) and have faster and more irregular rhythms. These differences reflect the fact that the populations of cells giving rise to the EEG waves are much more diverse than the muscle cells in the heart.

Figure 25.12 summarizes these various lines of evidence regarding the cellular basis of the EEG waves. The thalamic nucleus below generates the rhythmic output of the thalamocortical cells projecting to the cortex. The rhythms arise as a consequence of the intrinsic pacemaker property of cells within the nucleus and the network of ex-

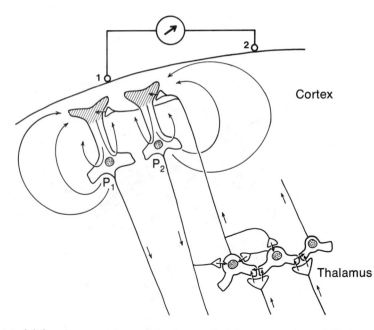

Fig. 25.12   Model for the synaptic organization underlying generation of EEG waves. The model depicts the local circuits of the thalamus, which generate a rhythmic output to the cortex. Within the cortex, the model depicts synchronous EPSPs (shaded) in the distal dendrites of cortical pyramidal cells P_1 and P_2. This generates pathways of electrical current flow as indicated by the arrows. The flow of extracellular current past electrodes 1 and 2 generates a voltage drop which is recorded as a potential difference between the two electrodes, resulting in the EEG.

citatory and inhibitory synaptic connections as discussed above.

In the cortex, the thalamic input causes rhythmic synaptic depolarization (EPSPs) of the apical dendrites of cortical pyramidal cells. This gives rise to current flows within the dendrites (the electrotonic spread of the EPSPs toward the cell bodies, to affect impulse generation). It also gives rise to flows of extracellular current, some of which follow a return path just outside the dendrites. The more synchronous the activity and densely packed the dendrites, the more return current will be pushed out into the surrounding tissue, including the cranium and scalp. As indicated in the diagram of Fig. 25.12, the difference between the amount of current flowing past recording electrode 1 compared with recording electrode 2 is registered as a voltage deflection in the EEG. If pyramidal cell P1 and cell P2 are both active in synchrony, their currents will summate, and the waves will be large. This is the situation in S sleep, and

also applies to alpha rhythms and other prominent waves. On the other hand, if the thalamic nucleus drives cell P1 in a way different from that of P2, the two cells will be asynchronous in their activity and their currents will not summate. This would be the situation during arousal or during D sleep.

This schema should be regarded as a working hypothesis for bringing together the main elements contributing to EEG waves, as an aid for understanding the application of the EEG to the study of waking and sleeping, discussed in the following section.

Early Studies of Sleep and Arousal

Sleep as a Passive State

Like circadian rhythms, sleep invited no close study until very recently. The first experimental investigations of brain mechanisms were carried out by the Belgian

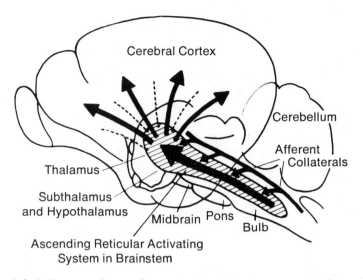

Ascending Reticular Activating
System in Brainstem

Fig. 25.13 Simplified diagram of ascending reticular activating system in the cat brain. (From Starzl et al., 1951)

neurologist Frederick Bremer, in the 1930s. He performed transections at many different levels of the brainstem in cats. Such lesions had been made for many years to produce different degrees of paralysis and hyperexcitability of spinal reflexes, but Bremer turned his attention to their effects on the head end of the animal. He found that with low transections, through the medulla and pons, a cat shows normal waking and sleeping cycles, but with high transections, through the midbrain, permanent somnolence ensues. These experiments pointed to the importance of the midbrain–pontine region for mechanisms of arousal.

Arousal and sleeping are behaviors involving the whole animal. As mentioned in the previous chapter, such behaviors require a central system with widespread connections. The first evidence for this came from experiments in which stimulating electrodes were placed in different parts of the thalamus. Stimulation of the specific sensory relay nuclei produced responses restricted to the appropriate sensory areas of the cortex. However, stimulation of other sites produced responses which were widespread throughout all cortical regions, and which increased in amplitude during repetitive stimulation. These sites were identified as the *nonspecific thalamic nuclei,* and the

responses were termed *recruiting responses.*

The brainstem system and its linkage to the thalamic system were discovered by Guiseppi Moruzzi of Italy and Horace Magoun of Los Angeles in 1949. They mapped the brainstem using electrical shocks, and showed that high-frequency simulation in the core of the brainstem produces arousal responses in the cortex. The sites of stimulation were correlated in general with the *reticular formation,* extending from the medulla to the diencephalon, as indicated in the well-known diagram of Fig. 25.13. Further experiments showed that lesions of the reticular formation produce a state of deep sleep, and that they also block the arousal that is usually produced by somatosensory stimulation. It was known that specific sensory fibers send collaterals to the brainstem reticular–nonspecific thalamus region. These studies thus suggested the very attractive hypothesis that arousal is mediated by the *reticular activating system,* stimulated by sensory collaterals, and activated through the nonspecific thalamic nuclei.

Sleep as an Active State

The idea that sleep is a simple state involving only a lack of arousal was soon disproven, however. In a classical study in 1953, Edward Aserinsky, a graduate student, and Nathaniel Kleitman, who had spent almost a lifetime amassing data on sleep, did a very simple experiment: they recorded the eye movements of sleeping subjects. This may seem a strange thing to do, but they explained the rationale in the beginning of their paper:

One is led to suspect that the activity of the extra-ocular musculature and the lids might be peculiarly sensitive indicators of CNS changes associated with the sleep–wakefulness cycle. The disproportionately large cortical areas involved in eye movements, the well-defined secondary vestibular pathways to the extra-ocular nuclei, and the low innervation ratio of the eye muscles point to at least a quantitative basis for their reflection of general CNS activity. A more specific relationship . . . is suggested by anatomical proximity of the oculomotor nuclei to a pathway involved in maintaining the waking state . . .

The reader may wish to review some of these points of anatomy in Chaps. 14, 16, and 22.

People had previously observed that the eyes rotate upward and outward, and that there are eye movements, during sleep. However, no one had studied the eye movements carefully and correlated them with the depth of sleep throughout an entire night. It is another of those experiments which could have been done, to some extent, by the ancients, but had to wait until modern times. Aserinsky and Kleitman found indeed that, after falling into deep sleep, subjects went through alternating periods of *light sleep* and *deep sleep;* that light sleep is associated with *rapid eye movements,* and that subjects awakened at these times reported that they had been *dreaming.* These findings showed that sleep contains alternating periods of light and deep sleep, and that light sleep is associated with a modified state of *arousal,* in which the heart rate increases, but skeletal muscles seem paralyzed. They showed that dreams occur during light sleep, and suggested that "the rapid eye movements are

directly associated with visual imagery in dreaming."

Stages of Sleep

These findings were soon independently confirmed by William Dement, then at Chicago. In 1957, Dement and Kleitman together then carefully characterized the different stages of the EEG and correlated them with the levels of sleep, as already indicated in Fig. 25.10. They could then follow the EEG patterns through a night of sleep, and relate them accurately to the occurrence of rapid eye movements, body movements, and dreaming. A typical correlation is shown in Fig. 25.14. Note that sleep always begins with an initial period of deep sleep, the deepest sleep of the night; there then ensues a sequence of light and deep sleep, in which deep sleep becomes less deep and light sleep becomes more prolonged; rapid eye movements are invariably associated with light sleep and a stage I EEG.

The terminology for light and deep sleep has evolved to reflect the associated changes in the EEG, eye movements, and other behavior. Thus, deep sleep is referred to as *S sleep* (for slow-wave EEG activity). Light sleep is referred to as *D sleep* (for desynchronized EEG activity; also for dreaming). Light sleep also has other names; *REM sleep* (for its associated rapid eye movements); *emergent stage I sleep* (because it emerges in the wake of deep sleep); and *paradoxical sleep* (because the EEG activity resembles that in the awake state, but the individual is hard to arouse).

Neuronal Systems Controlling Sleep and Waking

These studies in humans showed that sleep has a complicated internal structure which includes periods of arousal that share some properties with arousal during waking. It became clear that sleep involves more than a simple turning off of arousal, and likely involves the interaction of several neuronal subsystems. A great number of animal experiments (mostly in cats) ensued in the

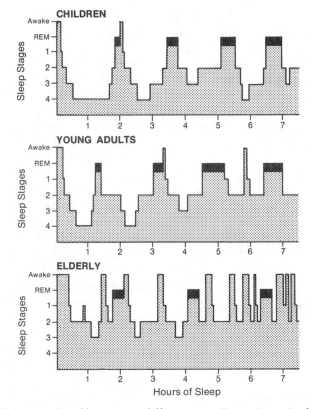

Fig. 25.14 Normal sleep cycles of humans at different ages. Dreaming episodes indicated by black bars. Note deeper sleep of children, more frequent periods of waking in the elderly. Sleep stages judged by EEG criteria. (From Kales and Kales, 1974)

1960s and 1970s in the attempt to identify these subsystems. Michael Jouvet in France, in particular, carried out an extensive series of studies on the effects of lesions of specific brainstem structures. These and other studies have combined assays for different transmitter substances, and the effects of transmitter agonists and antagonists. Other experiments have involved stimulation of specific brainstem and basal forebrain regions, and unit recordings from cells in these regions.

To review adequately all these studies would take an entire chapter in itself. Instead, we will summarize them in relation to Fig. 25.15. This diagram depicts the main regions that have been shown to be involved in either arousal or sleep. Let us review each region briefly.

Arousal Regions

High-frequency electrical stimulation is most effective in bringing about arousal and D sleep when it is applied to the *pontine reticular formation* (Pons, in Fig. 25.15) as in the experiments of Moruzzi and Magoun. The most effective sites are in the gigantocellular tegmental fields, whose neurons branch widely throughout the brainstem. A second arousal area is the *locus ceruleus*. As discussed in Chap. 24, this nucleus contains the noradrenergic neurons whose axons branch widely and innervate most of the forebrain, cerebellum, and spinal cord. Jouvet (1974) showed that destruction of the locus ceruleus selectively eliminates D sleep in cats. A third center related to arousal is the dopami-

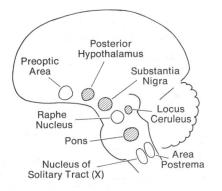

Fig. 25.15 Summary diagram showing regions of the brain that have been reported to be involved in controlling arousal or sleep. Arousal centers indicated by shaded areas, sleep centers by open areas.

nergic system of fibers arising in the *substantia nigra* and nearby midbrain. Lesions of these fibers in cats render the animals comatose. However, EEG arousal can still be elicited by sensory stimulation, and the effect of the lesions is not seen in rats, suggesting that the dopaminergic fibers may be more involved in the initiation of locomotor activity than with arousal itself. Finally, there is evidence that the *basal forebrain* also contributes to arousal mechanisms; stimulation in the hypothalamus is very effective in producing arousal, and ablations of the posterior hypothalamus, as first reported by Walle Nauta in Holland in 1946, produce prolonged somnolence. However, these effects may be due in part to the fibers of the median forebrain bundle, particularly the fibers in this bundle that connect brainstem nuclei and the forebrain.

Sleep Regions

A number of studies have pointed to the importance of the serotonergic cells of the brainstem *raphe nuclei* in mediating deep sleep. Destruction of the raphe nuclei produces cats that cannot sleep (i.e., insomnia). A parallel pharmacological experiment consists of blocking serotonin synthesis with the drug *p*-chlorophenylalanine (PCPA), which inhibits tryptophan hydrox-

ylase. This also produces insomnia, an effect which is alleviated by administration of serotonin. A second brainstem region is the *nucleus of the solitary tract,* which receives sensory fibers from the taste buds of the tongue (Chap. 11) as well as other visceral inputs. Stimulation of this region promotes a synchronization of the EEG. A related region is the *area postrema.* This area is special in that it has no blood–brain barrier, and thus can be stimulated directly by substances in the blood; toxic substances that enter the bloodstream elicit vomiting by acting on the cells in this region. Serotonin applied to this area modulates the influence of the nucleus of the solitary tract on sleep. The mechanisms of these two regions are not understood, but they may mediate some of the effects of feeding, metabolism, and visceral activities in inducing sleep.

Finally, in the *basal forebrain,* lesions of the *preoptic region* produce insomnia, and electrical stimulation of this region induces EEG synchrony and drowsiness leading to sleep. Bremer in 1970 showed that preoptic stimulation reduces the arousal induced by stimulation of the reticular activating system.

Neuronal Mechanisms: A Synthesis

The foregoing account does not indicate the numerous controversies that have arisen in attempting to assess the contributions of each of these regions to the control of sleeping and waking. At the very least, we can say that the regions depicted in Fig. 25.15 form a distributed system involved in this control. In this system, the three brainstem centers (pons, locus ceruleus, and raphe), each using a specific transmitter, seem to be of special importance. It is attractive to suggest, as Jouvet and others have done, that arousal is associated with activity in the noradrenergic fibers, and deep sleep is associated with activity in serotonergic fibers, but this by itself does not provide a satisfactory explanation.

A coherent explanation for the neural

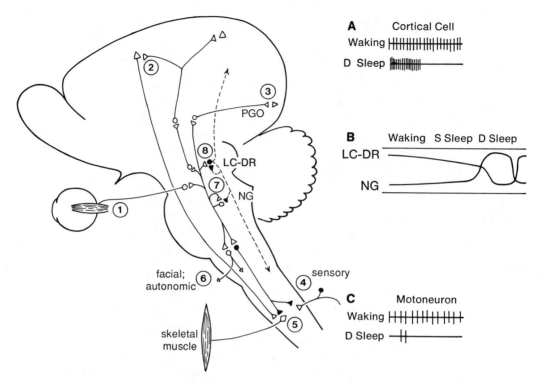

Fig. 25.16 Central circuits and neural activity involved in mediating D sleep, based on accumulated evidence from experiments in cats. The numbered sites ① through ⑧ are discussed in the text. **A.** Recordings from a cortical cell (site ②). **B.** Changes in impulse frequency of cells in locus ceruleus–dorsal raphe (LC-DR) ⑧ and nucleus gigantocellularis (NG) ⑦ during wake–sleep cycle. **C.** Recordings from a motoneuron (site ⑤). For full explanation, see text. (Based on Hobson and McCarley, 1977, and other sources)

basis of sleeping and waking states must characterize the specific changes in behavior, correlate these with different centers in the brain, and identify the circuits that connect the centers and thereby form the distributed systems for the different states. A proposal that attempts to do this for D sleep is summarized in Fig. 25.16. Each numbered site indicates a neural substrate that has been implicated in a function that is altered in D sleep. Let us consider each briefly:

① Phasic activation of motoneurons to the extraocular muscles produces rapid eye movements (REM).

② Generalized activation of the forebrain through the reticular formation produces bursting activity in forebrain re-

gions (see recordings in A); this may be associated with the production of dream images.

③ Phasic activation of the visual pathway by means of PGO spikes (i.e., pons–lateral geniculate–occipital cortex) possibly contributes to visual imagery.

④ Inhibition of sensory input raises the threshold for arousal; this is why a person who is dreaming is hard to awaken.

⑤ Inhibition of motoneurons raises the reflex threshold and suppresses internally generated movements by cortical and brainstem motor centers (see recordings in C); this is why we lie most quietly during dreaming.

⑥ Activation and inhibition of various brainstem neurons produces phasic fine movements of facial muscles (possibly expressing the emotional content of dreams); tonic autonomic contraction of the bladder and rectal sphincters; intermittent bursts of activity in the cardiovascular, respiratory, and other parts of the autonomic nervous system; and penile erection.

The cyclic relation between waking, S sleep, and D sleep is believed to involve interactions between the nucleus gigantocellularis (NG) neurons and neurons of the locus ceruleus (LC) and dorsal raphe (DR). In the model of Alan Hobson and Robert McCarley (1977):

⑦ NG neurons are reexcitatory to themselves; and

⑧ They also excite LC–DR neurons.

The LC–DR neurons are in turn inhibitory to themselves and to the NG neurons. With appropriate time delays for the onset and buildup of activity in these two neuronal populations, the activity in the two populations alternates in relation to the different stages of waking and sleeping, as indicated in the graph in B.

The centers and pathways summarized in Fig. 25.16 constitute the main outlines of the distributed system that is responsible for D sleep. The diagram provides a working hypothesis for understanding how the different physiological functions arise from properties of brainstem neurons and their synaptic connections, and how reciprocal interactions between brainstem centers could give rise to the sequence of waking and sleeping.

26

Visceral Brains:
Feeding

Among the many types of behavior in which animals engage, two in particular stand out: feeding and mating. Feeding is necessary for the survival of the individual organism, and mating is necessary for the reproduction and propagation of the species. A good proportion of other types of behavior, such as predation and flight, or grooming and courtship, have their significance as preludes or consequences of these two fundamental activities.

A basic distinction between animal and plant life is that animals procure their food and find their mates by *active* rather than passive means. Much of the sensory apparatus is tuned to receiving stimuli from sources of food or mates, and much of the motor apparatus is adapted for moving the animal to those sources and ingesting food or copulating with a mate. The motor behavior thus has two phases: an *appetitive* phase, during which the animal has an appetite for something and seeks to find it, and a *consummatory* phase, in which the goal is achieved and the appetite is satisfied. These phases, in fact, can be recognized in even the simplest kinds of motor acts; Sherrington (1906), for example, in studying the scratch reflex, noted that the cat first brings the leg to the site that itches (the appetitive phase) and then carries out the scratching (the consummatory phase). In the cases of complex behaviors like feeding and mating, the sensory and motor mechanisms for the two phases are of course quite different, and the temporal sequence may be quite prolonged. Although it is impossible to generalize adequately across all species, the sequence usually begins with waiting or search and proceeds through collection or capture, acceptance or rejection, and finally ingestion.

Ingested food typically enters an intestinal tract, where is is digested and the nutrient substances are absorbed into the bloodstream, in order to satisfy the needs of the body for hydration, mineral balance, and nutrition. These factors are kept in balance within the body by homeostatic mechanisms which maintain the "constancy of the internal milieu," one of the basic principles of body function first formulated by the great French physiologist, Claude Bernard, in the nineteenth century. The ingested foodstuffs provide the raw materials and sources of energy for these mechanisms. The whole sequence of feeding, from search to absorption, is under close control at every stage by a combination of nervous and hormonal mechanisms, and the parts of the central nervous system that mediate this control may be referred to as the "visceral nervous system" or "visceral brain." This is under control of the autonomic nervous system, as discussed in Chap. 18. The activities of the visceral brain are coordinated with the rest of the nervous system by a variety of centers which, in vertebrates, are called the limbic system. The relations between these systems will be discussed further in subsequent chapters in this section.

The fact that feeding is crucial for survival and requires a complicated series of actions means that each link in the chain is subject to the forces of natural selection. Each link can be adjusted for the greatest efficiency and advantage for a particular species, and the whole chain can undergo many permutations in different species. Therefore, when we study feeding, we are dealing with nervous mechanisms that, perhaps more than any others in the brain, most directly and vividly reflect the forces of evolution acting in the daily life of the animal.

The diversity of nervous mechanisms, which we have so often noted, is therefore nowhere more evident than in the control of feeding behavior. Animals have explored a wide range of food sources, and have devised the most clever strategies for catching and consuming them. In this chapter we will consider examples that have been particularly well studied and illustrate some of the more general principles of nervous control by central systems.

INVERTEBRATES

In introductory biology, we learn that the great chain of life begins with the simple plantlike microorganisms called phytoplankton, unicellular algae that float in the sea and are capable of capturing the energy of light and using it to manufacture organic compounds, the process called photosynthesis. The phytoplankton are present in enormous numbers in most bodies of water, and form what has been called an "aquatic pasture." The simplest animals, the amebalike zooplankton, feed on this pasture. The higher animals, the metazoans, thus have three possible sources of food. One is the nutrient-rich fluids secreted or contained within other organisms; these animals are called *fluid-feeders*. Another is the microorganisms of the sea; animals that feed on them are said to be *microphagous*. Larger animals may feed on each other, in which case they are said to be *macrophagous* (see Table 26.1).

One of the most efficient methods for microphagous feeding is to let seawater flow through the animal so that the plankton can be filtered out. This method is appropriately called *filter feeding*. In many invertebrates the microorganisms are trapped in secretions and moved to the digestive tract by ciliary motion. In small aquatic arthropods, which generally lack cilia, filter feeding is achieved by an ingenious use of the limbs. As shown in Fig. 26.1, the swimming motions of the limbs create currents which cause the water to circulate through

Table 26.1 Types of feeding by animals

Fluid feeding	Microphagy (small particles)	Macrophagy (large particles)
Bacterial	Filter feeding (some sponges; some arthropods)	Herbivores (cows, horses)
Planktonic		
Scavenging (some nematodes)	Deposit feeding (some annelid worms)	Carnivores (predators such as many molluscs, arthropods, vertebrates)
Predatory (some arachnids; some insects, such as flies and mosquitoes)		

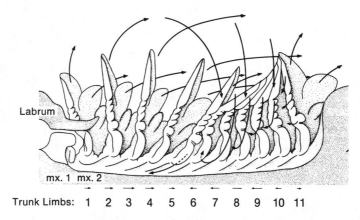

Fig. 26.1 Currents of water created by swimming and feeding movements of the simmerets of a crustacean *Branchinella*. Arrows below show direction and relative strength of limb movements; in this example, limb 5 is just completing its backward stroke, while limb 6 is just beginning to move forward. Hairlike setae on surface of limbs are not shown. The motor mechanisms controlling swimmeret movements are discussed in Chap. 21. (From Cannon, in Barrington, 1979)

the limbs and over the opening of the mouth, before passing backward to propel the animal forward. The food is trapped by fine hairlike setules, and then passed forward to be filtered out by the mucus-covered setae around the mouth.

This provides a very nice example of how motor mechanisms serve multiple uses. We previously described in Chap. 20 the neural mechanisms for generating the orderly beating of the crustacean swimmerets. This metachronal rhythm is equally efficient for moving food and for propelling the animal. As E. J. W. Barrington pointed out in 1979:

. . . the mechanisms involved (in filter feeding) are unexcelled for the precision and beauty of their adaptive organization. . . . The animal economically employs the limbs simultaneously for feeding as well as locomotion, while their delicate structure enables them also to serve for respiratory exchange.

Stomatogastric Nervous System of the Lobster

Filter feeding is widespread among small aquatic animals, especially crustacea and molluscs. It has been estimated that an oyster may filter up to 40 liters of water in an hour, from which it obtains less than a tenth of a gram of nutrients. Larger animals obviously need more ample sources of nourishment, and many species acquire this by consuming other large animals. This sets up one of the fundamental polarizations of animal life—the predator and its prey. Successful predation requires adequate size, speed, strength, and other capabilities, and therefore has been one of the main pressures leading to complex behaviors mediated by complex nervous systems. Since animals do not particularly enjoy being eaten, the same pressures work on animals that are prey. The behaviors must be almost evenly matched, in order to maintain the ecological balance that is necessary between predators and their food supply.

Feeding on large bodies is called macrophagy (Table 26.1). It is well-exemplified by our old friend, the lobster, and its freshwater cousin, the crayfish. The claws of the lobster are specialized for grasping, cutting, and crushing prey, and bringing the pieces to the mouth. The food is thus highly variable in its composition, containing many hard parts as well as soft tissue. The foregut is adapted for dealing with this mixture of ingested material. As shown in Fig. 26.2, the stomach is divided into three parts.

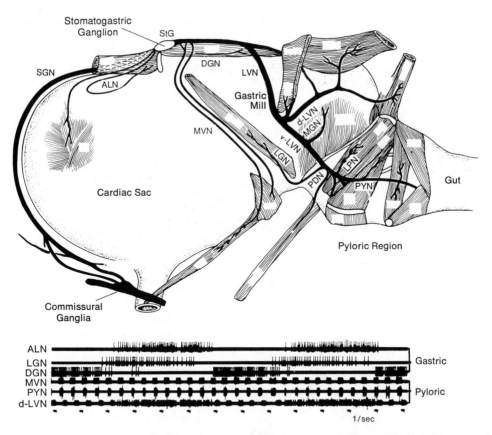

Fig. 26.2 The main regions of the lobster stomatogastric system, together with their nerve supply and some of the muscles. Recordings from nerves labeled in the diagram are shown in the traces below. These are extracellular recordings in the deafferented stomatogastric ganglion of impulse activity in motoneurons supplying their respective nerves. Abbreviations: ALN, anterior lateral nerve; DGN, dorsal gastric nerve; LGN, lateral gastric nerve; LPN, lateral pyloric nerve; LVN, lateral ventricular nerve (d. dorsal; v, ventral); MVN, median ventricular nerve; PDN, pyloric dilator nerve; PYN, pyloric constrictor nerve; SGN, stomatogastric nerve. (Modified from Selverston, 1976)

Foodstuff passing through the esophagus first enters the *cardiac sac,* which is mainly a large storage area. From here it passes to the *gastic mill,* which contains three calcified ossicles which function like sharp teeth. Muscles of the gastric mill wall move the teeth, to grind, macerate, and chew the food. In this way, the gastric mill functions like the vertebrate jaw. The food then passes to the *pyloric region,* where it is further churned by muscular contractions, squeezed between platelike ossicles, and subjected to the actions of digestive enzymes, before passing into the remainder of the gut where the nutrients are absorbed into the blood-

stream and the waste materials are eliminated.

The muscles of the gastric mill and pyloric region are under control of nerves that originate in neurons of the *stomatogastric ganglion.* This ganglion has an unusual location, being plastered against the inside wall of the nearby ophthalmic artery that runs to the eye. There seems to be no special significance to this location other than that it is near the stomach. Experimentally, the ganglion can be exposed by making a slit in the artery from above, removing the wall beneath the ganglion, and dissecting away the periganglionic sheath. Under the dissecting microscope the nerve cell bodies can be seen to be quite large, between 40 and 90 μm in diameter; like so many invertebrate ganglia, many of the cells are identifiable by size and location, and can be recorded from using intracellular electrodes.

The attractiveness of this preparation for studying the nervous control of the stomach rhythms was recognized by Don Maynard, and has been exploited by Allan Selverston and his colleagues at San Diego to the extent that it is one of the best understood of all invertebrate neuronal systems. The synaptic connections between neurons within the ganglion have already been mentioned in Chap. 4; as discussed there, the connections include microcircuits between neighboring dendrites that are similar to those seen in other systems, including the vertebrate retina and olfactory bulb.

There are two main rhythms in the stomach, related to the gastric mill and the pyloric region. Recordings from the nerves to the gastric mill muscles (ALN, LGN, and DGN in Fig. 26.2) show slow prolonged impulse discharges lasting several seconds, and occurring at intervals of 6–8 seconds. The discharges to antagonist muscles controlling the teeth alternate with each other, as shown in Fig. 26.2. In contrast, the nerves to pyloric muscles (MVN, PYN, and d-LVN) fire in briefer bursts of impulses, at more frequent intervals of less than a second.

The main focus of experimental work has been on understanding the nature of these rhythms. With regard to the *gastric mill,* it has been found that there are 10 motoneurons and 2 interneurons within the stomatogastric ganglion that are involved in generating the slow rhythm of impulse firing the muscle contractions. In completely isolated ganglia, the rhythmic firing is usually abolished, indicating that it is normally dependent on excitatory input from sensory fibers. Intracellular analysis has enabled the main functional connections between the 12 cells to be identified. No spontaneous bursting cell has been found, suggesting that the gastric rhythms are a property of the whole network, of the type that we discussed in Chap. 20.

The neural system controlling the *pyloric muscles* is composed of 13 motoneurons and one interneuron. Their names, numbers, and abbreviations are given in Table 26.2. John Miller and Allan Selverston (1985) were able to dissect apart this circuit and identify the contributions of each cell type to the pyloric rhythm, by using a photoinactivation procedure. This consists of injecting a fluorescent dye, such as Lucifer Yellow, into a cell; after the dye diffuses throughout the cell, a laser microbeam is aimed through the preparation at a specific part of the neuron or its dendritic tree. In this way the effect of inactivation of an entire neuron or a dendritic branch on the generation of a circuit property such as a rhythm can be assessed.

The neural basis of the pyloric rhythm was reconstructed on the basis of this method and the known synaptic connec-

Table 26.2 Pyloric neurons in the stomatogastric ganglion

Neuron	Number	Axon location	Function	Approximate phase
Anterior burster (AB)	1	stomatogastric nerve (SGN)	?	0
Pyloric dilator (PD)	2	pyloric dilator nerve (PDN)	dilates pylorus	0
Lateral pyloric (LP)	1	lateral pyloric nerve (LPN)	constricts pylorus	0.5
Ventricular dilator (VD)	1	median ventricular nerve (MVN)	dilates ventricle	0.75
Inferior cardiac (IC)	1	median ventricular nerve (MVN)	?	0.5
Pyloric (PY)[a]	8	pyloric nerve (PYN)	constricts pylorus	0.65

[a]Two classes.

From Miller and Selverston, in Selverston (1985)

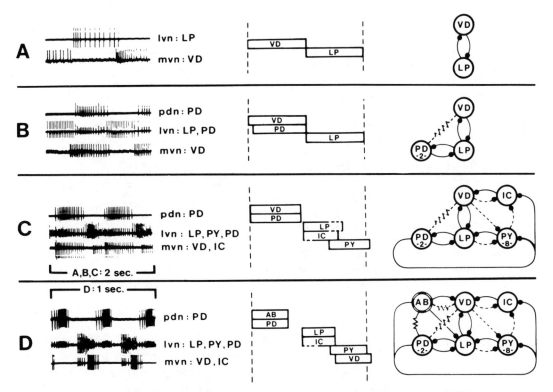

Fig. 26.3 Idealized reconstruction of the pyloric central pattern generator, based on selective inactivation of identified neurons by the dye-sensitized photoinactivation technique. **A.** System reduced to only ventricular dilator (VD) and lateral pyloric (LP) neuron (right) generates spontaneous rhythm (middle and left). **B.** System includes pyloric dilator (PD) cells. **C.** System enlarged to include IC and PY cells, which reinforce the pacemaker activity. **D.** Complete system includes anterior burster (AB) cells, which add further precision and overall control to the firing patterns. All abbreviations in Fig. 26.2 and Table 26.2. In the diagrams on the right, inhibitory chemical synapses are small filled terminals, electrical synapses are zig-zag lines, weak connections are dashed lines. (From Miller and Selverston, 1982)

tions between the cells, as summarized in Fig. 26.3. In A, all cells but the VD and LP cells were inactivated. These two cells nonetheless generated a rhythm of alternating bursts due to their mutual inhibitory connections. This is an example of the reciprocal inhibitory half-center model (see Fig. 20.3). In B, one of the PD cells is added, so to speak, to the circuit. It fires in synchrony with VD, because it is also connected to LP with reciprocal inhibition, and has in addition weak electrical coupling with VD. In C, the system includes IC and PY neurons. The IC cell is not connected to LP and therefore fires out of phase with it, but its timing is variable because of the

weaker inhibitory inputs from VD and PY (dashed lines) and the inhibition from the more distant PD cell. The PY cells fire slightly later than LP–IC because they do not fire until their inhibition of LP has worn off. Finally, the entire circuit includes the interneuron AB, as shown in D, which is electrotonically coupled to PD.

This analysis allowed three basic properties of the pyloric rhythm to be understood in terms of their neuronal basis. As summarized by Miller and Selverston (1985):

. . . The *existence* of the pyloric pattern results from oscillatory membrane properties of the individual neurons in combination with the multiple reciprocally inhibitory interactions within the network. The precise *phase relationships* derive from the synaptic connectivity circuit and depend on relative synaptic efficacies, postinhibitory rebound properties, and the kinetics of the plateau potential and BPP generation mechanisms [BPP = "bursting pacemaker potentials"; cyclic voltage changes due to cyclic conductance changes]. The overall *cycle frequency* is determined largely by the AB interneuron via its strong intrinsic oscillatory currents and its very strong synapses with the rest of the pyloric neurons.

It is clear that the pyloric pattern produced by an isolated nervous system represents the fundamental pattern. However, the *in vivo* behavior of the pyloric region is strongly influenced by sensory feedback and endogenous modulatory substances. The identification and physiological action of these factors on the well-characterized pyloric network promises to yield important insights into the problem of how centrally generated patterns can be modified by the environment.

Feeding in the Blowfly

One of the best understood species with respect to feeding behavior is the blowfly. Taste receptors in the blowfly have been discussed in Chap. 13, and the motor control of the proboscis was discussed in Chap. 22. The blowfly obtains all its nutrients by sucking them in through the labellum (see Fig. 26.4). The pharynx is lined with muscles which form what is called the "cibarial pump." The ingested fluid is moved through the pharynx and into the esophagus by rhythmic contractions of the cibarial muscles. These contractions are controlled by a neuronal rhythm generator located in the brain. The food passes by peristalsis from the esophagus into both the midgut and the crop, a storage region. As food is absorbed from the midgut into the blood, it is replenished by movement of stored fluid from the crop through the crop valve and cardiac valves into the midgut.

What are the mechanisms that initiate feeding behavior? This has been studied in flies that are starved for several days. Deprivation generally enhances the locomotor

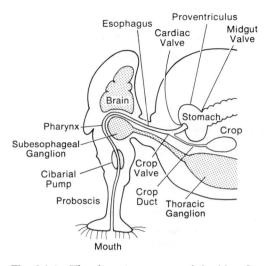

Fig. 26.4 The digestive system of the blowfly. (Modified from Dethier, 1976)

activity of the fly, which engages in bursts of activity (flying about in search of food) alternating with periods of rest. This represents a balance between maximizing the chances of finding food and the need to conserve the dwindling energy stores. When food, such as a sugar solution, is encountered, excitation of chemoreceptors on the legs (tarsae) stimulates proboscis extension, and excitation of chemoreceptors on the labellum of the proboscis stimulates sucking movements. These chemosensory stimuli are believed to be the sole excitatory inputs driving feeding behavior.

What are the mechanisms involved in terminating feeding? In order to identify these factors, many experiments have been carried out in which nerves to different part of the gut have been cut, and in which nutrients have been placed directly in different parts of the gut or removed through artificial fistulae. The outcome of these experiments appears to be that feeding is inhibited by three factors: first, the amount of peristalsis in the foregut, as sensed by stretch receptors in the gut wall; second, distention of the crop, as sensed by stretch receptors in the crop wall; and third, the amount of locomotor activity mediated by limb motoneurons in the thoracic ganglion.

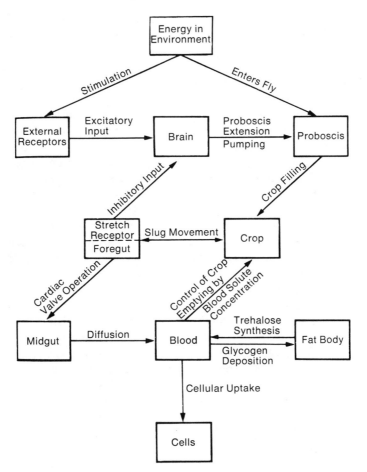

Fig. 26.5 Multiple mechanisms for regulating feeding behavior and metabolism in the blowfly. (From Gelperin, in Dethier, 1976)

These factors have the effect of raising the central threshold for incoming chemosensory stimuli, so that they become less and less effective in eliciting proboscis extension and sucking. Some of these factors, and their interrelations, are indicated in Fig. 26.5.

The surprising result emerging from these studies has been summarized by Vincent Dethier (1976) in the following way:

At no stage in ingestion does the nutritive value of food regulate intake. . . . The initiation of feeding depends on stimulating properties; the termination of feeding depends on mechanoreceptors; the emptying of the crop is regulated by osmotic properties. In the laboratory each one of these can be varied independently of the other and of caloric value. In nature the different properties tend to be correlated.

In conclusion, feeding in the insect is controlled by relatively few factors, which impinge immediately and directly on the regulation of food intake. We will see that this contrasts with most vertebrates, in which multiple factors and contingencies are involved.

VERTEBRATES

Vertebrates show interesting similarities and differences in feeding behavior among various species. Fish, for example, move about in a medium that contains their food; thus, their feeding is more or less continuous. Some terrestrial animals have similar habits; herbivores—like cows, for example—have their food literally under their noses all the time, and spend much of their waking hours ingesting or chewing. The cow munching its way through its terrestrial pasture seems rather similar to a crustacean or mollusc filter-feeding on its aquatic pasturage. In the case of the cow, the almost continuous eating makes it difficult to characterize its feeding behavior in terms of *meal size* and *meal frequency,* two of the variables we are most familiar with in our own daily lives. Nor does a third variable, *food preferences* or *aversions,* appear to be very relevant; it seems that the cow, which consumes enormous quantities of plant material in the course of a day, may simply dilute any noxious or poisonous plants to the level of harmlessness, without needing to pick and choose the way we do. Like many other terrestrial animals, especially carnivores, humans eat only intermittently. Thus meal size, meal frequency, and food preferences are important variables in our eating habits; indeed, they largely determine the rhythm of daily life.

Among vertebrates, no species has been studied more intensively with regard to all aspects of feeding behavior than the laboratory rat; in fact, the studies of the rat probably outnumber those of all other species combined. Much of this is due to the possible implications of the rat as a model of mammals in general, and humans in particular. In the practical realm, the laboratories of drug companies and government agencies test rats for the possible harmful effects of food additives or substitutes, under the premise that the effects will be relevant to humans. At the research level, psychologists for almost a century have focused their concepts (and controversies) about drives and motivation on behavioral studies of the rat, much of it in relation to feeding. Since the late 1940s, neuroscientists have exerted considerable efforts to identify the main nervous pathways and mechanisms involved. We will summarize some of this evidence first, and then discuss some implications for motivated behavior.

Feeding in the Infant Rat

Although most attention has traditionally been given to the adult, a new field of interest concerned with the development of feeding in the infant rat has emerged in recent years. This work is significant for several reasons. First, it has shown that the infant is not simply a small adult; it is a very special creature, living in a very special world, during the first few weeks of life. Second, the change from the infant to the adult pattern gives insight into processes of development and learning that provide the basis for adult feeding behavior and their neuronal mechanisms. Third, suckling at a mammary gland is the defining characteristic of all mammals, and this form of feeding is therefore important for understanding this class of animals. Finally, studies in subprimates may contribute to better understanding of suckling and infant–mother relations that are so crucial in the first days and weeks of human development.

The baby rat, called a pup, is born after about three weeks' gestation. At birth the mother occupies herself with a complex series of interrelated behaviors that create the transitional environment from womb to outside world. She consumes the placenta, licks her ventrum and nipples, and also vigorously licks the infants. Her behavior has two main functions. It imprints her ventrum and nipples with olfactory substances in her saliva, and it serves to warm, protect, and arouse the infants. The aroused infants search for and find the nipples, and begin sucking.

The act of sucking involves an extraordinary close relations between mother and infant. As shown in Fig. 26.6A, the nipple fills the mouth, and milk is ejected deep into the pharynx. Although the muscles for posture and locomotion are weak and poorly coordinated, the facial and neck muscles

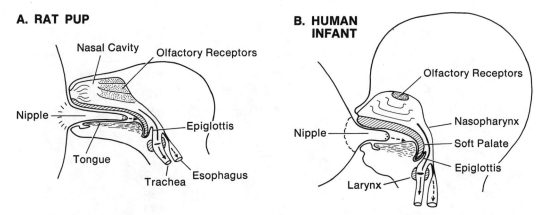

A. RAT PUP

Nasal Cavity   Olfactory Receptors

Nipple

Epiglottis

Tongue

Trachea   Esophagus

B. HUMAN INFANT

Olfactory Receptors

Nasopharynx

Nipple

Soft Palate

Epiglottis

Larynx

Fig. 26.6 Suckling in the rat pup (**A**) and in the human infant (**B**). Note that in both cases, the tip of the soft palate drops behind the back of the tongue and is held there by the epiglottis. This permits air flow between nose and trachea, while milk passes laterally around the epiglottis and into the esophagus. By this means, both the rat pup and the human infant can breathe while suckling. The high position of the larynx is maintained in the adult rat, an obligate nose breather. In the human, during infancy and childhood the pharynx grows in length and the larynx descends to its position in the neck in the adult. This elongation of the pharynx is crucial to our ability to form the different vowel sounds in human speech, as discussed in Chap. 24. (Diagram A based in part on J. Alberts, P. E. Pedersen, J. Laitman, and E. S. Crelin, personal communications; B adapted from Crelin, 1976)

involved in suckling are well developed at birth; it is, in fact, the one coordinated motor act that the infant can perform on its environment. In some mammals, the sucking contractions are so strong that the infants remain attached despite locomotion of the mother, an obvious advantage if the mother has to flee from danger. The rat pup suckles virtually continuously throughout the first two weeks of life, and intermittently for the next week or two until weaning occurs. It could well be asserted that suckling must be among the most intimate and sustained (to say nothing of beneficial) relations between two organisms to be found in the animal world.

The Odor Link in Suckling Behavior

The close proximity of the nose to the mouth suggests that the sense of smell may be an important factor in suckling, and this has been found to be the case in many species. Ablation of the olfactory bulbs at birth in rats and kittens eliminates suckling. Infants must therefore be able to smell some odor in order to suckle. Following this lead,

Elliott Blass and Martin Teicher at Johns Hopkins University washed the nipples of lactating mothers and found that this too eliminated attachment to the nipples by the pups. Dabbing the washing fluid back on the nipples reinstated suckling, as did samples of the amniotic fluid and the mother's salvia, but not saliva of virgin females. This suggests the presence of a substance in the saliva that is dependent on the hormonal status of the mother. After suckling has begun, the pups' own saliva contains the odor cue necessary to maintain suckling.

The vital link in establishing and maintaining suckling in the rat pup is thus an odor cue on the nipple. In order to analyze the kind of activity in the olfactory pathway that mediates this response, radioactively labeled 2-deoxyglucose was injected into suckling pups and autoradiographs of the olfactory bulbs were obtained by the Sokoloff method (see Chap. 8). As shown in Fig. 26.7, the most intense activity pattern in these olfactory bulbs was a small focus at the extreme dorsomedial margin of the main olfactory bulb, near its junction

A. 10 DAY OLD-SUCKLING

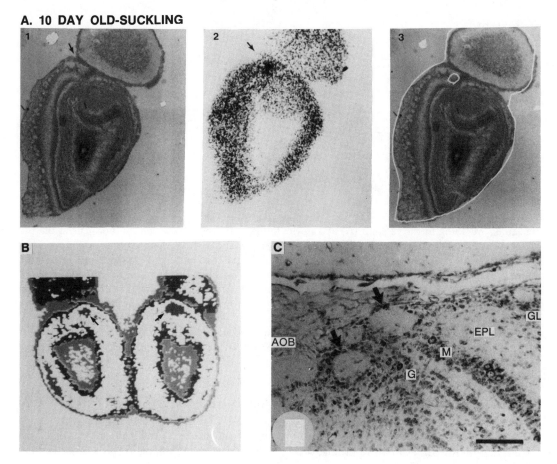

Fig. 26.7 Mapping of 2-deoxyglucose uptake in the olfactory bulb of the suckling rat pup. **A.** This 10-day-old pup was injected with [¹⁴C]2-deoxyglucose and allowed to suckle for 45 minutes. The autoradiogram (2) shows a focus at one site in the olfactory bulb; the histological correlation (1,3) shows that the site is a modified glomerulus adjacent to the accessory olfactory bulb. **B.** Computerized image analysis of an autoradiogram of 2DG uptake in the olfactory bulbs of another suckling rat pup, age 6 days. Note the bilateral foci (arrows), shown by histological correlation to be located in the modified glomerular complex. **C.** Higher-power view of the modified glomerular region in the olfactory bulb of a 12-day-old rat pup. Arrows indicate two glomeruli within the modified complex. Accessory olfactory bulb (AOB) is to the left, layers of the main olfactory bulb are to the right. Abbreviations: G, granule layer; M, mitral cell body layer; EPL, external plexiform layer; GL, glomerular layer. Bouin's fixation, stained with cresyl violet. Bar is 85 μm. (A from Teicher et al., 1980; B,C from Greer et al., 1982)

with the accessory olfactory bulb. Closer examination revealed that this is a site where the usual small, round glomeruli of the bulb are replaced by a large, irregular complex of glomeruli, an anatomically distinct region that had not previously been recognized. This was the first instance of a specific odor stimulus correlated with ac-

tivity in a specific, anatomically identified, glomerulus.

As discussed in Chap. 12, olfactory stimulation gives rise to patterns of activity in the olfactory bulb characterized by distinct foci associated with more widespread, less intense patterns. The activity shown in Fig. 26.7A,2, conforms to this pattern. One assumes that information about the suckling odor is carried both in the dense foci and the widespread pattern; by analogy, visual recognition of someone's face can be made not only from the most distinctive features (bushy eyebrows, toothy grin) but also from subtle aspects of the contours of the cheeks or wrinkles of the skin. The finding of a dense focus in the modified glomerular complex is of further interest with regard to the macroglomerular complex in the antennal lobes of insects, which is involved in processing male responses to female sexual attractant odors (Chap. 27); in both, it is hypothesized that a crucial olfactory-mediated behavior appears to have a "labeled line" to the brain.

Mother–Infant Interactions

Although the rat pup suckles continuously in the first two weeks, it does not receive milk continuously; milk is ejected from the nipple only intermittently. This process is called *milk letdown*. It is under the control of the hypothalamus. Neurons in the paraventricular (PV) and supraoptic nuclei synthesize *oxytocin*, an undecapeptide hormone (see Chap. 8) and transport it through their axons to their terminals in the posterior lobe of the pituitary. Single-cell recordings from PV cells in lactating mother rats show a background spontaneous discharge. Periodically, the neurons fire bursts of impulses, followed some 10–15 seconds later by ejection of milk (see Fig. 26.8). These results indicate that sensory inputs to the PV cells produce synaptic depolarization and increased impulse generation; that the impulses invade and depolarize the terminals in the posterior pituitary and cause release of oxytocin stored there; and that oxytocin acts on the smooth muscle of the mammary gland after a delay due to the time for circulation of the hormone through the blood circulation, from pituitary to nipple. Parts of this circuit are depicted in Fig. 26.8.

For their part, the rat pups are not just passive receptacles for the ejected milk. Letdown lasts only a few seconds, and the pup must be able to detect the engorgement of the nipple and respond with vigorous sucking. From these considerations it has been realized that the state of arousal of pups is very important in their ability to thrive. It appears that nipple attachment and ingestive control are exquisitely dependent on the level of arousal; a deprived pup with an empty stomach is more alert than a satiated pup, and therefore is more responsive to nipple engorgement and more active in sucking.

Arousal is mediated by the brainstem reticular system (Chap. 25), activated by the vigorous licking by the mother as described above. It is also mediated by activity in afferents from the empty stomach. The importance of arousal in initiating feeding appears to be similar to the higher activity levels of the adult blowfly after food deprivation, discussed earlier in this chapter. If rat pups are persistently aroused by experimental manipulation, they ingest milk beyond the normal capacity of the stomach. It is not until the age of 15 days that adultlike controls of ingestion begin to appear, and the rat begins to adjust intake to need.

Feeding in the Adult Rat

There was no clear idea about the neural pathways involved in adult feeding until Anand and Brobeck showed in 1951 that small, bilateral lesions in the lateral hypothalamic area (LHA) cause a rat to stop eating (aphagia) and stop drinking (adipsia), leading to death within a few days. The lesions did not appear to interrupt specific sensory or motor pathways. These workers suggested that the LHA could therefore be regarded as the center for the control of feeding (and drinking) behavior. The location of this area is shown in the drawing of Fig. 26.9. The cross-sectional view in A indicates the insertion of the lesioning electrode in this area. The LHA lies within, and is traversed by, fibers of the medial forebrain bundle (MFB), the massive population of fibers which serves

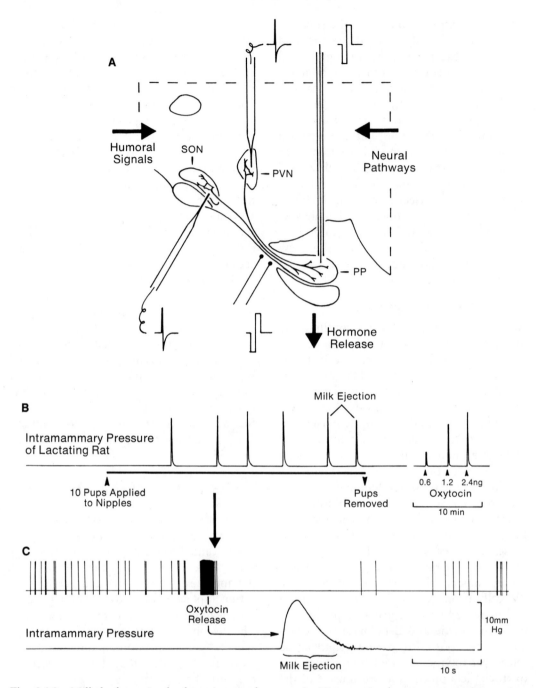

Fig. 26.8 Milk letdown in the lactating mother rat. **A.** Neurons in the paraventricular nucleus (PVN) and supraoptic nucleus (SON) in the hypothalamus and their connections to the posterior lobe (PP) of the pituitary. **B.** Intermittent pattern of milk ejection, as shown by recordings of intramammary pressure. The slow, long-duration trace shows milk ejections by an anesthetized mother rat in response to suckling by her litter. The slow, short-duration trace shows the mammary response to intravenous pulse injections of increasing concentrations of oxytocin. **C.** Unit activity recorded from a PVN neuron, showing the correlation of intense burst activity, oxytocin release, and subsequent mammary response and milk ejection. Note the much faster trace speed in C than in B. (Courtesy of D. W. Lincoln; see also Wakerly and Lincoln, 1973)

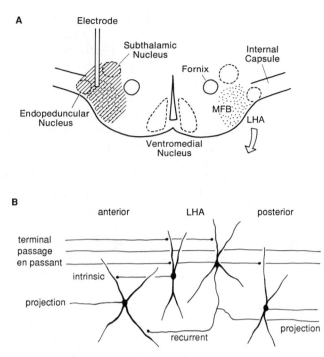

Fig. 26.9 A. Diagram of a cross section through the rat hypothalamus. Fibers of the medial fore-brain bundle (MFB) are shown by dots. Note the electrode used to make electrolytic lesions. Sites of lesions of the lateral hypothalamic area (LHA) indicated by shading. **B.** Sagittal section of the rat brain, showing neurons in the lateral hypothalamic area (LHA) and some aspects of their synaptic organization. (A after Epstein, 1971; B after Millhouse, in Stellar and Stellar, 1985)

as the main conduction pathway linking areas of the brainstem–hypothalamus–basal forebrain into a common system.

Since that time, it has been realized that control of feeding is mediated through the hypothalamic–MFB system, but *how* this control is exerted has been the subject of continuing controversy. Most of the experiments have involved traditional methods of making lesions or stimulating electrically in different parts of the hypothalamic–MFB system. In order to understand the limitations of these methods and the interpretations that have been placed upon them, the student first needs to become acquainted with the anatomy of the system.

Anatomy of the Hypothalamus– MFB System

In contrast to many other regions of the brain, the hypothalamus is not organized into a discrete region with distinct layers.

This is particularly true of the lateral hypothalamic area. As indicated in Fig. 26.9A, the LHA has no clear boundaries; lesions aimed at the LHA therefore commonly impinge on neighboring areas such as the subthalamus, endopeduncular nucleus, and medial part of the internal capsule, causing more widespread and variable affects.

The intrinsic organization of the LHA is characterized by a diffuse arrangement of neurons, as illustrated in Fig. 26.9B. The triad of elements—input fibers, output neurons, and intrinsic neurons—that make up synaptic organization has been difficult for neuronanatomists to identify. There is not a clear differentiation of projection and intrinsic neurons, a feature shared with other parts of the reticular core. A more serious problem is the mass of fibers of the MFB that passes through the LHA. Some of these fibers are afferents that have terminal boutons on the LHA dendrites and cell bodies;

some are afferents that make en passant synapses, on their way to other regions; some are fibers of passage, making no synapses on their way to other regions; and, finally, some are axons arising within the LHA, either projection axons joining the MFB and destined for outside targets, or intrinsic axons within the LHA. These different types are illustrated in Fig. 26.9B.

Because of the close association of the MFB with the LHA, we must next determine the connections made by the MFB. As shown in Fig. 26.10A, in the forebrain the *inputs* are mainly from olfactory cortex, amygdala, striatum, hippocampus, and prefrontal cortex (other areas of neocortex are conspicuously absent). Caudally, the main sources of inputs are the brainstem monoamine systems [locus ceruleus (LC), dorsal raphe (DR), and ventral tegmental area (VTA)], and reticular regions. The MFB *output* targets are summarized in Fig. 26.10B. In the forebrain, these are most of the input sites mentioned above, with, in addition, most of the neocortex. Caudally, the same principle of reciprocal relations applies, with, in addition, the central taste pathway (nucleus of the solitary tract, NTS) and spinal cord.

These aspects of anatomy are important for the following reasons. The synaptic organization of the LHA shows that any lesion of this area is bound to have variable effects due to loss of intrinsic circuits, and also have widespread effects through interruption of fibers providing passage of the MFB. Similarly, electrical stimulation in the LHA must activate (or inactivate) intrinsic circuits in unpredictable ways, as well as cause orthodromic activation of MFB output fibers and antidromic activation of MFB input fibers.

From this, the student may well conclude that the LHA–MFB system for control of feeding could stand as a model for the limitations of traditional lesion and stimulation methods in the analysis of central systems. Modern studies have recognized these limitations, and have added new and better methods, including single-unit re-

cordings, microionophoresis of transmitters and peptides, receptor localization by ligand binding studies, and sites of mRNA expression by in situ hybridization. We will first review the main results of the traditional methods, and then incorporate more recent findings into a model that represents a modern consensus of the neural system involved in feeding control.

The Lateral Hypothalamus and Feeding

In 1954, Phillip Teitlebaum and Eliot Stellar, at the University of Pennsylvania, showed that lesioned rats do not die if they are tube-fed, and that they subsequently recover and are able to regulate their food and water intake. The recovery process could be divided into four stages. In stage I, the animals are profoundly aphagic and adipsic. In stage II, the animals begin to accept wet, highly palatable food, but still will not drink. In stage III, the animals are less finicky: they eat a wider variety of food, and will drink sweetened water with a meal. In stage IV, the animal regulates its food intake, though it ingests water only with a meal.

These general results have been replicated many times in the intervening years, with many variations practiced on the exact sites and extents of lesions, the means of producing them, and the relations of other parts of the brain to the LHA–MFB. In addition, experiments in which the LHA has been stimulated electrically have generally shown increased eating. Unit recordings from the LHA have shown increased impulse firing under conditions of deprivation. From all these results it seems clear that the LHA–MFB is intimately involved in control of feeding behavior, but there has been much disagreement on the actual pathways involved and the nature of the control.

Despite the many controversies that have arisen, two major themes have emerged. The first theme is that, despite the remarkable recovery that can take place, LHA-lesioned animals show a number of permanent deficits, not only related to feeding

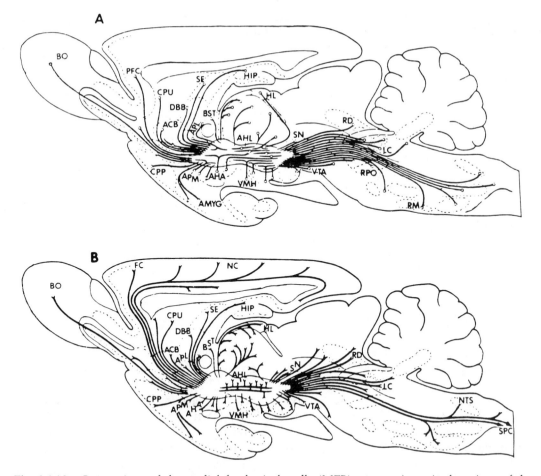

Fig. 26.10 Connections of the medial forebrain bundle (MFB), as seen in sagittal sections of the rat brain. **A.** Inputs to the MFB from different parts of the brain. **B.** Different regions of the brain that receive MFB fibers. Abbreviations: ACB, nucleus accumbens; AHA, anterior hypothalamic area; AHL, lateral hypothalamic area; AMYG, amygdala; APL, lateral preoptic area; APM, medial preoptic area; BO, olfactory bulb; BCA, bed nucleus of the anterior commissure; BST, bed nucleus of the stria terminalis; CPA, periamygdaloid cortex; CPP, prepiriform cortex; CPU, caudate–putamen; DBB, nucleus of the diagonal band (Broca); FC, frontal cortex; HIP, hippocampus; HL, lateral habenula; LC, locus ceruleus; NC, neocortex; NTS, nucleus of the tractus solitarius; PFC, prefrontal cortex; RD, dorsal raphe; RM, raphe magnus; RPO, raphe pontis; SE, septum; SN, substantia nigra; SO, supraoptic nucleus; SPC, spinal cord; VMH, ventromedial hypothalamus; VTA, ventral tegmental area; ZI, zone incerta. (From Niewenhuys et al., in Stellar and Stellar, 1985)

behavior but also profoundly affecting general behavior. Some of these effects are summarized in Table 26.3. Under *Ingestive behaviors*, it can be seen that the recovered rat, though able to survive, is far from normal. These defects all place serious limitations on feeding behavior; the depression of salivation, for example, could by itself explain much of the inability of an animal

to eat after lesioning. (Electrical stimulation of the LHA causes, on the contrary, copious salivation.) Under *General behaviors*, it can be seen that the lesion has serious consequences, leaving an animal that is lethargic, generally akinetic, emotionally depressed, and with limited tolerance for stress. These effects obviously contribute to the depression of feeding.

Table 26.3   Long-lasting deficits in feeding behavior of rats after bilateral ablation of LHA or destruction of catecholamine-containing neurons by injection of 6-hydroxydopamine

	LHA ablation	6-HDA
Ingestive behaviors		
No feeding response to glucoprivation (insulin or 2-deoxyglucose)	+	+
Lower body weight set point	+	+
Depressed drinking response to dehydration	+	+
Depressed salivary reflexes	+	−
Depressed feeding response to sodium deficiency	+	−
Depressed taste aversion learning	+	−
General behaviors		
Depressed arousal	+	+
Motor impairment	+	+
Depressed affect	+	+
Depressed tolerance for stress ("central sympathectomy")	+	+

The second theme, related to the first, is that many systems, not just an isolated one, are affected by an LHA lesion, and conversely, that many parts of the nervous system have inputs to and effects on the LHA. The LHA–MFB is simply a locus, a common path, for many *overlapping distributed systems,* as is implied by the diagrams of Fig. 26.10, above. Recent work has shown that these systems include the ascending DA and NE pathways from the brainstem. As shown in Table 26.3, intraventricular injection of 6-hydroxydopamine, which selectively destroys catecholamine-containing neurons, produces a syndrome very similar to that of the LHA-lesioned animal. Parts of the syndrome can also be produced by selective lesions or cuts at various places in the brainstem, at the borders of the hypothalamus, and in the basal ganglia, cortex, and olfactory pathway.

A summary of all the lesion and stimulation experiments shows, in essence, that all of the regions to which the MFB connects are involved in some aspect of the control of feeding. A crucial fact is that the MFB (and its associated regions) also controls other closely related behaviors. It includes the pathways for arousal which we discussed in the previous chapter. It also

forms the core for systems mediating aggressive and emotional behavior, as we will see in Chap. 28. Finally, it includes the sites at which electrical stimulation has rewarding effects; rats readily learn to press a bar to receive electrical stimulation in these central areas, as first shown by James Olds and Peter Milner in 1954. This phenomenon of self-stimulation has been demonstrated in many species, including even humans; neurosurgical patients receiving electrical stimulation in these regions report feelings of pleasure and euphoria. All of this evidence indicates that the core regions interconnected by the medial forebrain bundle are parts of distributed systems concerned with coordinating neural activity underlying arousal, feeding, and emotion in complex ways.

The Medial Hypothalamus and Satiety

Thus far, we have discussed the possible neural substrates that activate feeding. What causes the animal to terminate feeding? Two processes seem to be involved. One process is *satiation,* which can be measured as the duration of a meal: the shorter the meal, the faster the process of satiation. The other process is *satiety,* which can be measured as the duration from the end of

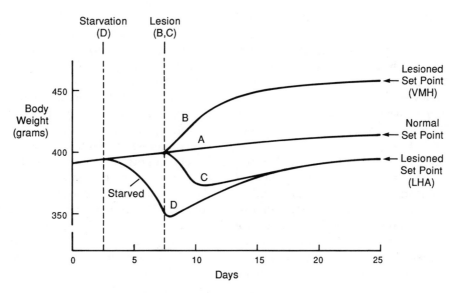

Fig. 26.11 Experimental analysis of feeding in the rat, illustrating the concept of set point for control of body weight. **A.** Curve for gradual increase of body weight in the normal adult rat, determined by a gradually increasing set point. **B.** After selective lesion of the ventral medial hypothalamus (VMH), the animal gains weight and then continues to feed at a higher set point. **C.** After selective lesion of the lateral hypothalamic area (LHA), the animal loses weight and then continues to feed at a lower set point. **D.** If the animal is initially starved, the response to an LHA lesion may be to gain weight before settling in at the new set point. (Adapted from Keesey et al., in Kandel and Schwartz, 1985)

a meal to the time when feeding begins again: the shorter the duration, the lower the level of satiety. These terms of course apply mainly to episodic feeders like rats and humans; grazers such as cows appear to have a more continuous monitoring of the rate of satiation or the level of satiety.

What are the neural mechanisms mediating satiety? The first evidence was obtained by Brobeck and his colleagues in the 1940s. They found that bilateral lesions of the ventromedial nucleus of the hypothalamus (VMH) produce an animal that grossly overeats and becomes enormously obese. This implied that normally this nucleus has a restraining influence on the feeding centers. This idea was supported by experiments showing that electrical stimulation in this area causes a reduction in eating.

Theories of the Neural Basis of Feeding Control

Dual Center Hypothesis. The evidence from the two classical lines of work, on LHA

and VMH, was first combined by Eliot Stellar in 1957 into the *dual center hypothesis.* This stated that feeding is due to LHA activity; satiety, to VMH activity; and the cycle of feeding and satiety, to interactions between these two centers. It was recognized that both centers receive several types of input, both neural and humoral, so that the whole system is under multifactorial control.

Set-Point Theory. The next major step toward a synthesis of views came in the 1970s, when it was realized that the dual centers are involved in inhibitory feedback pathways that maintain energy balance and body weight at a specific level; this is referred to as the *set-point theory.* It arose from experiments such as those illustrated in Fig. 26.11. Normally, a rat eats at a rate which moves its weight along a curve such as A. In rats with small lesions of VMH (curve B), the satiety controls are impaired; the animal increases its food intake in relation to a higher set-point. In rats with small lesions of the LHA (curve C), the animal reduces its feeding until it reaches a lower set point, which it thereafter maintains. If animals are first starved, given the same LHA lesions, and then allowed to feed, they actually gain weight initially, as shown in curve D, until they reach the same set point.

Multistage, Multifactor Concept. The set-point theory has given a more satisfactory conceptual framework for understanding feeding mechanisms, particularly in terms of systems control theory, but it does not by itself give further insight into the mechanisms themselves. Recent studies have suggested that no single theory or mechanism is likely to be adequate; rather, that feeding is actually a series of behaviors, each dependent on the stage before and contingent on a number of factors. For convenience, we may refer to this as the *multistage, multifactor concept.*

This concept may be summarized in relation to the diagram of Fig. 26.12. For simplification, we will focus on only two steps, the initiation of a feeding episode, and the termination of feeding.

Initiation of feeding. A bout of feeding by a rat is initiated in response to several main factors. In general, they can be divided into two types, humoral and neural. The *humoral* factors are due to the late stages of the state of satiety induced by the previous meal. The digestion of the meal gives rise to the postabsorption state, in which blood insulin levels are high (due to enhance glucose uptake) and blood glucose levels are low (due to uptake). Together, these changes stimulate hypothalamic feeding centers.

For rats, these changes are especially marked near nightfall, when the nocturnal rat begins to forage, and so are tied to the circadian rhythm generator (see previous chapter). At this time, a pancreatic polypeptide (neuropeptide Y, NPY) released from the pancreas and possibly from hypothalamic cells themselves, also stimulates hypothalamic cells; injections of NPY and the related peptide YY into the hypothalamus have been shown to cause satiated rats to begin eating voraciously. Another important humoral factor is corticosterone, released from the adrenal cortex in response to activation of the feedback loop through the hypothalamic–pituitary axis (Chap. 24).

Among the *neural* factors, an increased level of arousal, tied to the circadian rhythm, is very important in activating the animal to initiate foraging (just as in the insect, as discussed above). The low glucose/high insulin levels stimulate the locus ceruleus to increase NE release onto hypothalamic neurons, where it binds to α receptors. Corticosterone potentiates this action by upregulation of α receptors. NE is believed to act not directly by stimulating neurons that are excitatory for feeding pathways, but indirectly by inhibiting satiety neurons that are inhibitory to the hypothalamic neurons that activate feeding pathways. Opioid fibers acting directly on hypothalamic neurons, or indirectly by means of interactions with GABAergic and DAergic fibers, also stimulate feeding. Additional neural factors are the signals from the olfactory and taste pathways that direct the search for food and its ingestion.

Termination of feeding. Termination of feeding (B in Fig. 26.11) is similarly dependent on a coordination of humoral and neural factors. As feeding proceeds and absorption of nutrients from the gut into the bloodstream occurs, a variety of humoral substances are released. Blood glucose levels rise, while insulin levels fall. As the food makes its way through the gut, a variety of peptides are released. These include CCK, neurotensin, calcitonin, and bombesin. The previously high levels of insulin promote uptake of tryptophan, the precursor of 5HT; this neurotransmitter has actions which induce sleep (Chap. 25) and reduce feeding. Other neural factors are the activation of DAergic fibers to the hypothalamus, and sensory input from the gut due to distension of the gut walls.

As in the case of stimulation of feeding, termination of feeding depends on all these

A. HUNGER: INITIATION OF FEEDING

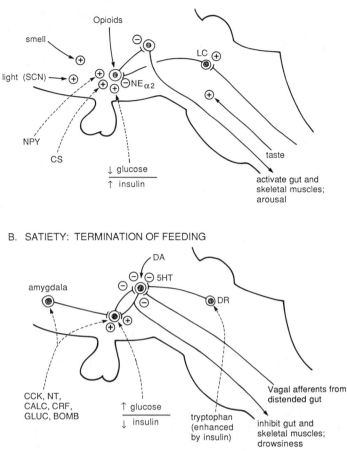

Fig. 26.12 Multiple factors involved in the neural control of feeding, based on experiments in the rat. Two stages in feeding are illustrated: hunger and satiety. **A.** Hunger initiates feeding. Neural pathways are shown by continuous lines; humoral factors, by dashed lines; stimulation, by +; inhibition, by −. Abbreviations: LC, locus ceruleus; NEα_2, α_2-adrenergic receptor; NPY, neuropeptide Y; SCN, suprachiasmatic nucleus; CS, corticosteroids. **B.** Satiety terminates feeding. Abbreviations: DA, dopamine; DR, dorsal raphe nucleus; CCK, cholecystokinin; NT, neurotensin; CALC, calcitonin; CRF, corticotropin releasing factor; GLUC, glucagon; BOMB, bombesin. These central feeding pathways through the hypothalamus may be compared with those of the neuroendocrine and immune systems (Chap. 24). (Based on Stricker, Hoebel, in Stellar and Stellar, 1985; see also Liebowitz, 1986; Bray, 1986; and Hoebel, 1986)

signals being integrated in the hypothalamus. The process may involve direct action on hypothalamic output neurons, or an indirect effect—for example, stimulation of satiety center neurons which are inhibitory to the output neurons. The hypothalamic output has two main targets. One is motoneurons to skeletal muscles, to reduce their activity. This often involves a stereo-typed sequence of motor behaviors, involving grooming, drinking, lying down and sleeping, a sequence found in rats and not unknown to humans! The other target is autonomic motoneurons, to facilitate digestion of the ingested foodstuffs.

In conclusion, the concept of multiple stages and multiple factors is of practical use in breaking down the mechanisms for feeding control into understandable parts. The previous notions of dual centers and set points are incorporated into this more comprehensive framework. Thus, as R. Hoebel (1986) has pointed out, it is recognized that there are excitatory and inhibitory controls in both medial and lateral hypothalamuses. The outputs from these regions are involved, directly or indirectly, in control of both parasympathetic and sympathetic parts of the autonomic nervous system. Humoral and neural factors can have different types of actions, including up- and down-regulation of receptors.

To conclude this discussion, it is appropriate to quote Jacques LeMagnen (1971) of Paris, a pioneer in the physiological and behavioral analysis of feeding, and a wise observer of both laboratory animals and his fellow countrymen:

> Food intake is not . . . separately regulated. . . . This field . . . represents perhaps the most advanced point in the study of a multifactorial physiological regulation. . . . A multifactorial system of regulation, in which the play of a network of positive and negative feedback mechanisms enables a body of variables to be simultaneously causes and effects, requires from the experimenter a kind of new mental program for collecting and processing data, and yet difficult to build and handle.

Drinking

Closely allied to feeding is drinking. Cells universally contain water, and metazoan animals universally consist of cells bathed in extracellular fluid. Maintenance of the fluid composition of both cells and extracellular fluid is therefore basic to animal life. As animals evolved from aquatic to terrestrial environments, homeostatic mechanisms became necessary for ensuring adequate fluid intake to offset dehydration and excretion. The need for intake is expressed as thirst, and is met by drinking.

In an animal deprived of water, the extracellular fluid begins to become more concentrated, and one says it is hyperosmotic; since the extracellular and intracellular compartments are in equilibrium across the cell wall, the cell cytoplasm also becomes hyperosmotic. In 1953, Bengt Andersson in Sweden showed that injections of hyperosmotic solutions into the hypothalamic region of goats induces drinking, suggesting that there are *osmoreceptors*, sensitive to cellular dehydration, in that region. This is a logical place to expect such receptors, near the location of the cells to the posterior pituitary that secrete antidiuretic hormone (ADH), which stimulates the kidney to retain water. Subsequent experiments by Elliott Blass and Alan Epstein at the University of Pennsylvania in 1971 showed that the osmoreceptors are distributed rather widely throughout the hypothalamus, especially in the preoptic and lateral hypothalamic areas (see Fig. 26.13A). These and other workers have found that microinjections of mildly hypertonic saline into these areas readily induces drinking, as do injections into the carotid arteries which supply these areas; conversely, lesions of these areas impair drinking behavior.

In addition to cellular dehydration, a loss of extracellular fluid volume is also a stimulus to drinking. This involves the *angiotensin* system. Knowledge of this system began with the finding that a reduction of blood volume stimulates cells of the kidney to release the enzyme renin into the bloodstream. Renin acts on a circulating peptide, angiotensinogen, to make angiotensin I, which in turn is converted to angiotensin II (A II) (see Fig. 26.13B). In 1970, Epstein and his colleagues made microinjections of A II into the hypothalamus, and showed that this is a powerful stimulus for drinking. Subsequent experiments have shown that all the components of the reinin—A II system are also present in the hypothalamus. The preoptic area is particularly sensitive to A II, as are several sites along the cerebral ventricles; these are indicated in Fig. 26.13B.

What are the relative contributions of osmoreceptors and A II receptors to normal

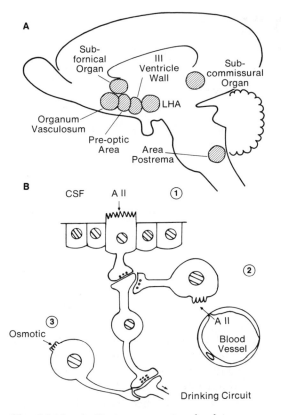

Fig. 26.13 **A.** Brain centers involved in control of drinking. **B.** Microcircuit of central receptors for angiotension. Site ①, receptor in the wall of the cerebral ventricle. Site ②, receptor in circumventricular organ, where there is no blood-brain barrier. Site ③, osmoreceptor in the hypothalamus. Drinking circuit includes cells projecting to the neural lobe of the pituitary, where vasopressin (antidiuretic hormone) is released. (B from Phillips et al., 1977)

drinking? In experiments carried out by Barbara Rolls, Ed Rolls, and Roger Wood at Oxford, it was found that about 65% of the drinking following water deprivation is due to cellular dehydration, and about 25% is due to blood volume reduction.

This is in the rat; in the monkey, the proportions were 85% and 5%, respectively. These and other experiments have supported the idea that the osmoreceptors are more important, and that the A II receptors are supplementary, perhaps acting as an emergency system invoked under conditions of extreme deprivation or blood loss.

Water deprivation is an easy variable for the experimenter to manipulate. An animal deprived of water has a strong *drive*, or *motivation*, to correct the deficit by drinking. In behavioral experiments, the drive can be quantitated by testing how hard the animal will work, or how intense the aversive shocks it will sustain, in order to obtain water and correct the deficit. Water deprivation is thus a convenient variable for studying both physiological and behavioral mechanisms.

Among humans, much of our water intake in daily life is actually guided by other factors. We drink fluids with our meals; we drink coffee because it is time for a coffee break; we drink at cocktail hour to be sociable; we drink when our mouths feel dry; we drink because it tastes good; we drink because we are bored. These different behavioral states depend on different kinds of receptors: taste receptors in the mouth and pharynx; somatosensory receptors in the mouth, pharynx, and esophagus; stretch receptors that sense the amount of distention in the stomach and duodenum; stretch receptors and osmoreceptors in the hepatic portal veins that return blood from the liver to the heart. There is thus a complex array of signals that determines the pattern of normal drinking. This pattern is shaped by our learned habits, habits that in effect anticipate need, and keep our bodies well hydrated so that we do not have to respond in situations of need or emergency.

27

Visceral Brains: Mating

As mentioned at the beginning of the previous chapter, mating is the function that is necessary for the propagation of the species. The object of mating is characteristically a copulatory union which brings the sexual organs of male and female together, so that fertilization of the female's egg or eggs by the male's sperms can occur. This requires maturation of the gonads and the copulatory organs, and timing of the preparedness of the male and receptivity of the female. In those animals in which fertilization occurs within the female, a series of internal body changes then takes place during gestation, in preparation for birth. The diagram in Fig. 27.1 shows the relation of mating to those other phases in the reproductive cycle of a social insect and a mammal.

Mating, like feeding, takes place under a combination of nervous and hormonal control. Much of this control is mediated by parts of the nervous system within the visceral brain. In the case of feeding, we saw that this part of the brain is responsible for a variety of different control mechanisms. Similarly, in the case of mating, the visceral brain mediates the most delicate and ingenious mechanisms for bringing about copulatory unions and the mixing of genes. This part of the brain also is involved in controlling other aspects of the reproductive cycle shown in Fig. 27.1, such as the maturation of gonads, and behavior related to maternal care. In this chapter we will focus on the functions of mating, and mention these related functions where relevant.

Reproductive Strategies

To begin with, let us get a perspective on the strategies of sexual reproduction. In some organisms, each individual is a hermaphrodite, which means it contains both male and female sexual organs. This has the advantage that any two individuals can meet and reproduce. Examples include the earthworm, the sea hare *(Aplysia)*, and, among vertebrates, a number of species of fish. In these cases, nervous mechanisms appropriate for both male and female mating behavior must be present. This has the disadvantage of limiting the degree of specialized sexually related behavior that is possible, which may be part of the explanation for why this form of sexual reproduction is not more widespread.

Among vertebrates, the potential for hermaphroditism is expressed in the ability of certain species to undergo sex reversal.

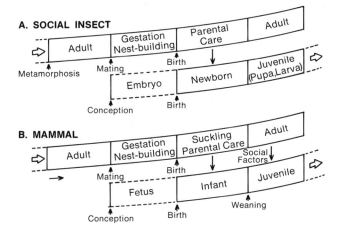

Fig. 27.1 Life cycles of a social insect and a mammal, to show timing of events related to reproduction.

For example, Robert Goy and Bruce McEwen, in their book on *Sexual Differentiation of the Brain* (1980), cite studies in which genetically female fish, frogs, or salamanders grown in water containing testosterone develop into males that mate with normal females, and, conversely, males grown in water containing estradiol develop into females that mate with normal males. Even more amazing are studies of certain species of fish that live in social groups; all the members of the group develop as females, and only a few differentiate into males. If an adult male is lost, within a week or two one of the adult females differentiates into a male to take its place! A contrasting species of fish is also known, in which a group has a single female; if this female is lost from the group, a male differentiates into a female to take its place. These studies have thus provided evidence for the ability of social factors to control the differentiation of sexes, presumably through effects on nervous mechanisms and the organizational actions of sex hormones.

Among higher invertebrates and vertebrates, the common pattern is for sexual differentiation to occur early in development, and for the male and female forms to be stable throughout life. This reflects the adaptive advantages to be gained from specialization of each sex for its role in the reproductive behaviors revolving around courtship, mating, and care of the young. We have already mentioned an example of specialized nervous mechanisms in the pathways for control of singing in male birds (Chap. 23), and we will discuss several further examples below. We will also discuss the mechanisms for development of these differences in neural circuits and see that they involve a series of changes under control of the organizational effects of hormones.

INVERTEBRATES

Given the importance of reproduction for the species, mating is not an activity that is entirely left to chance. As indicated already in connection with Fig. 27.1, it requires a careful orchestration in the development of the male and female partners. During development and maturity, animals of course spend much of their time looking for food and trying to avoid being eaten themselves. As a general rule, mating is not a part of this daily business of survival. Instead, it takes place at very prescribed times. The time is set by the biorhythm generators, the maturation and readiness of the gonads and secondary sex organs, and the differentiation of the parts of the neural pathways for controlling the appropriate behavior. These are basic principles that apply more or less to all animals, invertebrates and vertebrates.

Courtship

A crucial task for the neural apparatus is the control of an appropriate series of behaviors that will bring the male and female together. A basic problem is that in their daily business of survival, animals spend much of their time engaging in behaviors that are either aggressive or defensive. In order to mate, the male and female must overcome these attitudes and, at least briefly, trust each other. Furthermore, there must be an opportunity for each of the partners to test the other for its attractiveness as a source of sound genes; it is a waste to mate with a partner that is sick, weak, or maladapted, but an advantage to combine one's genes with those of a partner that is healthy, strong, and with optimal abilities to survive and flourish.

For these reasons, it is common for mating to involve a sequence of interactions between the prospective partners, during which the aggressive and defensive instincts are subdued, and attractiveness as partners is tested. Many species are every bit as meticulous in this process of choosing mates as humans are. Since we view this through human eyeglasses, we call it "courtship." Ethologists have studied these sequences in many species, and have developed flow charts for representing them. An example of the mating behavior of the cockroach is shown in Fig. 27.2. Each one of the behaviors can be identified as a distinct entity— one that is a necessary prelude to the behavior that follows it. Each requires a response from the partner. Each gives rise to a sensory stimulus or a set of stimuli that call forth the next response. The whole sequence involves a number of specific motor acts and sensory stimuli that, taken together, are specific for this species, and ensure the suitability of the partners.

Reaction Chains

In the language of ethologists, a sequence such as that in Fig. 27.2 is called a *reaction chain*. Each behavior in the sequence is thought to be activated or "released" by a set of neuronal centers and their connections, called an *innate releasing mechanism*. The stimuli that activate these mechanisms are called *releasing stimuli*, or *releasers*. It can be further realized that each behavior has the character of a *fixed-action pattern* (FAP), that is, a particular pattern of postural attitude, glandular secretion, or motor activity, such as that discussed in Chap. 19. Each of these motor acts in turn generates the stimuli which release the next act in the chain. The details of each step in the sequence are summarized in Fig. 27.3.

A reaction chain such as that in Fig. 27.2 involves a prescribed sequence of behaviors, but it should be emphasized that any given step is a probabilistic, not a rigidly determined, event. This, in fact, is the whole point of the sequence: any given step serves as a test for whether conditions are just right, so that the next step can take place. This is the means for assuring optimum gene transmission, as described above.

The releasing stimuli for a given behavior act on sensory receptors which in turn set up input in sensory pathways, as already discussed in previous chapters in sensory systems. In some cases it is the whole pattern of stimulation that is important, such as visual recognition of a partner or a prominent marking in a partner. In other cases, it is a conjunction of two or more sensory modalities, such as tactile and chemosensory stimuli in the cockroach in Fig. 27.2. In many cases it involves stimulation only of a specific type of receptor, as in tactile stimulation of specific parts of the body in the cockroach.

Role of Olfactory System

A dramatic example of a specific sensory pathway involved in mating behavior is

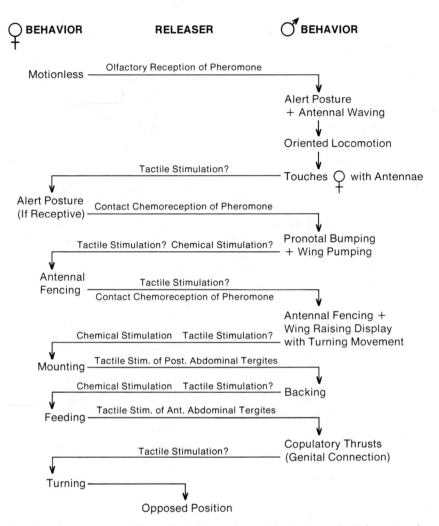

♀ BEHAVIOR **RELEASER** **♂ BEHAVIOR**

Motionless ——— Olfactory Reception of Pheromone ———→

Alert Posture
+ Antennal Waving

Oriented Locomotion

——— Tactile Stimulation? ——— Touches ♀ with Antennae

Alert Posture
(If Receptive) ——— Contact Chemoreception of Pheromone ———→

Pronotal Bumping
——— Tactile Stimulation? Chemical Stimulation? ——— + Wing Pumping

Antennal
Fencing ——— Tactile Stimulation? ———
——— Contact Chemoreception of Pheromone ———→

Antennal Fencing +
——— Chemical Stimulation Tactile Stimulation? ——— Wing Raising Display
with Turning Movement

Mounting ——— Tactile Stim. of Post. Abdominal Tergites ———

——— Chemical Stimulation Tactile Stimulation? ——— Backing

Feeding ——— Tactile Stim. of Ant. Abdominal Tergites ———

Copulatory Thrusts
——— Tactile Stimulation? ——— (Genital Connection)

Turning ———————————————

Opposed Position

Fig. 27.2 Reaction chain underlying mating behavior of the cockroach. Behaviors of male and female are shown in outside columns; releasing stimuli shown in center columns. (After Barth, in Gordon, 1972) *– a deterministic model!*

Fig. 27.3 Details of one step in a reaction train. (Adapted from Tinbergen, 1951)

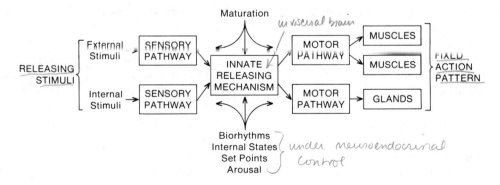

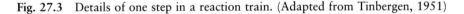

found in the insect olfactory system. As can be seen in Fig. 27.2, many of the steps leading to mating in the cockroach depend on chemical cues, a very general finding in many species. Such cues are mediated by pheromones (Chap. 7). The narrowly tuned responses of certain receptor cells in the male silk moth to the pheromone bombykol, emitted by the female, were described in Chap. 11.

Recently it has been discovered that these special receptors make connections to a special part of the antennal lobe. Careful studies by Jurgen Boeckh and his colleagues in Germany have shown that this part consists of a distinctive complex of glomerular structures, termed a macroglomerulus or macroglomerular complex (Fig. 27.4). Steve Matsumoto and John Hildebrand at Harvard succeeded in recording intracellularly from antennal lobe cells and marking them with HRP injections. They found cells that respond preferentially to bombykol; these cells are present only in the male; and they always have neurites which connect to the macroglomerulus. An example of this type of cell is shown in Fig. 27.4. The central connections of antennal lobe cells have not yet been determined; possible targets are the higher interpretive centers in the mushroom bodies (see Chap. 11) or other central neurons that command motor output to the wing motoneurons.

The involvement of pheromones and other chemical cues in mating and other types of behavioral reaction chains reflects the fact that they provide for very sure means of identification of individuals between and within species. In addition, the olfactory sensory pathways characteristically have direct access to parts of the visceral brain that contain innate releasing mechanisms. We will meet these same principles again in the mating and maternal behavior of vertebrates.

Role of Neuroendocrine Changes

An important aspect of mating behavior is the crucial role played by the neuroendo-crine system in preparing the body and the nervous system. As indicated in Fig. 27.3, the actions of nervous centers and pathways are contingent on internal factors such a maturation and internal state, and these are typically under neuroendocrine control. This control also involves a sequence of carefully orchestrated actions.

An overall scheme for the control of reproduction in insects is shown in Fig. 27.5. These sequence begins with sensory stimuli ① which activate neurosecretory cells in the brain. This causes the corpora allata ② to release their gonadotropin hormone. Gonadotropin promotes yolk formation in the ovum and stimulates the accessory sex glands ③. The ovary containing its maturing eggs releases ovarian hormone ④, which suppresses secretion of gonadotropin from the corpora allata, and also stimulates neurosecretion from the corpora cardiaca ⑤. The neurosecretion from the corpora cardiaca promotes ⑥ oviposition (the movement of the eggs into position for fertilization), possibly by acting through the central nervous system. This terminates the cycle, and the animal is ready to begin anew.

Of course the details in this sequence vary in different insects. Also, the hormones have actions on other parts of the body economy not shown in the diagram, such as metabolism; neurosecretions from the corpora cardiaca, for example, contribute to the preparation for mating by regulating the metabolism of fat tissue, so that proteins and other nutrients are provided for the developing oocyte. It should also be noted that the control of reproduction by the corpora allata in the adult follows in sequence the control of development through pupal stages to the adult by this same organ. It is of considerable interest in this regard that juvenile hormone and gonadotropin hormone in fact appear to be the same, or very similar, molecules. There appears to be an economy in having different effects depend on the stage of development of receptor molecules in target organs, rather than requiring the added job of synthesiz-

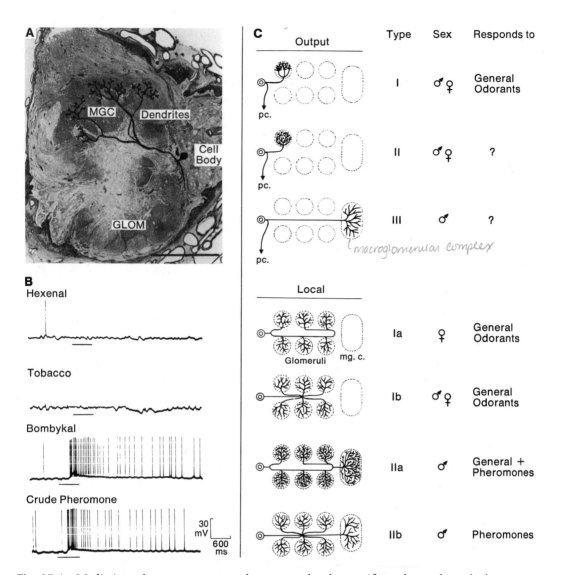

Fig. 27.4 Mediation of responses to sex pheromones by the specific pathway through the macroglomerulus in insects. **A.** Antennal lobe of a male Saturniid moth *Antheraea*. An olfactory neuron has been stained after injection of cobalt from an extracellular electrode. The tracing of the stained neuron is here superimposed on a corresponding histological section. The dendrites of this neuron connect to the macroglomerulus (MGC; above), but not to the common glomeruli (GLOM; below). This unit responded to stimulation by the sex attractant pheromone emitted by the female. **B.** Intracellular responses recorded from a neuron in a male hawkmoth *Manduca*. Note the specific response to bombykal, a major component of the sex pheromone emitted by the female, and to the pheromone itself. **C.** Correlation between the responsiveness of antennal lobe neurons and their dendritic connections, as revealed by intracellular HRP staining of recorded neurons. The antennal lobe neurons pictured here all receive inputs in the glomeruli from the antennal receptor cells; the output cells project to the mushroom bodies and other central regions, as described in Chap. 12. Abbreviations: mg. c., macroglomerular complex; pc., corpora pedunculata. (A from Boeckh and Boeckh, 1979; B, C from Matsumoto and Hildebrand, 1981)

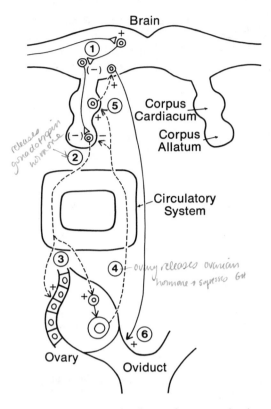

releases gonadotropin hormone

ovary releases ovarian hormone + supresses GH

Fig. 27.5 General scheme for control of reproduction in insects. Sequence of actions (1–7) is described in text. (Adapted from Tombes, 1970)

ing a different hormone at each stage. This expresses a principle of *multiaction hormonal effects in temporal sequence,* which is complementary to multiple actions of a given hormone on more than one target at the same time (Chap. 8).

VERTEBRATES

Most of the principles underlying mating behavior in invertebrates apply also to vertebrates. Thus, mating requires proper maturation of the reproductive organs and the nervous and neuroendocrine mechanisms for controlling them. Mating in vertebrates is characteristically preceded by courtship maneuvers every bit as complicated as that depicted in Fig. 27.2. The sequences of

behavior in most species involve fixed-action patterns, released by innate neural mechanisms under appropriate endogenous conditions and external stimulations as depicted in Fig. 27.3.

Our knowledge of neural mechanisms mediating mating behavior in vertebrates draws on work in many fields. There is a long tradition of biochemical work, beginning early in this century, on isolation and characterization of the hormones secreted by the reproductive organs and the hypothalamopituitary region. There is an enormous literature on the behavioral effects of removal of these organs in experimental animals, and the effects of diseases of these organs in human patients. In recent years, the identification of hypothalamic releasing factors and the localization of these and related peptides in many parts of the nervous system has greatly extended our concepts of the extent of neural systems involved in control of reproductive processes. Neuroanatomical studies have revealed a number of sites at which the organizational effects of hormone actions bring about sexually dimorphic regions. Neurophysiological studies have begun to reveal the time course and mode of action of nerve cells that mediate reproductive control. Finally, the genes for the hormones are being cloned and sequenced, and the sites of hormone synthesis localized by in situ hybridization.

Against this background of multidisciplinary studies, let us consider first the ways by which male and female animals achieve their final adult forms, and then consider examples of mating in several species.

Sexual Differentiation

Sexual differentiation is brought about by a sequence of steps. As summarized in Fig. 27.6, the general scheme is that the chromosomes carry the code for male or female, which determines the type of gonad, male or female. The gonad synthesizes and secretes hormones which organize the secondary sex characteristics of the body. In addition, the hormones act on the brain to

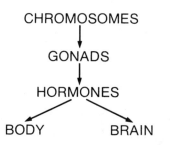

Fig. 27.6 Steps involved in sexual differentiation.

organize or modify circuits for appropriate nervous control of the sex organs and related behaviors.

An important generalization for understanding sexual differentiation is that, in higher vertebrates at least, all individuals will develop as one sex unless the chromosomal condition for the opposite sex is present and is expressed during a critical period on development. In birds, the sex chromosomes of the male are ZZ, whereas in the female they are ZO; hence birds are regarded as basically male (in computer terminology, the "default condition" is male), unless one of the sex chromosomes is missing. It is believed that ZZ inhibits the primordial ovary, allowing the testes to develop; in the case of ZO, the ovary develops while suppressing the primordial testis. In contrast, in mammals the sex chromosomes of the female are XX, whereas in the male they are XY; hence, mammals are regarded as basically female (the default condition is female), unless the Y chromosome is present.

Development of the Gonads

The differentiation of the sexes begins early in fetal life. We can illustrate the sequence of changes for the rat, a well-studied vertebrate (Fig. 27.7). The rat has a gestation period of about 21 days. By day 11, a genital ridge has formed in the lower abdomen (A). Germ cells, male or female, which have been lurking in the wall of the gut, migrate into this ridge, and bring about a proliferation of cells to form a primitive though undifferentiated gonad (B). The germ cells are grouped here into clusters, called *primary sex cords*. At about 13 days, the gonad begins to differentiate. In a genetic female, the primary sex cords migrate to the inner, medullary part of the gonad and degenerate. They are replaced in the outer, cortical part by secondary sex cords, which give rise to the egg cells *(oocytes)* (D). In the genetic male, the primary sex cords give rise to the seminiferous tubules, which contain in their walls the germ cells which give rise to spermatozoa (C).

Critical Period

As soon as the male gonad begins to differentiate into a testis, interstitial cells within the testis begin to synthesize and secrete the hormone testosterone. Synthesis in the rat has been detected as early as day 13. Testosterone levels peak twice during development, just before (E18–19) and just after birth; both of these peaks are lacking in the female (reviewed by MacLusky et al., 1985). These bursts of testosterone defines what is called a *critical period*, during which the message of the genetic sex is carried to the body; the testosterone acts on intracellular receptors, and causes the development of male secondary sex organs, and the differentiation of certain parts of the brain responsible for male behavior patterns.

Experimental manipulations, such as castration or hormone injections, have profound and enduring effects on both the sex organs and the brain if carried out during the critical period, up to about day 5 postnatally; after this, they have little effect. This critical period is relatively brief in the rat; in species with longer gestation periods, such as the guinea pig (67 days) or monkey (160), the period may be longer, and occur mostly before birth. In some species the end of the critical period occurs at about the time postnatally when the eyes open, which has been taken to indicate that sexual differentiation takes place before neural pathways in the brain are fully functional, and hence still more readily modifiable.

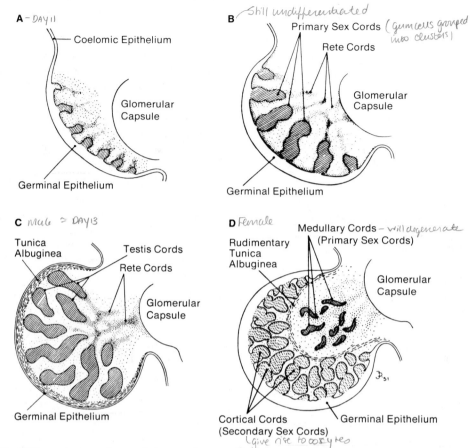

Fig. 27.7 Differentiation of gonads in vertebrates. See text. (From Burns, in Romer and Parsons, 1977)

Fred Naftolin and his colleagues proposed in 1975 that much of the masculinization effects produced by testosterone are actually due to conversion of testosterone to estradiol (reviewed by MacLusky and Naftolin, 1981). The conversion involves, biochemically, the aromatization of the hormone molecule (Fig. 27.8), and one says therefore that estrogen can act as an androgen through aromatization.

Within the brain there is a sex difference in aromatase activity during development: during the first few days of postnatal life, the levels of aromatase activity in the corticomedial amygdala and the hypothalamus are higher in males than in females. It is speculated that "early sex differences in testosterone levels could sensitize the male to subsequent androgen exposure," and that

"such sensitization could occur at least in part through increased estrogen formation" in these regions (MacLusky et al., 1985). Thus, the testosterone peaks may have a "priming effect" of inducing the aromatase enzyme in the cell cytoplasm, so that these cells would be more sensitive to further testosterone actions in the male. In addition, the several pathways for metabolizing testosterone (Fig. 27.8) yield a variety of active metabolites within the target cell. As Goy and MacEwen have pointed out (1980), this may be viewed

. . . as a means to diversify the action of a single hormone by producing . . . agents able to interact at different points in intracellular metabolism. It may provide a mechanism for achieving high concentrations of specific metab-

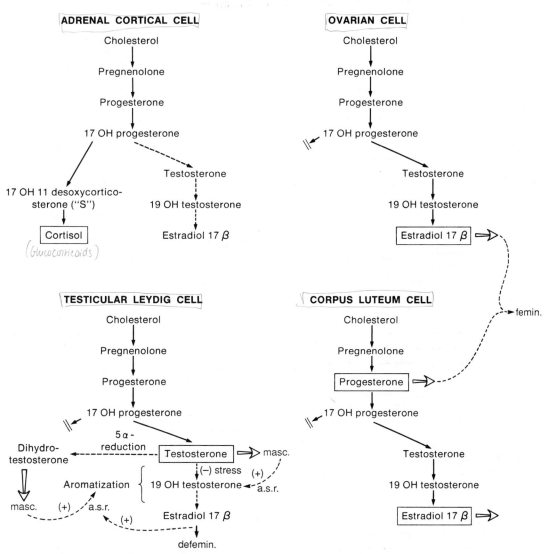

Fig. 27.8 Metabolic pathways for sex hormones. a.s.r., androgen steroid receptor; femin., feminization; defemin., defeminization; masc., masculinization (Based on Keele and Sampson, in Gordon, 1972; N. MacLusky, personal communication)

olites at discrete sites and for modulating hormone action through the regulation of the activity of the metabolizing enzymes. Not surprisingly, the CNS may prove to be the target organ in which these possibilities are most extensively exploited.

These mechanisms provide means not only for diversifying the effects of testosterone, but also for protecting the male embryo from circulating estrogens from the mother.

Sexual Dimorphisms

The previous section indicates that there is considerable biochemical evidence for sexual differentiation of the brain. We next consider how this produces differences in brain structures and sexual behavior.

The behaviors of male and female organisms are necessarily different during mating. The earlier idea (the "peripheral hypothesis") was that these behaviors reflect the differences in the sexual organs and their hormonal control through the pituitary. In this view, the decrease in male sexual behavior induced by castration of a newborn male rat, for example, is due to the underdeveloped penis rather than any effects on the brain. In contrast is the idea that there are differences in brain mechanisms in the two sexes (the "central hypothesis"). The first evidence for this was obtained by a closer examination of the behaviors of young animals.

It is typical of many mammalian species that the young engage in rough-and-tumble play among themselves. This play includes attempts at *mounting,* and receptive displays involving downward bending of the back and exposure of the bottom, termed *lordosis.* Both sexes engage in these behaviors, but normally males tend to be more active in mounting, and females in showing lordosis.

In 1959, Charles Phoenix and his collaborators at the University of Kansas reported studies in which they injected a small dose of testosterone into pregnant guinea pigs, and observed a reduction in lordotic behavior in the females progeny. This they interpreted as a *defeminizing* effect of the androgenic hormone on central brain mechanisms. In addition, guinea pigs ovariectomized at birth and subsequently injected with testosterone showed more mounting behavior, which was interpreted as a *masculinizing* effect of the hormone on the brain. Since that time, numerous studies have confirmed the generality of these two types of effects of male hormones on behavior patterns (see also Chaps. 28 and 30).

If behavior is mediated by the brain, then it should be possible to find differences in brain structure in the centers and pathways that mediate male or female behavior. At first the possibility of identifying such differences seemed remote, but the pioneering work of Geoffrey Raisman and Pauline Field, then at Oxford, in the early 1970s, showed that such differences could be found, and

at the level of resolution of the electron microscope. They studied the preoptic nucleus, a region in the basal forebrain that is involved in control of biorhythms, including the estrous cycle (see Chap. 27). The nucleus receives inputs from the amygdala, a structure in the limbic system (see next chapter) as well as from other sources. After placing lesions in the amygdala, they found more nonamygdalar nondegenerating synapses on dendritic spines in the nucleus of females than in males. These results are summarized in Fig. 27.9A. This study thus showed a difference in synaptic connections in males and females, a difference that depends on exposure to sex hormones early in life. The preoptic area is involved in control of the surge in secretion of LH that underlies the estrous cycle in females (see below), and the differences in synaptic connections may be related to this control.

Stimulated by these results, research workers have looked for and found differences between males and females in several other parts of the brian. These differences in brain structure are referred to as *sexual dimorphisms.* We have already mentioned in Chap. 23 the differences in binding of sex hormones and in the size of certain centers in the pathways controlling singing in male song birds. In the mammal, various nuclei of the hypothalamus show differences in cell size and sex hormone binding. Study of Golgi-impregnated neurons in the preoptic area of the hamster has suggested that neurons in the male have dendrites more oriented toward the center of this area, whereas in the female they are more oriented toward the periphery (see Fig. 27.9B). In another part of this area, there is a nucleus of cells that is up to eight times larger in males than in females (Fig. 27.9C). In addition to these structural dimorphisms, differences in functional properties of neurons have also been found; for example, amygdalar stimulation is more effective in driving preoptic cells in males than in females.

There is thus ample evidence that the brains of males and females are different

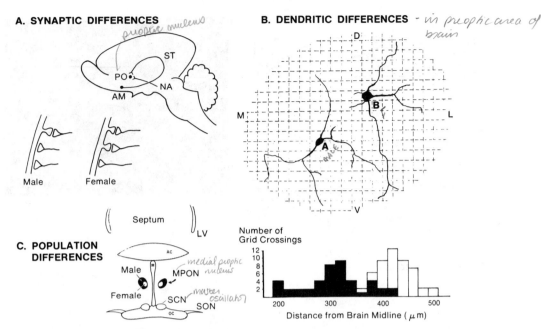

(handwritten annotations in figure: "preoptic nucleus" pointing to A. SYNAPTIC DIFFERENCES; "- in preoptic area of brain" next to B. DENDRITIC DIFFERENCES; "medial preoptic nucleus" next to MPON; "master oscillator" next to SCN)

Fig. 27.9 Sexual dimorphisms in the mammalian brain. **A.** Summary of experiments in the rat, showing that nonamygdalar (NA) fibers make more synapses on dendritic spines in the preoptic (PO) nucleus of females than males. AM, amygdala; ST, stria terminalis. **B.** Two Golgi-impregnated neurons in the preoptic area of hamster brain, illustrating that neurons in males (A) have dendrites more oriented toward the center of the area, whereas in females (B) the dendrites tend to be oriented toward the periphery. **C.** Medial preoptic nucleus (MPON) on the rat, showing that this region is larger in the male than in the female. AC, anterior commissure; LV, lateral ventricle; OC, optic chiasm; SCN, suprachiasmatic nucleus; SON, supraoptic nucleus. (A based on Raisman and Field, 1971; B from Greenough et al.; C from Gorski et al., in Goy and McEwen, 1980)

in certain very specific ways. Let us next examine how the differences relate to specific mating behavior.

Brain Mechanisms in Mating

Among the behaviors that are essential for mating to occur in many vertebrates are *mounting* by the male and *lordosis* by the female. Recent studies have begun to identify the specific nervous pathways that are involved in the control of these behaviors.

Mounting by the Male Frog

Mating in the frog takes place in the following manner. After suitable courtship preliminaries, the sexually mature male mounts the receptive female from behind so that their pelvises come together and

fertilization can occur, a position known as amplexus (see Fig. 27.10A). The transfer of sperm takes many hours, which puts the male at risk because other males may come along and try to dislodge him, and the female may try to throw him over for more attractive paramours. In order to maintain his position, the male clasps the female firmly with his forelimbs. This clasp is a remarkable reflex, which can be maintained for up to 30 hours. The spinal nature of the reflex is shown by the fact that after decapitation a male may continue to clasp for several hours, an experimental observation that was first made in the eighteenth century.

A team headed by Darcey Kelley at Princeton and Sol Erulkar at the University of Pennsylvania has carried out a multidis-

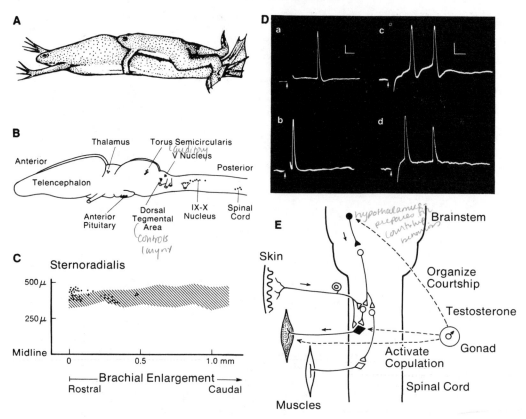

Fig. 27.10 Neural mechanisms mediating the clasp reflex of the male frog *Xenopus laevis*. **A.** Diagram of male clasping the female. **B.** Sites of binding of dihydrotestosterone to neurons in the central nervous system of the male frog. Binding in the auditory pathway (torus semicircularis) and the motor pathway controlling the larynx (dorsal tegmental area and IX–X nucleus) is related to mate calling during courtship. **C.** Localization of testosterone binding in the spinal cord. The shaded area indicates the distribution of the entire population of motoneurons innervating the sternoradialis muscle of the forelimb; dots indicate androgen-concentrating cells within that population. **D.** Intracellular recordings from a single sternoradialis motoneuron. a, b: Responses in spinal cord of castrated male to single stimulus delivered to dorsal root (a) and sternoradialis nerve (b). c, d: Response in spinal cord of a clasping male. **E.** Neural circuit mediating the male clasp reflex, showing sites of organizational and activational actions of androgen hormones. (A from Russell, 1964; B from Kelley, 1980; C, D from Erulkar et al., 1981)

ciplinary study of the spinal circuits. The results may be summarized as follows:

Anatomy. The main muscles used by the male in clasping are the sternoradialis and flexor carpi radialis of the forelimbs. HRP injections into these muscles showed their motoneurons to be localized in the brachial enlargement of the spinal cord.

Steroid Uptake. Castrated males were injected with dihydrotestosterone (DHT), one of the active metabolites of testosterone (see above). In addition to uptake in cells of the hypothalamus, uptake was found in cells of the spinal cord, among the motoneuron populations that mediate the clasp reflex (Fig. 27.10B,C).

Facilitation of Motoneuron Activity. Intracellular recordings were obtained from sternoradialis motoneurons in males induced to clasp by injection of gonadotropin, and compared with recordings from these motoneurons in castrated males. As shown in Fig. 27.10D, in clasping males the responses showed larger EPSPs and multiple spiking. This effect of androgens may be due to facilitation of transmitter actions, or to increased excitability of the membrane. Related experiments showed that the facilitation is blocked by cycloheximide, a protein synthesis inhibitor, suggesting that the androgen action is mediated through protein synthesis.

Enzyme Localization. The criteria for identifying neuroactive hormones parallel those for neurotransmitters (see Chap. 8). One of the criteria is the presence of appropriate enzymes. A search was therefore carried out for the presence of *5α-reductase,* the enzyme that converts testosterone to DHT (see above). Segments of the spinal cord were homogenized and incubated with tritiated testosterone. Thin-layer chromatography showed substantial *5α-reductase* activity in the spinal segments innervating the clasping muscles. The results are consistent with the idea that testosterone may affect clasping motoneurons by conversion to DHT.

Muscle Types. The types of muscle fibers in clasping muscles have been characterized by observing the binding of antibodies to fast myosin (present in fast twitch muscles) and slow myosin (present in slow twitch muscles). The proportion of slow myosin increases in males during the breeding season. This may be due in part to a direct action of androgens on the muscles, but Erulkar and his colleagues speculate that the changes induced in motoneuron activity by the binding of androgen, as described above, may be the main determinant of the myosin type in the muscles which these motoneurons innervate.

A summary of the neural and hormonal elements involved in male clasping behavior is shown in Fig. 27.10E. Note the two main neural targets of androgens, one in the hypothalamus to prepare the male for courtship behavior, the other in the spinal cord to prepare for clasping and copula-

tion. In this way the spinal circuits are primed for mediating the clasp reflex; in ethological terms, the fixed-action pattern (clasping) is released by appropriate releasing stimuli (tactile stimulation). Clasping behavior is thus programed into the spinal circuits, much as we have seen to be the case with motor activities related to posture and locomotion. The circuits thus appear to be constructed along the same principles as those controlling other motor behavior.

Lordosis in the Female Rat

Mating in the rat also involves mounting by the male, but copulation, by contrast, is extremely rapid: the entire sequence of mounting, thrusting, ejaculation, and release may take less than a second! The female's cooperation is critical, and the main motor activity which she must coordinate with mounting is lordosis. It has been known since the pioneering experiments of Frank Beach, then at Yale, in the 1940s, that lordosis is under control of female gonadal hormones. The neural circuits that mediate lordosis have been extensively studied by Don Pfaff and his collaborators at Rockefeller University. This work has also demonstrated the usefulness, indeed the necessity, of a multidisciplinary approach. The results will be summarized briefly, with reference to Fig. 27.11.

Lordosis is a reflex response to tactile stimulation by the male's body against the female's rump region ①. The main tactile receptors are believed to be Ruffini endings, responding to pressure stimulation with a slowly adapting barrage of impulses in the sensory fibers to the spinal cord.

Since lordosis does not occur if the spinal cord is transected (in contrast to frog clasping discussed above), the reflex requires supraspinal connections. The ascending information is carried in fibers in the anterolateral columns ② to three sites: the lateral vestibular nucleus, and the medullary and midbrain reticular formations.

Lordosis depends on estrogen; fully developed lordosis normally occurs only in mature females adequately primed by estrogens. The estrogens are primarily in neu-

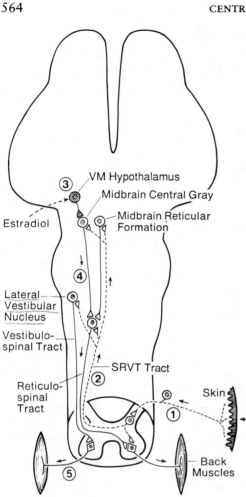

Fig. 27.11 Neural circuits mediating lordosis in the female rat. Sequence of actions (1–5) is described in text. SRVT, spino-reticular-vestibular tract (After Pfaff and Modianos, in Pfaff, 1980)

rons in the ventromedial hypothalamus and related regions (③; see also next section). The effect on these cells is to raise the level of tonic impulse activity, thereby facilitating the midbrain neurons to which these cells project.

When adequately facilitated by hypothalamic inputs, the midbrain neurons respond to the sensory inputs. Through a relay in the medullary reticular formation, this descending pathway ④ completes the reflex pathway to the spinal cord. The descending excitation is combined with sensory inputs to control the muscles of the back that

execute lordosis ⑤. The lateral vestibular nucleus contributes to this control by raising the tone of postural muscles.

In this system we see again the principle of hierarchical organization; the basic circuit for controlling the pattern of motor activity is present at the spinal level, and is modulated, gated, or activated by the higher centers. It is also worth pointing out that lordosis involves primarily axial muscles; thus, as in the case of respiratory and vocal activity, a delicate control of axial muscles is necessary, that rivals that of fine control of the extremities.

Neural Control of Gonadotropin Secretion in the Female Rat

It remains to consider the neural factors that affect the hormonal status of the female, and its preparedness for mating.

In mammals, most females upon reaching maturity undergo cyclic changes in their preparedness to mate and produce offspring. This is termed the *estrous cycle.* It reflects changes in the levels of the gonadal hormones, estrogens and progestins, secreted in the ovary, which in turn reflect changes in stimulation of the ovary by gonadotropin (FSH and LH) secreted by the pituitary. The way these levels change during the estrous cycle of the rat is shown in Fig. 27.12. Mating behavior must be critically timed in relation to the cycle; as indicated in the figure, mating must occur within several hours after the LH surge, and several hours before the actual time of ovulation.

The estrous cycle is thus one of the most important of the biorhythms we discussed in Chap. 25. Its duration varies considerably in different mammals. In contrast to rats, for example, are species in which the cycle lasts a year. Many primates are intermediate; in the case of humans, of course, the cycle lasts approximately 28 days, and is called the menstrual cycle.

The cyclic changes in gonadotropin secretion from the pituitary are determined by changes in levels of releasing factors secreted in the hypothalamus, as we dis-

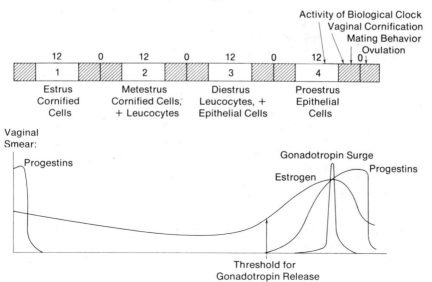

DIAGRAM OF FOUR DAY ESTROUS CYCLE IN RAT

Fig. 27.12 The estrous cycle in the laboratory rat. (After Gordon, 1972)

cussed in Chap. 23. What then determines the secretion of these factors? Part of the answer lies in the gonadal hormones themselves, which, as we have seen, are taken up and bound by specific cells in the hypothalamus. Negative feedback control is achieved in this way: increased hormone uptake suppresses production of releasing factors, decreasing the level of hormone, which in turn means less suppression and increased hormone levels, and so on. Part of the answer lies in the suprachiasmatic nucleus (SCN), which plays its role as the master oscillator in the brain; removal of the SCN abolishes the estrous cycle.

Many other regions of the brain make their contributions to the estrous cycle. These areas have been identified by a variety of studies. One approach is to stimulate electrically different regions, and observe the effects on blood levels of LH; conversely, the effects of ablation of different regions can be observed. Biochemical analysis of different regions has been carried out. Localization of sex hormones has been studied using intracerebral implants of hormones, and sites of steroid uptake and steroid receptors have been identified by

autoradiography. Finally may be added studies of sexual dimorphisms.

The results of these various studies are summarized in Fig. 27.13. These regions and the pathways that connect them may be said to form a distributed system, as we defined it in Chap. 24, for the neural control of the estrous cycle. At the heart of the system is the median eminence where the releasing factors are secreted (see Fig. 24.5). Feeding into this are the mammillary body, preoptic area (PO), the dopamine neurons of the median eminence, and the SCN (see Fig. 24.5). Next are regions of the limbic system such as the amygdala, septal region, thalamus, hippocampus, and mesencephalic reticular formation (see Chap. 28). Finally are the sensory pathways, especially olfactory, tactile, and visual, that have inputs to different regions. Within this distributed system, different regions are more or less closely related to the final control of releasing factors, and thus provide multiple ways in which nervous influences can be integrated and can have an influence on circulating hormonal levels. In some species, as in the rodent, the neural controls may be relatively powerful. In other spe-

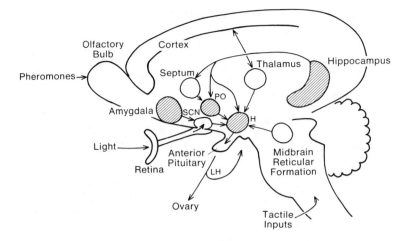

Fig. 27.13 Brain centers involved in the control of gonadotropin secretion and the estrous cycle in the female rat. Shaded areas indicate regions showing sexual dimorphism. H, hypothalamus; LH, luteinizing hormone; PO, preoptic area; SCN, suprachiasmatic nucleus. (Adapted from Harlan et al., 1979)

cies, such as the primate, they are less powerful, and hormonal levels are more dominated by pituitary–gonadal interactions.

Variety and Adaptability of Nervous Controls

No species better illustrates the powerful influences that the nervous system can exert on reproductive processes than the common house mouse. This is one of the most adaptable and opportunistic of all mammalian species, as attested by its distribution throughout the world. A key to this dispersion is the tendency of male mice to be aggressive toward each other, an aspect of behavior which we will discuss further in the next chapter. For now, we note that the result of this aggressiveness is for dominant mice to establish their territories, and for subordinate mice to be forced to seek elsewhere for mates.

Importance of Odor Cues

One of the main ways through which mice interact is through odor cues. When you put a mouse into a new cage, the first thing it does is to go around and mark it everywhere with urine. Figure 27.14 illustrates how this can be documented by simply taking a photograph under ultraviolet light. The urine caries odor cues (pheromones) that are like a fingerprint of that mouse, conveying specific information about its species, sex, sexual maturity, and social rank. By this means, a dominant male establishes his territory. The amount of pheromone in the urine is directly dependent on the high levels of circulating androgen that are present in a dominant male. The biochemical identity of the pheromone substance is still unknown.

The development of timing of ovulation in the female is critically dependent on the pheromones in the urine. The way this comes about is summarized in Fig. 27.15. Urine deposited by other females has an inhibiting effect on the development of puberty in a young female ①. This is viewed as a protection against pregnancy while the females are crowded and still growing, and before there is maximal opportunity for dispersion. By contrast, mature male urine odors act as powerful priming pheromones, which accelerate and indeed help to organize the processes of puberty, ovulation, mating, and pregnancy. The direct stimu-

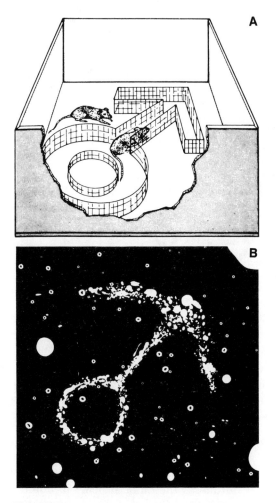

Fig. 27.14 **A.** Demonstration of urine marking by the house mouse. Diagram shows cage containing a fence in the form of the male symbol. Male mouse is inside cage, female mouse outside. **B.** Photograph of cage taken with UV light; white areas are sites of urine deposit. Picture was taken after mice had been in cage for 20 minutes (From Bronson, 1979)

latory effect on LH secretion is indicated at ②. This ability of males to bring a female into ovulation is obviously an important adaptive advantage in ensuring the success of mating. It is also known that female urinary pheromones can stimulate the secretion of LH and testosterone in males ③. This effect is independent of the reproductive status of the female. By this means

there is a positive feedback loop between the two sexes that ensures the greatest chances for ovulation and reproduction.

These experiments thus attest to the powerful effects of pheromones in regulating mating and reproductive behavior. These effects are found, to a greater or lesser degree, in most mammals. Many of the effects require or are enhanced by other factors, such as appropriate tactile stimulation by other animals, or adequate nutrition, or the ambient temperature.

Natural Rhythms of Ovulation

It should be stressed that most of our information comes from studies on laboratory animals living in crowded conditions, and the mechanisms of reproduction may be much modified compared with conditions in the wild. According to Frank Bronson (1979), one of the main contributors to the above account:

. . . we really have no idea whether or not the estrous cycle that has been so well delineated in the laboratory ever occurs with any regularity in the field. . . . house mice in natural populations (may) not routinely ovulate every fourth or fifth day . . . They may ovulate only when the probability of a successful, ensuing pregnancy is high. Thus ovulation may be a relatively rare event in the life of a mouse . . . It may be more adaptive for wild animals to concentrate on survival rather than reproduction unless the time for reproduction is truly propitious.

The fact that ovulation may be a relatively rare event in the mouse under some natural conditions has an interesting parallel among humans. Throughout most of human history, in many societies women have typically spent most of their childbearing years either pregnant or breast-feeding. Under these conditions, a woman ovulates only at irregular intervals, perhaps no more than a few dozen times in her entire lifetime. An interesting example of this is seen in the present-day 'Kung tribe in Africa, in which the mother breast-feeds her babies for several years. Suckling stim-

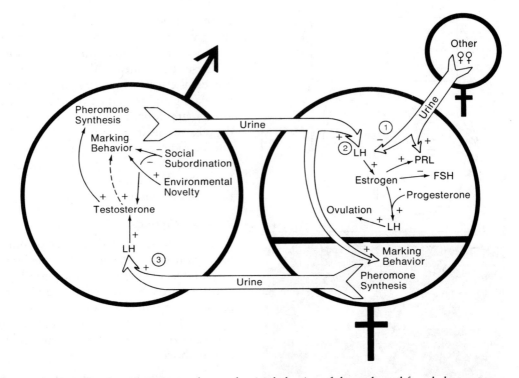

Fig. 27.15 Coordination of mating and reproductive behavior of the male and female house mouse through pheromones in the urine. ① Female–female inhibition; ② male–female stimulation; ③ female–male stimulation. FSH, follicle-stimulating hormone; LH, luteinizing hormone; PRL, prolactin; +, stimulation; −, inhibition. (From Bronson, 1979)

ulates the release of prolactin from the pituitary, which not only stimulates lactation but also suppresses ovulation. Prolactin thus acts as a natural contraceptive, and a 'Kung woman may become pregnant only a few times. Roger Short of Edinburgh, who has studied the 'Kung people, points out that we should consider infrequent and irregular ovulation and menstruation as just as normal as the modern belief in uninterrupted regular cycles. Thus, in humans as well as other mammals, there is evidence of the adaptability of the reproductive apparatus, and its ability to be shaped and modified by social and cultural factors mediated through the brain.

28

Emotion

Human beings have speculated about the nature of their emotions since earliest recorded history. The Pythagorian philosophers of ancient Greece believed that the universe is composed of four elements: fire and water, earth and air. Hippocrates and his followers deduced that the body is similarly composed of four corresponding humors: blood and phlegm (mucous discharge), black bile and yellow bile. A person's temperament was believed to express an excess of one or more of these humors. Thus, an excess of blood rendered a person sanguine: ruddy-complexioned, courageous, hopeful, amorous. An excess of phlegm made a person phlegmatic: dull, cold, even-tempered. An excess of black bile made a person melancholic and sad, whereas an excess of yellow bile made a person choleric, or angry. These ideas were so believable that they lasted until the seventeenth century.

Even though we regard this scheme now as a prescientific fairy tale, it is nonetheless sobering to realize that these terms are still used to describe human emotions. And when we try to define emotions, we find that we have made little progress, despite all our science. Shakespeare never used the word *emotion;* Hamlet, for example praised his friend Horatio as a man

. . . whose blood and judgment are so well co-mingled . . .

Today we would say that Horatio's thoughts and emotions were in good balance, but what have we gained?

According to the *Oxford English Dictionary,* the word *emotion* is derived from the French word *mouvoir,* "to move." It came into use in the seventeenth century to describe mental feelings (pain, desire, hope, etc.) that are distinct from thoughts, or cognitions. Within this broad and rather vague definition are three types of emotion, which are illustrated in Fig. 28.1. First are complex behaviors of an animal, such as predation, feeding, copulation, and related actions, which appear to us, through our human eyes, to be *emotional actions* (A), but which may actually have no emotional component for the animal itself. Second are specialized motor actions—*emotional expressions* (B)—in lower animals as well a humans which seem to express directly some inner feeling or emotion. Third are *inner emotions* or subjective feelings (C) which are entirely felt or perceived within

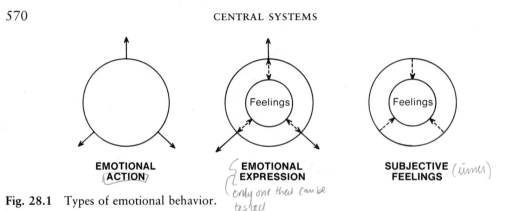

EMOTIONAL ACTION   **EMOTIONAL EXPRESSION**   **SUBJECTIVE FEELINGS** *(inner)*

(only one that can be tested)

Fig. 28.1 Types of emotional behavior.

us, and therefore known only to humans.

The neurobiological study of these three types of emotions has been rather limited. On the one hand, most complex behaviors are simply too complex to analyze, particularly when their emotional component is not obvious. On the other hand, our inner emotions are known only to ourselves. Most scientists rule out such subjective phenomena as objects of scientific study. That leaves us with only emotional expression as the type of emotion that is observable and amenable to precise analysis.

A Brief History

The subject of emotional expression was begun as a scientific study in 1806 by Sir Charles Bell of England, the same remarkable man responsible for the discovery of the sensory functions of the spinal nerves (Chap. 12), and for one of the first monographs on the structure and function of the hand (Chap. 22). In his book *Anatomy and Physiology of Expression* (Bell, 1837), he discussed the detailed relations between the facial muscles and many different expressions, such as laughter or grief. Various nineteenth-century authors added their observations, but the subject was little more than popular science, a branch of phrenology, until Charles Darwin published his book *On The Expression of Emotions in man and Animals,* in 1872:

Sir C. Bell's view (wrote Darwin), that man had been created with certain muscles specially adapted for the expressions of his feelings, struck

me as unsatisfactory. It seemed probable that the habit of expressing our feelings by certain movements, though now rendered innate, had been in some manner gradually acquired . . . expressions, such as the bristling of hair (during terror), or the uncovering of teeth (during rage), can hardly be understood, except on the belief that man once existed in a much lower and animal-like condition. . . . He who admits . . . that the structure and habits of all animals have been gradually evolved, will look on the whole subject of Expression in a new and interesting light.

Darwin based much of his study on comparisons between humans and domestic animals, and he analyzed the expressions of these animals as meticulously as he had the beaks of finches. One of his conclusions was that opposite emotions, such as hostility or affection, may be expressed by oppositely directed movements, and the illustration of Darwin's dog displaying these two attitudes (Fig. 28.2) has been often reproduced.

After Darwin there could be little doubt that humans express emotions by motor and muscular mechanisms that have evolved out of similar mechanisms present in ancestral forms and exemplified in present-day vertebrates, most particularly domesticated mammals. This provided the necessary rationale for scientific exploration of the neurobiological basis of emotions, using animals as experimental subjects. The techniques for doing these experiments did not become available until the 1920s and 1930s, and much of our present understanding of brain mechanisms had its origins

Fig. 28.2 Darwin's dogs, displaying the contrasting expressions of hostility and affection (the latter to a somewhat abject degree). Can you tell which is which? (From Darwin, 1872)

in that era. Before discussing this work in mammals, however, we need first to discuss the interesting question of whether emotions occur in invertebrates and lower vertebrates.

Invertebrates and Lower Vertebrates

The question of whether lower animals have, or express, emotions, has been the subject of lively debate. The view prevailing until the nineteenth century was well-summarized by Bell: ". . . with lower creatures there is no expression but what may be referred, more or less plainly, to their acts of volition or necessary instincts." Note that Bell was willing to grant lower creatures volition while denying them emotions! These acts or instincts fall into our first category of emotional behavior (see Fig. 28.1).

In contrast, Darwin was quite willing to extend his view of emotional expression in animals to lower forms. He wrote that "Even insects express anger, terror, jealousy, and love by their stridulation." In Chap. 23 it was noted that insects use stridulation to communicate with each other, with songs that signal "calling," "hostility," and "courtship." But whether or not these are accompanied by emotions, in the sending or receiving insect, remains unanswerable.

One test for the presence of an emotion is whether a given perception or motor act is accompanied by changes in the autonomic nervous system, such as faster heart beat or increased perspiration. This, for example, is the basis for the lie detector used to test whether suspects in a legal proceeding are telling the truth. It was stated in Chap. 18 that invertebrates have nerve ganglia that innervate their visceral organs, but that this innervation is relatively simple compared to that of vertebrates. The contrast has been summarized by Alan Epstein:

. . . like all other invertebrates (the molluscs) do not have an autonomic nervous system with which so much of affective expression is achieved. They do employ the same or very similar biogenic amines in their nervous systems and their viscera is innervated by peripheral ganglia, but this is hardly an autonomic nervous system which is an anatomically widespread and highly reactive system that provides duplex and functional antagonistic innervation to the viscera, smooth muscles, and glands, and is complemented by an adrenal gland.

Epstein notes the observation of Wells, that during sexual arousal and copulation, the octopus shows no changes in heart rate.

Later in this chapter it will be shown how important the vertebrate autonomic nervous system is for the expression of emotions in mammals.

Another feature of arthropods is their rigid exoskeleton, which limits their ability to express inner states by local muscular movements on their body surface. Nonetheless, arthropods do express different behavioral states in their displays and actions related to courtship, predation, and terri-

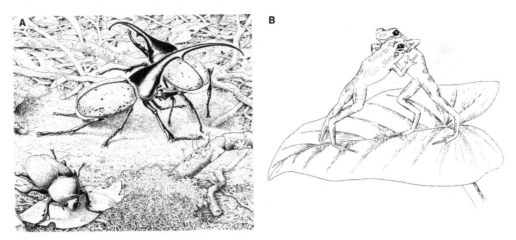

Fig. 28.3 Displays of aggressive behavior. **A.** Fight between two male Hercules beetles for dominance and access to female in lower left. **B.** Fight between two male frogs *(Dendrobates)* for possession of a territory. (A by Sarah Landry, B from Duellman, in Wilson, 1975)

tory. An example of a fierce struggle for dominance between two male beetles is depicted in Fig. 28.3A. However, these are signals conveyed by whole-body movements; there is no associated specialized system for conveying the emotional intensity or tone behind the actions. Nor is it entirely due to the limitations of an exoskeleton; frogs engaged in a struggle for territory similarly reveal little of the intensity of their efforts in their facial expressions (Fig. 28.3B).

We must conclude that a complex innervation of the internal viscera, and a complex set of muscles which can independently signal autonomic and other internal states, are two components that are necessary for the expression of emotion in animals. These two components are almost entirely lacking in invertebrates and lower vertebates. Therefore, we conclude that these animals can express behavioral states through whole-body actions, but they lack the ability to express emotions in any of the three ways defined in relation to Fig. 28.1 above.

Mammals

The fact that the expression of emotion seems to be a special ability of mammals is

a clue that it may play an important role in the development of higher nervous functions in mammals. Let us consider the evidence for the neural basis of emotions, and then discuss its implications, particularly with regard to motivated behavior.

Hypothalamic Mechanisms

The success of Ferrier and his contemporaries in mapping out the motor areas of the cortex in the late nineteenth century (see Chap. 21) prompted others to investigate the effects of electrical shocks to deep structures of the brain. This early phase culminated in the demonstration by W. R. Hess of Zurich in 1928 that attack behavior, including expressions of rage, and defensive behavior, including expressions of fear, can be elicited in cats by stimulation within the hypothalamus (see Fig. 28.4).

Sham Rage. At about this time, Walter Cannon and his student Philip Bard, at Harvard, carried out a complementary series of studies in which they examined the behavior of cats after transections of the brain at different levels. They found that removal of the forebrain (cortex and basal ganglia + thalamus, but sparing the hypothalamus) yields an animal that is irritable, and can be triggered into a display of rage

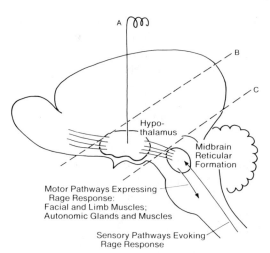

Fig. 28.4 Diagram of brain illustrating experimental demonstrations of various emotional
behaviors in the cat. Electrode (A) used to stimulate hypothalamus and produce expressions of
rage or fear. Transection (B) removing the forebrain and leaving the hypothalamus (hypothalamic animal) produces sham rage; transection
(C) below hypothalamus results in animal that
does not display sham rage.

nervous system). With regard to the autonomic responses, the displays of intense
emotional behaviors are one of the best
ways to bring out the actions of the sympathetic, as compared with the parasympathetic, divisions, as was first described
by Cannon. Thus, displays of rage or fear
are accompanied by increased levels of epinephrine and norepinephrine; in addition
to increased heart rate and piloerection,
blood is shunted to the muscles and the
brain, the eyes dilate, and so forth. These
changes bring the animal to the highest
level of alertness, and prepare it for the
most extreme levels of physical action which
may be necessary for ensuring its survival.

(baring of teeth, hissing, clawing) at the
slightest provocation (see Fig. 28.4). The
display is accompanied by autonomic
changes, such as increased heart rate and
bristling of the fur. However, because of
its low threshold, and uncoordinated and
undirected nature, the display lacks the
conscious dimension of normal attack behavior, and it was therefore termed "sham
rage." This is a useful concept; after all, it
is reasonable to expect a certain emptiness
of meaning in the behavior of a cat that
lacks its entire forebrain! When the transection occurs just below the hypothalamus, the sham rage response is lost (see
Fig. 28.4).

Autonomic Changes. These two lines of
evidence thus firmly established the importance of the hypothalamus for the expression of emotional behavior. This importance is seen both with respect to the somatic
component (control of facial and limb muscles) and the visceral component (control
of glands and muscles in the autonomic

Aggressive Behavior. Subsequent studies
have added some details to this general
picture. An important advance was the series of studies which John Flynn and his
associates at Yale initiated in the 1960s. By
selective stimulation of sites in the hypothalamus of awake, behaving cats, combined with careful behavioral observation,
they were able to distinguish between emotional and unemotional attack behaviors.
The behavioral test was to put a cat and a
rat into a cage and test the effects of hypothalamic stimulation on the cat. Stimulation could induce two basic types of attack. In *affective attack* (see Fig. 28.5), the
animal displays most of the signs of sympathetic arousal, emotional excitement, and
rage. The cat attacks the rat, with clawing
and hissing, though it does not usually
proceed to biting the rat unless stimulation
is prolonged. In contrast, in *quiet biting*,
the cat makes no sound nor shows any
emotion, but proceeds to capture the rat
and bite it (see Fig. 28.5). This is actually
similar to the normal predatory behavior
of the cat. If you have seen films of cheetahs
stalking and pursuing Thomson's gazelles
in the Serengeti of Africa, you will recall
the similar lack of emotional expression as
they go about their business.

It thus appears that one can distinguish
between *predation*, which has autonomic
activation but may proceed without the

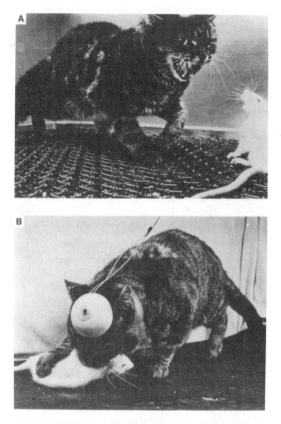

Fig. 28.5 Two types of aggression shown by a cat toward a rat. **A.** Affective attack. **B.** Quiet biting. (From Flynn, 1967)

expressive components, and *aggressive displays,* in which some of the components of predatory behavior are displayed in heightened form and used as threats to achieve dominance or defend territory.

Overlapping Distributed Systems. We have previously seen that the hypothalamus contains neural elements and mechanisms that are involved in several types of behavior: feeding, thirst, sexual activities, and hormonal and autonomic functions. To this we now can add mechanisms that are essential for the expression of emotions.

To some extent it is logical for these mechanisms to be closely related to emotions. Behaviors may be accompanied by emotions (such as attack accompanied by

rage), may lead to emotions (such as eating leading to satisfaction or dissatisfaction), or emotions may be the primary motivating force leading to the behaviors (such as fear leading to flight) (see below). However, it should be emphasized that the mechanisms are to some extent distinct; thus, animals stimulated to attack and bite prey do not also eat the prey. Close analysis of these relations is difficult, because of the close proximity of different centers within the hypothalamus, and the many systems of fibers that pass through it, as we have previously noted.

For the expression of emotion, we can therefore consider the hypothalamus as one center, or group of centers; in our previous terminology, it is one node, or collection of nodes, in a distributed system. Let us now consider the rest of that system.

The "Limbic" System

The region most closely related to the hypothalamus for the expression of emotion is the *midbrain,* just posterior to it (see Fig. 28.4). Attack behavior elicited by hypothalamic stimulation is blocked by lesions of the midbrain. Midbrain stimulation by itself can elicit attack behavior, even after surgical isolation of the hypothalamus from the rest of the brain. These results have indicated that much of the neural mechanism for the control of aggressive actions is present in the midbrain and lower levels. In line with the hierarchical view of motor organization, it appears that the motor control mechanisms are delegated to the brainstem and the spinal cord, and the hypothalamus may be mainly involved in initiating and coordinating these mechanisms.

The close relations of the hypothalamus and midbrain in these respects suggested to Walle Nauta, then at Walter Reed, that this part of the neuraxis has a functional unity in mediating visceral and emotional behavior. He has termed it the *"septo–hypothalamic–mesencephalic* continuum" (see Chap. 24). It is virtually identical with

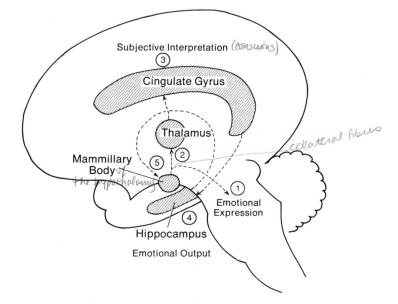

Fig. 28.6 Schematic diagram illustrating the Papez (1937) circuit for emotions. For explanation, see text.

the regions embraced by the medial fore-brain bundle.

Papez Circuit. What are the relations of this core system with other parts of the brain? The only coherent scheme of these numerous and complicated relations was put forward by James Papez of Chicago in 1973. We will discuss this scheme first, before reviewing more recent studies.

Papez was a neurologist who had noted reports of emotional outbursts in patients with damage to the hippocampus and to the cingulate gyrus. He carefully considered the known anatomy of the brain, and came up with a brilliant hypothesis for the neural circuit underlying emotions. The circuit starts with the mammillary body of the hypothalamus as the site of output for expression of the emotions, through its projections to the midbrain (see ① in Fig. 28.6). Collateral fibers pass to the anteroventral nucleus of the thalamus ②, where they connect to cells that project to the area of the cerebral cortex known as the cingulate syrus ③. Here it was proposed that conscious, subjective emotional expe-

rience arises; the cingulate gyrus was considered to be the cortical receptive region for emotional input relayed through the thalamus, in analogy with the visual cortex as the receptive region for visual input relayed through the thalamus. The cingulate gyrus, in turn, projects to the hippocampus ④. The hippocampus was proposed to combine this and other inputs and organize this information for output to its main projection site (it was believed), the mammillary bodies in the hypothalamus ⑤, thus completing the circuit. The pathway from cingulate to hippocampus to hypothalamus provided a means whereby the subjective experiences at the cortical level could be combined with the emotional content of the hypothalamic output.

No one had previously conceived of how these structures of the brain might be meaningfully related, and the Papez circuit was taken up with great enthusiasm and became a powerful stimulus to further research. An attractive feature was that it gave an interesting function to the hippocampus, which up to then had been considered to be part of the rhinencephalon (nose brain) and related in some unknown way to olfaction.

Broca's Brain. It was soon recognized that Papez's circuit was reminiscent of "The Great Limbic Lobe" of Broca. In 1879, Paul Broca, the great French neurologist, had noted how the cingulate gyrus and hippocampus seem to encircle or border the base of the forebrain. He imagined that this border, "placed at the entrance and exit of the cerebral hemisphere," was like the threshold of a door; hence, the term *limbic,* the Latin for threshold being "limen." He imagined that this limbic lobe is the seat of lower faculties compared with the higher faculties in the rest of the cerebral cortex. In 1952, Paul MacLean, then at Yale, and one of the foremost workers on the visceral functions of the brain, suggested the term "limbic system" for Papez's circuit and the other regions related to it, and the term stuck.

The idea that there is a distinct "limbic system" for emotions, just as there is a visual pathway for visual perception, is of course very attractive. But over 30 years later, it increasingly appears that this is a case of a beautiful theory at the mercy of some stubborn facts. Studies have indeed upheld the role of the hypothalamus and the cingulate gyrus in emotional behavior. But the essential roles of the remaining two regions in the Papez circuit, the thalamus and the hippocampus, remain uncertain. Ablation or stimulation of these regions has given variable or conflicting results in different species. In addition, several other regions have been shown to have powerful effects on emotional behavior. Foremost among these regions is the amygdala.

The Amygdala. This structure is a complex of related cells located in the cortex, at the base of the forebrain in lower mammals, and on the medial wall of the base of the temporal lobe in higher mammals. In the same year that Papez published his circuit, Heinrich Klüver and Paul Bucy at Chicago reported the results of experiments in which

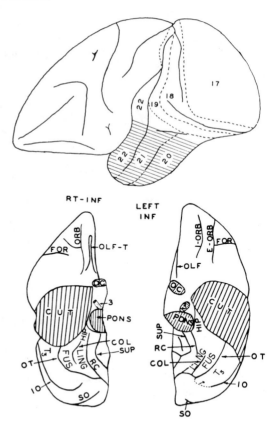

Fig. 28.7 Area of monkey temporal lobes removed (bilaterally) to produce the Klüver-Bucy syndrome. (From Bucy and Klüver, 1955)

they bilaterally remove the temporal lobe in higher mammals (see Fig. 28.7). They noted five main effects:

1. Overattentiveness: the animals are restless; they have an urge to orient toward or respond to all stimuli.
2. Hyperorality: the animals compulsively examine all objects by putting them in their mouths.
3. Psychic blindness: the animals see but do not understand; they indiscriminately approach and examine objects even though harmful (such as a lighted match).
4. Sexual hyperactivity: the animals increase their sexual activity, also indiscriminately, even toward inanimate objects.

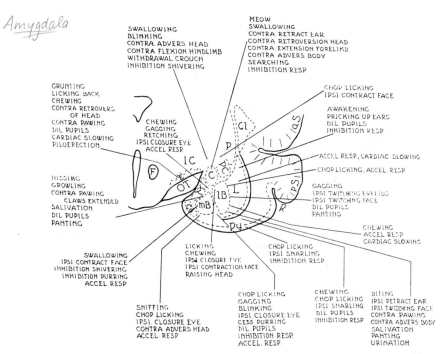

Fig. 28.8 Behavioral effects produced in the awake monkey by focal electrical stimulation at the sites shown. Abbreviations for nuclei of the amygdalar complex: C, central; PC, paracentral; M. medial; co, cortical; mB, mediobasal; lB, lateral basal; L, lateral. Other regions: IC, internal capsule; OT, optic tract; P, putamen; Cl, claustrum; aS, anterior sylvian; pS, posterior sylvian; R, rhinal sulcus; Py, pyriform cortex; F, fornix. (From MacLean and Delgado, 1953)

5. Emotional changes: monkeys previously wild and aggressive are rendered tame and placid, and can be handled easily.

This complex of features has come to be known as the *Klüver-Bucy syndrome*. The psychic blindness has subsequently been shown to be due to loss of temporal lobe neocortex (see Chap. 30). The hyperactivity may be due in part to discharging neurons on the borders of the lesion. The sexual hyperactivity (which originally was one of the most sensational aspects of the syndrome) seems to be so undirected as to be part simply of the general hyperactivity of these animals. Finally, the emotional changes in the Klüver-Bucy syndrome have been especially linked to the amygdala. However, the changes vary, depending on the species; cats, for example, are rendered savage after amygdala destruction. Some research has connected the hypersexuality with

the increased aggression in these cases. However, ablation is such a crude tool, and there are so many uncertainties about the extent of damage in different studies, that no firm conclusion can be reached.

Another approach in the study of the amygdala has been to use focal electrical stimulation. Some typical results are summarized in Fig. 28.8. Although these effects are quite dramatic, and seem relatively localized to the amygdala, a number of uncertainties limit the interpretation. For example, repeated shocks are often delivered over many seconds, or even minutes, to elicit these responses, raising questions about how much spread of seizure activity there is within the brain. Or the site stimulated may actually be suppressed by excessive currents, with activity being elicited only in surrounding areas.

To understand better the functions of the amygdala, we need to know to what it is

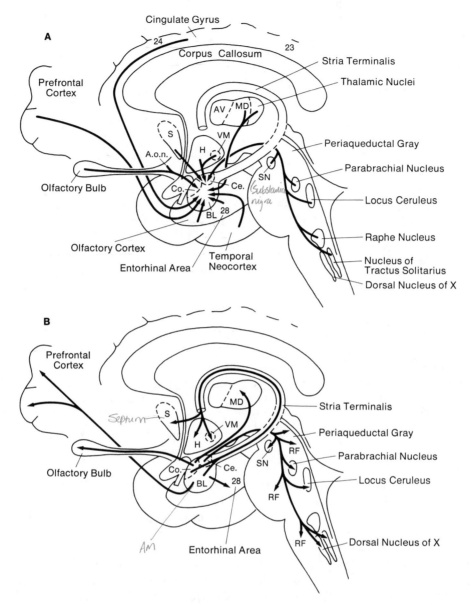

Fig. 28.9 Parts of the brain with connections to the amygdala. **A.** Inputs to the amygdala. **B.** Outputs from the amygdala. Abbreviations: A.o.n., anterior olfactory nucleus; AV, anteroventral thalamic nucleus; BL, basolateral amygdaloid nucleus; Ce., central amygdaloid nucleus; Co., cortical amygdaloid nucleus; H, hypothalamus; MD, dorsomedial thalamic nucleus; RF, reticular formation; S, septum; SN, substantia nigra; VM, ventromedial hypothalamic nucleus. (From Brodal, 1981)

connected. By studying transport of horseradish peroxidase (HRP), dyes, and radioactively labeled amino acids, neuroanatomists have shown that the amygdala has connections with a number of brain re-

gions. These results are summarized in Fig. 28.9. There are, first, projections from the two parts of the olfactory pathway (see Chap. 11). Then, starting from the forebrain, there are connections to cerebral cor-

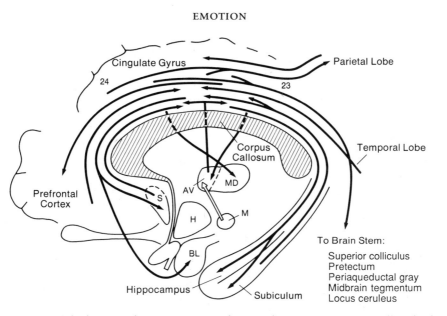

Fig. 28.10 Parts of the brain with connections to the cingulate gyrus. M, mammillary body. (From Brodal, 1981) For other abbreviations, see legend of Fig. 28.9.

tex (frontal lobe and cingulate gyrus), thalamus (mediodorsal nucleus), septal region, hypothalamus (through a long, looping tract, the stria terminalis, as well as short, direct ventral fibers), and numerous sites in the brainstem (fibers from the taste pathway—see Chap. 11—and from the raphe and locus ceruleus). Many of these connections are reciprocal, so that the amygdala gets feedback information from the sites to which it projects.

It should be emphasized that the amygdala is actually a complex of a number of nuclei (see Figs. 28.8 and 28.9). The *cortical and medial nuclei* form one main division, concerned with olfactory and taste information. As we have learned in Chap. 27, this information is used in the control of feeding, by the connections of the amygdala to the hypothalamus. The other main division of the amygdala, the *basolateral group of nuclei*, is much expanded in higher mammals. It seems likely that the connections of this division to the cortex and thalamus, as well as those to the "septo–hypothalamo–midbrain continuum," are involved in the expression of emotional behavior. Finally, it is likely that the microcircuits within different amygdaloid nuclei mediate special modes of local processing that the amygdala provides to the systems for emotional behavior.

Cingulate Gyrus. Similar studies have been carried out on other regions of the limbic system. The results of studies on the *cingulate gyrus* are summarized in Fig. 28.10. These results have fully confirmed the input pathway from the mammillary bodies through the anterior-ventral nucleus of the thalamus, and the output to the hippocampus, as postulated in the Papez circuit. However, they have shown further that the cingulate gyrus has connections to many other structures. Particularly important are connections to amygdala, subiculum (a cortical region neighboring the hippocampus), septum, and several sites within the midbrain (superior colliculi, for example, and locus ceruleus). In addition, there are connections to other areas of cortex, in the frontal, parietal, and temporal lobes. Many of the relations are reciprocal.

From these results it appears that the

cingulate gyrus may well have connections to a greater variety of subcortical and cortical structures than any other region in the brain. What is the significance of this great variety? Why should there be connections, for example, to the superior colliculus, which is involved in the precise sensorimotor coordination of visual tracking, as well as to the locus ceruleus, whose diffuse projections throughout the brain are involved in biorhythms and mechanisms of consciousness (Chap. 25)? We do not know why, but part of the answer may be that emotional expression requires extensive coordination of both visual and somatic behavior, and the cingulate gyrus is a center for this coordination.

Summary. In conclusion, we may summarize present concepts of the limbic system in the following manner. There is a series of structures, extending from the midbrain through the hypothalamus and into the basal forebrain, a phylogenetically ancient core system following the route of the medial forebrain bundle, that is concerned not only with visceral motor functions but also with related displays of motor behavior expressing emotion. These displays require the coordinated action of other brain centers. Some of these, such as the amygdala and the cingulate gyrus, are closely related to this core system. Others, such as the hippocampus and parts of the thalamus and midbrain, are related in limited, though specific, ways. Each of these regions acts as a nodal point in a distributed system, processing unique combinations of inputs and sending this information to unique combinations of output sites. By this means is achieved the coordination of visceral and somatic motor output to the whole body that is required for the expression of emotional behavior. Thus, it is still useful to think of a limbic system in terms of a core with many internal and outlying integrative centers; however, the borders of this system are not sharp, and the system overlaps with many other systems in the brain. In Chap.

30, we will discuss the particular contribution of the cerebral cortex to this system.

☀ Dermal Muscles

Most of the observations derived from studies of mammals appear to apply to the control of emotional behavior in humans as well. However, we would not want to leave the subject without discussing further the special motor apparatus that humans have for expressing emotions: the muscles of the face.

These have an interesting phylogenetic history. Snakes have small muscles that insert into their scales, and can hold the scale at different angles to help regulate how smoothly it moves; birds similarly have small muscles that regulate the angle of the feathers. Most mammals have a relatively loose skin, and there is characteristically a sheet of *dermal muscles* that inserts into the skin over most of the body. When a horse twitches the skin of its back to shake off the flies, it is using dermal muscles. The dermal muscles in the face are called *facial muscles,* and they serve a variety of obvious functions, such as moving whiskers (vibrissae) on the snout, pricking up ears, moving the mouth to form different sounds, or moving the mouth during oral exploration or eating.

In higher mammals, such as the dog, and especially in primates and humans, the facial muscles have become adapted for the expression of emotions. This was recognized by the earliest writers on the subject, and the diagram in Fig. 28.11, which was taken from Bells' book, shows the detailed picture of these muscles that had been obtained by anatomists by the nineteenth century. If, as Darwin put it, "expression is the language of the emotions," then movements of the facial muscles provide the vocabulary for that language. Although whole-body movements and gestures are important in the expression of many emotions, the facial muscles represent a special apparatus for this function.

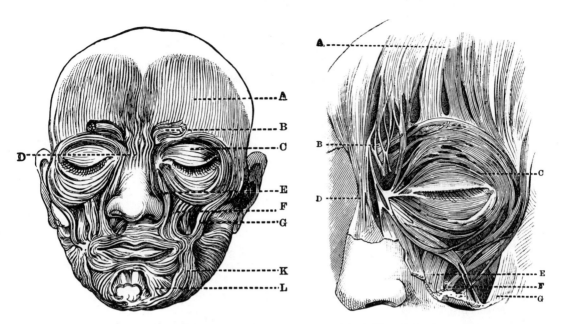

Fig. 28.11 Dermal muscles of the human face, as portrayed by Bell and Henle, in Darwin (1872). A, Occipitofrontalis, or frontal muscle; B, corrugator muscle; C, orbicular muscle of the eyelid; D, pyramidal muscle of the nose; E, medial lip-raising muscle; F, lateral lip-raising muscle; G, zygomatic muscle; K, mouth depressor muscle; L, chin muscle.

The degree of fine control exercised by the brain over these muscles is reflected in the large extent of their representation in the map of the motor cortex. It will be recalled from Chap. 21 that, in the homunculus of the body surface, the area of cortex involved in control of the facial muscles is greater even than the area for fine control of the hand. The pathways for this control are shown in Fig. 28.12. The fibers arising from pyramidal neurons in the facial area of the cortex connect bilaterally to the facial nuclei in the brainstem, there making monosynaptic and polysynaptic connections onto motoneurons that innervate the facial muscles through cranial nerve VII.

For the display of emotions by humans, we must therefore add this motor pathway to our limbic system. Detailed studies have shown that certain facial signals can be traced from primitive mammals through primates to humans. An example is shown

Fig. 28.12 Neural circuit mediating control of the dermal muscles of the face. RN, reticular nucleus.

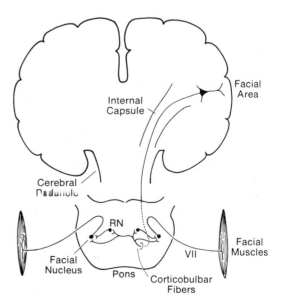

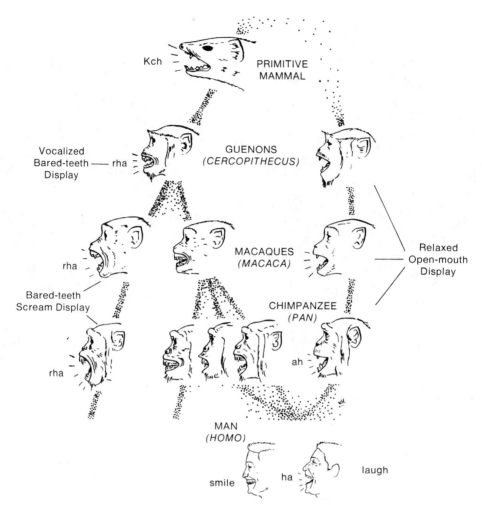

Fig. 28.13 Comparison of human expressions of smiling and laughter with the bared-teeth displays of lower primates and primitive mammals. (From van Hooff, in Wilson, 1975)

in Fig. 28.13, for the baring of teeth combined with vocalization.

Emotion and Motivation

In our previous discussion of motivation (Chap. 26), we noted that the behavior of most animals, certainly of higher animals, is not governed simply by reflex responses to deficits or immediate needs. We saw that most behavior starts with the internal generation of behavior patterns by the brain itself. This intrinsic activity of nervous centers produces instinctual patterns of behavior, that may be triggered or guided by appropriate environmental cues and feedback circuits. The intensity of these patterns varies by a complex set of factors, that include habits, incentives and rewards, learning and experience, as well as actual bodily needs. This set of factors is thought of as determining the amount of drive, or *motivation*, behind a given behavior pattern.

To this set of factors we now can add emotion. Emotion can be seen to be one of the key variables determining the kind of motor activity we engage in, and the strength or intensity of that activity. It is one of the primary factors responsible for the individuation of responses, for bringing out individual differences in behavior patterns among members of a species. We have seen that many of the neural mechanisms involved in the mediation of emotional behavior are found in the visceral part of the brain, and in the limbic system which coordinates visceral with somatic activities. Although we tend to think of these as lower functions, compared with higher functions such as learning or cognition, from an evolutionary point of view these mechanisms are among the most crucial to the success of individuals of a species, and for the adaptive survival of the species. This importance of emotions for motivated behavior has been eloquently stated by Alan Epstein (1980):

> Motivated behavior is laden with affect and its performance is accompanied by overt expressions of internal affective states. Affect is expressed by very young animals, is often full-fledged when first exhibited, and is typically species-specific . . . it does not depend on learning . . . These are not simply changes in limb movement or in the intensity of locomotion, but are true displays, organized into recognizable patterns, and sufficiently diversified to express a variety of internal states . . . in other words, motivated behavior is hedonic. . . . It arises from mood, is performed with feeling, and results in pleasure or the escape from pain, and although the moods, feelings, and satisfactions themselves are private and beyond our reach as scientists, their overt expression is a necessary characteristic of motivation.

The "hedonic" properties of behavior, mentioned above, are those that relate to our conscious judgments about whether a given sensation or action gives us pleasure or pain. How does the limbic system provide for this? Papez presumed that it depends on the cingulate gyrus. Modern concepts include the contributions of other regions, especially of the cerebral cortex, as we shall see in Chap. 30.

29

Learning and Memory

The Nature of Learning and Memory

Thus far we have assembled most of the major components needed by a central system to mediate behavior. A very rough idea of how these components vary across phyla is conveyed by Fig. 29.1. It can be seen that reflexes and instincts govern the lives of most invertebrates and lower vertebrates, with increasing contribution of motivated behavior in more complex verte-

Fig. 29.1 Schematic portrayal of the relative development of different modes of adaptive behavior in phylogeny. (Modified from Dethier and Stellar, 1964)

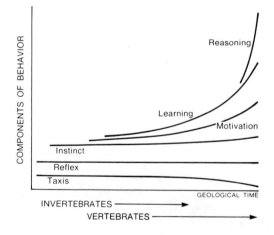

brates. We now consider an additional ability, and an essential one for most animals, the ability to learn, and remember what is learned. We shall discuss first the nature of learning and memory, and then consider what is known thus far about mechanisms, in invertebrates and vertebrates.

Definition of Learning

The word "learning" shares with other words we have used like "instinct" and "motivation," the problem of being a term in wide daily use. The ethologist S. A. Barnett (1981) maintained that

> colloquial terms with many . . . definitions, such as learning, are useful only as labels for general . . . categories of phenomena. . . . On this view it is inappropriate to ask what is the essence or the definition of learning.

This valid criticism notwithstanding, neurobiologists go right ahead and work on what they believe to be the problem of learning, so we need an appropriate definition for what they believe they are working on.

A very broad definition would state that *learning is an adaptive change in behavior caused by experience.* For the neurobiologist, the usefulness of this statement lies in a careful definition of each of the terms within it:

1. *Adaptive* indicates that the change must have some *meaning* for the behavior of the animal and the survival of the species.
2. By *change,* we mean that there must be a measurable *difference* between the behavior before and after some identifiable or imposed event. The change must be *selective* for the parts of the nervous system mediating the specific behavior, not just some general change in the animal, like increased metabolism or growing bigger. By the same token it must be independent of ongoing development or maturation. It should not be simply a reflection of fatigue, damage, or injury, or the normal adaptational properties of receptors and nerves.
3. The *behavior* must involve control by *central* systems of the whole organism. It should not be confined to a part of the peripheral nervous system, or a point in a sensory or motor pathway.

Although these qualifications may seem unduly burdensome, we shall see that each one has meaning when we come to the experimental analysis of mechanisms.

Definition of Memory

Closely allied to learning is *memory.* Memory may be defined as *the storage and recall of previous experiences.*

This is a definition that applies as easily to computers as to animals. Memory is necessary for learning; it is the mechanism whereby an experience is incorporated into the organism, so that it can later cause the adaptive change in behavior. In lower organisms, the mechanism for storage of information may involve almost any cellular or neuronal process that can be perturbed by experience or actions of the environment. In higher vertebrates, and especially humans, we usually think of memories as those experiences that are subject to conscious recall. In many cases these recollec-

tions may be of the nature of impressions of the passing world, and bear no obvious relation to learning. In this sense, memory may include more than the mechanisms specific for learning.

Although everyone agrees that the mechanisms for learning and memory are found in the nervous system, there has been considerable debate about whether one could ever learn anything about them. Many psychologists, for example, believe that theories about learning and memory should be self-consistent and self-sufficient, without recourse to neuronal mechanisms. In this view, psychologists and physiologists should each have their own theories; if one tries to join the two, it can only result, in the opinion of B. F. Skinner, in "bad physiology and bad psychology." For most neurobiologists, this view is outdated, and one of the goals of modern research is to join the two levels into a coherent framework.

In Search of the Engram

A more powerful voice in the debate was that of the psychologist Karl Lashley. In 1950, he published a paper entitled "In Search of the Engram." Engram is another word for memory trace. Lashley had spent most of a lifetime carrying out experiments designed to reveal the presence of memory traces in different parts of the brain. He concluded that engrams do not exist; that memories are not localized in any one structure within the brain, but are distributed diffusely throughout the brain.

In a way, this was the reticular theory reincarnated with a vengeance. Just as the reticular theory made rational investigation of neuronal organization seem hopeless, so the idea of functions spread diffusely throughout the brain seemed also to deny that they could be experimentally revealed. Lashley even observed, only half humorously that, after lifetime of studying learning, he was beginning to doubt it could exist! Lashley's famous essay had a powerful influence on the field, and it took a generation to reveal the shortcomings of his experiments and interpretations, and supplant them with a more optimistic view based on modern techniques.

Cell Assemblies and Synapses

The conceptual framework for the approach of modern neurobiologists to the study of the neuronal mechanisms underlying learning and memory was laid down by two other psychologists, Donald Hebb of Montreal and Jerzy Konorski of Poland, in the late 1940s. Both drew on notions dating back to Cajal that learning and memory must involve changes in nervous circuits. Hebb, in his book on *The Organization of Behavior* (1949), hypothesized that a psychological function, like memory (or emotion or thought), is due to activity in a *cell assembly,* in which the cells are connected together in specific *circuits.* He suggested that when a cell is active, its synaptic connections become more effective (see Fig. 29.2). This effectiveness may be a relatively short-lived increase in excitability, as in short-term memory, or it may involve some long-lasting structural *change in the synapse,* as in long-term memory. Konorski's ideas were similar. The concept that brain functions are mediated by cell assemblies and neuronal circuits has become widely accepted, as will be obvious to the reader of this book, and most neurobiologists believe that plastic changes at synapses are the underlying mechanisms of learning and memory.

Since the 1940s, there has been an outpouring of work by anatomists, biochemists, and electrophysiologists searching for clues to the postulated changes in synapses. Some of the main types of approaches that have been used are summarized in Table 29.1. We cannot review all this work here, and for further information the student will want to refer to textbooks and reviews in behavior, psychobiology, and physiological psychology. Much of this work was carried out before modern methods of cell biology were available. Also, many of the most sensational results have been found, on reexamination, to require more modest, or alternative, interpretations.

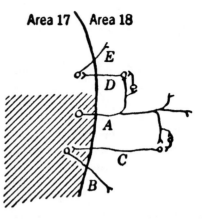

Fig. 29.2 The original concept of the "cell assembly" and the "Hebb synapse" (Hebb, 1949):

. . . perceptual integration would not be accomplished directly, but only as a slow development, and, for the purposes of exposition, at least, would involve several distinct stages, with the first of which we shall now be concerned.

The general idea is an old one, that any two cells or systems of cells that are repeatedly active at the same time will tend to become "associated," so that activity in one facilitates activity in the other . . .

The proposal is most simply illustrated by cells A, B, and C in [the] figure. . . . A and B, visual-area cells, are simultaneously active. The cell A synapses . . . with a large number of cells in 18, and C . . . happens to lead back into 17. . . . The cells in the region of 17 to which C leads are being fired by the same massive sensory excitation that fires A, and C would almost necessarily make contact with some cell B that also fires into 18. . . . With repetition of the same massive excitation in 17 the same firing relations would recur and, according to the assumption made, growth changes would take place at synapses AC and CB. This means that A and B, both afferent neurons of the same order, would no longer act independently of each other.

At the same time, . . . A would also . . . synapse . . . with a cell D which leads back into an unexcited part of 17, and there synapses with still another cell E. . . . The synapse DE, however, would be unlikely to be traversed, since it is not, like CB, exposed to concentrated afferent bombardment. Upon frequent repetition of the particular excitation in area 17, a functional relationship of activity in A and B would increase much more than a relationship of A to E.

A prime example is the recognition of the crucial importance of arousal. When an animal is tested in a learning task, its level of arousal, attention, motivation, and distraction are critical determinants of its

Table 29.1 Historical overview of some of the experiments that have provided evidence for mechanisms of learning and memory

Anatomical	
1. Environmental enrichment leading to bigger brains, dendrites, and synapses	Bennett et al., 1964
2. Effects of use on synapses	many authors, 1960s to present
Biochemical	
1. Increased neuronal activity leading to increased RNA	Hyden, 1959
2. Memory transfer between animals	
A. Cannibalism in *Planaria*	McConnell, 1962
B. Injections of brain extracts from trained animals into untrained animals	Babich et al., Fjerdingstad et al., Reinin et al., 1960s
3. Susceptibility to antimetabolite drugs (memory consolidation requires protein synthesis)	Flexner et al., 1960s
4. Cellular biochemistry of effects of use on synapses	many authors, 1960s to present
Electrophysiological	
1. Resistance to electroconvulsive shock	Duncan, 1949
2. Changes in EEG activity with learning	
A. Changes in hippocampal theta rhythms	Adey, 1960; Grastyan, 1966
B. High-frequency EEG rhythms in forebrain	Sheer, 1970
C. Slow potentials related to arousal or attention	Rowland, 1968
3. Changes in single neuron activity with learning	
A. During self-stimulation reinforcement	Olds and Olds, 1961
B. In relation to hippocampal theta rhythms	Ranck, 1973
C. In relation to amygdala and reward vs. aversive training	Fuster and Uyeda, 1971
4. Cellular electrophysiology of membrane properties at synaptic terminals	many authors (see Table 29.3)

For references, see Bennett (1977)

performance. Many of the findings in studies of interanimal transfer of learning (see item 2 under *Biochemical* in Table 29.1) have turned out to be attributable to nonspecific effects of the injected extracts on arousal, rather than on specific pathways in learning. Similar interpretations apply to several of the items under *Electrophysiological* in the table. This identification of the pervasive role of arousal and attention in learning is itself a valuable result, and is in accord with the importance we have placed on these functions for many aspects of behavior.

With regard to specific mechanisms of learning, most of the approaches listed in Table 29.1 may be regarded mainly as a historical background. For the remainder of this chapter, we will focus on modern research of recent years, which has shown that the postulated mechanisms of plastic changes at synapses can indeed be investigated at the cellular and molecular level. Thus, the field of learning and memory holds out some of the best prospects for understanding how cells and synaptic circuits provide the basis for behavior.

Types of Learning and Memory

Since behavior takes a variety of forms, it should not be surprising that there are a number of different types of learning and memory. Table 29.2 lists the main categories. The plan of this chapter is to consider each of these types in turn. One of the main accomplishments of recent research has been to show that many types

Table 29.2 Main categories of learning and memory

Types of learning	Types of memory
Simple	immediate
habituation	short-term
sensitization	long-term
	specific
Associative	
passive (classical)	
operant (instrumental)	
one-trial (aversion)	
Complex	
imprinting	
latent	
vicarious	

of learning have their counterparts in invertebrates as well as vertebrates. We will illustrate each type with examples.

SIMPLE LEARNING

Nerve cells have a number of properties that change with stimulation. For example, sensory receptors adapt, as already mentioned; their response tends to fade with continued or repeated stimulation (Chap. 10). Similarly, on the motor side, repeated stimulation of a motor nerve may cause a muscle to give either stronger (facilitation) or weaker (depression) responses. As we learned in Chap. 17, these changes are due to differences in the mobilization and release of the neurotransmitter at the neuromuscular junction. Table 29.3 lists some of the many studies of peripheral synapses that have laid the foundation for our understanding of the plastic changes that occur at synapses as a consequence of activity.

This raises an interesting question: do we say that the neuromuscular junction "learns" or has "memory"? The answer lies in the way we qualified our definitions in the previous section. Thus, we recognize that plastic changes may occur at many sites in the nervous system; these changes may contribute to learning and memory, and may serve as valuable models for their mechanisms. However, learning and memory are basically properties of *central systems* that control the behavior of the whole organism, and it is therefore within the central nervous system that we must ultimately seek the underlying mechanisms.

Habituation

Closely related to the plastic properties we have just discussed are habituation and sensitization. Habituation is defined as *the de-*

Table 29.3 Historical overview of some of the experiments that provided first evidence for molecular and membrane properties of synapses as a basis for plastic changes underlying learning and memory

Posttetanic potentiation at neuromuscular junction	Feng, 1941
Posttetanic potentiation in sympathetic ganglion	Larrabee and Bronk, 1947
Posttetanic potentiation in spinal cord	Lloyd, 1949
Quantal release of transmitter correlated with posttetanic potentiation and depression at the neuromuscular junction	del Castillo and Katz, 1954
Heterosynaptic interactions and presynaptic modulation	Dudel and Kuffler, 1961
Voltage dependence of transmitter release	Hagiwara and Tasaki; Takeuchi and Takeuchi, 1958–62
Calcium dependence of transmitter release, voltage dependence of calcium channels	Katz and Miledi, 1967
$[Ca^{2+}]$ (internal) and synaptic plasticity	Rahamimoff, 1968
I_{Ca} and synaptic plasticity	Zucker, 1974
Membrane potential effects of synaptic potential	Shinahara and Tauc; Nicholls and Wallace; Erulkar and Weight, 1970s

For reference, see Klein et al. (1980)

crease in behavioral response that occurs during repeated presentation of a stimulus. It may be seen that inclusion of the term *behavioral* helps to make this response fit our definition of learning. However, habituation is a universal phenomenon, and the term gets applied to many isolated components of behavior. In addition, habituation involves only a change in the intensity of a response, not in the nature of the response itself; and some workers, particularly psychologists, therefore do not consider it to be real learning. However, to the extent that habituation is of adaptive value, it is valid to consider it as an elementary form of learning.

The Spinal Cord

Habituation is usually observed as a change in the strength of a reflex response. Reflexes, as we have seen, are readily amenable to experimental analysis. Much of the early work on habituation was carried out on reflexes in mammals. This work showed that habituation occurs in a number of neural systems. Some of the best studied were spinal reflex pathways in the cat, and the reticular system of the brainstem. From these studies, Phillip Groves and Richard Thompson at the University of California elaborated a general scheme that accounts for the neuronal circuits that underlie habituation and sensitization (see below), and delineates the way the two processes are related. As shown in Fig. 29.3, it is envisaged that habituation is a property of relatively specific neural pathways, whereas sensitization involves a separate and more extensive set of connections which includes mechanisms for setting the "state" of the system. In Chap. 24, we discussed the significance of central systems with this property, and we shall see that this has provided a useful framework for considering sensitization in invertebrates as well as vertebrates.

In order to extend the studies summarized in Table 29.3 to habituation of central systems, what one wants ideally is a very simple response, a carefully controlled

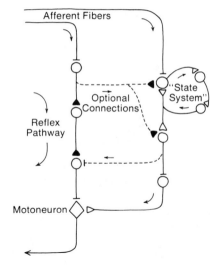

Fig. 29.3 Formal scheme to account for habituation and sensitization in a neural system, as exemplified by the mammalian spinal cord. Nonplastic synapses are indicated by bar terminal, habituating synapses by filled terminals. (Modified from Groves and Thompson, 1970)

stimulus, and a neuron along the central pathway that can be analyzed with intracellular recordings. These conditions are met in simple organisms with large, identifiable neurons.

Aplysia

The use of *Aplysia* for this purpose has been brilliantly exploited by Eric Kandel and his colleagues at Columbia University. They have studied the defensive withdrawal reflex of the siphon and gill (Fig. 29.4). The stimulus is a jet of water that activates tactile receptors in the siphon and gill and causes their reflex withdrawal. With repeated stimulation there is less withdrawal, and with sufficient repetition this depression of responsiveness may last for several weeks (A). Thus, both short-term and long-term habituation appear to occur.

For electrophysiological analysis, the sensory neuron mediating this response was stimulated electrically, while intracellular recordings were obtained from the motoneuron to the gill muscles (B). These experiments showed that the EPSP elicited in

A. THE REFLEX BEHAVIOR

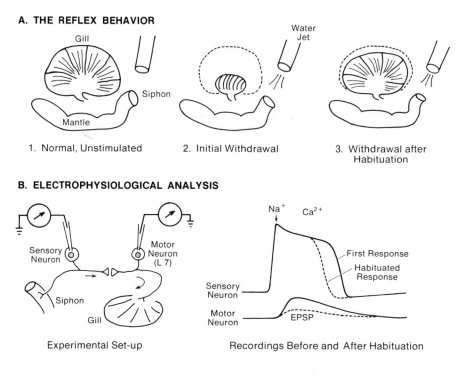

1. Normal, Unstimulated   2. Initial Withdrawal   3. Withdrawal after Habituation

B. ELECTROPHYSIOLOGICAL ANALYSIS

Experimental Set-up   Recordings Before and After Habituation

C. CONCEPTUAL MODELS

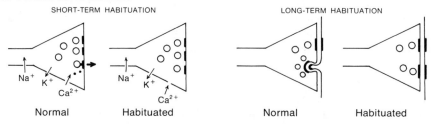

SHORT-TERM HABITUATION   LONG-TERM HABITUATION

Normal   Habituated   Normal   Habituated

Fig. 29.4 Summary of studies of habituation of the gill withdrawal reflex in *Aplysia*. **A.** The observed behavior. **B.** Intracellular recordings showing shortening of sensory action potential and decrement in motoneuron EPSP with repeated stimulation of sensory input. **C.** *Left:* Simplified model of synapse to account for habituation by depression of inward calcium current at the terminal. *Right:* Changes in structure of synaptic terminals during long-term habituation. (Adapted from Kandel, 1979; long-term habituation in C from Bailey and Chen, 1983)

the motoneurons by the sensory synapse underwent a decrease in amplitude with repeated stimulation that paralleled the habituation of the reflex. By analyzing the miniature EPSPs, it was found that the decrease in EPSPs with repeated stimulation was due to a decrease in the number of transmitter quanta released by the synapse; the response of the postsynaptic membrane to each quantum was unaffected.

What causes the decrease in number of transmitter quanta released? We know that Ca^{2+} is a critical factor controlling release at the neuromuscular junction, but how can one examine this at central synapses, which are too small to record from directly? Mark Klein and Kandel used the clever tactic of analyzing the Ca^{2+} channels of the cell body of the sensory neurons, and, by careful consideration of indirect evidence, inferring the properties of the Ca^{2+} channels in the synaptic terminal of this neuron. They blocked the Na^+ channels with TTX in the medium bathing the sensory ganglia, and showed that the TTX-insensitive part of the action potential, presumably mediated by Ca^{2+}, decreased in amplitude in parallel with the habituation. They concluded that depression of the Ca^{2+} current plays a critical part in short-term habituation. The model for this mechanism is depicted in C of Fig. 29.4.

Additional changes were found to be related to long-term habituation. In this case, it was found that a large proportion of sensory neurons produced no detectable EPSPs in motoneurons, as if a functional disconnection had occurred. The basis for this finding has been studied by injecting the neurons with HRP and examining their axonal varicosities, which make the synapses, under the electron microscope after long-term habituation (Bailey and Chen, 1983). In normal animals, 40% of the varicosities contain synaptic active zones, whereas in the habituated animals this was reduced to 10%, and the active zones were smaller and flatter (see Fig. 29.4C). Thus, long-term habituation may involve a decrease in numbers of active synapses as well as decreased output at a given synapse.

Sensitization

Sensitization may be defined as *the enhancement of a reflex response by the introduction of a strong or noxious stimulus.* Although it appears to be the opposite of habituation, it differs in several respects. It depends on a stimulus different from that which elicits the reflex in question. Any strong stimulus activates general arousal mechanisms (Chaps. 24, 25), and so do noxious stimuli (Chap. 12). Thus, sensitization involves activation of general arousal systems, which affect the intensity of reflex response. For example, if you are startled by a loud noise, you are more sensitive to a subsequent soft sound. It is a widespread phenomenon; it alerts animals to predators and other potentially harmful stimuli, and thus is of important adaptive value.

The cellular basis for sensitization has also been investigated in the gill withdrawal reflex of *Aplysia*. Noxious stimulation can be produced by delivering a train of strong electrical shocks to the skin of the animal. The effect of this stimulation is to restore partially the original amplitude of a habituated gill withdrawal reflex response (Fig. 29.5A,B). Analysis of the quantal EPSPs shows that the restoration results from an increase in the number of transmitter quanta released by each impulse in the sensory terminal.

The nociceptors activated by these shocks make connections onto the presynaptic terminals of the sensory neurons in the gill reflex pathway. A variety of studies by James Schwartz and Kandel and colleagues have shown that sensitization via this pathway involves a series of steps at the molecular level. These include (1) action in the nociceptor pathway, by release of serotonin and other transmitters or neuropeptides, to activate a specific receptor in the membrane of the sensory neuron terminals; (2) coupling of the receptor to adenylate cyclase, with production of cAMP; (3) activation of a cAMP-dependent protein kinase; (4) phosphorylation of a K^+ channel (S channel) to reduce K^+ currents during the impulse; (5) subsequent broadening of the impulse (as in Fig. 29.5B), leading to increased Ca^{2+} influx and therefore increased transmitter release (see Fig. 29.5C).

Sensitization thus works in a manner that is opposed to habituation, to increase the amount of transmitter released, increasing thereby the strength of each active synapse. The essence of this mechanism is control of K^+ channels, which in turn affects Ca^{2+} influx and transmitter release. It is important to note that the mechanism involves interactions between several types of

A. EXPERIMENTAL SET-UP DEMONSTRATING SENSITIZATION

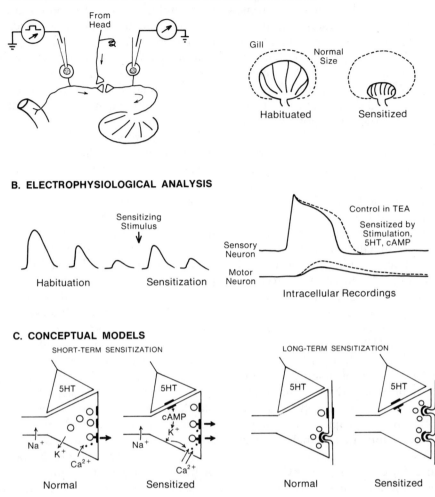

Fig. 29.5 Summary of studies of sensitization of the gill withdrawal reflex in *Aplysia*. **A.** Intracellular recordings from gill motoneuron, showing habituation to sensory input and sentitization by stimulation of nociceptors from the head. **B.** *Left:* Amplitude of the gill response during habituation and sensitization. *Right:* Broadening of the sensory action potential and facilitation of the motoneuron EPSP during sensitization of gill reflex. **C.** *Left:* Simplified model of the synapse to account for sensitization (see text). *Right:* Model of structural changes underlying long-term sensitization. (Adapted from Kandel, 1979, Shapiro et al., 1980, and Bailey and Chen, 1983)

properties: second messenger, ionic currents, membrane potential, and neurosecretion.

Long-term training can produce longlasting sensitization. This has been studied by election microscopic analysis of HRP-injected sensory neurons (Bailey and Chen, 1983). In contrast to the decrease in inci-

dence of active zones after long-term habituation (see above), long-term sensitization increases the incidence to 65%, and the active zones are larger and more complex (see Fig. 29.5C). The number of varicosities is also increased, indicating that sprouting of the terminal axonal branches has occurred. These experimental results imply that a second messenger (such as cAMP) not only has local effects in the nerve terminals underlying the short-term changes, but also stimulates protein synthesis to produce the long-lasting increases in sprouting and synaptic structure. Recent experiments have in fact demonstrated that treatment of the preparation with protein synthesis inhibitors can block the long-term morphological changes, and the long-term sensitization, without affecting short-term sensitization. We will discuss the molecular mechanisms underlying these changes further below.

Sensitization also occurs in the neural circuits that control feeding and heart rate in *Aplysia*, as well as in a variety of other invertebrate preparations. The three systems in *Aplysia* are similar in that sensitization appears to be mediated by serotonergic and/or peptidergic fibers, acting through cAMP to control voltage-dependent K^+ conductances, which in turn affect Ca^{2+} conductances. However, the points at which sensitization occurs are different in the three systems. The serotonergic fibers function to mediate arousal, and the different sites of connection are believed to reflect the differing significance of arousal for short-term sensitization, and for long-term plastic changes underlying learning in the case of the gill withdrawal and feeding reflexes. These arousal systems in *Aplysia* have their counterparts in vertebrates, as we discussed in Chaps. 24 and 26.

From these results, Kandel (1979) has postulated that

. . . Ca^{2+} current modulation may prove a general mechanism for learning and memory. The changes in Ca^{2+} influx can control the instantaneous level of transmitter release. . . . [M]odulation of Ca^{2+} channels . . . (might) be capable of contributing to long-term memory . . . by producing simple geometric changes in the shape of the synaptic apposition.

Similar mechanisms of synaptic modification have been proposed by others to underlie the changes that occur during neu-ronal development (see Chap. 9), and Kandel has speculated whether in this light one ". . . can conceive of learning as being a late . . . stage in neuronal differentiation." Thus, Cajal's belief that development and learning share common processes of neuronal remodeling seems a step nearer realization.

The work on habituation and sensitization therefore illustrates nicely how neurobiologists, by isolating for study a very simple and elementary function, can progress through a series of experiments to arrive at results of considerable general interest. Much more work remains, of course, in applying these concepts to the behaving animal. Despite these results showing synaptic plasticity, the learning ability of *Aplysia* in behavioral tasks is in fact rather limited. We shall consider this question further below.

ASSOCIATIVE LEARNING

In associative learning, an animal makes a connection through its behavioral response between a neutral stimulus and a second stimulus that is either a reward or punishment. The best known example is the way a dog, which normally salivates when presented with a piece of meat, will salivate at the sound of a neutral stimulus like a bell, after the bell has been paired with the presentation of the meat. This is called a *conditional reflex*. It was discovered in the early 1900s by Ivan Pavlov. By force of tradition it has come to be called *classical conditioning*.

With the advent of single-cell recording techniques, it became possible to test for the physiological mechanisms at the neuronal level. Table 29.4 summarizes some of the model systems that have been introduced for this purpose. Remarkably, a consensus is beginning to emerge on some of the cellular mechanisms that are common to classical conditioning in the different systems. For simplicity, we will consider

Table 29.4   Some model central systems which have been introduced for study
of the neuronal basis of associative learning

EEG alpha blocking	Jasper and Shagass, 1941; John, 1967
Electrical stimulation of the brain	Olds and Milner, 1954
Single neurons	Olds and Olds, 1961
Flexion reflex	Buchwald et al., 1965
Motor cortex neurons	Fetz, 1961
Leg position in cockroach	Horridge, 1960s
Heart rate in pigeon	Cohen, 1969
Auditory tones	Woody, 1972
Shortening response in the leech	Henderson and Strong, 1972
Odor learning in *Drosophila* mutants	Dudai et al., 1976
Sensory stimulation in *Hermissenda*	Crow and Alkon, 1978
Sugar-odor learning in honeybees	Erber, 1978
Odor learning in *Limax*	Gelperin et al., 1978
Feeding in *Pleurobranchia*	Davis and Gillette, 1978
Withdrawal reflexes in *Aplysia*	Walters et al., 1979
Eyeblink response	Gormezano, 1972; Thompson, 1976

For references, see Woody (1982).

these mechanisms by extending our discussion of *Aplysia* from the previous section.

Invertebrates

Tom Carew, Kandel, and their colleagues have shown that the siphon–gill reflex can be classically conditioned, and the mechanism is similar to the underlying sensitization. The system is depicted in Fig. 29.6A. Gill withdrawal can be elicited by stimulation of the tail (middle); the siphon (below); or a nearby region, the mantle shelf (above). A strong shock to the tail was an unconditional stimulus (US in A,B), whereas a weak shock to the mantle shelf was a conditional stimulus (CS$^+$ in A,B). When the two were paired, the monosynaptic response recorded in the motoneurons in response to the conditioned stimulus was increased (see asterisk in C). As required in classical conditioning, the timing was critical; the conditional stimulus had to precede the unconditional stimulus (see B), and by an interval of no more than 1 second. Stimulation of another pathway (the siphon; see A, CS$^-$) without this temporal specificity (see B, CS$^-$) produced no conditioning [see C, unpaired (CS$^-$)].

At the molecular level, the mechanism is believed to be similar to that of sensitization. Thus, the normal sequence of events in the synaptic terminal onto motoneurons in either the mantle or siphon pathway (the conditional pathway) involves invasion of the impulse into the terminal; the depolarization activates a limited Ca^{2+} influx, bringing about a low level of vesicle exocytosis, transmitter release, and postsynaptic response. During conditioning, the temporally specific pairing of action potentials (CS) with synaptic input (US) leads to a greater influx of Ca^{2+} with each action potential. The Ca^{2+} binds to calmodulin which activates adenylate cyclase to produce cAMP; thus, the conditioned terminals produce more cAMP, leading to activation of more cAMP-dependent protein kinase, and thus to phosphorylation and closing of K^+ (S) channels; broadening of the preterminal spike; more Ca^{2+} influx at the synaptic active zone; more transmitter release; and a larger postsynaptic response. These steps may be reviewed in the diagrams of Fig. 29.5C.

As a result of this mechanism, the weak CS in effect accesses the same second messenger system employed by the strong synaptic input of the US, and replaces the US in activating this system. These changes all take place in the terminals onto the motoneurons; activity in the motoneurons is neither necessary nor sufficient for condition-

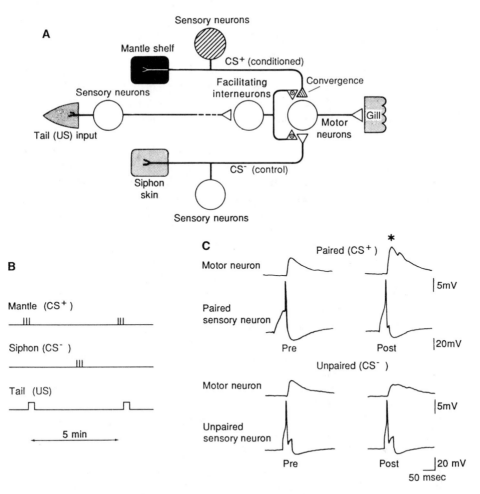

Fig. 29.6 Analysis of mechanisms of classical conditioning in *Aplysia*. **A.** Neural system controlling the gill reflex. The unconditional stimulus (US) consists of strong electrical shocks to the sensory nerves from the tail; it always elicits gill withdrawal. The conditional stimulus (CS⁺) consists of weak electrical shocks to the sensory neurons of the mantle; by itself it does not elicit a response. Weak electrical shocks to the sensory neurons to the siphon skin serve as a control conditional stimulus (CS⁻). **B.** The classical conditioning paradigm. CS⁺ is paired with US; CS⁻ is unpaired. **C.** Intracellular recordings from sensory neurons and gill motoneurons before conditioning (Pre) and one hour after (Post) a series of conditioning trials. The paired (CS⁺) trials produced a potentiation of the EPSPs in the motoneurons (asterisk), whereas the unpaired (CS⁻) trials did not. (From Kandel and Schwartz, 1985)

ing to occur. It would appear therefore that classical conditioning of this reflex is based entirely on a *presynaptic* mechanism, and that this differs from a Hebb-type mechanism, in which changes are postulated to occur in both pre- and postsynaptic sites (see above). However, while the mechanism is *presynaptic* with relation to the motoneuron, it is *postsynaptic* with relation to the synaptic input from the tail. Further experiments will be necessary to determine if changes also occur in the presynaptic terminals of the tail pathway.

In comparing these results with those in other invertebrate models (see Table 29.4), Tom Carew and Chris Sahley (1986) have noted some "common themes and convergent ideas [that] provide a framework for further investigations." First, experience causes changes in previously existing circuits; "in no case have novel synapses or new biophysical properties been introduced by learning." Second, modulation of K^+ conductance is involved in memory storage. Third, second messengers such as Ca^{2+} and cAMP are important in modulating the K^+ conductances. These second messengers may mediate local changes underlying short-term memory, or they may link local changes to the genome and regulation of protein synthesis related to long-term memory. Finally, although storage mechanisms (2 and 3 above) may be common, acquisition mechanisms may be variable. For example, acquisition in *Hermissenda* involves a cumulative sensory-induced depolarization that is primarily monosynaptic, whereas in *Aplysia* it involves, as we have seen, heterosynaptic enhancement.

A final point is that in most of the model systems examined thus far (see Table 29.4), the pathways are either primary sensory (e.g., *Hermissenda*) or sensorimotor reflexes (e.g., *Aplysia*). We began this chapter by noting that learning and memory need to be viewed primarily as properties of central systems. Therefore, in order to relate these model systems to learning and memory, there is a need to develop models of central systems to bridge this gap and address more directly the way central circuits mediate these functions. We turn next to some models in the mammalian brain.

Vertebrates

Mechanisms underlying associative learning have been pursued at the single cell level in many parts of the mammalian brain. In reviewing recent studies, Thompson (1986) has observed that memory traces do not appear to be localized to lower reflex centers in the brainstem and spinal cord; the most likely structures under current investigation are the cerebellum, hippocampus, amygdala, and cerebral cortex. We will summarize recent evidence obtained in the cerebellum and cerebral cortex, and

later in this chapter consider the hippocampus.

Cerebellum. A useful model for investigating the role of the cerebellum in learning at the cellular level has been the eyeblink reflex, introduced by I. Gormezano in 1972 and developed by Richard Thompson and his colleagues. An air puff to the cornea of a rabbit elicits an unconditional eyeblink reflex; this can be classically conditioned to an auditory tone. By making ablations of many different regions, it has been shown that the ipsilateral cerebellum is essential for learning and remembering this conditioned response, though not for the unconditioned reflex itself. The crucial site has been further localized to the lateral interpositus nucleus, one of the group of deep cerebellar nuclei (see Chap. 21).

The main afferent pathway for the unconditional reflexes is via the inferior olive, and the main efferent pathway is via the red nucleus (Fig. 29.7, diagram in upper left). The interpositus nucleus receives climbing fiber input from the inferior olive, and in turn sends its output fibers to the red nucleus (Chap. 21). Single-cell recording from microelectrodes chronically implanted in the interpositus nucleus have documented the learning-related changes in neuronal activity. As shown in Fig. 29.7, the animal was first given separate random unpaired presentations of the conditional stimulus (CS), which elicited no significant eyelid response or change in neural activity, and the unconditional stimulus (US), which elicited the blink and a small change in neural activity. The stimuli were then paired; as training progressed through day 1 and day 2, the CS elicited an increased eyeblink response and an increased cell response (see Day 2, Fig. 29.7). The cell activity is associated in time with the CS, suggesting that it represents a "model" of the conditioned, that is, learned, response.

The pathway for the conditional response has been shown to be, on the sensory side, through the auditory pathway to

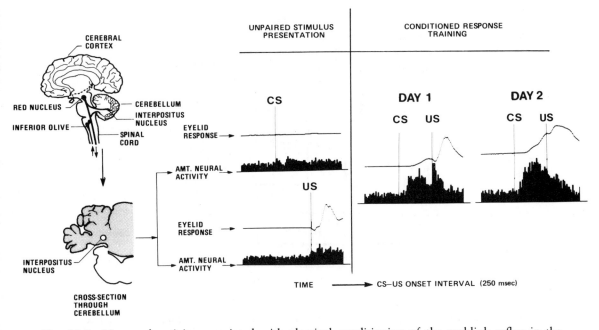

Fig. 29.7 Neuronal activity associated with classical conditioning of the eyeblink reflex in the rabbit. *Left:* The upper diagram shows the main pathway for the unconditional eyeblink in response to an air puff to the eye; the lower diagram shows the recording site in the interpositus nucleus. On *Right:* Histograms of the neural activity together with a monitor of the eyelid movement. The pretraining control tests consisted of 104 trials with each stimulus (US air puff and CS auditory tone). Training sessions consisted of 117 trials each day. In the histograms, each bar represents the numbers of spikes in 9-msec bins. Note that the increased responses during training are related to the CS rather than the US. See text. (From Thompson et al., 1984, and R. F. Thompson, personal communication)

pontine nuclei, where mossy fibers to the cerebellum arise. Electrical stimulation of the mossy fibers is effective as a CS, producing rapid learning when paired with a US air puff. Thus, at the level of the cerebellum, the climbing fibers act as the US and the mossy fibers act as the CS. Many years ago, David Marr deduced that climbing fibers and mossy fibers could function in this way. The entire circuit identified thus far is summarized in Fig. 29.8. Although this particular circuit applies to the eyeblink response, the cerebellar components are more generally involved in learning; it has been suggested that "the cerebellum is essential for the learning of all discrete, adaptive motor responses, at least for classical conditioning with an aversive UCS" (Thompson et al., 1984).

Cerebral Cortex. The cerebral cortex is crucial for mechanisms of learning and memory, particularly in mammals and, of course, humans. Single-cell recordings have shown that single cortical neurons can be classically conditioned, and the use of intracellular techniques has permitted analysis of membrane properties that may underlie the acquisition of the learned responses.

A series of experiments of this type have been carried out in the cat by Charles Woody and his colleagues at UCLA. Typical results are illustrated in Fig. 29.9. The experiment consisted first of conditioning the eyeblink response while recording extracellular spike activity from a single neuron in the motor cortex of the cat. The conditioning responses to an auditory "click" are shown

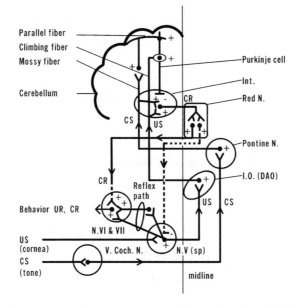

Fig. 29.8 Pathways that represent the memory trace circuit for the eyeblink response. The unconditional stimulus (US) is an air puff to the cornea. This activates the sensory fiber of the trigeminal nerve to the spinal nucleus of the trigeminal nerve [N. V (sp)]. From here the output fibers divide. Some mediate an immediate unconditional response (UR) at the brainstem level. Others ascend to the dorsal accessory portion of the inferior olive (IO, DAO), which projects through climbing fibers to the interpositus nucleus (Int.) and to the cerebellar cortex to connect there to Purkinje cells. By contrast, the auditory conditional stimulus (CS) activates the ventral cochlear nucleus (V. Coch. N.) which projects to the pontine nuclei, from which mossy fibers arise that connect to the interpositus nucleus and cerebellar cortex. The output pathway from the interpositus nucleus goes through the red nucleus to the brainstem output nuclei. The dashed line shows an inhibitory connection from the red nucleus to the spinal nucleus of V, which is presumed to enable the red nucleus to dampen US activation of climbing fibers after the CR eyelid closure. +, synaptic excitation; −, inhibition. The cerebellar components of this circuit are believed to be involved in many other learned aversive behaviors. (From Thompson, 1986)

in A. A period of time then passed without stimulation; the conditioning response became much weaker, a phenomenon known as extinction (B). Upon retraining, the response returned (C). The loss with extinction and return with reconditioning are summarized in (D).

In some cells, these trials were carried out using intracellular recordings, so that the cells could be identified and the membrane properties analyzed. In E is shown a layer V pyramidal neuron, injected with HRP, which displayed the properties shown in A–D. Intracellular recordings from this cell in F show the response to injected current (monitor below) before (left) and after (right) the extracellular application of ACh. As can be seen, the effect of ACh is to increase the input resistance (as shown by the larger depolarizing transient on the right); the raised excitability leads to an increased spike discharge. A similar effect is induced by intracellular application of cGMP or cGMP-dependent protein kinase. It is postulated that similar changes could be part of the molecular mechanisms underlying the increased probability of impulse activity after conditioning, by altering

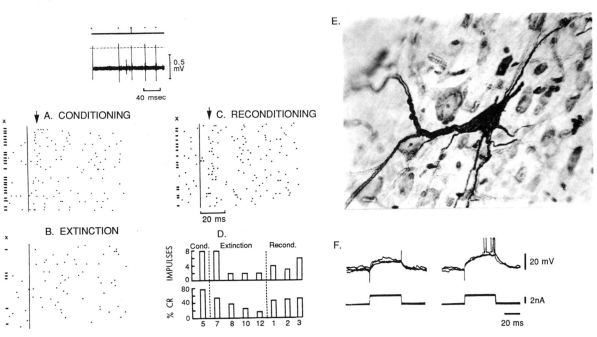

Fig. 29.9 Classical conditioning of neurons in the motor cortex of the cat to the eye blink response. *Upper left:* Extracellular spike recording of a cortical cell; dashed line shows cutoff for dot display of spike activity. **A.** A 32-sweep raster display of spike activity evoked by click CS in a conditioned animal. Each dot shows one spike; each row shows one trial. The initial horizontal bar designates a conditioned blink response in that trial; the large arrow indicates the initial spike response. **B.** Activity after extinction (see D for extinction times). **C.** Activity after reconditioning. **D.** Number of impulses above the resting level in the period 8–28 msec after the conditioning click, averaged for each time interval during extinction (B) and reconditioning (C), and compared with the corresponding percent change in the conditioned response (CR) eye blink (bottom graph). **E.** HRP-injected pyramidal neuron in layer V of the cat motor cortex. This cell showed properties of A–D and F. **F.** Responses of this cell to intracellular current pulses before (left) and after (right) extracellular application of ACh. See text. (From C. Woody, personal communication; see also Woody, 1982)

the weighting of EPSPs elicited in the cell by the CS (C. Woody, personal communication).

Operant Conditioning

In classical conditioning, the animal is a passive participant. By contrast, an animal may be asked to learn a task or solve a problem, such as escaping from a box, or pressing a lever, or running a maze. This experimental method was introduced by Edward Thorndike in 1898. Since the animal learns to solve the problem and get the reward (or avoid the punishment) by operating on its environment, it is called *operant conditioning,* or *instrumental conditioning;* since the animal usually makes mistakes before learning the task, it is also called *trial-and-error learning.*

In both classical and instrumental conditioning, the strength of the response depends on the amount of reward or punishment. Particularly in the case of instrumental conditioning, the strength of the response can be used as a measure of the animal's "drive" to obtain the reward or escape the punishment. These experiments have thus

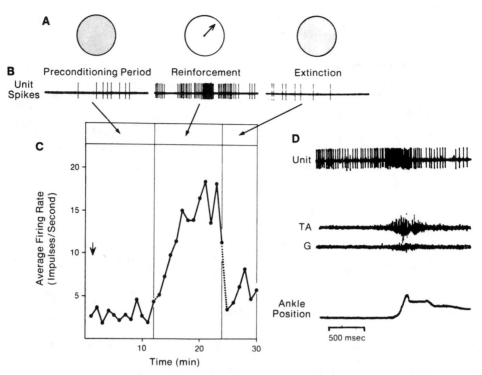

Fig. 29.10 Operant conditioning of a single neuron in the motor cortex of an awake, behaving monkey. **A.** Meter registering rate of impulse firing; when firing rate exceeded a preset level, dial became illuminated, and food reward was given. **B.** Representative records of impulse activity. **C.** Graph of impulse firing rate during successive experimental periods. **D.** Relation of muscle activity [EMG of tibialis anticus (TA) and gastrocnemius (G) muscles] and ankle movement to operant impulse burst of a reinforced motor cortical neuron. (Modified from Fetz and Baker, 1973)

provided the basis for studies of motivation, as discussed in Chap. 26.

One of the most surprising results of these studies has been the ability to condition single neurons in the brain by operant techniques. This was first demonstrated by James and Marianne Olds at Michigan in 1961 (see Table 29.1). Figure 29.10 illustrates such an experiment on neurons in the motor cortex of the monkey, conducted by Eb Fetz and Mary Ann Baker (1973) of the University of Washington. The recordings were made using implanted microelectrodes in awake animals. The rate of impulse firing was registered on an illuminated dial, and when the rate exceeded a preset level, a few drops of tasty fruit juice were given as a reward. During the training period, the increase in activity took the form of bursts of impulses; as conditioning proceeded, the bursts became more frequent and more intense. When the reward was withheld, the rate of firing fell rapidly to its former level, a property called extinction. Occasionally, two units could be recorded from the same electrode; in some cases the firing patterns were similar, indicating coactivation; in other cases they were inversely correlated, indicating differential control of neighboring cortical cells. The relation of the neuronal activity to muscle movement was studied by recording the electrical activity of the muscles (electromyograph) and muscle movement. As shown in Fig. 29.10D, the impulse bursts tended to precede slightly the onset of muscle activity and muscle movement, suggesting that the bursts were part of the motor activity initiating motor performance during reinforcement, rather than simply a result of sensory feedback to the cortex from the moving muscles. The student should review Chaps. 12, 22, and 24 to appreciate the sensory, motor, and central circuits involved in this motor activity.

Aversion Learning

For most of this century, classical and operant conditioning have dominated our concepts of how learning may occur. Each seemed to have such obvious value to an animal that it was impossible for most behavioral scientists to conceive of any other mechanism. However, it has become clear that there are indeed other very important forms of learning. The problem first is to recognize them, and then to figure out how to study them experimentally.

An excellent example of this is aversion learning. In the 1960s, John Garcia and Robert Koelling (1966) were interested in how rats learn to associate tastes with sickness. They used the fact that strong X-irradiation of an animal damages the gastrointestinal tract and induces sickness after a period of several hours. The rats were given distinctively tasty solutions of water to drink, paired with X-irradiation. After recovering from the sickness, the rats refused to drink the tasty water. This is a laboratory demonstration of a phenomenon we all recognize: when we suspect that a food has made us sick, we lose our "taste" for the food and avoid it. In field studies of animals it is called "bait-shyness." Because it requires only one episode of sickness, it is also called "one-trial learning."

Although the pairing of an unconditional stimulus (sickness) and a conditional stimulus (taste) satisfies the criteria for associative learning, there are several differences from the situation in classical conditioning. In classical conditioning, many trials are usually needed for transfer from the unconditional to the conditional response, and the unconditional and conditional stimuli must be timed very closely together, usually within a second or two, or else the animal cannot make the association between the two. By contrast, in aversion learning, only one trial is necessary, and the association between taste and sickness is made after a delay of several hours. These differences are so dramatic that at first few psychologists would even believe the results; one of them has been quoted as commenting "These findings are no more likely than bird droppings in a cuckoo clock!" (quoted in Chance, 1979).

By now the basic findings have been repeatedly documented and extended to many different species. It has been found that many agents can serve as the unconditional aversive stimuli; these include lithium chloride solutions, psychoactive drugs like amphetamine and apomorphine, and certain poisons. However, many agents are surprisingly ineffective; these include toxic substances like strychnine, and general factors such as stress. Electric shocks, which are so effective for classical or operant conditioning when paired with visual and auditory stimuli, have little effect. Parallel studies of the conditional stimulus have shown that one-trial learning can be demonstrated only by using stimulation of the tongue. The learning is strongest when the inputs come from the taste buds, but aversion can also be demonstrated with tactile stimulation of the tongue.

Many fascinating questions are raised by these findings, but we will consider only two here. First, what are the neural pathways for aversion learning? The taste part of the system was discussed in Chap. 11, and is reproduced in Fig. 29.11. The other pathway, mediating the aversive input, is more difficult to specify, because of the diversity of agents that may serve as unconditional stimuli. However, it is believed that much of this input is carried in visceral afferent fibers. These fibers convey sensory input from the intestines and other internal organs to the brainstem, through the tenth cranial nerve. Among the sites of termination within the brainstem is the nucleus of the solitary tract, the main sensory relay

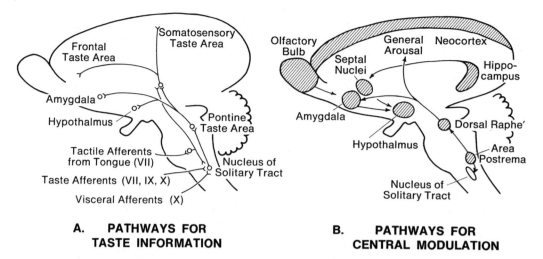

**A.   PATHWAYS FOR
        TASTE INFORMATION**

**B.   PATHWAYS FOR
        CENTRAL MODULATION**

Fig. 29.11   Neural pathways mediating taste aversion learning in the mammal. (Based in part on Ashe and Nachman, 1980)

nucleus in the taste pathway. The explanation of aversion learning requires a site, or sites, at which the taste and aversive pathways meet, and the nucleus of the solitary tract appears to be a likely candidate.

In addition to the two pathways mediating the sensory inputs, a variety of other brain regions have been found to have an influence on aversion learning. These have been identified by ablation and stimulation experiments, which, as we have emphasized, are rather crude tools. Some of the main regions identified by these means are shown in Fig. 29.11B. The diversity of these regions is remarkable. Note that many of them have been encountered before, as nodal points in limbic systems involved in mediation of feeding, arousal, and sexual functions. Each region is an integrative center that makes its special contribution to these different functions. Thus, the *nucleus of the solitary tract* is itself significant not only as the convergence point for taste and visceral inputs, but also as a region involved in arousal, as discussed in Chap. 25. As another example, lesions of the *amygdala* produce deficits in several types of learning. In the case of aversion learning, the rats seem to have difficulty in recognizing the significance of different taste stim-

uli, which has been interpreted as a perceptual deficit. In addition, animals with amygdalar lesions are unable to orient normally, which is believed to represent deficits in motivation.

From these considerations, the study of the neural circuits involved in aversion learning has led to a much broader perspective on learning processes in general. This new view has been expressed by John Ashe and Marvin Nachman (1980) in the following way:

When an animal undergoes an experience, learning is only one of a wider complex of physiological responses that may occur. Arousal, attention, stress, and motor responses are (also) . . . initiated, and it is . . . likely that these responses are coupled to associative mechanisms . . . One of the major by-products of learned taste aversion research has been the reemphasis on the importance of understanding the total animal in elucidating principles of associative formation. In neurobiological terms . . . stimuli that initiate internal consequences that are smoothly coupled to the on-going physiology of the animal should result in robust learning and thus the animal will appear to be especially "prepared" for the acquisition of this learning.

It can thus be seen that considerable progress has been made toward understanding the neural circuits involved in aversion learning. By contrast, we know almost nothing about the cellular mechanisms that mediate these remarkably long-lasting effects. As a working hypothesis, one can speculate that the mechanisms that have been invoked for long-term changes in habituation and sensitization may be involved—that is, changes at synapses involving phosphorylation of channel proteins, modulation of K^+ and Ca^{2+} conductances, and possibly changes in DNA expression.

Invertebrates also show one-trial learning (see Table 29.4), and therefore offer the opportunity for analysis. The land slug *Limax* is a good example. *Limax* not only learns rapidly to avoid food containing a bitter substance (quinine), but also has been shown to avoid a specific food after a single meal in which an essential amino acid (methionine) was missing from it (Delaney and Gelperin, 1986). Gelperin and his colleagues at Bell Laboratories have developed an isolated preparation of the *Limax* cerebral ganglion, buccal ganglion, and lips. They have identified several types of nerve cells that form the circuit for the feeding motor programs, and found that the program can be modulated by a serotonergic interneuron. Thus, at the cellular level there may be mechanisms that are shared with models of associative learning in other species, as we have discussed above. At the systems level, circuits for aversion learning, as well as for taste sensation, appetitive behavior (locomotion), and consummatory behavior (feeding), may be seen to be common to all animals.

COMPLEX LEARNING

The types of learning we have discussed thus far are those that have received the greatest attention from behaviorists and that have been most amenable to experimental analysis by neurobiologists. In order to have an adequate perspective, it is necessary to recognize that these by no means exhaust

the types of learning that occur. As indicated in Table 29.2, several additional types may be grouped under the general heading of *Complex Learning*.

Imprinting

Imprinting is the process whereby a young animal forms a behavioral attachment to a parent. It was discovered by ethologists, who found that the attachment usually depended on some special stimulus, such as the shape of the parent's body, or a particular colored spot on the plumage. A young animal can often be induced to form its attachment to an individual or object that sufficiently resembles the specific stimulus; hence, the famous picture of young geese following Konrad Lorenz on his daily walk. Imprinting usually occurs during some early *critical period* in the young animal's life, and if it does not occur, the subsequent normal development of behavior is irretrievably lost. Thus, songbirds fail to learn their song (see Chap. 23), and animals fail to develop their adult social and sexual behaviors. Imprinting is thus an essential kind of learning in many species.

Some evidence for the brain mechanisms that are involved in imprinting has been obtained by Gabriel Horn and his colleagues at Cambridge. They have studied young chicks, which become attached to a visually conspicuous object (normally the mother hen) early in life. Experimentally, the chicks can become attached to a rotating disc. In animals trained in this manner, it was found that the incorporation of radioactive uracil into RNA was selectively increased in a part of the forebrain called the medial part of the hyperstriatum ventrale (MHV). This could reflect a growth of synaptic boutons in this region, requiring synthesis of proteins and increased RNA. Electron microscopic measurements of the synapses in the MHV showed an increase in the area of contact of about 20% over controls. Studies in other laboratories have shown changes in 2-deoxyglucose (2DG) uptake in this region during training. Thus, several lines of evidence suggest that increases in synaptic activity and synaptic effectiveness are associated with processes of imprinting in this species.

Latent Learning

Another type of complex learning occurs when an animal is introduced to an experimental environment, like a maze, and allowed to run about in it without being trained or rewarded. Although there is no evidence of learning at the time, the animal later learns an operant task in the maze much faster than an unexposed animal. This effect of experience is called latent learning.

Mechanisms of latent learning have been studied by exposing animals to a maze and then testing the effect of different brain lesions on their ability to run the maze. Daniel Kimble and his colleagues at Oregon found that animals with hippocampal lesions initially show a benefit from previous unrewarded exposure to the maze, but do not improve their performance with subsequent trials (Kimble et al., 1981). This suggests that the brain circuits that store spatial information in latent learning are distinct from those that form "cognitive maps" in learning (see Hippocampus, under Memory, below).

There is evidence that experiences such as maze running or social interactions with other animals lead to larger brains, increases in the numbers of cortical dendritic branches and spines, and even the sizes of individual synapses (Table 29.1). These findings recall the observations of Darwin on the larger brains of wild compared with domesticated animals (see Chap. 30).

In the light of the perspective taken above with regard to aversion learning, familiarity with a training apparatus could facilitate learning through various ways, including alleviating stress, reducing fear, and enhancing attention and orienting mechanisms; in other words, we learn better in comfortable surroundings.

Observational Learning

The final type of learning we will mention is called *vicarious,* or *observational, learning.* This occurs when an animal observes another animal performing a task, and then learns the task more rapidly. This is obviously extremely important in humans; it covers the way we imitate and follow examples, learn from experiences of others, and follow symbolic directions to achieve skills and attain goals. It is more difficult to demonstrate in other mammals, and, in fact, for a long time behaviorists denied that vicarious learning occurs in subhumans. There is no evidence that observational learning takes place in lower vertebrates or invertebrates.

It is believed by many behaviorists that observational learning goes beyond associative conditioning, and involves *cognitive* processes: attention, retention, and thinking. Behaviorists are only beginning to form a coherent view of these processes. Neurobiologists may soon be able to contribute their information about neural mechanisms to these emerging concepts.

MEMORY

As mentioned in the preceding section, memory, the capacity to store and recall information, is a necessary component of learning. Animals as low on the evolutionary scale as the flatworms (*Planaria;* see Table 29.1) can show classical conditioning, which implies that there is a memory mechanism present. Whether this is distributed throughout the peripheral nerves or body cells of this animal, as some of the more sensational experiments imply, is still a controversial question. In higher invertebrates and vertebrates, it is clear that memory mechanisms related to behavioral experiences depend on the brain.

Invertebrates

The octopus has the largest brain among the invertebrates. It also has highly developed eyes and a highly developed tactile system in its tentacles. J. Z. Young and his colleagues in London have shown that the octopus can readily learn visual discrimination tasks, such as distinguishing between vertical and horizontal lines. By making ablations of different parts of the brain, they showed that visual memory is stored in the vertical lobe (see Fig. 22.3). Octopuses can also learn tactile discriminations with their tentacles (though, as we discussed in Chap. 22, they cannot learn proprioceptive discriminations). It was found that tactile memories are stored in the inferior frontal and subfrontal lobes. Thus, the visual and tactile memory systems are mostly separate, though there is some overlap in the vertical lobe.

This separation of memory systems is more distinct than is the case in vertebrates, at least as far as is known at present. The vertical lobe is packed with millions of very small neurons; many of these lack axons, and thus appear to form microcircuits by means of dendrodendritic interactions (see Chap. 3). Young (1978) has hypothesized that these "microneurons" are crucial for memory; during learning they inhibit unwanted pathways, leaving others open to be used selectively in the learned task. This is an interesting hypothesis that deserves further study.

Vertebrates: The Hippocampus

The brain structure that has attracted most attention as a possible repository of memories in the vertebrate is the hippocampus. This was first dramatically demonstrated by the accidental and unfortunate discovery that bilateral removal of the hippocampus in neurosurgical operations results in almost total loss of recent memory in humans. Complementing this was the finding that brief electrical shocks applied to the hippocampal area elicit fleeting memories in awake patients undergoing neurosurgical operations for the relief of epilepsy.

The hippocampus is certainly one of the most intriguing regions in the brain. It ful-

fills all our criteria for a central system: a well-defined region, remote from specific sensory and motor pathways. What does it do, and how is it related to memory?

Anatomy and Synaptic Organization

The hippocampus derives its name from its curving shape, which reminded some early neuroanatomist of a sea horse (and others of a ram's horn). This is an ancient part of the brain; as one of the first areas of the wall of the forebrain to become differentiated in primitive vertebrates, it is called the archicortex (see Fig. 29.12A). Its functions are unknown, but they appear to depend on the nearby septum, to which it is closely connected. As the forebrain expanded during evolution, the hippocampus got pushed and dragged around. It got particularly attached to the temporal lobe, and so as this lobe enlarged, the hippocampus got pulled along in a loop through the dorsal forebrain to the temporal lobe (B), and eventually ended up entirely within that lobe (C) in primates, snuggled up against the amygdala. It retains its primitive connection with the septum through a thick tract called the fornix, whose graceful arc describes the trajectory of evolution.

The hippocampus is one of those regions, like the cerebellum and olfactory bulb, whose internal circuits are organized in a highly distinctive manner. This by itself is an interesting fact: stereotyped microcircuits and local circuits are used not just for processing sensory information, but also for processing information related to higher brain functions. The circuits in the hippocampus were described briefly in Chap. 7, and are shown in more detail in Fig. 29.13. The main specific inputs come from the entorhinal cortex and septum, and the contralateral hippocampus. The inputs are excitatory, as are two pathways (the mossy fibers and Schaffer collaterals) for internal transfer of information. Pitted against this in the control of the output neurons are local inhibitory interneurons. A delicate balance is thus set up between excitation and inhibition, a balance that can be upset

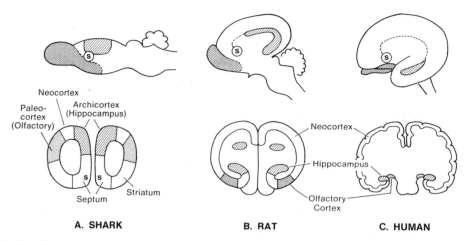

A. SHARK   B. RAT   C. HUMAN

Fig. 29.12 Evolution of the hippocampus, as exemplified in a lower vertebrate (shark), a mammal (rat), and the human. Above, longitudinal views; below, cross-sectional views. (Based on Sarnat and Netsky, 1981)

by too much excitation or too little inhibition, either of which leads to uncontrolled discharges which become manifest in humans as certain kinds of epileptic seizures.

Long-Term Potentiation (LTP)

If the hippocampus is to have a role in memory, one would expect these synapses to have properties that change with use, and in fact this has turned out to be one of the outstanding characteristics of this region. In 1973, Tim Bliss and Terje Lømo in London reported studies in the intact, anesthetized rabbit, in which they recorded the field potentials evoked in the dentate fascia by a shock to the entorhinal cortex (which activates pathway d in Fig. 29.13).

Fig. 29.13 Neuronal organization of the hippocampus. Abbreviations: A, entorhinal cortex; B, subiculum; C, hippocampus; D, dentate fascia; E, fornix; F, fibers to entorhinal cortex; G, alveus; H, periventricular gray matter; a, pyramidal cell axon; b, axon terminals; c, deep perforant fibers; d, superficial perforant fibers; e, deep perforant bundle; f, fimbria fibers; g, pyramidal neuron; h, apical dendrite of a hippocampal pyramidal neuron; i, Schaffer collateral; j, mossy fibers arising from dentate granule cell; r, recurrent axon collateral of a pyramidal neuron. (From Cajal, 1911)

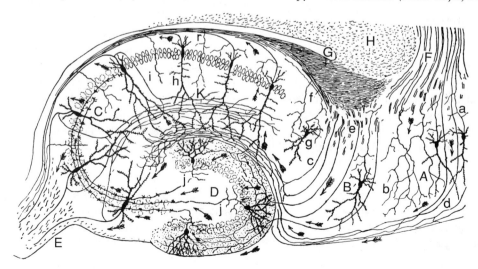

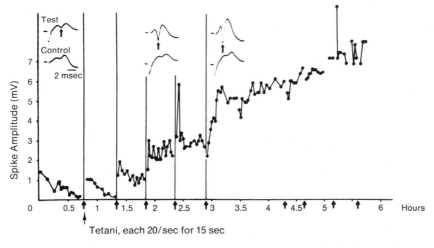

Fig. 29.14 Long-lasting potentiation of the granule cell response of the dentate fascia. Electrical stimulation was applied to the perforant fibers, at a rate of 20 per second for 15 seconds; this was repeated at times marked by arrows in the graph. The amplitude of the sharp wave in the field potential (due to granule cell responses) grew, as shown in insets (arrows); the time course of the increase over a period of 6 hours is plotted in the graph. (From Bliss and Lømo, 1973)

they stimulated at high frequency (tetanically) for several seconds, and then tested with a single shock at various intervals after that, they found that the part of the recording due to the synaptic response of the granule cells grew to a much greater amplitude than normal (Fig. 29.14). This phenomenon is called long-term potentiation (LTP). It is similar to, though much more powerful than, the posttetanic potentiation that is seen at the neuromuscular junction (Chap. 17). In the dentate cells, LTP persists for a surprisingly long time; as shown in Fig. 29.14, it characteristically lasts for several hours, and can even be demonstrated over periods of days and weeks. It has subsequently been demonstrated in hippocampal pyramidal cells as well.

Bliss and Lømo suggested several possible mechanisms for LTP, such as increased release of transmitter by the input synapses, or increased postsynaptic response. It can be seen that these are the types of mechanisms implied in Hebb's and Konorski's original concepts of the effects of use on neural circuits.

In the ensuing years, LTP in the hippocampus has generated an enormous amount of interest as a model for mechanisms involved in learning and memory. Much of the interest has focused on whether the site of potentiation is pre- or postsynaptic. A crucial test would be a quantal analysis of synaptic transmission before and during LTP, but this is not yet available. In its absence, evidence for both sites has been obtained.

In favor of a presynaptic locus, it has been found that LTP is accompanied by a prolonged increase in the release of radioactively labeled glutamate (see Fig. 29.15). It has been further postulated that, in analogy with *Aplysia*, phosphorylation of ion channels may be involved, and evidence has been obtained for phosphorylation of a number of proteins, some of which are known to be concentrated in presynaptic terminals.

In favor of a postsynaptic locus, increased binding of radioactively labeled glutamate has been reported in the hippocampus during LTP. There may be activation of proteases, which leads to the exposure of more glutamate receptors (see Lynch, 1986). At the single-cell level, development of LTP can be blocked either by intracellular injection of the Ca^{2+} chelator

EGTA or by hyperpolarizing current. Anatomical studies have reported that LTP is accompanied by an increase in the diameter of the dendritic spine stem, which would allow for increased current flow from the spine synapses into the dendritic branches. An important development has been the implication that the voltage-dependent NMDA channel, when depolarized by spread from neighboring sites, permits Ca^{2+} influx. This mechanism may be reviewed in Chap. 8.

From this brief summary, it can be seen that the issue of a pre- or postsynaptic site for LTP in the hippocampus is unresolved. The most likely explanation is that both sites are involved. In fact, the mechanisms probably involve many of the interactions between pre- and postsynaptic terminals during development, which were discussed in Chap. 17. Further work is needed to throw light on the relation between mechanisms of LTP and those underlying learning in the simple models discussed earlier in this chapter.

Axonal Sprouting

The plasticity inherent in hippocampal circuits is also expressed in the response to loss of an input pathway. Normally, the dentate fascia is innervated by several types of fibers, each of which has its special level of termination in the granule dendritic tree. When the predominant input, the perforant pathway, is removed on one side, there is massive degeneration of its synapses in the outer three-quarters of the granule cell dendrites. This is followed after several weeks by the appearance of new synapses on the dendrites. A series of experiments by Gary Lynch and Carl Cotman and their colleagues in California has shown that these new terminals result from sprouting and migration of other types of fibers, which take over the vacated synaptic sites (see Fig. 29.16). The hippocampus is not unique in this respect; we have had ample opportunity to note the astonishing abilities for plasticity of connections in many parts of the nervous system. However, the hippo-

campus is certainly a favorable site for demonstrating these properties.

Behavioral Studies

If the hippocampus has properties at the cellular level appropriate for playing a role in memory, what evidence is there for this role at the behavioral level? The most dramatic evidence was provided in 1953 by William Scoville and Brenda Milner at the Montreal Neurological Institute. They reported that one of their patients, a 27-year-old skilled mechanic known as H.M., in whom bilateral hippocampal removal had been performed for relief of epilepsy, had lost the ability to remember recent events, without any significant impairment of other intellectual abilities. Needless to say, this operation was never performed again. H.M. has become perhaps the most studied patient in history. In a recent thorough reexamination 28 years after the operation, Suzanne Corkin and her colleagues in Boston report (1981):

> He still exhibits a profound anterograde amnesia, and does not know where he lives, who cares for him, or what he ate at his last meal. . . . Nevertheless, he has islands of remembering, such as knowing that an astronaut if someone who travels in outer space. . . . A typical day's activities include doing crossword puzzles and watching television.

Corkin's studies have shown that H.M. cannot recall words that are presented to him verbally, but he can show improvement in the ability to solve puzzles and acquire perceptual skills in repeated trials. This has contributed to a variety of evidence that memory is not just one global entity, but rather consists of many subsystems, as will be discussed further below. Other interesting results in the recent studies are that H.M. has a diminished perception of pain, a lack of feelings of hunger or satiety, and an inability to identify different odors.

Learning and Memory: A Synthesis

The case of the patient H.M. stimulated workers to reproduce the symptoms in pri-

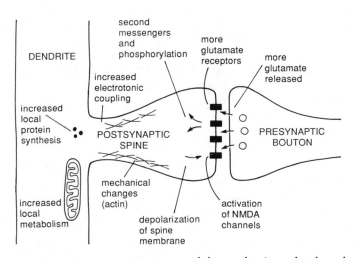

Fig. 29.15 Schematic diagram summarizing some of the mechanisms that have been implicated in the mediation of long-term potentiation (LTP) in hippocampus. NMDA, N-methyl-D-aspartate. The postulated mechanisms include increased presynaptic glutamate release (Bliss), increased glutamate receptors (Baudry and Lynch), activation of NMDA receptors (Ascher; Jahr and Stevens, and many authors), second messengers (Routtenberg, and many authors), actin-mediated structural changes (Fifkova; Crick), changes in electrotonic coupling (Rall and Rinzel; Fifkova), changes in polyribosomes and protein synthesis (Steward). (For references, see Bliss, 1985; Lynch, 1986; Smith, 1987)

Fig. 29.16 Plasticity of synaptic connections onto dentate granule cells after a lesion of the ipsilateral entorhinal cortex, destroying the perforant fibers. Note the sprouting and migration of the fibers from the contralateral entorhinal cortex, the septal nucleus, and the commissural–associational projection. (Modified from Cotman and McGaugh, 1980)

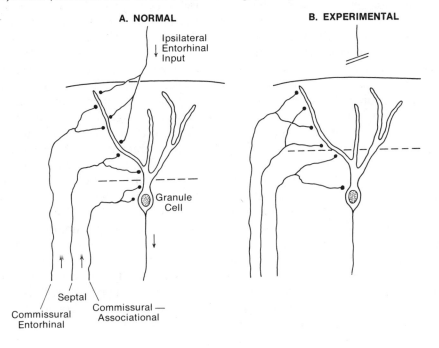

mates, in order to gain insight into the nature of the circuits that subserve memory. The first experiments in the monkey involved bilateral ablations confined to the hippocampus; these showed surprisingly limited effects. The same was true of lesions confined to the amygdala. However, H.M. lost both hippocampus and amygdala, and lesions of both these regions (the so-called medial temporal animal) in monkeys reproduced more closely the severe amnesia.

These experiments had the benefit of showing that memory is not a unitary and global process. First, memory involves distinct *steps;* there are at least three main stages: (1) a stage of acquisition, in which information is encoded in central circuits that include microcircuits in specific regions such as the hippocampus; (2) a stage of storage, in which the information is retained in those circuits, presumably dependent on changes in the synapses as postulated by Hebb; and (3) a stage of recall, in which the information is recalled to produce a perceptual or motor output. Stage 2 is usually recognized to consist of an early labile period of short-term memory, which then passes into a later stable period of long-term memory by a process known as consolidation.

A second important advance is the recognition of different *types* of information, stored as different types of memory. Among the many types that have been suggested, a useful distinction is between "knowing how" and "knowing that." "Knowing how" information is just what its name implies: knowing how to do a skilled act, such as writing or riding a bicycle, which one has learned to do successfully. "Knowing that" information, by contrast, is about specific facts or dates; it does require conscious attention and recall. These distinctions were pointed out by the philosopher, Gilbert Ryle, in 1949, and have been elaborated subsequently by neuroscientists. In a formulation of Larry Squire and Neal Cohen, of San Diego (see Square and Butters, eds., 1984), "knowing how" memory is termed "procedural memory" and "knowing that"

memory is termed "declarative memory."

These distinctions have been useful in characterizing more accurately the types of memory and identifying the types of circuits that mediate them. For instance, the learning demonstrated in *Aplysia* falls in the category of "procedural memory." The reflex circuit itself is the site of the memory; there is no separate representation of the learning change elsewhere. By contrast, the amnesia of H.M. does not prevent him from learning perceptual–motor skills of the "knowing how" variety. His defect, and that of primates with similar lesions, is in retention of recent "knowing that," declarative memories. Recent tests show that this defect involves an abnormally rapid rate of forgetting, that can be ascribed to inability to transfer newly acquired information to storage, or to consolidate it. In this view, the hippocampus is an essential part of the distributed circuits involved in acquisition and consolidation, but the sites of permanent memory storage must be elsewhere, because long-term memory remains and can be retrieved despite loss of the hippocampus.

The hippocampus has thus served as a useful focus for work in learning and memory. This work now extends from the level of molecular mechanisms at the synaptic level, through several levels of circuit organization within the hippocampus and between it and other regions, to the level of behavioral analysis of primate models and psychological testing in the human. The goal is to assemble a coherent framework embracing all these levels, equivalent to that for the visual task represented at the beginning of this book (Fig. 1.1), and for the many other systems that have been discussed.

While the hippocampus is a valuable model in this respect, it must be emphasized that it is only one of many regions of the brain with specific memory functions. In the next chapter we will assess further the contributions of neocortical regions to these functions.

30

The Cerebral Cortex
and Human Behavior

In previous chapters we have noted many areas of the mammalian cortex given over to specific functions related to sensory processing, control of motor outputs, and integration of centrally mediated behaviors. The diagram in Fig. 30.1 provides a summary view of the human. Specific sensory and motor areas are present in lower mammals, and are further elaborated in primates and humans. While these specific areas are important in the evolution of human attributes, it is the other parts of the cortex that have undergone the greatest expansion. Some idea of this expansion can be grasped by realizing that the area of the cortex of a cat is about 100 cm², or about ¼ the size of this page, whereas that of the human is about 2400 cm², or about 6 times the size of this page. The specific areas discussed thus far account for only a small part of this total (see Fig. 30.1). It is therefore to these vast tracts of neural landscape, with billions of neurons and hundreds of billions of synapses, that we now turn to identify the circuits and mechanisms that make us uniquely human.

What Makes Us Human?

It is appropriate to begin by asking, what is it that makes humans unique? The attri-

butes that are commonly regarded as distinctive of humans are listed in Table 30.1. *Erect posture* and walking on *hind legs* allowed the *forelimbs* to be free for other functions. Recall that locomotion by the minimum number of legs expresses a trend present also in the invertebrates, as discussed in Chap. 20. The important feature was that the forelimbs did not become dedicated to other obligatory tasks, like flying birds or swinging through trees in monkeys, but rather were free to work on the environment in new and novel ways. The most crucial way was provided by the *prehensile hand*, which led to *tools* and *technology*.

The parallel development of *speech* and *language* gave rise to more adaptable modes of communication, and ultimately to *symbolic thought*. These attributes involved changes in the musculoskeletal system, and associated adaptations in neural systems for sensorimotor control of posture, locomotion, throwing, grasping, vocalization, and related activities. In addition, a *prolonged childhood* provided the basis for complex social organization and an enduring *culture*. Finally, human beings express themselves as *individuals*. The ingredients in this include emotion, motivation, and imagination; their testing ground is play;

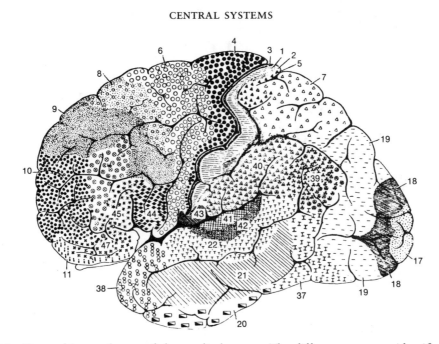

Fig. 30.1 Cytoarchitectural map of the cerebral cortex. The different areas are identified by the thickness of their layers and types of cells within them. Some of the most important specific areas are as follows. Motor cortex: motor strip, area 4; premotor area, area 6; frontal eye fields, area 8. Somatosensory cortex: areas 3, 1, 2. Visual cortex: areas 17, 18, 19. Auditory cortex: areas 41 and 42. Wernicke's speech area: approximately area 22. Broca's speech area: approximately area 44 (in the left hemisphere). (From Brodmann, in Brodal, 1981)

they realize themselves to the fullest in the supremely human qualities of *scientific* and *artistic expression* and *spiritual experience*.

Phylogeny of Cerebral Cortex

The human attributes listed in Table 30.1 depend on the cerebral cortex. In order to gain insight into how the human cortex has evolved, we need to consider the phylogeny of the vertebrate forebrain.

As histological stains for visualizing nerve cells and fiber tracts became available around 1900, neuroanatomists applied them across the vertebrate spectrum and attempted to identify corresponding centers and pathways in the brains of different species. This work culminated in 1936 in the monumental tome by Kappers, Huber, and Crosby entitled *The Comparative Anatomy of the Nervous System of Vertebrates, Including Man.* The view emerging from this survey was of a gradual "linear" increase in size

of the forebrain and differentiation of the cortex as one ascends from fish to mammals. In fish, it seemed that the cortex was very primitive, devoted mainly to olfactory inputs (paleocortex) and higher-order olfactory processing (archicortex). In amphibians, and especially in reptiles, a new cortex (neocortex) appeared; in reptiles and birds, other sensory systems began to proj-

Table 30.1 Human characteristics

1. Locomotion on hind legs: forelimbs free for other functions
2. Prehensile hand: making of tools and development of technology
3. Enlargement of brain relative to body size
4. Development of speech and language
5. Development of social interactions and culture: prolonged youth; division of labor in society; controls on sex and aggression
6. Individual artistic and spiritual expression

Modified from Isaac and Leakey (1979)

Table 30.2 Evolution of the forebrain (telecephalon): a comparison of old and new ideas

Old ideas	New ideas
1. There is a linear increase in size through the vertebrate series.	1. There are independent increases in size among several radiations.
2. There is early olfactory dominance and later dominance by ascending thalamic inputs.	2. There are early restricted olfactory inputs plus early restricted thalamic inputs.
3. Lower vertebrates have only a primitive cortex.	3. Main divisions of cortex are present in all vertebrates.
4. Lower vertebrates lack long descending tracts from cortex.	4. Long descending tracts are present in all vertebrate groups.
5. Functionally specific tracts are stable across different groups.	5. The same function may be mediated by different tracts in different species ("phylogenetic plasticity"). There is no truly "typical" tract or center for a given function.
6. Similar structures in different groups are homologous (evolved from a common ancestral form).	6. Similar structures in different groups are often homoplastic (they evolved independently: convergent evolution).

Based on Northcutt (1981) and others

ect to the cortex through a thalamus. In mammals the neocortex, together with its thalamic inputs and closely related basal ganglia, greatly expanded. This sequence was supposed to mirror the events that lay behind the evolution of the primate cortex. It was a satisfying view, and is summarized in Table 30.2 under "Old Ideas."

So satisfying was this view that the comparative anatomy of the nervous system came to be regarded as a rather stodgy subject, like an old exhibit in a museum. It is only since the 1970s that neuroanatomists have returned in force to rejuvenate this whole field by new studies. The surprising outcome is that most of the old ideas have had to be discarded, in the face of new evidence that significantly alters the interpretation of the evolution of the forebrain.

One of the most important new findings is that the forebrain and cortex have not undergone a gradual, linear increase, but rather there have been independent offshoots of forebrain expansion at several stages; examples of this are certain fish, and the dolphin. This phenomenon should not be surprising to the reader of this book; we have already noted in Chap. 21 the enormous expansion of the cerebellum in certain species of electric fish. Similar but independently evolved structures are referred to as "homoplastic," in contrast to similar structures in a linearly evolved series, which are referred to as "homologous." The case of the dolphin illustrates that cortical enlargement by itself confers only limited adaptive abilities; it is the whole constellation of adaptations in Table 30.1 that is necessary for human behavior.

Another important finding has been that olfactory projections to the forebrain are much more specific than formerly believed, and that other sensory modalities are represented already in fishes by projections through thalamic relays. In studies of the visual pathway from the retina through the thalamus to the cortex, considerable variation has been found among lower vertebrates; according to R. Glenn Northcutt of Michigan, in different species the visual pathway may project ipsilaterally or bilaterally, through different central tracts, to different cortical sites. This may be regarded as a kind of "phylogenetic plasticity," reflecting in part the flexibility of the nervous system in its routing of information through central pathways. The "New Ideas" emerging from these and related studies are summarized in Table 30.2.

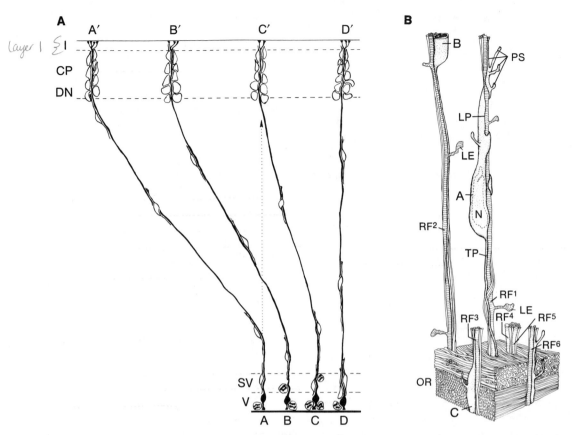

Layer 1

Fig. 30.2 **A.** Diagram showing how radial glia provide guides for the migration of neurons (N) from ventricular (V) and subventricular (SV) zones to the cortical plate (CP). Within the CP, the new neurons migrate past deeper neurons (DN) to layer I (I). Note that despite shift of cortical position (A′–D′) relative to prolilferative zones (A–D), the radial glia preserve the topographical relations. **B.** Relations between migrating neuron and radial glia fiber, based on electron microscopy. Six radial fibers (RF[1–6]) are shown traversing the packed fibers of the optic radiation (OR). Three neurons (A–C) are shown at various stages of migration. Neuron A is shown with nucleus (N), leading process (LP), and pseudopodia (PS). (A from Rakic, 1981; B from Rakic, in Jacobson, 1978)

Ontogeny of Cerebral Cortex

In Chap. 9, we discussed the stages involved in the development of the nervous system; we can now apply those principles to the cortex.

Neuronal Migration

Neurons characteristically migrate from their site of birth (the last mitosis) to their final position, and the neocortex is no exception. The precursor cells are located in the proliferative zones that line the surface of the cerebral ventricles. As shown by studies in which animals are sacrificed shortly after radioactively labeled thymidine injections are given, all of the final mitoses take place in the proliferative zones. The neurons must therefore migrate to the primitive cortical plate. They are guided in this by a special type of cell, the radial glia, which spans the distance between the proliferative zone and the cortical plate. This mechanism has been elucidated by the elegant studies of Pasko Rakic, at Harvard and at Yale, and is illustrated in Fig. 30.2. The neurons are all generated within a period of about 60 days in the monkey (100 days in the human), and the migration is complete in the monkey by day 100 (gestation lasts 165 days).

Within the cortex, the first neurons are laid down in the deepest layers, with later neurons migrating to more superficial layers; hence, there is an "inside-out" sequence of cortical development. Thus, according to the timing of its last mitosis, each neuron appears to be destined as a specific cell type in a specific layer. According to Rakic (1981):

> The redistribution of such a vast number of cells during development undoubtedly provides opportunities for establishment of essential relationships and key contacts that eventually determine the radial and tangential coordinates of each neuron in the 3-dimensional map of the neocortex. Thus, the separation of proliferative centers from the final residence of neurons is of great biological significance.

Neuronal Maturation

Within the cortex, the larger pyramidal neurons (projection neurons) mature first, followed by the smaller interneurons (local circuit neurons). In comparison with the relatively brief period for cell birth, maturation is a much more prolonged process. An indication of this is given in Fig. 30.3. Note the small sizes of the cells in the newborn and their limited dendritic branches, and the subsequent growth and differentiation of the cells. It is apparent from this evidence alone that early childhood is a time of rapid and profound maturation of the cells in the cortex.

Maturation of Synapses

The maturation of cortical neurons is associated with maturation of cortical circuits. This can be documented and quantitated by counting. One might assume that the maturation of synaptic circuits would proceed linearly in parallel with the maturation of neuronal form shown in Fig. 30.3. One might have further predicted that the synaptic circuits would be laid down first in the primary sensory and motor areas (because they mediate lower levels of cortical sensory and motor processing) followed by secondary areas and lastly the association areas (which mediate higher levels of cortical processing).

Surprisingly, none of these expectations has been borne out. A direct test has been carried out by a team under Pasko Rakic

Fig. 30.3 Growth and differentiation of the dendritic trees and axon collaterals of cortical pyramidal cells in the human, from fetus to adult. (Courtesy of P. Rakic)

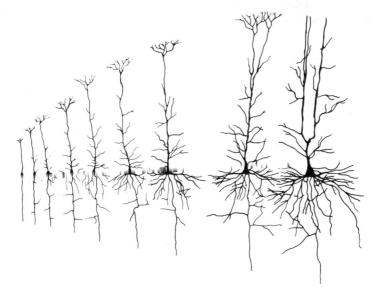

at Yale; they measured under the electron microscope the density of synapses in different cortical areas of the monkey at different ages during development (Rakic et al., 1986). This mammoth undertaking, involving the identification of over 500,000 synapses in 25,000 electron micrographs from 22 monkeys, revealed that the density of synapses followed a very similar time course during development of different regions. The basic pattern (see Fig. 30.4) was a steady increase in density during fetal life, reaching approximately adult levels at birth. The density continued to increase, however, reaching a peak at two to four months of age and then declining, at first rapidly and then slowly to the adult level at two to four years. Regardless of whether the region was primary sensory, primary motor, association, or limbic, the results were very similar, as shown in Fig. 30.4.

These results indicate, first, that synapses in cortex are formed as elsewhere in the nervous system, with an overproduction followed by elimination (cf. Chaps. 9 and 17). With synaptic maturation comes the formation of functioning cortical circuits. Second, the similar time course of overproduction and subsequent decline to a similar neuronal density in all cortical regions suggests that "the cortex develops as a whole rather than regionally" (Rakic et al., 1986); in other words, there may be a basic cortical plan under common genetic control. We will explain this basic plan further below. Finally, the early development of association areas is in accord with behavioral studies showing the early development of certain cognitive functions, such as ability to perform delayed-response tests.

It is important to realize that maturation does not occur in a vacuum; in addition to the timetable prescribed by the genetic program, a neuron reaches its final form under the influence of its environment. The old debate of nature vs. nurture has been rendered obsolete, and we now recognize that both factors shape the neuron. To speak of one without the other is like asking what is the sound of one hand clapping. Fur-

thermore, the question is not just whether a neuron by itself will mature, but whether it will survive in the competition for available nutrients, synaptic connections, and functional validation. Thus, the competition of organisms for survival in the external world mirrors a competition in the inner world among neurons to fashion the circuits that will be most effective in the external world. We shall see clear evidence of the relations between the two worlds when we discuss the organization of cortical circuits.

We may summarize this section by noting that ontogeny, like phylogeny, is not a simple linear process. It involves a series of stages, in which the organism at one stage gives rise to the next stage through the complex interaction of a number of factors. This is evident at the cellular level in the development of the cortex, and it is also evident in the behavior of the developing fetus and child. This has been summarized elegantly by Myron Hofer of Albert Einstein College of Medicine as follows (1981):

Development is characterized by transformations in which certain functional patterns come into being that are not found in previous or even in subsequent stages. Functionally as well as structurally, it is not the same creature at two different stages of its own development. The differences between stages of development in a single animal are almost as profound as those between species of vertebrates. The implications of this fact are difficult for adults to fully grasp, accustomed as we are to relative stability in our remembered past experience. It means that we cannot generalize about the mechanism of an action, the effect of a stimulus, or the long-term impact of an experience from one stage of development to another. We have to understand exactly how the developing infant interacts with its environment separately at each age.

Levels of Cortical Organization

We are now in a position to tackle the key question: What are the cortical mechanisms that underlie our uniquely human abilities? The nineteenth-century idea was that ideas and other higher human faculties

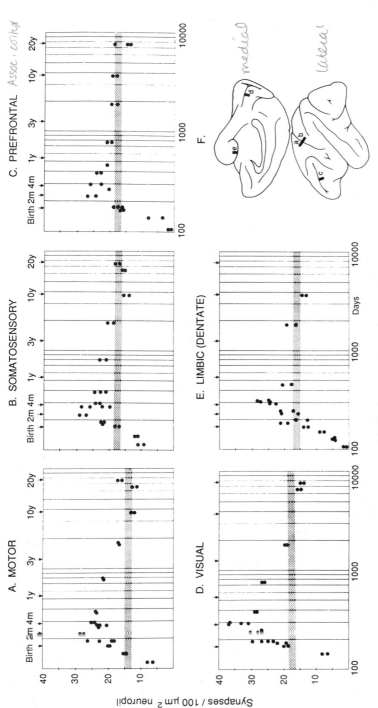

Fig. 30.4 The time course of development of synapses in five different regions of the cerebral cortex in the monkey is depicted in A–E: A. Motor cortex. B. Somatosensory cortex. C. Prefrontal cortex. D. Visual cortex. E. Limbic cortex (dentate molecular layer). The inset (F) shows lateral (below) and medial (above) views of the left cerebral hemisphere, depicting the regions examined: a, motor cortex (area 4); b, somatosensory cortex (area 1); c, prefrontal association cortex (area 9); d, visual cortex (area 17); e, molecular layers of dentate gyrus. The numbers identify the areas in the human according to Brodmann (see Fig. 30.1). In each of these areas, a track of cortical tissue that passed through all layers (I–VI) was examined with 100 serial electron micrographs in order to count all the synapses along that track. This yields a value for number of synapses/100 μm^2 of neuropil (defined as cortical tissue minus cell bodies, blood vessels). Each point is the value obtained from a single track. The horizontal stippled stripe denotes the average value in the adult as a reference. Note the logarithmic scale, spanning from conception to 20 years. Parts A–E are graphs of the data for animals of different ages before and after birth. (From Rakic et al., 1986)

617

actually reside in the cortex, and constitute a kind of supreme executive council which hands down orders to its neural minions. These faculties were believed to be embedded in some fashion in the billions of cells distributed throughout the cortex.

It should be obvious to the reader of this book that the modern view is radically different. Rather than being like a self-contained college of bishops and cardinals, the cortex actually contains many areas that function at middle levels of management, being involved in signal processing within specific sensory and motor systems. Furthermore, there is increasing evidence that higher functions are mediated by distributed systems, in which the cortex is only one part. Thus, the significance of any given region in the cortex is to be found in the internal organization of its synaptic circuits, and the external organization of its connections to other regions, cortical and subcortical. The synaptic circuits generate particular functional properties, and the external connections determine the contributions of these properties to the distributed systems of which they are a part.

In order to understand how cortical circuits function, we must use the concept of levels of organization that was introduced in Chap. 1 and has been a central theme in discussing systems throughout this book. The main levels of cortical organization thus far characterized are summarized in Table 30.3. Each of these is a specific example of one of the levels of system organization, extending from molecule to behavior, depicted previously in Fig. 1.1. We will discuss each of these specific levels in turn, with the ultimate goal of obtaining insight into the relations between them and human mental activity.

Molecules and Channels

The first two levels in the cortex correspond to the same levels in other systems. The properties of ion channels may be reviewed in Chaps. 4 and 6, and the properties of receptors for neurotransmitters and neuromodulators in Chap. 8. The specific

Table 30.3 Functional units at different levels of system and cortical organization

General neural systems levels	Specific cortical systems levels
System	Distributed system
Pathway	Multiple cortical representation
	Lobes
	Hemispheres
Local region	Cortical area
Local circuit	Basic cortical circuit
	Cortical modules
Microcircuit	Multiple spine units
Synapse	Spine unit
Channels and receptors	Channels and receptors
Molecules and ions	Molecules and ions

Compare this table with the diagrams in Fig. 1.1. Each level is defined by one or more molecular, structural, or functional units that provide the basis for the organization of the level above.

relation of these properties to cortical functions such as memory has already been discussed in Chap. 29, and we will discuss further examples below. As far as is known, the significance of these two levels of organization lies not in unique properties of the molecules, receptors, or channels in the cortex, but rather in their integrative context within cortical circuits.

Synapses and Spines

At the first level of circuit organization is the individual synapse and its associated pre- and postsynaptic structures. Although one may think of a single synapse as a simple link, or circuit element, we have seen (cf. Chaps. 5, 8, and 29) that it is a complex functional unit in its own right, with a variety of time- and use-dependent controls.

This is demonstrated vividly by synapses in the cortex, especially those made onto the dendritic spines of pyramidal cells. The increase in cortical synapses during development is largely associated with spines; as shown in Fig. 30.5, the spines in a 7-month-old human fetus are few in number and irregular in shape, whereas the stouter dendrite of even an 8-month-old infant is bristling with well-formed lollipop-shaped spines. Each of these spines is the site of a

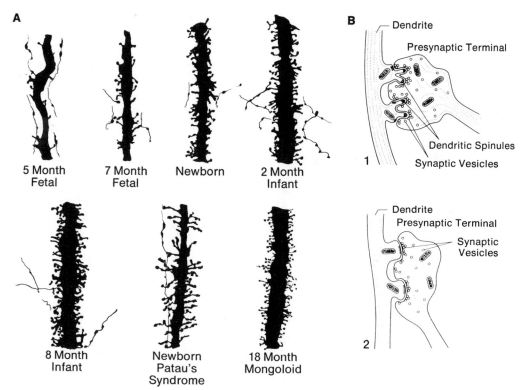

Fig. 30.5 **A.** Increase in number of spines on apical dendrites of large pyramidal neurons of layer V of human cortex, at five different ages before and after birth. In a disease known as Patau's syndrome, the spines are fewer, elongated, and irregular in form. In mongolism, the spines are thin and tiny. **B.** Effects of deprivation on spines in the lateral geniculate nucleus of the dog. 1, normal; 2, animal reared in the dark. (A from Marin-Padilla, in Lund, 1979; B from Hamori, in Hofer, 1981)

synapse, usually a type I synapse (see Chap. 4) with an excitatory action. Synapses on spines account for up to 70% of all synapses in the cortex of rhesus monkey; during development, the ratio of type I (mostly spine) to type II (mostly soma and dendritic shaft) synapses increases during the overproduction phase and then decreases during the elimination phase, suggesting that overproduction and elimination mainly involve the spine synapses (see Rakic et al., 1986).

Cortical synapses have been shown to be extraordinarily sensitive to a number of environmental influences. In the visual cortex, the number of spines on dendritic shafts of deep pyramidal cells is reduced following removal of one eye in newborn rodents.

This could be due to several factors, including loss of spines already formed, or failure of dendrites to mature. A reduction in visual experience, caused by raising animals in the dark, also leads to a reduction in numbers of synapses in visual areas, and to reduction in sizes of individual synapses.

Even more dramatic results are seen in experiments comparing the cortices of animals raised in enriched environments, containing lots of toys to play with and mazes to run in, with those raised in barren cages (see Table 29.1 and Greenough, 1984). The animals raised in enriched environments have thicker cortices, and bigger synaptic contacts. Similarly, the cortex may be up to one-third thicker in wild animals compared with those that have been domesticated. The fact that the brain is reduced in size in domesticated animals was actually first noted by Darwin. Finally, we may note that dendritic spines are affected in certain kinds of neurological diseases that produce mental retardation; the derangements of spines that occur in Patau's syndrome and in Down's syndrome (mongolism) are shown in Fig. 30.5A.

The fact that cortical synapses, and especially those on spines, are sensitive to environmental influences, should not be surprising. Spines in the lateral geniculate nucleus are also sensitive to visual deprivation, as shown in Fig. 30.5B, and many examples could be cited in other systems. Among the most interesting are spines of neurons in the corpora pedunculata, the highest integrative centers in the brains of insects (see Chap. 23). Brandon and Coss (1982) made careful measurements of the dimensions of these spines in honeybees just before and just after their first orientation flight from the hive; they found that the spine necks become significantly limper after this single flight.

These findings begin to suggest why synapses are so often situated in spines. Building on our previous discussions in Chaps. 4 and 29, each spine can be conceived of as creating a microenvironment, wherein the postsynaptic response is modulated by use, and exerts its first and most immediate effects on its neighbors (see Fig. 30.6). Each spine thus acts as a miniature input–output unit, whose properties depend on its history, its metabolic machinery, its inputs, and its interactions with its neighbors. These multiple factors which control synaptic efficacy in the spine are indicated in the diagram of Fig. 30.6 and are discussed further in the legend.

Multiple Spine Units

The next level of organization is the microcircuit level, in which the pattern of synaptic connections and the interactions they mediate give rise to basic operations of information processing. Many instances have been cited in this book of such operations,

which include spatial summation, temporal summation, and feedforward and feedback inhibition. It has been emphasized that there are two main neuronal substrates where these operations are carried out. The predominant site is within dendritic trees, with local output either through dendrodendritic output synapses or by means of intradendritic spread to control impulse output in the axon. The other site is within axonal terminals, where output can be modulated by axoaxonic synapses.

In the cerebral cortex, most of the synapses are on spines of dendritic trunks and branches, so it may be assumed that dendritic microcircuits provide the main substrate for synaptic interactions. Since much of this dendritic substrate is remote from the cell body, our knowledge of the basic properties that are involved is limited. However, information has been obtained by recording intracellularly from dendrites in isolated cortical slices (cf. Chap. 7). These experiments have supported previous evidence suggesting that cortical dendrites, like dendrites of many other types of neurons, contain ionic membrane channels that are voltage sensitive. It has been believed that these sites are located at branch points, where they serve to boost the responses of distal dendrites.

The ubiquitousness of voltage-dependent channels (see Chap. 6) has suggested that they may also be present in spines. The way that this would contribute to spine responses and spine interactions has been explored in computer simulations by Wilfrid Rall and his colleagues, and Don Perkel and his colleagues. A simulation consists in representing a portion of a dendritic tree with its spines by a system of compartments (see Fig. 30.7A,B), each compartment comprising the electrical properties of a dendritic segment or spine as discussed in Chap. 6 (see Fig. 30.7C,D). It was shown that an active response in a spine would boost the amplitude of the synaptic response spreading out of the spine (Fig. 30.7E). It was further shown that current spreading passively out of one spine readily

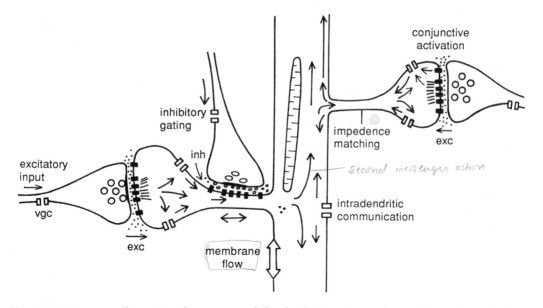

Fig. 30.6 Diagram illustrating the concept of the dendritic spine as the smallest neuronal micro-compartment capable of providing for a complete input–output operation of a synapse. Two spines are shown, arising from a dendritic branch. Excitatory (exc) input on the left, coming through impulses (voltage-gated channels: vgc) in presynaptic axons, activates the spine. The synaptic response can be amplified by voltage-gated channels and gives rise to second-messenger actions. Its transmission to the dendritic branch can be gated by inhibitory (inh) synapses on the spine stem. The spread of the response into the dendritic branch and from there into neighboring spines, as on the right, can depolarize those spines. By this means, electrotonic depolarization of spines receiving excitatory synaptic input can provide for conjunctive activation of Hebb-like mechanisms, such as NMDA receptors, as discussed previously in Chap. 29. Communication between spines and parent dendrite depends on impedance matching of electrotonic properties (Rall and Rinzel, 1973); activity-dependent changes in these properties could contribute to mechanisms for learning and memory. Proteins move within the plasma membrane, and may distribute differentially between dendrite and spine (Horwitz). (For reviews of spine properties and complete references, see Coss and Perkel, 1985; Shepherd and Greer, 1987)

enters neighboring spines, where it can trigger further active responses; thus, distal responses can be brought much closer to the cell body by a process resembling saltatory conduction in axons.

A third interesting property is that the interactions between active spines can be readily characterized in terms of logic operations. Thus, an AND operation is performed when two spines must be synaptically activated simultaneously in order to generate spine responses (E). An OR operation is performed when either one spine or another can be activated by a synaptic input. Finally, a NOT-AND operation occurs when a response can be generated by

an excitatory synapse if an inhibitory synapse is not simultaneously active (F).

The interest of these simulations is that these three logic operations, together with a level of background activity, are sufficient for building a computer. This result of course does *not* mean that the cortex *is* a computer; rather, it helps to define more clearly the nature of the synaptic interactions that take place at the microcircuit level. Defining these interactions more clearly is a step toward identifying the basic operations underlying the functions of higher levels of circuit organization. One can speculate that interactions of this nature may underlie some of our higher cognitive functions, such

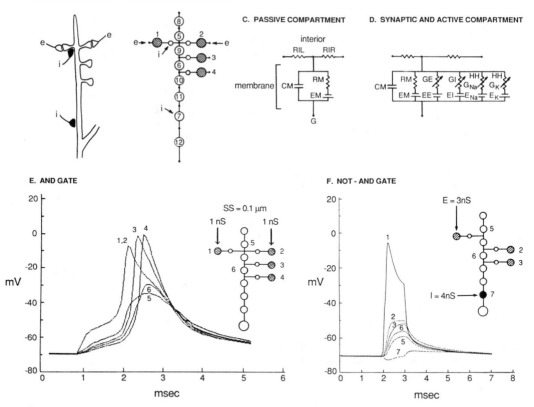

Fig. 30.7 Multiple spine interactions could generate logic operations in dendrites of cortical neurons. **A.** A distal dendritic segment of a cortical neuron is depicted in simplified form, consisting of a branch with four spines. Four possible synaptic inputs are shown: two excitatory (e), and two inhibitory (i). **B.** Compartmental representation of the system in A. Compartments with passive membrane properties are shown by open circles; those with synaptic and active properties are shaded. **C.** Equivalent electrical circuit of a passive compartment in B. Abbreviations: RIL, RIR, left and right limbs of internal resistance; CM, membrane capacitance; RM, membrane resistance; EM, membrane potential; G, electrical ground. **D.** Equivalent circuit of a synaptic and/or active compartment in B. Abbreviations: GE, excitatory synaptic conductance; EE, excitatory equilibrium potential; GI, inhibitory synaptic conductance; EI, inhibitory equilibrium potential; HH, Hodgkin-Huxley model for nerve impulse; G_{Na}, Na conductance; E_{Na}, Na equilibrium potential; G_K, K conductance; E_K, K equilibrium potential. **E.** Computer simulation of the response of the system when simultaneous excitatory inputs are delivered to spines 1 and 2 (see insert). Each synaptic response consists of an increase in the excitatory conductance (GE) of 1 nS. The spine stem diameter, which controls the spread of electric current between the spine head and dendritic branch, is 0.1 μm. With these parameters, spine heads 1 and 2 generate simultaneous impulses, which spread passively through the dendritic branch (compartments 5 and 6) to trigger impulses in spines 3 and 4. The system thus functions as an AND gate in logic terms. **F.** Computer simulation of the response of the system when an excitatory input to spine head 1 (with conductance changes of 3 nS) is paired with an inhibitory input (conductance change of 4 nS), sited at a distance on the dendritic branch. By itself, this excitatory input was sufficient to generate an impulse in spine head 1, which then spread passively to elicit impulses in spines 2 and 3 (not shown). The effect of the inhibition was to block the impulse in 2 and 3, but not in 1; the blocked impulse spread only passively throughout the system, as shown by the transients 2–7. This provides the basis for this system to function as a NOT-AND gate. Not shown are simulations of the system functioning as an OR gate. The simulations were run on an electrical circuit analysis program (ASTAP). (From Shepherd and Brayton, 1987)

as logical and abstract reasoning. If so, the precise deployment of active ionic channels in the membranes of distal dendrites and dendritic spines of cortical neurons could be added to the list of attributes contributing to the unique qualities of humans (see Table 30.1, above).

Local Circuits

As in every other region in the brain, the synaptic circuits in the cortex are built up out of the triad of neural elements: input fibers, output neurons, and intrinsic neurons. By combining methods for intracellular staining and recording with cellular identification of transmitters, it has been possible to begin to construct the basic circuits that characterize each of the three main types of cerebral cortex: palaeocortex (olfactory cortex), archicortex (hippocampus), and neocortex.

The Basic Cortical Circuit. Insight into the complexities of neocortex can be gained by considering the simple types of cortex first. We discussed olfactory cortex in Chap. 11 and hippocampus in Chaps. 7 and 29. Careful consideration of the organization of these regions shows that each consists of a basic circuit constructed of three types of connections: (1) afferent input fibers (IN) make excitatory synapses onto distal apical dendritic spines of pyramidal neurons; (2) intrinsic axon collaterals are reexcitatory (RE) to pyramidal neurons over long distances; and (3) local interneurons are activated by afferents to give feedforward inhibition (FI) and/or axon collaterals to give lateral inhibition (LI). These connections can be identified in the basic circuit diagram of Fig. 30.8B.

In view of the fact that submammalian vertebrates have a cortex (Fig. 29.12), and it is of interest to know its fundamental plan. Recent studies (see Kriegstein and Connors, 1986) have yielded a basic circuit which is in fact very similar to that for olfactory and hippocampal cortex. This is significant because submammalian cortex is believed to be similar to the phylogenetic precursor of neocortex (see Fig. 29.12A).

These facts suggest that the basic circuit for olfactory–hippocampal–general cortex may represent a framework that has been elaborated into the neocortex in the course of mammalian evolution. The way this might have come about is indicated in Fig. 30.8. As shown in B, agranular association cortex is closely similar to simple cortex. The primary input (IN), by definition, is from other parts of cortex, and this terminates mainly in the most superficial layers. Pyramidal cells mediate reexcitation of pyramidal cells through direct connections of their axon collaterals (RE). Feedforward inhibition (FI) and lateral inhibition (LI) are also mediated much as in simple cortex.

In primary sensory cortex, such as visual cortex, the afferent input ends mainly in a specific population of stellate cells that defines a new layer, lamina IV, midway through the cortex (see IN in Fig. 30.8C). This population of cells can be seen to function as a kind of intracortical relay, receiving the thalamic input and transferring it to the pyramidal neurons, providing thereby a more complex preprocessing of information prior to its input to the pyramidal neurons. This is part of the evolutionary process of encephalization, in which functions carried out in peripheral centers in earlier species are transferred to central centers in order to enhance the complexity of processing by interactions with other central centers.

What Makes Neocortical Circuits Unique? We can now begin to get a perspective on the properties that are special about the neocortex. First, it is placed where it is accessible to every major sensory input, arriving either directly (from the olfactory cortex) or relayed from below through the brainstem and thalamus. Second, it is a layered structure doubled back on itself, so that inputs arrive from the depths and outputs exit through the depths. This leaves the cells in every layer potentially accessible to every input. When the local circuits through collaterals and interneurons are added to the picture, the potential ways by which information can be integrated, stored,

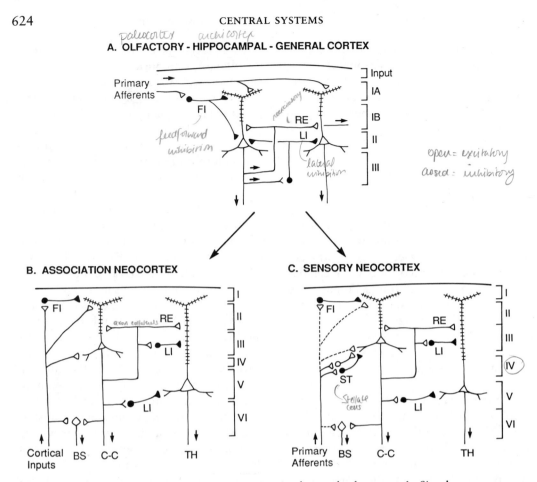

Fig. 30.8 Principles of local circuit organization in the cerebral cortex. **A.** Simple cortex, as represented by olfactory cortex, hippocampus, and reptilian dorsal (general) cortex. Layers indicated on right. Abbreviations: FI, feedforward inhibition; LI, lateral (and feedback) inhibition; RE, recurrent (and lateral) excitation. **B.** Agranular association areas of neocortex. Layers on right. Output sites below: BS, brainstem; C–C, corticocortical; TH, thalamus. **C.** Primary sensory areas of neocortex. Note that the main difference from the circuit in B is the predominance of primary afferents from the thalamus which project to an intracortical relay through stellate (ST) cells in layer IV. Connections to other layers are still present, but less prominent (dashed lines). Excitatory connections shown by open profiles; inhibitory, by closed profiles. (Modified from Shepherd, 1987)

and recombined become enormous. Such a structure is no longer dominated by the operational sequence demanded of a particular input or output. Third, rather than there being one type of output cell, as is common in so many centers, there are several types. In fact, each layer is the source of output fibers; some fibers go only to other layers (such as outputs from layer I and IV), others go to different distant targets (such as outputs from layers II, III, V, and VI; see Fig. 30.8). As a result, each

layer, in effect, acts as a semi-independent unit, defined by its particular inputs, outputs, intrinsic connections, and relations to its neighboring layers. Finally, give this structure the chance to expand, through some property of its not-quite-rigid braincase, and one has the opportunity to go on enlarging individual areas, or adding on new ones, in order to combine information from new combinations of inputs or control different combinations of output targets.

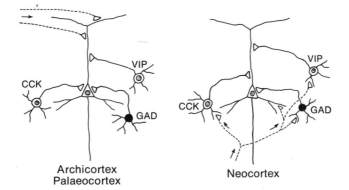

Fig. 30.9 Diagrams summarizing the localization of neurons and terminals in different types of cortex, as shown by immunocytochemical staining methods for the peptides cholecystokinin (CCK) and vasoactive intestinal polypeptide (VIP), and for glutamic acid decarboxylase (GAD), the enzyme that synthesizes GABA. (Adapted from Emson and Hunt, 1981)

An interesting example illustrating some of these principles is provided by work on peptides in the cortex. Using immunocytochemical methods, P. C. Emson and S. P. Hunt of Cambridge University have localized two peptides, cholecystokinin (CCK) and vasoactive intestinal polypeptide (VIP), as well as GABA, in neurons of different cortical regions. Figure 30.9 summarizes their findings. In primitive cortex (paleocortex and archicortex), immunoreactive terminals for both CCK and glutamic acid dehydragenase (GAD) were found on the cell bodies of large pyramidal (output) neurons, whereas terminals positive for VIP were found on the apical dendrites. The results in neocortex were similar for GAD and VIP, but CCK terminals were found predominately on the proximal portions of apical dendrites. In interpreting their results, Emson and Hunt (1981) noted that the main excitatory input through specific afferents connects directly to the apical dendrites of the pyramidal (output) neurons in primitive cortex, but is mostly relayed indirectly through interneurons in sensory neocortex (compare Fig. 30.9 with Fig. 30.8A and C). They speculated:

The altered position of the CCK terminals on the neocortical neurons may reflect the altered role of the CCK neuron from providing a *parallel* excitatory input, for example in the hippocampal pyramidal neurons, to providing the *principal* excitatory input in certain neocortical neurons.

Local Circuit Modules. In our studies of nervous systems, both invertebrate and vertebrate, we have seen that local circuits tend to be arranged not diffusely, but rather in discrete clusters, or modules. The ganglia of invertebrates, and the discrete regions of neuropil called glomeruli in the vertebrate olfactory bulb, are perhaps the clearest anatomical expressions of this modularization. In the cortex, modularization is expressed in many ways; some of them are summarized in Table 30.4.

Modules are not static, hard-wired enti-

Table 30.4 Modules in cerebral cortex

Hippocampus	transverse lamellae
Somatosensory cortex	modality-specific columns
	glomeruli (barrels)
Visual cortex	ocular dominance columns
	orientation columns
	hypercolumns
Motor cortex	colonies
	"columns"
Entorhinal cortex (fetal human)	glomeruli
Frontal association cortex	columns

References in Shepherd (1979), Goldman-Rakic (1981); for entorhinal cortex, I. Kostovic (personal communication)

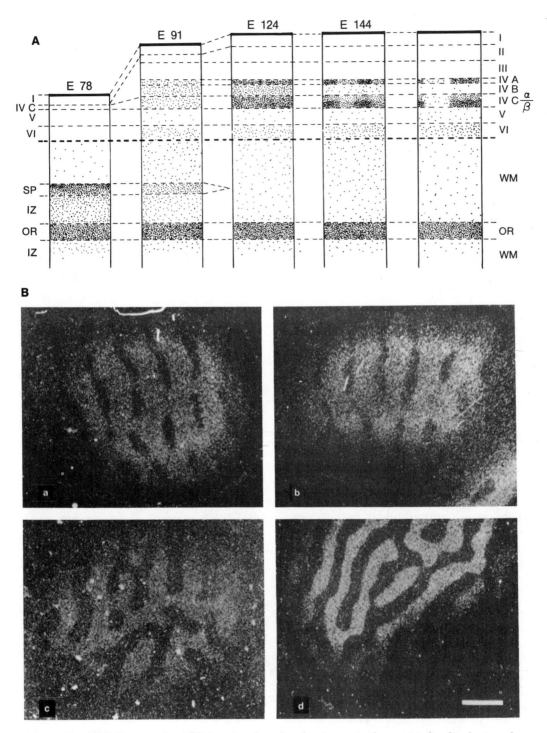

Fig. 30.10 **A.** Summary of establishment of ocular dominance columns in the developing rhesus monkey. The five diagrams start at embryonic day 78 and end with the adult. For each age, a monkey had been injected with radioactively labeled amino acids into one eye 14 days previously; the amino acid was incorporated into protein by the ganglion cells in the retina of that eye and transported by axonal transport to the lateral geniculate, where interneuronal transfer took place

ties. We have noted that individual neurons and synapses must compete for functional validation and survival, and it should not be surprising therefore to learn that the same applies to the populations within modules. This has been seen most clearly in the visual cortex.

In the monkey, the fibers from the two lateral geniculate nuclei first project during development in a diffuse and overlapping manner to the visual cortex; as Rakic has shown, it is only about two weeks before birth that segregation into columns dominated by input from one or the other eye is first seen. This process of establishment of ocular dominance columns is complete in the monkey by about three to six weeks after birth (Fig. 30.8A).

Hubel and Wiesel showed in the early 1960s that if one eye is closed at birth, the ocular dominance columns of the normal eye expand. They demonstrated this with unit recordings, and it has recently been documented by injecting radioactively labeled amino acids into the spared eye and making autoradiographs of the distribution of the transported material in the cortex. As shown in Fig. 30.10B, the terminal fields of the fibers from the normal eye have expanded, at the expense of the neighboring fields from the deprived eye. Moreover, the fact that this can be demonstrated with deprivation beginning at 5½ weeks, when the normal adult ocular dominance columns are already established, suggests that the expansion of the fields from the normal eye involves an actual sprouting of the fibers. There is evidence that this plasticity after monocular deprivation depends on the presence of norepinephrine in the cortex, with the implication that this might be one of the "state-setting" functions of the NE fibers from the brainstem to the cortex.

Plasticity in cortical modules has also been implicated in the orientation selectivity of cells in the visual cortex. In kittens exposed only to a pattern of vertically oriented stripes, the recordings from the cortex show units that tend to respond maximally only to stimulation with vertically oriented stripes. This implies that the circuit connections within orientation columns are dependent to some extent on visual experience.

Cortical Areas and Lobes

At the next higher level of organization are areas and lobes. The mammalian cortex consists of four main lobes: occipital, parietal, frontal, and temporal (Fig. 30.11). These terms are already familiar. You already know that the occipital lobe receives visual input, the parietal lobe receives somatosensory input, the temporal lobe receives auditory input, and the frontal lobe is the origin of many motor pathways.

The areas of each lobe that are not directly related to a specific sensory or motor function have traditionally been termed *association areas*. Since these are the areas that have undergone greatest expansion in the human brain, it has been commonly assumed that they have a large role to play in the attributes that are distinctly human. Three main functions have been ascribed to these association areas. First, a surprisingly large expanse of what appeared to be "association" cortex is actually given over

to geniculate cells that projected to the visual cortex. The diagrams show how the pattern of termination within the cortex changed from diffuse (E 91) to columnar (E 144 and adult). Cortical layers 1–6 are indicated at the side. IZ, intermediate zone; SP, subplate layer; OR, optic radiation; WM, white matter. **B.** Experiments showing effects of long-term monocular deprivation on ocular dominance columns at different ages in the rhesus monkey. Deprivation was begun at 2 weeks (a), 5½ weeks (b), 10 weeks (c), and in the adult (d). In each case, the normal (nondeprived) eye was injected with radioactive amino acids. In the photomicrographs, the sites of label appear white. Note the expansion of the terminal fields of the geniculate input from the nondeprived eye up to 5½ weeks. (A from Rakic, 1981; B from LeVay et al., 1981)

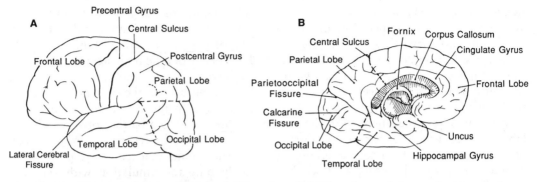

Fig. 30. 11 Diagrams showing the lateral (**A**) and medial (**B**) surfaces of the cerebral hemispheres. Note the division of the lateral hemisphere into four major lobes. The main gyri and sulci are also indicated. Compare with the more detailed cytoarchitectonic map of cortical areas in Fig. 30.1. (Modified from Daube et al., 1986)

to multiple representations of sensory or motor fields. This was a common theme in our discussion of visual, somatosensory, auditory, and motor cortex. Second, increasingly complex processing takes place within these multiple sensory areas; this is seen clearly, for example, in the abstraction of visual information in the occipital lobe. Third, the higher association areas are increasingly concerned with multimodal integration of information from other lobes. The capacity to integrate higher-order sensory information and use it to control different kinds of motor outputs lies at the heart of many of our higher cognitive functions.

Distributed Cortical Systems

It would be convenient if each lobe subserved one of the higher mental functions, but this is not generally the case. Most cortically mediated behavior depends on interactions between areas in different lobes. This is nicely illustrated by the very first type of behavior considered in this book, the act of reading from a page. As shown in Fig. 1.1, this involves visual input to the occipital lobe, processing of the visual information in areas of the occipital lobe and the neighboring parietal and temporal lobes, and control of eye movements and other motor output through the frontal lobe. Thus, cortical circuits in all the lobes must be

engaged in a coordinated manner in order to carry out this simple act.

From these considerations the old idea that cerebral functions are organized in terms of lobes is giving way to the new idea that cerebral functions are organized in terms of distributed systems. Each area within a lobe contributes the special operational properties mediated within its local circuits, the centers being tied together by multiple long tracts, collateral branches, and feedback connections. A crucial feature is that different areas of the cortex are accessible to each other, so that there are maximal opportunities for the areas to interact. Within each area there is maximal opportunity for different inputs to tap or utilize specific properties of the local-circuit machinery, as we have already described above.

There is increasing experimental evidence for the pathways that connect the areas of different lobes to form distributed systems, and for the cognitive functions which they mediate. We will consider several of these distributed systems, involved in higher visual processing, memory for representational knowledge, personality, and language.

Higher Visual Processing

Processing of visual information is not limited to the visual association areas of the occipital lobe. By tracing connections be-

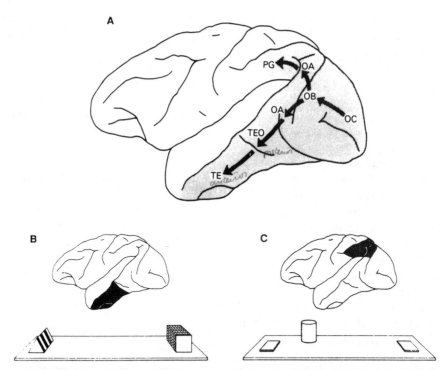

Fig. 30.12 Distributed cortical systems for higher visual processing. **A.** Diagram of lateral surface of the rhesus monkey brain. Shading indicates cortical areas involved in visual processing. Arrows show dorsal and ventral pathways that have been identified by anatomical and behavioral studies. Abbreviations: OC, primary visual area (area 17; V1); OB, secondary visual area (V2); OA in ventral pathway represents tertiary visual areas (V₃, V₄); OA in dorsal pathway represents tertiary visual areas (area MT; see Fig. 16.20); PG, inferior parietal cortex; TEO, posterior temporal area; TE, inferior temporal cortex. TE connects through the amygdala to many other regions (see Chap. 28). Both PG and TE have connections with the frontal lobe (see below). (From Mishkin et al., 1983)

tween areas, it has been found in the monkey that the connections from the primary visual cortex diverge in two main pathways. As illustrated in Fig. 30.12A, the ventral pathway passes from primary visual cortex (OC) to successive association areas (OB, OA) and thence to the temporal lobe (cf. Fig. 16.20). Within the temporal lobe, there are connections from the posterior (TEO) to the anterior (TE) part.

The functions mediated by this pathway have been revealed by behavioral tests such as that illustrated in Fig. 30.12B. In this test, the animal is first familiarized with one object, and then is presented with a second object and rewarded for selecting it if it is different from the first. This requires synthesis of the physical properties of the first object (size, color, texture, shape), storing of a central representation of that combined information, and discrimination of the second object with that representation. According to Mortimer Mishkin at NIH, monkeys can carry out this type of recognition after only one exposure to the test object, even after a delay of several minutes (see Mishkin et al., 1983) Lesions of area TE render the monkey unable to perform the recognition.

By contrast, a dorsal pathway diverges within occipital cortex (OB, OA) to reach inferior parietal cortex (PG) (See Fig. 30.12A). The type of visual information processed by this pathway is illustrated in Fig. 30.12C. In this test, a "landmark" object, such as a tall cylinder, is positioned randomly in successive trials between two identical rectangular food wells; the monkey is rewarded for choosing the feed well closer to the landmark. Lesions of the inferior parietal area severely disrupt this type of spatial vision. Mishkin et al. conclude that "posterior parietal cortex seems to be concerned with the perception of the spatial relations among objects," in contrast to inferior temporal cortex, which is concerned with the intrinsic qualities of an object, not its position in space (cf. Fig. 16.20). In addition, the dorsal pathway is a polysensory area, mediating "a supramodal spatial ability that subsumes both the macrospace of vision and the (tactile) microspace encompassed by the hand."

What are the mechanisms whereby visual and tactile information are integrated in the posterior parietal area in controlling the hand? Vernon Mountcastle and his colleagues have succeeded in recording from units in this area in awake, behaving monkeys (see Fig. 30.13). Most of these neurons responded to one or another submodality of muscle, joint, or skin stimulation, similar to neurons in the primary somatosensory cortex (see Chap. 14). However, some units showed complex properties. One type was active only when the animal performed a movement of the arm or a manipulation of the hand—in other words, movement in the immediate extrapersonal space. Another type was active only when the animal visually fixated on an object in which it had an obvious interest, such as an item of food when the monkey was hungry. The activity continued even when the object was moved in space. These experiments thus gave evidence of higher levels of abstraction, in which the mutual effects of location in space of a limb, location in space of an object, and the motivational state of the animal, combine to specify the activity of a single cortical cell. Dependence of activity on multiple contingencies is one of the defining characteristics of higher abstraction. It was concluded that the kind of sensory integration displayed by this type of neuron could serve as a basis for higher

abstraction, and be concerned with spatially orienting the animal toward behavioral goals.

In conclusion, we may note that already by the eighteenth century, philosophers had postulated a "sensorium commune," where sensory information comes together to form a coherent representation of our perceptual world. The discussion above indicates that we are making progress toward understanding the neural mechanisms involved in this process. Indeed, Mountcastle (1986) has stated the modern credo of this endeavor: "Any aspect of perception identified in the behavior of a non-human primate and brought under quantitative experimental control can be studied directly at the level of mechanism."

Internal Representations and the Frontal Lobes

If the brain constructs internal representations of the external world, the question arises of how it uses those representations to guide the behavior of the animal. Study of this problem has implicated the frontal lobes.

In 1937, Carlyle Jacobson, working in John Fulton's laboratory at Yale, studied the effects of frontal lobe lesions. The experimental paradigm was the "delayed-response" test. As illustrated in Fig. 30.14A, the monkey first watches as the experimenter puts food in one of the wells and then covers both wells. There is then a delay period (middle diagram) during which an opaque panel is lowered. The panel is then raised, and the monkey is tested for its ability to select the well with the food. Jacobson showed that lesions of the prefrontal area of the frontal lobe disrupt the ability to remember the location of the food. This loss of "delayed response" learning is quite specific; the performance on other complex learning tasks is unaffected.

A simple way to characterize these results is: "out of site, out of mind." The results imply that the frontal lobe is in-

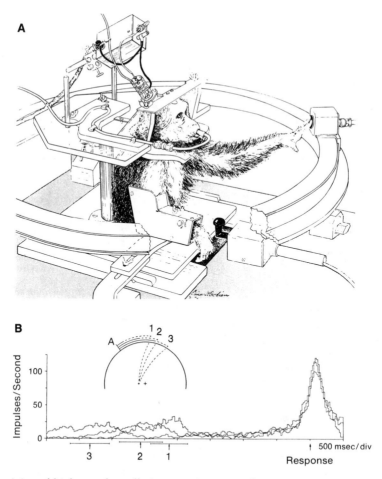

Fig. 30.13 Activity of higher-order cells in posterior parietal association cortex related to control of purposive movement. **A.** Monkey sitting in recording and test apparatus. The small box containing a signal light moves along the circular rail. The monkey starts by resting its left hand on the signal key (see black knob), then releases and projects the hand to touch the moving signal light when it is illuminated, as shown. **B.** Activity of an arm projection neuron. In this experiment, the signal light moved through three different arcs (inset); solid lines show the movement before, dashed lines the movement after, the signal came on. The trajectories of the hand, from the starting position (+) to the final points (1–3) at which the finger contacted the signal light, are also shown by dashed lines. Histograms of the firing frequency of this neuron are superimposed in the graph, aligned on the instant at which the finger touched the signal light (Response). Horizontal bars (1–3) below the abscissa indicate the detection times for the different trials. The similar firing patterns of this neuron during different arm trajectories indicate that the activity of this neuron is related to command signals for this type of purposive movement, rather than to detailed instructions for individual muscle contractions. (From Mountcastle et al., 1975)

volved in circuits which construct an internal representation of the visual information about the place of an object, and then read out that information to control a motor response at an appropriate later time. There is a direct and interesting parallel with hu-

mans in this regard; human infants show the same inability to perform the delayed-response test as frontal-lobe-lesioned monkeys. The ability to perform the test is not manifest until around one year of age. The implication from the animal experiments is

A. DELAYED RESPONSE TEST

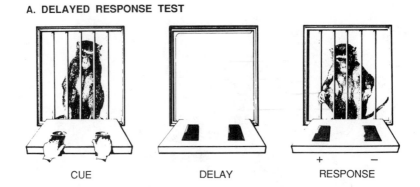

CUE   DELAY   RESPONSE

B. PREFRONTAL - PARIETAL CONNECTIONS

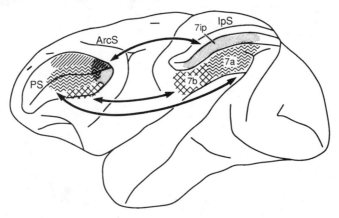

Fig. 30.14 The delayed response and its mediation by the prefrontal–parietal distributed system. **A.** The delayed response test, consisting of three stages: "cue" (the monkey is shown food being put into one of two wells); "delay" (an opaque panel hides the monkey's view of the wells for 1–10 minutes); "response" (the monkey selects the well with the food). Lesions of the prefrontal cortex selectively disrupt the ability to perform this task (see text). **B.** Lateral view of the monkey brain, showing the connections between prefrontal and parietal cortex that mediate spatial memory underlying the delayed response. Note the parallel and reciprocal connections between subareas in each cortex. Abbreviations: ArcS, arcuate sulcus; IpS, intraparietal sulcus; PS, principal sulcus; 7ip, 7a, 7b, subareas of area 7 of parietal cortex. (From Goldman-Rakic, 1987)

therefore that the prefrontal cortex is responsible for

. . . the capacity to recognize that an object exists in time and space when it is not in view. In children such a basic function may be a building block for object internalization and symbolic reasoning, crucial components of cognitive capacity. [Goldman-Rakic, 1984]

What are the pathways that mediate these crucial functions? Neuroanatomists have used a variety of tract-tracing methods to investigate the connections between the prefrontal cortex and other parts of the brain. The results of a recent study by Goldman-Rakic and Carmen Cavada are summarized in Fig. 30.14B. Note first the strong connections between prefrontal and parietal association cortex; these provide the pathways whereby supramodality spatial and visual information is transferred to the frontal lobe. Second, each connection is reciprocal, so that the parietal areas receive input from the prefrontal areas; this provides a means whereby prefrontal cortex can "participate in the regulation of the attentional and motor commands for the task" (Goldman-Rakic, 1987). Third, there are multiple parallel pathways between the subareas in the two lobes; this implies that each pathway is distinctive in the type of information that is processed. Here again we see an expression of the parallel architecture of the brain, even as one approaches the highest levels of information processing.

Personality and the Frontal Lobes

The role of the frontal lobe in reading out internal representations of stored information is only part of a larger role involving, in humans, the entire personality of an individual. This was first indicated by the sad case of Phineas P. Gage in the early nineteenth century. Following a deep wound to his frontal lobes in a railroad construction accident, his personality changed from that of a responsible foreman to being erratic and undependable.

A century passed before the experiments of Jacobson revived an interest in the neural basis of this change. In his animals, the prefrontal lesions not only disrupted the specific ability to perform on the delayed response test, but also induced changes such as reducing the expression of agitation in frustrating situations. This result led to the introduction of operations for frontal lobotomy (surgical undercutting of the frontal lobes) in schizophrenia patients who displayed uncontrolled aggressive behavior. Unfortunately, the results of these operations were inconsistent, and the attendant changes in personality, many of them remindful of the Gage case, were generally unacceptable.

These results made clear the need for much more research on the neural basis of frontal lobe function in relation to normal personality and to psychotic illness. A review of this large body of work, and the theories it has spawned, is beyond the scope of the present account. At present, there is considerable interest in the roles of specific neurotransmitters and neuromodulators, especially dopamine. Abnormalities in dopamine neurotransmission have long been suspected in schizophrenia, and the discovery of the mesocortical dopaminergic innervation of the frontal lobes (cf. Thierry et al., 1973; see Chap. 24) has therefore been significant. A variety of neuropharmacological manipulations have documented the antipsychotic effects of neuroleptic drugs on dopaminergic systems, including the prefrontal cortex (cf. Bunney, 1984). These studies support the belief that psychotic behavior is due to malfunctioning of specific brain circuits, and the hope that normal function can be restored by drugs acting on the synapses of these circuits.

Hemispheres: Laterality and Dominance

All of the lobes together constitute a hemisphere, and the whole forebrain thus consists of two hemispheres. Just as each hemisphere is differentiated into lobes, so are the two himespheres differentiated from each other in mediating the highest levels of cerebral function.

The first evidence that the hemispheres are different came from the French neurologist Paul Broca; in 1863 he described a patient with the inability to speak (aphasia) who turned out to have a tumor in the left frontal lobe. Broca deduced that this is the area of cortex that controls speech; in his words, "We speak with the left hemisphere." In 1875, Carl Wernicke, a 26-year-old German neurologist, reported that aphasia can also be caused by a lesion in the temporal lobe. He showed the difference between sensory aphasia, the lack of ability to formulate words due to temporal lobe damage, and motor aphasia, the inability to produce words (speak) due to frontal lobe damage. His diagram of the way these two regions are involved in the control of speech (Fig. 30.15) was one of the first attempts to identify the brain circuits underlying specific behavioral functions.

This work thus clearly established that

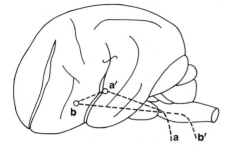

Fig. 30.15 Wernicke's original drawing in 1874, illustrating his concept of the brain circuits involved in language. Sounds received in the ears are converted into neural signals and transmitted through the auditory pathway (a) to the brain, where the sound "images" are stored in Wernicke's area (a'). These neural images are transferred to Broca's area (b) where they activate the descending pathway for motor control of speech (b'). The diagram indicates how lesions in a' give rise to sensory aphasia (an inability to understand spoken words or organize words coherently), whereas lesions in b give rise to motor aphasia (an inability to articulate spoken words). (From Kolb and Whishaw, 1985)

the left hemisphere is "dominant" for a specific function, speech. And there the matter rested. Until the 1950s, this stood as an isolated exception to what appeared to be the general equivalence of the two hemispheres in all their other functions, sensory and motor. Then R. D. Myers and Roger Sperry carried out a series of elegant experiments in cats, in which they cut the corpus callosum, the thick band containing millions of fibers that connect the two hemispheres. Until that time, no significant function had been ascribed to these fibers. When visual stimuli were presented to both eyes, the animals behaved as competently as normal cats. However, when the decussating fibers in the optic chiasm were cut and each eye was tested separately, it was found that each hemisphere functioned independently; visual learning in one hemisphere was not transferred to the other hemisphere.

Sperry and Michael Gazzaniga then ex-

amined a series of human patients in whom the callosum had been cut to prevent spread of epileptic seizures. These studies confirmed that, with independent visual input to one hemisphere or the other, the hemispheres also functioned and learned independently of one another. This work, which earned Sperry the Nobel Prize in 1981, led to our present concepts of the laterality of higher functions in the human brain. The left hemisphere is dominant for control of speech, language, complex voluntary movement, reading, writing, and arithmetic calculations. The right hemisphere is specialized for mainly nonlinguistic functions: complex pattern recognition in vision, audition, and the tactile senses; the sense of space, spatial shapes, and direction in space; the sense of intuition (see Fig. 30.16).

There have been many attempts to read a lot into these differences, such as the idea that the left hemisphere is scientific whereas the right is artistic. A useful generalization is that the left hemisphere is specialized for certain specific kinds of motor output, whereas the right is more specialized for global relations of the body in space, something akin to the perceptual Gestalt referred to in Chap. 10. Recalling our previous discussion of different types of information and their storage as memories (Chap. 29), it further appears that the right hemisphere is specialized for handling procedural information, and the left hemisphere for declarative information. No matter how one characterizes the two hemispheres, it is important to realize that neither one is "dominant" in the absolute sense; each constellation of functions is of adaptive value, and the human brain attempts to optimize both by letting the hemispheres specialize in these two directions.

In recent years, lateralization of function has been found in a number of species, invertebrate as well as vertebrate; we have noted several instances in this book. It may well be that it is an inherent tendency in an animal with bilaterally organized body and brain.

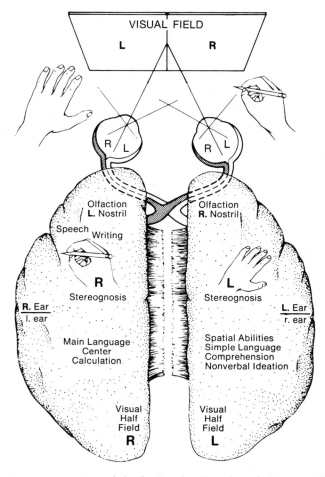

Fig. 30.16 Schematic representation of the brain, showing the relative specialization of the two hemispheres and their relations to sensory inputs and motor outputs. Cutting of the corpus collosum is shown in the midline. (From Sperry, 1974)

Language

The simple circuit first proposed by Wernicke as the basis for cortical mechanisms in language still holds, but it has been considerably elaborated by recent studies. An important finding has been the discovery that there is an anatomical asymmetry associated with the functional asymmetry of language in the human brain. This simple fact had escaped most neuroanatomists and neuropathologists, in their examinations of the brains of humans obtained post mortem, until 1968.

In that year, Norman Geschwind and W. Levitsky at Harvard reported that measurements of the right and left temporal lobes showed a striking difference. In most brains, an area called the "planum temporale," located on the upper border of the temporal lobe and extending deep into the Sylvian fossa, is considerably larger on the left. This is shown diagrammatically in Fig. 30.17. The planum temporale contains Wernicke's speech area. It is tempting to conclude that the larger speech area on the left is correlated with left-hemispheric dominance for language in most humans. This, of course, does not explain how Wernicke's area mediates language, but it indicates that one of the mechanisms for obtaining greater complexity of information processing, that of increasing the num-

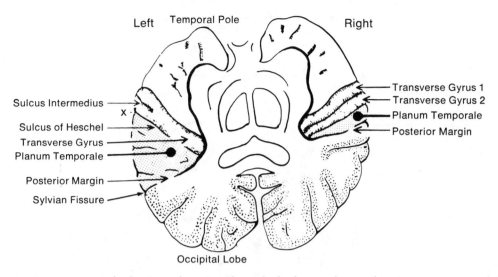

Fig. 30.17 Diagram of a horizontal section through the human brain, showing asymmetry of the temporal lobe upper surface, and the larger area called planum temporale on the left. (From Geschwind and Levitsky, in Geschwind, 1980)

ber of neurons and extent of local circuits, has been utilized in this case.

An expanded view of the distributed system for language is shown in Fig. 30.18. This is based on the results from electrical stimulation of speech areas in human patients, as well as on anatomical studies in monkeys and humans. The diagram em-

phasizes the connections involved in one language task: naming a seen object. Visual information is first received in area 17, and elaborated in areas 18 and 19. From here, the perceptual image of the object is transferred to a large "posterior speech area," which includes area 39 (of parietal cortex) as well as the classical Wernicke's area.

Fig. 30.18 Summary of the main pathways believed to be involved in seeing an object and saying its name. **A.** Lateral view of left hemisphere. **B.** Overhead view of both hemispheres. Bilateral inwardly pointing arrows represent the descending corticospinal motor pathway. AF, arcuate fasciculus; CC, corpus callosum. (A from Popper and Eccles, 1977; B modified from Geschwind, 1980)

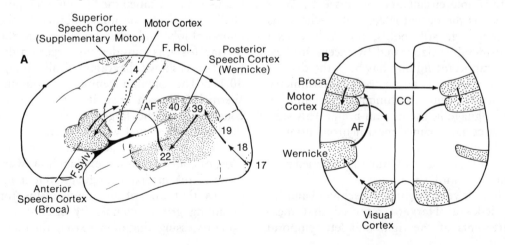

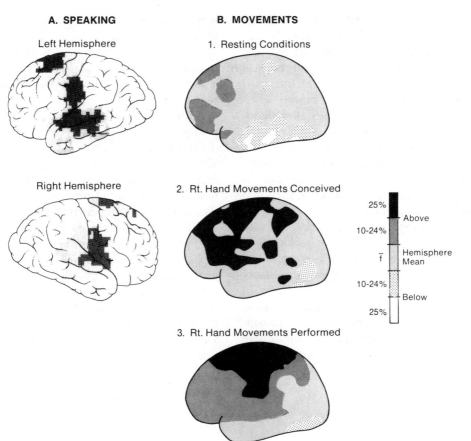

Fig. 30.19 Computerized images of differences in regional blood flow in the human brain during different behaviors. **A.** Regions active during speaking. These images represent averages from nine different subjects. Squares indicate the resolution of the multiple detector array aimed at the side of the head. Regions of high blood flow (and increased cortical activity) are indicated by darkest shading; regions of light shading indicate background levels; unshaded regions indicate below-average activity. **B.** Comparison between regions active during the conceptualization of a motor act and the performance of that act. **1.** Resting condition (note activity in frontal poles). **2.** The subject was asked to imagine rhythmic clenching movements of the right hand (note active regions in frontal, parietal, and temporal lobes, but largely sparing the motor strip along the central sulcus). **3.** When the movements were actually performed, activity was centered over the motor strip. Drawings are adapted from data plots like those in A; results were from six subjects. (A from Lassen et al., 1978, in Kolb and Whishaw, 1980; B from Ingvar and Phillipsson, in Yarovsky and Ingvar, 1981)

Area 39 transfers the visual representation of the object to its auditory representation in area 22. From area 22, the information is transferred to Broca's speech area, where the motor programs for speech are located. These programs are then "read out" to the face area of the motor cortex, where they control the complex spatiotemporal coordination of the muscles of speech, so that

the name of the observed object can be articulated.

The Thinking Brain

The circuits described above have been inferred from traditional methods of anatomy and physiology. Activity in these circuits can now be directly visualized by new methods for mapping cerebral function. We have previously described the Sokoloff method for mapping brain activity by autoradiography. A related method is based on the fact that when different cortical regions are active, they receive an increased blood flow, much as does a muscle when it is active. By injecting into the bloodstream a substance (xenon$_{133}$) whose concentration can be monitored by radioactivity detectors placed on the skull, the activity of different cortical regions can be mapped in awake subjects while they perform specific mental tasks.

In the example in Fig. 30.19A, the subject was asked to speak. The peaks of activity occur over the mouth–tongue–larynx area of the motor and somatosensory cortex, the supplementary motor area in the frontal lobe, and the auditory cortex, including Wernicke's area. There is considerably more activity in the left hemisphere than in the right, as expected since the left hemisphere is dominant for speech. Figure 30.19B shows that these methods can reveal not only the patterns associated with performance of a motor task, but also those associated with the conceptualization of that task.

Results such as these confirm the general postulates regarding the contributions of different areas to specific higher functions. When combined with electrophysiological recordings and molecular analysis, these new methods should provide a firm foundation for analyzing cortical systems at the cellular level. An understanding of the nature of cortical function, and the nature of our own being, seems a bit closer to our grasp; our progress, as always, will depend on our ingenuity in devising new methods, our imagination in interpreting the results, and our wisdom in maintaining a balanced view of humankind among the creatures of this planet.

Literature Cited

Adams, D. J., J. S. Smith, and S. H. Thompson (1980). Ionic currents in molluscan soma. *Annu. Rev. Neurosci.* 3:141–168.

Adrian, E. D., and Y. Zotterman (1926). The impulses produced by sensory nerve endings. 2. The response of a single end-organ. *J. Physiol. (London)* 61:151–171.

Aghajanian, G. K., and B. S. Bunney (1976). Dopamine "autoreceptors": pharmacological characterization by microiontophoretic single cell recording studies. *Naunyn-Schmiedeberg's Arch. Pharmacol.* 297:1–7.

Aghajanian, G. K., and K. Rasmussen (1988). Basic electrophysiology. In *Psychopharmacology: The Third Generation of Progress* (H. Meltzer, ed.). New York: Raven Press.

Aguayo, A. J. (1985). Axonal regeneration from injured neurons in the adult mammalian central nervous system. In *Synaptic Plasticity* (C. E. Cotman, ed.). New York: Guilford Press, pp. 457–484.

Aidley, D. J. (1978). *The Physiology of Excitable Cells.* Cambridge: Cambridge University Press.

Alberts, B., D. Bray, J. Lewis, M. Raff, K. Roberts, and J. D. Watson (1983). *Molecular Biology of the Cell.* New York: Garland.

Alcock, J. (1979). *Animal Behavior: An Evolutionary Approach.* Sunderland, MA: Sinauer.

Alexander, R. McN. (1979). *The Invertebrates.* Cambridge: Cambridge University Press.

Alexandrowicz, J. S. (1951). Muscle receptor organs in the abdomen of *Homarus vulgaris* and *Palinrus vulgaris. Q. J. Microsc. Sci.* 92:163–199.

Andersen, P., and S. A. Andersson (1968). *Physiological Basis of the Alpha Rhythm.* New York: Appleton-Century-Crofts.

Andersen, P. S., S. H. Sundberg, O. Sveen, and H. Wigström (1977). Specific long-lasting potentiation of synaptic transmission in hippocampal slices. *Nature* 266:736–737.

Anderson, D. J. (1984). New clues to protein localization in neurons. *Trends Neurosci.* 7:355–357.

Armstrong, C. M. (1981). Sodium channels and gating currents. *Physiol. Rev.* 61:644–683.

Art, J. J., R. Fettiplace, and P. A. Fuchs (1984). Synaptic hyperpolarization and inhibition of turtle cochlear hair cells. *J. Physiol. (London)* 356:525–530.

Asanuma, H. (1981). Functional role of sensory inputs to the motor cortex. *Prog. Neurobiol.* 16:241–262.

Aserinsky, E., and N. Kleitman (1953). Two types of ocular motility occurring during sleep. *J. Appl. Physiol.* 8:1–10.

Ashe, J. H., and M. Nachman (1980). Neural mechanisms in taste aversion learning. *Prog. Psychobiol. Physiol. Psychol.* 9:233–262.

Atwood, H. L. (1973). An attempt to account for the diversity of crustacean muscle. *Am. Zool.* 13:357–378.

Atwood, H. L. (1977). Crustacean neuromuscular systems: past, present, and future. In *Identified Neurons and Behavior of Arthropods* (G. Hoyle, ed.). New York: Plenum Press, pp. 9–29.

Augustine, G. J., M. P. Charlton, and S. J. Smith (1987). Calcium action in synaptic transmitter release. *Annu. Rev. Neurosci.* 10:633–693.

Baehr, W., and M. L. Applebury (1986). Exploring visual transduction with recombinant DNA techniques. *Trends Neurosci.* 9:198–203.

Bailey, C. H., and M. Chen (1983). Morphological basis of long-term habituation and sensitization in *Aplysia. Science* 220:91–93.

Baitinger, C., R. Cheney, D. Clements, M. Glicksman, N. Hirokawa, J. Levine, K. Meiri, C. Simon, P. Skene, and M. Willard (1983). Axonally transported proteins in axon development, maintenance, and regeneration. *Cold Spring Harbor Symp. Quant. Biol.* 48:791–802.

Baker, R., and R. Llinás (1971). Electrotonic coupling between neurones in the rat mesencephalic nucleus. *J. Physiol. (London)* 212:45–63.

Bard, P. (1934). On emotional expression after decortication with some remarks on certain theoretical views: parts I and II. *Psychol. Rev.* 41:309–329, 434–439.

Barker, D. (1974). The morphology of muscle receptors. In *Handbook of Sensory Physiology,* Vol. 3, Part 2: *Muscle Receptors* (C. C. Hunt, ed.). New York: Springer-Verlag, pp. 1–190.

Barlow, R. B., S. C. Chamberlain, and L. Kass (1984). Circadian rhythms in retinal function. In *Molecular and Cellular Basis of Visual Acuity: Cell and Developmental Biology of the Eye* (S. R. Hilfer and J. B. Sheffield, eds.). New York: Springer-Verlag, pp. 31–53.

Barnett, S. A. (1981). *Modern Ethology: The Science of Animal Behavior.* New York: Oxford University Press.

Barrington, E. J. W. (1979). *Invertebrate Structure and Function.* New York: John Wiley.

Bartoshuk, L. M. (1978). Gustatory system. In *Handbook of Behavioral Neurobiology,* Vol. 1: *Sensory Integration* (R. B. Masterton, ed.). New York: Plenum Press, pp. 503–567.

Baylor, D. A., T. D. Lamb, and K.-W. Yau (1979a). The membrane current of single rod outer segments. *J. Physiol. (London)* 288:589–611.

Baylor, D. A., T. D. Lamb, and K.-W. Yau (1979b). Responses of retinal rods to single photons. *J. Physiol. (London)* 288:613–634.

Beidler, L. M. (1980). The chemical senses: gustation and olfaction. In *Medical Physiology,* Vol. 1 (V. B. Mountcastle, ed.). St. Louis: C. V. Mosby, pp. 586–602.

Bell, C. (1833/37). *The Hand.* London: Pickering.

Bender, W. (1985). Homeotic gene products as growth factors. *Cell* 43:559–560.

Bennett, M. V. L. (1977). Electrical transmission: a functional analysis and comparison with chemical transmission. In *Handbook of Physiology,* Sec. 1: *The Nervous System,* Vol. 1: *Cellular Biology of Neurons* (E. R. Kandel, ed.). Bethesda, MD: Am. Physiol. Soc. pp. 367–416.

Bennett, M. V. L. (1984). Escapism: some startling revelations. In *Neural Mechanisms of Startle Behavior* (R. C. Eaton, ed.). New York: Plenum Press, pp. 353–363.

Bennett, T. L. (1977). *Brain and Behavior.* Belmont, CA: Wadsworth.

Bentley, D., and R. R. Hoy (1974). The neurobiology of cricket song. *Sci. Am.* 231:34–44.

Bentley, D., and M. Konishi (1978). Neural control of behavior. *Annu. Rev. Neurosci.* 1:35–59.

Berridge, M. J. (1985). The molecular basis of communication within the cell. *Sci. Am.* 253:142–152.

Blalock, J. E., and E. M. Smith (1985). The immune system: our mobile brain? *Immunol. Today* 6:115–117.

Blass, E. M., and A. N. Epstein (1971). A lateral preoptic osmosensitive zone for thirst in the rat. *J. Comp. Physiol. Psychol.* 76:378–394.

Blass, E. M., W. G. Hall, and M. N. Teicher (1979). The ontogeny of suckling and ingestive behaviors. *Prog. Psychobiol. Physiol. Psychol.* 8:243–300.

Bliss, T. V. P., and A. C. Dolphin (1984). Where is the locus of long-term potentiation? In *Neurobiology of Learning and Memory* (G. Lynch, J. L. McGaugh, and N. M. Weinberger, eds.). New York: Guilford Press, pp. 451–458.

Bliss, T. V. P., and T. Lømo (1973). Long-lasting potentiation of synaptic transmission in the dentate area of the anaesthetized rabbit following stimulation of the perforant path. *J. Physiol. (London)* 232:331–356.

Bloom, W., and D. W. Fawcett (1975). *A Textbook of Histology.* Philadelphia: W. B. Saunders.

Bodian, D. (1967). Neurons, circuits, and neuroglia. In *The Neurosciences: A Study Program* (G. C. Quarton, T. Melnechuk, and F. O. Schmitt, eds.). New York: Rockefeller, pp. 6–24.

Bodian, D. (1972). Synaptic diversity and characterization by electronmicroscopy. In *Structure and Function of Synapses* (G. D. Pappas and D. P. Purpura, eds.). New York: Raven Press, pp. 45–66.

Boeckh, J. (1980). Sinne. In *Allgemeine Zoologie* (R. Siewing, ed.). Stuttgart: Gustav Fischer Verlag, pp. 345–387.

Boeckh, J., and V. Boeckh (1979). Threshold and odor specificity of pheromone-sensitive neurons in the deutocerebrum of *Antheraea pernyi* and *A. polyphemus* (Saturnidae). *J. Comp. Physiol.* 132:234–242.

Boeckh, J., K.-D. Ernst, H. Sass, and U. Waldow (1975). Coding of olfactory quality in the insect olfactory pathway. In *Ofaction and Taste V* (D. Denton, ed.). New York: Academic Press, pp. 239–245.

Borg, G., H. Diamant, L. Ström, and Y. Zotterman (1967). The relation between neural and perceptual intensity: a comparative study on the neural and psychophysical response to taste stimuli. *J. Physiol. (London)* 192:13–20.

Boring, E. G. (1950). *A History of Experimental Psychology.* New York: Appleton.

Brandon, J. G., and R. G. Coss (1982). Rapid dendritic spine stem shortening during one-trial learning: the honey bee's first orientation flight. *Brain Res.* 252:51–61.

Bray, G. A. (1986). Autonomic and endocrine factors in the regulation of energy balance. *Fed Proc.* 45:1404–1410.

Brazier, M. A. B. (1970). *The Electrical Activity of the Nervous System.* London: Pitman.

Brodal, A. (1981). *Neurological Anatomy in Relation to Clinical Medicine,* 3rd ed. New York: Oxford University Press.

Bronson, F. H. (1979). The reproductive ecology of the house mouse. *Q. Rev. Biol.* 54:265–299.

Brooks, V. B., and T. T. Thach (1981). Cerebellar control of posture and movement. In *Handbook of Physiology,* Sec. 1: *The Nervous System,* Vol. 2: *Motor Control* (V. B. Brooks, ed.). Bethesda, MD: Am. Physiol. Soc., pp. 877–946.

Brown, R. M., A. M. Crane, and P. S. Goldman (1979). Regional distribution of monamines in the cerebral cortex and subcortical structures of the rhesus monkey: concentrations and in vivo rates. *Brain Res.* 168:133–150.

Bucy, P. C., and H. Klüver (1955). An anatomical investigation of the temporal lobe in the monkey (*Macaca mulatta*). *J. Comp. Neurol.* 103:151–252.

Bulloch, K. (1985). Neuroanatomy of lymphoid tissue: a review. In *Neural Modulation of Immunity* (K. Guillemin, M. Cohn, and T. Melnechuk, eds.). New York: Raven Press, pp. 111–142.

Bullock, T. H. (1976). *Introduction to Neural Systems.* San Francisco: Freeman.

Bunge, R. P. (1968). Glial cells and the central myelin sheath. *Physiol. Rev.* 48:197–251.

Bunney, B. S. (1984). Antipsychotic drug effects on the electrical activity of dopaminergic neurons. *Trends Neurosci.* 7:212–215.

Burgess, P. R., J. Y. Wei, F. J. Clark, and J. Simon (1982). Signalling of kinesthetic information by peripheral sensory receptors. *Annu. Rev. Neurosci.* 5:171–187.

Burrows, M. (1978). Local interneurones and integration in locust ganglia. *Verb. Dtsch. Zool. Ges.* Stuttgart: Gustav Fischer Verlag, pp. 68–79.

Bush, B. M. H. (1981). Non-impulsive stretch receptors in crustaceans. In *Neurons Without Impulses* (A. Roberts and B. M. H. Bush, eds.). Cambridge: Cambridge University Press, pp. 147–176.

Byrne, J. H. (1980). Analysis of ionic conductance mechanisms in motor cells mediating inking behavior in *Aplysia californica. J. Neurophysiol.* 43:630–650.

Cahalan, M. D., K. G. Chandy, T. E. DeCoursey, and S. Gupta (1985). A voltage-gated potassium channel in human T lymphocytes. *J. Physiol. (London)* 358:197–237.

Cajal, S. Ramón y (1911). *Histologie du Système Nerveux de l'Homme et des Vertèbres.* Paris: Maloine.

Calabrese, R. L., and E. A. Arbas (1985). Modulation of central and peripheral rhythmicity in the heartbeat system of the leech. In *Model Neural Networks and Behavior* (A. I. Selverston, ed.). New York: Plenum Press, pp. 69–86.

Caldwell, P. C., A. L. Hodgkin, R. D. Keynes, and T. I. Shaw (1960). The effects of injecting "energy-rich" compounds on the active transport of ions in the giant axons of Loligo. *J. Physiol. (London)* 152:561–590.

Cannon, W. B. (1929). *Bodily Changes in Pain, Hunger, Fear, and Rage.* New York: Appleton.

Cantley, L. (1986). Ion transport systems sequenced. *Trends Neurosci.* 9:1–3.

Carew, T. J., and C. L. Sahley (1986). Invertebrate learning and memory: from behavior to molecules. *Annu. Rev. Neurosci.* 9:435–487.

Carpenter, M. B. (1976). *Human Neuroanatomy.* Baltimore: Williams & Wilkins.

Carr, W. E. S. (1986). The molecular nature of chemical stimuli in the aquatic environment. In *Sensory Biology of Aquatic Organisms* (J. Atema, R. R. Fay, A. N. Popper, and W. N. Tanolga, eds.). New York: Springer-Verlag, pp. 1–36.

Caviness, V. S., Jr., and P. Rakic (1978). Mechanisms of cortical development: a view from mutations in mice. *Annu. Rev. Neurosci.* 1:297–326.

Chance, P. (1979). *Learning and Behavior.* Belmont, CA: Wadsworth.

Changeux, J.-P., A. Devillers-Thiéry, and P. Chemovilli (1984). Acetylcholine receptor: an allosteric protein. *Science* 225:1335–1345.

Cheney, P. D., E. E. Fetz, and S. S. Palmer (1985). Patterns of facilitation and suppression of antagonist forelimb muscles from motor cortex sites in the awake monkey. *J. Neurophysiol.* 53:805–820.

Claudio, T. (1986). Recombinant DNA technology in the study of ionic channels. *Trends Pharmacol. Sci.* 7:308–312.

Claudio, T., M. Ballivet, J. Patrick, and S. Heinemann (1983). Nucleotide and deduced amino acid sequences of *Torpedo californica* acetylcholine receptor subunit. *Proc. Natl. Acad. Sci. USA* 80:1111–1115.

Cooper, J. R., F. E. Bloom, and R. H. Roth (1987). *The Biochemical Basis of Neuropharmacology,* 5th ed. New York: Oxford University Press.

Corey, D. P. (1983). Patch clamp: current excitement in membrane physiology. *Neurosci. Comment.* 1:99–110.

Corkin, S., E. V. Sullivan, R. E. Twitchell, and E. Grove (1981). The amnesic patient H.M.: clinical observations and test performance 28 years after operation. *Soc. Neurosci. Abstr.* 7:235.

Coss, R. G., and D. H. Perkel (1985). The function of dendritic spines: a review of theoretical issues. *Behav. Neural Biol.* 44:151–185.

Cotman, C. W., and J. L. McGaugh (1980). *Behavioral Neuroscience.* New York: Academic Press.

Crawford, A. C., and R. Fettiplace (1985). The mechanical properties of ciliary bundles of turtle cochlear hair cells. *J. Physiol. (London)* 364:359–379.

Crelin, E. S. (1974). Development of the nervous system. *Ciba Clin. Symp.* 26:1–32.

Crelin, E. S. (1976). Development of the upper respiratory system. *Ciba Clin. Symp.* 28:1–30.

Cull-Candy, S. G., and M. M. Usowicz (1987). Multiple-conductance channels activated by excitatory amino acids in cerebellar neurons. *Nature* 325:525–528.

Dale, H. H. (1935). Pharmacology and nerve endings. *Proc. R. Soc. Med.* 28:319–332.

Dallos, P. (1985). The role of outer hair cells in cochlear function. In *Contemporary Sensory Neurobiology* (M. J. Correia and A. A. Perachio, eds.). New York: Alan R. Liss, pp. 207–230.

Daube, J. R., T. J. Reagan, B. A. Sandole, and B. F. Westmoreland, eds. (1986). *Medical Neuroscience*, 2nd ed. Boston: Little, Brown.

Darwin, C. A. (1872). *On the Expression of the Emotions in Man and Animals.* London: Murray.

David, S., and A. J. Aguayo (1981). Axonal regeneration after crush injury of rat central nervous system innervating peripheral nerve grafts. *J. Neurocytol.* 14:1–12.

Davies, A. M., C. Bandtlow, R. Heumann, S. Korsching, H. Rohrer, and H. Thoenen (1987). Timing and site of nerve growth factor synthesis in developing skin in relation to innervation and expression of the receptor. *Nature* 326:353–358.

Davis, H., and S. R. Silverman (1970). *Hearing and Deafness.* New York: Holt, Rhinehart and Winston.

Davis, W. J. (1976). Behavioral and neuronal plasticity in mollusks. In *Simpler Networks and Behavior* (J. C. Fentress, ed.). Sunderland, MA: Sinauer, pp. 224–238.

Delaney, K., and A. Gelperin (1986). Post ingestive food-aversion learning to amino acid deficient diets by the terrestrial slug *Limax maximus. J. Comp. Physiol. [A]* 159:281–295.

DeLong, M. R., and A. P. Georgopoulos (1981). Motor functions of the basal ganglia. In *Handbook of Physiology,* Sec. 1: *The Nervous System,* Vol. 2: *Motor Control* (V. B. Brooks, ed.). Bethesda, MD: Am. Physiol. Soc., pp. 1017–1061.

DeYoe, E. A. and Van Essen, D. C. (1987) Parallel processing streams in monkey visual cortex. *Trends Neurosci.*

Dement, W., and N. Kleitman (1957). Cyclic variations in EEG during sleep and their relation to eye movements, body motility, and dreaming. *Electroencephal. Clin. Neurophysiol.* 9:673–690.

Denis-Donini, S., J. Glowinski, and A. Prochiantz (1983). Specific influence of striatal target neurons on the in vitro outgrowth of mesencephalic dopaminergic neurites: a morphological quantitative study. *J. Neurosci.* 3:2292–2299.

Dethier, V. G. (1976). *The Hungry Fly.* Cambridge, MA: Harvard University Press.

Dethier, V. G., and E. Stellar (1984). *Animal Behavior: Its Evolutionary and Neurological Basis.* Englewood Cliffs, NJ: Prentice-Hall.

Diamond, I. T. (1979). The subdivisions of neocortex: a proposal to revise the traditional view of sensory, motor, and association areas. In *Progress in Psychobiology and Physiological Psychology* (J. M. Sprague and A. N. Epstein, eds.). New York: Academic Press, pp. 2–44.

Doty, R. W. (1976). The concept of neural centers. In *Simpler Networks and Behavior* (J. C. Fentress, ed.). Sunderland, MA: Sinauer, pp. 251–265.

Dowling, J. E. (1979). Information processing by local circuits: the vertebrate retina as a model system. In *The Neurosciences: Fourth Study Program* (F. O. Schmitt and F. G. Worden, eds.). Cambridge, MA: MIT Press, pp. 163–182.

Dowling, J. E., and B. B. Boycott (1966). Organization of the primate retina: electron microscopy. *Proc. R. Soc. Lond. [B]* 166:80–111.

Dunant, Y., and M. Israel (1985). The release of acetylcholine. *Sci. Am.* 252:58–66.

Dunlap, K., and G. D. Fischbach (1978). Neurotransmitters decrease the calcium component of sensory neurone action potentials. *Nature* 276:837–839.

Eagles, E. I., ed. (1975). *The Nervous System, Human Communication and Its Disorders.* New York: Raven Press.

Eakin, R. M. (1965). Evolution of photoreceptors. *Cold Spring Harbor Symp. Quant. Biol.* 30:363–370.

Easter, S. S., Jr., D. Purves, P. Rakic, and N. C. Spitzer (1985). The changing view of neural specificity. *Science* 230:507–511.

Eaton, R. C., and J. T. Hackett (1984). The role of the Mauthner cell in fast-starts involving escape in teleost fishes. In *Neural Mechanisms of Startle Behavior* (R. C. Eaton, ed.). New York: Plenum Press, pp. 213–266.

Eaton R. C., R. A. Bombardieri, and D. L. Meyer (1977). The Mauthner-initiated startle response in teleost fish. *J. Exp. Biol.* 66:65–81.

Eccles, J. C. (1957). *The Physiology of Nerve Cells.* Baltimore: Johns Hopkins.

Elsner, N., and A. V. Popov (1978). Neuroethology of acoustic communication. In *Advances in Insect Physiology,* Vol. 13 (J. E. Treherne, M. J. Berridge, and V. B. Wigglesworth, eds.). New York: Academic Press, pp. 229–355.

Emson, P. C., and S. P. Hunt (1981). Anatomical chemistry of the cerebral cortex. In *The Organization of the Cerebral Cortex* (F. O. Schmitt, F. G. Worden, G. Adelman, and S. G. Dennis, eds.). Cambridge, MA: MIT Press, pp. 325–345.

Epstein, A. N. (1971). The lateral hypothalamic syndrome: its implications for the physiological psychology of hunger and thirst. *Prog. Psychobiol. Physiol. Psychol.* 4:263–317.

Epstein, A. N. (1980). A comparison of instinct and motivation with emphasis on their differences. In *Neural Mechanisms of Goal-Directed Behavior and Learning* (R. Thompson and L. Hicks, eds.). New York: Academic Press, pp. 119–126.

Epstein, A. N., J. T. Fitsimons, and B. J. Rolls (1970). Drinking induced by injection of angiotensin into the brain of the rat. *J. Physiol (London)* 210:457–474.

Erulkar, S. D., and A. Fine (1979). Calcium in the nervous system. *Rev. Neurosci.* 4:179–232.

Erulkar, S. D., B. Kelley, M. E. Jurman, F. P. Zemlan,

G. T. Schneider, and N. R. Krieger (1981). Modulation of the neural control of the clasp reflex in male *Xenopus laevis* by androgens: a multidisciplinary study. *Proc. Natl. Acad. Sci. USA* 78:5876–5880.

Evarts, E. V. (1981). Functional studies of the motor cortex. In *The Organization of the Cerebral Cortex* (F. O. Schmitt, F. G. Worden, G. Adelman, and S. G. Dennis, eds.). Cambridge, MA: MIT Press, pp. 199–236.

Fain, G. L., H. M. Gerschenfeld, and F. N. Quandt (1980). Calcium spike in toad rods. *J. Physiol. (London)* 303:495–514.

Fahrenbach, W. H. (1985). Anatomical circuitry of lateral inhibition in the eye of the horseshoe crab, *Limulus polyphemus. Proc. R. Soc. Lond. [B]* 225:219–249.

Farbman, A. I. (1986). Prenatal development of mammalian olfactory receptor cells. *Chem. Senses* 11:3–18.

Fernandez, C., and J. M. Golberg (1976). Physiology of peripheral neurons innervating otolith organs of the squirrel monkey. III. Response dynamics. *J. Neurophysiol.* 39:996–1008.

Fetz, E., and M. A. Baker (1973). Operantly conditioned patterns of precentral unit activity and correlated responses in adjacent cells and contralateral muscles. *J. Neurophysiol.* 36:179–204.

Finer-Moore, J., and R. M. Stroud (1984). Amphipathic analysis and possible formation of the ion channel in acetylcholine receptor. *Proc. Natl. Acad. Sci. USA* 81:155–159.

Flynn, J. P. (1967). The neural basis of aggression in cats. In *Neurophysiology and Emotion* (D. C. Glass, ed.). New York: Rockefeller, pp. 40–69.

Forbes, A. (1939). Problems of synaptic functions. *J. Neurophysiol.* 2:465–472.

Foster, M. (1897). *A Textbook of Physiology.* London: Macmillan.

Frohlich, A. (1985). Freeze-fracture study of an invertebrate multiple-contact synapse: the fly photoreceptor tetrad. *J. Comp. Neurol.* 241:311–326.

Frank, E., and G. D. Fischbach (1979). Early events in neuromuscular junction formation in vitro: induction of acetylcholine receptor clusters in the post synaptic membrane and morphology of newly formed synapses. *J. Cell Biol.* 83:143–158.

Furshpan, E. J., and D. D. Potter (1959). Transmission at the giant motor synapses of the crayfish. *J. Physiol. (London)* 145:289–325.

Gainer, H., and M. J. Brownstein (1981). Neuropeptides. In *Basic Neurochemistry.* (G. J. Siegel, R. W. Albers, B. W. Agranoff, and R. Katzman, eds.). Boston: Little, Brown, pp. 269–296.

Galambos, R., and H. Davis (1943). The response of single aduitory-nerve fibers to acoustic stimulation. *J. Neurophysiol.* 6:39–57.

Gallistel, C. R. (1980). *The Organization of Action: A New Synthesis.* New York: Wiley.

Ganong, W. F. (1985). *The Nervous System.* Los Altos, CA: Lange.

Garcia, J., and R. A. Koelling (1966). Relation of cue to consequence in avoidance learning. *Psychonomet. Sci.* 4:123–124.

Geschwind, N. (1980). Some special functions of the human brain. In *Medical Physiology* (V. B. Mountcastle, ed.). St. Louis: C. V. Mosby, pp. 647–665.

Gesteland, R. D. (1986). Speculations on receptor cells as analyzers and filters. *Experientia* 42:287–291.

Getchell, T. V., and G. M. Shepherd (1978). Responses of olfactory receptor cells to step pulses of odour at different concentrations in the salamander. *J. Physiol. (London)* 282:521–540.

Getting, P. A., and M. S. Dekin (1985). *Tritonia* swimming: a model system for integration within rhythmic motor systems. In *Model Neural Networks and Behavior* (A. I. Selverston, ed.). New York: Plenum Press, pp. 3–20.

Gilbert, C. D., and J. P. Kelly (1975). The projections of cells in different layers of the cat's visual cortex. *J. Comp. Neurol.* 163:81–106.

Glowinski, J., J. P. Tassin, and A. M. Thierry (1984). The mesocortico-prefrontal dopaminergic neurons. *Trends Neurosci.* 7:415–418.

Gobel, S., W. M. Falls, G. J. Bennett, M. Abdelmoumene, H. Hayashi, and E. Humphrey (1980). An EM analysis of the synaptic connections of horseradish peroxidase-filled stalked cells and islet cells in the substantia gelatinosa of adult cat spinal cord. *J. Comp. Neurol.* 194:781–807.

Goldman, P. S. (1976). Maturation of the mammalian nervous system and the ontogeny of behavior. In *Advances in the Study of Behavior,* Vol. 7 (J. S. Rosenblatt, R. A. Hinde, E. Shaw, and C. Beer, eds.). New York: Academic Press, pp. 1–90.

Goldman-Rakic, P. S. (1981). Development and plasticity of primate frontal association cortex. In *The Organization of the Cerebral Cortex* (F. O. Schmitt, F. G. Worden, G. Adelman, and S. G. Dennis, eds.). Cambridge, MA: MIT Press, pp. 69–97.

Goldman-Rakic, P. S. (1984). The frontal lobes: uncharted provinces of the brain. *Trends Neurosci.* 7:711.

Goldman-Rakic, P. S. (1987). Circuitry of the prefrontal cortex and the regulation of behavior by representational knowledge. In *Handbook of Physiology, Sec. 1: The Nervous System,* Vol. 5: *Higher Cortical Function* (F. Plum and V. Mountcastle, eds.). Bethesda, MD: Am. Physiol. Soc., pp. 373–417.

Goldsmith, T. H. (1980). Hummingbirds see near ultraviolet light. *Science* 207:706–700.

Goodman, C. S., and Bate, M. (1981). Neuronal development in the grasshopper. *Trends Neurosci.* 4:163–169.

Goodman, C. S., M. Bate, and N. C. Spitzer (1981). Embryonic development of identified neurons: origin and transformation of the H cell. *J. Neurosci.* 1:94–102.

Goodwin, G. M., D. I. McCloskey, and P. B. C. Matthews (1972). The contribution of muscle afferents to kinesthesia shown by vibration induced illusions of movement and by the effects of paralysing joint afferents. *Brain* 95:705–748.

Gordon, M. S. (1970). *Animal Physiology: Principles and Adaptations*. New York: Macmillan.

Gormezano, I. (1972). Investigations of defense and reward conditioning in the rabbit. In *Classical Conditioning*, Vol. II: *Current Research and Theory* (A. H. Black and F. Prokasy, eds.). New York: Appleton-Century-Crofts, pp. 151–181.

Gouras, P. (1985). Color vision. In *Principles of Neural Science*, 2nd ed. (E. R. Kandel and J. H. Schwartz, eds.). New York: Elsevier, pp. 384–395.

Goy, R. W., and B. S. McEwen (1980). *Sexual Differentiation of the Brain*. Cambridge, MA: MIT Press.

Gray, J. (1968). *Animal Locomotion*. New York: Norton.

Graziadei, P. P. C., and G. A. Monti-Graziadei (1978). Continuous nerve cell renewal in the olfactory system. In *Handbook of Sensory Physiology*, Vol. 9 (M. Jacobson, ed.). New York: Springer-Verlag, pp. 55–83.

Greenberg, M. J., and D. A. Price (1983). Invertebrate neuropeptides: native and naturalized. *Annu. Rev. Physiol.* 45:271–288.

Greenough, W. T. (1984). Possible structural substrates of plastic neural phenomena. In *Neurobiology of Learning and Memory* (G. Lynch, J. L. McGaugh, and N. M. Weinberger, eds.). New York: Guilford Press, pp. 470–478.

Greer, C. A., W. B. Stewart, M. H. Teicher, and G. M. Shepherd (1982). Functional development of the olfactory bulb and a unique glomerular complex in the neonatal rat. *J. Neurosci.* 2:1744–1759.

Gregory, R. L. (1966). *Eye and Brain: The Psychology of Seeing*. London: Weidenfeld and Nicolson.

Grillner, S. (1985). Neurobiological bases of rhythmic motor acts in vertebrates. *Science* 228:143–149.

Grillner, S., and P. Zangger (1984). The effect of dorsal root transection on the efferent motor pattern in the cat's hindlimb during locomotion. *Acta Physiol. Scand.* 120:393–405.

Grinvald, A., and I. C. Farber (1981). Optical recording of calcium action potentials from growth cones of cultured neurons with a laser microbeam. *Science* 212:1164–1167.

Grossman, Y., D. L. Alkon, and E. Heldman (1979). A common origin of voltage noise and generator potentials in statocyst hair cells. *J. Gen. Physiol.* 73:23–48.

Groves, P. M., and R. F. Thompson (1970). Habituation: a dual-process theory. *Psychol. Rev.* 77:419–450.

Groves, P. M., D. A. Staunton, C. J. Wilson, and S. J. Young (1979). Sites of action of amphetamine intrinsic to catecholaminergic nuclei: catecholaminergic presynaptic dendrites and axons. *Prog. Neuropsychopharmacol.* 3:315–335.

Gurney, M. E., and M. Konishi (1980). Hormone-induced sexual differentiation of brain and behavior in zebra finches. *Science* 208:1380–1383.

Guyton, A. C. (1976). *Textbook of Medical Physiology*. Philadelphia: W. B. Saunders.

Gwilliam, G. F., and M. Burrows (1980). Electrical characteristics of the membrane of an identified insect motor neurone. *J. Exp. Biol.* 86:49–61.

Hall, N. R., and A. L. Goldstein (1985). Neurotransmitters and host defense. In *Neural Modulation of Immunity* (R. Guillemin, M. Cohn, and T. Melnechuk, eds.). New York: Raven Press, pp. 143–160.

Hall, N. R., J. P. McGillis, B. L. Spangelo, D. L. Healy, G. P. Chronsos, H. M. Schultz, and A. L. Goldstein (1985). Thymic hormone effects on the brain and neuroendocrine circuits. In *Neural Modulation of Immunity* (R. Guillemin, M. Cohn, and T. Melnechuk, eds.). New York: Raven Press, pp. 179–196.

Hansen, K. (1978). Insect chemoreception. In *Taxis and Behavior: Receptors and Recognition*, Series B, Vol. 5 (G. I. Hazelbauer, ed.). London: Chapman and Hall, pp. 231–292.

Harlan, R. E., J. H. Gordon, and R. A. Gorski (1979). Sexual differentiation of the brain: implications for neuroscience. *Rev. Neurosci.* 4:31–61.

Harris, G. W. (1955). *Neural Control of the Pituitary Gland*. London: Edward Arnold.

Harrison, R. G. (1907). Observations on the living developing nerve fiber. *Anat. Rec.* 1:116–118.

Hauri, P. (1977). *The Sleep Disorders*. Kalamazoo, MI: Upjohn.

Haymaker, W., ed. (1953). *The Founders of Neurology*. Springfield, IL: Charles C. Thomas.

Hebb, D. O. (1949). *The Organization of Behavior*. New York: John Wiley.

Heck, G. L., S. Mierson, and J. A. DeSimone (1984). Salt taste transduction occurs through an amiloride-sensitive sodium transport pathway. *Science* 223:403–405.

Heimer, L. (1983). *The Human Brain and Spinal Cord: Functional Neuroanatomy and Dissection Guide*. New York: Springer-Verlag.

Henneman, E. (1980a). Organization of the spinal cord and its reflexes. In *Medical Physiology* (V. B. Mountcastle, ed.). St. Louis: C. V. Mosby, pp. 762–786.

Henneman, E. (1980b). Motor functions of the cerebral cortex. In *Medical Physiology* (V. B. Mountcastle, ed.). St. Louis: C. V. Mosby, pp. 859–891.

Heuser, J. E. (1977). Synaptic vesicle exocytosis revealed in quick-frozen frog neuromuscular junctions treated with 4-aminopyridine and given a single electrical shock. In *Soc. for Neurosci. Symp.*, Vol. 2 (W. M. Cowan and J. A. Ferrendelli, eds.). Bethesda, MD: Soc. for Neurosci., pp. 215–239.

Heuser, J. E., and T. S. Reese (1977). Structure of the synapse. In *Handbook of Physiology*, Sec. 1: *The Nervous System*, Vol. 1: *Cellular Biology of Neurons* (E. R. Kandel, ed.). Bethesda, MD: Am. Physiol. Soc., pp. 261–294.

Hille, B. (1977). Ionic basis of resting potentials and action potentials. In *Handbook of Physiology*, Sec.

1: *The Nervous System*, Vol. 1: *Cellular Biology of Neurons* (E. R. Kandel, ed.). Washington, DC: Am. Physiol. Soc., pp. 99–136.

Hille, B. (1981). Excitability and ion channels. In *Basic Neurochemistry*. (G. J. Siegel, R. W. Albers, B. W. Agranoff, and R. Katzman, eds.). Boston: Little, Brown.

Hille, B. (1984). *Ionic Channels of Excitable Membranes*. Sunderland, MA: Sinauer.

Hobson, J. A., and R. W. McCarley (1977). The brain as a dream state generator: an activation-synthesis hypothesis of the dream process. *Am. J. Psychiatry* 134:1335–1348.

Hockfield, S., R. D. McKay, S. H. C. Hendry, and E. G. Jones (1983). A surface antigen that identifies ocular dominance columns in the visual cortex and laminar features of the lateral geniculate nucleus. *Cold Spring Harbor Symp. Quant. Biol.* 48:877–889.

Hodgkin, A. L., and A. F. Huxley (1952). A quantitative description of membrane current and its application to conduction and excitation in nerve. *J. Physiol. (London)* 117:500–544.

Hodgkin, A. L., and B. Katz (1949). The effect of sodium ions on the electrical activity of the giant axons of the squid. *J. Physiol. (London)* 108:37–77.

Hoebel, B. G. (1986). Neuropsychology of motivation: peptides and pathways that define motivational systems. In *Handbook of Experimental Psychology*, 2nd ed. (R. C. Atkinson, B. J. Herrnstein, G. Lindzey, and R. D. Luce, eds.). New York: John Wiley.

Hofer, M. A. (1981). *The Roots of Human Behavior*. San Francisco: Freeman.

Hökfelt, T., O. Johansson, A. Llungdahl, J. M. Lundberg, and M. Schultzberg (1980). Peptidergic neurones. *Nature* 284:515–521.

Hökfelt, T., O. Johansson, and M. Goldstein (1984). Chemical anatomy of the brain. *Science* 225:1326–1334.

Homick, J. L., M. F. Reschke, and E. F. Miller, II (1977). The effects of prolonged exposure to weightlessness on postural equilibrium. In *Biomedical Results from Skylab* (R. S. Johnston and L. F. Dietlein, eds.). Washington, DC: NASA, pp. 104–112.

Hopkins, W. G., and M. C. Brown (1984). *Development of Nerve Cells and Their Connections*. London: Cambridge University Press.

Horn, G. (1979). Imprinting in search of new mechanisms. *Trends Neurosci.* 2:219–222.

Hoyle, G. (1982). *Muscles and Their Nervous Control*. New York: Wiley.

Hubbard, J. I., R. Llinás, and D. M. J. Quastel (1969). *Electrophysiological Analysis of Synaptic Transmission*. Baltimore: Williams & Wilkins.

Hubbell, W. L., and M. D. Bownds (1979). Visual transduction in vertebrate photoreceptors. *Annu. Rev. Neurosci.* 2:17–34.

Hubel, D. H., and T. N. Wiesel (1974). Sequence

regularity and geometry of orientation columns in the monkey striate cortex. *J. Comp. Neurol.* 158:267–294.

Hubel, D. H., T. N. Wiesel, and M. P. Stryker (1978). Anatomical demonstration of orientation columns in macaque monkey. *J. Comp. Neurol.* 177:361–380.

Hudspeth, A. J. (1985). The cellular basis of hearing: the biophysics of hair cells. *Science* 230:745–752.

Hudspeth, A. J., and R. Jacobs (1979). Stereocilia mediate transduction in vertebrate hair cells. *Proc. Natl. Acad. Sci. USA* 76:1506–1509.

Isaac, G., and R. E. F. Leakey (1979). *Human Ancestors*. San Francisco: W. H. Freeman.

Ito, M. (1985). *The Cerebellum and Neural Control*. New York: Raven Press.

Iversen, L. (1979). Chemistry of the brain. *Sci. Am.* 241:118–129.

Jack, J. J. B., D. Noble, and R. W. Tsien (1975). *Electric Current Flow in Excitable Cells*. Oxford: Clarendon Press.

Jacklet, J. W. (1981). Circadian timing by endogenous oscillators in the nervous system: toward cellular mechanisms. *Biol. Bull.* 160:199–227.

Jacklet, J. W. (1985). Neurobiology of circadian rhythm generators. *Trends Neurosci.* 8:69–73.

Jacobson, M. (1978). *Developmental Neurobiology*. New York: Plenum Press.

Jahnsen, H., and R. Llinás (1985). Ionic basis for the electroresponsiveness and oscillatory properties of guinea-pig thalamic neurones in vitro. *J. Physiol. (London)* 349:227–247.

Jahr, C. E., and C. F. Stevens (1987). Glutamate activates multiple single channel conductances in hippocampal neurons. *Nature* 325:522–525.

Jan, L. Y., Y. N. Jan, and S. W. Kuffler (1979). A peptide as a possible transmitter in sympathetic ganglia of the frog. *Proc. Natl. Acad. Sci. USA* 76:1501–1505.

Johannson, O., T. Hökfelt, B. Pernow, S. L. Jeffcoate, N. White, H. W. M. Steinbusch, A. J. Verhofstad, P. C. Emson, and E. Spindel (1981). Immunohistochemical support for three putative transmitters in one neuron: coexistence of 5-hydroxytryptamine-, substance P- and thyrotropin releasing hormone-like immunoreactivity in medullary neurons projecting to the spinal cord. *Neuroscience* 6:1857–1881.

Johansson, R. S., and G. Westling (1984). Roles of glabrous skin receptors and sensorimotor memory in automatic control of precision grip when lifting rougher or more slippery objects. *Exp. Brain Res.* 56:550–564.

Johnson, J. W., and P. Ascher (1987). Glycine potentiates the NMDA response in cultured mouse brain neurons. *Nature* 325:529–531.

Jones, E. G. (1981). Anatomy of cerebral cortex: columnar input–output organization. In *The Organization of the Cerebral Cortex* (F. O. Schmitt, F. G. Worden, G. Adelman, and S. G. Dennis, eds.). Cambridge, MA: MIT Press, pp. 199–235.

Jones, E. G. (1986). Neurotransmitters in the cerebral cortex. *J. Neurosurg.* 65:135–153.

Jones, E. G., and S. P. Wise (1977). Size, laminar and columnar distribution of the efferent cells in the sensory-motor cortex of monkeys. *J. Comp. Neurol.* 175:391–438.

Jones, S. W., and P. R. Adams (1987). The M-current and other potassium currents of vertebrate neurons. In *Neuromodulation: The Biochemical Control of Neuronal Excitability* (L. K. Kaczmarek and I. B. Levitan, eds.). New York: Oxford University Press, pp. 159–186.

Jouvet, M. (1974). Monoaminergic regulation of the sleep–waking cycle in the cat. In *The Neurosciences: Third Study Program* (F. O. Schmitt and F. G. Worden, eds.). Cambridge, MA: MIT Press, pp. 499–508.

Jürgens, U., and D. Ploog (1981). On the neural control of mammalian vocalization. *Trends Neurosci.* 4:135–137.

Kaissling, K. E., and J. Thorson (1979). Insect olfactory sensilla: structural, chemical and electrical aspects of the functional organization. In *Receptors for Neurotransmitters, Hormones, and Pheromones in Insects* (D. B. Satelle, L. M. Hall, and J. G. Hildebrand, eds.). Amsterdam: Elsevier, pp. 261–282.

Kales, A., and J. D. Kales (1974). Sleep disorders. *N. Engl. J. Med.* 290:487–499.

Kandel, E. R. (1976). *Cellular Basis of Behavior*. San Francisco: W. H. Freeman.

Kandel, E. R. (1979). Cellular insights into behavior and learning. *Harvey Lectures* 73:19–92.

Kandel, E. R. (1985). Cellular mechanisms of learning and the biological basis of individuality. In *Principles of Neural Science* (E. R. Kandel and J. H. Schwartz eds.). New York: Raven Press, pp. 243–255.

Kaplan, E., and R. B. Barlow, Jr. (1980). Circadian clock in *Limulus* brain increases response and decreases noise of retinal photoreceptors. *Nature* 286:393–395.

Kappers, C. U. A., G. C. Huber, and E. Crosby (1936). *The Comparative Anatomy of the Nervous Ssytem of Vertebrates, Including Man*. New York: Macmillan.

Kasamatsu, T., J. D. Pettigrew, and M. Ary (1979). Restoration of visual cortical plasticity by local microperfusion of norepinephrine. *J. Comp. Neurol.* 185:163–182.

Kater, S. B. (1977). Calcium electroresponsiveness and its relationship to secretion in molluscan exocrine gland cells. In *Soc. for Neurosci. Symp.*, Vol. II (W. M. Cowan and J. A. Ferrendelli, eds.). Bethesda, MD: Soc. for Neurosci., pp. 195–214.

Katz, B. (1950). Deplorization of sensory terminals and the initiation of impulses in the muscle spindle. *J. Physiol. (London)* 111:261–282.

Katz, B. (1962). The transmission of impulses from nerve to muscle, and the subcellular unit of synaptic action. *Proc. R. Soc. Lond. [B]* 195:455–477.

Katz, B. (1966). *Nerve, Muscle and Synapse*. New York: McGraw-Hill.

Kauer, J. S. (1974). Response patterns of amphibian olfactory bulb to odour stimulation. *J. Physiol. (London)* 243:675–715.

Kelley, D. B. (1981). Social signals—an overview. *Am. Zool.* 21:111–116.

Kemp, D. T. (1978). Stimulated acoustic emissions from within the human auditory system. *J. Acoust. Soc. Am.* 64:1386–1391.

Kennedy, D. (1976). Neural elements in relation to network function. In *Simple Networks and Behavior* (J. C. Fentress, ed.), Sunderland, MA: Sinauer, pp. 65–81.

Kenshalo, D. R. (1976). In *Sensory Functions of the Skin in Primates* (Y. Zotterman, ed.). Oxford: Pergamon, pp. 305–330.

Kerwin, J. P. (1977). Skylab 2 crew observations and summary. In *Biomedical Results from Skylab* (R. S. Johnston and L. F. Dietlein, eds.). Washington, DC: Sci. and Tech. Info. Office, NASA, pp. 27–29.

Kien, J. (1983). The initiation and maintenance of walking in the locust: an alternative to the command concept. *Proc. R. Soc. Lond. [B]* 219:137–174.

Kimble, D. P., W. P. Jordan, and R. Bremiller (1982). Further evidence for latent learning in hippocampal-lesioned rats. *Physiol. Behav.* 29:401–407.

Kimmel, C. B., and R. M. Varga (1986). Tissue-specific cell lineages originate in the gastrula of the zebrafish. *Science* 231:365–368.

Kistler, J., R. Stroud, R., M. Klymkowsky, R. Lalancette, and R. Fairclough (1982). Structure and function of an acetylocholine receptor. *Biophys. J.* 37:371–383.

Kitai, S. T. (1981). Anatomy and physiology of the neostriatum. In *GABA and the Basal Ganglia* (G. Di Chiara and G. L. Gessa, eds.). New York: Raven Press, pp. 1–21.

Klein, D. C. (1974). Circadian rhythms and indole metabolism in the rat pineal gland. In *The Neurosciences: Third Study Program* (F. O. Schmitt and F. G. Worden, eds.). Cambridge, MA: MIT Press, pp. 509–515.

Klein, M., E. Shapiro, and E. R. Kandel (1980). Synaptic plasticity and the modulation of the Ca^{2+} current. *J. Exp. Biol.* 89:117–157.

Klüver, H., and P. C. Bucy (1937). "Psychic blindness" and other symptoms following bilateral temporal lobectomy in rhesus monkeys. *Am. J. Physiol.* 119:352–353.

Knowles, A., and J. A. Dartnall (1977). The photobiology of vision. In *The Eye*, Vol. 2B (H. Dawson, ed.). New York: Academic Press, pp. 1–13.

Kolb, B., and I. Q. Whishaw (1985). *Fundamentals of Human Neuropsychology*. San Francisco: W. H. Freeman.

Konopka, R. J., and S. Benzer (1971). Clock mutants of *Drosophila melanogaster. Proc. Natl. Acad. Sci. USA* 68:2112–2115.

Korn, H., C. Sotelo, and F. Crepel (1973). Electrotonic coupling between neurons in rat lateral vestibular nucleus. *Exp. Brain Res.* 16:255–275.

Koshland, D. E., Jr. (1980). Bacterial chemotaxis in relation to neurobiology. *Annu. Rev. Neurosci.* 3:43–76.

Krasne, F. B., and J. J. Wine (1984). The production of crayfish tailflip escape responses. In *Neural Mechanisms of Startle Behavior* (R. C. Eaton, ed.). New York: Plenum Press, pp. 179–212.

Kravitz, E. A., B. S. Beltz, S. Glusman, M. Goy, R. M. Harris-Warwick, M. F. Johnston, M. S. Livingstone, and T. L. Schwarz (1983). Neurohormones and lobsters: biochemistry to behavior. *Trends Neurosci.* 6:346–349.

Kravitz, E. A., B. S. Beltz, S. Glusman, M. Goy, R. Harris-Warwick, M. Johnston, M. Livingston, T. Schwarz, and K. K. Siwicki (1985). The well-modulated lobster: the roles of serotonin, octopamine, and proctolin in the lobster nervous system. In *Model Neural Networks and Behavior* (A. I. Selverston, ed.). New York: Plenum Press, pp. 339–360.

Kreutzberg, G. W., P. Schubert, and H. D. Lux (1975). Neuroplasmic transport in axons and dendrites. In *Golgi Centennial Symposium* (M. Santini, ed.). New York: Raven Press, pp. 161–166.

Kriegstein, A. R., and B. W. Connors (1986). Cellular physiology of the turtle visual cortex: synaptic properties and intrinsic circuitry. *J. Neurosci.* 6:178–191.

Kubo, T., K. Fukuda, A. Mikami, A. Maeda, H. Takahashi, M. Mishina, T. Haga, K. Haga, A. Ichiyama, K. Kangawa, M. Kojima, H. Matsuo, T. Hirose, and S. Numa (1986). Cloning, sequencing and expression of complementary DNA encoding the muscarine acetylcholine receptor. *Nature* 323:411–416.

Kuffler, S. W. (1953). Discharge patterns and functional organization of mammalian retina. *J. Neurophysiol.* 16:37–68.

Kuffler, S. W. (1958). Synaptic inhibitory mechanisms: properties of dendrites and problems of excitation in isolated sensory nerve cells. *Exp. Cell Res. [Suppl.]* 5:493–519.

Kuffler, S. W., and C. Eyzaguirre (1955). Synaptic inhibition in an isolated nerve cell. *J. Gen. Physiol.* 39:155–184.

Kuffler, S. W., J. G. Nicholls, and A. R. Martin (1984). *From Neuron to Brain.* Sunderland, MA: Sinauer.

Kupfermann, I., and K. R. Weiss (1978). The command neuron concept. *Behav. Brain Sci.* 1:3–39.

Kuypers, H. G. J. M. (1985). The anatomical and functional organization of the motor system. In *Scientific Basis of Clinical Neurology* (M. Swash and C. Kennard, eds.). London: Churchill Livingstone, pp. 3–18.

LaMotte, R. H., J. G. Thalhammer, H. E. Torebjork, and C. G. Robinson (1982). Peripheral nerval mechanisms of cutaneous hyperalgesia following mild injury by heat. *J. Neurosci.* 2:765–781.

Lampson, L. A. (1984). Molecular basis of neuronal individuality: lessons from anatomic and biochemical studies with monoclonal antibodies. In *Monoclonal Antibodies and Functional Cell Lines* (R. H. Kennett, K. B. Bechtol, and T. J. McKearn, eds.). New York: Plenum Press, pp. 153–189.

Lancet, D. (1986). Vertebrate olfactory reception. *Annu. Rev. Neurosci.* 9:329–355.

Lancet, D., and U. Pace (1987). The molecular basis of odor recognition. *Trends Biochem. Sci.* 7:1–4.

Lancet, D., C. A. Greer, J. S. Kauer, and G. M. Shepherd (1982). Mapping of odor-related activity in the olfactory bulb by high resolution 2-deoxyglucose autoradiography. *Proc. Natl. Acad. Sci. USA* 79:670–674.

Land, M. F. (1981). Optics and vision in invertebrates. In *Handbook of Sensory Physiology*, Vol. 7, Sec. 6: *Comparative Physiology and Evolution of Vision in Invertebrates*, Part B: *Invertebrate Visual Centers and Behavior* (H. Autrum, ed.). New York: Springer-Verlag, pp. 471–594.

Landis, D. M. D., and T. S. Reese (1974). Differences in membrane structure between excitatory and inhibitory synapses in the cerebellar cortex. *J. Comp. Neurol.* 155:93–126.

Landmesser, L. T. (1980). The generation of neuromuscular specificity. *Annu. Rev. Neurosci.* 3:279–302.

Lashley, K. S. (1950). In search of the engram. *Symp. Soc. Exp. Biol.* 4:454–482.

Lassen, N. A., D. H. Ingvar, and E. Skinhoj (1978). Brain function and blood flow. *Sci. Am.* 239:62–71.

Laughlin, S. (1981). Neural principles in the visual system. In *Handbook of Sensory Physiology*, Vol. 7, Sec. 6: *Comparative Physiology and Evolution of Vision in Invertebrates*, Part B: *Invertebrate Visual Centers and Behavior* (H. Autrum, ed.). New York: Springer-Verlag, pp. 133–280.

Lehninger, A. L. (1982). *Principles of Biochemistry.* New York: Worth.

LeMagnen, J. (1971). Advances in studies on the physiological control and regulation of food intake. *Prog. Psychobiol. Physiol. Psychol.* 4:203–261.

Lemon, R. N., and R. Porter (1976). Afferent input to movement-related precentral neurones in conscious monkeys. *Proc. R. Soc. Lond. [B]* 194:313–339.

Lentz, T. (1968). *Primitive Nervous Systems.* New Haven: Yale University Press.

Leon, M., R. Coopersmith, S. Lee, R. M. Sullivan, D. A. Wilson, and C. Woo (1987). Neural and behavioral plasticity induced by early olfactory experience. In *Perinatal Development: A Psychobiological Perspective* (N. Krasnegor, E. Blass, M. Hofer, and W. Smotherman, eds.). New York: Academic Press, pp. 145–167.

LeVay, S., T. N. Wiesel, and D. H. Hubel (1981). The postnatal development and plasticity of ocular dominance columns in the monkey. In *The Organization of the Cerebral Cortex* (F. O. Schmitt, F. G.

Worden, G. Adelman, and S. G. Dennis, eds.). Cambridge, MA: MIT Press, pp. 29–46.

Lewis, D. B., and D. M. Gower (1980). *Biology of Communication*. New York: Wiley.

Liddell, E. G. T. (1960). *The Discovery of Reflexes*. Oxford: Oxford University Press.

Lieberman, P., E. S. Crelin, and D. H. Klatt (1972). Phonetic ability and related anatomy of the newborn and adult human, Neanderthal man, and the chimpanzee. *Am. Anthropol.* 74:287–307.

Liebowitz, S. F. (1986). Brain monoamines and peptides: roles in the control of eating behavior. *Fed. Proc.* 45:1396–1403.

Lindstrom, J. (1983). Using monoclonal antibodies to study acetylcholine receptors and myasthenia gravis. *Neurosci. Comment.* 1:135–156.

Llinás, R., and M. Sugimori (1980). Electrophysiological properties of in vitro Purkinje cell somata in mammalian cerebellar slices. *J. Physiol. (London)* 305:171–195.

Llinás, R., R. Baker, and C. Sotelo (1974). Electronic coupling between neurons in the cat inferior olive. *J. Neurophysiol.* 37:560–571.

Llinás, R., T. L. McGuiness, C. S. Leonard, M. Sugimori, and P. Greengard (1985). Intraterminal injection of synapsin I or calcium/calmodulin-dependent protein kinase II alters neurotransmitter release at the squid giant synapse. *Proc. Natl. Acad. Sci. USA* 82:3035–3039.

Lockerbie, R. O. (1987). The neuronal growth cone: a review of its locomotory, navigational and target recognition capabilities. *Neurosci.* 20:719–730.

Loewenstein, O. E. (1974). Comparative morphology and physiology. In *Handbook of Sensory Physiology*, Vol. 6: *Vestibular System*, Part 1: *Basic Mechanisms* (H. H. Kornhuber, ed.). New York: Springer-Verlag, pp. 75–123.

Loewenstein, W. R. (1971). Mechano-electric transduction in the Pacinian corpuscle: initiation of sensory impulses in mechano-receptors. In *Handbook of Sensory Physiology*, Vol. 1: *Principles of Receptor Physiology* (W. R. Loewenstein, ed.). New York: Springer-Verlag, pp. 269–290.

Loewenstein, W. R. (1981). Junctional intercellular communication: the cell-to-cell membrane channel. *Physiol. Rev.* 61:829–913.

Logothetis, D. E., Y. Kurachi, J. Galper, E. J. Neer, and D. E. Clapham (1987). The subunits of GTP-binding proteins activate the muscarinic K$^+$ channel in heart. *Nature* 325:321–326.

Lømo, T., and J. Rosenthal (1972). Control of ACh sensitivity by muscle activity in the rat. *J. Physiol. (London)* 221:453–513.

Lorenz, K. (1950). The comparative method in studying innate behavior patterns. *Symp. Soc. Exp. Biol.* 4:221–268.

Lorenz, K. Z. (1981). *The Foundations of Ethology*. New York: Springer-Verlag.

Lund, R. D. (1979). Tissue transplantation: A useful tool in mammalian neuroembryology. *Trends Neurosci.* 3:XII–XIII.

Lund, R. D. (1978). *Development and Plasticity of the Brain*. New York: Oxford University Press.

Lynch, G. (1986). *Synapses, Circuits, and the Beginnings of the Memory*. Cambridge, MA: MIT Press.

MacLean, P. D., and J. M. R. Delgado (1953). Electrical and chemical stimulation of frontotemporal portion of limbic system in the waking animal. *EEG Clin. Neurophysiol.* 5:91–100.

MacLusky, N. J., A. Philip, C. Hurlburt, and F. Naftolin (1985). Estrogen formation in the developing rat brain: sex differences in aromatase activity during early post-natal life. *Psychoneuroendocrinology* 10:355–361.

Maddrell, S. H. P., and J. J. Nordmann (1979). *Neurosecretion*. New York: Wiley.

Makowski, L., D. L. D. Casper, W. C. Phillips, D. A. Goodenough (1977). Gap junction structure. II. Analysis of the x-ray diffraction data. *J. Cell Biol.* 74:629–645.

Markl, H. (1974). The perception of gravity and of angular acceleration in invertebrates. In *Handbook of Sensory Physiology*, Vol. 6, *Vestibular System*, Part 1: *Basic Mechanisms* (H. Kornhuber, ed.). New York: Springer-Verlag, pp. 17–74.

Marler, P. (1976). Sensory templates in species-specific behavior. In *Simpler Networks and Behavior* (J. E. Fentress, ed.). Sunderland, MA: Sinauer, pp. 314–329.

Marty, A., M. G. Evans, Y. P. Tan, and A. Trautmann (1986). Muscarinic response in rat lacrimal glands. *J. Exp. Biol.* 124:15–32.

Marx, J. (1983). Synthesizing the opioid peptides. *Science* 220:395–396.

Matsumoto, S. G., and J. G. Hildebrand (1981). Olfactory mechanisms in the moth *Manduca sexta*: response characteristics and morphology of central neurons in the antennal lobes. *Proc. R. Soc. Lond. [B]* 213:249–277.

Matthews, B. H. C. (1931). The response of a single end organ. *J. Physiol. (London)* 71:64–110.

Matthews, P. B. C. (1972). *Mammalian Muscle Receptors and Their Central Actions*. London: Arnold.

Matthews, P. B. C. (1982). Where does Sherrington's "muscular sense" originate? Muscles, joints, corollary discharge. *Annu. Rev. Neurosci.* 5:189–218.

Maturana, H. R., J. Y. Lettvin, W. S. McCulloch, and W. H. Pitts (1960). Anatomy and physiology of vision in the frog *(Rana pipiens)*. *J. Gen. Physiol.* 43:129–175.

McDonald, D. M., and R. A. Mitchell (1975). The innervation of glomus cells, ganglion cells and blood vessels in the rat carotid body: a quantitative ultrastructural analysis. *J. Neurocytol.* 4:177–220.

Meinertzhagen, J. A. (1977). Development of neuronal circuitry in the insect optic lobe. In *Soc. for Neurosci. Symp. II* (W. H. Cowan and J. A. Ferrendelli, eds.). Bethesda, MD: Soc. for Neurosci., pp. 92–119.

Melzack, R., and P. D. Wall (1965). Pain mechanisms: a new theory. *Science* 150:971–979.

Menaker, M., J. S. Takahaski, and A. Eskin (1978). The physiology of circadian pacemakers. *Annu. Rev. Physiol.* 40:501–526.

Merlie, J. P., R. Sebbane, S. Gardner, E. Olson, and J. Lindstrom (1983). The regulation of acetylcholine receptor expression in mammalian muscle. *Cold Spring Harbor Symp. Quant. Biol.* 48:135–146.

Merzenich, M. M., and J. H. Kaas (1980). Principles of organization of sensory–perceptual systems in mammals. In *Progress in Psychobiology and Physiological Psychology* (J. M. Sprague and A. N. Epstein, eds.). New York: Academic Press, pp. 2–43.

Michael, C. R. (1985). Serial processing color in the monkey's striate cortex. In *Models of the Visual Cortex* (D. Rose and V. G. Dobson, eds.). New York: John Wiley, pp. 301–309.

Miller, J. A. (1980). A song for the female finch. *Sci. News* 117:58–59.

Miller, J. A. (1983). Molecular hardware of cell communication: describing the acetylcholine receptor. *Neurosci. Comment.* 1:98–98.

Miller, J. P., and A. I. Selverston (1982). Mechanisms underlying pattern generation in lobster stomatogastric ganglion as determined by selective inactivation of identified neurons. IV. Network properties of pyloric system. *J. Neurophysiol.* 48:1416–1432.

Miller, J. P., and A. I. Selverston (1985). Neural mechanisms for the production of the lobster pyloric motor pattern. In *Model Neural Networks and Behavior* (A. I. Selverston, ed.). New York: Plenum Press, pp. 37–48.

Miller, S. G. and M. B. Kennedy (1986). Regulation of brain type Ca^{2+}/calmodulin-dependent protein kinase by autophosphorylation: a calcium triggered molecular switch. *Cell* 44:861–870.

Mishina, M., T. Takai, K. Imoto, M. Noda, T. Takahashi, S. Numa, C. Methfessel, and B. Sakmann (1986). Molecular distinction between fetal and adult forms of muscle acetylcholine receptor. *Nature* 321:406–411.

Mishkin, M., L. G. Ungerleider, and K. A. Macko (1983). Object vision and spatial vision: two cortical pathways. *Trends Neurosci.* 6:414–417.

Moore, J. K., and K. K. Osen (1979). The human cochlear nuclei. In *Experimental Brain Research*, Suppl. II: *Hearing Mechanisms and Speech* (O. Creutzfeld, H. Scheich, and C. Schreiner, eds.). New York: Springer-Verlag, pp. 36–44.

Moore, R. Y. (1982). The suprachiasmatic nucleus and the organization of a circadian system. *Trends Neurosci.* 5:404–407.

Mountcastle, V. B., ed. (1980). *Medical Physiology.* St. Louis: C. V. Mosby.

Mountcastle, V. B. (1986). The neural mechanisms of cognitive functions can now be studied directly. *Trends Neurosci.* 9:505–508.

Mountcastle, V. B., J. C. Lynch, A. Georgopolous, H. Sakata, and C. Acuna (1975). Posterior parietal association cortex of the monkey: command functions for operation within extra-personal space. *J. Neurophysiol.* 38:871–908.

Mrosovsky, N. (1986). Sleep researchers caught napping. *Nature* 319:536–537.

Murray, R. G. (1973). The ultrastucture of taste buds. In *The Ultrastructure of Sensory Organs* (I. Friedmann, ed.). New York: Elsevier, pp. 1–81.

Muybridge, E. (1957). *Animals in Motion.* Reprinted from *Animal Locomotion, 1887.* New York: Dover.

Nakamura, T., and G. H. Gold (1987). A cyclic nucleotide-gated conductance in olfactory receptor cilia. *Nature* 325:442–444.

Nauta, W. J. M. (1972). The central visceromotor system: a general survey. In *Limbic System Mechanisms and Autonomic Function* (C. H. Hockman, ed.). Springfield, MA: C. C. Thomas, pp. 21–38.

Neher, E., and J. H. Steinbach (1978). Local anaesthetics transiently block currents through single acetylcholine-receptor channels. *J. Physiol. (London)* 227:153–176.

Nestler, E. J., and P. Greengard (1984). *Protein Phosphorylation in the Nervous System.* New York: John Wiley.

Neyton, J., and A. Trautmann, A. (1985). Single-channel currents of an intercellular junction. *Nature* 317:331–335.

Nicoll, R. A. (1982). Neurotransmitters can say more than yes or no. *Trends Neurosci.* 5:369.

Nilsson, B. (1984). Master class. *The New Yorker,* December 10, pp. 44–45.

Noble, D. (1985). Ionic mechanisms in rhythmic firing of heart and nerve. *Trends Neurosci.* 8:499–504.

Noda, M., T. Ikeda, T. Kayano, H. Suzuki, H. Takeshima, M. Kurasaki, H. Takahashi, and S. Numa (1986). Existence of distinct sodium channel messenger RNAs in rat brain. *Nature* 320:188–192.

Noma, A. (1986). GTP-binding proteins couple cardiac muscarinic receptors to potassium channels. *Trends Neurosci.* 8:142–143.

Norgren, R. (1980). Neuroanatomy of gustatory and visceral afferents systems in rat and monkey. In *Olfaction and Taste VII* (H. van der Starre, ed.). London: IRL Press, p. 288.

Northcutt, R. G. (1981). Evolution of the telencephalon in non-mammals. *Annu. Rev. Neurosci.* 4:301–350.

Nottebohm, F. (1975). Vocal behavior in birds. In *Avian Biology,* Vol. 5 (D. S. Farner and J. R. King, eds.). New York: Academic Press, pp. 287–332.

Nottebohm, F. (1980). Brain pathways for vocal learning in birds. In *Prog. Psychobiol. Physiol. Psychol* (J. M. Sprague and A. N. Esptein, eds.). New York: Academic Press, pp. 86–125.

Nowak, L., P. Bregestovski, P. Ascher, A. Herbet, and A. Prochiantz (1984). Magnesium gates glutamate-activated channels in mouse central neurones. *Nature* 307:462–465.

Nowycky, M. C., and R. H. Roth (1978). Dopaminergic neurons: role of presynaptic receptors in the regulation of transmitter biosynthesis. *Prog. Neuropsychopharmacol.* 2:139–158.

Nowycky, M. C., A. P. Fox, and R. W. Tsien (1985). Three types of neuronal calcium channel into different calcium against sensitivity. *Nature* 310:440–443.

Numa, S., M. Noda, H. Takahashi, T. Tanabe, M. Toyasato, Y. Furatani, and S. Kikyotani (1983). Molecular structure of the nicotinic acetylcholine receptor. *Cold Spring Harbor Symp. Quant. Biol.* 48:57–69.

Olds, M. E., and J. Olds (1961). Emotional and associative mechanisms in the rat brain. *J. Comp. Physiol. Psychol.* 54:120–126.

Olson, L. (1985). On the use of transplants to counteract the symptoms of Parkinson's disease: background experimental models, and possible clinical applications. In *Synaptic Plasticity.* (C. Cotman, ed.). New York: Guilford Press, pp. 485–506.

Otsuka, M., and Z. W. Hall (1979). Preface. In *Neurobiology of Chemical Transmission* (M. Otsuka and Z. W. Hall, eds.). New York: John Wiley, p. vii.

Ottoson, D., and G. M. Shepherd (1971). Transducer properties and integrative mechanisms in the frog's muscle spindle. In *Handbook of Sensory Physiology,* Sec. 1: *The Nervous System,* Vol. 1: *Principles of Receptor Physiology* (W. R. Loewenstein, ed.). New York: Springer-Verlag, pp. 443–499.

Palade, G. E., and M. G. Farquhar (1981). Cell biology. In *Pathophysiology: The Biological Principles of Disease* (L. H. Smith and S. O. Thie, eds.). Philadelphia: W. B. Saunders, pp. 1–56.

Papez, J. W. (1937). A proposed mechanism of emotion. *Arch. Neurol. Psychiatry* 38:725–743.

Patlak, J., and R. Horn (1982). Effect of N-bromoacetamide on single sodium channel currents in excised membrane patches. *J. Gen. Physiol.* 79:333–351.

Patton, H. D., J. W. Sundsten, W. E. Crill, and P. D. Swanson, eds. (1976). *Introduction to Basic Neurology.* Philadelphia: W. B. Saunders.

Pearson, K. (1976). The control of walking. *Sci. Am.* 235:72–86.

Pedersen, P. E., and E. M. Blass (1982). Prenatal and postnatal determinants of the first suckling episode in the albino rat. *Dev. Psychobiol.* 15:349–356.

Penfield, W., and T. Rasmussen (1952). *The Cerebral Cortex of Man.* New York: Macmillan.

Peters, A., and E. G. Jones, eds. (1985). *Cerebral Cortex,* Vol. 1: *Cellular Components of the Cerebral Cortex.* New York: Plenum Press.

Petersen, O. H. (1980). *The Electrophysiology of Gland Cells.* London: Academic Press.

Petersen, O. H., and Y. Maruyama (1984). Calcium-activated potassium channels and their role in secretion. *Nature* 307:693–696.

Peterson, E. L. (1983). Visual processing in the leech visual system. *Nature* 303:240–242.

Pfaff, D. W. (1980). *Estrogens and Brain Function.* New York: Springer-Verlag.

Pfaffman, C., M. Frank, L. M. Bartoshuk, and T. C. Snell (1976). Coding gustatory information in the squirrel monkey chorda tympani. In *Progress in Psychobiology and Physiological Psychology* (J. M. Sprague and A. N. Epstein, eds.). New York: Academic Press, pp. 1–27.

Pfeiffer, R. R. (1966). Classification of response patterns of spike discharges for units in the cochlear nucleus: tone burst stimulation. *Exp. Brain Res.* 1:220–235.

Pfenninger, K.-H. (1986). Of nerve growth cones, leukocytes and memory: second messenger systems and growth-regulated proteins. *Trends Neurosci.* 8:562–565.

Phillips, C. G., and R. Porter (1977). *Cortico-Spinal Neurones: Their Role in Movement.* London: Academic Press.

Phillips, I. M., D. Felix, W. E. Hoffman, and D. Ganten (1977). Angiotensin-sensitive sites in the brain ventricular system. In *Soc. for Neurosci. Symposia,* Vol. 2 (W. M. Cowan and J. A. Ferrendelli, eds.). Bethesda, MD: Soc. for Neurosci., pp. 308–339.

Phoenix, C. H., R. W. Goy, A. A. Gerall, W. C. Young (1959). Organizational action of prenatally administered testosterone propionate on the tissues mediating behavior in the female guinea pig. *Endocrinology* 65:369–382.

Pittendrigh, C. S. (1974). Circadian oscillation in cells and the circadian organization of multicellular systems. In *The Neurosciences: Third Study Program* (F. O. Schmitt and F. G. Worden, eds.). Cambridge, MA: MIT Press pp. 437–458.

Poggio, J. F. (1980). Central neural mechanisms in vision. In *Medical Physiology* (V. B. Mountcastle, ed.). pp. 544–585.

Popper, K. R., and J. C. Eccles (1977). *The Self and Its Brain.* New York: Springer-Verlag.

Potter, D. D., E. J. Furshpan, and S. C. Landis (1981). Multiple-transmitter status and "Dale's principle." *Neurosci. Comment.* 1:1–9.

Powell, T. P. S., and V. B. Mountcastle (1959). Some aspects of the functional organization of the cortex of the postcentral gyrus of the monkey: a correlation of findings obtained in a single unit analysis with cytoarchitecture. *Bull. John Hopkins Hosp.* 105:133–162.

Proctor, D. F. (1980). *Breathing, Speech and Song.* New York: Springer-Verlag.

Purves, D., and J. W. Lichtman (1985). *Principles of Neural Development.* Sunderland, MA: Sinauer.

Raisman, G. (1969). Neuronal plasticity in the septal nuclei of the adult rat. *Brain Res.* 14:25–48.

Raisman, G., and P. M. Field (1971). Sexual dimorphism in the preoptic area of the rat. *Science* 173:731–733.

Rakic, P. (1976). *Local Circuit Neurons.* Cambridge, MA: MIT Press.

Rakic, P. (1981). Developmental events leading to laminar and areal organization of the neocortex. In *The Organization of the Cerebral Cortex*. (F. O. Schmitt, F. G. Worden, G. Adelman, and S. G. Dennis, eds.). Cambridge, MA: MIT Press, pp. 7–28.

Rakic, P., J.-P. Bourgeois, M. F. Eckenhoff, N. Zecevic, and P. S. Goldman-Rakic (1986). Concurrent overproduction of synapses in diverse regions of the primate cerebral cortex. *Science* 232:232–235.

Rall, W., and J. Rinzel (1973). Branch input resistance and steady attenuation for input to one branch of a dendritic neuron model. *Biophys. J.* 13:648–688.

Rall, W., and G. M. Shepherd (1968). Theoretical reconstruction of field potentials and dendrodendritic synaptic interactions in olfactory bulb. *J. Neurophysiol.* 31:884–915.

Rall, W., G. M. Shepherd, T. S. Reese, and M. W. Brightman (1966). Dendrodendritic synaptic pathway for inhibition in the olfactory bulb. *Exp. Neurol.* 14:44–56.

Ratliff, F. (1965). *Mach Bands: Quantitative Studies on Neural Networks in the Retina*. San Francisco: Holden-Day.

Ratnam, M., D. L. Nguyen, J. Rivier, P. B. Sargent, and J. Lindstrom (1986). Transmembrane topography of nicotinic acetylcholine receptor: immunochemical tests contradict theoretical predictions based on hydrophobicity profiles. *Biochemistry* 25:2633–2643.

Reichelt, K. L., and P. D. Edminson (1977). Peptides containing probable transmitter candidates in the central nervous system. In *Peptides in Neurobiology* (H. Gainer, ed.). New York: Plenum Press, pp. 171–181.

Renaud, L. P. (1977). TRH, LHRH, and somatostatin: distribution and physiological action in neural tissue. In *Soc. for Neurosci. Symp.*, Vol. 2 (W. M. Cowan and J. A. Ferrendelli, eds.). Bethesda, MD: Soc. for Neurosci. pp. 265–290.

Ribak, C. E., J. E. Vaughn, K. Saito, R. Barber, and E. Roberts (1977). Glutamate decarboxylase localization in neurons of the olfactory bulb. *Brain Res.* 126:1–18.

Ripley, S. H., B. M. H. Bush, and A. Roberts (1968). Crab muscle receptor which responds without impulses. *Nature* 218:1170–1171.

Roberts, A., and M. H. Bush (1981). *Neurones Without Impulses: Their Significance for Vertebrate and Invertebrate Nervous System*. Cambridge: Cambridge University Press.

Robertson, R. M., and K. G. Pearson (1985). Neural networks controlling locomotion in locusts. In *Model Neural Networks and Behavior* (A. I. Selverston, ed.). New York: Plenum Press, pp. 21–36.

Romer, A. S., and T. S. Parsons (1977). *The Vertebrate Body*. Philadelphia: W. B. Saunders.

Römer, H. (1983). Tonotopic organization of the auditory neuropile in the bushcricket *Tettigonia viridissima. Nature* 306:60–62.

Routtenberg, A. (1984). Brain phosphoproteins, kinase C and protein F1: protagonists of plasticity in particular pathways. In *Neurobiology of Learning and Memory* (G. Lynch, J. McGaugh, and N. Weinberger, eds.). New York: Guilford Press, pp. 479–490.

Sakmann, B., and E. Neher (1983). *Single-Channel Recording*. New York: Plenum Press.

Sarnat, H. B. and M. G. Netsky (1981). *Evolution of the Nervous System*. New York: Oxford University Press.

Schmidt, R. F., ed. (1978). *Fundamentals of Sensory Physiology*. New York: Springer-Verlag.

Schmidt, R. F., and G. Thewes, eds. (1983). *Human Physiology*. New York: Springer-Verlag.

Schneider, D. W., A. Kafka, M. Beroza, and B. A. Bierl (1977). Odor receptor responses of male gypsy and nun moths (Lepidoptera, Lymantriidae) to disparlure and its analogues. *J. Comp. Physiol.* 113:1–15.

Schwartz, W. J., and H. Gainer (1977). Suprachiasmatic nucleus: use of ^{14}C-labeled deoxyglucose uptake as a functional marker. *Science* 197:1089–1091.

Scoville, W. B., and B. Milner (1957). Loss of recent memory after bilateral hippocampal lesions. *J. Neurol. Neurosurg. Psychiatry* 20:11–21.

Sellick, P. M., R. Patuzzi, and B. M. Johnstone (1982). Measurement of basilar membrane motion in the guinea pig using the Mossbauer technique. *J. Acoust. Soc. Am.* 72:131–141.

Selverston, A. (1976). A model system for the study of rhythmic behavior. In *Simpler Networks and Behavior* (J. C. Fentress, ed.) Sunderland, MA: Sinauer, pp. 82–98.

Selverston, A. I., D. F. Russell, J. P. Miller, D. G. King (1976). The stomatogastric nervous system: structure and function of a small neural network. *Prog. Neurobiol.* 7:215–289.

Shapiro, E., V. F. Castellucci, and E. R. Kandel (1980). Presynaptic inhibition in *Aplysia* involves a decrease in the Ca^{2+} current of the presynaptic neuron. *Proc. Natl. Acad. Sci. USA* 77:1185–1189.

Shepherd, G. M. (1972). The neuron doctrine: a revision of functional concepts. *Yale J. Biol. Med.* 45:584–599.

Shepherd, G. M. (1978). Microcircuits in the nervous system. *Sci. Am.* 238:92–103.

Shepherd, G. M. (1979). *The Synaptic Organization of the Brain*. New York: Oxford University Press

Shepherd, G. M. (1981). The nerve impulse and the nature of nervous function. In *Without Impulses* (A. Roberts and B. M. H. Bush, eds.). Cambridge: Cambridge University Press, pp. 1–27.

Shepherd, G. M. (1985). Welcome whiff of biochemistry. *Nature* 316:214–215.

Shepherd, G. M. (1986). Neurobiology: microcircuits to see by. *Nature* 319:452–453.

Shepherd, G. M. (1987). The basic circuit for cortical

organization. In *Perspectives in Memory Research* (M. S. Gazzaniga, ed.). Cambridge, MA: MIT.

Shepherd, G. M., and R. K. Brayton (1987). Logic operations are properties of computer-simulated interactions between excitable dendritic spines. *Neurosci.* 21:151–165.

Shepherd, G. M., and C. A. Greer (1987). The dendritic spine: adaptations of structure and function for different types of synaptic integration. In *Intrinsic Determinants of Neuronal Form* (R. Lassek, ed.). New York: Alan R. Liss.

Shepherd, G. M., P. E. Pedersen, and C. A. Greer (1987). Development of olfactory specificity in the albino rat: a model system. *In Perinatal Development: A Psychobiological Perspective* (N. A. Krasnegor, E. M. Blass, M. A. Hofer, and W. P. Smotherman, eds.). New York: Academic Press, pp. 127–144.

Shepherd, J. T., and P. M. Vanhoutte (1979). *The Human Cardiovascular System.* New York: Raven.

Sherrington, C. S. (1906). *The Integrative Action of the Nervous System.* New Haven: Yale University Press.

Sherrington, C. S. (1935). Santiago Ramón y Cajal, 1852–1934. *Obituary Notices of the Royal Society of London* 4:425–441.

Sholl, D. A. (1956). *The Organization of the Cerebral Cortex.* London: Methuen.

Shull, G. E., L. K. Lane and J. B. Lingrel (1986). Amino-acid sequence of the β-subunit of the (Na+ +K+) ATPase deduced from a cDNA. *Nature* 321:429–431.

Siegler, M. V. S., and M. Burrows (1979). The morphology of local nonspiking interneurones in the metathoracic ganglia of the locust. *J. Comp. Neurol.* 183:121–148.

Siggins, G. R., B. J. Hoffer, and F. E. Bloom (1971). Studies on norepinephrine-containing afferents to Purkinje cells of rat cerebellum: III. Evidence for mediation of norepinephrine effects by cyclic 3′, 5′-adenosine monophosphate. *Brain Res.* 25:535–553.

Sims, S. M., J. J. Singer, and J. V. Walsh, Jr. (1986). A mechanism of muscarinic excitation in dissociated smooth muscle cells. *Trends Pharmacol. Sci [Suppl.]* 7:28–32.

Skoglund, S. (1973). Joint receptors and kinaesthesis. In *Handbook of Sensory Physiology,* Vol. 2: *Somatosensory System* (A Iggo, ed.) New York: Springer-Verlag, pp. 111–136.

Smith, D. S. (1965). The flight muscles of insects. *Sci. Am.* 212:76–88.

Smith, S. J. (1987). Progress on LTP at hippocampal synapses: a post-synaptic Ca^{2+} trigger for memory storage? *Trends Neurosci.* 10:142–144.

Smith, S. J., L. R. Osses, and G. J. Augustine (1987). Imaging of localized calcium accumulation within squid 'giant' presynaptic terminals. *Biophys. Soc. Abstr.* 51:66a.

Snyder, S. H. (1984). Drug and neurotransmitter receptors in the brain. *Science* 224:22–31.

Sokoloff, L. (1977). Relation between physiological function and energy metabolism in the central nervous system. *J. Neurochem.* 27:13–26.

Somjen, G. (1972). *Sensory Coding in the Mammalian Nervous System.* New York: Appleton-Century-Crofts.

Sperry, R. W. (1974). Lateral specialization in the surgically separated hemispheres. In *The Neurosciences: Third Study Program* (F. O. Schmitt and F. G. Worden, eds.). Cambridge, MA: MIT Press, pp. 5–19.

Spitzer, N. C. (1979). Ion channels in development. *Annu. Rev. Neurosci.* 2:363–397.

Spoendlin, H. (1969). Innervation patterns in the organ of Corti of the cat. *Acta Otolaryngol. (Stockholm)* 67:239–254.

Squire, L. R. (1986). Mechanisms of memory. *Science* 232:1612–1619.

Squire, L., and N. Butters (1984). *Neuropsychology of Memory.* New York: Guilford Press.

Starzl, T. E., C. W. Taylor, and H. Magoun (1951). Collateral afferent excitation of the reticular formation of the brain stem. *J. Neurophysiol.* 14:479–496.

Stellar, J. R., and E. Stellar (1985). *The Neurobiology of Motivation and Reward.* New York: Springer-Verlag.

Stent, G. S., W. J. Thompson, and R. L. Calabrese (1979). Neural control of heartbeat in the leech and in some other invertebrates. *Physiol. Rev.* 59:101–136.

Stent, G. S. (1981). Strength and weakness of the genetic approach to the development of the nervous system. *Annu. Rev. Neurosci.* 4:163–194.

Stevens, C. F. (1980). Ionic channels in neuromembranes: methods for studying their properties. In *Molluscan Nerve Cells: From Biophysics to Behavior.* (J. Koester and J. H. Byrne, eds.). Cold Spring Harbor, NY: Cold Spring Harbor Laboratories, pp. 11–31.

Stewart, W. B., J. S. Kauer, and G. M. Shepherd (1979). Functional organization of rat olfactory bulb analysed by the 2-deoxyglucose method. *J. Comp. Neurol.* 185:715–734.

Storer, T. I. (1943). *General Zoology.* New York: McGraw-Hill.

Strausfeld, N. J., and P. R. Nässel (1981). Neuroarchitecture of brain regions that subserve the compound eyes of crustacea and insects. In *Handbook of Sensory Physiology,* Vol. 7: *Comparative Physiology and Evolution of Vision in Invertebrates,* Part B: *Invertebrate Visual Centers and Behavior* (H. Autrum, ed.). New York: Springer-Verlag, pp. 1–132.

Stretton, A. O. W., and E. A. Kravitz (1968). Neuronal geometry: determination with a technique of intracellular dye injection. *Science* 162:132–134.

Strumwasser, F. (1974). Neuronal principles organizing periodic behaviors. In *The Neurosciences: Third Study Program* (F. O. Schmitt and F. G. Worden, eds.). Cambridge, MA: MIT Press, pp. 459–478.

Suga, N. (1978). Specialization of the auditory system for reception and processing of species-specific sounds. *Fed. Proc.* 37:2342–2354.

Sugden, D., J. Vanecek, D. C. Klein, T. P. Thomas, and W. B. Anderson (1985). Activation of protein kinase C potentiates isoprenaline-incuded cyclic AMP accumulation in rat pinealocytes. *Nature* 314:359–362.

Sulston, J., E. Schierenberg, J. White, and N. Thomson (1983). The embryonic lineage of the nematode *Caenorhabditis elegans*. *Dev. Biol.* 100:64–119.

Sutcliffe, J. G., R. J. Milner, J. M. Gottesfeld, and W. Reynolds (1984). Control of neuronal gene expression. *Science* 225:1308–1315.

Szekely, G (1968). Development of limb movements: embryological, physiological and model studies. In *Ciba Found. Symp. on Growth of the Nervous System* (G. E. W. Wolstenholme and M. O'Connor, eds.). London: Churchill, pp. 77–93.

Teeter, J., M. Funakoshi, K. Kurihara, S. Roper, T. Sato, and K. Tonosaki (1987). Generation of the taste cell potential. In *Chemical Senses*. Washington, D.C.: Irl Press, pp. 217–234.

Teicher, M. H., W. B. Stewart, J. S. Kauer, and G. M. Shepherd (1980). Suckling pheromone stimulation of a modified glomerular region in the developing rat olfactory bulb revealed by the 2-deoxyglucose method. *Brain Res.* 194:530–535.

Thomas, R. C. (1972). Electrogenic sodium pump in nerve and muscle cells. *Physiol. Rev.* 52:563–594.

Thompson, R. F. (1986). The neurobiology of learning and memory. *Science* 233:941–947.

Thompson, R. F., G. A. Clark, N. H. Donegan, D. G. Lavond, J. Madden, IV, L. A. Mamounas, M. D. Mauk, and D. A. McCormick (1984). Neuronal substrates of basic associative learning. In *Neuropsychology of Memory* (L. R. Squire and N. Butters, eds.). New York: Guilford Press, pp. 424–442.

Thompson, S. H., and R. W. Aldrich (1980). Membrane potassium channels. In *The Cell Surface and Neuronal Function* (C. W. Cotman, G. Poste, and G. L. Nicolson, eds.). New York: Elsevier/North-Holland, pp. 49–85.

Thompson, W., D. P. Kuffler, and J. K. S. Jansen (1979). The effect of prolonged, reversible block of nerve impulses on the elimination of polyneuronal innervation of new-born rat skeletal muscle fibers. *Neuroscience* 4:271–281.

Tinbergen, N. (1951). *The Study of Instinct*. Oxford: Oxford University Press.

Tombes, A. S. (1970). *An Introduction to Invertebrate Endocrinology*. New York: Academic Press.

Triller, A., F. Cluzeaud, and H. Korn (1987). GABA-containing terminals can be apposed to glycine receptors at central synapses. *J. Cell Biol.* 104:947–956.

Trotier, D., and P. MacLeod (1986). Intracellular recordings from salamander olfactory receptor cells. *Brain Res.* 268:225–237.

Truman, J. W., and L. M. Schwartz (1980). Peptide hormone regulation of programmed death of neurons and muscle in an insect.In *Peptides: Integrators of Cell and Tissue Function*,Soc. Gen. Physiol. Series, Vol. 35 (F. E. Bloom, ed.). New York: Raven Press, pp. 55–68.

Tsien, R. W. (1987). Calcium currents in heart cells and neurons. In *Neuromodulation: The Biochemical Control of Neuronal Excitability* (L. K. Kaczmarek and I. B. Levitan, eds.). New York: Oxford University Press, pp. 206–242.

Tunturi, A. (1944). Audio frequency localization in the acoustic cortex of the dog. *Am. J. Physiol.* 141:397–403.

Vale, R. D., T. S. Reese, and M. P. Sheetz (1985). Identification of a novel force generating protein (kinesin) involved in microtubule-based motility. *Cell* 41:39–50.

Vallbo, A. B., and R. S. Johansson (1984). Properties of cutaneous mechanoreceptors in the human hand related to touch sensation. *Hum. Neurobiol.* 3:3–14.

van Essen, D. C. (1985). Functional organization of primate visual cortex. In *Cerebral Cortex* (A. Peters and E. G. Jones, eds.). New York: Plenum, pp. 259–330.

Viancour, T. A. (1979). Peripheral electrosense physiology: a review of recent findings. *J. Physiol. (Paris)* 75:321–333.

Vincent, S. R., T. Hökfelt, L. R. Steinboll, and J.-Y. Wu (1983). Hypothalamic α-aminobutyric acid neurons project to neocortex. *Science* 220:1309–1311.

von Békésy, G. (1960). *Experiments in Hearing*. New York: McGraw-Hill.

Wakerly, J. B., and D. W. Lincoln (1973). The milk-ejection reflex of the rat: a 20- to 40-fold acceleration in the firing of paraventricular neurones during oxytocin release. *J. Endocrinol.* 57:477.

Ward, S. (1977). Use of nematode behavioral mutants for analysis of neural function and development. In *Society for Neuroscience Symposia*, Vol. 2: *Approaches to the Cell Biology of Neurons* (W. M. Cowan and J. A. Ferrendelli, eds.). Bethesda, MD: Soc. for Neurosci., pp. 1–26.

Warwick, R., and P. L. Williams (1973). *Gray's Anatomy*. Philadelphia: W. B. Saunders.

Watson, J. D., J. Tooze, and D. T. Kurtz (1983). *Recombinant DNA: A Short Course*. New York: Sci. Am. Books; W. H. Freeman, distr.

Watt, D. G. D., E. K. Stauffer, A. Taylor, A., R. M. Reinking, and D. G. Stuart (1976). Analysis of muscle receptor connections by spike-triggered averaging. 1. Spindle primary and tendon organ afferents. *J. Neurophysiol.* 39:1375–1392.

Welker, W. I., and S. Seidenstein (1959). Somatic sensory representation in the cerebral cortex of the raccoon (*Procyon loter*). *J. Comp. Neurol.* 111:469–501.

Wells, M. (1968). *Lower Animals*. New York: McGraw-Hill.

Werblin, F. S., and J. E. Dowling (1969). Organization of the retina of the mudpuppy, *Necturus maculosus*. II. Intracellular recording. *J. Neurophysiol.* 32:339–355.

Wersäll, J., and D. Bagger-Sjöbäck (1974). Morphology of the vestibular sense organ. In *Handbook of Sensory Physiology*, Vol. 6: *Vestibular System*, Part 1: *Basic Mechanisms* (H. H. Kornhuber, ed.). New York: Springer-Verlag, pp. 123–170.

Wetzel, M. C., and D. G. Stuart (1976). Ensemble characteristics of cat locomotion and its neural control. *Prog. Neurobiol.* 7:1–98.

Wiesel, T. N., D. H. Hubel, and D. M. K. Lam (1974). Autoradiographic demonstration of ocular-dominance columns in the monkey striate cortex by means of transneuronal transport. *Brain Res.* 79:273–279.

Wilson, E. O. (1975). *Sociobiology*. Cambridge, MA: Harvard.

Wilson, V. J., and G. Melvill-Jones (1979). *Mammalian Vestibular Physiology*. New York: Plenum Press.

Wine, J. J., and T. B. Krasne (1982). The cellular organization of crayfish escape behavior. In *The Biology of Crustacea*, Vol. 4 (D. C. Sandman and H. Atwood, eds.). New York: Academic Press, pp. 241–292.

Wood, J. D. (1975). Neurophysiology of Auerbach's plexus and control of intestinal motility. *Physiol. Rev.* 55:307–324.

Woodbury, J. W. (1965). The cell membrane: ionic and potential gradients and active transport. In *Physiology and Biophysics* (T. C. Ruch and H. D. Patton, eds.). Philadelphia: W. B. Saunders, pp. 1–25.

Woody, C. D. (1982). *Memory, Learning, and Higher Function*. New York: Springer-Verlag.

Woolsey, T. A., and H. van der Loos (1970). The structural organization of layer IV in the somatosensory region (SI) of mouse cerebral cortex. The description of a cortical field composed of discrete cytoarchitectonic units. *Brain Res.* 17:205–242.

Yamamoto, C., and H. McIlwain (1966). Electrical activities in thin sections from the mammalian brain maintained in chemically defined media in vitro. *J. Neurochem.* 13:1333–1343.

Yarowsky, P. J., and D. H. Ingvar (1981). Neuronal activity and energy metabolism. *Fed. Proc.* 40:2353–2362.

Young, M. W., F. R. Jackson, H. S. Shin, and T. A. Bargiello (1985). A biological clock in *Drosophila*. *Cold Spring Harbor Symp. Quant. Biol.* 50:865–875.

Young, J. Z. (1964). *A Model of the Brain*. Oxford: Oxford University Press.

Young, J. Z. (1978). *Programs of the Brain*. Oxford: Oxford University Press.

Zemlin, W. R. (1968). *Speech and Hearing Science: Antomy and Physiology*. Englewood Cliffs, NJ: Prentice-Hall.

Further Reading

Altner, H., H. Sass, and I. Altner (1977). Relationship between structure and function of antennal chemo-, hygro-, and thermoreceptive sensilla in *Periplaneta americana*. *Cell Tiss. Res.* 176:389–405.

Bell, P. R. (1959). *Darwin's Biological Work*. Cambridge: Cambridge University Press.

Bennet-Clark, H. C. (1975). Sound production in insects. *Sci. Prog. Oxford* 62:263–283.

Boeckh, J. (1980b). Ways of nervous coding of chemosensory quality at the input level. In *Olfaction and Taste VII* (H. van der Starre, ed.). London: IRL Press, pp. 113–122.

Burrows, M. (1980). The control of sets of motoneurones by local interneurones in the locust. *J. Physiol. (London)* 298:213–233.

Cajal, S. Ramón y (1937). *Recollections of My Life* (E. H. Craigie and J. Cano, trans.). Philadelphia: University of Pennsylvania.

Chapman, R. F. (1977). *The Insects: Structure and Function*. New York: American Elsevier.

Delcomyn, F. (1980). Neural basis of rhythmic behavior in animals. *Science* 210:492–498.

Eccles, J. C., M. Ito, and J. Szentágothai (1967). *The Cerebellum as a Neuronal Machine*. New York: Springer-Verlag.

Edwards, C., and D. Ottoson (1958). The site of impulse initiation in a nerve cell of a crustacean stretch receptor. *J. Physiol. (London)* 143:138–148.

Ewert, J.-P. (1981). Neural coding of "worms" and "antiworms" in the brains of toads: the question of hard-wired and soft-wired systems. In *Brain Mechanisms of Behavior in Lower Vertebrates* (P. R. Laming, ed.). Cambridge: Cambridge University Press, pp. 137–170.

Faber, D. S., and H. Korn (1978). *Neurobiology of the Mauthner Cell*. New York: Raven Press.

Fawcett, D. W. (1981). *The Cell*. Philadelphia: W. B. Saunders.

Fitsimons, J. T. (1979). *The Physiology of Thirst and Sodium Appetite*. London: Cambridge University Press.

Flicker, C., R. W. McCarley, and J. A. Hobson (1981). Aminergic neurons: state control and plasticity in three model systems. *Cell. Mol. Neurobiol.* 1:123–166.

Frank, E., and G. D. Fischbach (1979). Early events in neuromuscular junction formation in vitro: induction of acetylcholine receptor clusters in the postsynaptic membrane and morphology of newly formed synapses. *J. Cell Biol.* 83:143–158.

Friesen, W. O., and G. S. Stent (1978). Neural circuits for generating rhythmic movements. *Annu. Rev. Biophys. Bioeng.* 7:37–61.

Gershon, M. D. (1981). The enteric nervous system. *Annu. Rev. Neurosci.* 4:227–272.

Hamill, O. P., A. Marty, E. Neher, B. Sakmann, and F. J. Sigworth (1981). Improved patch-clamp techniques for high-resolution current recording from cells and cell-free membrane patches. *Pflugers Arch.* 391:85–100.

Heitler, W. J., and M. Burrows (1977). The locust jump. 1. The motor programme. *J. Exp. Biol.* 66:203–219.

Hodgkin, A. L., and P. Horowicz (1959). The influence of potassium and chloride ions on the membrane potential of single muscle fibers. *J. Physiol. (London)* 1148:127–160.

Hubel, D. H., T. N. Wiesel, and M. P. Stryker (1978). Anatomical demonstration of orientation columns in macaque monkey. *J. Comp. Neurol.* 177:361–380.

Huxley, H. E. (1973). Muscular contraction and cell mobility. *Nature* 243:445–449.

Keesey, R. E., P. C. Boyle, J. W. Kemnitz, and J. S. Mitchell (1976). The role of the lateral hypothalamus in determining the body weight set point. In *Hunger: Basic Mechanisms and Clinical Implications*. (D. Novin, W. Wyricka and G. A. Bray, eds.). New York: Raven Press, pp. 243–255.

Konishi, M. (1985). Birdsong: from behavior to neuron. *Annu. Rev. Neurosci.* 8:125–170.

Kruger, L., and J. C. Liebeskind, eds. (1984). *Neural Mechanisms of Pain*. New York: Raven Press.

Landmesser, L. T. (1980). The generation of neuromuscular specificity. *Annu. Rev. Neurosci.* 3:279–302.

Lewis, D. B., and D. M. Gower (1980). *Biology of Communication*. New York: John Wiley.

Locy, W. A. (1915). *Biology and Its Makers*. New York: Henry Holt.

Lømo, T., and J. Rosenthal (1972). Control of ACh sensitivity by muscle activity in the rat. *J. Physiol. (London)* 221:453–513.

MacLusky, N. J., and F. Naftolin (1981). Sexual differentiation of the central nervous system. *Science* 211:1294–1303.

Napier, J. (1979). The evolution of the hand. In *Human Ancestors* (G. Isaac and R. E. F. Leakey, eds.). San Francisco: W. H. Freeman, pp. 43–49.

Nicoll, R. A. (1982). Neurotransmitters can say more than just 'yes' or 'no'. *Trends Neurosci.* 5:369–373.

Niewenhuys, R., L. M. G. Geeraedts, and J. G. Veening (1982). The medial forebrain bundle of the rat. I. General introduction. *J. Comp. Neurol.* 206:49–81.

O'Keefe, J., and L. Nadel (1978). *The Hippocampus as a Cognitive Map*. Oxford: Oxford University Press.

Pearson, K. G., W. J. Heitler, and J. D. Steeves (1980). Triggering of locust jump by multimodal inhibitory interneurons. *J. Neurophysiol.* 43:257–278.

Peters, A. S., L. Palay, and H. de F. Webster (1976). *The Fine Structure of the Nervous System*. New York: Harper & Row.

Rall, W. (1977). Core conductor theory and cable properties of neurons. In *Handbook of Physiology*, Sec. 1: *The Nervous System*, Vol. 1: *Cellular Biology of Neurons* (E. R. Kandel, ed.). Bethesda, MD: Am. Physiol. Soc., pp. 39–98.

Schiller. F. (1979), *Paul Broca: Founder of French Anthropology, Explorer of the Brain*. Berkeley: University of California Press.

Shaw, S. (1981). Anatomy and physiology of identified non-spiking cells in the photoreceptor–lamina complex of the compound eye of insects, especially *Diptera*. In *Neurones Without Impulses* (A. Roberts and B. M. H. Bush, eds.). Cambridge: Cambridge University Press, pp. 61–116.

Smith, D. S. (1968). *Insect Cells: Their Structure and Function*. Edinburgh: Oliver and Boyd.

Stein, P. S. G. (1978). Motor systems, with specific reference to the control of locomotion. *Annu. Rev. Neurosci.* 1:61–81.

Stein, R. B. (1980). *Nerve and Muscle: Membranes, Cells and Systems*. New York: Plenum Press.

Stone, J., B. Dreher, and A. Levinthal (1979). Hierarchical and parallel mechanisms in the organization of visual cortex. *Brain Res. Rev.* 1:345–394.

Stricker, E. M. (1983). Brain neurochemistry and the control of food intake. In *Handbook of Behavioral Neurobiology*, Vol. 6: *Motivation* (E. Satinoff and P. Teitlebaum, eds.). New York: Plenum Press, pp. 329–366.

Sukhanov, V. B. (1974). *General System of Symmetrical Locomotion of Terrestrial Vertebrates and Some Features of Movement of Lower Tetrapods*. New Delhi: Amerind.

Teicher, M. H., and E. M. Blass (1980). Suckling. *Science* 210:15–22.

Tolbert, L. R., and J. G. Hildebrand (1981). Organization and synaptic ultrastructure of glomeruli in the antennal lobes of the moth *Manduca sexta:* a study using thin sections and freeze-fracture. *Proc. R. Soc. Lond. [B].* 213:279–301.

Waldeyer, W. (1891). Uber einige neuere Forschungen in Gebiete der Anatomie des Centralnervensystems. *Dtsch. Med. Wochenschr.* 17:1352–1356.

Wasserman, G. S., G., Felstein, and G. S. Easland (1979). The psychophysical function: harmonizing Fechner and Stevens. *Science* 204:85–87.

Weight, F. F., and J. Votava (1970). Slow synaptic excitation in sympathetic ganglion cells: evidence for synaptic inactivation of potassium conductance. *Science* 170:755–758.

Werman, R. A. (1966). Criteria for identification of a central nervous sytem transmitter. *Comp. Biochem. Physiol.* 18:745–766.

Appendixes

Appendix A: Study Guide for Selected Topics

This list provides a guide to topics that are covered in several different chapters. It can be used as an outline for a one-semester course.

Topic	Chapters	Topic	Chapters
Synapses		*Sensory systems*	
1 Neuromuscular junction	2, 3, 7, 9, 17	11 Olfactory system organization	4, 7, 10, 11, 24, 26, 30
2 Squid giant synapse	8, 19		
3 Central synapses	4, 7, 8, 9, 17, 19, 24, 29, 30	12 Somatosensory system organization	9, 10, 12
4 Neurotransmitters	4, 7, 8, 17, 24, 29	13 Auditory system organization	15, 16, 23
5 Neuropeptides	8, 17, 18, 24, 29	14 *Limulus* eye	10, 16, 25
6 Second messengers	8, 10, 16, 17, 18, 25, 29	15 Visual system organization	4, 10, 12, 15, 16, 24, 25, 30
7 Dendritic spines	3, 4, 8, 29, 30	*Behavior*	
Action potentials		16 Leech	12, 16, 18, 20
8 Rhythmic action potentials	6, 18, 25	17 Escape responses	7, 10, 13, 20
Development and learning		18 Rhythm-generating networks	19, 20, 25, 26
9 Neural development	2, 9, 17, 23, 26, 30	19 Motor control in awake monkey	12, 21, 22, 30
10 Learning	4, 8, 29, 30	20 Cerebral cortex	4, 11–16, 22–25, 29, 30

Appendix B: Reference Table for Amino Acids

Each amino acid has a carbon atom attached to a hydrogen, an amino group, a carboxyl group, and a variable sidechain called an R group. The amino acids are classified in the table according to properties of their R groups. The size and composition are indicated in parentheses (C, carbon; O, oxygen, N, nitrogen; S, sulfur). At right are the three-letter and one-letter abbreviations used to represent the amino acid sequences in peptides and proteins.

Amino acid classification	Abbreviations		Amino acid classification	Abbreviations	
Acidic (negatively charged R group)			Serine (1 C, 1 O)	Ser	S
Aspartic acid (Aspartate) (2 C, 2 O)	Asp	D	Threonine (2 C, 1 O)	Thr	T
Glutamic acid (Glutamate) (3 C, 2 O)	Glu	E	Tyrosine (1 C, 1 benzene ring, 1 N)	Tyr	Y
Basic (positively charged R group)			*Nonpolar (hydrophobic R group)*		
Arginine (1 C, 3 N)	Arg	R	Alanine (1 C)	Ala	A
Histidine (4 C, 3 N)	His	H	Isoleucine (4 C)	Ile	I
Lysine (4 C, 1 N)	Lys	K	Leucine (4 C)	Leu	L
Polar (uncharged R group)			Methionine (3 C, 1 S)	Met	M
Asparagine (2 C, 1 O, 1 N)	Asn	N	Phenylalanine (1 C, 1 benzene ring)	Phe	F
Cysteine (1 C, 1 S: forms disulfide bonds)	Cys	C	Proline (3 C)	Pro	P
			Tryptophan (1 C, 1 indole)	Trp	W
Glutamine (3 C, 1 O, 1 N)	Gln	Q	Valine (3 C)	Val	V
Glycine	Gly	G			

Author Index

Subject Index

Page numbers in *italics* indicate illustrations. Page numbers followed by *t* indicate tables.